Not For Tourists™ Guide to **BOSTON**

P9-DXR-684

2009

Not For Tourists Inc

Published and designed by:
Not For Tourists, Inc.
NFT.—Not For Tourists_ Guide to BOSTON 2009
www.notfortourists.com

Publisher
Jane Pirone

Information Design
Jane Pirone
Rob Tallia
Scot Covey
Ben Bray

Managing Editor
Craig Nelson

Database Manager
Ben Bray

City Editor
Todd Strauss

Writing and Editing
Leah Bagas
Patrick Hellen
Craig Nelson
Todd Strauss

Research
Melissa Burgos
Ben Bray
Michael Dale
Lea Garrett

Contributors
Colleen Nugent
Sydney Yang

Research
Melissa Burgos
Ben Bray
Michael Dale
Lea Garrett

Graphic Design/Production
Scot Covey
Bethany Covey
Yumi Endo
Aaron Schielke
Carolyn Thomas

Editorial Intern
Rebecca Katherine Hirsch

Proofing
Sho Spaeth

Sales & Marketing
Sarah Hocevar
Annie Holt
Sho Spaeth
Jennifer Wong

Web Guru
Juan Molinari

All rights reserved. No portion of this book may be reproduced without written permission from the publisher.

Printed in China
ISBN# 978-0-9814887-3-8 $16.95
Copyright © 2008 by Not For Tourists, Inc.

Every effort has been made to ensure that the information in this book is as up-to-date as possible at press time. However, many details are liable to change—as we have learned. The publishers cannot accept responsibility for any consequences arising from the use of this book.

Not For Tourists does not solicit individuals, organizations, or businesses for listings inclusion in our guides, nor do we accept payment for inclusion into the editorial portion of our book; the advertising sections, however, are exempt from this policy. We always welcome communications from anyone regarding ANYTHING having to do with our books; please visit us on our website at www.notfortourists.com for appropriate contact information.

Dear NFT User,

Welcome to the 2009 edition of NFT Boston. We don't know what you did last year, but we spent a good chunk of our days running around the streets of the city to see what this book needed to make it even better than last year's. We trimmed some listings and added a bunch of new ones that we know you will like. As you flip through the pages, you'll discover tons of places to go for delicious cheap eats, romance, drinks, shows, dancing, more drinks, shopping splurges, and culture.

We're helped by the generous Bostonian contributors called out on the facing page, who sent in their suggestions and corrections to make this book absolutely amazing. All of this means that NFT Boston helps you navigate just about anything. We love it—and if you're reading a display copy of this book right now, you really should buy it.

As always, we want to get your feedback. If there is anything that you would like to see in the next edition of NFT Boston, please visit our website at www.notfortourists.com and let us know. Your feedback is important to us and contributes mightily to the integrity of this book.

While you're there, check out the new and improved website to search the online database, sign up for the weekly Boston newsletter, and read the daily " On Our Radar" articles for tips on more restaurants, events, and other goings-on about Beantown.

Here's hoping you find what you need,

Jane, Rob, Craig, & Todd

Table of Contents

Boston Area Driving Map
and **Downtown Boston Map**
foldout, last page

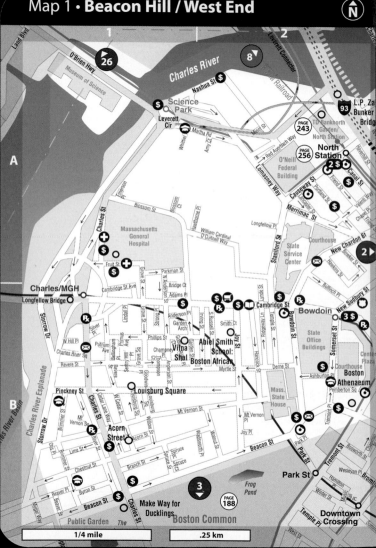

Map 1 • **Beacon Hill / West End**

Essentials

Map 1

Beacon Hill is still home to some of the most expensive real estate in America. Charming brick row houses reflect a long and storied history; where the State House stands, John Hancock once grazed cows. Full gentrification has yet to reach the West End, where government buildings, hospitals, and tucked-away burrito joints mingle fairly harmoniously.

$ Banks

- **Bank of America** • 104 Canal St [Valenti]
- **Bank of America** • 161 Cambridge St [Joy St]
- **Bank of America** • 3 Center Plz [Cambridge St]
- **Bank of America (ATM)** • 125 Nashua St [Storrow]
- **Bank of America (ATM)** • 200 Portland [Valenti]
- **Bank of America (ATM)** • 243 Charles St [Fruit]
- **Bank of America (ATM)** • 45 Charles St [Chestnut St]
- **Banknorth Massachusetts (ATM)** • 126 Causeway St [Canal St]
- **Cambridge Trust** • 65 Beacon St [Charles St]
- **Citizens Bank** • 1 Center Plz [Cambridge St]
- **Citizens Bank (ATM)** • 122 Cambridge St [Temple St]
- **Citizens Bank (ATM)** • 250 Cambridge St [Garden St]
- **Citizens Bank (ATM)** • 55 Fruit St [N Grove]
- **Citizens Bank (ATM)** • Boston Museum of Science • Science Park [Monsignor O'Brien Hwy]
- **Sovereign Bank** • 1 Beacon St [Tremont St]
- **Sovereign Bank** • 125 Causeway St [Canal St]
- **Sovereign Bank** • 67 Beacon St [Charles St]
- **Sovereign Bank (ATM)** • 1 Ashburton Pl [Somerset St]
- **Sovereign Bank (ATM)** • CVS/Pharmacy • 191 Cambridge St [S Russell]
- **Sovereign Bank (ATM)** • CVS/Pharmacy • 2 Center Plz [Somerset St]
- **Sovereign Bank (ATM)** • 27 Beacon St [Park St]

◉ Donuts

- **Dunkin' Donuts** • 106 Cambridge St [Bowdoin]
- **Dunkin' Donuts** • 111 Causeway St [Friend]
- **Dunkin' Donuts** • 125 Nashua St [Storrow]
- **Dunkin' Donuts** • 16 Tremont St [Court]
- **Dunkin' Donuts** • 180 Canal St [Causeway]
- **Dunkin' Donuts** • 22 Beacon St [Bowdoin]
- **Dunkin' Donuts** • 59 Causeway St [Lancaster St]

➕ Emergency Rooms

- **Massachusetts Eye and Ear Infirmary** • 243 Charles St [Fruit]
- **Massachusetts General Hospital** • 55 Fruit St [N Grove]

O Landmarks

- **Abiel Smith School** • 46 Joy St [Smith Ct]
- **Acorn Street** • b/w West Cedar St & Willow St, running parallel to Chestnut St
- **Boston Athenaeum** • 10 1/2 Beacon St [Somerset St]
- **Leonard P Zakim Bunker Hill Bridge** • I-93 & Charles River
- **Longfellow Bridge** • Cambridge St & Charles St
- **Louisburg Square** • b/w Mt Vernon St & Pinckney St
- **Make Way for Ducklings** • Charles St & Beacon St
- **Massachusetts General Hospital** • 55 Fruit St [N Grove]
- **TD Banknorth Garden** • 150 Causeway St [Beverly]
- **Vilna Shul** • 18 Phillips St [Garden St]

📖 Libraries

- **West End** • 151 Cambridge St [Lynde]

℞ Pharmacies

- **Rite Aid** • 100 Cambridge St [Bowdoin]
- **CVS** • 155 Charles St [Silver Pl]
- **CVS** • 191 Cambridge St [S Russell]
- **CVS** • 2 Center Plz [Cambridge St]
- **Gary Drug** • 59 Charles St [Mount Vernon St]

👮 Police

- **District A-1** (Temorariy relocated to 152 North End St)• 40 New Sudbury St [Bulfinch]

✉ Post Offices

- **Charles Street Station** • 136 Charles St [Revere St]
- **John F Kennedy Station** • 25 New Chardon St [Bulfinch]
- **State House Station** • 24 Beacon St [Park St]

🎓 Schools

- **Advent School** • 15 Brimmer St [Pinckney]
- **Boston Children's School** • 8 Whittier Pl [Martha]
- **Park Street School** • 67 Brimmer St [Chestnut St]
- **Suffolk University** • 8 Ashburton Pl [Somerset St]

🛒 Supermarkets

- **Whole Foods Market** • 181 Cambridge St [Joy St]

Map 1 • **Beacon Hill / West End**

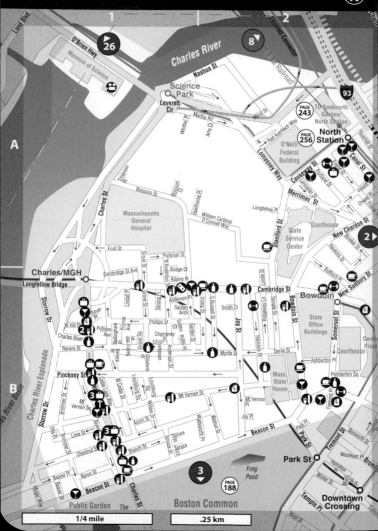

Sundries / Entertainment

Map 1

Locals praise the community feel of the square mile that constitutes Beacon Hill. Pubs like Seven's and The Four's cater to sports fans, and the crispy pizza at Upper Crust causes mini sidewalk traffic jams. The Public Garden and Boston Common function as the neighborhood's backyard.

☕ Coffee

• **Bagels Etc** • 70 Staniford St [Longfellow Pl]
• **Capital Coffee House** • 122 Bowdoin St [Ashburton]
• **Starbucks** • 1 Charles St [Beacon St]
• **Starbucks** • 222 Cambridge St [Irving St]
• **Starbucks** • 97 Charles St [Pinckney]
• **Tammy's Place** • 25 New Sudbury St [Bulfinch]

🖨 Copy Shops

• **Copy Clone** • 31 Mt Vernon St [Hancock St]
• **FedEx Kinko's** • 2 Center Plz [Cambridge St] ♿
• **Johnson's Printing** • 15 Tremont Pl [Beacon St]
• **The UPS Store** • 139 Charles St [Revere St]

🏋 Gyms

• **Beacon Hill Athletic Club** • 261 Friend St [Causeway]
• **Beacon Hill Athletic Club** • 3 Hancock St [Cambridge St]
• **Boston Sports Club** • 1 Bulfinch Pl [Bowdoin]
• **Fitcorp** • 1 Beacon St [Tremont St]

🔧 Hardware Stores

• **Charles Street Supply** • 54 Charles St [Mount Vernon St]

🍾 Liquor Stores

• **Beacon Capitol Market** • 32 Myrtle St [Joy St]
• **Beacon Hill Wine & Spirits** •
  63 Charles St [Mount Vernon St]
• **Charles Street Liquors** • 143 Charles St [Silver Pl]
• **DeLuca's Market** • 11 Charles St [Branch]
• **Demetri Brothers Liquor & Gifts** •
  53 Revere St [Grove St]
• **Jobi's Liquors** • 170 Cambridge St [Joy St]
• **Mccormack's Liquors** • 82 Hancock St [Mount Vernon St]
• **Simmons Liquor Store** • 210 Cambridge St [S Russell]
• **Swetts Liquors** • 3 Somerset St [Beacon St]

🎬 Movie Theaters

• **Mugar Omni Theatre** • Science Park [Monsignor O'Brien Hwy]

🍸 Nightlife

• **21st Amendment** • 150 Bowdoin St [Mount Vernon St]
• **6B** • 6 Beacon St #B [Tremont Pl]
• **Beacon Hill Pub** • 149 Charles St [Silver Pl]
• **Cheers** • 84 Beacon St [Brimmer]
• **The Four's** • 166 Canal St [Causeway]
• **Greatest Bar** • 262 Friend St [Causeway]
• **The Harp** • 85 Causeway St [Portland]
• **Hill Tavern** • 228 Cambridge St [Irving St]
• **Seven's** • 77 Charles St [Mount Vernon St]
• **Sullivan's Tap** • 168 Canal St [Causeway]

🍽 Restaurants

• **75 Chestnut** • 75 Chestnut St [River St]
• **Artu** • 89 Charles St [Pinckney]
• **Beacon Hill Bistro** • 25 Charles St [Chestnut St]
• **The Federalist** • XV Beacon Hotel •
  15 Beacon St [Somerset St]
• **Figs** • 42 Charles St [Chestnut St]
• **Grotto** • 37 Bowdoin St [Somerset St]
• **Harvard Gardens** • 316 Cambridge St [Grove St]
• **Hungry I** • 71 1/2 Charles St [Mount Vernon St]
• **King & I** • 145 Charles St [Silver Pl]
• **Lala Rokh** • 97 Mt Vernon St [W Cedar]
• **Ma Soba** • 156 Cambridge St [Hancock St]
• **Panificio** • 144 Charles St [Silver Pl]
• **The Paramount** • 44 Charles St [Chestnut St]
• **Phoenicia** • 240 Cambridge St [Garden St]
• **Pierrot** • 272 Cambridge St [Anderson St]
• **Upper Crust** • 20 Charles St [Branch]

🛍 Shopping

• **Black Ink** • 101 Charles St [Pinckney]
• **DeLuca's Market** • 11 Charles St [Branch]
• **Eugene Galleries** • 76 Charles St [Mount Vernon St]
• **The Flat of the Hill** • 60 Charles St [Mount Vernon St]
• **Good** • 88 Charles St [Pinckney]
• **Hilton's Tent City** • 272 Friend St [Causeway]
• **Moxie** • 51 Charles St [Mount Vernon St]
• **The Red Wagon** • 69 Charles St [Mount Vernon St]
• **Savenor's Market** • 160 Charles St [Cambridge St]
• **Wish** • 49 Charles St [Mount Vernon St]

🎲 Video Rental

• **Mike's Movies** • 250 Cambridge St [Garden St]

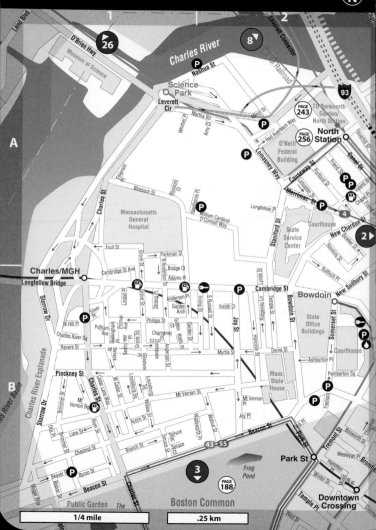

Map 1 · **Beacon Hill / West End**

Public transit (or your own two feet) remains the best way to travel in this parking-scarce neighborhood. A walk down Charles Street from the Charles/MGH Red Line T station to the Boston Common is an especially stress-free way to experience the area. If you simply must drive, be prepared for the havoc wreaked by never-ending construction.

Subway

- Bowdoin
- Charles/MGH
- Downtown Crossing
- North Station
- Park Street
- Science Park

Bus Lines

4 • North Station—World Trade Center via Federal Courthouse
43 • Ruggles Station—Park & Tremont Streets
55 • Jersey & Queensberry Streets—Copley Square or Park & Tremont Streets

Car Rental

- **Avis** • 3 Center Plz [Cambridge St] • 617-534-1400
- **Dollar** • Government Ctr • 209 Cambridge St [S Russell] • 617-723-8312

Car Washes

- **Professional Auto Detailers** • 1 Center Plz [Cambridge St]

Gas Stations

- **Arthur's Sunoco** • 70 River St [Mount Vernon St]
- **Exxon** • 239 Cambridge St [Blossom St] ✿
- **Gulf** • 296 Cambridge St [Strong]
- **Mobil** • 150 Friend St [Valenti]
- **Sunoco** • 70 River St [Mt Vernon St]

Parking

Map 2 • **North End / Faneuil Hall**

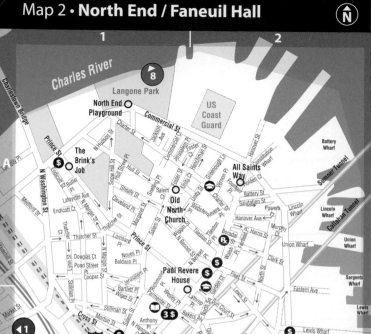

Boston's version of Little Italy, the North End is a maze of narrow streets and brick buildings with a decidedly European air. The first parks in the Rose Kennedy Greenway are seeded and waiting for spring to bloom, and with the Big Dig finally "done," the End is connected to Boston again for the first time in decades.

$ Banks

- **Bank of America** · 260 Hanover St [Parmenter]
- **Bank of America** · 60 State St [Kilby St]
- **Bank of America (ATM)** · 2 Atlantic Ave [High St]
- **Bank of America (ATM)** · 283 Causeway St [Endicott St]
- **Bank of America (ATM)** · 4 Commercial St [State]
- **Bank of America (ATM)** · 48-50 Salem St [Morton St]
- **Century Bank** · 136 State St [India St]
- **Century Bank** · 275 Hanover St [Richmond St]
- **Citizens Bank** · 28 State St [Congress]
- **Citizens Bank** · 315 Hanover St [Prince]
- **Citizens Bank** · 53 State St [Congress]
- **Citizens Bank (ATM)** · 1 Boston Pl [Court]
- **Citizens Bank (ATM)** · 1 Cambridge St [Sudbury]
- **Citizens Bank (ATM)** · 1 State St [Washington St]
- **Citizens Bank (ATM)** · 100 City Hall Plz [Cambridge St]
- **Citizens Bank (ATM)** · 177 State St [McKinley]
- **Citizens Bank (ATM)** · 342 Hanover St [N Bennet St]
- **Citizens Bank (ATM)** · 92 State St [Broad]
- **First National Bank of Ipswich** · 33 State St [Congress]
- **Sovereign Bank** · 287 Hanover St [Richmond St]
- **Sovereign Bank** · 75 State St [Kilby St]
- **Sovereign Bank (ATM)** · 1 Union St [North St]
- **Sovereign Bank (ATM)** · Central Wharf [Central St]
- **Sovereign Bank (ATM)** · CVS · 218 Hanover St [Cross St]

Donuts

- **Dunkin' Donuts** · 1 Congress St [North St]
- **Dunkin' Donuts** · 1 Fleet Ctr [Hanover St]
- **Dunkin' Donuts** · 100 City Hall Plz [Cambridge St]
- **Dunkin' Donuts** · 111 State St [Broad]
- **Dunkin' Donuts** · 2 City Hall Sq [Cambridge St]
- **Dunkin' Donuts** · 20 North St [Scott Aly]

O Landmarks

- **All Saints Way** · Battery St & Hanover St
- **The Boston Stone** · Marshall St [Hanover St]
- **Boston Tea Kettle** · 63 Court St [Cambridge St]
- **The Brink's Job** · 165 Prince St [Causeway]
- **Christopher Columbus Park** · Atlantic Ave
- **City Hall** · 1 City Hall Plz [Cambridge St]
- **Faneuil Hall** · Congress St & North St
- **Holocaust Memorial** · Congress St at Union St [Congress]
- **New England Aquarium** · Central Wharf [Central St]
- **North End Playground** · Commercial St & Foster St
- **Old North Church** · 193 Salem St [Hull St]
- **Paul Revere House** · 19 North Sq [Garden Ct St]
- **Union Oyster House** · 41 Union St [Marshall St]

Libraries

- **North End** · 25 Parmenter St [Hanover St]

Pharmacies

- **CVS** · 218 Hanover St [Cross St]
- **Green Cross Pharmacy** · 393 Hanover St [Clark St]

Post Offices

- **Hanover Street Station** · 217 Hanover St [Cross St]
- **Post Offices** · Faneuil Hall Retail Unit · 1 Faneuil Hall Sq [S Market]

Schools

- **Eliot Elementary** · 16 Charter St [Unity St]
- **St John** · 9 Moon St [Lewis St]

Map 2 • North End / Faneuil Hall

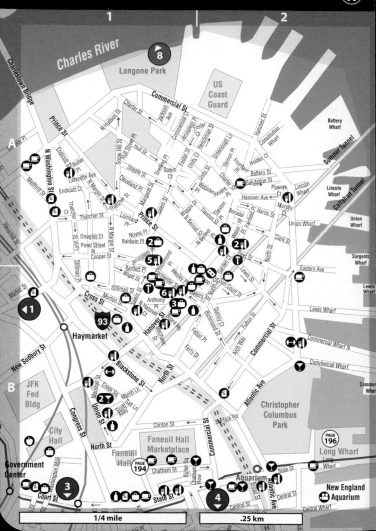

Sundries / Entertainment

Map 2

It would take some effort to find a bad meal in the North End; keep it real at L'Osteria or up the ante at Maurizio's. By night, young professionals reemerge from Faneuil Hall and hit the clubs—hard. Night owls stop by Bova's Bakery for a tasty pastry at 3 am.

☕ Coffee

- **Anne-Marie's Place** •
  251 Causeway St [Medford St]
- **Boston Bean Stock Coffee** •
  97 Salem St [Wiget]
- **Caffe Paradiso** •
  255 Hanover St [Richmond St]
- **Caffe Victoria** • 296 Hanover St [Prince]
- **Causeway Café** •
  239 Causeway St [Medford St]
- **Contrata's** • 396 Hanover St [Salutation]
- **Polcari's Coffee Shop** •
  105 Salem St [Parmenter]
- **Red Barn Coffee Roasters** •
  1 Faneuil Hall Sq [S Market]
- **Starbucks** • 2 Atlantic Ave [High St]
- **Starbucks** • 2-4 Faneuil Hall
  Marketplace [Commercial St]
- **Starbucks** • Boston Long Wharf Marriott
  • 296 State St [Atlantic Ave]
- **Starbucks** • 63 Court St [Cambridge St]
- **Starbucks** • 63 Court St [Kilby St]

📋 Copy Shops

- **AlphaGraphics** • 74 Canal St [Valenti]
- **FedEx Kinko's** • 60 State St [Kilby St]
- **Sir Speedy Printing Center** • 123 N
  Washington St [Medford St]
- **Staples** • 25 Court St [Tremont St]
- **The UPS Store** •
  71 Commercial St [Cross St]

🌾 Farmers Markets

- **City Hall Plaza**
  (May–Nov, Mon 11–6, Wed 11–6) •
  City Hall Plz at Cambridge St [Cambridge St]

🏋 Gyms

- **Beacon Hill Athletic Club** •
  85 Atlantic Ave [High St]
- **Fitness Together** •
  145 Hanover St [Blackstone]

🔧 Hardware Stores

- **Boston Hardware** •
  16 Fleet St [Garden Ct St]
- **Salem Street True Value** •
  89 Salem St [Wiget]

🍾 Liquor Stores

- **Cirace's Liquor** • 173 North St [Moon]
- **Federal Wine & Spirits** •
  29 State St [Devonshire]

- **Hanover Liquors** • 363 Hanover St [N
  Bennet St]
- **Martignetti Liquors** • 64 Cross St
  [Morton St]
- **Wine Bottega (wine only)** • 341
  Hanover St [Prince]
- **Wine Cave** • 33 Union St [Marshall St]

🎬 Movie Theaters

- **Simons IMAX Theatre** • Central Wharf
  [Central St]

🎤 Nightlife

- **Bell in Hand Tavern** •
  45 Union St [Marshall St]
- **Black Rose** • 160 State St [Commercial St]
- **Boston Beer Works** •
  112 Canal St [Valenti]
- **Boston Rocks** • 245 Quincy Market
- **Boston Sail Loft** •
  80 Atlantic Ave [High St]
- **Green Dragon Tavern** •
  11 Marshall St [Hanover St]
- **The Hong Kong** •
  65 Chatham St [Chatham Row]
- **McFadden's** • 148 State St [India St]
- **Paddy O's** • 33 Union St [Marshall St]
- **Parris** • Quincy Market [S Market]
- **Purple Shamrock** • 1 Union St [North St]
- **Sanctuary** • 189 State St [McKinley]
- **Tia's on the Waterfront** •
  200 Atlantic Ave [State]
- **Vertigo** • 126 State St [Broad]

🍴 Restaurants

- **Al's State Street Café** •
  110 State St [Broad]
- **Antico Forno** • 93 Salem St [Wiget]
- **Billy Tse** •
  240 Commercial St [Atlantic Ave]
- **Boston Sail Loft** • 80 Atlantic Ave [High St]
- **Bova's Bakery** • 134 Salem St [Prince]
- **Bricco** • 241 Hanover St [Cross St]
- **Caffe Paradiso** •
  255 Hanover St [Richmond St]
- **The Daily Catch** •
  323 Hanover St [Prince]
- **Galleria Umberto** •
  289 Hanover St [Richmond St]
- **Green Dragon Tavern** •
  11 Marshall St [Hanover St]
- **Haymarket Pizza** •
  106 Blackstone St [Hanover St]
- **Il Panino Express** •
  11 Parmenter St [Hanover St]
- **L'Osteria** • 104 Salem St [Bartlett Pl]
- **La Famiglia Giorgio's** •
  112 Salem St [Cooper]
- **La Summa** • 30 Fleet St [McClellan Hwy]

- **Lucca** • 226 Hanover St [Cross St]
- **Lulu's Bake Shoppe** •
  227 Hanover St [N Hanover]
- **Mamma Maria** • 3 North Sq [Garden Ct St]
- **Massimino's Cucina Italiana** •
  207 Endicott St [Lafayette]
- **Maurizio's** • 364 Hanover St [N Bennet St]
- **McCormick & Schmick's** • Faneuil Hall
  Marketplace [S Market]
- **Neptune Oyster** • 63 Salem St [Morton St]
- **Pizzeria Regina** •
  11 1/2 Thacher St [N Margin]
- **Prezza** • 24 Fleet St [Garden Ct St]
- **Sel de la Terre** •
  255 State St [Atlantic Ave]
- **Taranta** • 210 Hanover St [Cross St]
- **Theo's Cozy Corner** •
  162 Salem St [Tileston St]
- **Trani** • 111 Salem St [Cooper]
- **Union Oyster House** •
  41 Union St [Marshall St]
- **Wagamama Faneuil Hall** •
  Quincy Market Building

🛍 Shopping

- **Bova's Bakery** • 134 Salem St [Prince]
- **Brooks Brothers** • 75 State St [Kilby St]
- **Dairy Fresh Candies** •
  57 Salem St [Morton St]
- **Fresh Cheese** • 81 Endicott St [Stillman St]
- **Green Cross Pharmacy** •
  393 Hanover St [Clark St]
- **Holbrows Flowers** •
  100 City Hall Plz [Cambridge St]
- **Karma** • 26 Prince St [Hanover St]
- **Maria's Pastry Shop** •
  46 Cross St [Morton St]
- **Mike's Pastry** • 300 Hanover St [Prince]
- **Modern Pastry** •
  257 Hanover St [Richmond St]
- **Monica's Salumeria** •
  130 Salem St [Prince]
- **Newbury Comics** •
  1 Washington Mall [Court]
- **Salumeria Italiana** •
  151 Richmond St [North St]
- **Salumeria Toscana** •
  272 Hanover St [Parmenter]
- **Stanza dei Sigari** •
  292 Hanover St [Prince]
- **Staples** • 25 Court St [Tremont St]

📹 Video Rental

- **North End Video** • 292 North St [Moon]

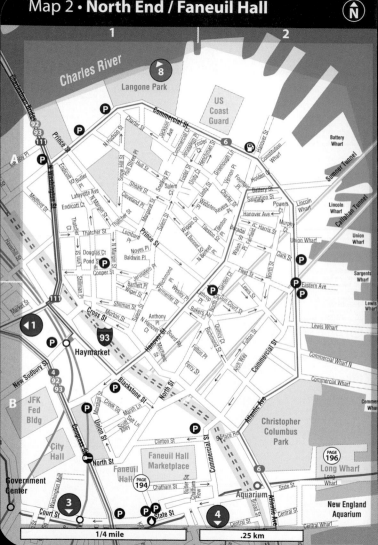

Map 2 · North End / Faneuil Hall

Take the T. Just take the T. Honestly. If you're one of those people who can afford to valet, or doesn't mind parking at one of the garages along Atlantic, so be it. Most of the charm of the North End involves walking around and eating and looking for parking for 45 minutes tends to kill the mood.

Subway

- **· Aquarium**
- **· Haymarket**
- **· State**

Bus Lines

- **4** · North Station—World Trade Center via Federal Courthouse
- **6** · Boston Marine Industrial Park—South Station/ Haymarket Station
- **92** · Assembly Square Mall—Downtown via Sullivan Square Station, Main Street
- **93** · Sullivan Square Station—Downtown via Bunker Hill Street & Haymarket Station
- **111** · Woodlawn or Broadway & Park Ave— Haymarket Station via Mystic River/Tobin Bridge

Car Rental

· **Enterprise** · 1 Congress St [North St] · 617-723-8077

Car Washes

· **Bradford Auto Park & Wax** · 75 State St [Kilby St]

Gas Stations

· **Mobil** · 420 Commercial St [Holden Ct]

Parking

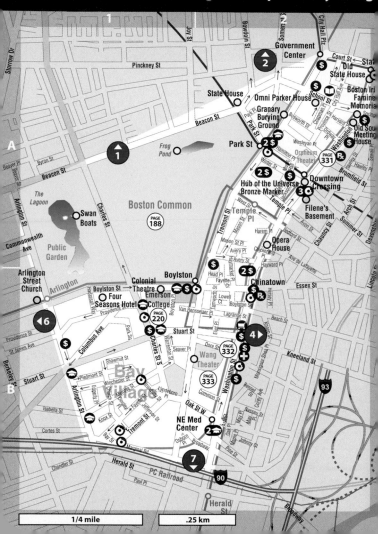

Essentials

Downtown Crossing is abuzz with pedestrians from all walks of life. You'll find a lively mixture of financial types, shoppers, New England Medical Center doctors, and the down-and-out. High-end development continues, but remnants of the old Combat Zone remain. Bay Village, a tiny 19th-Century enclave, is pleasantly serene after a snowstorm.

$ Banks

- **Bank of America** · 157 Stuart St [Warrenton St]
- **Bank of America** · 315 Washington St [Milk St]
- **Bank of America** · 6 Tremont St [Court]
- **Bank of America** · 710 Washington St [Kneeland]
- **Bank of America (ATM)** · 11 Winter St [Winter Pl]
- **Bank of America (ATM)** · 175 Tremont St [Avery St]
- **Bank of America (ATM)** · 58 Winter St [Tremont St]
- **Bank of America (ATM)** · 630 Washington St [Essex]
- **Bank of America (ATM)** · 80 Boylston St [Tremont St]
- **Cathay Bank** · 621 Washington St [Hayward Pl]
- **Citizens Bank** · 73 Tremont St [Beacon St]
- **Citizens Bank (ATM)** · 1 Milk St [Washington St]
- **Citizens Bank (ATM)** · 630 Washington St [Kneeland]
- **Sovereign Bank** · 30 Winter St [Winter Pl]
- **Sovereign Bank** · 61 Arlington St [St James Ave]
- **Sovereign Bank (ATM)** ·
  600 Washington St [Hayward Pl]
- **Sovereign Bank (ATM)** ·
  769 Washington St [Kneeland]

⊙ Donuts

- **Dunkin' Donuts** · 1 Summer St [Washington St]
- **Dunkin' Donuts** · 127 Tremont St [Park St]
- **Dunkin' Donuts** · 130 Broadway [Melrose St]
- **Dunkin' Donuts** · 235 Washington St [Devonshire Pl]
- **Dunkin' Donuts** · 357 Tremont St [Church St]
- **Dunkin' Donuts** · 363 Tremont St [Marginal Rd]
- **Dunkin' Donuts** · 417 Washington St [Winter St]
- **Dunkin' Donuts** · 426 Washington St [Winter St]
- **Dunkin' Donuts** · 630 Washington St [Essex]
- **Dunkin' Donuts** · 750 Washington St [Kneeland]
- **Dunkin' Donuts** · 8 Park Plz [Boylston St]
- **Dunkin' Donuts** · 80 Boylston St [Tremont St]

✚ Emergency Rooms

- **Tufts-New England Medical Center** ·
  750 Washington St [Kneeland]

○ Landmarks

- **Arlington Street Church** ·
  351 Boylston St [Arlington St]
- **Boston Irish Famine Memorial** ·
  School St & Washington St
- **Boston Opera House** ·
  539 Washington St [Ave de Lafayette]
- **Colonial Theatre** · 106 Boylston St [Tremont St]
- **Four Seasons Hotel** · 200 Boylston St [Charles St]
- **Frog Pond** · Boston Common
- **Granary Burying Ground** · Tremont St & Park St
- **Harriet Tubman Square** · Columbus Sq
- **Hub of the Universe Bronze Marker** ·
  Washington St & Summer St
- **John Hancock's Phallic Gravestone** ·
  Tremont St & Park St
- **Old South Meeting House** ·
  310 Washington St [Milk St]
- **Old State House** · 206 Washington St [Court]
- **Omni Parker House** · 60 School St [Chapman]
- **Opera House** · 539 Washington St [Ave de Lafayette]
- **State House** · Beacon St & Park St
- **Swan Boats** · Arlington St & Boylston St
- **Wang Theater** · 270 Tremont St [Hollis St]

📖 Libraries

- **Kirstein Business** · 20 City Hall Ave [Pi]

℞ Pharmacies

- **CVS** · 631 Washington St [Essex]

🎓 Schools

- **Boston Renaissance Charter** ·
  250 Stuart St [Church St]
- **Emerson College** · 120 Boylston St [Boylston Pl]
- **Josiah Quincy Elementary** ·
  885 Washington St [Oak St W]
- **Josiah Quincy Upper School** ·
  900 Washington St [Pine St]
- **New England School of Law** ·
  154 Stuart St [Warrenton St]
- **Quincy Upper** ·
  152 Arlington St [Melrose]
- **Suffolk University Law School** ·
  120 Tremont St [Hamilton Pl]
- **Transportation Children's Center** ·
  10 Park Plz [Providence]

🛒 Supermarkets

- **C-Mart** · 692 Washington St [Kneeland]

Map 3

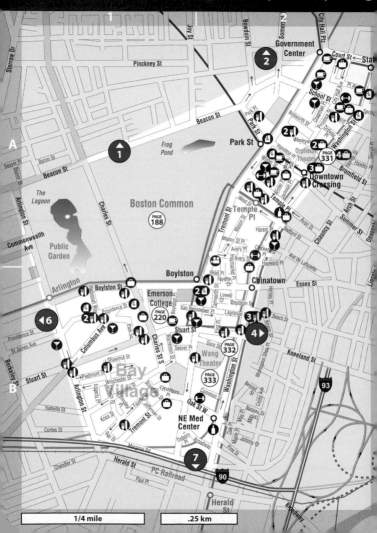

Map 3 · Downtown Crossing/Park Square/Bay Village

Sundries / Entertainment

Map 3

Locals still mourn the loss of Jordan Marsh. It's hard to get excited about TJ Maxx and Marshall's. The best way to finish a weekday shopping excursion here is with a scrumptious Chilean sandwich from Chacarero (take-away only). For a top-end meal, try Aujourd'hui, Excelsior, or No. 9 Park across the Common.

Coffee

- **Café** • 1 City Hall Plz [Court]
- **Rachel's Kitchen** •
  12 Church St [Fayette St]
- **Starbucks** • 12 Winter St [Washington St]
- **Starbucks** • 143 Stuart St [Warrenton St]
- **Starbucks** •
  240 Washington St [Water]
- **Starbucks** • 27 School St [Province St]
- **Starbucks** • 62 Boylston St [Tremont St]
- **Tremont Tea Room (tea only)** •
  48 Winter St [Tremont St]

Copy Shops

- **BFS Business Printing** •
  10 Park Plz [Providence]
- **Copy Cop** •
  260 Washington St [Water]
- **Emerson College Print Copy Center** • 80 Boylston St [Tremont St]
- **FedEx Kinko's** •
  125 Tremont St [Park St]
- **Mail Boxes Etc** •
  276 Washington St [Spring Ln]
- **Staples** • 25 Winter St [Winter Pl]
- **The UPS Store** •
  198 Tremont St [Boylston St]

Gyms

- **Bally Total Fitness** •
  17 Winter St [Winter Pl]
- **Sports Club LA** •
  4 Avery St [Washington St]
- **Wang YMCA of Chinatown** •
  8 Oak St W [Tremont St]
- **Women's Fitness of Boston** •
  27 School St [Province St]

Liquor Stores

- **Boston Liquor Depot** •
  861 Washington St [Oak St W]
- **Wine Cellar** •
  497 Washington St [Temple Pl]

Movie Theaters

- **AMC Loews Boston Common** •
  175 Tremont St [Avery St]

Nightlife

- **Aria** • 246 Tremont St [Stuart]
- **Felt** •
  533 Washington St [Ave de Lafayette]
- **Jacque's** • 79 Broadway [Winchester St]
- **Limelight Stage and Studios** •
  204 Tremont St [Lagrange]
- **Matrix** • 275 Tremont St [Hollis St]
- **MJ O'Connor's** •
  27 Columbus Ave [Park Sq]
- **Mojitos Lounge** •
  48 Winter St [Tremont St]
- **Parker's Bar** • 60 School St [Chapman]
- **Roxy** • 279 Tremont St [Common]
- **Rumor** • 100 Warrenton St [Stuart]
- **The Tam** • 222 Tremont St [Stuart]
- **Venu** • 100 Warrenton St [Stuart]
- **Whiskey Park** •
  64 Arlington St [Providence]

Restaurants

- **Aujourd'hui** •
  200 Boylston St [Charles St]
- **Bonfire** • Park Plaza Hotel •
  50 Park Plz [Providence St]
- **Buddha's Delight** •
  5 Beach St [Washington St]
- **Chacarero** •
  426 Washington St [Winter St]
- **Dedo** • 69 Church St [Piedmont]
- **Emperor's Garden** •
  690 Washington St [Lagrange]
- **Excelsior** • 272 Boylston St [Hadassah]
- **Herrera's Mexican Grille** •
  11 Temple Pl [Tremont St]
- **Intermission Tavern** •
  228 Tremont St [Stuart]
- **Jacob Wirth** •
  31 Stuart St [Dartmouth St]
- **Know Fat!** •
  530 Washington St [Ave de Lafayette]
- **Legal Sea Foods** •
  26 Park Plz [Hadassah]
- **Locke-Ober** • 3 Winter Pl [Winter St]
- **Lu's Sandwich Shop** •
  2 Knapp St [Monsignor Shea Rd]
- **Mantra** • 52 Temple Pl [Tremont St]
- **McCormick & Schmick's** •
  34 Columbus Ave [Park Sq]
- **Montien** • 63 Stuart St [Tremont St]
- **New Saigon Sandwich** •
  696 Washington St [Kneeland]
- **New York Pizza** •
  224 Tremont St [Lagrange]
- **No. 9 Park** • 9 Park St [Beacon St]
- **Penang** •
  685 Washington St [Lagrange]
- **Pigalle** • 75 Charles St S [Stuart]
- **Rachel's Kitchen** •
  12 Church St [Fayette St]
- **Sam LaGrassa's** •
  44 Province St [Bosworth]
- **Silvertone Bar & Grill** •
  69 Bromfield St [Tremont St]
- **Smith & Wollensky** •
  101 Arlington St [Stuart]
- **Teatro** • 177 Tremont St [Head]
- **Tequila Mexican Grill** •
  55 Bromfield St [Tremont St]
- **Via Matta** • 79 Park Plz [Hadassah]
- **Viga** • 304 Stuart St [Arlington St]

Shopping

- **Beacon Hill Skate Shop** •
  135 Charles St [Fayette St]
- **Borders** • 10 School St [Washington St]
- **Bromfield Camera & Video** •
  10 Bromfield St [Washington St]
- **City Antiques** •
  362 Tremont St [Jefferson St]
- **City Sports** •
  11 Bromfield St [Washington St]
- **DSW** • 385 Washington St [Bromfield]
- **Eddie Bauer Outlet** •
  500 Washington St [West St]
- **H&M** • 350 Washington St [Franklin St]
- **Lambert's** •
  Washington St & Summer St
- **LJ Peretti** • 2 1/2 Park Sq
- **Macy's** • 450 Washington St [Temple Pl]
- **Marshall's** •
  350 Washington St [Franklin St]
- **Roche-Bobois** •
  2 Avery St [Washington St]
- **Staples** • 25 Winter St [Winter Pl]
- **TJ Maxx** •
  350 Washington St [Franklin St]
- **Windsor Buttons** •
  35 Temple Pl [Tremont St]

Video Rental

- **Kung Fu Video** •
  365 Washington St [Bromfield]

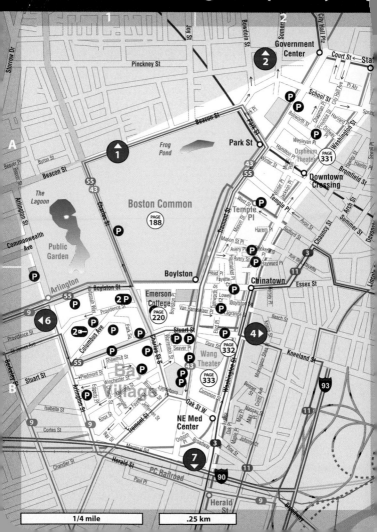

Map 3 • Downtown Crossing/Park Square/Bay Village

1/4 mile   .25 km

Transportation

Map 3

This area is well served by the T and buses, and there's little reason to drive around here. Note that Tremont Street runs in only one direction until it intersects with, uh, Tremont Street, and that Washington Street north of Temple Place in Downtown Crossing is a pedestrian mall closed to traffic.

Subway

- **Arlington**
- **Boylston**
- **Chinatown**
- **Downtown Crossing**
- **Government Center**
- **NE Medical Center**
- **Park Street**

Bus Lines

3 • Boston Marine Industrial Park—South Station/
   Haymarket Station

9 • City Point—Copley Square via Broadway
   Station

11 • City Point—Downtown, Bayview Route

43 • Ruggles Station—Park & Tremont Streets

55 • Jersey & Queensberry Streets—Copley Square
   or Park & Tremont Streets

Car Rental

- **Budget** • Motor Mart Garage •
  28 Park Plz • 617-497-3669
- **Hertz** • 30 Park Plz • 617-338-1500

Parking

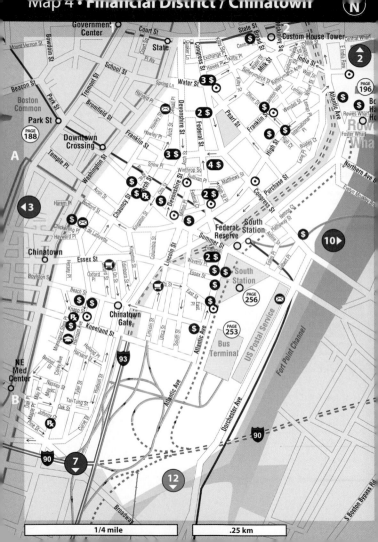

Essentials

Map 4

With the Big Dig finally over, attention has turned to the Rose Kennedy Greenway, a mixed-use green space that will pull together the heart of the Financial District and buildings along the waterfront. In the meantime, Boston's Chinatown bustles. For an introduction, stroll and window-shop along Beach Street and its cross-streets.

$ Banks

- **Asian American Bank & Trust** •
  68 Harrison Ave [Beach St]
- **Bank of America** • 100 Federal St [Franklin St]
- **Bank of America** • 125 High St [Pearl St]
- **Bank of America** • 175 Federal St [High St]
- **Bank of America** • 65 Franklin St [Arch St]
- **Bank of America (ATM)** • 0 Post Office Sq [Congress]
- **Bank of America (ATM)** • 1 Financial Ctr [Summer]
- **Bank of America (ATM)** • 1 Post Office Sq [Water]
- **Bank of America (ATM)** • 175 Federal St [High St]
- **Bank of America (ATM)** • 30 Rowes Wharf [High St]
- **Bank of America (ATM)** • 730 Atlantic Ave [Beach St]
- **Bank of America (ATM)** • 79 Summer St [Otis St]
- **Banknorth Massachusetts** • 15 Broad St [Doane]
- **Banknorth Massachusetts** •
  75 Federal St [Franklin St]
- **Boston Private Bank & Trust** •
  10 Post Office Sq [Water]
- **Century Bank** • 24 Federal St [Milk St]
- **Century Bank** • 280 Atlantic Ave [Central St]
- **Citizens Bank** • 1 Financial Ctr [Summer]
- **Citizens Bank** • 40 Summer St [Arch St]
- **Citizens Bank** • 6 Ave de Lafayette [Chauncy St]
- **Citizens Bank** • 77 Franklin St [Arch St]
- **Citizens Bank (ATM)** •
  2 Delafayette Ave [Harrison Ave]
- **Citizens Bank (ATM)** • 650 Atlantic Ave [Essex]
- **Citizens Bank (ATM)** • 700 Atlantic Ave [Last St]
- **Eastern Bank** • 101 Federal St [Matthews]
- **Eastern Bank** • 265 Franklin St [Oliver]
- **One United Bank** • 133 Federal St [Milton Pl]
- **Sovereign Bank** • 1 Federal St [Milk St]
- **Sovereign Bank** • 100 Oliver St [High St]
- **Sovereign Bank** • 125 Summer St [Bedford]
- **Sovereign Bank** • 2 South Station Concourse [Essex]
- **Sovereign Bank** • 43 Kneeland St [Harrison Ave]
- **Sovereign Bank** • 61 Harrison Ave [Beach St]
- **Sovereign Bank (ATM)** • 160 Federal St [Milton Pl]
- **Sovereign Bank (ATM)** • CVS/Pharmacy •
  55 Summer St [Arch St]
- **Sovereign Bank (ATM)** • CVS/Pharmacy •
  81 Milk St [Congress]
- **Wainwright Bank & Trust** • 63 Franklin St [Arch St]

⊙ Donuts

- **Dunkin' Donuts** • 10 Winthrop Sq [Devonshire]
- **Dunkin' Donuts** • 101 Summer St [Lincoln St]
- **Dunkin' Donuts** • 16 Kneeland St [Shea]
- **Dunkin' Donuts** • 176 Federal St [High St]
- **Dunkin' Donuts** • 265 Franklin St [Oliver]
- **Dunkin' Donuts** • 3 Post Office Sq [Water]
- **Dunkin' Donuts** • 70 E India Row [Atlantic Ave]
- **Honey Dew Donuts** • South Station •
  700 Atlantic Ave [East St]

O Landmarks

- **Boston Harbor Hotel** • 70 Rowes Wharf [High St]
- **Chinatown Gate** • Beach St & Hudson St
- **Custom House Tower** • 3 McKinley Sq [Central St]
- **Federal Reserve** • 600 Atlantic Ave [Summer]
- **South Station** • Atlantic Ave & Summer St

℞ Pharmacies

- **CVS** • 340 Washington St [Bromfield]
- **CVS** • 55 Summer St [Chauncy St]
- **PharmaCare Specialty Pharmacy** •
  35 Kneeland St [Harrison Ave]
- **Tai Tung Pharmacy** • 256 Harrison Ave [Johnny]

✉ Post Offices

- **Fort Point Station** • 25 Dorchester Ave [Summer]
- **Lafayette Station** • 7 Ave de Lafayette [Chauncy St]
- **Milk Street** • 31 Milk St [Arch St]

🎓 Schools

- **Tufts University School of Medicine** •
  136 Harrison Ave [Harvard St]

🛒 Supermarkets

- **C-Mart** • 109 Lincoln St [Tufts]
- **Super 88** • 73 Essex St [Oxford St]

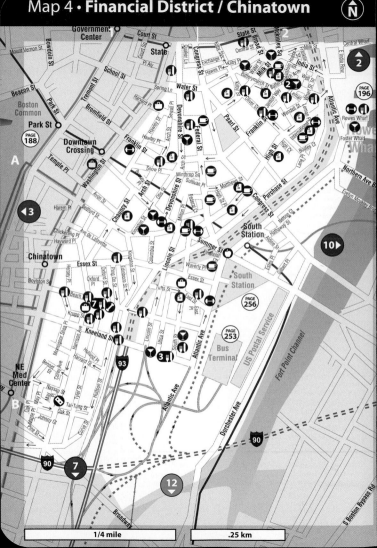

Map 4 • **Financial District / Chinatown**

Sundries / Entertainment

Map 4

Chinatown = Chau Chow City for dim sum, Taiwan Café for the real deal, Ocean Wealth for seafood, or Shabu-Zen for Japanese hot pot. For late-night bites, remember that neighbors News and South Street Diner serve well into the night. Some of Boston's top restaurants, including Radius, Julien, and Meritage, call the Financial District home.

☕ Coffee

• **Bean & Leaf Company** • 20 Custom House St [India St]
• **Peet's Coffee & Tea** • 176 Federal St [High St]
• **Starbucks** • 1 Federal St [Milk St]
• **Starbucks** • 1 Financial Ctr [Summer]
• **Starbucks** • 1 International Pl [High St]
• **Starbucks** • 101 Federal St [Matthews]
• **Starbucks** • 211 Congress St [High St]
• **Starbucks** • 125 Summer St [High St]

🖨 Copy Shops

• **Air Graphics** • 89 Broad St [Franklin St]
• **BFS Business Printing** • 76 South St [Tufts]
• **Boston Business Printing** • 115 Broad St [Wendell St]
• **Copy Cop** • 125 High St [Pearl St]
• **Copy Cop** • 05 Franklin St [Devonshire]
• **FedEx Kinko's** • 10 Post Office Sq [Water]
• **FedEx Kinko's** • 211 Congress St [High St]
• **Litigation Document Productions** •
  61 Batterymarch St, Fl 4 [Wendell St]
• **News Clips Etc Inc** • 42 Chauncy St [Summer]
• **Sir Speedy Printing** • 1 Milk St [Washington St]

🌽 Farmers Markets

• **Dewey Square**
  (May–Nov; M,W,Th; 11:30 am–6:30 pm) •
  Atlantic Ave & Summer St

🏋 Gyms

• **Boston Sports Club** • 10 Franklin St [Washington St]
• **Boston Sports Club** • 695 Atlantic Ave [East St]
• **Boston Racquet Club** • 100 Summer St [Bedford]
• **Fitcorp** • 125 Summer St [Bedford]
• **Fitness International** • 1 International Pl [High St]
• **Langham Hotel Health Club** • 250 Franklin St [Oliver]
• **Rowes Wharf Health Club & Spa** •
  70 Rowes Wharf [High St]

🍸 Nightlife

• **An Tain** • 31 India St [Milk St]
• **Aqua** • 120 Water St [Kilby St]
• **Elephant & Castle** • 161 Devonshire St [Milk St]
• **Good Life** • 28 Kingston St [Bedford]
• **JJ Foley's** • 21 Kingston St [Summer]
• **Jose McIntyre's** • 160 Milk St [India St]
• **Les Zygomates** • 129 South St [Tufts]
• **Mr Dooley's Boston Tavern** • 77 Broad St [Custom]
• **News** • 150 Kneeland St [Utica St]

• **Rowes Wharf Bar** • Boston Harbor Hotel •
  70 Rowes Wharf [High St]
• **Times Restaurant and Bar** • 112 Broad St [Wendell St]
• **Umbria** • 295 Franklin St [Batterymarch St]

🐾 Pet Shops

• **Aqua World (fish only)** • 20 Tyler St [Kneeland]

🍴 Restaurants

• **Chau Chow City** • 83 Essex St [Ping]
• **China Pearl** • 9 Tyler St [Beach St]
• **Ginza** • 16 Hudson St [Kneeland]
• **Hei La Moon** • 88 Beach St [Lincoln St]
• **The Hong Kong Eatery** • 79 Harrison Ave [Knapp]
• **J Pace & Son** • 1 Federal St [Devonshire]
• **Julien** • Langham Hotel • 250 Franklin St [Oliver]
• **King Fung Garden** • 74 Kneeland St [Hudson St]
• **Les Zygomates** • 129 South St [Tufts]
• **Mei Sum Inc** • 40 Beach St [Harrison Av]
• **Meritage** • 70 Rowes Wharf [High St]
• **Milk Street Café** • 50 Milk St [Devonshire]
• **New Shanghai** • 21 Hudson St [Kneeland]
• **News** • 150 Kneeland St [Utica St]
• **Noodle Alcove** • 10 Tyler St [Beach St]
• **Ocean Wealth** • 8 Tyler St [Beach St]
• **Osushi** • 101 Arch St [Snow Pl]
• **Peach Farm** • 4 Tyler St [Beach St]
• **Pho Hoa** • 17 Beach St [Shea]
• **Pizza Oggi** • 131 Broad St [Wendell St]
• **Pressed Sandwiches** • 2 Oliver St [Milk St]
• **Radius** • 8 High St [Summer]
• **Sakurabana** • 57 Broad St [Broad]
• **Shabu-Zen** • 16 Tyler St [Beach St]
• **South Street Diner** • 178 Kneeland St [South St] ☼
• **Sultan's Kitchen** • 116 State St [Broad]
• **Taiwan Café** • 34 Oxford St [Oxford Pl]
• **Umbria** • 295 Franklin St [Batterymarch St]
• **Xinh Xinh** • 7 Beach St [Monsignor Shea Rd]

🛍 Shopping

• **Anna's Dessert House** • 66 Harrison Ave [Beach St]

📀 Video Rental

• **Top Ten Video Music (Chinese)** • 219 Harrison Ave [Oak St]

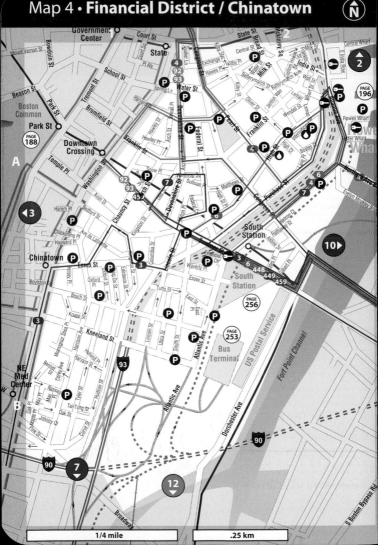

Map 4 • **Financial District / Chinatown**

Map 4

The Dig may be over, and all of the lanes in O'Neill Tunnel may finally be open, but there's still some surface road construction in the Financial District. If you don't need to drive here, don't, especially during rush hour. There is street parking on weeknights/weekend nights if you look hard enough.

Subway

- · Chinatown
- · Downtown Crossing
- · Park Street
- · South Station
- · State

Bus Lines

- **3** · Boston Marine Industrial Park—South Station/ Haymarket Station
- **4** · North Station—World Trade Center via Federal Courthouse
- **6** · Boston Marine Industrial Park—South Station/ Haymarket Station
- **7** · City Point—Otis & Summer Streets via Northern Avenue & South Station
- **92** · Assembly Square Mall—Downtown via Sullivan Square Station, Main Street
- **93** · Sullivan Square Station—Downtown via Bunker Hill Street & Haymarket Station
- **448** · Marblehead—Haymarket, Downtown Crossing, or Wonderland
- **449** · Marblehead—Haymarket, Downtown Crossing, or Wonderland
- **459** · Marblehead—Haymarket, Downtown Crossing, or Wonderland

Car Rental

- · **Alamo** · 270 Atlantic Ave [Central St] · 617-557-7179
- · **Dollar** · Boston Harbor Hotel · 30 Rowes Wharf [High St] · 617-367-2654
- · **Hertz** · 2 International Pl [Purchase] · 617-204-1165
- · **Hertz** · South Station Amtrak · Summer St & Atlantic Ave · 617-338-1503
- · **National** · 270 Atlantic Ave [E India] · 617-557-7179

Car Washes

- · **Executive Car Care** · 125 High St [Pearl St]

Parking

Map 5 · **Back Bay (West) / Fenway (East)** Ⓝ

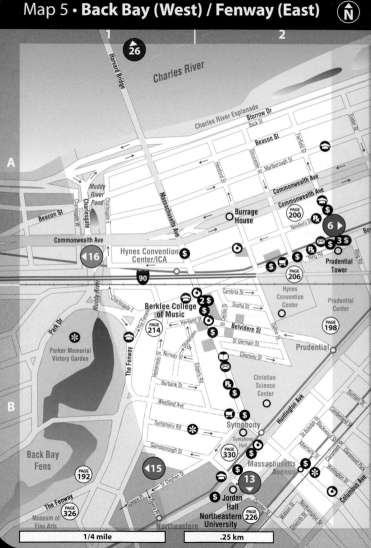

Essentials

Traffic on Mass Ave! MassPIRG on Newbury Street! Berklee students between classes! This area is fraught with minor perils, but that's because there's a lot going on here. The striking group of buildings that comprises the Christian Science Center, together with the Pru and 111 Huntington (the "Daily Planet"), looks great at night.

$ Banks

- **Bank of America** •
  133 Massachusetts Ave [Boylston St]
- **Bank of America** •
  285 Huntington Ave [Gainsborough]
- **Bank of America** • 855 Boylston St [Gloucester]
- **Bank of America** •
  133 Massachusetts Ave [Boylston St]
- **Bank of America (ATM)** •
  161 Massachusetts Ave [Belvidere St]
- **Bank of America (ATM)** •
  221 Massachusetts Ave [Clearway]
- **Bank of America (ATM)** •
  285 Huntington Ave [Gainsborough]
- **Bank of America (ATM)** •
  393 Massachusetts Ave [St Botolph St]
- **Bank of America (ATM)** •
  346 Huntington Ave [Opera]
- **Bank of America (ATM)** •
  800 Boylston St [Fairfield St]
- **Bank of America (ATM)** •
  90 Massachusetts Ave [Comm Ave]
- **Citizens Bank (ATM)** •
  141 Massachusetts Ave [Boylston St]
- **Citizens Bank (ATM)** • 800 Boylston St [Fairfield St]
- **Citizens Bank (ATM)** • 900 Boylston St [Gloucester]
- **Sovereign Bank** • 279 Massachusetts Ave [Westland]
- **Sovereign Bank** • 800 Boylston St [Fairfield St]
- **Sovereign Bank (ATM)** • CVS/Pharmacy •
  240 Newbury St [Fairfield St]
- **Sovereign Bank (ATM)** • 799 Boylston St [Fairfield St]

✴ Community Gardens

◉ Donuts

- **Dunkin' Donuts** • 1108 Boylston St [Hemenway St]
- **Dunkin' Donuts** •
  153 Massachusetts Ave [Belvidere St]
- **Dunkin' Donuts** • 283 Huntington Ave [Gainsborough]
- **Dunkin' Donuts** • 333 Newbury St [Hereford]
- **Dunkin' Donuts** • 434 Massachusetts Ave [Columbus]

○ Landmarks

- **Burrage House** • 314 Commonwealth Ave [Hereford]
- **Christian Science Center** •
  175 Huntington Ave [W Newton]
- **Hynes Convention Center** •
  900 Boylston St [Gloucester]
- **Jordan Hall** • 30 Gainsborough St [Huntington]
- **Prudential Tower** • 800 Boylston St [Fairfield St]
- **Symphony Hall** •
  301 Massachusetts Ave [Huntington]

📖 Libraries

- **The Mary Baker Eddy Library** •
  200 Massachusetts Ave [Clearway]

℞ Pharmacies

- **CVS** • 231 Massachusetts Ave [Clearway]
- **CVS** • 240 Newbury St [Fairfield St]
- **Walgreens** • 841 Boylston St [Fairfield St] 🕐

✉ Post Offices

- **Astor Station** • 207 Massachusetts Ave [Clearway]
- **Prudential Center Post Office** •
  800 Boylston St [Fairfield St]

🏫 Schools

- **Berklee College of Music** •
  1140 Boylston St [Hemenway St]
- **Boston Conservatory** • 8 The Fenway [Boylston St]
- **City on a Hill Charter** • 320 Huntington Ave [Opera]
- **Kingsley Montessori** • 30 Fairfield St [Comm Ave]
- **New England Conservatory** •
  290 Huntington Ave [Gainsborough]
- **Newman Preparatory** • 247 Marlborough St [Exeter St]

🛒 Supermarkets

- **Trader Joe's** • 899 Boylston St [Gloucester]
- **Whole Foods Market** • 15 Westland Ave [Edgerly Rd]

31

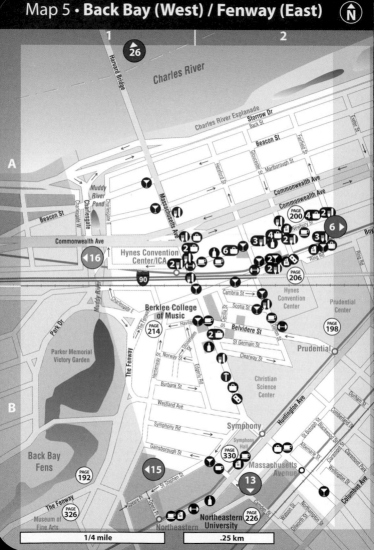

Map 5 • **Back Bay (West) / Fenway (East)** Ⓝ

Sundries / Entertainment

Map 5

Trident Booksellers and Café is a terrific spot for brunching and browsing. Get earthy (or just drink) at Other Side Cosmic Café. Beer drinkers who can handle Tunnel-level stereo volume and a touch of attitude should try Bukowski's. Berklee students often sit in at Wally's, joining more established musicians to play live jazz most nights of the week.

Coffee

- **Café Golden Horn** • 334 Massachusetts Ave [St Botolph]
- **Espresso Royale** • 286 Newbury St [Gloucester]
- **Espresso Royale** • 44 Gainsborough St [Huntington]
- **Starbucks** • 151 Massachusetts Ave [Haviland St]
- **Starbucks** • 273 Huntington Ave [Gainsborough]
- **Starbucks** • 346 Huntington Ave [Opera Pl]
- **Starbucks** • 350 Newbury St [Mass Ave]
- **Starbucks** • Sheraton Hotel • 39 Dalton St [Scotia]
- **Trident Booksellers & Café** • 338 Newbury St [Hereford]

Copy Shops

- **FedEx Kinko's** • 900 Boylston St [Gloucester]
- **Gnomon Copy** • 325 Huntington Ave [Opera]
- **Sir Speedy Printing Center** • 827 Boylston St [Fairfield St]
- **The UPS Store** • 263 Huntington Ave [Gainsborough]
- **The UPS Store** • 304 Newbury St [Hereford]

Gyms

- **Atlantis Sports Club** • 39 Dalton St [Scotia St]
- **Boston Sports Club** • 361 Newbury St [Mass Ave]
- **Central YMCA** • 316 Huntington Ave [Gainsborough]
- **Tennis & Racquet Club** • 939 Boylston St [Hereford]

Hardware Stores

- **Economy Hardware** • 219 Massachusetts Ave [Clearway]

Liquor Stores

- **Bauer Wine & Spirits** • 330 Newbury St [Hereford]
- **Choice Mart** • 181 Massachusetts Ave [St Germain]
- **DeLuca's Market** • 239 Newbury St [Fairfield St]
- **Huntington Wine & Spirits** • 301 Huntington Ave [Gainsborough]

Nightlife

- **Bukowski's** • 50 Dalton St [Scotia]
- **Crossroads** • 495 Beacon St [Mass Ave]
- **Dillon's** • 955 Boylston St [Hereford]
- **Kings** • 10 Scotia St [Dalton St]
- **The Last Drop** • 421 Marlborough St [Mass Ave]
- **Lir** • 903 Boylston St [Gloucester]
- **Match** • 94 Massachusetts Ave [Newbury St]
- **Our House East** • 52 Gainsborough St [St Stephen]
- **Pour House** • 907 Boylston St [Gloucester]
- **Sonsie** • 327 Newbury St [Hereford]
- **TC's Lounge** • 1 Haviland St [Mass Ave]
- **Top of the Hub** • 800 Boylston St [Fairfield St]
- **Wally's Café** • 427 Massachusetts Ave [Columbus]

Restaurants

- **Bangkok City** • 167 Massachusetts Ave [Belvidere St]
- **Bhindi Bazaar** • 95 Massachusetts Ave [Newbury St]
- **Bukowski's** • 50 Dalton St [Scotia]
- **Café Jaffa** • 48 Gloucester St [Boylston St]
- **Capital Grille** • 359 Newbury St [Mass Ave]
- **Casa Romero** • 30 Gloucester St [Newbury St]
- **Chilli Duck** • 829 Boylston St [Fairfield St]
- **Clio** • 370A Commonwealth Ave [Mass Ave]
- **India Samraat Restaurant** • 51 Massachusetts Ave [Marlborough St]
- **Island Hopper** • 91 Massachusetts Ave [Newbury St]
- **Kashmir** • 279 Newbury St [Gloucester]
- **L'Espalier** • 30 Gloucester St [Newbury St]
- **Other Side Cosmic Café** • 407 Newbury St [Mass Ave]
- **Pour House** • 907 Boylston St [Gloucester]
- **Sonsie** • 327 Newbury St [Hereford]
- **Spike's Junkyard Dogs** • 1076 Boylston St [Mass Ave]
- **Tapeo** • 266 Newbury St [Gloucester]
- **Top of the Hub** • 800 Boylston St [Fairfield St]
- **Trident Booksellers & Café** • 338 Newbury St [Hereford]

Shopping

- **Army Barracks** • 328 Newbury St [Hereford]
- **Back Bay Bicycle** • 366 Commonwealth Ave [Mass Ave]
- **Bön Bön** • 197 Massachusetts Ave [Clearway St]
- **The Compleat Strategist** • 201 Massachusetts Ave [Clearway St]
- **Daddy's Junky Music** • 159 Massachusetts Ave [Belvidere St]
- **DeLuca's Market** • 239 Newbury St [Fairfield St]
- **Economy Hardware** • 219 Massachusetts Ave [Clearway]
- **Emack & Bolio's** • 290 Newbury St [Gloucester]
- **Firefly Jewelry & Gifts** • 270 Newbury St [Gloucester]
- **John Fluevog** • 302 Newbury St [Hereford]
- **Johnny Cupcakes** • 279 Newbury St [Gloucester]
- **Johnson Artist Materials** • 355 Newbury St [Mass Ave]
- **JP Licks** • 352 Newbury St [Mass Ave]
- **Luna Boston** • 286 Newbury St [Gloucester]
- **Matsu** • 259 Newbury St [Fairfield St]
- **Orpheus** • 362 Commonwealth Ave [Mass Ave]
- **Sephora** • 800 Boylston St [Fairfield St]
- **Sweet-N-Nasty** • 90 Massachusetts Ave [Comm Ave]
- **Trident Booksellers & Café** • 338 Newbury St [Hereford]
- **Urban Outfitters** • 361 Newbury St [Mass Ave]
- **Utrecht Art Supply Center** • 333 Massachusetts Ave [St Botolph]

Video Rental

- **Blockbuster** • 235 Massachusetts Ave [Clearway]
- **Hollywood Video** • 899 Boylston Ave [Gloucester]

Map 5 • **Back Bay (West) / Fenway (East)** Ⓝ

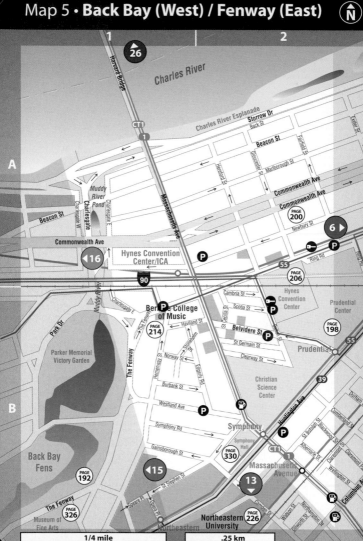

1/4 mile .25 km

Map 5

Traffic is always nasty on Mass Ave during the week. On weekends it becomes a parking lot, so avoid driving around here on Saturdays and Sundays if at all possible. And remember: there's no left turn from inbound Boylston Street onto Mass Ave. Few spots in Boston make it so easy for traffic cops to fill their quotas.

Subway

- **Massachusetts Avenue**
- **Hynes Convention Center (B,C,D)**
- **Prudential (E)**
- **Symphony (E)**

Bus Lines

- **CT1** · Central Square, Cambridge—BU Medical Center/BU Medical Campus
- **1** · Harvard/Holyoke Gate—Dudley Station via Massachusetts Avenue & BU Medical Center
- **9** · City Point—Copley Square via Broadway Station
- **39** · Forest Hills Station—Back Bay Station via Huntington Avenue
- **55** · Jersey & Queensberry Streets—Copley Square or Park & Tremont Streets

Car Rental

- **Enterprise** · 800 Boylston St [Fairfield St] · 617-262-8222
- **Select Car Rental** · 39 Dalton St [Scotia] · 617-236-6088

Gas Stations

- **Shell** · 584 Columbus Ave [Mass Ave] ✪
- **Sunoco** · 266 Massachusetts Ave [Westland Ave]

Parking

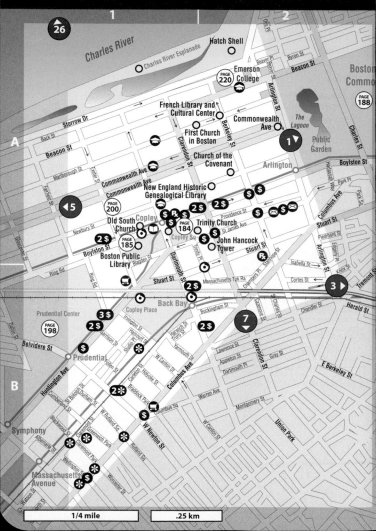

Map 6 • **Back Bay (East) / South End (Upper)**

Charles River

Hatch Shell

Charles River Esplanade

PAGE 26

PAGE 220

Emerson College

Storrow Dr

French Library and Cultural Center

Back St

Beacon St

Commonwealth Ave

The Lagoon

PAGE 188

Boston Common

Beacon St

Berkeley St

First Church in Boston

Marlborough St

Clarendon St

Church of the Covenant

Arlington

Public Garden

Charles St

A

Exeter St

Commonwealth Ave

Boylston St

Fairfield St

Commonwealth Ave

New England Historic Genealogical Library

Gloucester St

PAGE 200

PAGE 5

Newbury St

Old South Church

Copley

PAGE 185

PAGE 184

Trinity Church

Providence St

St. James Ave

Columbus Ave

Stuart St

2 $

$ $

Boylston St

Boston Public Library

Copley Sq

Bladgen St

John Hancock Tower

Piedmont St

Arlington St

Isabella St

2 $

Dartmouth St

Stuart St

Stanhope St

Cortes St

3

Tremont St

Ring Rd

Ring Rd

Stuart St

Massachusetts Tpk Rd

Chambers Pl

Herald St

Back Bay

Buckingham St

7

Chandler St

Prudential Center

Copley Place

3 $

Clarendon St

E Berkeley St

PAGE 198

2 $

Trinton St

Harcourt St

Yarmouth St

Lawrence St

2 $

Gray St

Belvidere St

$

Prudential

Clearway St

Garrison St

Carleton St

Holyoke St

Appleton St

Dartmouth Pl

Montgomery St

B

Huntington Ave

Cumberland St

W Canton St

Columbus Ave

Warren Ave

Union Park

2 $

Braddock Park

Columbus Sq

W Canton St

Symphony

Blackwood St

W Rutland Sq

W Newton St

Albemarle St

Wellington St

Claremont Park

Greenwich St

Irvington St

Massachusetts Avenue

Watson St

Wellington St

Wooster St

1/4 mile

.25 km

Map 6

The eastern end of Back Bay features the "top" of Newbury Street, with its mix of locals, tourists, and international students keeping its mainly highbrow merchants busy. The upper regions of the South End---especially Columbus Avenue---are now home to excellent restaurant upon excellent restaurant, with a culturally-correct number of galleries thrown in as well.

$ Banks

- **Bank of America** · 210 Berkeley St [St James Ave]
- **Bank of America** · 699 Boylston St [Exeter St]
- **Bank of America (ATM)** ·
  101 Huntington Ave [Garrison St]
- **Bank of America (ATM)** ·
  110 Huntington Ave [Harcourt]
- **Bank of America (ATM)** ·
  130 Dartmouth St [Columbus]
- **Bank of America (ATM)** · 145 Dartmouth St [Stuart]
- **Bank of America (ATM)** · 31 St James Ave [Arlington St]
- **Bank of America (ATM)** ·
  465 Columbus Ave [W Newton]
- **Bank of America (ATM)** ·
  557 Boylston St [Clarendon St]
- **Bank of America (ATM)** · 745 Boylston St [Exeter St]
- **Banknorth Massachusetts** ·
  579 Boylston St [Dartmouth St]
- **Boston Private Bank & Trust** ·
  500 Boylston St [Clarendon St]
- **Citizens Bank** · 426 Boylston St [Berkeley St]
- **Citizens Bank** · 535 Boylston St [Clarendon St]
- **Citizens Bank** · 607 Boylston St [Dartmouth St]
- **Citizens Bank (ATM)** · 101 Huntington Ave [Garrison St]
- **Citizens Bank (ATM)** · 111 Huntington Ave [Garrison St]
- **Citizens Bank (ATM)** · 145 Dartmouth St [Stuart]
- **Citizens Bank (ATM)** · 200 Clarendon St [St James Ave]
- **Citizens Bank (ATM)** · 717 Boylston St [Exeter St]
- **Sovereign Bank** · 575 Boylston St [Dartmouth St]
- **Sovereign Bank (ATM)** ·
  100 Huntington Ave [Harcourt]
- **Sovereign Bank (ATM)** ·
  Prudential Center Shoppe ·
  111 Huntington Ave [W Newton St]
- **Sovereign Bank (ATM)** ·
  200 Clarendon St [St James Ave]
- **Sovereign Bank (ATM)** ·
  United Settlement House ·
  566 Columbus Ave [Wellington St]
- **Sovereign Bank (ATM)** · CVS/Pharmacy ·
  587 Boylston St [Dartmouth St]
- **Wainwright Bank & Trust** ·
  155 Dartmouth St [Stuart]

❊ Community Gardens

◉ Donuts

- **Dunkin' Donuts** · 145 Dartmouth St [Stuart]
- **Dunkin' Donuts** · 2 Copley Pl [Dartmouth St]
- **Dunkin' Donuts** · 430 Stuart St [Trinity]
- **Dunkin' Donuts** · 715 Boylston St [Exeter St]

○ Landmarks

- **Boston Public Library** · 700 Boylston St [Exeter St]
- **Charles River Esplanade** · n/a
- **Church of the Covenant** · 67 Newbury St [Berkeley St]
- **Commonwealth Ave** · Arlington St to Mass Ave
- **Copley Square** · Boylston St & Dartmouth St
- **First Church in Boston** ·
  66 Marlborough St [Clarendon St]
- **French Library and Cultural Center** ·
  53 Marlborough St [Berkeley St]
- **Hatch Shell** · Esplanade [Congress]
- **John Hancock Tower** · 200 Clarendon St [St James Ave]
- **New England Historic Genealogical Library** ·
  101 Newbury St [Clarendon St]
- **Old South Church** · 645 Boylston St [Dartmouth St]
- **Trinity Church** · 206 Clarendon St [St James Ave]

🏛 Libraries

- **Boston Public Library** · 700 Boylston St [Exeter St]

℞ Pharmacies

- **Bioscrip Pharmacy** · 21 Stanhope St [Berkeley St]
- **CVS** · 587 Boylston St [Dartmouth St] ♿

✉ Post Offices

- **Back Bay Annex Station** ·
  31 St James Ave [Arlington St]
- **Post Offices** · Back Bay Retail Unit ·
  31 St James Ave [Arlington St]

🎓 Schools

- **Commonwealth** ·
  151 Commonwealth Ave [Dartmouth St]
- **Fisher College** · 118 Beacon St [Berkeley St]
- **Learning Project Elementary** ·
  107 Marlborough St [Clarendon St]
- **Snowden International High** ·
  150 Newbury St [Dartmouth St]

🛒 Supermarkets

- **Shaw's** · 53 Huntington Ave [Exeter St]
- **South End Food Emporium** ·
  469 Columbus Ave [W Newton]

Map 6 · **Back Bay (East) / South End (Upper)**

Sundries / Entertainment

Grab a great sandwich at Parish Café, a curry at House of Siam, or, if you're operating on an expense account, a steak at Grill 23. If you're just thirsty, you can hit the roof-deck at Rattlesnake, or if you need to be seen while seeing, stop off at Saint.

Coffee

- **L'Aroma Café** •
  85 Newbury St [Clarendon St]
- **Starbucks** • Westin Hotel •
  10 Huntington Ave [Dartmouth St]
- **Starbucks** • Copley Place •
  110 Huntington Ave [Harcourt]
- **Starbucks** •
  165 Newbury St [Dartmouth St]
- **Starbucks** • 441 Stuart St [Trinity]
- **Starbucks** • 443 Boylston St [Berkeley St]
- **Starbucks** • 755 Boylston St [Fairfield St]
- **Surreal Image Café** •
  300 Boylston St [Arlington St]
- **Tealuxe** • 108 Newbury St [Clarendon St]
- **Uptown Espresso Cafe** •
  563 Columbus Ave [W Springfield]

Copy Shops

- **BFS Printers** • 320 Stuart St [Columbus]
- **Copy Cop** •
  601 Boylston St [Fairfield St]
- **FedEx Kinko's** •
  187 Huntington St [St James Ave]
- **FedEx Kinko's** •
  575 Boylston St [Dartmouth St]
- **Printing Plus** •
  31 St James Ave [Arlington St]
- **Pro Print** • 410 Boylston St [Berkeley St]
- **The UPS Store** •
  110 Huntington Ave [Harcourt]
- **The UPS Store** •
  398 Columbus Ave [W Canton]

Farmers Markets

- **Copley Square**
  (May–Nov; Tues 11 am–6 pm.
  Fri 11 am–6 pm) •
  Copley Sq & St James Ave

Gyms

- **Body Evolver Health Fitness Center** •
  364 Boylston St [Arlington St]
- **Boston Sports Club** •
  505 Boylston St [Clarendon St]
- **Fitcorp** •
  111 Huntington Ave [Garrison St]
- **Fitcorp** • 197 Clarendon St [St James Ave]
- **Fitcorp** • 800 Boylston St [Fairfield St]
- **Fitness Together** •
  36 Newbury St [Berkeley St]
- **HealthWorks Fitness Center**
  (Women Only) • 441 Stuart St [Trinity]
- **Revolution Fitness** •
  209 Columbus Ave [Berkeley St]

Hardware Stores

- **Park True Value Hardware** •
  233 Newbury St [Fairfield St]

Liquor Stores

- **Best Cellars (Wine Only)** •
  745 Boylston St [Exeter St]
- **Clarendon Wine** •
  563 Boylston St [Clarendon St]
- **The Wine Emporium** •
  474 Columbus Ave [W Newton]

Nightlife

- **Anchovies** • 433 Columbus Ave [Braddock]
- **Champions** • Marriott •
  110 Huntington Ave [Harcourt]
- **City Bar** • Lenox Hotel •
  61 Exeter St [Boylston St]
- **Clery's** • 113 Dartmouth St [Columbus]
- **Club Café** • 209 Columbus Ave [Columbus]
- **Rattlesnake** • 384 Boylston St [Berkeley St]
- **Rise** • 306 Stuart St [Columbus]
- **Saint** • 90 Exeter St [Blagden]
- **Vox Populi** • 755 Boylston St [Fairfield St]

Restaurants

- **33** • 33 Stanhope St [Clarendon St]
- **Abe & Louie's** •
  793 Boylston St [Fairfield St]
- **b.good** • 131 Dartmouth St [Columbus]
- **Bouchee** • 159 Newbury St [Dartmouth St]
- **Brasserie Jo** •
  120 Huntington Ave [W Newton]
- **Charlie's Sandwich Shoppe** •
  429 Columbus Ave [Holyoke St]
- **Claremont Café** •
  535 Columbus Ave [Claremont Pk]
- **Davio's** • 75 Arlington St [Stuart]
- **Domani** • 51 Huntington Ave [Exeter St]
- **Grill 23 & Bar** • 161 Berkeley St [Stuart]
- **House of Siam** •
  542 Columbus Ave [Worcester St]
- **L'Aroma Café** •
  85 Newbury St [Clarendon St]
- **Laurel** • 142 Berkeley St [Columbus]
- **Legal Sea Foods** •
  800 Boylston St [Fairfield St]
- **Mistral** • 223 Columbus Ave [Cahners]
- **The Oak Room** •
  138 Saint James Ave [Trinity]
- **Osushi** • 10 Huntington Ave [Dartmouth St]
- **Parish Café** • 361 Boylston St [Arlington St]
- **Petsi Pies** • 285 Beacon St [Exeter St]
- **Shino Express Sushi** •
  144 Newbury St [Dartmouth St]

Shopping

- **All Things Chocolate** •
  31 St James Ave [Arlington St]
- **Amazing Express** •
  57 Stuart St [Huntington]
- **Anthropologie** •
  799 Boylston St [Fairfield St]
- **Best of Scotland** •
  115 Newbury St, Ste 202 [Clarendon St]
- **Brooks Brothers** •
  46 Newbury St [Berkeley St]
- **City Sports** •
  480 Boylston St [Clarendon St]
- **Crate & Barrel** •
  777 Boylston St [Fairfield St]
- **First Act Guitar Studio** •
  745 Boylston St [Exeter St]
- **Hempest** • 207 Newbury St [Exeter St]
- **International Poster Gallery** •
  205 Newbury St [Exeter St]
- **Kitchen Arts** •
  161 Newbury St [Dartmouth St]
- **Lindt Master Chocolatier** •
  704 Boylston St [Exeter St]
- **Lord & Taylor** •
  760 Boylston St [Fairfield St]
- **Louis Boston** •
  234 Berkeley St [Newbury St]
- **Luna Boston** •
  205 Newbury St [Exeter St]
- **Lush** • 166 Newbury St [Dartmouth St]
- **Marc Jacobs** •
  81 Newbury St [Clarendon St]
- **Marshall's** •
  500 Boylston St [Clarendon St]
- **Neiman Marcus** •
  5 Copley Pl [Dartmouth St]
- **O & Co.** • 161 Newbury St [Dartmouth St]
- **Paper Source** •
  338 Boylston St [Arlington St]
- **Saks Fifth Avenue** • 1 Ring Rd [Waltham]
- **Second Time Around** •
  176 Newbury St [Exeter St]
- **Shreve, Crump & Low** •
  440 Boylston St [Berkeley St]
- **Stil** • 170 Newbury St [Dartmouth St]
- **Teuscher Chocolates** •
  230 Newbury St [Fairfield St]
- **Tweeter Etc** •
  350 Boylston St [Arlington St]
- **Winston Flowers** •
  131 Newbury St [Dartmouth St]

Map 6

39

Map 6 · **Back Bay (East) / South End (Upper)**

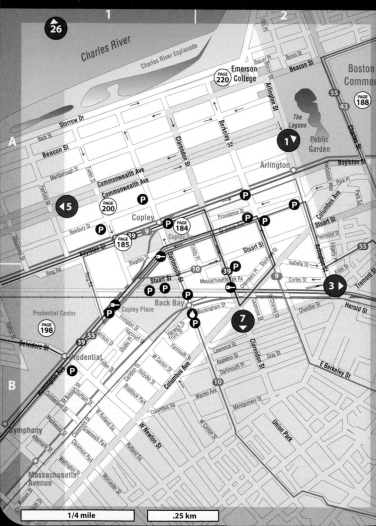

In Boston, jaywalking is a time-honored pastime, especially around the Pru and along Boylston and Newbury Streets. Back Bay is generally well-served by public transportation, even though (somewhat unusually) no buses actually run down Commonwealth Ave. Street parking? Good luck.

Subway

- **· Arlington**
- **· Copley**
- **· Back Bay**

Bus Lines

- **9** · City Point—Copley Square via Broadway Station
- **10** · City Point—Copley Square via Andrew Station & BU Medical Area
- **39** · Forest Hills Station—Back Bay Station via Huntington Avenue
- **43** · Ruggles Station—Park & Tremont Streets
- **55** · Jersey & Queensberry Streets—Copley Square or Park & Tremont Streets

Car Rental

- **Avis** · 100 Clarendon St [Stanhope] · 617-534-1404
- **Dollar** · Marriott Copley Place · 110 Huntington Ave [Harcourt] · 617-578-0025
- **Hertz** · 10 Huntington Ave [Dartmouth St] · 617-338-1506
- **Hertz** · Back Bay Station Amtrak · 145 Dartmouth St [Stuart] · 617-338-1500

Car Washes

- **Magic Touch** · 131 Dartmouth St [Columbus]

Parking

Map 7 • **South End (Lower)**

The South End is America's largest Victorian neighborhood, has the city's largest gay population, and, after years of gentrification, is now a "destination" spot. All this hipness, of course, makes the South End more expensive than it was a decade ago. Ultra-trendy boutiques rub shoulders with family-friendly brasseries (especially on happening Tremont Street).

💲 Banks

- **Bank of America** · 557 Tremont St [Waltham]
- **Century Bank (ATM)** · BU Dental School · 100 E Newton St [Harrison Ave]
- **Century Bank (ATM)** · BU Parking Garage · 710 Albany St [E Concord]
- **Century Bank (ATM)** · BU Med School · 715 Albany St [E Concord]
- **Citizens Bank** · 1355 Washington St [Waltham]
- **Citizens Bank (ATM)** · 840 Harrison Ave [E Springfield]
- **Mercantile Bank** · 1320 Washington St [Rollins St]
- **Sovereign Bank** · 521 Tremont St [Dwight]
- **Sovereign Bank (ATM)** · CVS · 400 Tremont St [Herald]
- **Sovereign Bank (ATM)** · Boston Center for the Arts · 539 Tremont St [Hanson St]
- **Sovereign Bank (ATM)** · 818 Harrison Ave [Worcester St]

❇️ Community Gardens

⭕ Donuts

- **Dunkin' Donuts** · 1138 Washington St [E Berkeley]
- **Dunkin' Donuts** · 616 Massachusetts Ave [Shawmut Ave]

➕ Emergency Rooms

- **Boston Medical Center** · 1 Boston Medical Ctr Pl [Mass Ave]

⭕ Landmarks

- **Cathedral of the Holy Cross** · 1400 Washington St [Union Pk St]
- **SoWa Building** · 450 Harrison Ave [Thayer St]

📖 Libraries

- **South End** · 685 Tremont St [W Newton]

℞ Pharmacies

- **Boston Medical Outpatient Pharmacy** · 720 Harrison Ave [E Brookline]
- **CVS** · 400 Tremont St [Herald]
- **Tremont Drug** · 610 Tremont St [W Dedham]
- **Walgreens** · 1603 Washington St [Rutland]

🚓 Police

- **District D-4** · 650 Harrison Ave [E Dedham]

✉️ Post Offices

- **Cathedral Station** · 59 W Dedham St [Shawmut Ave]

🏫 Schools

- **Cathedral Grammar** · 595 Harrison Ave [Malden]
- **Cathedral High** · 74 Union Park St [Harrison Ave]
- **Joseph J Hurley Elementary** · 70 Worcester St [Tremont St]
- **William Blackstone Elementary** · 380 Shawmut Ave [W Dedham]
- **William McKinley** · 90 Warren Ave [Columbus]

🛒 Supermarkets

- **Foodie's Urban Market** · 1421 Washington St [Upton]
- **Ming's Supermarket** · 1102 Washington St [E Berkeley]
- **Super 88** · 50 Herald St [Washington St]

Map 7 · **South End (Lower)**

1/4 mile

.25 km

Sundries / Entertainment

Map 7

Start your night at Delux, a beloved neighborhood bar complete with Elvis shrine. Then head to Joe V's for Italian, or Aquitaine for French. After a few bottles of wine, hit up Pho Republique. The morning after, treat your stomach to Mike's City Diner or the pajama brunch at Tremont 647. If you're still alive after all that, call us.

Coffee

- **Francesca's** • 564 Tremont St [Union Pk St]
- **Haley House Bakery & Café** • 23 Dartmouth St [Montgomery St]
- **Starbucks** • 627 Tremont St [W Canton]

Copy Shops

- **FedEx Kinko's** • 715 Albany St [E Concord]
- **Stratografix** • 1200 Washington St [Perry St]

Farmers Markets

- **South End at the Open Market** (May 23—Oct: Sun 10am—4pm) • 540 Harrison Ave [Savoy St]

Gyms

- **Boston Sports Club** • 560 Harrison Ave [Rollins St]

Hardware Stores

- **Warren Hardware** • 470 Tremont St [E Berkeley]

Liquor Stores

- **Brix Wine Shop** • 1284 Tremont St [Savoy St]
- **The Wine Emporium** • 607 Tremont St [Dartmouth St]

Nightlife

- **Beehive** • 541 Tremont St [Hanson St]
- **Delux Café** • 100 Chandler St [Clarendon St]
- **Eagle** • 520 Tremont St [Dwight]
- **Franklin Café** • 278 Shawmut Ave [Hanson]
- **Pho Republique** • 1415 Washington St [Union Pk St]

Pet Shops

- **The Pet Shop Girls** • 12 Union Park St [Shawmut Ave]
- **Polka Dog Bakery** • 256 Shawmut Ave [Milford]
- **s'Poochies Spa & Boutique** • 400 Tremont St [Herald]

Restaurants

- **Addis Red Sea** • 544 Tremont St [Waltham]
- **Appleton Bakery & Café** • 123 Appleton St [Appleton St]
- **Aquitaine** • 569 Tremont St [Union Pk St]
- **B&G Oysters** • 550 Tremont St [Waltham]
- **Delux Café** • 100 Chandler St [Clarendon St]
- **Dish** • 253 Shawmut Ave [Milford]
- **El Triunfo** • 147 E Berkeley St [Harrison Ave]
- **flour bakery + café** • 1595 Washington St [Rutland]
- **Franklin Café** • 278 Shawmut Ave [Hanson]
- **Garden of Eden** • 571 Tremont St [Union Pk St]
- **Gaslight 560** • 560 Harrison Ave [Waltham St]
- **Hamersley's Bistro** • 553 Tremont St [Waltham]
- **Joe V's** • 315 Shawmut Ave [Union Pk St]
- **Masa** • 439 Tremont St [Appleton St]
- **Metropolis Café** • 584 Tremont St [Upton]
- **Mike's City Diner** • 1714 Washington St [W Springfield]
- **Morse Fish** • 1401 Washington St [Union Pk St]
- **Oishii** • 1166 Washington St [E Berkeley]
- **Orinoco** • 477 Shawmut Ave [W Concord St]
- **Pho Republique** • 1415 Washington St [Union Pk St]
- **Picco** • 513 Tremont St [E Berkeley]
- **Red Fez** • 1222 Washington St [Perry St]
- **Sage** • 1395 Washington St [Union Pk St]
- **Sibling Rivalry** • 523 Tremont St [Dwight]
- **Stella** • 1525 Washington St [E Brookline]
- **Tremont 647** • 647 Tremont St [W Brookline]
- **Union Bar and Grille** • 1357 Washington St [Waltham]

Shopping

- **Aunt Sadie's** • 18 Union Park St [Shawmut Ave]
- **Bobby from Boston** • 19 Thayer St [Harrison Ave]
- **Brix Wine Shop** • 1284 Washington St [Savoy St]
- **The Butcher Shop** • 552 Tremont St [Waltham]
- **Community Bicycle Supply** • 496 Tremont St [E Berkeley]
- **Ilex** • 73 Berkeley St [Chandler St]
- **Lekker** • 1317 Washington St [Rollins St]
- **Lionette's** • 577 Tremont St [Union Pk St]
- **Picco** • 513 Tremont St [E Berkeley]
- **Posh** • 557 Tremont St [Waltham]
- **South End Buttery** • 314 Shawmut Ave [Union Pk St]
- **South End Formaggio** • 268 Shawmut Ave [Milford]
- **Uniform** • 511 Tremont St [E Berkeley]
- **Urban Living Studio** • 58 Clarendon St [Chandler St]

Video Rental

- **Mike's Movies** • 630 Tremont St [W Canton]

Map 7 · **South End (Lower)**

1/4 mile

.25 km

Transportation

Map 7

Street parking north of Washington Street is a disaster, a situation compounded by the paucity of parking lots and garages. Visitors should strongly consider using the Silver Line, particularly to go to any spot on or near Washington Street. Check Gaslight 560 for the food and the huge parking lot for diners.

Subway

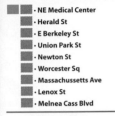

- **NE Medical Center**
- **Herald St**
- **E Berkeley St**
- **Union Park St**
- **Newton St**
- **Worcester Sq**
- **Massachussetts Ave**
- **Lenox St**
- **Melnea Cass Blvd**

Bus Lines

- **CT1** • Central Square, Cambridge—BU Medical Center/BU Medical Campus
- **CT3** • Beth Israel Deaconess Medical Center—Andrew Station via BU Medical Center
- **1** • Harvard/Holyoke Gate—Dudley Station via Mass Ave & BU Medical Center
- **8** • Harbor Point/UMass—Kenmore Station via South End Medical Area
- **9** • City Point—Copley Square via Broadway Station
- **10** • City Point—Copley Square via Andrew Station & BU Medical Area
- **43** • Ruggles Station—Park & Tremont Streets
- **47** • Central Square, Cambridge—Broadway Station via South End Medical Area

Gas Stations

- **Mobil** • 273 E Berkeley St [Albany St] ⌚
- **Stop N Gas** • 970 Washington St [Herald]
- **Sunoco** • 976 Washington St [Herald]

Parking

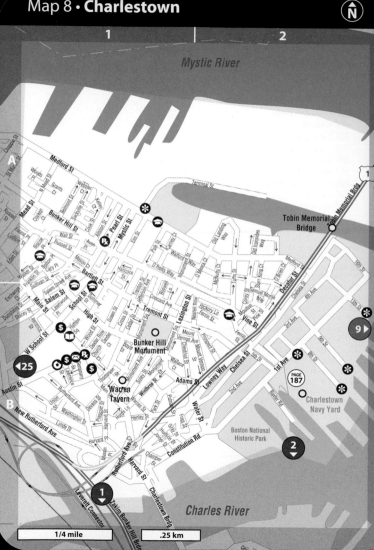

Map 8 • **Charlestown**

Looking at Charlestown now, it's hard to believe that this small (one square mile) neighborhood was once the stolen car capital of the entire country (and home to many of Boston's infamous Irish gangsters). Despite the public housing blocks that still sit along the edge of town, Charlestown is now an upscale, quaint community.

$ Banks

- **Citizens Bank** · 5 Austin St [Warren St]
- **Citizens Bank (ATM)** · 140 Main St [Church Ct]
- **Co-Operative Bank** · 201 Main St [Hathon]

❋ Community Gardens

◉ Donuts

- **Dunkin' Donuts** · 11 Austin St [Warren St]

○ Landmarks

- **Bunker Hill Monument** · Monument Ave [High St]
- **Charlestown Navy Yard** ·
  Constitution Rd & Warren St
- **Tobin Memorial Bridge** · US-1
- **Warren Tavern** · 2 Pleasant St [Main]

📖 Libraries

- **Charlestown** · 179 Main St [Wood St]

℞ Pharmacies

- **CVS** · Bunker Hill Mall · 5 Austin St [Warren St]
- **High Pharmacy** · 54 High St [Green St]

✉ Post Offices

- **Charlestown** · 23 Austin St [Lawrence St]

🎓 Schools

- **Charlestown High** · 240 Medford St [Polk]
- **Clarence R Edwards Middle** · 28 Walker St [High St]
- **Harvard-Kent Elementary** ·
  50 Bunker Hill St [Moulton St]
- **The Holden School** · 8 Pearl St [Wesley St]
- **Warren Prescott Elementary** ·
  50 School St [Bartlett St]

Map 8 · Charlestown

Mystic River

Charles River

Charlestown Navy Yard

Boston National Historic Park

Tobin Memorial Brdg

1/4 mile   .25 km

Sundries / Entertainment

Two notable restaurants along Charlestown's City Square are Olives and Tangierino. On Flagship Wharf, views of the city can't be beat while eating oysters at the recently upscaled Tavern on the Water. For history buffs, nothing's better than the Warren Tavern, one of the oldest bars in the country.

Map 8

☕ Coffee

- **Coffee Shop** · 1 Thompson Square [Austin]
- **Sorelle** · 100 City Sq [Park St]

🍎 Farmers Markets

- **Charlestown (July—Oct; Wed 2 pm—7 pm)** · Main St & Austin St

🏋 Gyms

- **Boston Young Men's Christian Union** · 48 Boyle St [Pleasant St]

🍾 Liquor Stores

- **Bunker Hill Liquors** · 200 Bunker Hill St [Green St]
- **Charlestown Liquors** · 10 Thompson Sq [Austin]
- **McCarthy Brothers Liquors** · 9 Moulton St [Bunker Hill St]

🍸 Nightlife

- **Goody Glovers** · 50 Salem St [High St]
- **Sullivan's Pub** · 85 Main St [Monument Ave]
- **Tavern on the Water** · 1 Pier 6 at E 8th St
- **Warren Tavern** · 2 Pleasant St [Main]

🍴 Restaurants

- **Figs** · 67 Main St [Monument Ave]
- **Ironside Grill** · 25 Park St [Warren St]
- **Jenny's Pizza** · 320 Medford St [Allston St]
- **Navy Yard Bistro & Wine Bar** · 1 1st Ave [3rd St]
- **Ninety Nine** · 29 Austin St [Lawrence St]
- **Olives** · 10 City Sq [Main]
- **Paolo's Trattoria** · 251 Main St [Lawnwood]
- **Sorelle** · 1 Monument Ave [Main]
- **Sorelle** · 100 City Sq [Park St]
- **Tangierino** · 83 Main St [Monument Ave]
- **Warren Tavern** · 2 Pleasant St [Main]

🛍 Shopping

- **A Wild Flower** · 73 Main St [Monument Ave]
- **Bunker Hill Florist** · 1 Thompson Sq [Austin]
- **Doherty's Flowers** · 223 Main St [School St]
- **The Joy of Old** · 85A Warren St [Pleasant St]
- **Serenade Chocolates** · 5 Harvard Sq [Andem Pl]

Map 8 · **Charlestown**

Mystic River

Charles River

Boston National
Historic Park

Charlestown
Navy Yard

1/4 mile   .25 km

Transportation

Map 8

In the middle of winter, it's a long, bitter hike into Charlestown from the Orange Line at Community College or Sullivan Square. Driving is ill-advised, but cabs are a quick hop from downtown. Warmer options are buses 92 or 93. A great summer alternative is the City Water Taxi from Long Wharf.

Bus Lines

- **92** • Assembly Square Mall—Downtown via Sullivan Square Station, Main St
- **93** • Sullivan Square Station—Downtown via Bunker Hill Street & Haymarket Station
- **111** • Woodlawn or Broadway & Park Ave— Haymarket Station via Mystic River/Tobin Bridge

Gas Stations

- **Shell** • 1 Rutherford Ave [N Washington] ⏰

P Parking

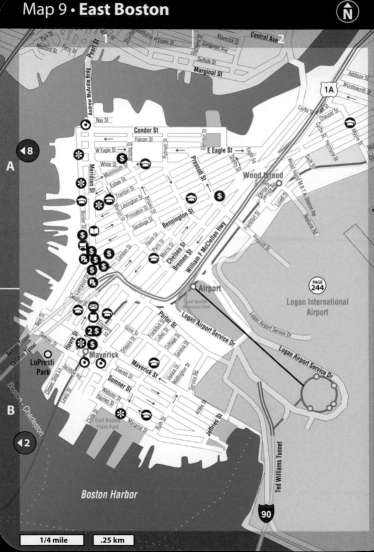

Map 9 · **East Boston**

Isolated from the city by water and the airport, Eastie's tree-lined streets and copious three-deckers are home to a diverse and vibrant Latin American community. Maverick Square is busy, but you'll want to make the walk up to Day Square to get a better sense of the turf.

$ Banks

- **Bank of America (ATM)** · 3-11 Porter St [Central Sq]
- **Bank of America (ATM)** · 47 Maverick Sq [Sumner St]
- **Citizens Bank** · 26 Central Sq [Bennington]
- **Citizens Bank (ATM)** · 49 White St [Monmouth]
- **East Boston Savings Bank** ·
  1 Bennington St [Porter St]
- **East Boston Savings Bank** ·
  10 Meridian St [Maverick St]
- **East Boston Savings Bank (ATM)** ·
  294 Bennington St [Chelsea St]
- **Eastern Bank (ATM)** · 246 Border St [Lexington St]
- **Sovereign Bank** · 2 Meridian St [Maverick St]
- **Sovereign Bank (ATM)** · 1 Porter St [Bennington St]
- **Sovereign Bank (ATM)** · CVS/Pharmacy ·
  210 Border St [Saratoga St]

✳ Community Gardens

◎ Donuts

- **Dunkin' Donuts** · 13 Maverick Sq [Sumner St]
- **Honey Dew Donuts** · 12 Maverick Sq [Sumner St]
- **Honey Dew Donuts** · 470 Meridian St [Condor]

○ Landmarks

- **LoPresti Park** · Summer St & Jeffries St

Libraries

- **East Boston** · 276 Meridian St [Princeton St]

℞ Pharmacies

- **CVS** · 210 Border St [Saratoga St] ⌖
- **Walgreens** · 1 Central Sq [Meridian St] ⌖

Police

- **District A-7** · 69 Paris St [Emmons St]

✉ Post Offices

- **East Boston Station** · 50 Meridian St [Paris St]

Schools

- **Dante Alighieri Elementary** · 37 Gove St [Paris St]
- **Donald McKay Elementary/Middle** ·
  122 Cottage St [Maverick St]
- **East Boston Central Catholic** ·
  69 London St [McClellan Hwy]
- **East Boston High** · 86 White St [Eutaw]
- **Hugh Roe O'Donnell Elementary** ·
  33 Trenton St [Marion St]
- **James Otis Elementary** · 218 Marion St [Morris]
- **Patrick J Kennedy Elementary** ·
  343 Saratoga St [Putnam St]
- **Samuel Adams Elementary** · 165 Webster St [Ruth]
- **St Mary Star of the Sea Elementary** ·
  58 Moore St [London St]
- **Umana/Barnes Middle** · 312 Border St [Eutaw]

Supermarkets

- **Shaw's** · 246 Border St [Lexington St]

Map 9 · **East Boston**

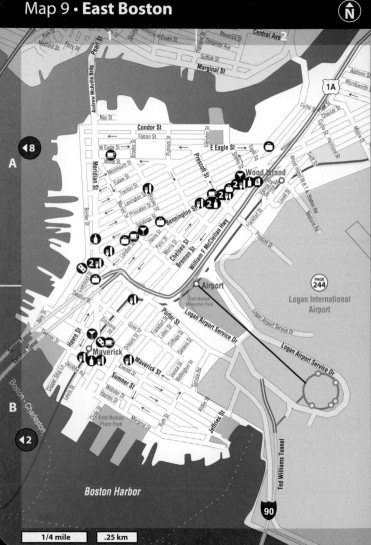

Sundries / Entertainment

Santarpio's Pizza is regionally-renowned, but it's the pañerias, rotisseries, and taquerias that dominate the dining scene. Try the Peruvian chicken at the Rincon Limeno in Day Square, or the refined Salvadoran fare at El Buen Gusto. Small Latin American shops abound, selling piñatas, saint votives, and soccer kits.

Coffee

- **Café Zing** · 25 White St [Marion St]
- **La Sultana** · 40 Maverick Sq [Winthrop St]
- **Peaches & Cream** · 73 Bennington St [London St]
- **Spinelli's** · 282 Bennington St [Prescott St]

Copy Shops

- **The UPS Store** · 2 Neptune Rd [Bennington]

Liquor Stores

- **Castillo Liquors** · 228 Meridian St [Saratoga St]
- **Clipper Ship Wine & Spirits** ·
  17 Maverick Sq [Sumner St]
- **Day Square Liquor** · 288 Bennington St [Chelsea St]
- **Neptune Liquors** · 1 Neptune Rd [Bennington]

Nightlife

- **Kelly Square Pub** · 84 Bennington St [Marion St]
- **Trainor's Café** · 127 Maverick St [Paris St]

Restaurants

- **Angela's Café** · 131 Lexington St [Brooks St]
- **Café Belo** · 254 Bennington St [Prescott St]
- **Café Italia** · 150 Meridian St [London St]
- **Café Meridian** · 271 Meridian St [Princeton St]
- **El Buen Gusto** · 295 Bennington St [Chelsea St]
- **El Chalan** · 405 Chelsea St [Shelby St]
- **Jeveli's** · 387 Chelsea St [Bennington]
- **La Frontera** · 290 Bennington St [Chelsea St]
- **La Terraza** · 19 Bennington St [Porter St]
- **Rincon Limeno** · 409 Chelsea St [Shelby]
- **Santarpio's Pizza** · 111 Chelsea St [Porter St]
- **TacoMex** · 65 Maverick Sq [Sumner St]
- **Taqueria Cancun** · 192 Sumner St [Maverick Sq]

Shopping

- **Brazilian Soccer House** · 110 Meridian St [London St]
- **Globos y Fiesta** · 52A Bennington St [London St]
- **Lilly's Flower Shop** · 512 Saratoga St [Chelsea St]
- **Lolly's Bakery** · 158 Bennington St [Brooks]
- **Studium Spanish Bookstore** ·
  268 Bennington St [Prescott St]

Video Rental

- **Blockbuster** · 184 Border St [Central Sq]
- **Maverick Audio & Video** ·
  25 Maverick Sq [Sumner St]

Map 9 · **East Boston**

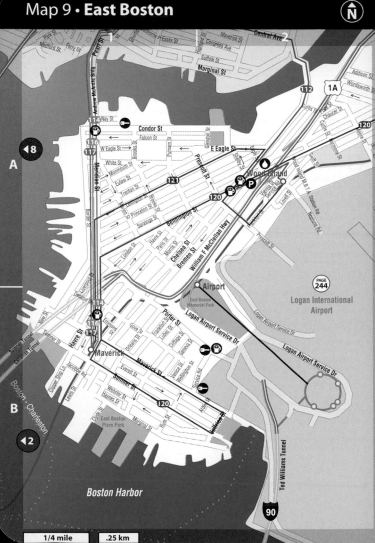

Map 9

Driving means the Callahan Tunnel—stay in the right lane as you exit the tunnel. When leaving, keep a map handy; there are few roads out of Eastie and they're not always easy to locate. For public transportation, take the Blue line to the Maverick or Wood Island stops.

Subway

■ · **Maverick**
■ · **Airport**
■ · **Wood Island**

Bus Lines

112 · Wellington Station—Wood Island Station via Central Ave, Mystic Mall & Admiral's Hill

116 · Wonderland Station—Maverick Station via Revere St

117 · Wonderland Station—Maverick Station via Revere St

120 · Orient Heights Station—Maverick Station via Bennington St

121 · Wood Island Station—Maverick Station via Lexington

Car Rental

· **Affordable Auto Rental** ·
84 Condor St [Brooks] · 617-561-7000
· **Alamo** · 2 Tomahawk Dr [Lamson St] · 617-561-4100

Car Washes

· **Squikee Clean** · 452 Bremen St [Bennington]

Gas Stations

· **Citgo** · 110 Service Rd [Mass Tpke]
· **Getty** · 331 Bennington St [Bremen St]
· **Mobil** · 396 Chelsea St [Shelby]
· **Mobil** · 470 Meridian St [Condor] ⊗
· **Shell** · 52 Meridian St [Paris St] ⊗

Parking

Map 10 · **South Boston (West) / Fort Point** ⊕

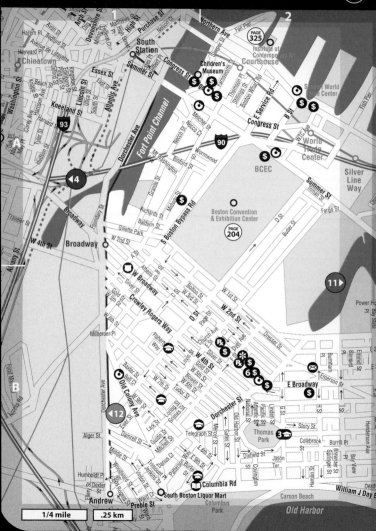

Map 10

Southie seems to be in its renaissance. The formerly locals-only neighborhood has attracted yuppies, artists, and college students with a flurry of new condos, restaurants, and a short commute downtown. Even the Mayor wants in, by planning to rebuild City Hall in the Seaport district.

$ Banks

- **Bank of America** · 460 W Broadway [Dorchester St]
- **Bank of America (ATM)** · 332 Congress St [Sleeper]
- **Boston Private Bank & Trust** · 157 Seaport Blvd [B]
- **Citizens Bank** · 441 W Broadway [F]
- **Citizens Bank (ATM)** · 405 W Broadway [F]
- **Citizens Bank (ATM)** · 415 Summer St [D]
- **Citizens Bank (ATM)** · 482 W Broadway [Dorchester St]
- **Citizens Bank (ATM)** · 555 E Broadway [H]
- **Eastern Bank** · 470 W Broadway [Dorchester St]
- **Mt Washington Bank** · 430 W Broadway [F]
- **Mt Washington Bank** · 455 W Broadway [Dorchester]
- **Sovereign Bank** · 474 W Broadway [Dorchester St]
- **Sovereign Bank (ATM)** · 200 Seaport Blvd [WTC]
- **Sovereign Bank (ATM)** · 300 Congress St [Dorchester]
- **Sovereign Bank (ATM)** · 330 Congress St [Sleeper]
- **Sovereign Bank (ATM)** · CVS/Pharmacy · 423 W Broadway [F]

✳ Community Gardens

⊙ Donuts

- **Dunkin' Donuts** · 268 Summer St [A St]
- **Dunkin' Donuts** · 330 Congress St [Sleeper]
- **Dunkin' Donuts** · 415 Summer St [WTC]
- **Dunkin' Donuts** · 482 W Broadway [Dorchester St]
- **Dunkin' Donuts** · 75 Old Colony Ave [C]

O Landmarks

- **Boston Children's Museum** · 300 Congress St [Sleeper]
- **Boston Convention & Exhibition Center** · 415 Summer St [D]
- **Institute of Contemporary Art** · 100 Northern Ave [E Service]
- **South Boston Liquor Mart** · 295 Old Colony Ave [Jenkins]

📖 Libraries

- **Washington Village** · 1226 Columbia Rd [Mercer St]

℞ Pharmacies

- **CVS** · 423 W Broadway [F]
- **Prescription Shoppe** · 378 W Broadway [E]

⬤ Police

- **District C-6** · 101 W Broadway [A St]

✉ Post Offices

- **South Boston Station** · 444 E 3rd St [Emerson St]

🎓 Schools

- **Excel High** · 95 G St [E 6th]
- **James Condon Elementary** · 200 D St [W 5th]
- **Michael J Perkins Elementary** · 50 Burke St [Pilsudski]
- **Monument High** · 95 G St [E 6th]
- **Odyssey High** · 95 G St [E 6th]
- **Patrick F Gavin Middle** · 215 Dorchester St [W 5th]
- **St Augustine's** · 209 E St [Baxter]

Map 10 · **South Boston (West) / Fort Point**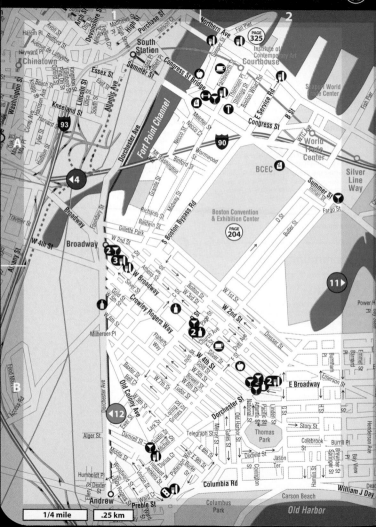

1/4 mile   .25 km

Sundries / Entertainment

Map 10

Tourists and locals mix it up at Barking Crab. Drinkin' establishments are great here—especially Lucky's and Shenanigans. Finish your new pad with retro pieces from Machine Age. To get a dose of culture, catch a flick at the new ICA.

Coffee

- **Café Arpeggio** • 398 W Broadway [F]
- **Yada Yada Café** • 34 Farnsworth St [Congress St]

Copy Shops

- **FedEx Kinko's** • 415 Summer St [D]
- **Sir Speedy Printing Centers** • 266 Summer St [A St]

Farmers Markets

- **Children's Museum (July–Oct; Tues 4 pm–7 pm)** (In front of Children's Museum) • 300 Congress St [Sleeper]
- **South Boston (July–Oct; Mon 12 pm–6 pm)** • 444 W Broadway [F]

Gyms

- **Focus Fitness** • 303 Congress St [Dot Ave]

Hardware Stores

- **Seaport Hardware** • 369 Congress St [Stillings]

Liquor Stores

- **Al's Liquors** • 226 W Broadway [C]
- **Leonid Wine Company** • 341 W Broadway [E]
- **New Bay View Liquors** • 108 Dorchester St [W 2nd]
- **O'Donoghue's Liquor Store** • 341 West Broadway [D]
- **Old Colony Wine** • 259 Dorchester Ave [W 5th]

Movie Theaters

- **Institute of Contemporary Art** • 100 Northern Ave [B]

Nightlife

- **Blackthorn Pub** • 471 W Broadway [Dorchester St]
- **The Cornerstone** • 16 W Broadway [Dot Ave]
- **The Junction** • 110 Dorchester St [W 2nd]
- **Lucky's** • 355 Congress St [A St]
- **The Quiet Man** • 11 W Broadway [Dot Ave]
- **Shenanigans** • 332 W Broadway [D]
- **Stadium** • 232 Old Colony Ave [Mitchell]

Restaurants

- **6 House** • 28 W Broadway [Dot Ave]
- **Amrheins** • 80 W Broadway [A St]
- **Anthony's Pier 4** • 140 Northern Ave [Seaport Blvd]
- **Barking Crab** • 88 Sleeper St [Northern Ave]
- **The Daily Catch** • 2 Northern Ave [Sleeper]
- **Fresh Tortillas** • 475 W Broadway [Dorchester St]
- **Lucky's** • 355 Congress St [A St]
- **Mul's Diner** • 80 W Broadway [A St]
- **R&L Delicatessen** • 313 Old Colony Ave [Jenkins]
- **Salsa's Mexican Grill** • 118 Dorchester St [W B'way]
- **Stadium** • 232 Old Colony Ave [Mitchell]
- **Teriyaki House** • 32 W Broadway [Dot Ave]

Shopping

- **Machine Age** • 645 Summer St [Fargo]

Video Rental

- **Blockbuster** • 267 Old Colony Ave [Patterson]

Map 10 · **South Boston (West) / Fort Point** (N)

1/4 mile   .25 km

Map 10

Parking here is hard to find and mostly residential. The Red Line and the Silver Line graze this area, and don't get you very close to Broadway, so to get to Broadway from Back Bay or the South End, consider taking the 9 bus.

Subway

- **South Station**
- **Broadway**
- **Andrew**
- **Courthouse**
- **World Trade Center**
- **Silver Line Way**
- **BCEC**

Bus Lines

- **CT3** · Beth Israel Deaconess Medical Center— Andrew Station via BU Medical Center
- **3** · Boston Marine Industrial Park—South Station/ Haymarket Station
- **4** · North Station—World Trade Center via Federal Courthouse
- **5** · City Point—McCormack Housing via Andrew Station
- **6** · Boston Marine Industrial Park— South Station/Haymarket Station
- **9** · City Point—Copley Square via Broadway Station
- **10** · City Point—Copley Square via Andrew Station & BU Medical Area
- **11** · City Point—Downtown, Bayview Route
- **47** · Central Square, Cambridge—Broadway Station via South End Medical Area

🚗 Car Rental

· **Select Car Rental** · Seaport Hotel · 1 Seaport Ln [Northern Ave] · 617-345-0203

💧 Car Washes

· **Super Shine Auto Wash** · 39 Old Colony Ave [C]

⛽ Gas Stations

· **Exxon** · 79 W Broadway [A St]
· **Shell** · 302 W Broadway [D]

🅿 Parking

Map 11 · **South Boston (East)**

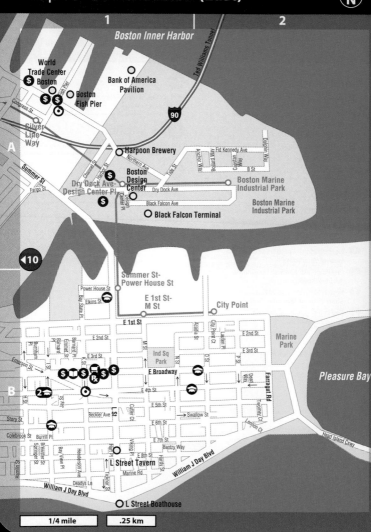

Boston Inner Harbor

2

World
Trade Center
$ Boston

Fish Pier

$ Boston
Fish Pier

Bank of America
Pavilion

Ted Williams Tunnel

Congress St

90

Silver
Line
Way

Summer St

Fargo St

A

Harpoon Brewery

Northern Ave

Channel St

Harbor St

Dry Dock Ave-
Design Center Pl

$

Design Center Pl

$

Boston
Design
Center

Dry Dock Ave

Anchor Way

Boston Marine
Industrial Park

Fid Kennedy Ave

Bolivar Way

B St

Dolphin Way

Cristian Way

Boston Marine
Industrial Park

Black Falcon Ave

Black Falcon Terminal

◀10

Summer St-
Power House St

Power House St

Bay State Pl

Elkins St

E 1st St

Summer St-
Power House St

E 1st St-
M St

City Point

Burnham
Pl

Emerson St

I St

Barnard Pl

Emmet Pl

K St

E 2nd St

E 3rd St

M St

N St

Acadia St

Taulden Pl

Old Point Ct

E 2nd St

E 3rd St

Marine
Park

Pleasure Bay

$ $ $

Rx

B

2

H St

Ind Sq
Park

E Broadway

Dorchester

E 4th St

O St

P St

Q St

Farragut Rd

Dresser
Way

Twomey Ct

Story St

Colebrook St

Burrill Pl

Beckler Ave

Caller St

E 5th St

Swallow St

E 6th St

E 7th St

Vinton St

Bantry Way

Lennon Ct

Head Island Cswy

Brewster St
Springer St

Bay View Pl

Heisterson Ave

Hardy St

L Street Tavern

Marine Rd

N St

H St

Flint Pl

E 8th St

William J Day Blvd

N Smith St

Deadys Ln

William J Day Blvd

L Street Boathouse

1/4 mile   .25 km

Well-known as a working class Irish 'hood in a very Irish city, Southie's ethnic and socioeconomic makeup is slowly changing. Many young professionals, swayed by Southie's charm and priced out of other neighborhoods, are renovating triple-deckers.

$ Banks

· **Bank of America** · 636 E Broadway [Emerson St]
· **Citizens Bank (ATM)** · 713 E Broadway [K St]
· **First Trade Union Bank** · 1 Harbor St [Dry]
· **First Trade Union Bank** ·
  10 Drydock Ave [Design Ctr Pl]
· **First Trade Union Bank** · 753 E Broadway [L]
· **Mt Washington Bank** · 708 E Broadway [K St]
· **Sovereign Bank (ATM)** · 1 Seaport Ln [Northern Ave]
· **Sovereign Bank (ATM)** · 2 Seaport Ln [Northern Ave]

Donuts

· **Dunkin' Donuts** · 1 Fish Pier [Northern Ave]
· **Dunkin' Donuts** · 200 Seaport Blvd [WTC]
· **Joseph's Bakery** · 258 K St [E 4th St]

Landmarks

· **Bank of America Pavilion** ·
  290 Northern Ave [Mass Tpke]
· **Black Falcon Terminal** ·
  1 Black Falcon Ave [Design Ctr Pl]
· **Boston Design Center** ·
  1 Design Center Pl [Black]
· **Boston Fish Pier** · 212 Northern Ave [D]
· **Harpoon Brewery** · 306 Northern Ave [Harbor St]
· **L Street Bathhouse** · William J Day Blvd & L St
· **L Street Tavern** · 658 E 8th St [L]
· **World Trade Center Boston** ·
  200 Seaport Blvd [WTC]

Libraries

· **South Boston** · 646 E Broadway [Emerson St]

Pharmacies

· **Rite Aid** · 710 E Broadway [K St]

Schools

· **Gate of Heaven** · 609 E 4th St [I St]
· **Joseph P Tynan Elementary** · 640 E 4th St [I St]
· **Oliver Hazard Perry Elementary** · 745 E 7th St [N]
· **St Brigid's** · 866 E Broadway [O St]
· **St Peter's** · 518 E 6th St [I St]
· **Uphams Corner Charter** · 7 Elkins St [Summer]

Supermarkets

· **Stop & Shop** · 713 E Broadway [K St]

Map 11 · **South Boston (East)**

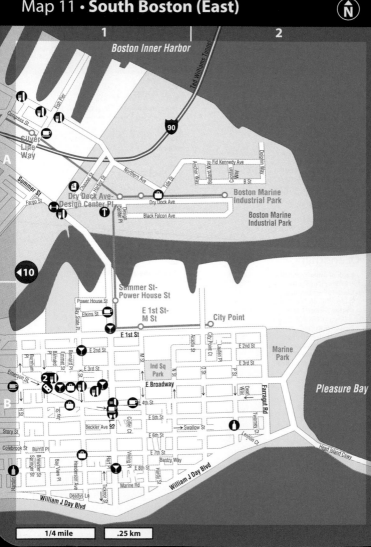

Sundries / Entertainment

During the summer, sea-bathers gather at the beaches along Dorchester Bay while Bank of America Pavilion hosts big-name entertainers. Good beer spots abound—take a tour of Harpoon Brewery for the samples of the freshest possible ale—and you can count on No Name Restaurant for reliable seafood.

Map 11

Coffee

- **Java House** · 566 E Broadway [H]
- **Margaret's Coffee Shop** · 11 Elkins St [Summer]
- **Sidewalk Café** · 764 E 4th St [M St]
- **Starbucks** · 601 Congress St [D]

Copy Shops

- **Copy Cop** · 12 Channel St [Harbor]

Gyms

- **Boston Athletic Club** · 653 Summer St [W 1st]

Hardware Stores

- **Backstage True Value** · 21 Drydock Ave [Tide]

Liquor Stores

- **East Side Market** · 474 E 8th St [Winfield]
- **Jimmy's Korner** · 143 P St [E 6th]

Nightlife

- **Boston Beer Garden** · 732 E Broadway [L]
- **Corner Tavern** · 645 E 2nd St [K St]
- **L Street Tavern** · 658 E 8th St [L]
- **Murphy's Law** · 837 Summer St [E 1st]
- **Playwright** · 658 E Broadway [K St]

Restaurants

- **Aura** · Seaport Hotel · 1 Seaport Ln [Northern Ave]
- **Boston Beer Garden** · 732 E Broadway [L]
- **Café Porto Bello** · 672 E Broadway [K St]
- **Going my Way Café** · 87 L St [Emerson St]
- **Kelly's Landing** · 81 L St [E 4th]
- **L Street Diner** · 108 L St [E 5th]
- **LTK (Legal Test Kitchen)** · 225 Northern Ave [D]
- **No Name Restaurant** · 15 Fish Pier Rd [Northern Ave]
- **Playwright** · 658 E Broadway [K St]
- **Summer Street Grille** · 653 Summer St [W 1st]
- **Terrie's Place** · 676 E Broadway [K St]

Shopping

- **EP Levine** · 23 Drydock Ave [Tide]
- **Ku De Ta** · 663 E Broadway [K St]
- **Miller's Market** · 336 K St [E 7th]
- **Stapleton Floral** · 635 E Broadway [Emerson St]

Video Rental

- **Hub Video** · 604 E Broadway [Emerson St]

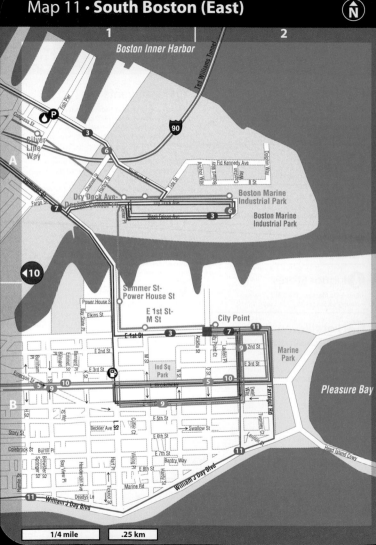

The addition of Silver Line stops in the neighborhood has made Southie much more accessible. If you drive, you'll have to find visitor parking, as the majority of the neighborhood is now resident only. Move a cone from a shoveled out parking spot, and be prepared to lose tires/windshield/wipers.

Subway

- **Silver Line Way**
- **Northern Ave - Harbor St**
- **Northern Ave - Tide St**
- **Dry Dock Ave - Design Center Pl**
- **Summer St - Power House St**
- **E 1st St - M St**
- **City Point**

Bus Lines

3 · Boston Marine Industrial Park—
South Station/Haymarket Station

5 · City Point—McCormack Housing via
Andrew Station

6 · Boston Marine Industrial Park—
South Station/Haymarket Station

7 · City Point—Otis & Summer Streets via
Northern Avenue & South Station

9 · City Point—Copley Square via
Broadway Station

10 · City Point—Copley Square via
Andrew Station & BU Medical Area

11 · City Point—Downtown, Bayview Route

Car Washes

· **Mr Perfection** · 1 Seaport Ln [Northern Ave]

Gas Stations

· **Exxon** · 57 L St [E 3rd]

Parking

Map 12 • **Newmarket / Andrew Square**

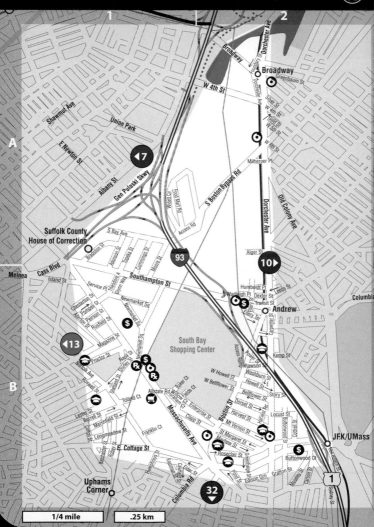

Essentials

Food distributors, u-store warehouses, and the big box chains at South Bay Shopping Center are the heart of this commercial and industrial area. Unless you've got a trip to Target, Home Depot, or are visiting family at the Suffolk County House of Correction, you'll find only the fraying edges of Southie, Dorchester, and Roxbury worth a deeper look.

Map 12

$ Banks

- **Bank of America** •
  1104 Massachusetts Ave [Newmarket]
- **Bank of America (ATM)** •
  150 Mt Vernon St [Morrissey]
- **Citizens Bank** • 60 Newmarket Sq [Mass Ave]
- **Citizens Bank (ATM)** • 863 Columbia Rd [Buttonwood]
- **Mt Washington Bank** • 501 Southampton St [Ellery St]

Donuts

- **Doughboy Deli** • 220 Dorchester Ave [W 5th]
- **Dunkin' Donuts** •
  1100 Massachusetts Ave [Newmarket]
- **Dunkin' Donuts** • ?? W Broadway [Dot Ave]
- **Dunkin' Donuts** • 256 Boston St [Roseclair]
- **Dunkin' Donuts** • 510 Southampton St [Ellery St]
- **Dunkin' Donuts** • 847 Dorchester Ave [Mount Vernon St]

O Landmarks

- **Suffolk County House of Correction** •
  20 Bradston St [Southampton]

Rx Pharmacies

- **Stop & Shop** • 1100 Massachusetts Ave [Newmarket]
- **Target** • 7 Allstate Rd [Mass Ave]

Schools

- **Boston Collegiate Charter** •
  11 Mayhew St [Boston St]
- **Community Academy Middle** •
  76 Shirley St [Roswell]
- **Roger Clap Elementary** • 35 Harvest St [Boston St]
- **Samuel W Mason Elementary** •
  150 Norfolk Ave [Proctor]
- **St Mary's Elementary** • 52 Boston St [Father Songin]
- **William E Russell Elementary** •
  750 Columbia Rd [Pond St]

Supermarkets

- **Super 88** • 101 Allstate Rd [Mass Ave]

Map 12 • **Newmarket / Andrew Square** Ⓝ

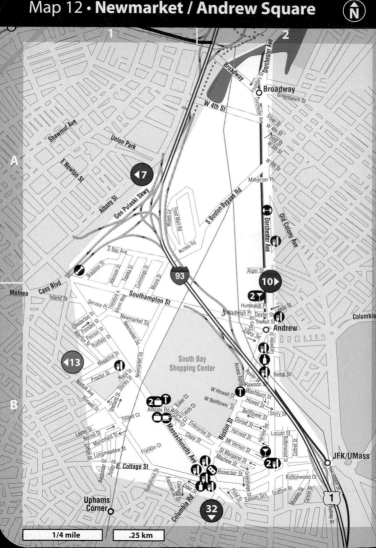

Sundries / Entertainment

Map 12

Treat your date at an out-of-the-way den of romance. Cozy 224 Boston Street fits that bill, with reasonable prices to boot. So does Cape Verdean Restaurante Laura with live fado, despite its high-crime exterior. It would be a shame to overlook the authentic Polish cuisine of tiny Café Polonia.

Coffee

- **Starbucks** · Target · 7 Allstate Rd [Mass Ave]
- **Sugar Bowl** · 837 Dorchester Ave [Mount Vernon St]

Gyms

- **Gold's Gym** · 323 Dorchester Ave [W 7th]

Hardware Stores

- **Home Depot** · 5 Allstate Rd [Mass Ave]
- **PJ O'Donnell & Co** · 115 Boston St [Washburn St]

Liquor Stores

- **Andrew Square Liquors** · 605 Dorchester Ave [Boston St]
- **Cape Verdean Liquors** · 690 Columbia Rd [Elder]

Nightlife

- **Aces High** · 551 Dorchester Ave [Dexter St]
- **Dot Tavern** · 840 Dorchester Ave [Harvest St]
- **Sports Connection Bar** · 560 Dorchester Ave [Leeds]

Pet Shops

- **Skipton Kennel & Pet Center** · 70 Southampton St [Bradston]

Restaurants

- **224 Boston Street** · 224 Boston St [St Margaret]
- **Alex's Pizza** · 580 Dorchester Ave [Leeds]
- **Avenue Grille** · 856 Dorchester Ave [Mount Vernon St]
- **Baltic Deli & Café** · 632 Dorchester Ave [Father Songin]
- **Café Polonia** · 611 Dorchester Ave [Boston St]
- **Restaurante Laura** · 688 Columbia Rd [Elder]
- **Singh's Roti Shop** · 692 Columbia Rd [Elder]
- **Taqueria Casa Real** · 860A Dorchester Ave [Mount Vernon St]
- **Venetian Garden** · 1269 Massachusetts Ave [Columbia Rd]
- **Victoria** · 1024 Massachusetts Ave [Newmarket]
- **World Seafood Restaurant** · 400 Dorchester Ave [D]

Shopping

- **Home Depot** · 5 Allstate Rd [Mass Ave]
- **Marshall's** · 8D Allstate Rd [Mass Ave]

Video Rental

- **North End Video** · 292 Boston St [Roseclair St]

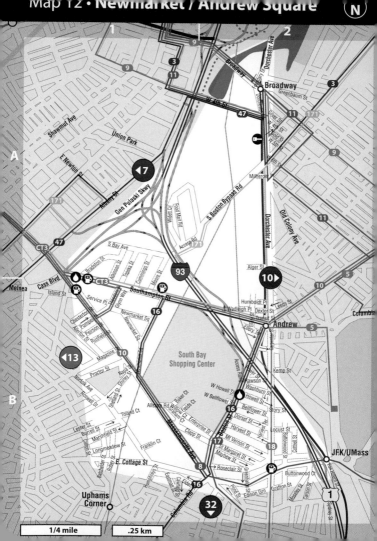

Map 12 • **Newmarket / Andrew Square**

Transportation

Map 12

This largely commercial and industrial area isn't well served by public transportation. If you need to get to the South Bay Shopping Center without driving, take the 10 bus from Andrew Square or Copley. If you're out for a stroll, make sure to leave the JFK/UMass T stop to the north onto Columbia Road.

Subway

- **Broadway**
- **Andrew**
- **JFK/UMass**

Bus Lines

- **CT3** · Beth Israel Deaconess Medical Center—Andrew Station via BU Medical Center
- **3** · Boston Marine Industrial Park—South Station/Haymarket Station
- **5** · City Point—McCormack Housing via Andrew Station
- **8** · Harbor Point/UMass—Kenmore Station via South End Medical Area
- **9** · City Point—Copley Square via Broadway Station
- **10** · City Point—Copley Square via Andrew Station & BU Medical Area
- **11** · City Point—Downtown, Bayview Route
- **16** · Forest Hills Station—Andrew Station or UMass via Columbia Road
- **17** · Fields Corner Station—Andrew Station via Uphams Corner & Edward Everett Square
- **18** · Ashmont Station—Andrew Station via Fields Corner Station
- **47** · Central Square, Cambridge—Broadway Station via South End Medical Area
- **171** · Dudley Station—Logan Airport via Andrew Station

Car Rental

- **Enterprise** · 230 Dorchester Ave [W 5th] · 617-268-1411

Car Washes

- **Bubbles Car Wash** · 90 Southampton St [Mass Ave]
- **Scrubadub** · 25 W Howell St [Boston St]

Gas Stations

- **Gulf** · 888 Dorchester Ave [Columbia Rd] ⏰
- **Independent** · 150 Southampton St [Topeka] ⏰
- **Mobil** · 85 Southampton St [Bradston]
- **Sunoco** · 895 Massachusetts Ave [Island]

Map 13 · **Roxbury**

Museum of Fine Arts

Northeastern

Northeastern University

Massachusetts Avenue

1. Hammond Ter
2. Sussex St
3. Greenwich Ct
4. Westminster St
5. Sojourner Truth Ct

Columbus Ave

Massachusetts Ave

Ruggles

Ruggles St

Lenox St

1. Fellows St
2. Lenox Ct
3. Connolly St

Harrison Ave

Roxbury Crossing

Islamic Cultural Center

Tremont St

Whittier St

Malcolm X Blvd

Melnea Cass Blvd

Melnea Cass Blvd

Island St

Roxbury St

Washington St

Dudley Sq

Roxbury Center For the Arts

Dudley St

1. Nathan St
2. Greenville Park

Highland Park

Warren St

Warren Pl

1. St James Ter
2. Regent Pl
3. Mewes St

Hampden St

Jackson Square

Rockville Park

Circuit St

Ritchie St

Marcella St

Malcolm X Park

Martin Luther King Blvd

Malcolm X and Ella Little-Collins House

1. S Charlame Ct
2. N Charlame Ct
3. N Charlame Ter

Humboldt Ave

Townsend St

National Center for Afro-American Artists

Quincy St

Blue Hill Ave

1/2 mile   .5 km

There's a beauty to Roxbury, despite its roughness. Dudley Square is Roxbury's commercial center, but businesses are also finding opportunity closer to the busy Orange Line and along Blue Hill Avenue. Highlights include The National Center of Afro-American Art, the largest mosque in New England, and the view from Fort Hill.

$ Banks

- **Bank of America** · 114 Dudley St [Washington St]
- **Bank of America (ATM)** · 1762 Washington St [Mass Ave]
- **Bank of America (ATM)** · 39 Warren St [Ziegler]
- **Citizens Bank** · 2343 Washington St [Marvin St]
- **Sovereign Bank** · 3060 Washington St [Walnut Pk]
- **Sovereign Bank** · 330 Martin Luther King Blvd [Washington St]
- **Sovereign Bank (ATM)** · 1010 Harrison Ave [Melnea]
- **Sovereign Bank (ATM)** · Boston Medical Center · 850 Harrison Ave [Mass Ave]

✳ Community Gardens

- **Winthrop Street Garden** · 25 Winthrop St [Kearsarge Ave]

◉ Donuts

- **Dunkin' Donuts** · 1131 Tremont St [Ruggles St]
- **Dunkin' Donuts** · 1350 Tremont St [Prentiss]
- **Dunkin' Donuts** · 17 Melnea Cass Blvd [Hampden]
- **Dunkin' Donuts** · 2360 Washington St [Roxbury]

O Landmarks

- **Highland Park** · Fort Ave & Beech Glen St
- **Islamic Cultural Center** · 1 Malcolm X Blvd [Roxbury]
- **Malcolm X and Ella Little-Collins House** · 72 Dale St [Wakullah]
- **National Center for Afro-American Artists** · 300 Walnut Ave [Cobden]
- **Roxbury Center for Arts** · 182 Dudley St [Harrison Ave]
- **Shirley-Eustis House** · 33 Shirley St [Clifton St]

📖 Libraries

- **Dudley** · 65 Warren St [Dudley St]

℞ Pharmacies

- **Kornfield Drug** · 2121 Washington St [Williams St]
- **Ruggles Square Pharmacy** · 1123 Tremont St [Ruggles St]
- **Walgreens** · 2275 Washington St [Vernon]
- **Walgreens** · 416 Warren St [Townsend]

◉ Police

- **District B-2** · 135 Dudley St [Warren St]

✉ Post Offices

- **Roxbury Station** · 55 Roxbury St [Shawmut Ave]

🏫 Schools

- **826 Boston** · 3035 Washington St [W Walnut Park]
- **Boston Adult Academy** · 55 New Dudley St [King St]
- **Boston Day and Evening Academy** · 20 Kearsarge Ave [Warren St]
- **Boston Latin Academy** · 205 Townsend St [Humboldt Ave]
- **Carter Development Center** · 396 Northampton St [Columbus]
- **David A Ellis Elementary** · 302 Walnut Ave [Cobden]
- **Eliot Educational Center** · 56 Dale St [Walnut Ave]
- **George Lewis Middle** · 131 Walnut Ave [Dale]
- **Haynes Early Education Center** · 263 Blue Hill Ave [Dove St]
- **Henry Dearborn Middle** · 35 Greenville St [Dudley St]
- **Henry L Higginson Elementary** · 160 Harrishof St [Haley]
- **James P Timilty Middle** · 205 Roxbury St [Centre St]
- **John Winthrop Elementary** · 35 Brookford St [Dromey]
- **Madison Park Technical Vocational High School** · 75 Malcom X Blvd [Roxbury]
- **Nathan Hale Elementary** · 51 Cedar St [Hawthorne St]
- **O'Bryant School of Math & Science** · 55 Malcom X Blvd [Roxbury]
- **Orchard Gardens K-8** · 906 Albany St [Webber]
- **Paige Academy** · 40 Highland Ave [Centre St]
- **Ralph Waldo Emerson Elementary** · 6 Shirley St [Dudley St]
- **Roland Hayes School of Music** · 55 Malcom X Blvd [Roxbury]
- **Roxbury Community College** · 1234 Columbus Ave [Cedar St]
- **St Joseph School** · 18 Hulbert St [Regent St]
- **St Patrick Elementary** · 131 Mt Pleasant Ave [Blue Hill]
- **William Monroe Trotter Elementary** · 135 Humboldt Ave [Wyoming]

🛒 Supermarkets

- **Tropical Foods** · 2101 Washington St [Williams St]

Map 13 · **Roxbury**

Massachusetts Avenue

Northeastern

Museum of Fine Arts

PAGE 226

Northeastern University

15

Ruggles

A

Roxbury Crossing

Columbus Ave

Tremont St

Ruggles St

Shawmut Ave

Malcolm X Blvd

Washington St

Columbus Ave

Dudley Sq

Warren St

Jackson Square

14

Circuit St

Walnut Ave

B

Ritchie St

Marcella St

Malcolm X Park

Martin Luther King Blvd

Humboldt Ave

28

31

Columbus Ave

Townsend St

Massachusetts Ave

1. Hammond Ter
2. Switzer St
3. Greenwich Ct
4. Westminster St
5. Sojourner Truth Ct

Lenox St

1. Fellows St
2. Lennox Ct
3. Connolly St

Melnea Cass Blvd

Melnea Cass Blvd

12

1. St James Ter
2. Regent Pl
3. Hewes St

1. Natham St
2. Greenville Park

Dudley St

Hampden St

Shirl
Eust
Hous

1. S Charlame Ct
2. N Charlame Ter

1/2 mile   .5 km

Map 13

Lunch counters here serve soul food, jerk, and Latin American delicacies. Hankering for Dominican food? It doesn't get better than Merengue. Pepper Pot will hook you up Jamaican style. Grab a drink at local joints C&S or El Mondonguito.

Coffee

- **Blue Hill Coffee Shop** · 170 Blue Hill Ave [Clifford]

Farmers Markets

- **Dudley Town Common**
  (Jun—Oct; Tues & Thurs 4 pm—7 pm) ·
  Dudley St & Blue Hill Ave

Gyms

- **Body by Brandy Fitness Center** ·
  2181 Washington St [Ruggles St]
- **Roxbury Family YMCA** ·
  285 Martin Luther King Blvd [Walnut Ave]

Liquor Stores

- **Brothers Liquors** · 616 Shawmut Ave [Lenox]
- **Caribbean Liquors** · 527 Dudley St [North Ave]
- **Folgers Liquors** · 2665 Washington St [Cedar St]
- **Garden Liquors** · 276 Warren St [Waverly St]
- **Giant** · 2371 Washington St [Roxbury]
- **Hollywood Liquors** · 950 Tremont St [Davenport]
- **Liquor Land** · 874 Harrison Ave [Northampton St]
- **Simon's Liquor** · 2169 Washington St [Ruggles St]
- **Warren Liquors** · 368 Warren St [Maywood St]

Nightlife

- **C&S Tavern** · 380 Warren St [Maywood St]
- **El Mondonguito** · 221 Dudley St [Greenville St]
- **Slade's** · 958 Tremont St [Davenport]

Restaurants

- **Bob's Southern Bistro** ·
  604 Columbus Ave [Northampton St]
- **Breezeway Bar and Grill** · 153 Blue Hill Ave [Julian]
- **Merengue** · 156 Blue Hill Ave [Julian]
- **Pepper Pot** · 208 Dudley St [Winslow St]
- **Stash's Grille** · 150 Dudley St [Warren St]

Shopping

- **Bikes Not Bombs** · 18 Bartlett Sq [Washington St]

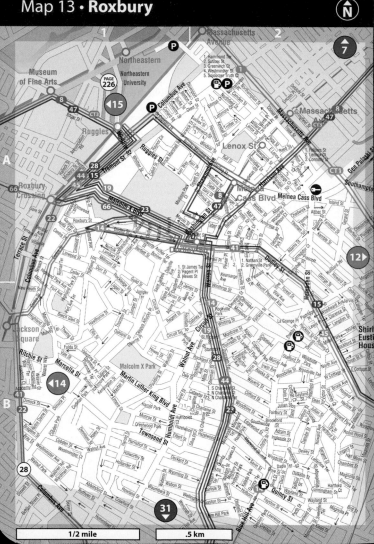

Map 13 · **Roxbury**

Transportation

Potholed and neglected, Roxbury's streets are fiendishly difficult to travel. Considering how many people call the neighborhood home, the public transportation is woefully inadequate. Unless you skirt the perimeter on the Orange Line or the pleasant Southwest Corridor bike trail, you'll likely head through Dudley Station, the busy bus hub packed with loiterers.

Subway

- **Massachusetts Ave**
- **Ruggles**
- **Roxbury Crossing**
- **Jackson Square**
- **Northeastern (E)**
- **Museum (E)**
- **Ruggles (E)**
- **Mass Ave**
- **Lenox St**
- **Melnea Cass Blvd**
- **Dudley Square**

Car Rental

- **Enterprise** ·
  17 Melnea Cass Blvd [Hampden] · 617-442-7500

Gas Stations

- **Citgo** · 294 Blue Hill Ave [Quincy St]
- **Ho Gas** · 57 Blue Hill Ave [Winthrop St]
- **Independent** · 67 Blue Hill Ave [Moreland]
- **Sunoco** · 785 Tremont St [Northampton St] ✪

Parking

Bus Lines

- **CT1** · Central Square, Cambridge—BU Medical Center/BU Medical Campus
- **CT3** · Beth Israel Deaconess Medical Center—Andrew Station via BU Medical Center
- **1** · Harvard/Holyoke Gate—Dudley Station via Massachusetts Ave & BU Medical Center
- **8** · Harbor Point/UMass—Kenmore Station via South End Medical Area
- **14** · Roslindale Square—Heath Street via Dudley Station, Grove Hall & American Legion Hwy
- **15** · Kane Square or Fields Corner Station—Ruggles Station via Uphams Corner
- **19** · Fields Corner Station—Ruggles Station via Grove Hall & Dudley Streets
- **22** · Ashmont Station—Ruggles Station via Talbot Ave & Jackson Square
- **23** · Ashmont Station—Ruggles Station via Washington Street
- **28** · Mattapan Station—Ruggles Station via Dudley Station
- **41** · Centre & Eliot Streets—JFK/Umass Station via Dudley Station, Centre Street & Jackson Square Station
- **44** · Jackson Square Station—Ruggles Station via Seaver Street & Humboldt Avenue

Map 13

19 27
16 5 6 3
7
17 15 12
13
14

Map 14 · **Jamaica Plain**

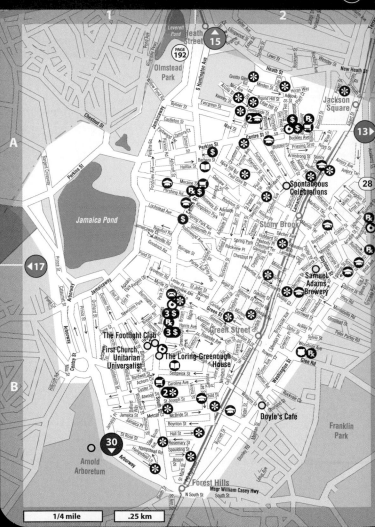

Essentials

Map 14

Despite the ongoing gentrification, Jamaica Plain is still home to a diverse population of artists, yuppies, students, lesbians, and immigrants. Stunning Jamaica Pond, the Arnold Arboretum, and the Franklin Park Zoo are all great reasons to head outside. Colorful festivals are a highlight of the summer months.

$ Banks

- **Bank of America** • 315 Centre St [Walden St]
- **Bank of America** • 677 Centre St [Seaverns]
- **Boston Private Bank & Trust (ATM)** • 403 Centre St [Barbara]
- **Citizens Bank** • 696 Centre St [Burroughs St]
- **Citizens Bank (ATM)** • 301 Centre St [Walden St]
- **Citizens Bank (ATM)** • 684 Centre St [Seaverns]
- **Hyde Park Cooperative Bank** • 733 Centre St [Harris Ave]
- **People's Federal Savings Bank** • 725 Centre St [Harris Ave]
- **Roxbury Highland Bank** • 515 Centre St [Spring Pk Ave]
- **Sovereign Bank (ATM)** • CVS/Pharmacy • 467 Centre St [Roseway]
- **Wainwright Bank & Trust** • 687 Centre St [Seaverns]

✳ Community Gardens

◉ Donuts

- **Dunkin' Donuts** • 1926 Columbus Ave [Walnut Pk]
- **Dunkin' Donuts** • 315 Centre St [Walden St]
- **Dunkin' Donuts** • 684 Centre St [Seaverns]
- **Dunkin' Donuts** • 757 Centre St [Thomas St]

O Landmarks

- **Arnold Arboretum** • 125 Arborway [Centre St]
- **Doyle's Café** • 3484 Washington St [Williams St]
- **First Church, Unitarian Universalist** • 6 Eliot St [Centre St]
- **The Footlight Club** • 7A Eliot St [Centre St]
- **The Loring-Greenough House** • 12 South St [Centre St]
- **Samuel Adams Brewery** • 30 Germania St [Brookside]
- **Spontaneous Celebrations** • 75 Danforth St [Boylston St]

📖 Libraries

- **Connolly** • 433 Centre St [Paul Gore St]
- **Jamaica Plain** • 12 Sedgwick St [South St]

℞ Pharmacies

- **CVS** • 467 Centre St [Boylston St]
- **CVS** • 704 Centre St [Burroughs St]
- **Egleston Square Pharmacy** • 3090 Washington St [Beethoven]
- **Samuels Pharmacy** • 46 Woodside Ave [Washington St]
- **Stop & Shop Pharmacy** • 301 Centre St [Johnson]
- **Walgreens** • 1890 Columbus Ave [Bray]

🛡 Police

- **District E-13** • 3345 Washington St [Green St]

✉ Post Offices

- **Jamaica Plain Station** • 655 Centre St [Myrtle St]

🎓 Schools

- **Blessed Sacrament Elementary** • 30 Sunnyside St [Westerly]
- **Compass** • 26 Sunnyside St [Westerly]
- **Egleston High** • 3134 Washington St [School St]
- **Ellis Mendell Elementary** • 164 School St [Copley]
- **English High** • 144 McBride St [Call]
- **Greater Egleston Community High** • 80 School St [Weld]
- **James Curley Elementary** • 40 Pershing Rd [Centre St]
- **John F Kennedy Elementary** • 7 Bolster St [Wyman St]
- **Louis Agassiz Elementary** • 20 Child St [South St]
- **Mary E Curley Middle** • 493 Centre St [Pershing]
- **Nativity Prep** • 39 Lamartine St [Roys]
- **Our Lady of Lourdes Elementary** • 54 Brookside Ave [Minton]

🛒 Supermarkets

- **Harvest Co-op Market** • 57 South St [Custer]
- **Hi-Lo** • 415 Centre St [Moraine]
- **Stop & Shop** • 301 Centre St [Walden St]

Map 14 · **Jamaica Plain**

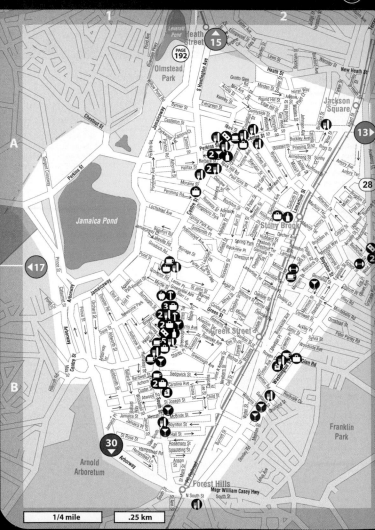

Sundries / Entertainment

Map 14

Centre Street functions as the main artery in JP, lined with restaurants and shops of all kinds. NFT picks = Brendan Behan Pub. La Pupusa Guanaca, Zon's, Midway Café, and James's Gate. Jackson Square and Washington Street offer the flavors of its Puerto Rican, Dominican, and Cape Verdean communities.

☕ Coffee

• **Canto 6** • 3346 Washington St [Green St]
• **Cha Fahn** • 763 Centre St [Greenough Ave]
• **Fiore's Bakery** • 55 South St [Carolina Ave]
• **June Bug Café** • 403A Centre St [Barbara]
• **Sweet Christophers Desserts** • 601 Centre St [Pond St]
• **Sweet Finnish** • 761 Centre St [Eliot St]
• **ULA Café** • 284 Amory St [New Minton]

🖨 Copy Shops

• **Fresh Copy** • 64 South St [Carolina Ave]
• **Schell Printing** • 3399 Washington St [Green St]

🌻 Farmers Markets

• **Jamaica Plain**
(July—Oct; Tues 12 pm—5 pm, Sat 12 pm—3 pm) •
677 Centre St [Seaverns]

💪 Gyms

• **Mike's Fitness** • 284 Amory St [Porter St]
• **YMCA Egleston Square Youth Center** •
3134 Washington St [School St]

🔧 Hardware Stores

• **Hardware City** • 656 Centre St [Myrtle St]
• **Yumont True Value Hardware** •
702 Centre St [Burroughs St]

🍾 Liquor Stores

• **Blanchard Liquors** • 741 Centre St [Harris Ave]
• **Chauncy Liquor Mart** • 3100 Washington St [Beethoven]
• **Egleston Liquors** • 3086 Washington St [Beethoven]
• **Foerster's Market & Liquors** • 78 Boylston St [Danforth St]
• **Hyde Square Wine & Liquor** • 391 Centre St [Sheridan St]

🍸 Nightlife

• **Alchemist Lounge** • 435 S Huntington Ave [Centre St]
• **Brendan Behan Pub** • 378 Centre St [Sheridan St]
• **Costello's Tavern** • 723 Centre St [Harris Ave]
• **Doyle's Café** • 3484 Washington St [Williams St]
• **Drinking Fountain** • 3520 Washington St [Rossmore]
• **James's Gate** • 5 McBride St [South St]
• **Jeanie Johnston Pub** • 144 South St [Hall St]
• **Midway Café** • 3496 Washington St [Williams St]

• **Milky Way Lounge & Lanes** • 403 Centre St [Barbara]
• **Samuel Adams Brewery** • 30 Germania St [Brookside]

🍴 Restaurants

• **Alex's Chimis** • 358 Centre St [Forbes]
• **Bukhara** • 701 Centre St [Burroughs St]
• **Café D** • 711 Centre St [Burroughs St]
• **Centre Street Café** • 699 Centre St [Burroughs St]
• **Cha Fahn** • 763 Centre St [Greenough Ave]
• **Dogwood Café** • 3712 Washington St [Arborway]
• **Doyle's Café** • 3484 Washington St [Williams St]
• **El Oriental de Cuba** • 416 Centre St [Paul Gore St]
• **Fredy's Pastelito** • 3381 Washington St [Green St]
• **The Galway House** • 720 Centre St [Burroughs St]
• **Great Wall** • 779 Centre St [Eliot St]
• **James's Gate** • 5 McBride St [South St]
• **JP Seafood Café** • 730 Centre St [Harris Ave]
• **La Pupusa Guanaca** • 378 Centre St [Sheridan St]
• **Miami Restaurant** • 381 Centre St [Sheridan St]
• **Sorella's** • 388 Centre St [Sheridan St]
• **Tacos El Charro** • 349 Centre St [Westerly]
• **Ten Tables** • 597 Centre St [Pond St]
• **Vee Vee** • 763 Centre St [Eliot St]
• **Wonder Spice Café** • 697 Centre St [Burroughs St]
• **Yely's Coffee Shop** • 284 Centre St [Chestnut Ave]
• **Zon's** • 2 Perkins St [Perkins Sq]

🛍 Shopping

• **Boing! JP's Toy Shop** • 729 Centre St [Harris Ave]
• **Boomerangs** • 716 Centre St [Burroughs St]
• **Canto 6** • 3346 Washington St [Green St]
• **City Feed and Supply** • 66 Boylston St [Chestnut Ave]
• **Eye Q Optical** • 7 Pond St [Centre St]
• **Fat Ram's Pumpkin Tattoo** • 380 Centre St [Sheridan St]
• **Ferris Wheels Bicycle Shop** • 66 South St [Carolina Ave]
• **Fire Opal** • 683 Centre St [Seaverns]
• **Gadgets** • 671 Centre St [Seaverns]
• **Honeyspot** • 48 South St [Essex St]
• **JP Licks** • 659 Centre St [Starr Ln]
• **Petal & Leaf** • 461 Centre St [Moraine]
• **Salmagundi** • 765 Centre St [Eliot St]

🎬 Video Rental

• **Columbus Video** • 1967 Columbus Ave [Washington St]
• **Video Underground** • 385 Centre St [Sheridan St]

Map 14 · **Jamaica Plain**

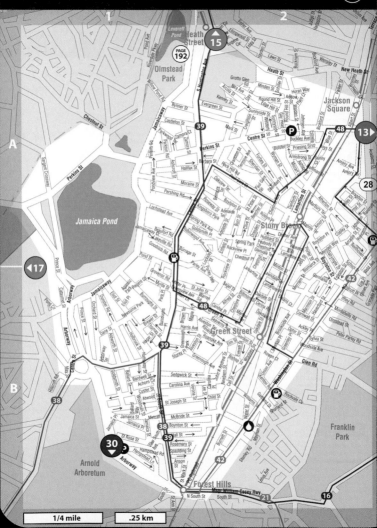

Map 14

Driving is fairly convenient in JP, thanks to the quick flow of traffic on the Riverway and the abundance of free parking. Locals use the 39 bus as often as the Orange Line. Make Al Gore proud—take the bike trail in Southwest Corridor Park alongside the Orange Line all the way downtown.

Subway

- · **Jackson Square**
- · **Stony Brook**
- · **Green St**
- · **Forest Hills**
- · **Heath St (E)**

Bus Lines

16 · Forest Hills Station—Andrew Station or UMass via Columbia Road

21 · Ashmont Station—Forest Hills Station via Morton Street

38 · Wren Street—Forest Hills Station via Centre & South Streets

39 · Forest Hills Station—Back Bay Station via Huntington Avenue

42 · Forest Hills Station—Ruggles Station via Washington Station & Dudley Square

48 · Jamaica Plain Loop Monument— Jackson Square Station via Green Street

Car Washes

· **Jamaica Plain Car Wash** ·
3530 Washington St [Rossmore]

Gas Stations

- · **Citgo** · 3055 Washington St [Walnut Pk]
- · **Hatoff's** · 3440 Washington St [Union Ave]
- · **Independent** · 581 Centre St [Goodrich]

Parking

Map 15 · **Fenway (West) / Mission Hill**

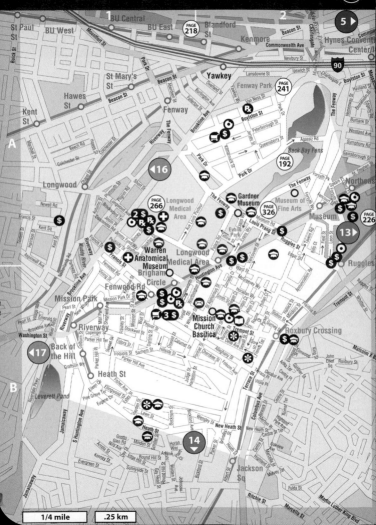

Map 15

Essentials

The place where culture, education, and sports meet, you can wander among fine art museums, green parks, eclectic colleges, top medical centers, and historic Fenway Park. While high-rise condos are changing the face of Fenway, Mission Hill is still a funky mix of students, families, and young professionals.

$ Banks

- **Bank of America** • 1614 Tremont St [Wigglesworth]
- **Bank of America** • 333 Longwood Ave [Binney St]
- **Bank of America (ATM)** • 1643 Tremont St [Wigglesworth]
- **Bank of America (ATM)** • Ruggles St MBTA • 249 Ruggles St [Leon]
- **Bank of America (ATM)** • 300 The Fenway [Palace]
- **Bank of America (ATM)** • 360 Huntington Ave [Opera]
- **Bank of America (ATM)** • 550 Huntington Ave [Ruggles St]
- **Bank of America (ATM)** • 610 Huntington Ave [St Alphonsus]
- **Bank of America (ATM)** • 621 Huntington Ave [Tetlow]
- **Bank of America (ATM)** • MBTA Roxbury Crossing • Tremont St & Columbus Ave
- **Citizens Bank** • 1628 Tremont St [Wigglesworth]
- **Citizens Bank (ATM)** • 1 Francis St [Kent St]
- **Citizens Bank (ATM)** • 1620 Tremont St [Wigglesworth]
- **Citizens Bank (ATM)** • Boston Children's Hospital • 300 Longwood Ave [Blackfan]
- **Citizens Bank (ATM)** • 33 Kilmarnock St [Boylston St]
- **Citizens Bank (ATM)** • 75 Francis St [Vining]
- **Sovereign Bank** • 6 Francis St [Huntington]
- **Sovereign Bank (ATM)** • 350 Longwood Ave [Brookline Ave]
- **Sovereign Bank (ATM)** • 58 Forsyth St [Greenleaf]

✳ Community Gardens

◐ Donuts

- **Dunkin' Donuts** • 115 Forsyth St [Greenleaf]
- **Dunkin' Donuts** • 1420 Boylston St [Kilmarnock]
- **Dunkin' Donuts** • 1620 Tremont St [Wigglesworth]
- **Dunkin' Donuts** • 1631 Tremont St [Wigglesworth]
- **Dunkin' Donuts** • 350 Longwood Ave [Brookline Ave]
- **Dunkin' Donuts** • 360 Huntington Ave [Opera]
- **Mike's Donuts** • 1524 Tremont St [Carmel]

✚ Emergency Rooms

- **Brigham and Women's Hospital** • 75 Francis St [Vining]
- **Children's Hospital** • 300 Longwood Ave [Blackfan]

O Landmarks

- **Isabella Stewart Gardner Museum** • 280 The Fenway [Palace]
- **Mission Church Basilica** • 1545 Tremont St [Pontiac]
- **Museum of Fine Arts** • 465 Huntington Ave [Museum Rd]
- **Warren Anatomical Museum** • 10 Shattuck St [Binney St]

📖 Libraries

- **Parker Hill** • 1497 Tremont St [Burney]

℞ Pharmacies

- **Rite Aid** • 1295 Boylston St [Yawkey]
- **CVS** • 300 Longwood Ave [Blackfan]
- **CVS** • 350 Longwood Ave [Brookline Ave]
- **Walgreens** • 1630 Tremont St [Wigglesworth]

✉ Post Offices

- **Mission Hill Station** • 1575 Tremont St [S Whitney]

🚌 Schools

- **Boston Latin School** • 78 Ave Louis Pasteur [Longwood]
- **David Farragut Elementary** • 10 Fenwood Rd [Huntington]
- **ELC - West Zone** • 200 Heath St [Schiller]
- **Emmanuel College** • 400 The Fenway [Ave Louis Pasteur]
- **Harvard Medical** • 25 Shattuck St [Binney St]
- **Harvard School of Dental Medicine** • 188 Longwood Ave [Palace]
- **Harvard School of Public Health** • 677 Huntington Ave [Washington St]
- **Health Careers Academy** • 360 Huntington Ave [Opera]
- **James Hennigan Elementary** • 200 Heath St [Schiller]
- **Manville School** • 3 Blackfan Cir [Longwood]
- **Massachusetts College of Art** • 621 Huntington Ave [Tetlow]
- **Massachusetts College of Pharmacy and Health Sciences** • 179 Longwood Ave [Palace]
- **Mission Hill** • 67 Alleghany St [Parker St]
- **New Mission High School** • 67 Alleghany St [Parker St]
- **Northeastern University** • 360 Huntington Ave [Opera]
- **Roxbury Preparatory Charter** • 120 Fisher Ave [Hayden St]
- **School of the Museum of Fine Arts** • 230 The Fenway [Evans Rd]
- **Simmons College** • 300 The Fenway [Palace]
- **Wentworth Institute of Technology** • 550 Huntington Ave [Ruggles St]

🛒 Supermarkets

- **Shaw's** • 33 Kilmarnock St [Boylston St]
- **Stop & Shop** • 1620 Tremont St [Wigglesworth]

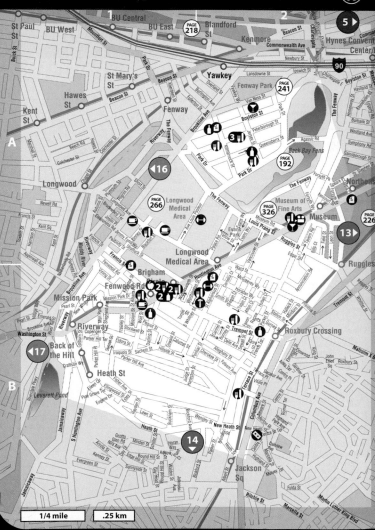

Map 15 • **Fenway (West) / Mission Hill**

Sundries / Entertainment

Map 15

The New Fenway developments continue to bring upscale shops and restaurants, but head out of the fray to neighborhood favorites like El Pelon Taqueria and Rod Dee II. In Mission Hill, Penguin Cafe makes delicious pizzas with creative toppings, and the best pints flow at Flann O'Briens.

Coffee

- **Brigham Circle Diner** ·
  737 Huntington Ave [Francis St]
- **Red Bean Coffee Roasters** ·
  350 Longwood Ave [Brookline Ave]
- **Starbucks** · Children's Hospital ·
  283 Longwood Ave [Blackfan]

Copy Shops

- **FedEx Kinko's** · 1373 Boylston St [Kilmarnock St]
- **The Print House** · 660 Huntington Ave [Washington St]
- **The Print House** · 75 Francis St [Vining]
- **USP** · 360 Huntington Ave [Opera]

Farmers Markets

- **Mission Hill (June—Oct; Thurs 11:30 am—6 pm)**
  · Huntington Ave & Tremont St

Gyms

- **Custom Fitness** · 75 St Alphonsus St [Smith St]
- **Fitcorp** · 77 Ave Louis Pasteur [Longwood]

Hardware Stores

- **AC Hardware** · 1562 Tremont St [St Alphonsus]

Liquor Stores

- **Bradley Liquors** · 1383 Boylston St [Kilmarnock]
- **Brigham Liquors** · 732 Huntington Ave [Calumet]
- **Dara's Wine & Spirits** ·
  750 Huntington Ave [Fenwood]
- **Fuentes Market and Liquor Store** ·
  680 Parker St [Gurney]
- **Jersey Street Liquors** · 48 Queensberry St [Jersey]
- **Mission Hill Liquors** · 1623 Tremont St [Wigglesworth]

Movie Theaters

- **Museum of Fine Arts** ·
  465 Huntington Ave [Museum Rd]

Nightlife

- **Baseball Tavern** · 1270 Boylston St [Jersey]
- **Flann O'Brien's** · 1619 Tremont St [Wigglesworth]
- **Machine** · 1256 Boylston St [Yawkey]
- **Punter's Pub** · 450 Huntington Ave [Parker St]
- **Ramrod** · 1254 Boylston St [Yawkey]

Restaurants

- **Bravo** · 465 Huntington Ave [Museum Rd]
- **Brigham Circle Diner** ·
  737 Huntington Ave [Francis St]
- **Brown Sugar Café** · 129 Jersey St [Queensberry]
- **Chacho's** · 1502 Tremont St [Rumey]
- **El Pelon Taqueria** · 92 Peterborough St [Kilmarnock]
- **Huntington Pizza & Café** ·
  764 Huntington Ave [Wait]
- **Longwood Grille & Bar** ·
  342 Longwood Ave [Brookline Ave]
- **Mississippi's** · 103 Terrace St [Cedar St]
- **Penguin Café** · 735 Huntington Ave [Francis St]
- **Rod Dee II** · 94 Peterborough St [Kilmarnock]
- **Solstice Café** · 1625 Tremont St [Wigglesworth]
- **Sorento's** · 86 Peterborough St [Kilmarnock]
- **Squealing Pig** · 134 Smith St [Washington St]

Video Rental

- **Blockbuster** · 171 Centre St [Nathanial Askia Way]

Map 15 · **Fenway (West) / Mission Hill**

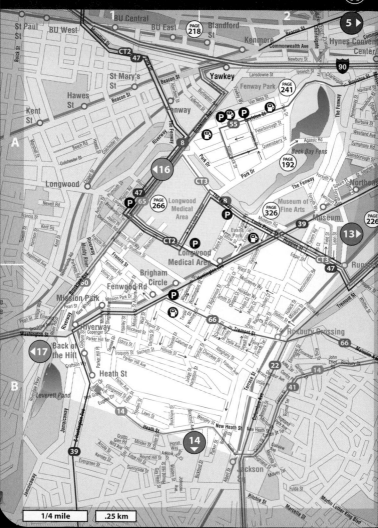

Map 15

Avoid driving around Fenway during Sox games, Huntington Avenue during rush hour, and Longwood at any time. Street parking is never easy. Fenway and Longwood have garages (beware of game day price hikes), but are also served by the Green Line D train. The Green Line E tram runs up Huntington.

Subway

- **Northeastern (E)**
- **Museum of Fine Arts (E)**
- **Longwood Medical Area (E)**
- **Brigham Circle (E)**
- **Fenwood Rd (E)**
- **Mission Park (E)**
- **Riverway (E)**
- **Back of the Hill (E)**
- **Heath (E)**
- **Roxbury Crossing**

Gas Stations

- **Citgo** • 914 Huntington Ave [S Huntington]
- **Exxon** • 1420 Boylston St [Kilmarnock]
- **Getty** • 1600 Tremont St [Wigglesworth]
- **Mobil** • 1301 Boylston St [Yawkey]
- **Shell** • 1241 Boylston St [Yawkey]

Parking

Bus Lines

- **CT2** • Sullivan Station—Ruggles Station via Kendall/MIT
- **CT3** • Beth Israel Deaconess Medical Center—Andrew Station via BU Medical Center
- **8** • Harbor Point/UMass—Kenmore Station via South End Medical Area
- **8** • Roslindale Square—Heath Street via Dudley Station, Grove Hall & American Legion Hwy
- **22** • Ashmont Station—Ruggles Station via Talbot Avenue & Jackson Square
- **39** • Forest Hills Station—Back Bay Station via Huntington Avenue
- **41** • Centre & Eliot Streets—JFK/UMass Station via Dudley Station, Centre Street & Jackson Square Station
- **47** • Central Square, Cambridge—Broadway Station via South End Medical Area
- **60** • Chestnut Hill—Kenmore Station via Brookline Village & Cypress Street
- **65** • Brighton Center—Kenmore Station via Washington Street, Brookline Village
- **66** • Harvard Square—Dudley Station via Allston & Brookline

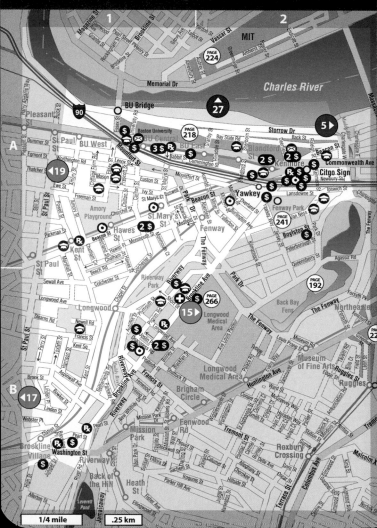

Map 16 • **Kenmore Square / Brookline (East)**

1

2

MIT

PAGE 224

Charles River

Memorial Dr

BU Bridge

27

PAGE 218

90

Boston University

Storrow Dr

5

Back St

St Paul St

BU West

BU Central

Essex St

3 $

BU East

Blandford St

2 $

Kenmore

Beacon St

Commonwealth Ave

Citgo Sign

Newbury St

19

Worthington Rd

Mountfort St

Lenox St

Cummington St

Babbit St

Bay State Rd

Yawkey

Lansdowne St

Mason St

Euston St

Mountfort St

Beacon St

Ipswich St

Freeman St

Clifton St

Ivy St

Buswell St

St Mary's Ct

Overland St

Fenway Park

PAGE 241

Van Ness St

Ewe St

Hawes St

2 $

St Mary's St

Fenway

Boylston St

Kent St

Beacon St

Park Dr

Burlington Ave

The Fenway

Peterborough St

Agassiz Rd

Chatham St

Monmouth St

Fullerton St

Queensberry St

St Paul St

Beech Rd

Colchester St

Riverway Park

PAGE 192

Sewall Ave

Coolidge

The Fenway

Back Bay Fens

Northeastern

Longwood Ave

Riverway

Brookline Ave

PAGE 266

Stearns Rd

Longwood

15

Longwood Medical Area

Newell Rd

Museum Rd

Francis St

Kent Sq

Louis Prang St

Museum of Fine Arts

Perry St

2 $

Peabody St

Sherlock St

Longwood Medical Area

Ruggles St

Ruggles

17

Brook St

Francis St

Brigham Circle

Huntington Ave

Tremont St

Webster St

Linden St

Aspinwall Ave

Mission Park

Fenwood Rd

Roxbury Crossing

Station St

Pearl St

Washington St

Brookline Village

Riverway

Back of the Hill

Heath St

Leverett Pond

Jamaicaway

Columbus Ave

1/4 mile

.25 km

Under the watchful triangular eye of the revamped Citgo sign, the Kenmore Square area is notable for sprawling Boston University, the nightclub scene on Lansdowne Street, and, of course, Fenway Park. Beyond Fenway and the core of Kenmore Square, urban bustle gives way to the more serene residential neighborhoods of affluent Brookline.

$ Banks

- **Bank of America** • 410 Brookline Ave [Longwood]
- **Bank of America** •
  540 Commonwealth Ave [Kenmore]
- **Bank of America** •
  771 Commonwealth Ave [St Mary's St]
- **Bank of America (ATM)** •
  1024A Beacon St [St Mary's St]
- **Bank of America (ATM)** • 201 Brookline Ave [Park Dr]
- **Bank of America (ATM)** • 4 Brookline Pl [Brookline Ave]
- **Bank of America (ATM)** •
  540 Commonwealth Ave [Brookline Ave]
- **Bank of America (ATM)** • 660 Beacon St [Comm Ave]
- **Bank of America (ATM)** • BU - Warren Towers • 700
  Commonwealth Ave [Cummington]
- **Bank of America (ATM)** •
  BU - George Sherman Union •
  775 Commonwealth Ave [University Rd]
- **Brookline Savings Bank** • 1016 Beacon St [St Mary's St]
- **Brookline Savings Bank** •
  160 Washington St [White Pl]
- **Century Bank** • 512 Commonwealth Ave [Kenmore]
- **Century Bank** • 771 Commonwealth Ave [St Mary's St]
- **Century Bank (ATM)** • Barnes & Noble •
  660 Beacon St [Comm Ave]
- **Century Bank (ATM)** •
  770 Commonwealth Ave [St Mary's St]
- **Citizens Bank** • 435 Brookline Ave [Longwood]
- **Citizens Bank** • 560 Commonwealth Ave [Beacon St]
- **Citizens Bank (ATM)** • 1 Deaconess Rd [Pilgrim Rd]
- **Citizens Bank (ATM)** • 49 Lansdowne St [Ipswich St]
- **Citizens Bank (ATM)** •
  542 Commonwealth Ave [Brookline Ave]
- **Citizens Bank (ATM)** • Barnes & Noble •
  660 Beacon St [Commonwealth Ave]
- **Mercantile Bank** • 61 Brookline Ave [Lansdowne]
- **People's Federal Savings Bank** •
  160 Washington St [White Pl]
- **Sovereign Bank** •
  552 Commonwealth Ave [Brookline Ave]
- **Sovereign Bank (ATM)** • CVS •
  1249 Boylston St [Ipswitch St]
- **Sovereign Bank (ATM)** • CVS •
  730 Commonwealth Ave [St Mary's St]

◎ Donuts

- **Dunkin' Donuts** • 1008 Beacon St [St Mary's St]
- **Dunkin' Donuts** • 1108 Beacon St [Hawes St]
- **Dunkin' Donuts** • 330 Brookline Ave [Short St]
- **Dunkin' Donuts** • 457 Brookline Ave [Longwood]
- **Dunkin' Donuts** •
  530 Commonwealth Ave [Brookline Ave]

➕ Emergency Rooms

- **Beth Israel Deaconess Medical Center** •
  330 Brookline Ave [Short St]

O Landmarks

- **BU Bridge** • Essex St & Mountfort St
- **Citgo Sign** • Commonwealth Ave & Beacon St
- **Fenway Park** • 4 Yawkey Wy [Brookline Ave]

℞ Pharmacies

- **CVS** • 730 Commonwealth Ave [St Mary's St]
- **PharmaCare Specialty Pharmacy** •
  350 Longwood Ave [Brookline Ave]
- **Pierce Apothecary** • 1180 Beacon St [Kent St]
- **Village Pharmacy** • 1 Brookline Pl [Brookline Ave]

✉ Post Offices

- **Boston University** •
  775 Commonwealth Ave [Mountfort]
- **Kenmore Station** • 11 Deerfield St [Comm Ave]

⌂ Schools

- **Amos A Lawrence** • 27 Francis St [St Albans]
- **Ansin Religious School of Ohabei Shalom** •
  1187 Beacon St [Marshall St]
- **Boston Arts Academy** • 174 Ipswich St [Lansdowne]
- **Boston University** • 1 Sherborn St [Comm Ave]
- **Boston University Academy** •
  1 University Rd [Comm Ave]
- **Fenway High** • 174 Ipswich St [Lansdowne]
- **Ivy Street** • 200 Ivy St [Essex]
- **Kids Are People Elementary** •
  656 Beacon St [Comm Ave]
- **Neha/Lubavitch School for Girls** •
  9 Prescott St [Lenox]
- **New England Hebrew Academy** •
  9 Prescott St [Lenox]
- **New England School of Photography** •
  537 Commonwealth Ave [Brookline Ave]
- **Wheelock College** • 200 Riverway [Short St]
- **The Winsor School** • 103 Pilgrim Rd [Short St]

Map 16 • **Kenmore Square / Brookline (East)**

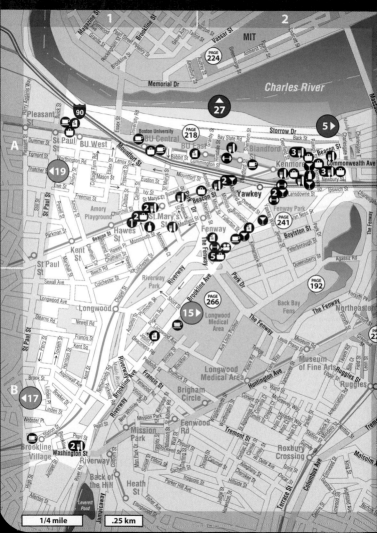

Sundries / Entertainment

Map 16

Even while some of the biggest nightspots on Lansdowne Street are changing hands—not to mention the construction—there's still an ample selection of clubs and bars. For non-clubbers, Elephant Walk or Taberno de Haro are excellent dining options. For those lucky enough to score tickets, the best entertainment in the world is at Fenway Park.

Coffee

- **Espresso Royale** • 736 Commonwealth Ave [St Mary's St]
- **Java Stop** • 4 Brookline Pl [Brookline Ave]
- **Starbucks** • Beth Israel Hospital • 364 Brookline Ave [Short St]
- **Starbucks** • 148 Brookline Ave [Kilmarock St]
- **Starbucks** • 595 Commonwealth Ave [Sherborn St]
- **Starbucks** • 775 Commonwealth Ave [Mountfort]
- **Starbucks** • 874 Commonwealth Ave [Armory]

Copy Shops

- **FedEx Kinko's** • 115 Cummington St [Babbitt]
- **Minuteman Press** • 870 Commonwealth Ave [Amory St]
- **Staples** • 401 Park Dr [Brookline Ave]
- **The UPS Store** • 423 Brookline Ave [Longwood]

Gyms

- **Boston Sports Club** • 201 Brookline Ave [Park Dr]
- **Boston University Nutrition & Fitness Center** • 635 Commonwealth Ave [Hinsdale]
- **Gold's Gym** • 71 Lansdowne St [Brookline Ave]

Hardware Stores

- **Economy Hardware** • 1012 Beacon St [St Mary's St]

Liquor Stores

- **Wine Gallery** • 516 Commonwealth Ave [Kenmore]
- **Wine Press** • 1024 Beacon St [St Mary's St]

Movie Theaters

- **Regal Fenway Stadium 13** • 201 Brookline Ave [Park Dr]

Nightlife

- **An Tua Nua** • 835 Beacon St [Munson]
- **Audubon Circle** • 838 Beacon St [Munson]
- **Axis** • 13 Lansdowne St [Ipswich St]
- **Bill's Bar and Lounge** • 5 1/2 Lansdowne St [Ipswich St]
- **Boston Billiard Club** • 126 Brookline Ave [Burlington]
- **Cask 'n' Flagon** • 62 Brookline Ave [Lansdowne]
- **The Dugout** • 722 Commonwealth Ave [St Mary's St]
- **Embassy** • 36 Lansdowne St [Ipswich St]
- **Foundation Lounge** • 500 Commonwealth Ave [Kenmore]
- **Game On!** • 82 Lansdowne St [Brookline Ave]
- **Lucky Strike Lanes** • 145 Ipswich St [Lansdowne]
- **The Modern** • 36 Lansdowne St [Ipswich St]
- **Tequila Rain** • 3 Lansdowne St [Ipswich St]
- **Who's on First?** • 19 Yawkey Wy [Brookline Ave]

Restaurants

- **Ankara Café** • 472 Commonwealth Ave [Kenmore]
- **Audubon Circle** • 838 Beacon St [Munson]
- **Boston Beer Works** • 61 Brookline Ave [Lansdowne]
- **Café Belo** • 636 Beacon St [Raleigh]
- **Cornwall's** • 654 Beacon St [Comm Ave]
- **Eastern Standard** • 520 Commonwealth Ave [Kenmore]
- **Elephant Walk** • 900 Beacon St [Park Dr]
- **Ginza** • 1002 Beacon St [St Mary's St]
- **Great Bay** • 500 Commonwealth Ave [Kenmore]
- **India Quality** • 484 Commonwealth Ave [Kenmore]
- **New England Soup Factory** • 2 Brookline Pl [Brookline Ave]
- **Noodle Street** • 627 Commonwealth Ave [Sherborn St]
- **O'Leary's Pub** • 1010 Beacon St [St Mary's St]
- **Petit Robert Bistro** • 468 Commonwealth Ave [Kenmore]
- **Taberno de Haro** • 999 Beacon St [St Mary's St]
- **Uburger** • 636 Beacon St [Raleigh]

Shopping

- **Bed Bath & Beyond** • 401 Park Dr [Brookline Ave]
- **Best Buy** • 401 Park Dr [Brookline Ave]
- **Blick Art Materials** • 401 Park Dr [Brookline Ave]
- **Boston Bicycle** • 842 Beacon St [Arundel]
- **Economy Hardware** • 1012 Beacon St [St Mary's St]
- **Guitar Center** • 750 Commonwealth Ave [St Mary's St]
- **Hunt's Photo and Video** • 520 Commonwealth Ave [Kenmore]
- **Japonaise Bakery** • 1020 Beacon St [St Marys St]
- **Nantucket Natural Oils** • 508 Commonwealth Ave [Kenmore]
- **Nuggets** • 486 Commonwealth Ave [Kenmore]
- **REI** • 401 Park Dr [Brookline Ave]
- **Ski Market** • 860 Commonwealth Ave [Armory]
- **University Computers** • 533 Commonwealth Ave [Brookline Ave]

Map 16 · **Kenmore Square / Brookline (East)**

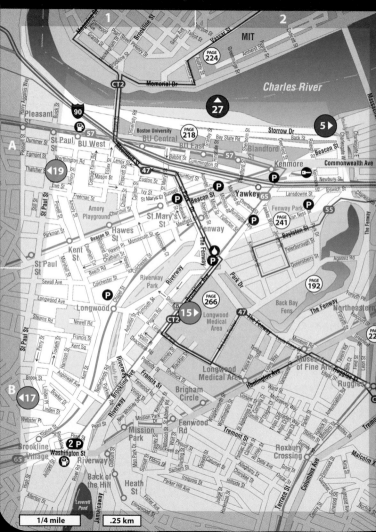

Transportation

Map 16

The Green Line T stops around Kenmore Square and BU are frequently overrun by students and baseball fans, so B train riders might prefer the 57 bus during peak school and game hours. For parking, trawl Bay State Road and Cummington Street or head further west on Commonwealth Ave.

Subway

- **Kenmore**
- **Blandford St** (B)
- **BU East** (B)
- **BU Central** (B)
- **BU West** (B)
- **St Paul St** (B)
- **St Mary's St** (C)
- **Hawes St** (C)
- **Kent St** (C)
- **St Paul St** (C)
- **Fenway** (D)
- **Longwood** (D)
- **Brookline Village** (D)

Bus Lines

- **CT2** · Sullivan Station—Ruggles Station via Kendall/MIT
- **55** · Jersey & Queensberry Streets—Copley Square or Park & Tremont Streets
- **57** · Watertown Yard—Kenmore Station via Newton Corner & Brighton Center
- **65** · Brighton Center—Kenmore Station via Washington Street, Brookline Village

Car Rental

- **Select Car Rental** · 500 Commonwealth Ave
  [Kenmore] · 617-532-5060

Car Washes

- **Advance Auto Detailing** · 401 Park Dr [Brookline Ave]

Gas Stations

- **Gulf** · 25 Washington St [Brooklin Pl] ☉
- **Sunoco** · 850 Commonwealth Ave [Amory St]

Parking

Map 17 · **Coolidge Corner / Brookline Hills**

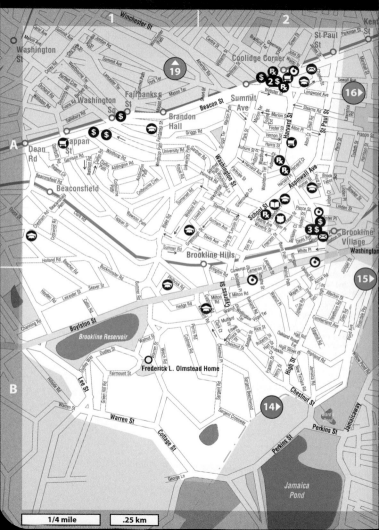

Essentials

Map 17

This neighborhood is a vibrant mix of old and new, urban and suburban, old-fashioned and eclectic. Long-time residents in stately Victorian homes share quiet neighborhood parks, diverse restaurants and shops, and a buzzing nightlife with transient college students and well-paid young professionals.

$ Banks

- **Bank of America** • 1319 Beacon St [Harvard St]
- **Bank of America (ATM)** • 1624 Beacon St [Washington St]
- **Bank of America (ATM)** • 225 Washington St [Snow]
- **Banknorth Massachusetts** • 1641 Beacon St [University Rd]
- **Brookline Cooperative Bank** • 264 Washington St [Davis Ave]
- **Brookline Savings Bank** • 1340 Beacon St [Harvard St]
- **Brookline Savings Bank** • 1661 Beacon St [Winthrop Rd]
- **People's Federal Savings Bank** • 254 Washington St [Harvard St]
- **Sovereign Bank** • 1 Harvard St [Kent St]
- **Sovereign Bank** • 1341 Beacon St [Harvard St]

Donuts

- **Dunkin' Donuts** • 1316 Beacon St [Harvard St]
- **Dunkin' Donuts** • 20 Boylston St [High St]
- **Dunkin' Donuts** • 265 Boylston St [Cameron St]
- **Dunkin' Donuts** • 8 Harvard St [Kent St]

O Landmarks

- **Frederick Olmstead Home** • 99 Warren St [Welch]

Libraries

- **Brookline Main Library** • 361 Washington St [Goodwin Pl]

Pharmacies

- **CVS** • 1322 Beacon St [Harvard St]
- **CVS** • 294 Harvard St [Green St]
- **CVS** • 400 Washington St [Cypress St]
- **Walgreens** • 1324 Beacon St [Harvard St]
- **Walgreens** • 99 Harvard St [School St]

Police

- **Brookline Police Department** • 350 Washington St [Thayer St]

Post Offices

- **Brookline Branch** • 1295 Beacon St [Pleasant St]
- **Brookline Village Branch** • 207 Washington St [Station]

Schools

- **Boston Graduate School of Psychoanalysis** • 1581 Beacon St [Washington St]
- **Brookline High** • 115 Greenough St [Davis Ave]
- **Israeli Complementary School** • 50 Sewall Ave [Charles St]
- **John D Runkle** • 50 Druce St [Buckminster]
- **Maimonides** • 34 Philbrick Rd [Boylston St]
- **Pierce** • 50 School St [Washington St]
- **St Mary of the Assumption** • 67 Harvard St [Kent St]
- **William H Lincoln** • 19 Kennard Rd [Boylston St]

Supermarkets

- **Star Market** • 1717 Beacon St [Tappan]
- **Stop & Shop** • 155 Harvard St [Harris St]
- **Trader Joe's** • 1317 Beacon St [Harvard St]

Map 17 · Coolidge Corner / Brookline Hills

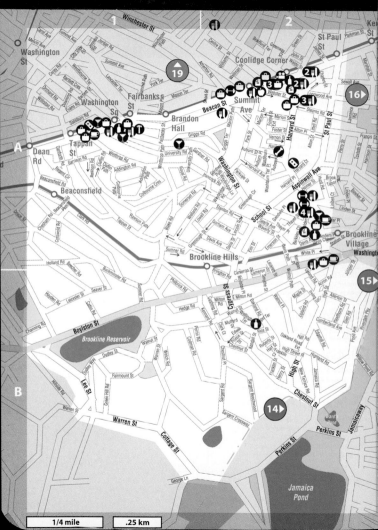

Sundries / Entertainment

Map 17

Brookline is a place where specialty shops mingle with chain stores, and an ethnic array of food spans from the inexpensive Rani Indian Bistro and Boca Grande to the upscale Fireplace and Fugakyu. The popular Art Deco Coolidge Corner Theater shows first-run, repertory, midnight movies, and occasional burlesque.

Coffee

- **Athan's Bakery** • 1621 Beacon St [Washington St]
- **Heney's Resa** • 220 Washington St [Davis Ct]
- **Starbucks** • 15 Harvard St [Webster Pl]
- **Starbucks** • 1655 Beacon St [Winthrop Rd]

Copy Shops

- **FedEx Kinko's** • 1370 Beacon St [Centre St]
- **Mail Boxes Etc** • 258 Harvard St [Beacon St]
- **The UPS Store** • 288 Washington St [Holden St]

Farmers Markets

- **Brookline (June–Oct; Thurs 1:30 pm–dusk)** •
  Centre St at Beacon St [Beacon St]

Gyms

- **Beacon Hill Athletic Club** • 279 Washington St [Holden St]
- **Fitness Together** • 1404 Beacon St [Winchester St]
- **Fitness Unlimited** • 62 Harvard St [Kent St]

Hardware Stores

- **Connelly's Hardware** • 706 Washington St [Beacon St]

Liquor Stores

- **Best Cellars (wine only)** • 1327 Beacon St [Harvard St]
- **Foley's Liquor Store** • 228 Cypress St [Rice St]
- **Food Center Liquors** • 10 Harvard Sq [Andem]
- **Gimbel's Liquors** • 1637 Beacon St [University Rd]
- **Wine Gallery** • 375 Boylston St [Brington]

Movie Theaters

- **Coolidge Corner Theatre** • 290 Harvard St [Green St]

Nightlife

- **Matt Murphy's Pub** • 14 Harvard St [Webster Pl]
- **The Publick House** • 1648 Beacon St [Washington St]
- **Washington Square Tavern** •
  714 Washington St [Beacon St]

Pet Shops

- **Brookline Grooming & Pet Supplies** •
  148 Harvard St [Harris St]

Restaurants

- **Boca Grande** • 1294 Beacon St [Pleasant St]
- **Bottega Fiorentina** • 41 Harvard St [Andem]
- **Brookline Family Restaurant** •
  305 Washington St [Holden St]
- **Dok Bua** • 411 Harvard St [Fuller St]
- **Fireplace** • 1634 Beacon St [Washington St]
- **Fugakyu** • 1280 Beacon St [Pleasant St]
- **Gourmet India** • 1335 Beacon St [Harvard St]
- **Khao Sarn** • 250 Harvard St [Longwood]
- **La Morra** • 48 Boylston St [High St]
- **Matt Murphy's Pub** • 14 Harvard St [Webster Pl]
- **Martin's Coffee Shop** • 35 Harvard St [Linden St]
- **Michael's Deli** • 256 Harvard St [Longwood]
- **Orinoco** • 22 Harvard St [Pierce St]
- **Pho Lemongrass** • 239 Harvard St [Webster St]
- **Rani Indian Bistro** • 1353 Beacon St [Webster St]
- **Rod Dee** • 1430 Beacon St [Summit Ave]
- **Shawarma King** • 1383 Beacon St [Park St]
- **Village Fish** • 22 Harvard St [Webster Pl]
- **Washington Square Tavern** •
  714 Washington St [Beacon St]

Shopping

- **Athan's Bakery** • 1621 Beacon St [Washington St]
- **Bowl & Board** • 1354 Beacon St [Webster St]
- **EC Florist & Gifts** • 224 Washington St [Davis Ct]
- **Emack & Bolio's** • 1663 Beacon St [Winthrop Rd]
- **Eureka Puzzles** • 1349 Beacon St [Centre St]
- **Madras Masala** • 191 Harvard St [Marion St]
- **Marathon Sports** • 1638 Beacon St [University Rd]
- **Paper Source** • 1361 Beacon St [Webster St]
- **Party Favors** • 1356 Beacon St [Webster St]
- **Petropol** • 1428 Beacon St [Summit Ave]
- **Pier 1 Imports** • 1351 Beacon St [Webster St]
- **Russian Village** • 1659 Beacon St [Winthrop Rd]
- **Ten Thousand Villages** • 226 Harvard St [Sewall Ave]
- **Wild Goose Chase** • 1431 Beacon St [Summit Ave]

Video Rental

- **Hollywood Video** • 111 Harvard St [Harvard Ct]
- **Movieworks** • 1658 Beacon St [Winthrop Rd]

Map 17 · **Coolidge Corner / Brookline Hills**

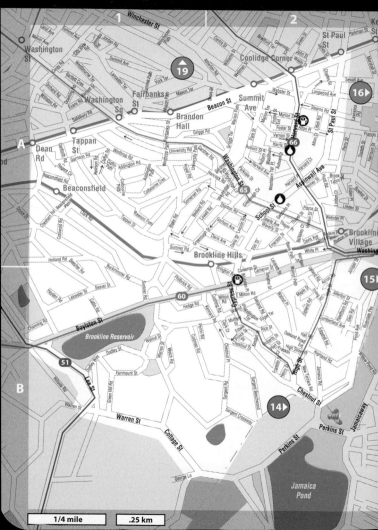

Brookline welcomes visitors, but as with any house guest, you aren't expected to stay too long. A two-hour parking limit is strictly enforced, and overnight street parking is forbidden. The alternative? The maddeningly slow and crowded Green Line C train and 66 bus. The D train serves Brookline Hills.

Subway

- ■ · **Kent St (C)**
- ■ · **St Paul St (C)**
- ■ · **Coolidge Corner (C)**
- ■ · **Summit Ave (C)**
- ■ · **Brandon Hall (C)**
- ■ · **Fairbanks St (C)**
- ■ · **Washington Sq (C)**
- ■ · **Tappan St (C)**
- ■ · **Dean Rd (C)**
- ■ · **Brookline Village (D)**
- ■ · **Brookline Hills (D)**
- ■ · **Beaconsfield (D)**

Bus Lines

- **60** · Chestnut Hill—Kenmore Station via Brookline Village & Cypress Street
- **65** · Brighton Center—Kenmore Station via Washington Street, Brookline Village
- **66** · Harvard Square—Dudley Station via Allston & Brookline

◆ Car Washes

- **Effective Car Detail** · 40 Aspinwall Ave [Harvard St]
- **Scrubadub** · 143 Harvard St [Harris St]

⬢ Gas Stations

- **Mobil** · 198 Harvard St [Marion St]
- **Mobil** · 345 Boylston St [Cypress St] ⏰

Map 18 · **Brighton**

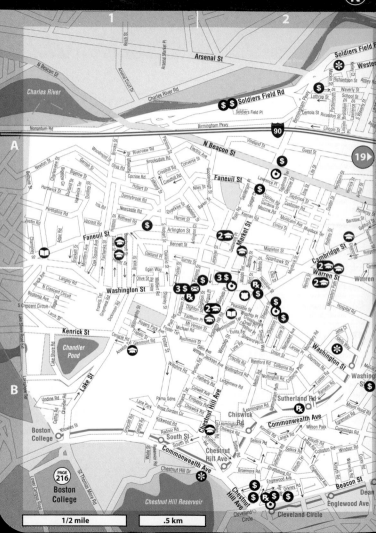

Brighton is the more sedate half of the Allston-Brighton duo but, like its rowdier neighbor, it attracts plenty of college students and young folk. Narrow, tangled, residential streets surround the cluster of shops and restaurants on Washington Street in Brighton Center.

💲 Banks

- **Bank of America** • 350 Chestnut Hill Ave [Englewood]
- **Bank of America** • 5 Chestnut Hill Ave [Washington St]
- **Bank of America (ATM)** •
  1650 Soldiers Field Rd [Soldiers Field Pl]
- **Bank of America (ATM)** • 175 Market St [N Beacon]
- **Bank of America (ATM)** • 401 Washington St [Dighton]
- **Cambridge Trust (ATM)** •
  2 Soldiers Field Rd [Soldiers Field Pl]
- **Citizens Bank** • 2000 Beacon St [Sutherland]
- **Citizens Bank** • 35 Washington St [Monastery]
- **Citizens Bank** • 414 Washington St [Parsons]
- **Citizens Bank (ATM)** • 1912 Beacon St [Ayr]
- **Citizens Bank (ATM)** • 241 Market St [Cypress Rd]
- **Mercantile Bank** • 423 Washington St [Parsons]
- **People's Federal Savings Bank** •
  435 Market St [Surrey]
- **People's Federal Savings Bank (ATM)** •
  236 Faneuil St [Arlington St]
- **Sovereign Bank** • 30 Birmingham Pkwy [Waverly St]
- **Sovereign Bank** • 415 Market St [Henshaw]
- **Sovereign Bank (ATM)** • CVS/Pharmacy •
  1927 Beacon St [Ayr]
- **Sovereign Bank (ATM)** •
  250 Washington St [Shepard St]
- **Sovereign Bank (ATM)** • CVS/Pharmacy •
  427 Washington St [Eastburn St]

✳️ Community Gardens

🎯 Donuts

- **Dunkin' Donuts** • 1955 Beacon St [Ayr]
- **Dunkin' Donuts** • 214 N Beacon St [Market St]
- **Dunkin' Donuts** • 350 Washington St [Academy Hill]

📖 Libraries

- **Brighton** • 40 Academy Hill Rd [Peaceable]
- **Faneuil** • 419 Faneuil St [Bigelow St]

℞ Pharmacies

- **CVS** • 1927 Beacon St [Ayr]
- **CVS** • 427 Washington St [Eastburn St]
- **Rite Aid** • 399 Market St [Henshaw]
- **Sutherland Pharmacy** •
  1690 Commonwealth Ave [Wilson Pk]

👮 Police

- **District D-14** • 301 Washington St [Wirt]

✉️ Post Offices

- **Brighton** • 424 Washington St [Parsons]

🎓 Schools

- **Alexander Hamilton Elementary** •
  198 Strathmore Rd [Lothian]
- **Another Course to College** • 20 Warren St [Nevins]
- **Boston Community Leadership Academy** •
  20 Warren St [Nevins]
- **Brighton High** • 25 Warren St [Monastery]
- **Conservatory Lab Charter** •
  25 Arlington St [Leicester]
- **James Garfield Elementary** •
  95 Beechcroft St [Hester]
- **Kennedy Day School Program** •
  30 Warren St [Monastery]
- **Mary Lyon Elementary/Middle** •
  50 Beechcroft St [Hester]
- **Mesivta High School of Greater** •
  34 Sparhawk St [Bentley]
- **Mount St Joseph Academy** •
  617 Cambridge St [Eleanor]
- **Shaloh House Hebrew Day** •
  29 Chestnut Hill Ave [Dighton]
- **St. Columbkille Elementary** •
  25 Arlington St [Leicester]
- **Thomas A Edison Junior High** •
  60 Glenmont Rd [Willoughby St]
- **William H Taft Middle** • 20 Warren St [Nevins]
- **Winship Elementary** •
  54 Dighton St [Chestnut Hill Ave]

Map 18 · **Brighton**

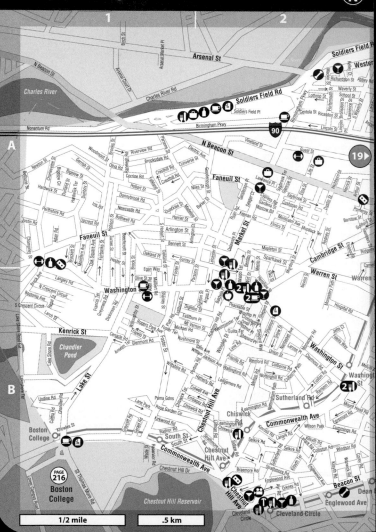

Sundries / Entertainment

Map 18

Meet a BC student at Mary Ann's or watch a soccer match at Roggie's. Want frills? Try Soho, a modern, two-level club that tries to emulate Manhattan chic. Hungry? Grab some tapas and, of course, sangria at Tasca. Late night, head to IHOP on Soldiers Field Road for boisterous times and reliable breakfast fare.

Coffee

- **Starbucks** · 1660 Soldiers Field Rd [Soldiers Field Pl]
- **Starbucks** · 470 Washington St [Allen St]

Copy Shops

- **FedEx Kinko's** · 252 Washington St [Shepard St]
- **Staples** · 1660 Soldiers Field Rd [Soldiers Field Pl]
- **The UPS Store** · 2193 Commonwealth Ave [Lake St]

Farmers Markets

- **Brighton** (July–Oct; Sat 12–4:30) · 5 Chestnut Hill Ave [Washington St]

Gyms

- **Bally Total Fitness** · 25 Guest St [Life]
- **Beacon Hill Athletic Club** · 1686 Commonwealth Ave [Colborne Ave]
- **Beacon Hill Athletic Club** · 470 Washington St [Allen Rd]
- **Oak Square YMCA** · 615 Washington St [Breck]

Hardware Stores

- **Cleveland Circle Hardware** · 1920 Beacon St [Ayr]

Liquor Stores

- **Dorr's Liquor Mart** · 354 Washington St [Chestnut Hill Ave]
- **Martignetti Liquors** · 1650 Soldiers Field Rd [Soldiers Field Pl]
- **Oak Square Liquors** · 610 Washington St [Breck]
- **Reservoir Wines & Spirits** · 1922 Beacon St [Ayr]
- **Walsh Wine & Spirits** · 313 Washington St [Waldo Ter]

Movie Theaters

- **National Amusements Circle Cinemas** · 399 Chestnut Hill Ave [Beacon St]

Nightlife

- **Cityside Bar & Grill** · 1960 Beacon St [Sutherland]
- **Green Briar** · 304 Washington St [Wirt]
- **Irish Village** · 224 Market St [Saybrook St]
- **Joey's** · 416 Market St [Henshaw]
- **The Last Drop** · 596 Washington St [Griggs Rd]
- **Mary Ann's** · 1937 Beacon St [Ayr]
- **Roggie's** · 356 Chestnut Hill Ave [Englewood]
- **Soho** · 386 Market St [Henshaw]

Pet Shops

- **No Bones About It** · 1786 Beacon St [Warwick Rd]
- **Toureen Kennels & Grooming Salon** · 503 Western Ave [Mackin]

Restaurants

- **Bamboo** · 1616 Commonwealth Ave [Washington St]
- **Bangkok Bistro** · 1952 Beacon St [Sutherland]
- **Bluestone Bistro** · 1799 Commonwealth Ave [Chiswick Rd]
- **Café Mirror** · 362 Washington St [Goodwin Pl]
- **Cityside Bar & Grill** · 1960 Beacon St [Sutherland]
- **Devlin's** · 332 Washington St [Waldo Ter]
- **Green Briar** · 304 Washington St [Wirt]
- **IHOP** · 1850 Soldiers Field Rd [N Beacon] ✪
- **Jasmine Bistro** · 412 Market St [Henshaw]
- **Roggie's** · 356 Chestnut Hill Ave [Englewood]
- **Soho** · 386 Market St [Henshaw]
- **Tasca** · 1612 Commonwealth Ave [Washington St]

Shopping

- **Amanda's Flowers** · 347 Washington St [Academy Hill]
- **CompUSA** · 205 Market St [Lawrence Pl]
- **New Balance Factory Store** · 40 Life St [Guest]
- **Staples** · 1660 Soldiers Field Rd [Soldiers Field Pl]

Video Rental

- **Blockbuster** · 358 Chestnut Hill Ave [Englewood]
- **Brighton Video** · 572 Washington St [Brackett]
- **Hollywood Video** · 103 N Beacon St [Arthur]

Map 18 · **Brighton**

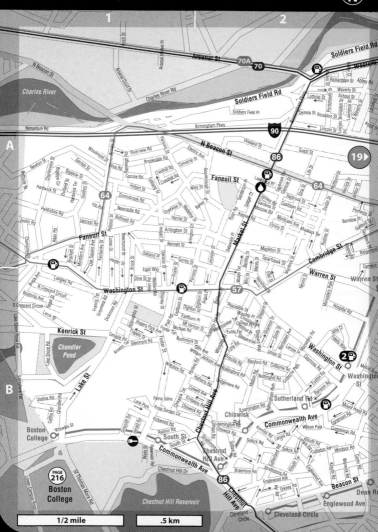

The bus dominates public transportation in Brighton—the 57 bus brings riders into Kenmore Square, and the 64 and 86 buses lead into Cambridge and Somerville. The Green Line's C train creeps along the southern edge of Brighton to Cleveland Circle.

Subway

- **Warren St (B)**
- **Washington St (B)**
- **Sutherland Rd (B)**
- **Chiswick Rd (B)**
- **Chestnut Hill Ave (B)**
- **South St (B)**
- **Boston College (B)**
- **Englewood Ave (C)**
- **Cleveland Circle (C)**

Bus Lines

- **57** • Watertown Yard—Kenmore Station via Newton Corner & Brighton Center
- **64** • Oak Square—Central Square, Cambridge, or Kendall/MIT
- **65** • Brighton Center—Kenmore Station via Washington Street, Brookline Village
- **70** • Cedarwood, N Waltham, or Watertown Square—University Park via Central Square
- **70A** • Cedarwood, N Waltham, or Watertown Square—University Park via Central Square
- **86** • Sullivan Square Station—Cleveland Circle via Harvard/Johnson Gate

Car Rental

- **Rent A Wreck** •
  2022 Commonwealth Ave [Gerald] • 617-254-9540

Car Washes

- **Scrubadub** • 235 Market St [Faneuil]

Gas Stations

- **Econogas** • 1550 Commonwealth Ave [Melvin Ave] ✿
- **Gulf** • 1650 Commonwealth Ave [Mt Hood]
- **Gulf** • 195 Market St [N Beacon]
- **Mobil** • 500 Western Ave [Mackin]
- **Shell** • 332 Chestnut Hill Ave [Englewood]
- **Sunoco** • 602 Washington St [Breck]

Map 19 · **Allston (South) / Brookline (North)**

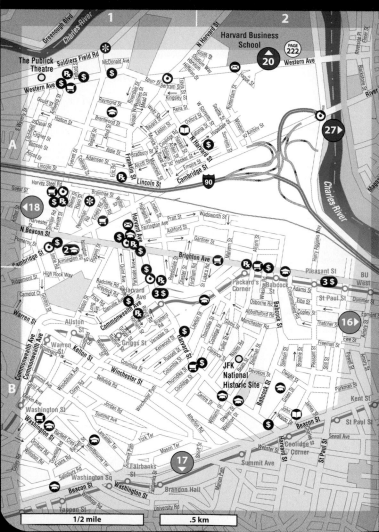

For most Bostonians, crowded living and rowdy students define Allston. There's no place in the city where so many cheap eats, dive bars, and used goods are crammed into so few blocks. It's a dirty mashup and the city is better for it.

💲 Banks

- **Bank of America** •
  1237 Commonwealth Ave [Harvard Ave]
- **Bank of America (ATM)** •
  1236A Commonwealth Ave [Harvard Ave]
- **Bank of America (ATM)** • 186 Brighton Ave [Quint]
- **Bank of America (ATM)** • 400 Western Ave [Litchfield St]
- **Bank of America (ATM)** • 881 Commonwealth Ave [Buick]
- **Bank of America (ATM)** •
  957 Commonwealth Ave [Harry Agganis]
- **Century Bank** • 300 Western Ave [Everett St]
- **Citizens Bank** • 315 Harvard St [Babcock]
- **Citizens Bank** • 429 Harvard St [Coolidge St]
- **Citizens Bank** • 60 Everett St [Harvester]
- **Citizens Bank (ATM)** • 1065 Commonwealth Ave [Alcorn]
- **Citizens Bank (ATM)** •
  1219 Commonwealth Ave [Harvard Ave]
- **Citizens Bank (ATM)** • 157 Brighton Ave [Harvard Ave]
- **Citizens Bank (ATM)** • 370 Western Ave [Telford]
- **Citizens Bank (ATM)** • 509 Cambridge St [Barrows]
- **People's Federal Savings Bank** •
  229 N Harvard St [Franklin St]
- **Sovereign Bank** • 487 Harvard St [Lawton]
- **Sovereign Bank (ATM)** • CVS/Pharmacy •
  1266 Commonwealth Ave [Gorham St]
- **Sovereign Bank (ATM)** • CVS/Pharmacy •
  900 Commonwealth Ave [St Paul]
- **UCB** • 230 Harvard Ave [Brainerd]
- **Wainwright Bank & Trust** • 301 Harvard St [Babcock]

❋ Community Gardens

⦿ Donuts

- **Dunkin' Donuts** • 100 Cambridge St [Soldiers Field Rd]
- **Dunkin' Donuts** • 179 Brighton Ave [Parkvale]
- **Dunkin' Donuts** • 209 N Harvard St [Western]
- **Dunkin' Donuts** • 210 Harvard Ave [Comm Ave]
- **Dunkin' Donuts** • 60 Everett St [Harvester]
- **Twin Do-Nuts** • 501 Cambridge St [Barrows]

○ Landmarks

- **JFK National Historic Site** • 83 Beals St [Harvard St]
- **The Publick Theatre** • 1400 Soldiers Field Rd [Western]

📖 Libraries

- **Coolidge Corner** • 31 Pleasant St [John St]
- **Honan-Allston** • 300 N Harvard St [Eatonia]

℞ Pharmacies

- **CVS** • 1266 Commonwealth Ave [Gorham St]
- **CVS** • 900 Commonwealth Ave [St Paul]
- **Osco** • Shaw's • 1065 Commonwealth Ave [Alcorn]
- **Osco** • 370 Western Ave [Telford]
- **Pelham Healthcare Services** • 280 Lincoln St [Eric]
- **Rite Aid** • 181 Brighton Ave [Parkvale]
- **Stop & Shop** • 60 Everett St [Harvester]

✉ Post Offices

- **Allston Station** • 47 Harvard Ave [Farrington]
- **Soldiers Field Station** • 117 Western Ave [Hague]

🏫 Schools

- **Bay Cove Academy** • 156 Lawton St [Abbottsford]
- **Beacon High** • 74 Green St [Dwight]
- **Congregation Kehillath Israel Religious School** •
  384 Harvard St [Beals]
- **Edward Devotion** • 345 Harvard St [Shailer]
- **Harriet Baldwin Elementary** • 121 Corey Rd [Washington St]
- **Horace Mann School for the Deaf and Hard of
  Hearing** • 40 Armington St [Webley]
- **Jackson Mann Elementary** • 40 Armington St [Webley]
- **Media and Technology Charter High** •
  1001 Commonwealth Ave [Babcock]
- **Michael Driscoll** • 64 Westbourne Ter [Bartlett St]
- **St Herman of Alaska Christian School** •
  62 Harvard Ave [Farrington]
- **Thomas Gardner Elementary** • 30 Athol St [Brentwood]
- **Torah Academy** • 11 Williston Rd [Salisbury]

🛒 Supermarkets

- **Bazaar** • 424 Cambridge St [Rugg]
- **The Butcherie** • 428 Harvard St [Coolidge St]
- **Osco** • Shaw's • 1065 Commonwealth Ave [Alcorn]
- **Shaw's** • 370 Western Ave [Telford]
- **Stop & Shop** • 60 Everett St [Harvester]
- **Super 88** • 1 Brighton Ave [Malvern St]
- **Whole Foods Market** • 15 Washington St [Corey Rd]

Map 19 · **Allston (South) / Brookline (North)**

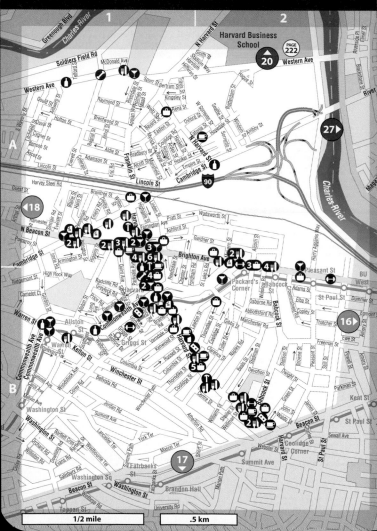

Sundries / Entertainment

Map 19

Allston Rock City! Clubs drive the scene here, with live music and DJs every night of the week. Check Paradise, Harper's Ferry, Great Scott, and even the velvet rope at Wonder Bar. Taps dominate Sunset Grill and Big City. As for food, we've been known to fantasize about Lebanese at Reef Café, Chinese at Gitlo's, and Bánh Mi at Super 88.

Coffee

- **Caffe LaScala** • 318 Harvard St [Babcock]
- **Peet's Coffee & Tea** •
  285 Harvard St [Green St]
- **Starbucks** • 277 Harvard St [Green St]
- **Starbucks** • 473 Harvard St [Lawton]

Copy Shops

- **Prinstant Press Inc** •
  15 North Beacon St [Cambridge St]
- **Signal Graphics** • 450 Cambridge St [Emery]
- **Staples** • 214 Harvard Ave [Comm Ave]
- **The UPS Store** •
  1085 Commonwealth Ave [Malvern St]

Gyms

- **Boston Sports Club** •
  15 Gorham St [Comm Ave]
- **Commonwealth Health** • 1079
  Commonwealth Ave [Malvern St]
- **Coolidge Corner Gym** •
  310 Harvard St [Babcock]
- **HealthWorks Fitness Center**
  (Women Only) •
  920 Commonwealth Ave [St Paul]

Hardware Stores

- **Aborn True Value** •
  438 Harvard St [Coolidge St]
- **Economy Hardware** •
  144 Harvard Ave [Glenville Ter]
- **Model Hardware** •
  22 Harvard Ave [Cambridge St]

Liquor Stores

- **Allston Food and Spirits** •
  223 Cambridge St [N Harvard]
- **Blanchard Liquors** •
  103 Harvard Ave [Brighton Ave]
- **Brookline Liquor Mart** •
  1354 Commonwealth Ave [Walbridge]
- **Hurley's** •
  1441 Commonwealth Ave [Warren St]
- **Mall Discount Liquors & Wines** •
  525 Harvard St [Verndale]
- **Marty's Liquors** •
  193 Harvard Ave [Comm Ave]
- **Wine Shop** • 370 Western Ave [Telford]

Nightlife

- **Avenue Bar & Grille** •
  1249 Commonwealth Ave [Royce Rd]
- **Big City** • 138 Brighton Ave [Harvard Ave]
- **Bus Stop Pub** • 252 Western Ave [N Harvard]
- **Common Ground** •
  85 Harvard Ave [Gardner St]
- **Great Scott** •
  1222 Commonwealth Ave [Harvard Ave]
- **Harper's Ferry** •
  156 Brighton Ave [Harvard Ave]
- **Harry's Bar & Grill** •
  1430 Commonwealth Ave [Kelton]
- **Joshua Tree** •
  1316 Harvard Ave [Redford]

- **The Kells** • 161 Brighton Ave [Harvard Ave]
- **Model Café** • 7 N Beacon St [Cambridge St]
- **O'Brien's** • 3 Harvard Ave [Cambridge St]
- **Our House** •
  1277 Commonwealth Ave [Spofford]
- **Paradise Rock Club & Lounge** •
  967 Commonwealth Ave [Harry Agganis]
- **Scullers Jazz Club** • Doubletree Hotel •
  400 Soldiers Field Rd [Cambridge St]
- **Silhouette Lounge** •
  200 Brighton Ave [Allston St]
- **Sports Depot** • 353 Cambridge St [Highgate]
- **Sunset Grill & Tap** •
  130 Brighton Ave [Linden St]
- **T's Pub** •
  973 Commonwealth Ave [Crowninshield Rd]
- **White Horse Tavern** •
  116 Brighton Ave [Linden St]
- **Wonder Bar** • 186 Harvard Ave [Glenville Ter]

Pet Shops

- **The Pet Shop** • 165 Harvard Ave [Glenville Ave]
- **Petco** • 304 Western Ave [Everett St]

Restaurants

- **Aneka Rasa** • 122 Harvard St [Brighton Ave]
- **Angora Café** •
  1024 Commonwealth Ave [Babcock]
- **Anna's Taqueria** •
  446 Harvard St [Thorndike]
- **Bagel Rising** •
  1243 Commonwealth Ave [Harvard Ave]
- **Big City** • 138 Brighton Ave [Harvard Ave]
- **Bottega Fiorentina** •
  313B Harvard St [Babcock]
- **Breakfast Club Diner** •
  270 Western Ave [McDonald]
- **Buk Kyung II** •
  151 Brighton Ave [Harvard Ave]
- **Café Brazil** • 421 Cambridge St [Denby]
- **Camino Real** • 48 Harvard St [Farrington]
- **Charlie's Pizza & Café** • 177 Allston St [Kelton]
- **Coolidge Corner Clubhouse** •
  307 Harvard St [Babcock]
- **El Cafetal** • 479 Cambridge St [Islington St]
- **Gitlo's** • 164 Brighton Ave [Parkvale Ave]
- **Grasshopper** • 1 N Beacon St [Cambridge St]
- **Grecian Yearning** •
  174 Harvard Ave [Glenville Ave]
- **Indian Dhaba Roadside Diner** •
  180 Brighton Ave [Parkvale]
- **La Mamma Pizza** • 190 Brighton Ave [Quint]
- **Mr Sushi Japanese Restaurant** •
  329 Harvard St [Babcock]
- **Nori Sushi** • 398 Harvard St [Naples]
- **Paradise Rock Club & Lounge** •
  967 Commonwealth Ave [Harry Agganis]
- **Paris Creperie** • 278 Harvard St [Green St]
- **Pho Viets** •
  1095 Commonwealth Ave [Brighton Ave]
- **Quan's Kitchen** •
  1026 Commonwealth Ave [Winslow Rd]
- **Rangoli** • 129 Brighton Ave [Linden St]
- **Redneck's Roast Beef** •
  140 Brighton Ave [Harvard Ave]
- **Reef Café** • 170 Brighton Ave [Harvard Ave]
- **Saigon** • 431 Cambridge St [Denby]
- **Saray** •
  1098 Commonwealth Ave [Brighton Ave]
- **Spike's Junkyard Dogs** •
  108 Brighton Ave [Linden St]

- **Steve's Kitchen** •
  120 Harvard St [Brighton Ave]
- **Sumi** • 182 Brighton Ave [Parkvale]
- **Sunset Grill & Tap** •
  130 Brighton Ave [Linden St]
- **Super 88 Food Court** •
  1095 Commonwealth Ave [Malvern St]
- **Upper Crust** • 286 Harvard St [Green St]
- **Victoria Seafood** •
  1029 Commonwealth Ave [Winslow Rd]
- **YoMa** • 5 N Beacon St [Cambridge St]
- **Zaftigs Delicatessen** •
  335 Harvard St [Shailer]

Shopping

- **Berezka International Food Store** •
  1215 Commonwealth Ave [Linden St]
- **Bicycle Bill's** • 253 N Harvard St [Easton]
- **Bob Smith's Wilderness House** •
  1048 Commonwealth Ave [Winslow Rd]
- **Brookline News and Gifts** •
  313 Harvard St [Babcock]
- **Catering by Andrew** •
  402 Harvard St [Naples]
- **City Housewares** •
  434 Harvard St [Coolidge St]
- **City Sports** •
  1035 Commonwealth Ave [Winslow Rd]
- **Clear Flour** • 178 Thorndike St [Lawton]
- **Coco Cosmetics** •
  192 Harvard St [Comm Ave]
- **Eastern Mountain Sports** •
  1041 Commonwealth Ave [Winslow Rd]
- **Economy Hardware** •
  144 Harvard Ave [Glenville Ter]
- **Herrell's Ice Cream** •
  155 Brighton Ave [Harvard Ave]
- **In Your Ear** •
  957 Commonwealth Ave [Harry Agganis]
- **International Bicycle Center** •
  89 Brighton Ave [Reedsdale]
- **Israel Bookshop** • 410 Harvard St [Fuller St]
- **JP Licks** • 311 Harvard St [Babcock]
- **Kolbo Fine Judaica** •
  437 Harvard St [Fuller St]
- **Kupel's Bake & Bagel** •
  421 Harvard St [Fuller St]
- **New England Comics** •
  131 Harvard Ave [Brighton Ave]
- **Re:Generation Records and Tattoo** •
  155 Harvard Ave [Glenville Ave]
- **Richman's Zipper Hospital** •
  318 Harvard St [Babcock]
- **Staples** • 214 Harvard Ave [Comm Ave]
- **Stingray Body Art** •
  1 Harvard Ave [Cambridge St]
- **TJ Maxx** • 525 Harvard St [Verndale]
- **Urban Renewals** •
  122 Brighton Ave [Linden St]
- **Vespa Boston** • 22 Brighton Ave [St Lukes]
- **Wulf's Fish Market** • 407 Harvard St [Fuller St]

Video Rental

- **Blockbuster** • 473 Harvard St [Lawton]
- **Cinemasmith** • 279 Harvard St [Green St]
- **Korean Book & Video**
  (Korean & Japanese) •
  156 Harvard Ave [Glenville Ter]

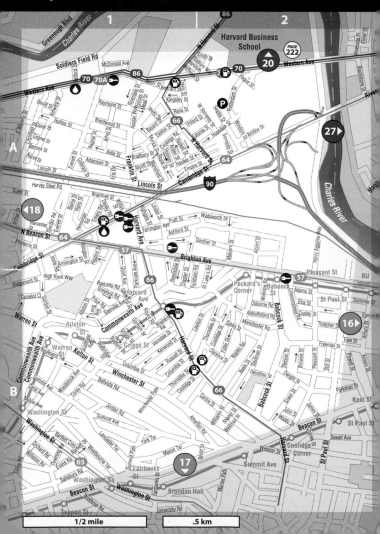

Map 19 • **Allston (South) / Brookline (North)**

Map 19

The Green Line doesn't get more crowded and unbearable than the B train to BC. Parking is notoriously difficult in Allston. Clubbing and busing go like this: 66 bus to Harvard, 64 bus to Central Square, and if you think it's faster than the T, 54 bus to Kenmore Square.

Subway

- **St Paul St** (B)
- **Pleasant St** (B)
- **Babcock St** (B)
- **Packard's Corner** (B)
- **Harvard Ave** (B)
- **Griggs St** (B)
- **Allston St** (B)
- **Warren St** (B)
- **Washington St** (B)

Bus Lines

- **57** • Watertown Yard—Kenmore Station via Newton Corner & Brighton Center
- **64** • Oak Square—Central Square, Cambridge, or Kendall/MIT
- **65** • Brighton Center—Kenmore Station via Washington Street, Brookline Village
- **66** • Harvard Square—Dudley Station via Allston & Brookline
- **70** • Cedarwood, N Waltham, or Watertown Square—University Park via Central Square
- **70A** • Cedarwood, N Waltham, or Watertown Square—University Park via Central Square
- **86** • Sullivan Square Station—Cleveland Circle via Harvard/Johnson Gate

Car Rental

- **Adventure Vehicle Rental** • 226 Harvard Ave [Brainerd] • 617-566-1018
- **Adventure Vehicle Rental** • 27 Harvard Ave [Cambridge St] • 617-783-3825
- **Budget** • 95 Brighton Ave [Linden St] • 617-497-3608
- **Enterprise** • 292 Western Ave [Everett St] • 617-783-2240
- **Enterprise** • 996 Commonwealth Ave [Babcock] • 617-738-6003
- **Hertz** • 414 Cambridge St [Denby] • 617-787-2894
- **U-Save Auto & Truck Rental** • 25 Harvard Ave [Cambridge St] • 617-254-1000

Car Washes

- **Allston Car Wash** • 434 Cambridge St [Rugg]
- **Shield System Cloth Car Wash** • 365 Western Ave [Telford]

Gas Stations

- **Citgo** • 580 Western Ave [Hague]
- **Exxon** • 198 Western Ave [N Harvard]
- **Gulf** • 226 Harvard Ave [Brainerd]
- **Independent** • 445 Harvard St [Thorndike]
- **Mobil** • 434 Cambridge St [Rugg]
- **Sunoco** • 454 Harvard St [Thorndike]

Parking

Map 20 · **Harvard Square / Allston (North)**

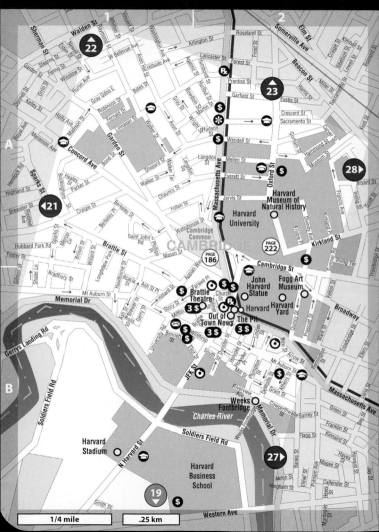

Essentials

Map 20

Despite an onslaught of retail chain stores, Harvard Square still retains some of its eccentric charm, with speed chess players, quirky stores, and eclectic eateries. Stroll up Brattle Street to admire the magnificent houses or step into Harvard Yard to escape into another world.

$ Banks

- **Bank of America** · 1414 Massachusetts Ave [JFK]
- **Bank of America (ATM)** · 1 Mifflin Pl [Mt Auburn]
- **Bank of America (ATM)** · 1663 Massachusetts Ave [Hudson St]
- **Bank of America (ATM)** · 28 Eliot St [Winthrop St]
- **Bank of America (ATM)** · 45 Quincy St [Kirkland St]
- **Bank of America (ATM)** · 47 Oxford St [Everett St]
- **Bank of America (ATM)** · 67 Mt Auburn St [Linden St]
- **Bank of America (ATM)** · Spangler Ctr [Hague]
- **Boston Private Bank & Trust (ATM)** · 104 Mt Auburn St [Brattle St]
- **Cambridge Savings Bank** · 1374 Massachusetts Ave [Holyoke St]
- **Cambridge Savings Bank (ATM)** · 36 JFK St [Mt Auburn]
- **Cambridge Trust** · 1336 Massachusetts Ave [Holyoke St]
- **Cambridge Trust** · 1720 Massachusetts Ave [Garfield St]
- **Cambridge Trust (ATM)** · 124 Mt Auburn St [University Rd]
- **Citizens Bank** · 6 JFK St [Brattle Sq]
- **Citizens Bank (ATM)** · 1 Bennett St [Eliot St]
- **Sovereign Bank** · 1420 Massachusetts Ave [Church St]
- **Sovereign Bank (ATM)** · 125 Mt Auburn St [University Rd]
- **Wainwright Bank & Trust** · 1 Brattle St [Story]

✺ Community Gardens

◉ Donuts

- **Dunkin' Donuts** · 1 Bow St [Mass Ave]
- **Dunkin' Donuts** · 65 JFK St [Eliot St]
- **Dunkin' Donuts** · Harvard MBTA · Massachusetts Ave & Brattle St
- **Nornie B's Sandwich & Donut Shop** · 61 Church St [Palmer St]

○ Landmarks

- **Brattle Theatre** · 40 Brattle St [Church St]
- **Fogg Art Museum** · 32 Quincy St [B'way]
- **Harvard Museum of Natural History** · 26 Oxford St [Kirkland St]
- **Harvard Stadium** · N Harvard St & Soldiers Field Rd
- **Harvard Yard** · b/w Broadway, Quincy St, Peabody St, & Massachusetts Ave
- **John Harvard Statue** · Harvard Yard [Peabody St]
- **Out of Town News** · 0 Harvard Sq [JFK]
- **The Pit** · 0 Harvard Sq [JFK]
- **Weeks Footbridge** · Memorial Dr & DeWolfe St

℞ Pharmacies

- **CVS** · 1426 Massachusetts Ave [Church St] ♿
- **Rite Aid** · 1740 Massachusetts Ave [Prentiss]

✉ Post Offices

- **Harvard Square Station** · 125 Mt Auburn St [University Rd]

🏫 Schools

- **Boston Archdiocesan Choir School** · 29 Mt Auburn St [Athens St]
- **Graham and Parks** · 44 Linnaean St [Avon St]
- **Harvard Business** · Soldiers Field Rd [Soldiers Field Rd]
- **Harvard Law** · 1563 Massachusetts Ave [Waterhouse]
- **Harvard University** · 1350 Massachusetts Ave [Holyoke St]
- **Lesley University** · 29 Everett St [Mass Ave]
- **Maria L Baldwin** · 28 Sacramento St [Sacramento Pl]
- **St Peter's** · 96 Concord Ave [Buckingham St]

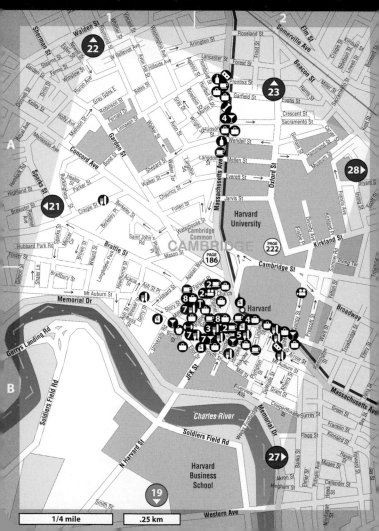

Map 20 • Harvard Square / Allston (North)

CAMBRIDGE

Harvard
University

Harvard

Charles River

Harvard
Business
School

1/4 mile   .25 km

If the people watching isn't enough, browse the Harvard Bookstore, grab a beer at Grendel's, or indulge in LA Burdick's justly celebrated hot chocolate. For meaty grub, nothing beats Bartley's Burger Cottage. If you want to dress up a little, try Chez Henri, then hit up Regattabar.

Coffee

- **Algiers** • 40 Brattle St [Story]
- **Au Bon Pain** •
  1360 Massachusetts Ave [Holyoke St]
- **Dado Tea (tea only)** •
  50 Church St [Palmer St]
- **LA Burdick** • 52 Brattle St [Farwell]
- **Peet's Coffee & Tea** •
  100 Mt Auburn St [JFK]
- **Simon's Coffee House** •
  1736 Massachusetts Ave [Prentiss]
- **Starbucks** •
  1662 Massachusetts Ave [Shepard St]
- **Starbucks** • 31 Church St [Palmer St]
- **Starbucks** • 36 JFK St [Mt Auburn]
- **Tealuxe** • 0 Brattle St [Hague]

Copy Shops

- **FedEx Kinko's** • 1 Mifflin Pl [Mt Auburn]
- **Flash Print** • 99 Mt Auburn St [JFK]
- **Gnomon Copy** •
  1308 Massachusetts Ave [Hollow Ln]
- **Staples** •
  57 John F Kennedy St [Winthrop St]

Farmers Markets

- **Cambridge/Charles Square**
  (May–Nov; Fri 1 pm–6 pm,
  Sun 10 am–3 pm) •
  1 Bennett St [Eliot St]

Gyms

- **Wellbridge Health and Fitness Center** •
  5 Bennett St [Eliot St]

Hardware Stores

- **Dickinson Brothers True Value** •
  26 Brattle St [Church St]

Liquor Stores

- **Harvard Wine** •
  1664 Massachusetts Ave [Shepard St]
- **University Wine Shop** •
  1739 Massachusetts Ave [Prentiss]

Movie Theaters

- **AMC Loews Harvard Square** •
  10 Church St [Mass Ave]
- **Brattle Theatre** • 40 Brattle St [Church St]
- **Harvard Film Archive** •
  24 Quincy St [B'way]

Nightlife

- **Cambridge Common** •
  1667 Massachusetts Ave [Hudson St]
- **Charlie's Kitchen** • 10 Eliot St [Winthrop St]
- **Club Passim** • 47 Palmer St [Church St]
- **The Comedy Studio** •
  1238 Massachusetts Ave [Plympton]
- **Grendel's Den** • 89 Winthrop St [JFK]
- **John Harvard's Brew House** •
  33 Dunster St [Mt Auburn]
- **Lizard Lounge** •
  1667 Massachusetts Ave [Hudson St]
- **Noir** • Charles Hotel • 1 Bennett St [Eliot St]
- **Redline** • 59 JFK St [Winthrop St]
- **Regattabar** • Charles Hotel •
  1 Bennett St [Eliot St]
- **Shay's Lounge** • 58 JFK St [South St]
- **Temple Bar** • 1688 Massachusetts Ave
  [Sacramento St]
- **Tommy Doyle's** •
  90 Winthrop St [Winthrop St]
- **West Side Lounge** •
  1680 Massachusetts Ave [Sacramento St]

Pet Shops

- **Cambridge Pet Care Center** •
  1724 Massachusetts Ave [Garfield St]

Restaurants

- **Algiers** • 40 Brattle St [Story]
- **b. good** • 24 Dunster St [Mass Ave]
- **Border Café** • 32 Church St [Palmer St]
- **Café Pamplona** • 12 Bow St [Arrow]
- **Caffe Paradiso** • Eliot Sq [Mt Auburn]
- **Cambridge, 1** • 27 Church St [Palmer St]
- **Casablanca** • 40 Brattle St [Story St]
- **Charlie's Kitchen** • 10 Eliot St [Winthrop St]
- **Chez Henri** • 1 Shepard St [Mass Ave]
- **Craigie Street Bistro** •
  5 Craigie Cir [Craigie St]
- **Crazy Doughs** • 36 JFK St [Mt Auburn]
- **Daedalus** • 45 Mt Auburn St [Plympton]
- **Darwin's Ltd** • 148 Mt Auburn St [Brewer]
- **Flat Patties** • 81 Mt Auburn St [Summer]
- **Grafton Street** •
  1230 Massachusetts Ave [Bow St]
- **Grendel's Den** • 89 Winthrop St [JFK]
- **Harvest** • 44 Brattle St [Story]
- **Hi-Rise Bread Company** •
  56 Brattle St [Hilliard St]
- **John Harvard's Brew House** •
  33 Dunster St [Mt Auburn]
- **Mr & Mrs Bartley's Burger Cottage** •
  1246 Massachusetts Ave [Plympton]
- **My Thai Vegetarian Café** •
  404 Harvard St [Prescott St]
- **OM** • 92 Winthrop St [JFK]
- **Pho Pasteur** • 35 Dunster St [Mt Auburn]
- **The Red House** • 98 Winthrop St [JFK]
- **Rialto** • 1 Bennett St [Eliot St]
- **Sabra Grill** • 20 Eliot Sq [JFK]
- **Sandrine's** • 8 Holyoke St [Mass Ave]
- **Shilla** • 57 JFK St [Winthrop St]

- **Tamarind Bay** • 75 Winthrop St [Dunster St]
- **UpStairs on the Square** •
  91 Winthrop St [JFK]
- **Veggie Planet** • 47 Palmer St [Church St]
- **Z Square Restaurant & Bar** •
  14 JFK St [Brattle St]

Shopping

- **Abodeon** • 1731 Massachusetts Ave [Prentiss]
- **Alpha Omega** •
  1380 Massachusetts Ave [Holyoke St]
- **Berk's Shoes** • 50 JFK St [Winthrop St]
- **Black Ink** • 5 Brattle St [Brattle Sq]
- **Bob Slate** •
  1288 Massachusetts Ave [Linden St]
- **Brattle Square Florist** •
  31 Brattle St [Eliot St]
- **Cardullo's Gourmet Shoppe** •
  6 Brattle St [Brattle Sq]
- **City Sports** • 14 Brattle St [Brattle Sq]
- **Colonial Drug** • 49 Brattle St [Farwell Pl]
- **Crate & Barrel** • 48 Brattle St [Story]
- **Harvard Bookstore** •
  1256 Massachusetts Ave [Plympton]
- **Harvard Coop** •
  1400 Massachusetts Ave [Dunster St]
- **Herrell's Ice Cream** •
  15 Dunster St [Mass Ave]
- **Hidden Sweets** • 25 Brattle St [Church St]
- **LA Burdick Homemade Chocolates** •
  52D Brattle St [Story]
- **Leavitt & Pierce** •
  1316 Massachusetts Ave [Holyoke St]
- **Little Tibet** •
  1174 Massachusetts Ave [DeWolfe St]
- **Lizzy's Ice Cream** • 29 Church St [Palmer St]
- **Lush** • 30 John F Kennedy St [Winthrop St]
- **Museum of Useful Things** •
  49 Brattle St [Farwell]
- **Newbury Comics** • 36 JFK St [Mt Auburn]
- **Nomad** • 1741 Massachusetts Ave [Prentiss]
- **On Church Street** • 54 Church St [Palmer St]
- **Oona's** • 1210 Massachusetts Ave [Bow St]
- **Out of Town News** • 0 Harvard Sq [JFK]
- **Planet Records** • 54B JFK St [Winthrop St]
- **Proletariat** • 36 JFK St [Mt Auburn]
- **Staples** •
  57 John F Kennedy St [Winthrop St]
- **Stereo Jack's** •
  1686 Massachusetts Ave [Sacramento St]
- **Tannery** • 11A Brattle St [Brattle Sq]
- **Tealuxe** • 0 Brattle St [Hague]
- **Tennis and Squash Shop** •
  67 Mt Auburn St [Brattle St]
- **Tess and Carlos** • 20 Brattle St [Church St]
- **Twisted Village** • 12B Eliot St [Winthrop St]
- **Urban Outfitters** • 11 JFK St [Brattle Sq]
- **ZIPA Jewelry** •
  1316 Massachusetts Ave [Holyoke St]

Video Rental

- **Hollywood Express** •
  1740 Massachusetts Ave [Prentiss]
- **Quick Flix** • 8 Bow St [Mass Ave]

Map 20 · **Harvard Square / Allston (North)**

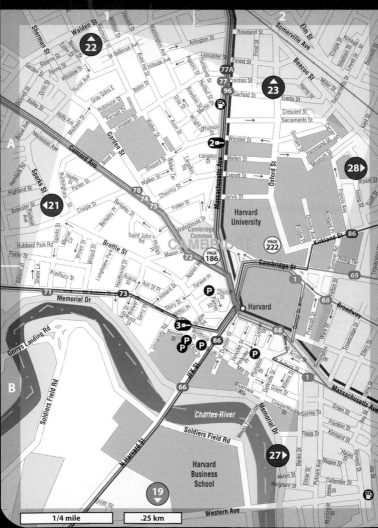

Map 20

All roads, or at least many bus routes and the Red Line, lead to Harvard Square. Throngs of pedestrians are sure to slow down those brave enough to drive, and parking is hard to find, though diligent circling—and a little bit of luck—usually yields results.

Subway

■ · **Harvard**

Bus Lines

1 · Harvard/Holyoke Gate—Dudley Station via Massachusetts Avenue & BU Medical Center

66 · Harvard Square—Dudley Station via Allston & Brookline

68 · Harvard/Holyoke Gate—Kendall/MIT via Broadway

69 · Harvard/Holyoke Gate—Lechmere Station via Cambridge Street

71 · Watertown Square—Harvard Station via Mt Auburn Street

72 · Huron Avenue—Harvard Station via Concord Avenue

73 · Waverley Square—Harvard Station via Trapelo Road

74 · Belmont Center—Harvard Station via Concord Avenue

75 · Belmont Center—Harvard Station via Concord Avenue

77 · Arlington Heights—Harvard Station via Massachusetts Ave

77A · North Cambridge—Harvard Station, Local

78 · Arlmont Village—Harvard Station via Park Circle

86 · Sullivan Square Station—Cleveland Circle via Harvard/Johnston Gate

96 · Medford Square—Harvard Station via George Street & Davis Square

🚗 Car Rental

· **Alamo** ·
1663 Massachusetts Ave [Hudson St] · 617-661-8747

· **Avis** · 1 Bennett St [Eliot St] · 617-534-1430

· **Hertz** · 24 Eliot St [Winthrop St] · 617-338-1520

· **National** ·
1663 Massachusetts Ave [Hudson St] · 617-661-8747

· **Thrifty** · Harvard Square Hotel ·
110 Mt Auburn St [Eliot St] · 617-876-2758

🅿 Gas Stations

· **Gulf** · 1725 Massachusetts Ave [Garfield St]

🅿 Parking

Map 21 · **West Cambridge**

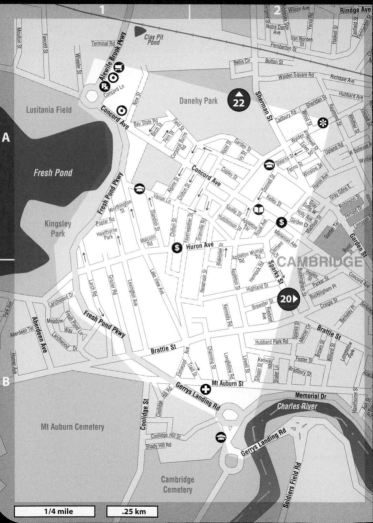

Tucked behind bustling Harvard Square, this hushed suburban community is nice for a pleasant, house-viewing stroll, but little else. Beautiful Mt. Auburn Cemetery is certainly a neighborhood highlight. Stop by and pay your respects to such long-ago dignitaries as Winslow Homer and Henry Cabot Lodge.

$ Banks

· **Cambridge Savings Bank (ATM)** ·
  168 Huron Ave [Manassas]
· **Cambridge Trust** · 353 Huron Ave [Chilton]

✸ Community Gardens

◎ Donuts

· **Dunkin' Donuts** · 201 Alewife Brook Pkwy [Terminal]
· **Dunkin' Donuts** · 517 Concord Ave [Concord Ln]

✚ Emergency Rooms

· **Mount Auburn** · 330 Mt Auburn St [Longfellow Rd]

📖 Libraries

· **Boudreau Public Library** ·
  245 Concord Ave [Donnell]

℞ Pharmacies

· **CVS** · 211 Alewife Brook Pkwy [Concord Ave] ♺

🏫 Schools

· **Buckingham Browne & Nichols** ·
  80 Gerrys Landing Rd [Greenough Blvd]
· **Cambridge Montessori** · 161 Garden St [Walden St]
· **John M Tobin** · 197 Vassal Ln [Standish]

🛒 Supermarkets

· **Whole Foods Market** ·
  200 Alewife Brook Pkwy [Concord Ave]

Map 21 · **West Cambridge**

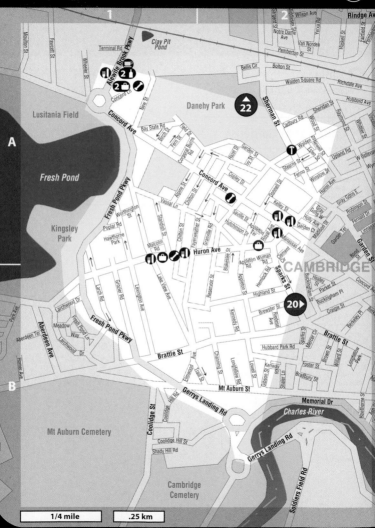

Sundries / Entertainment

Map 21

If you're a gourmand—and particularly if you're a cheese enthusiast—make the trip to Formaggio Kitchen. For a quick bite along Huron Avenue, grab a slice at Armando's. And for pastries galore, stop by Hi-Rise Bread Company, on the ever-engaging corner of Concord Avenue.

Coffee

- **Starbucks** · 220 Alewife Brook Pkwy [Concord Ave]

Hardware Stores

- **Masse's True Value Hardware** ·
  249 Walden St [Sherman St]

Liquor Stores

- **Kappy's Liquors** ·
  215 Alewife Brook Pkwy [Concord Ave]
- **Mall Discount Liquors & Wines** ·
  202 Alewife Brook Pkwy [Concord Ave]

Pet Shops

- **Jeana's Dirty Dog Salon** ·
  298 Concord Ave [Walden St]
- **Pet Supply Outlet Store** ·
  211 Alewife Brook Pkwy [Concord Ave]
- **Raining Cats and Dogs** · 368 Huron Ave [Standish]

Restaurants

- **Armando's** · 163 Huron Ave [Concord Ave]
- **Cheddars** · 201 Alewife Brook Pkwy [Concord Ln]
- **Full Moon** · 344 Huron Ave [Chilton]
- **Hi-Rise Bread Company** · 208 Concord Ave [Huron]
- **Il Buongustaio** · 369 Huron Ave [Standish]
- **Trattoria Pulcinella** · 147 Huron Ave [Concord Ave]

Shopping

- **Formaggio Kitchen** · 244 Huron Ave [Appleton St]
- **Henry Bear's Park** · 361 Huron Ave [Standish]
- **Newbury Comics** ·
  211 Alewife Brook Pkwy [Concord Ave]

Map 21 · **West Cambridge**

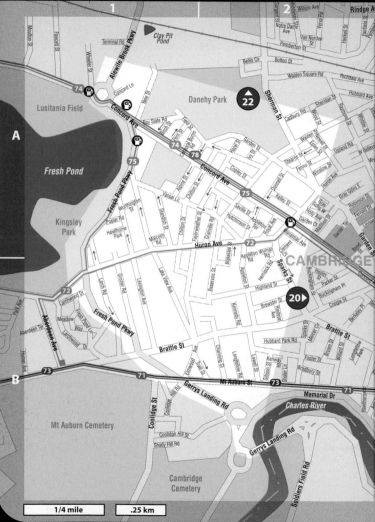

Transportation

Map 21

Unless you live here, you're not going to have an easy time parking. You might snag a space on Huron Avenue, but that's about it. Red Line stops are also far away; to get here by public transportation, take one of the buses that originate at Harvard Square.

Bus Lines

- **71** • Watertown Square—Harvard Station via Mt Auburn Street
- **72** • Huron Avenue—Harvard Station via Concord Avenue
- **73** • Waverley Square—Harvard Station via Trapelo Road
- **74** • Belmont Center—Harvard Station via Concord Avenue
- **75** • Belmont Center—Harvard Station via Concord Avenue
- **78** • Arlmont Village—Harvard Station via Park Circle

Gas Stations

- **Citgo** • 199 Concord Ave [Huron]
- **Mobil** • 343 Fresh Pond Pkwy [Lake View Ave] ⏰
- **Shell** • 603 Concord Ave [Wheeler]
- **Sunoco** • 515 Concord Ave [Concord Ln] ⏰

Map 22 • North Cambridge / West Somerville

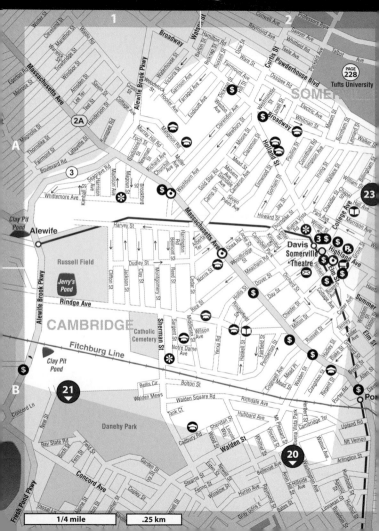

Over the years, the Cambridge contingent has pushed working-class Somerville back into Medford, and claimed Davis Square as its capital. Blending NPR culture with town-center appeal, there is a virtual Benetton ad of businesses, bars, restaurants, and bodegas—not to mention a diner and an ice cream shop.

$ Banks

- **Bank of America** • 406 Highland Ave [Grove St]
- **Bank of America (ATM)** • 1116 Broadway [Holland St]
- **Bank of America (ATM)** •
  2168 Massachusetts Ave [Rindge Ave]
- **Bank of America (ATM)** •
  2502 Massachusetts Ave [Cottage Pk]
- **Bank of America (ATM)** • 253 Elm St [Chester St]
- **Century Bank** • 2309 Massachusetts Ave [Meacham Rd]
- **Citizens Bank** • 212 Elm St [Bowers]
- **Citizens Bank (ATM)** • 1 Holland St [College]
- **Citizens Bank (ATM)** • 4 College Ave [Winter St]
- **East Cambridge Savings Bank** •
  2067 Massachusetts Ave [Walden St]
- **First National Bank of Ipswich** •
  2067 Massachusetts Ave [Walden St]
- **Middlesex Federal Savings** •
  1 College Ave [Highland Ave]
- **Middlesex Federal Savings** • 1196 Broadway [Hill]
- **Wainwright Bank & Trust** •
  176 Alewife Brook Pkwy [Terminal]
- **Wainwright Bank & Trust** • 250 Elm St [Chester St]

✺ Community Gardens

◎ Donuts

- **Dunkin' Donuts** • 244 Elm St [Chester St]
- **Dunkin' Donuts** •
  2480 Massachusetts Ave [Washburn Ave]
- **Verna's Donut Shop** •
  2344 Massachusetts Ave [Norris]

O Landmarks

- **Somerville Theatre** • 55 Davis Sq [Highland Ave]

📖 Libraries

- **O'Neill Public Library** • 70 Rindge Ave [Rindgefield]
- **Somerville West** • 40 College Ave [Morrison Ave]

℞ Pharmacies

- **Rite Aid** • 393 Highland Ave [Grove St]

✉ Post Offices

- **West Somerville** • 58 Day St [Herbert]

⌂ Schools

- **Benjamin Banneker Charter** •
  21 Notre Dame Ave [Middlesex St]
- **Cambridge Friends** • 5 Cadbury Rd [Wood St]
- **Ecole Bilingue, The French American
  International School** •
  45 Matignon Rd [Murray Hill Rd]
- **Matignon High** • 1 Matignon Rd [Churchill Ave]
- **North Cambridge Catholic High** •
  40 Norris St [Cedar St]
- **Peabody** • 70 Rindge Ave [Rindgefield]
- **Powder House Community** •
  1060 Broadway [Packard]
- **SCALE** • 167 Holland St [Cameron Ave]
- **St John the Evangelist** • 122 Rindge Ave [Rice St]
- **Tufts University** • 169 Holland St [Cameron Ave]

🛒 Supermarkets

- **Sessa's Cold Cuts & Italian Specialties** •
  414 Highland Ave [Grove St]

Map 22 • **North Cambridge / West Somerville**

Sundries / Entertainment

Whatever your taste in food and entertainment, you'll satisfy it here. Try Out of the Blue's delicious and inexpensive seafood, Redbones' barbecue, or belly-warming momo from House of Tibet. Live Music=Somerville Theatre or Johnny D's. Somerville Shuffle=Sligo Pub. The perfect Guinness=The Burren.

Coffee

- **Diesel Café** • 257 Elm St [Chester St]
- **Starbucks** • 260 Elm St [Chester St]

Copy Shops

- **Budget Copy** • 2449 Massachusetts Ave [Gold Star Rd]
- **Princeton Printing** • 260 Elm St [Chester St]
- **Staples** • 186 Alewife Brook Pkwy [Terminal]
- **The UPS Store** • 411 Highland Ave [Grove St]

Farmers Markets

- **Somerville (May—Nov; Wed 12 pm—6 pm)** • Day St & Herbert St

Hardware Stores

- **City Paint & Supply** • 2564 Massachusetts Ave [Newman St]

Liquor Stores

- **Downtown Wine & Spirits** • 225 Elm St [Grove St]
- **Norton Beverage** • 2451 Massachusetts Ave [Gold Star Rd]
- **Pemberton Fruit Market** • 2172 Massachusetts Ave [Rindge Ave]
- **Teele Square Liquor** • 1119 Broadway [Westminster St]

Movie Theaters

- **Entertainment Cinemas Fresh Pond** • 168 Alewife Brook Pkwy [Terminal]
- **Somerville Theatre** • 55 Davis Sq [Highland Ave]

Nightlife

- **The Burren** • 247 Elm St [Chester St]
- **Diva Lounge** • 246 Elm St [Chester St]
- **Johnny D's Uptown** • 17 Holland St [Winter St]
- **PJ Ryan's** • 239 Holland St [Broadway]
- **Redbones** • 55 Chester St [Herbert]
- **Sligo Pub** • 237A Elm St [Grove St]
- **Somerville Theatre** • 55 Davis Sq [Highland Ave]

Pet Shops

- **Animal Spirit** • 2348 Massachusetts Ave [Norris]

Restaurants

- **Anna's Taqueria** • 236 Elm St [Chester St]
- **Antonia's Italian Bistro** • 37 Davis Sq [Highland Ave]
- **Café Barada** • 2269 Massachusetts Ave [Dover]
- **Dave's Fresh Pasta** • 81 Holland St [Irving St]
- **Diesel Café** • 257 Elm St [Chester St]
- **Diva Indian Bistro** • 246 Elm St [Chester St]
- **Elephant Walk** • 2067 Massachusetts Ave [Walden St]
- **Gargoyles on the Square** • 219 Elm St [Grove St]
- **House of Tibet** • 235 Holland St [B'way]
- **Jasper White's Summer Shack** • 149 Alewife Brook Pkwy [Rindge Ave]
- **Jose's** • 131 Sherman St [Bellis Cir]
- **Joshua Tree** • 256 Elm St [Chester St]
- **Martsa on Elm** • 233A Elm St [Grove St]
- **Namaskar** • 236 Elm St [Chester St]
- **Out of the Blue** • 215 Elm St [Grove St]
- **Qingdao Garden** • 2382 Massachusetts Ave [Alberta]
- **Redbones** • 55 Chester St [Herbert]
- **Rosebud Diner** • 381 Summer St [Cutler Ave]
- **Rudy's Café** • 248 Holland St [Newbury St]
- **Sabur** • 212 Holland St [Moore]
- **Soleil Café** • 1153 Broadway [Curtis]
- **Spike's Junkyard Dogs** • 217 Elm St [Grove St]

Shopping

- **Bicycle Exchange** • 2067 Massachusetts Ave [Walden St]
- **Black & Blues** • 89 Holland St [Simpson Ave]
- **CD Spins** • 235 Elm St [Grove St]
- **China Fair** • 2100 Massachusetts Ave [Walden St]
- **Chinook Outdoor Adventure** • 93 Holland St [Simpson Ave]
- **Cibeline** • 85 Holland St [Irving St]
- **Magpie** • 416 Highland Ave [Grove St]
- **McKinnon's Choice Meat Market** • 239A Elm St [Grove St]
- **Modern Brewer** • 2304 Massachusetts Ave [Rice St]
- **Nellie's Wildflowers** • 72 Holland St [Buena Vista Rd]
- **Poor Little Rich Girl** • 255 Elm St [Chester St]
- **Staples** • 186 Alewife Brook Pkwy [Terminal]

Video Rental

- **Blockbuster** • 180 Alewife Brook Pkwy [Terminal]
- **Hollywood Express** • 238 Elm St [Chester St]
- **Palmer Video** • 2368 Massachusetts Ave [Nickerson Rd]

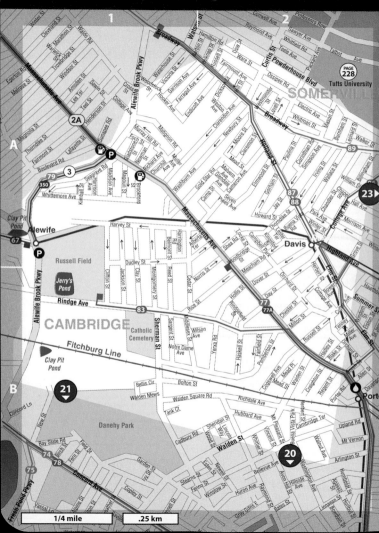

Map 22 · **North Cambridge / West Somerville**

Transportation

Map 22

Driving is no fun in Davis Square; parking is painful. Ditto for the area around Alewife. The Red Line serves both areas, but if you must drive, look for parking along Holland Avenue, a bit outside the Square. For North Cambridge haunts along Mass Ave and its side streets, get to know the 77 bus.

Subway

- **Davis**
- **Alewife**

Bus Lines

- **74** · Belmont Center—Harvard Station via Concord Avenue
- **75** · Belmont Center—Harvard Station via Concord Avenue
- **77** · Arlington Heights—Harvard Station via Massachusetts Avenue
- **77A** · North Cambridge—Harvard Station Local
- **78** · Arlmont Village—Harvard Station via Park Circle
- **79** · Arlington Heights—Alewife Station via Massachusetts Avenue
- **83** · Rindge Ave—Central Square, Cambridge via Porter Square Station
- **87** · Arlington Center or Clarendon Hill—Lechmere Station
- **88** · Clarendon Hill—Lechmere Station via Highland Avenue
- **89** · Clarendon Hill—Sullivan Square Station via Broadway
- **90** · Davis Square—Wellington Station via Sullivan Square Station
- **96** · Medford Square—Harvard Station via George Street & Davis Square
- **350** · North Burlington—Alewife Station via Burlington

Car Washes

- **Cambridge Car Wash** ·
  2013 Massachusetts Ave [Regent St]

Gas Stations

- **Independent** · 2535 Massachusetts Ave [Rindge Ave]
- **Mobil** · 2615 Massachusetts Ave [Alewife Brook]

Parking

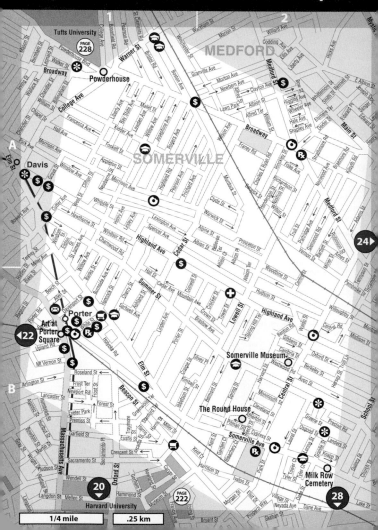

Map 23 • Central Somerville / Porter Square

Map 23

Porter Square feels less polished than Harvard and Davis, and living space here and in neighboring Somerville is slightly more affordable. Shops and restaurants are concentrated on Mass Ave, and a mix of young people, families, and townies populates the residential neighborhoods.

💲 Banks

- **Bank of America** • 1847 Massachusetts Ave [Upland]
- **Bank of America (ATM)** • 1815 Massachusetts Ave [Roseland]
- **Cambridge Savings Bank** • 53 White St [Elm St]
- **Cambridge Savings Bank (ATM)** • 36 White St [White St Pl]
- **Cambridge Savings Bank (ATM)** • 711 Somerville Ave [Elm St]
- **Central Bank** • 399 Highland Ave [Grove St]
- **Century Bank (ATM)** • 110 Medford St [Dexter St]
- **Citizens Bank (ATM)** • Somerville Ave & Massachusetts Ave
- **East Cambridge Savings Bank** • 285 Highland Ave [Cedar St]
- **Sovereign Bank** • 403 Highland Ave [Grove St]
- **Sovereign Bank (ATM)** • CVS/Pharmacy • 36 White St [Somerville Ave]
- **Winter Hill Bank** • 5 Cutter Ave [Elm St]
- **Winter Hill Bank** • 691 Broadway [Boston Ave]

✳️ Community Gardens

🔵 Donuts

- **Dunkin' Donuts** • 1 White St [Somerville Ave]
- **Dunkin' Donuts** • 154 Highland Ave [Central St]
- **Dunkin' Donuts** • 504 Broadway [Hinckley]
- **Dunkin' Donuts** • 519 Somerville Ave [Park St]
- **Russ' Donuts** • 2 Highland Rd [Morrison Ave]

➕ Emergency Rooms

- **Somerville Hospital** • 230 Highland Ave [Tower St]

⭕ Landmarks

- **Art at Porter Square** • Somerville Ave & Massachusetts Ave
- **Milk Row Cemetery** • 439 Somerville Ave [School St]
- **Powderhouse** • College Ave & Broadway
- **The Round House** • 36 Atherton St [Beech St]
- **Somerville Museum** • 1 Westwood Rd [Central St]

℞ Pharmacies

- **CVS** • 36 White St [White St Pl] ⏰
- **CVS** • 532 Medford St [Lowell St]
- **Rite Aid** • 530 Somerville Ave [Park St]

✉️ Post Offices

- **Porter Square** • 1953 Massachusetts Ave [Allen St]

🎓 Schools

- **Benjamin G Brown** • 201 Willow Ave [Kidder]
- **John F Kennedy** • 5 Cherry St [Elm St]
- **St Anthony Elementary** • 480 Somerville Ave [Loring]
- **St Catherine's of Genoa** • 192 Summer St [Belmont St]
- **St Clement's Elementary** • 589 Boston Ave [Warner]
- **St Clement's High** • 579 Boston Ave [Warner]

🛒 Supermarkets

- **Star Market** • 275 Beacon St [Sacramento St]
- **Star Market** • 49 White St [White St Pl]

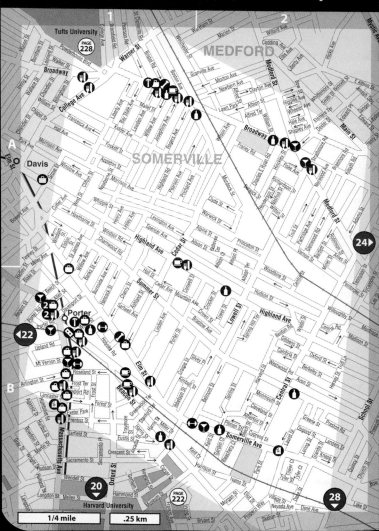

Map 23 · **Central Somerville / Porter Square**

Tufts University

PAGE 228

MEDFORD

Broadway

College Ave

Davis

SOMERVILLE

Broadway

24

Porter

22

20

Harvard University

PAGE 222

28

1/4 mile

.25 km

Sundries / Entertainment

Map 23

The best bet for nearby entertainment is to hop on the Red Line and head one stop in either direction (toward Davis or Harvard). If you do stay local, enjoy a low-key meal at Christopher's, or hit Toad, where there's live music almost every night. Also don't pass up a fresh, homemade taco at Anna's Taqueria.

Coffee

- **Café Rustica** · 356 Beacon St [Roseland]
- **Caffé Rossini** · 278 Highland Ave [Cedar St]
- **Starbucks** · 711 Somerville Ave [Elm St]
- **True Grounds** · 715 Broadway [Willow Ave]

Copy Shops

- **The UPS Store** · 1770 Massachusetts Ave [Lancaster St]
- **The UPS Store** · 519 Somerville Ave [Park St]

Gyms

- **Bally Total Fitness** · 1815 Massachusetts Ave [Roseland]
- **Curves For Women** · 622 Somerville Ave [Kent St]
- **HealthWorks Fitness Center (Women Only)** · 35 White St [White St Pl]

Hardware Stores

- **City Paint & Supply** · 729 Broadway [Bristol Rd]
- **Tags Hardware** · 29 White St [White St Pl]

Liquor Stores

- **Ball Square Fine Wines & Liquors** · 716 Broadway [Willow Ave]
- **Crowley's Liquors** · 152 Boston Ave [Highland Rd]
- **Liquor World** · 13 White St [Somerville Ave]
- **Seven Hills Wine & Spirits** · 288 Beacon St [Sacramento St]
- **Somerville Wine & Spirits** · 235 Highland Ave [Crocker]
- **Woody's Liquor** · 594 Somerville Ave [Garden Ct]
- **Woody's Liquors** · 523 Broadway [William St]

Nightlife

- **Christopher's** · 1920 Massachusetts Ave [Porter Rd]
- **Newtowne Grille** · 1945 Massachusetts Ave [Davenport]
- **Olde Magoun Saloon** · 518 Medford St [Lowell St]
- **On the Hill Tavern** · 499 Broadway [Medford St]
- **Samba Bar & Grill** · 608 Somerville Ave [Kent St]
- **Toad** · 1912 Massachusetts Ave [Porter Rd]

Pet Shops

- **Big Fish, Little Fish** · 55 Elm St [Cedar St]
- **Stinky's Kittens & Doggies Too** · 110 Bristol Rd [B'way]

Restaurants

- **Anna's Taqueria** · 822 Somerville Ave [Acadia Pk]
- **Blue Fin** · 1815 Massachusetts Ave [Roseland]
- **Broken Yolk** · 136 College Ave [B'way]
- **Café Mami** · Porter Exchange · 1815 Massachusetts Ave [Roseland St]
- **Café Rustica** · 356 Beacon St [Roseland]
- **Caffé Rossini** · 278 Highland Ave [Cedar St]
- **Christopher's** · 1920 Massachusetts Ave [Porter Rd]
- **Kelly's Diner** · 674 Broadway [Boston Ave]
- **Lil Vinny's** · 525 Medford St [Lowell St]
- **Lyndell's Bakery** · 720 Broadway [Willow Ave]
- **Passage to India** · 1900 Massachusetts Ave [Porter Rd]
- **RF O'Sullivan's** · 282 Beacon St [Sacramento St]
- **Sound Bites** · 708 Broadway [Willow Ave]
- **Sugar & Spice** · 1933 Massachusetts Ave [Davenport]
- **Tacos Lupita** · 13 Elm St [Porter St]
- **Tu y Yo** · 858 Broadway [Walker St]
- **Wang's Fast Food** · 509 Broadway [Hinckley]

Shopping

- **Ace Wheelworks** · 145 Elm St [Willow Ave]
- **Big Fish, Little Fish** · 55 Elm St [Cedar St]
- **Bob Slate** · 1975 Massachusetts Ave [Beech St]
- **Cambridge Music Center** · 1906 Massachusetts Ave [Porter Rd]
- **Cambridge Naturals** · 23 White St [Somerville Ave]
- **City Sports** · 1815 Massachusetts Ave [Roseland]
- **Greenward** · 1776 Massachusetts Ave [Lancaster St]
- **Joie de Vivre** · 1792 Massachusetts Ave [Arlington St]
- **Lyndell's Bakery** · 720 Broadway [Willow Ave]
- **Paper Source** · 1810 Massachusetts Ave [Arlington St]
- **Porter Square Books** · 25 White St [Somerville Ave]
- **Roach's Sporting Goods** · 1957 Massachusetts Ave [Allen St]

Video Rental

- **Blockbuster** · 1 Porter Sq [White St]

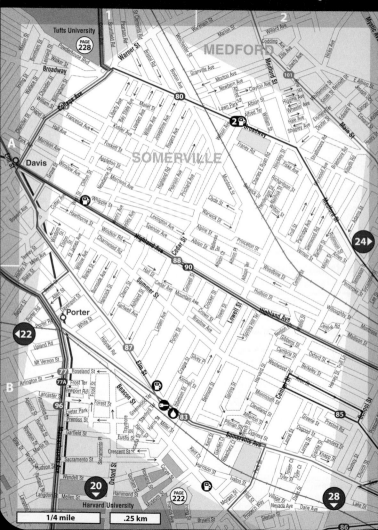

Map 23 · **Central Somerville / Porter Square**

Tufts University
PAGE 228
MEDFORD

Broadway
Somerville
Davis
Porter
Harvard University
PAGE 222
PAGE 228

1/4 mile
.25 km

Map 23

Guarded by a 46-foot steel kinetic sculpture (painted red to match the subway line), centrally located Porter Square T stop makes it easy to get from Porter to other corners of Cambridge or all the way into Boston. Street parking is generally plentiful.

Subway

■ · Porter

Bus Lines

77 · Arlington Heights—Harvard Station via Massachusetts Avenue

77A · North Cambridge—Harvard Station Local

80 · Arlington Center—Lechmere Station via Medford Hills

83 · Rindge Avenue—Central Square, Cambridge via Porter Square Station

85 · Spring Hill—Kendall/MIT Station via Summer Street & Union Square

96 · Sullivan Square Station—Cleveland Circle via Harvard/Johnson Gate

88 · Clarendon Hill—Lechmere Station via Highland Avenue

90 · Davis Square—Wellington Station via Sullivan Square Station

94 · Medford Square—Davis Square Station via W Medford & Medford Streets

96 · Medford Square—Harvard Station via George St & Davis Square

101 · Malden Center Station— Sullivan Square Station

Car Rental

· **Hertz** · 646 Somerville Ave [Lowell St] · 617-625-7958

Car Washes

· **Somerville Car Wash** · 680 Somerville Ave [Craigie St]

Gas Stations

· **Fortini's Service Station** · 225 Beacon St [Kent St]
· **Gulf** · 367 Highland Ave [West St]
· **Gulf** · 583 Broadway [Alfred St]
· **Gulf** · 701 Somerville Ave [Elm St]
· **Sunoco** · 541 Broadway [William St]

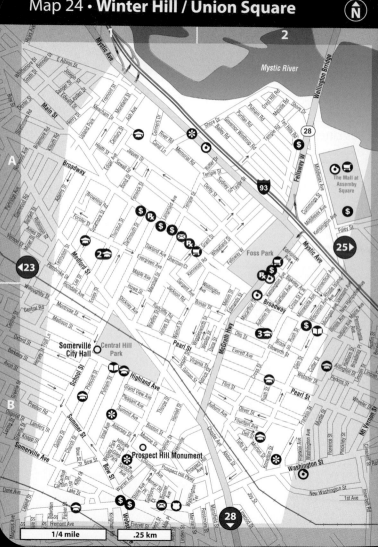

Essentials

Here you'll find remnants of Somerville's working-class neighborhoods, City Hall, and the 93-year-old library. Bypass residential Winter Hill for the livelier Union Square, and don't miss the view of Boston (and July 4 fireworks) from Prospect Hill, where America's first flag was raised in 1776.

$ Banks

- **Bank of America (ATM)** · 5 Middlesex Ave [Main]
- **Bank of America (ATM)** · 68 Union Sq [Stone Ave]
- **Century Bank** · 102 Fellsway W [Shore]
- **Citizens Bank** · 338 Broadway [School St]
- **Citizens Bank** · 40 Union Sq [Warren Ave]
- **Citizens Bank** · 779 McGrath Hwy [Mystic Ave]
- **Citizens Bank (ATM)** · 321 Broadway [Temple St]
- **Sovereign Bank** · 125 Broadway [Wisconsin]
- **Sovereign Bank (ATM)** ·
  77 Middlesex Ave [Kensington Ave]
- **Winter Hill Bank** · 342 Broadway [School St]

✹ Community Gardens

◉ Donuts

- **Dunkin' Donuts** · 220 Broadway [McGrath Hwy]
- **Dunkin' Donuts** · 498 Mystic Ave [Butler Dr]
- **Dunkin' Donuts** · 709 McGrath Hwy [Blakeley Ave]
- **Dunkin' Donuts** · 76 Middlesex Ave [Kensington Ave]
- **Dunkin' Donuts** · 90 Washington St [Franklin St]

O Landmarks

- **Prospect Hill Monument** ·
  Munroe St b/w Prospect Hill Ave & Walnut St
- **Somerville City Hall** · 93 Highland Ave [School St]

◫ Libraries

- **Somerville East** · 115 Broadway [Michigan]
- **Somerville Main Library** ·
  79 Highland Ave [Prescott St]

℞ Pharmacies

- **Rite Aid** · 299 Broadway [Marshall St]
- **Stop & Shop** · 779 McGrath Hwy [Mystic Ave]
- **Walgreens** · 343 Broadway [Dartmouth St]

◉ Police

- **Somerville Police Department** ·
  220 Washington St [Merriam St]

✉ Post Offices

- **Somerville Branch** · 237 Washington St [Bonner Ave]
- **Winter Hill Branch** · 320 Broadway [Marshall St]

◉ Schools

- **Arthur D Healey** · 5 Meacham St [Ash Ave]
- **Capuano Ecc** · 150 Glen St [Dell]
- **Cummings** · 42 Prescott St [Summer]
- **East Somerville Community** · 115 Pearl St [Rush]
- **Full Circle High** · 8 Bonair Pl [Royce Pl]
- **Lincoln Park Community** ·
  290 Washington St [Parker St]
- **Lincoln Park Community Edgerly** ·
  8 Bonair St [Royce Pl]
- **Lincoln Park Community Thurston** ·
  50 Thurston St [Evergreen Ave]
- **Little Flower Elementary** ·
  17 Franklin St [Arlington St]
- **Next Wave Middle** · 8 Bonair St [Royce Pl]
- **Somerville High** · 81 Highland Ave [School St]
- **St Ann's** · 50 Thurston St [Evergreen Ave]
- **Winter Hill Community** ·
  115 Sycamore St [Evergreen Ave]

◫ Supermarkets

- **Star Market** · 299 Broadway [Marshall St]
- **Stop & Shop** · 779 McGrath Hwy [Mystic Ave]

Map 24

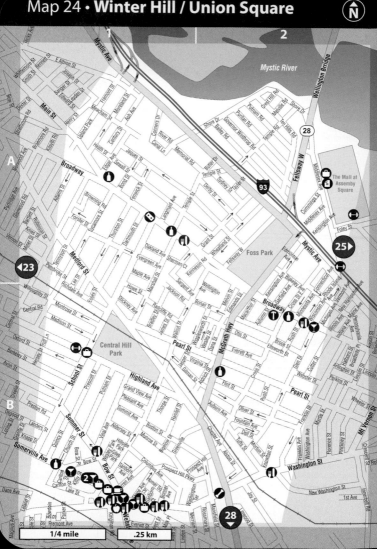

Map 24 • **Winter Hill / Union Square**

Sundries / Entertainment

Map 24

Perpetually up-and-coming, Union Square has a thriving dining and drinking scene, outdoor arts festivals, and a weekend farmers market. Free bands at PA's Lounge and Sally O'Brien's, Peruvian food at Machu Picchu, and the huge breakfasts at Neighborhood Restaurant can't be beat. If you want to go out, try the Independent.

Coffee

• **Sherman Café** • 257 Washington St [Webster Ave]

Copy Shops

• **Staples** • 165 Middlesex Ave [Cummings St]

Farmers Markets

• **Union Square (June—Oct; Sat 9 am—1 pm)** • Washington St & Somerville Ave

Gyms

• **Planet Fitness** • 5 Middlesex Ave [Mystic Ave]
• **YMCA** • 101 Highland Ave [School St]

Hardware Stores

• **Robi Tool Sales** • 168 Broadway [Cross St]

Liquor Stores

• **Jerry's Liquor** • 329 Somerville Ave [Hawkins]
• **Joe's Liquors** • 166 Broadway [Rush]
• **Paul Revere Beverage** • 10 Main St [Edgar Ave]
• **Trans Liquor Mart** • 545 McGrath Hwy [Pearl St]
• **Winter Hill Liquor Mart** • 313 Broadway [Temple St]

Nightlife

• **11th Chapter Saloon** • 366 Somerville Ave [Carlton]
• **The Independent** • 75 Union Sq [Stone Ave]
• **Khoury's State Spa** • 118 Broadway [Glen St]
• **PA's Lounge** • 345 Somerville Ave [Hawkins]
• **Sally O'Brien's** • 335 Somerville Ave [Hawkins]
• **Toast** • 70 Union Sq [Stone Ave]

Restaurants

• **Café Belo** • 120 Washington St [New Washington]
• **Fasika Ethiopian Restaurant** • 145 Broadway [Rush]
• **Great Thai Chef** • 255 Washington St [Bonner Ave]
• **Leone's** • 292 Broadway [Marshall St]
• **Machu Picchu** • 25 Union Sq [Webster Ave]
• **Neighborhood Restaurant & Bakery** • 25 Bow St [Walnut St]
• **Sherman** • 257 Washington St [Webster Ave]
• **Taqueria la Mexicana** • 247 Washington St [Bonner Ave]

Shopping

• **Bombay Market** • 359 Somerville Ave [Kilby St]
• **Bostonian Florist** • 92 Highland Ave [School St]
• **Christmas Tree Shops** • 177 Middlesex Ave [Cummings St]
• **Mudflat Studio** • 149 Broadway [Minnesota]
• **Reliable Market** • 45 Union Sq [Warren Ave]
• **Ricky's Flower Market** • 9 Union Sq [Stone Ave]

Video Rental

• **Palmer Video** • 345 Broadway [Dartmouth St]

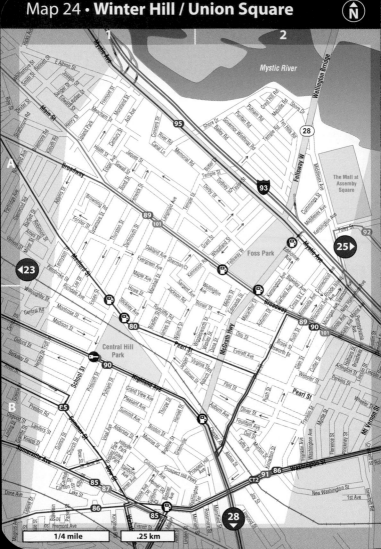

Map 24 · **Winter Hill / Union Square**

Transportation

Map 24

A pinwheel of converging roads, including the city's oldest, Washington Street, Union Square has preserved its ethnic diversity by remaining inaccessible by subway. Served by the 86, 87, and 91 buses, we hope a long-proposed T extension that could spoil the neighborhood flavor never sees the light of day.

Bus Lines

CT2 • Sullivan Station—Ruggles Station via Kendall/MIT

85 • Spring Hill—Kendall/MIT Station via Summer Street & Union Square

86 • Sullivan Sq Station—Cleveland Circle via Harvard/Johnson Gate

87 • Arlington Center or Clarendon Hill—Lechmere Station

89 • Clarendon Hill—Sullivan Square Station via Broadway

90 • Davis Square—Wellington Station via Sullivan Square Station

91 • Sullivan Square Station—Central Square, Cambridge via Washington

92 • Assembly Square Mall—Downtown via Sullivan Square Station, Main Street

95 • West Medford—Sullivan Square Station via Mystic Avenue

101 • Malden Center Station—Sullivan Square Station

Car Rental

• **Americar Auto Rental** •
90 Highland Ave [School St] • 617-776-4640

Gas Stations

• **Gulf** • 212 Broadway [McGrath Hwy]
• **Gulf** • 231 Washington St [Columbus]
• **Hess** • 709 McGrath Hwy [Blakeley] ✇
• **Mobil** • 360 Medford St [School St]
• **Sunoco** • 258 Broadway [Walnut St]
• **Sunoco** • 434 McGrath Hwy [Greenville St]
• **Vincente Brothers** • 345 Medford St [Pearl St]

Map 25 • **East Somerville / Sullivan Square**

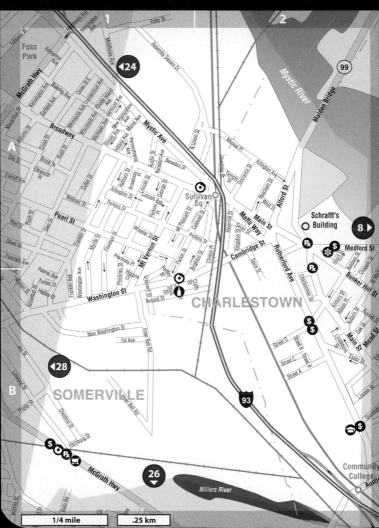

Essentials

Map 25

People go to Sullivan Square for the Orange Line or if they have a package at UPS. The historic Schrafft's Building, formerly the country's largest candy factory, looms over this throughway of a neighborhood from Cambridge/Somerville to Charlestown, Everett, and Malden.

$ Banks

- **Bank of America (ATM)** ·
  22 McGrath Hwy [Fitchburg]
- **Citizens Bank (ATM)** ·
  250 New Rutherford Ave [W School St]
- **East Cambridge Savings Bank (ATM)** ·
  534 Medford St [Short St]
- **Sovereign Bank** · 437 Rutherford Ave [Essex]

✳ Community Gardens

◉ Donuts

- **Dunkin' Donuts** · Sullivan Sq Station ·
  1 Broadway [Mystic Ave]
- **Dunkin' Donuts** · 14 McGrath Hwy [Fitchburg]
- **Dunkin' Donuts** · 99 Cambridge St [Carter St]

O Landmarks

- **Schrafft's Building** · 529 Main St [Mishawum]

℞ Pharmacies

- **Melrose Drug Center** · 462 Main St [Charbonnier]
- **Rite Aid** · 14 McGrath Hwy [Fitchburg] ♿
- **Teamsters Care Pharmacy** · 552 Main St [Mishawum]

🎓 Schools

- **Bunker Hill Community College** ·
  250 New Rutherford Ave [W School St]

🛒 Supermarkets

- **Shaw Market** · 14 McGrath Hwy [Fitchburg]

Map 25 · **East Somerville / Sullivan Square**

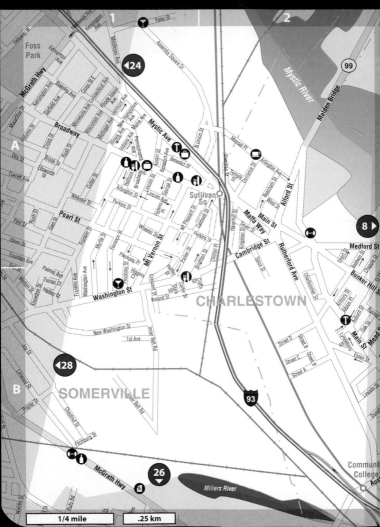

Sundries / Entertainment

Map 25

Vinny's at Night is the best reason to visit this part of town. Don't be fooled by the convenience store frontage: in back lies a treasure trove of unreal Sicilian food. Good Time Emporium is the ideal place for ping pong, free darts, or a good batting cage heart-to-heart à la Good Will Hunting.

Coffee

- **Ro-Lin's Breakfast & Lunch** ·
  78 Arlington Ave [Dorrance]

Copy Shops

- **Go Ape** · 21 McGrath Hwy [Rufo]

Gyms

- **Fitcorp** · 529 Main St [Mishawum]
- **Gold's Gym** · 14 McGrath Hwy [Fitchburg]

Hardware Stores

- **Everett Supply & True Value Hardware** ·
  403 Main St [Auburn St]
- **Home Depot** · 75 Mystic Ave [N Union]

Liquor Stores

- **Bairos Liquors** · 78 Broadway [Hathorn]
- **Blue Label Liquors** · 2 Carter St [Richerd St]
- **Middlesex Beverages** ·
  30 Broadway [Mount Vernon St]
- **Sav-Mor Discount Liquors** · 15 McGrath Hwy [Rufo]

Nightlife

- **Good Time Emporium** ·
  30 Assembly Square Dr [Foley]
- **Night Games** · 30 Washington St [Florence St]

Restaurants

- **Beijing Taste** · 99A Cambridge St [Brighton St]
- **Mount Vernon** · 14 Broadway [Mt Pleasant St]
- **Vinny's at Night** · 76 Broadway [Hathorn]

Shopping

- **Home Depot** · 75 Mystic Ave [N Union]
- **Vinny's Superette** · 76 Broadway [Hathorn]

Map 25 · **East Somerville / Sullivan Square**

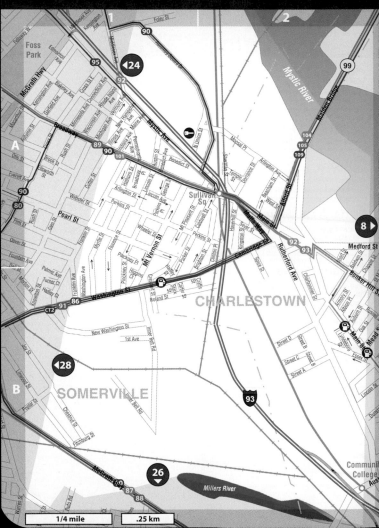

Sullivan Square Station is a major stop on the T's Orange Line and several bus routes. If driving, beware of the other drivers (true in all of Boston but must be highlighted here), confusing signage (ditto), multiple rotaries (ditto), and annoying traffic (you guessed it).

Bus Lines

- **CT2** · Sullivan Station—Ruggles Station via Kendall/MIT
- **80** · Arlington Center—Lechmere Station via Medford Hills
- **86** · Sullivan Square Station—Cleveland Circle via Harvard/Johnson Gate
- **87** · Arlington Center or Clarendon Hill—Lechmere Station
- **88** · Clarendon Hill—Lechmere Station via Highland Avenue
- **89** · Clarendon Hill—Sullivan Square Station via Broadway
- **90** · Davis Square—Wellington Station via Sullivan Square Station
- **91** · Sullivan Square Station—Central Square, Cambridge via Washington Street
- **92** · Assembly Square Mall—Downtown via Sullivan Square Station, Main Street
- **93** · Sullivan Square Station—Downtown via Bunker Hill Street & Haymarket Station
- **95** · West Medford—Sullivan Square Station via Mystic Avenue
- **101** · Malden Center Station—Sullivan Square Station
- **104** · Malden Center Station—Sullivan Square Station
- **105** · Malden Center Station—Sullivan Square Station
- **109** · Linden Square—Sullivan Square Station via Glendale Square

Car Rental

- **Enterprise** · 37 Mystic Ave [N Union] · 617-625-1766

Gas Stations

- **Hess** · 123 Cambridge St [Parker St] ✪
- **Independent** · 339 Main St [Eden]
- **Mobil** · 386 Main St [Lyndeboro St]

Map 26 · **East Cambridge/Kendall Square/MIT**

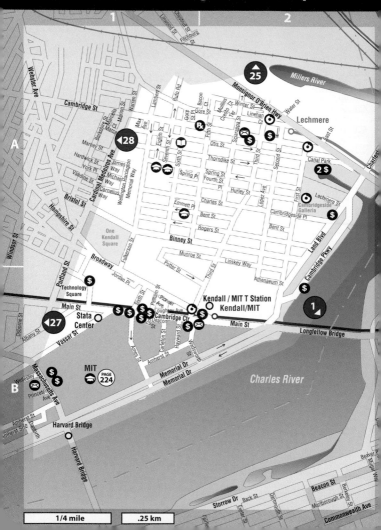

Essentials

Map 26

Once dominated by countless factories producing candy and candles, East Cambridge is now dominated by MIT and countless labs and tech companies. These eager beavers have a sweet tooth for sleek architecture; the most striking example being the Stata Center.

$ Banks

- **Bank of America** · 100 Cambridgeside Pl [Land]
- **Bank of America** · 226 Main St [Wadsworth St]
- **Bank of America** · 84 Massachusetts Ave [Vassar]
- **Bank of America (ATM)** ·
  150 Cambridge Park [Land]
- **Bank of America (ATM)** · 2 Canal Park [Land]
- **Bank of America (ATM)** · 4 Cambridge Ctr [Dock]
- **Bank of America (ATM)** · 600 Technology Sq [B'way]
- **Bank of America (ATM)** ·
  77 Massachusetts Ave [Amherst]
- **Boston Private Bank & Trust** ·
  1 Cambridge Ctr [Hayward St]
- **Cambridge Trust** · 326 Main St [Dock]
- **Citizens Bank** · 225 Cambridge St [3rd St]
- **East Cambridge Savings Bank** · 1 Canal Park [Land]
- **East Cambridge Savings Bank** ·
  292 Cambridge St [Sciarappa]
- **Sovereign Bank (ATM)** · 3 Cambridge Ctr [Dock]
- **Wainwright Bank & Trust** · 1 Broadway [Main]

◉ Donuts

- **Dunkin' Donuts** · Sullivan Sq Station ·
  1 Broadway [Main]
- **Dunkin' Donuts** · 100 Cambridgeside Pl [Land]
- **Dunkin' Donuts** · 5 Third St [Monsignor O'Brien Hwy]

○ Landmarks

- **Harvard Bridge** · Massachusetts Ave [Memorial Dr]
- **Kendall/MIT T Station** · Main St [B'way]
- **Stata Center** · 32 Vassar St [Main]

📖 Libraries

- **O'Connell Public Library** · 48 Sixth St [Thorndike]

℞ Pharmacies

- **Ciampa Apothecary** · 425 Cambridge St [5th St]

✉ Post Offices

- **East Cambridge Station** ·
  303 Cambridge St [Sciarappa]
- **Kendall Square Station** · 250 Main St [Hayward St]
- **MIT** · 84 Massachusetts Ave [Vassar]

🏫 Schools

- **Community Charter School of Cambridge** ·
  245 Bent St [5th St]
- **Kennedy-Longfellow** · 158 Spring St [7th St]
- **Massachusetts Institute of Technology** ·
  77 Massachusetts Ave [Amherst]

Map 26 · East Cambridge/Kendall Square/MIT

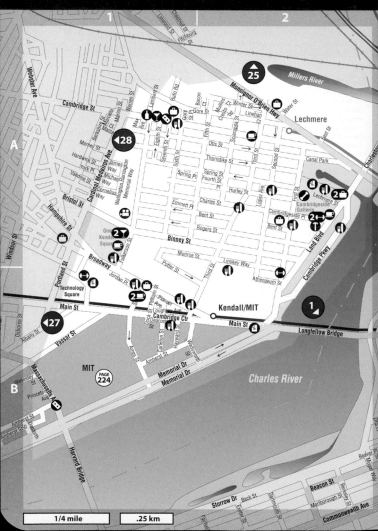

Sundries / Entertainment

Map 26

East Cambridge is home to the tasty Helmand Restaurant and the indie-chain Kendall Square Cinema. Grab a beer at Cambridge Brewing Company after a film (or before, if called for). The Apple Store at Cambridgeside Galleria is a chain store we can easily live with.

Coffee

- **Beantowne Coffee House** ·
  One Kendall Sq [Hampshire St]
- **Starbucks** · 100 Cambridgeside Pl [Land]
- **Starbucks** · Marriott Hotel ·
  2 Cambridge Ctr [Hayward St]
- **Starbucks** · 6 Cambridge Ctr [Dock]
- **Sweet Touch** · 241 Cambridge St [3rd St]

Copy Shops

- **Dmr Print** · 5 Cambridge Ctr [Dock]
- **FedEx Kinko's** · 600 Technology Sq [B'way]
- **Kendall Press** · 1 Main St [1st St]
- **The UPS Store** · One Kendall Sq [Hampshire St]

Gyms

- **Cambridge Racquet & Fitness Club** ·
  215 First St [Linskey]
- **Fitcorp** · 600 Technology Sq [B'way]

Hardware Stores

- **Sears** · 100 Cambridgeside Pl [Land]

Liquor Stores

- **660 Liquors** · 660 Cambridge St [Max]

Movie Theaters

- **Landmark Kendall Square Cinema** ·
  One Kendall Sq [Hampshire St]

Nightlife

- **Cambridge Brewing Company** ·
  One Kendall Sq, Bldg 100 [Hampshire St]
- **Flat Top Johnny's** ·
  One Kendall Sq, Bldg 200 [Hampshire St]
- **Pugliese's** · 635 Cambridge St [Lambert St]

Pet Shops

- **Petco** · 119 First St [Charles St]

Restaurants

- **Aceituna** · 605 W Kendall St [Athenaeum]
- **Bambara** · 25 Land Blvd [Cambridgeside]
- **Black Sheep Café** · 350 Main St [Dock]
- **The Blue Room** · One Kendall Sq [Hampshire St]
- **Court House Seafood** · 498 Cambridge St [6th St]
- **Desfina** · 202 Third St [Charles St]
- **Helmand Restaurant** · 143 First St [Bent St]
- **Legal Sea Foods** · 5 Cambridge Ctr [Dock]
- **Second Street Café** · 89 Second St [Spring]

Shopping

- **Apple Store** · 100 Cambridgeside Pl [Land]
- **Best Buy** · 100 Cambridgeside Pl [Land]
- **Calumet Photographic** · 65 Bent St [2nd St]
- **Cambridge Antique Market** ·
  201 Monsignor O'Brien Hwy [Water]
- **Mayflower Poultry** · 621 Cambridge St [8th St]

Video Rental

- **Hollywood Video** ·
  25 Massachusetts Ave [Memorial Dr]

Map 26 · **East Cambridge/Kendall Square/MIT**

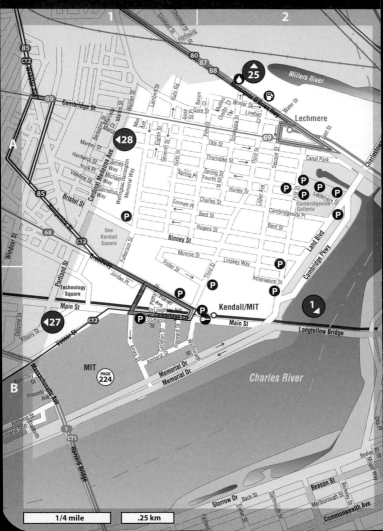

Parking at the Galleria is reasonably priced and handy if street parking is difficult to locate. Perennially confusing is the One Kendall Square complex not being located at Kendall Square—it's actually a few blocks up Broadway toward Cardinal Medeiros Avenue.

Subway

- **· Lechmere**
- **· Kendall/MIT**

Bus Lines

- **CT2** · Sullivan Square Station—Ruggles Station via Kendall/MIT
- **68** · Harvard/Holyoke Gate—Kendall/MIT via Broadway
- **69** · Harvard/Holyoke Gate—Lechmere Station via Cambridge Street
- **80** · Arlington Center—Lechmere Station via Medford Hills
- **85** · Spring Hill—Kendall/MIT Station via Summer Street & Union Square
- **87** · Arlington Center or Clarendon Hill—Lechmere Station
- **88** · Clarendon Hill—Lechmere Station via Highland Avenue

Car Rental

· **Enterprise** · 1 Broadway [Main] · 617-577-0404

Car Washes

· **Lechmere Auto Wash Centers** · 262 Monsignor O'Brien Hwy [Sciarappa]

Gas Stations

· **Shell** · 239 Monsignor O'Brien Hwy [Sciarappa]

Parking

Map 27 · **Central Square / Cambridgeport**

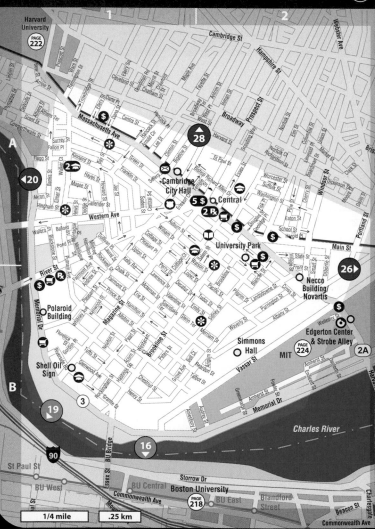

Central Square is a mix of MIT residences, biotech companies, rock clubs, and angry cab drivers. Sadly, the old Necco candy factory is now a Novartis research facility. However, the gorgeous Cambridge City Hall has not been converted to a biotech lab…yet. Find all your grocery needs (and tasty organic food supplies) at Harvest Co-op.

$ Banks

- **Bank of America** ·
  727 Massachusetts Ave [Pleasant St]
- **Bank of America (ATM)** ·
  1000 Massachusetts Ave [Ellery St]
- **Bank of America (ATM)** ·
  139 Massachusetts Ave [Vassar]
- **Bank of America (ATM)** · 235 Main St [Hayward St]
- **Bank of America (ATM)** ·
  622 Massachusetts Ave [Essex]
- **Bank of America (ATM)** · 820 Memorial Dr [River St]
- **Cambridge Savings Bank** ·
  630 Massachusetts Ave [Essex]
- **Cambridge Trust** · 350 Massachusetts Ave [Blanche]
- **Citizens Bank** · 689 Massachusetts Ave [Temple St]
- **Sovereign Bank** · 313 Massachusetts Ave [Norfolk St]
- **Wainwright Bank & Trust** ·
  647 Massachusetts Ave [Prospect St]

✱ Community Gardens

◑ Donuts

- **Dunkin' Donuts** · 84 Massachusetts Ave [Vassar]

O Landmarks

- **Cambridge City Hall** ·
  795 Massachusetts Ave [Bigelow St]
- **Edgerton Center & Strobe Alley** ·
  77 Massachusetts Ave, MIT [Vassar]
- **Necco Building/Novartis** ·
  250 Massachusetts Ave [Landsdowne]
- **Polaroid Building** · 784 Memorial Dr [Pleasant St]
- **Shell Oil Sign** · 187 Magazine St [Granite]
- **Simmons Hall** · 229 Vassar St [Concord Ave]
- **University Park** · Massachusetts Ave & Sidney St

📖 Libraries

- **Central Square Public Library** ·
  45 Pearl St [Franklin St]

℞ Pharmacies

- **CVS** · 624 Massachusetts Ave [Essex]
- **Rite Aid** · 330 River St [Blackstone]
- **Walgreens** · 625 Massachusetts Ave [Essex]

🛡 Police

- **Cambridge Police Department** ·
  5 Western Ave [Magazine St]

✉ Post Offices

- **Cambridge** · 770 Massachusetts Ave [Inman St]

🏫 Schools

- **Amigos Elementary** · 100 Putnam Ave [Magee]
- **Henry Buckner** ·
  85 Bishop Richard Allen Dr [Norfolk St]
- **James F Farr Academy** · 71 Pearl St [Auburn St]
- **Martin Luther King Jr** · 100 Putnam Ave [Magee]
- **Morse School** · 40 Granite St [Pearl St]

🛒 Supermarkets

- **Harvest Co-op Market** ·
  581 Massachusetts Ave [Essex]
- **Star Market** · 20 Sidney St [Green St]
- **Trader Joe's** · 748 Memorial Dr [Pleasant St]
- **Whole Foods Market** · 340 River St [Blackstone]

Map 27 · **Central Square / Cambridgeport**

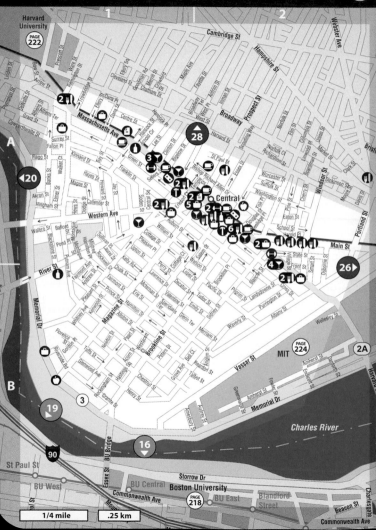

Sundries / Entertainment

Not the obvious place to frolic the day away, Central's full of funk-venture by night. Seeing a rock show at The Middle East earns you instant cool. The Field pours a perfect pint. River Gods is a sacrilegiously charming place to chill. Do Phoenix Landing for dancing on the weekends and Great Eastern Trading Company for vintage duds.

Map 27

Coffee

- **1369 Coffee House** •
757 Massachusetts Ave [Inman St]
- **Carberry's Bakery & Coffee House** •
74 Prospect St [St Paul]
- **Clear Conscience Café** •
581 Massachusetts Ave [Essex St]
- **Dado Tea (tea only)** •
955 Massachusetts Ave [Bay St]
- **Mariposa Bakery** •
424 Massachusetts Ave [Main]
- **Starbucks** •
655 Massachusetts Ave [Prospect St]

Copy Shops

- **Classic Copy & Printing** •
678 Massachusetts Ave [Western]
- **Reproman Reprographics** •
675 Massachusetts Ave [Temple St]
- **The UPS Store** •
955 Massachusetts Ave [Bay St]

Farmers Markets

- **Cambridgeport**
(June—Oct; Sat 10:30—3:30) •
Magazine St & Memorial Dr
- **Central Square**
(May—Nov; Mon 11:30am—6 pm)
• Bishop Richard Allen Dr at Norfolk St

Gyms

- **Boston Sports Club** •
625 Massachusetts Ave [Essex]
- **Cambridge Family YMCA** •
820 Massachusetts Ave [Bigelow St]
- **Athens Sports Club** •
350 Massachusetts Ave [Blanche]
- **Curves** • 614 Massachusetts Ave [Essex]

Hardware Stores

- **Economy Hardware** •
438 Massachusetts Ave [Main]
- **Pill Hardware** •
743 Massachusetts Ave [Pleasant St]

Liquor Stores

- **Dana Hill Liquors** •
910 Massachusetts Ave [Lee]
- **Libby's Liquors** •
575 Massachusetts Ave [Essex]
- **Whole Foods Market** •
340 River St [Blackstone]

Nightlife

- **All Asia** •
334 Massachusetts Ave [Blanche]
- **Cantab Lounge** •
738 Massachusetts Ave [Pleasant St]
- **The Cellar** •
991 Massachusetts Ave [Dana St]
- **Enormous Room** •
567 Massachusetts Ave [Pearl St]
- **The Field** • 20 Prospect St [Mass Ave]
- **Green Street Grill** •
280 Green St [Magazine St]
- **The Middle East** •
472 Massachusetts Ave [Douglas St]
- **Middlesex** •
315 Massachusetts Ave [State]
- **Miracle of Science** •
321 Massachusetts Ave [State]
- **People's Republik** •
880 Massachusetts Ave [Lee]
- **Phoenix Landing** •
512 Massachusetts Ave [Brookline St]
- **Plough & Stars** •
912 Massachusetts Ave [Hancock St]
- **River Gods** • 125 River St [Kinnaird]
- **TT the Bear's Place** •
10 Brookline St [Green St]
- **Western Front** •
343 Western Ave [Putnam Ave]

Restaurants

- **Asgard** •
350 Massachusetts Ave [Blanche]
- **Asmara** •
739 Massachusetts Ave [Pleasant St]
- **Brookline Lunch** •
9 Brookline St [Mass Ave]
- **Café Baraka** • 80 1/2 Pearl St [William St]
- **Carberry's Bakery & Coffee House** •
74 Prospect St [St Paul]
- **Central Kitchen** •
567 Massachusetts Ave [Norfolk St]
- **Cuchi Cuchi** • 795 Main St [Cherry St]
- **Dolphin Seafood** •
1105 Massachusetts Ave [Remington]
- **Green Street Grill** •
280 Green St [Magazine St]
- **Hi-Fi Pizza & Subs** •
496 Massachusetts Ave [Brookline St]
- **India Pavilion** •
17 Central Sq [Pleasant St]
- **La Groceria** •
853 Main St [Bishop Richard Allen Dr]
- **Mary Chung** •
464 Massachusetts Ave [Douglas St]
- **The Middle East** •
472 Massachusetts Ave [Douglas St]

- **Miracle of Science** •
321 Massachusetts Ave [State]
- **Moody's Falafel Palace** •
25 Central Sq [Pleasant St]
- **Picante Mexican Grill** •
735 Massachusetts Ave [Pleasant St]
- **Pu Pu Hot Pot** •
907 Main St [Columbia St]
- **Rendezvous** •
502 Massachusetts Ave [Brookline St]
- **Salts** • 798 Main St [Windsor St]
- **Zoe's** •
1105 Massachusetts Ave [Remington]
- **ZuZu!** •
474 Massachusetts Ave [Douglas St]

Shopping

- **Buckaroo's Mercantile** •
5 Brookline St [Mass Ave]
- **Cambridge Bicycle** •
259 Massachusetts Ave [Front]
- **Cheapo Records** •
538 Massachusetts Ave [Norfolk St]
- **Cremaldi's** • 31 Putnam Ave [Green St]
- **Economy Hardware** •
438 Massachusetts Ave [Main]
- **Great Eastern Trading Company** •
49 River St [Auburn St]
- **Hubba Hubba** •
534 Massachusetts Ave [Norfolk St]
- **Looney Tunes** •
1001 Massachusetts Ave [Ellery St]
- **Micro Center** •
730 Memorial Dr [Riverside Rd]
- **Pearl Art & Craft Supplies** •
579 Massachusetts Ave [Essex]
- **Shalimar** •
571 Massachusetts Ave [Pearl St]
- **Ten Thousand Villages** •
694 Massachusetts Ave [Western]
- **Toscanini's** • 899 Main St [Columbia St]
- **University Stationery** •
311 Massachusetts Ave [State]

Video Rental

- **Blockbuster** •
541 Massachusetts Ave [Norfolk St]
- **Hollywood Express** •
765 Massachusetts Ave [Inman St]

(165)

Map 27 • **Central Square / Cambridgeport** Ⓝ

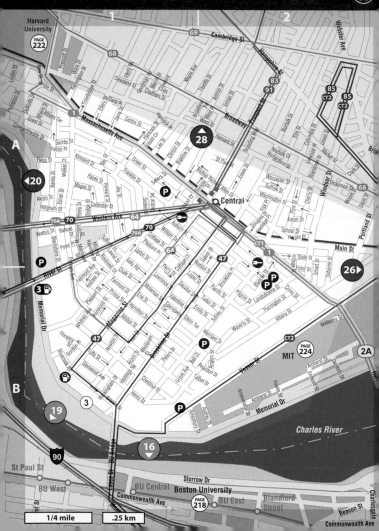

Map 27

Parking around Central Square is not easy. Drop a couple of bucks and the parking garages in University Park will get you close. The Cambridge Department of Public Works has a phone number you can call to "report a street or sidewalk" defect, tempting us to call them once a day to report "all of Mass Ave."

Subway

■ • Central

Bus Lines

CT1 • Central Square, Cambridge—BU Medical Center/BU Medical Campus

CT2 • Sullivan Station—Ruggles Station via Kendall/MIT

1 • Harvard/Holyoke Gate—Dudley Station via Massachusetts Avenue & BU Medical Center

47 • Central Square, Cambridge—Broadway Station via South End Medical Area

64 • Oak Square—Central Square, Cambridge, or Kendall/MIT

68 • Harvard/Holyoke Gate—Kendall/MIT via Broadway

69 • Harvard/Holyoke—Lechmere Station via Cambridge Street

70 • Cedarwood, N Waltham, or Watertown Square—University Park via Central Square

70A • Cedarwood, N Waltham, or Watertown Square—University Park via Central Square

83 • Rindge Avenue—Central Square, Cambridge via Porter Square Station

85 • Spring Hill—Kendall/MIT Station via Summer Street & Union Square

91 • Sullivan Square Station—Central Square, Cambridge via Washington

Car Rental

• **Budget** • Hotel at MIT • 20 Sidney St [Green St] • 617-577-7606
• **Enterprise** • 25 River St [Franklin St] • 617-547-7400

Gas Stations

• **Mobil** • 816 Memorial Dr [River St] ✪
• **Shell** • 207 Magazine St [Riverside Rd] ✪
• **Shell** • 820 Memorial Dr [River St] ✪
• **Sunoco** • 808 Memorial Dr [River St]

Parking

Map 28 · **Inman Square**

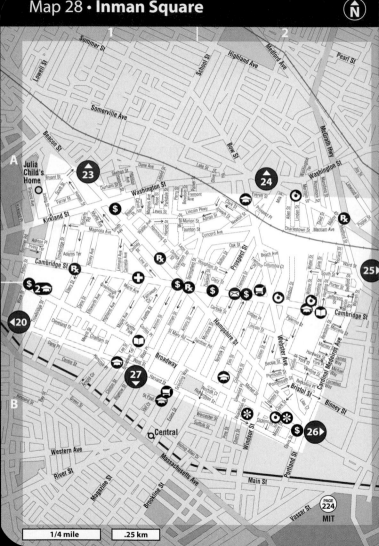

Essentials

Inman Square is an almost-hidden treasure at the center of the Cambridge/Somerville vortex. Folks from the rest of Boston are increasingly finding their way to Inman, particularly when they're hungry. We still miss seeing Julia Child walking around her old neighborhood.

Map 28

$ Banks

- **Bank of America (ATM)** ·
  120 Beacon St [Washington St]
- **Bank of America (ATM)** ·
  1400 Cambridge St [Antrim]
- **Cambridge Savings Bank** ·
  1378 Cambridge St [Hampshire St]
- **Cambridge Trust (ATM)** · 468 Broadway [Ware]
- **Citizens Bank** · 141 Portland St [B'way]
- **East Cambridge Savings Bank** ·
  1310 Cambridge St [Oak St]

✳ Community Gardens

◉ Donuts

- **Cambridge Coffee Shop** ·
  847 Cambridge St [Harding St]
- **Dunkin' Donuts** · Shell ·
  1001 Cambridge St [Windsor St]
- **Dunkin' Donuts** · 222 Broadway [Moore]
- **Dunkin' Donuts** · 282 Somerville Ave [Prospect St]

➕ Emergency Rooms

- **The Cambridge Hospital** ·
  1493 Cambridge St [Highland Ave]

O Landmarks

- **Julia Child's Home** · 103 Irving St [Bryant]

📖 Libraries

- **Cambridge Main Library** · 359 Broadway [B'way Ter]
- **Valente Public Library** ·
  826 Cambridge St [Harding St]

℞ Pharmacies

- **Inman Pharmacy** · 1414 Cambridge St [Antrim]
- **Skenderian Apothecary** ·
  1613 Cambridge St [Roberts Rd]
- **Target** · 180 Somerville Ave [Mansfield]
- **Walgreens** · 16 Beacon St [Concord Ave]

✉ Post Offices

- **Inman Square Station** · 1311 Cambridge St [Oak St]

🎓 Schools

- **Cambridge Rindge & Latin High** ·
  459 Broadway [Ware]
- **Cambridgeport** · 89 Elm St [Market St]
- **Castle** · 298 Harvard St [Lee]
- **Fletcher/Manyard Academy** ·
  225 Windsor St [Broadway]
- **King Open School** · 850 Cambridge St [Harding St]
- **Prospect Hill Academy Charter** ·
  15 Webster Ave [Everett St]
- **Rindge School of Technical Arts** ·
  459 Broadway [Ware]

🛒 Supermarkets

- **Farmer's Bounty** · 234 Elm St [Chester St]
- **Whole Foods Market** · 115 Prospect St [Harvard St]

Map 28 · **Inman Square**

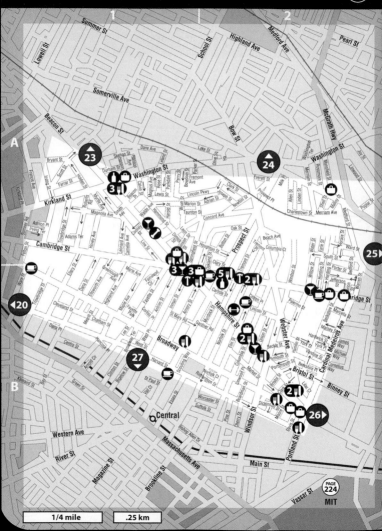

Sundries / Entertainment

Map 28

Eats and treats. Choose one of over a hundred beers at Bukowski's. Sample Dali's to-die-for tapas or East Coast Grill & Raw Bar's marvels from the sea. All-Star Sandwich Bar is a must for gourmet sandwiches. Curious shoppers will not be disappointed by Boutique Fabulous or The Garment District, a thrift megastore whose basement sells clothes at $1 per pound.

Coffee

- **1369 Coffee House** · 1369 Cambridge St [Springfield]
- **Cambridge Coffee Shop** · 847 Cambridge St [Harding St]
- **Peet's Coffee & Tea** · Whole Foods · 115 Prospect St [Harvard St]
- **Starbucks** · 468 Broadway [Ware]

Gyms

- **Fitness Together** · 143 Hampshire St [Norfolk St]

Hardware Stores

- **City Paint & Supply** · 1149 Cambridge St [Norfolk St]
- **Inman Square Ace Hardware** · 1337 Cambridge St [Springfield]

Liquor Stores

- **Prospect Liquor** · 1226 Cambridge St [Prospect St]
- **Wine Cask** · 407 Washington St [Beacon St]

Nightlife

- **Abbey Lounge** · 3 Beacon St [Dickinson St]
- **Atwood's Tavern** · 877 Cambridge St [Hunting]
- **B-Side Lounge** · 92 Hampshire St [Windsor St]
- **Bukowski's** · 1281 Cambridge St [Oakland St]
- **The Druid** · 1357 Cambridge St [Springfield]
- **Ryles Jazz Club** · 212 Hampshire St [Inman St]
- **Thirsty Scholar Pub** · 70 Beacon St [Cooney]

Pet Shops

- **Boston Dogs** · 70 Beacon St [Cooney]

Restaurants

- **All-Star Sandwich Bar** · 1245 Cambridge St [Prospect St]
- **Amelia's Trattoria** · 111 Harvard St [Davis St]
- **Atasca** · 50 Hampshire St [Webster Ave]
- **B-Side Lounge** · 92 Hampshire St [Windsor St]
- **Café Kiraz** · 119 Hampshire St [Columbia St]
- **City Girl Café** · 204 Hampshire St [Inman St]
- **Dali** · 415 Washington St [Beacon St]
- **East Coast Grill & Raw Bar** · 1271 Cambridge St [Oakland St]
- **Emma's Pizzeria** · 40 Hampshire St [Webster Ave]
- **EVOO** · 118 Beacon St [Washington St]
- **Koreana** · 154 Prospect St [B'way]
- **Magnolia's** · 1193 Cambridge St [Tremont St]
- **Midwest Grill** · 1124 Cambridge St [Norfolk St]
- **Montien** · 1287 Cambridge St [Oakland St]
- **O Cantinho** · 1128 Cambridge St [Norfolk St]
- **Ole Mexican Grill** · 11 Springfield St [Cambridge St]
- **Oleana** · 134 Hampshire St [Elm St]
- **Pho Lemon** · 228 Broadway [Clark St]
- **Punjabi Dhaba** · 225 Hampshire St [Cambridge St]
- **S&S Restaurant** · 1334 Cambridge St [Oak St]
- **Toscanini and Sons** · 406 Washington St [Beacon St]

Shopping

- **Boston Costume Company** · 200 Broadway [Davis St]
- **Boutique Fabulous** · 1309 Cambridge St [Oak St]
- **Central Bakery** · 732 Cambridge St [Marion St]
- **Christina's Homemade Ice Cream** · 1255 Cambridge St [Prospect St]
- **The Garment District** · 200 Broadway [Davis St]
- **Inman Square Market** · 1343 Cambridge St [Springfield]
- **Royal Pastry** · 738 Cambridge St [Marion St]
- **Sadye & Company** · 121 Hampshire St [Columbia St]
- **Target** · 180 Somerville Ave [Mansfield]
- **Urban Oasis** · 243 Hampshire St [Dickinson St]
- **Wine Cask** · 407 Washington St [Beacon St]

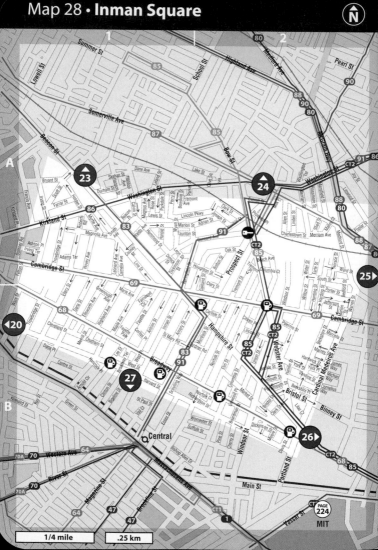

Map 28 · **Inman Square**

Can't get there by T, but it's easy enough to hop a bus or take a short walk from the Central or Kendall Square T stops. Parking is for the adventurous, though there are a couple of public lots. The neighborhood is a cyclists' mecca—drivers, take heed.

Bus Lines

CT1 • Central Square, Cambridge—BU Medical Center/BU Medical Campus

CT2 • Sullivan Station—Ruggles Station via Kendall/MIT

1 • Harvard/Holyoke Gate—Dudley Station via Massachusetts Avenue & BU Medical Center

47 • Central Square, Cambridge—Broadway Station via South End Medical Area

64 • Oak Square—Central Square, Cambridge, or Kendall/MIT

68 • Harvard/Holyoke Gate—Kendall/MIT via Broadway

69 • Harvard/Holyoke Gate—Lechmere Station via Cambridge Street

70 • Cedarwood, N Waltham, or Watertown Square—University Park via Central Square

70A • Cedarwood, N Waltham, or Watertown Square—University Park via Central Square

80 • Arlington Center—Lechmere Station via Medford Hills

83 • Rindge Avenue—Central Square, Cambridge via Porter Square Station

85 • Spring Hill—Kendall/MIT Station via Summer Street & Union Square

86 • Sullivan Square Station—Cleveland Circle via Harvard/Johnson Gate

87 • Arlington Center or Clarendon Hill—Lechmere Station

88 • Clarendon Hill—Lechmere Station via Highland Avenue

90 • Davis Square—Wellington Station via Sullivan Square Station

91 • Sullivan Square Station—Central Square, Cambridge via Washington

Car Rental

• **U-Save Auto & Truck Rental** •
70 Prospect St [Webster Ave] • 617-628-8800

Gas Stations

• **Citgo** • 277 Broadway [Elm St]
• **Exxon** • 209 Broadway [Moore]
• **Hess** • 287 Prospect St [Hampshire St] ♿
• **Mobil** • 320 Broadway [Prospect St]
• **Shell** • 1001 Cambridge St [Windsor St]

Map 29 · **West Roxbury**

1

2

Roxbury Pkwy Rotary

Walnut Hills Cemetery

VFW Pkwy

30▶

VFW Pky

A

Mt. Benedict Catholic Cemetery

Mt. Lebanon Cemetery

St. Joseph's Cemetery

Gethsemane Cemetery

1. Park Lane Dr
2. Ellswood St
3. Amesbury St
4. Long Ter
5. Dennell St
6. Jennett Ave
7. Pleasant Ave
8. Henshaw Ter
9. Francesca St
10. Porter St
11. Anderer Ln
12. Maple Ter
13. Theodore Parker Rd
14. Paulman Cir
15. Belgrade Ter
16. Anawan Ter
17. New Park Ave
18. Ardmore Rd
19. Cuthbert Rd
20. Pine Lodge Rd
21. Rockingham Ave
22. Westmoor Cir
23. Camp Rd
24. Maple Rd
25. Bartlett Ave
26. Billings Way
27. March Way
28. March Ter
29. Cypress St
30. Spring Valley Rd
31. Moloney St
32. Miami Ter
33. Miami Ave
34. Autumn St
35. Alta Crest Rd
36. Ashland St
37. Running Brook Rd
38. Trevore Deldord St
39. Peacock Ln
40. Stimson Rd

Millennium Park

Centre St

Belgrade Ave

W Roxbury Pkwy

Billings Field

Spring St

Centre St

33▶

Stony Brook State Reservation

Turtle Pond

B

Cutler Park

Cow Island Pond

Harvey Beach

VFW Pkwy

Needham St

Bridge St

VFW Pkwy

Charles River

Charles River

Welch Pond

Washington St

Stony Brook Cemetery

Enneking Pkwy

Lower East St

Grove St

Grove Street Cemetery

Stony Brook State Reservation

Motley Pond

Charles River

Draper Playground

Dedham Mall

Dedham Pkwy

Turtle Pond Pkwy

Map 29 • **West Roxbury**

Map 29

Essentials

West Roxbury is a suburb-within-the-city community, with selective shopping and some good food. Millennium Park has fields, paths, and playgrounds, and a drive along VFW can be nice when the construction isn't bad and the trees are in bloom. The area exists as a middle ground between suburban Newton and city communities like Roslindale. With supermarkets and places to park, West Roxbury is a good place to settle if you want to stay in the city and own an affordable house.

O Landmarks

- **Millennium Park** • VFW Pkwy & Gardner St

Sundries/Entertainment

For a tasty lunch, try a sandwich from Real Deal or a kabob from Samia Bakery. For a great Euro-South American take on dinner, try MaSoNa by the commuter rail on Corey Street.

Restaurants

- **Himalayan Bistro** • 1735 Centre St [Manthorne Rd]
- **MaSoNa Grill** • 4 Corey St [Park St]
- **Real Deal** • 1882 Centre St [Hastings St]
- **Samia Bakery** • 1894 Centre St [Hastings St]
- **Vintage** • 1430 VFW Pkwy [Caledonian Ave]
- **West on Centre** • 1732 Centre St [Manthorne Rd]

Shopping

- **Irish Cottage** • 1898 Centre St [Park St]
- **Jack Davis Florist** • 2097 Centre St [Temple St]

Transportation

The subway doesn't extend into West Roxbury, but you can use the Needham commuter rail line. Pick it up at the Forest Hills stop (on the T's Orange Line) and get off at either the Highland stop or the West Roxbury stop

Map 30 · **Roslindale**

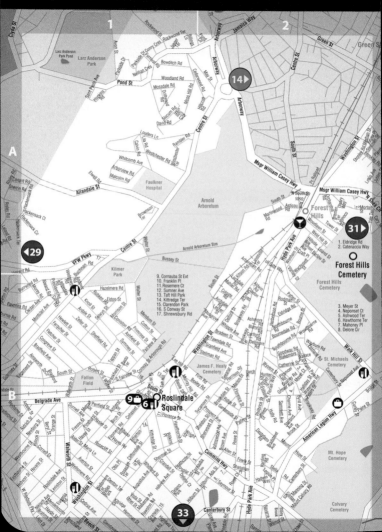

Larz Anderson
Park Pond
Larz Anderson
Park

Clyde St

Green St
Green S

Rockwood St
Rockwood Ter

Arborway
Jamaica Way

Centre St

Bowditch Rd

Pond St

Woodland Rd

Mossdale Rd

14▶

David Rd

Centre St

Arborway

Louders Ln

Whitcomb Ave

Arborview Rd
Malcolm Rd

Allandale St

Faulkner
Hospital

Msgr William Casey Hwy

A

Centre St

Arnold
Arboretum

Msgr William Casey Hwy

South St

South St

Forest
Hills

31▶

1. Eldridge Rd
2. Catenaccia Way

VFW Pkwy

Kilmer
Park

Centre St

Arnold Arboretum Stm

Bussey St

Hyde Park Ave

Weld Hill St

Tower St

◀29

Hazelmere Rd

Hazelwood Rd

**Forest Hills
Cemetery**

Forest Hills
Cemetery

9. Cornauba St Ext
10. Franklin Pl
11. Rosemere Ct
12. Sumner Ave
13. Taft Hill Park
14. Kittredge Ter
15. Clarendon Park
16. S Conway St
17. Shrewsbury Rd

3. Meyer St
4. Neponset Ct
5. Ashwood Ter
6. Hawthorne Ter
7. Mahoney Pl
8. Delore Cir

Weld Hill St

Washington St

James F. Healy
Cemetery

St. Michaels
Cemetery

B

Belgrade Ave

South St

9 **6** **Roslindale
Square**

Fallon
Field

American Legion Hwy

Mt. Hope
Cemetery

Washington St

Cummins Hwy

Hyde Park Ave

33

Canterbury St

Calvary
Cemetery

Map 30 · **Roslindale**

Map 30

Essentials

Over the last few decades, Roslindale Square (also known as Roslindale Village) has received awards for turning a virtual ghost town into a nice place to live through local shops and some great restaurants. The city subsidies didn't hurt either. Walking through the village area, one gets the sense of a community proud of itself. As a bonus, Roslindale Village is within walking distance of the Arnold Arboretum, the best park in Boston and possibly the best urban park in America.

O Landmarks

- **Forest Hills Cemetery** · 95 Forest Hills Ave [Morton St]
- **Roslindale Square** · Washington St & Belgrade Ave

Sundries/Entertainment

What Rozzie lacks in hip bars, it makes up for in restaurants like Delfino, shopping like Joanne Rossman and Pazzo, and a surprisingly large amount of bakeries like Fornax Bread Baking Company. If you wanna get your drink on, you'll have to hightail it for JP.

Nightlife

- **JJ Foley's Fireside Tavern** ·
  30 Hyde Park Ave [Weld Hill St]

Restaurants

- **Birch Street Bistro** · 14 Birch St [Corinth St]
- **Delfino** · 754 South St [Taft St]
- **Diane's Bakery** · 9 Poplar St [South St]
- **Geoffrey's Café** · 4257 Washington St [Corinth St]
- **John's Bakery** · 31 Poplar St [Washington St]
- **Pleasant Café** · 4515 Washington St [Cedrus Ave]
- **Primavera** · 289 Walk Hill St [Canterbury St]
- **Sophia's Grotto** · 22 Birch St [Corinth St]
- **Village Sushi & Grill** · 14 Corinth St [Birch St]
- **Yucatan Tacos** · 1417 Centre St [Knoll St]

Shopping

- **Atlas Liquors** · 591 Hyde Park Ave [Cummins Hwy]
- **Boston Cheese Cellar** · 18 Birch St [Corinth St]
- **Droubi Bakery** · 748 South St [Cohasset St]
- **Emack & Bolio's** · 2 Belgrade Ave [Birch St]
- **Exotic Flowers** ·
  609 American Legion Hwy [Canterbury St]
- **Fornax Bread Baking Company** ·
  27 Corinth St [Washington St]
- **Joanne Rossman: Purveyor of the Unnecessary
  & The Irresistible** · 6 Birch St [Corinth St]
- **Pazzo Books** · 4268 Washington St [Corinth St]
- **Roslindale Fish Market** ·
  389 Poplar St [Washington St]
- **Solera** · 12 Corinth St [Birch St]
- **Thrift Shop of Boston** · 17 Corinth St [Birch St]
- **Village Books** · 751 South St [Taft Ct]

Transportation

To get to Roslindale without driving, you can either take the T's Orange Line to the Forest Hills stop and from there take an MBTA bus, or you can ride the commuter rail to Roslindale Village or Bellevue.

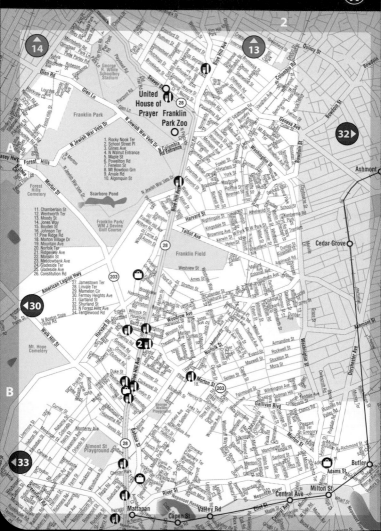

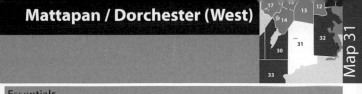
Essentials

Mattapan is mostly residential and home to about 40,000 people. It has a growing Haitian-American community (the largest in Massachusetts), and has smaller communities whose roots are in many of the nations of the Caribbean. This is reflected in the wealth of Caribbean restaurants located on Blue Hill Avenue.

Landmarks

- **Franklin Park Zoo Bear Cages** · 1 Franklin Park Rd [Blue Hill Ave]
- **United House of Prayer** · 206 Seaver St [Elm Hill Ave]

Sundries/Entertainment

Commercial activity in Mattapan clusters around Mattapan Square. Here you can argue with your friends about whether Haitian patties are tastier than Jamaican patties. Then, as you head towards Morton Street, you can stop arguing to stuff your mouths with roti at Ali's. Pit Stop Bar-B-Q, with its great ribs, represents.

Restaurants

- **Ali's Roti** · 1188 Blue Hill Ave [Morton St]
- **Bon Appetit** · 1138 Blue Hill Ave [Livingstone St]
- **Brothers** · 1638 Blue Hill Ave [Fairway St]
- **Flames** · 461 Blue Hill Ave [Georgia St]
- **Flames** · 663 Morton St [Rhoades Ave]
- **Lenny's Tropical Bakery** · 1195 Blue Hill Ave [Deering Rd]
- **P&R Ice Cream** · 1284 Blue Hill Ave [Evelyn St]
- **Picasso Creole Cuisine** · 1296 Blue Hill Ave [Fessenden St]
- **Pit Stop Bar-B-Q** · 888A Morton St [Cemetery Rd]
- **R&S Jamaican Restaurant** · 770 Blue Hill Ave [Wales St]
- **Simco's on the Bridge** · 1509 Blue Hill Ave [Regis Rd]
- **Tastee Jamaican Restaurant** · 522 River St [Cummins Hwy]
- **United House of Prayer** · 206 Seaver St [Elm Hill]

Shopping

- **Dark Horse** · 2297 Dorchester Ave [Adams St]
- **Le Foyer Bakery** · 132 Babson St [Fremont St]
- **Taurus Records** · 1282 Blue Hill Ave [Evelyn St]

Transportation

To get to the Mattapan T stop, choose an Ashmont-bound train. At the Ashmont station, the "it's not retro, it's old" Mattapan trolley will take you as far as Mattapan Square. The MBTA commuter rail's Fairmount line makes a stop at Morton Street.

Map 32 · **Dorchester (East)**

1

2

N

1. Cawfield St
2. Quincefield St
3. Wendover St
4. Dudley Ter
5. Humphreys Pl
6. Belden Sq
7. Dawes Ter
8. Sumner St
9. Bakersfield St
10. Annapolis St
11. Alvan Ter
12. Sumner Park
13. Sexagston Ter

14. Kevin Rd
15. Sumner Sq
16. Chase St
17. Dawes St
18. Uphams Ct
19. Whittemore Ter
20. Mount Cushing Ter
21. Wheelock Ave
22. Upham Ave
23. Wilbur St
24. Whitby Ter
25. Hesston Ter
26. Greenmount St

27. Island View Pl
28. Harbor Point Blvd
29. Westwood Rd
30. Ocean St
31. Oyster Bay Rd

James Blake House
Dorchester North Burying Ground
Strand Theatre
Commonwealth Museum
Savin Hill
Savin Park
JFK Library and Museum

PAGE 208
PAGE 210
PAGE 221

Columbus Park
Dorchester Bay
Dorchester Bay

32. Caspian Way
33. Heckmans St
34. Plainsfield Rd
35. Delroy St
36. Southview St
37. Wilkinson Park
38. Mirimiede Ter
39. Treadway Rd
40. Dunn St
41. Nuvillus Ter
42. Tovar St
43. Winter St
44. Marklin Way
45. Duncan Pl
46. Clayton St
47. Centervale Park
48. Levant St
49. Telonic St
50. Eunice St
51. Westville Ter
52. Dayton St
53. Remington St
54. Endicott Ter
55. Elindale St
56. Popes Hill St
57. Saint Clare Rd
58. Southwick St
59. Bloomington St
60. Lorenzo St
61. Berry St
62. Woodworth St
63. Walnut St
64. Taylor St
65. Ashmont Ct
66. Burgoyne St
67. Beaumont St
68. Westmoreland
69. Radford Ln St
70. Northam Park
71. Argyle St
72. Argyle Ter
73. Delvin St
74. Joseph St
75. Tilman St
76. Greenfield St

Fields Corner

Shawmut

Ashmont
All Saints Church

Map 32 · **Dorchester (East)**

Map 32

Essentials

(In)famous for protecting turf, Dorchester is a collection of distinct neighborhoods and ethnicities. Uphams Corner, Savin Hill, Fields Corner, Ashmont, Codman Square, and Grove Hall are but a few of the areas that comprise Boston's largest district. Sure, there's crime, but let's hope the gentrification creeping down Dot Ave doesn't entirely rob Dorchester of its cred.

O Landmarks

- **All Saints' Church** · 209 Ashmount St [Bushnell St]
- **Commonwealth Museum** · 220 Morrissey Blvd [Dominic J Bianculli]
- **Dorchester North Burying Ground** · Columbia Rd & Stoughton St [Stoughton St]
- **The James Blake House** · 735 Columbia Rd [Pond St]
- **John F Kennedy Library and Museum** · Morrissey Blvd & Columbia Pt
- **Strand Theatre** · 543 Columbia Rd [Dudley St]

Sundries/Entertainment

Irish bars line Dot Ave; they lack tourists and charge three bucks for Guinness. If you're looking for a trendier night spot, check out dBar. Mixed in are the city's best pho houses. You'll find excellent Caribbean cuisine along Blue Hill Avenue. Go to Grove Hall and Uphams Corner for soul food.

🍸 Nightlife

- **Banshee** · 934 Dorchester Ave [Edison Grn]
- **Boston Bowl** · 820 Morrissey Blvd [Tenean St]
- **dBar** · 1236 Dorchester Ave [Hoyt St]
- **Eire Pub** · 795 Adams St [Washington St]
- **Harp & Bard** · 1099 Dorchester Ave [Savin Hill Ave]

- **Ka' Carlos** · 33 Hancock St [Bird St]
- **Lucky Café** · 1107 Dorchester Ave [Saving Hill Ave]
- **O Ya** · 9 East St [South St]
- **Phillips Old Colony House** ·
  780 Morrissey Blvd [Freeport St]
- **Pho 2000** · 198 Adams St [Arcadia St]
- **Pho Hoa** · 1356 Dorchester Ave [Kimball St]
- **Restaurante Cesaria** · 266 Bowdoin St [Draper St]
- **Shanti: Taste of India** · 1111 Dorchester Ave [Savin Hill Ave]
- **Sunrise** · 1157 Dorchester Ave [Dunn St]

🍴 Restaurants

- **Ashmont Grill** · 555 Talbot Ave [Ashmont]
- **Ba-Le Restaurant** · 1052 Dorchester Ave [William St]
- **Blarney Stone** · 1505 Dorchester Ave [Park St]
- **Blasi's Café and Fat Belly Deli** · 762 Adams St [Minot St]
- **CF Donovan's** · 112 Savin Hill Ave [Sydney]
- **Charlie's Place** · 1740 Dorchester Ave [Semont Rd]
- **Chef Lee's II** · 554 Columbia Rd [Dudley St]
- **dBar** · 1236 Dorchester Ave [Hancock St]

🛍 Shopping

- **Asian Bookstore** · 1392 Dorchester Ave [Greenwich St]
- **Coleen's Flowershop** · 912 Dorchester Ave [Grafton St]
- **Greenhill's Irish Bakery** · 780 Adams St [Henderson Rd]

Transportation

In a word: Underserved! The Red Line tracks along the eastern side of Dorchester; roughly parallel to Dot Ave. From Ashmont, a trolley line wraps around to Mattapan Square. Buses run along Blue Hill Avenue; unfortunately, none of these buses directly connects Dorchester to Central Boston. The commuter rail's Fairmount line makes a stop at Uphams Corner and Morton Street.

Map 33 · Hyde Park

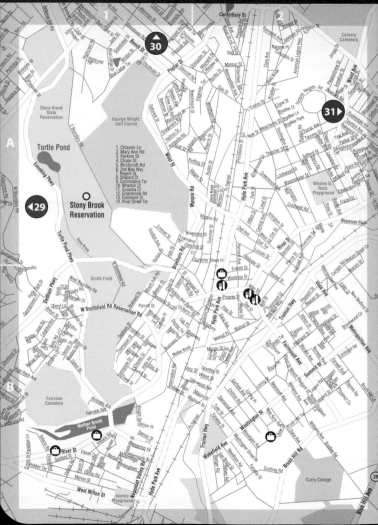

1. Chisolm Ln
2. Mary Ann Rd
3. Perkins St
4. Chase St
5. Birchcroft Rd
6. 2nd New Way
7. Regent St
8. Shepard Ct
9. Commodore Ter
10. Wharton Ct
11. Susanna Ct
12. Greenbrook Rd
13. Fieldmont St
14. River Street Ter

Map 33 · **Hyde Park**

Map 33

Essentials

Almost as large as Franklin Park, Stony Brook Reservation covers 475 acres and includes low hills, dense woods, rock outcroppings, and marshland. The park's largest feature is Turtle Pond, where you can fish for perch and sunfish. There are also several miles of bicycle paths and the most extensive hiking opportunities within the city limits. Among the park's many recreational facilities is the John F. Thompson Center, New England's first recreational facility designed specifically to accommodate handicapped visitors.

O Landmarks

- **Stony Brook Reservation** · Washington St & Turtle Pond Pkwy

Sundries/Entertainment

If you're hungry, check out the food at African Cuisine. If you're looking for entertainment, enjoy some bowling at Ron's. If you're not into bowling but you have pimped your ride, then you're at least able to cruise Hyde Park Avenue for hotties and doughnuts.

Restaurants

- **African Cuisine** · 1248 Hyde Park Ave [River St]
- **Dottie's Deli** · 5 Fairmount Ave [River St]
- **Rincon Caribeno** · 18 Fairmount Ave [River St]

Shopping

- **Capone Foods** · 14 Bow St [Garfield Ave]
- **Marascio's Market** · 1758 River St [Neponset Valley Pkwy]
- **Ron's Gourmet Ice Cream** · 1231 Hyde Park Ave [Everett St]
- **Tutto Italiano** · 1893 River St [Solaris Rd]

Transportation

To get to Hyde Park, take the MBTA commuter rail's Franklin line or Providence line. The Franklin line makes two stops in Hyde Park, Fairmount and Readville. You can get on the Franklin line at South Station, which is served by the T's Red Line. Use the Providence line to reach the Hyde Park stop or the Readville stop. The Providence line stops at Forest Hills, where you can transfer from the T's Orange Line.

Overview

Copley Square is named after Boston-born portrait painter John Singleton Copley (1738–1815), America's first great artist. His portraits of America's founding fathers are on display at the Massachusetts Historical Society, across the street from the square and at the Museum of Fine Arts. The Boston Marathon, held annually on Patriots Day (the third Monday in April), ends on Boylston Street. A BosTix outlet, the place to score discounted theater tickets, stands at the corner of Boylston Street and Dartmouth Street. The farmers market fills the square Tuesdays and Fridays from 11 am to 6 pm, late May through November. The Friends of Copley Square sponsors its annual Holiday Tree Lighting on the first Thursday after Thanksgiving. Summer months bring folk and swing dancing performances to the square on Tuesday evenings, as well as a bevy of sun-seeking loungers.

Architecture & Sculpture

The Boston Public Library is America's oldest public library. The Renaissance-revival style structure holds within it over seven million books, as well as busts of famous writers and prominent Bostonians. Big bonus: It offers wireless Internet access. Across the square you'll find the neo-Romanesque Trinity Church, designed by notable architect H.H. Richardson. The stained glass windows alone are worth a trip inside.

John Hancock Tower

The John Hancock Mutual Life Insurance Company, which already inhabited buildings on Clarendon Street and Berkeley Street, needed more space to house its employees, so it opted to build a 60-story black glass tower. What better place to put it than next to the Public Library and an old church? Designed by architect I. M. Pei, and completed in 1976, the John Hancock Tower became famous for being the tallest building in New England, and simultaneously infamous for falling apart.

Locals were upset when a foundation collapse in the early stages of construction nearly sucked Trinity Church into the ground. They became outraged when, in January 1973, one of the building's 10,000-plus glass windows "popped off" and shattered on the ground below, followed by dozens more 500-pound window panes. All told, 65 panes fell onto the roped-off area below the building before workers changed the solder used to mount the windows. In the meantime, locals had dubbed the Hancock "The Plywood Palace," in reference to the black plywood sheets put in place to substitute for the fallen panes. Not long after, engineers discovered the building was in danger of being sheared in half by the wind, resulting in another expensive fix. Today, the Hancock Tower stands sturdy, tall, and proud, and locals have even grown to love it. (Classic Boston photo op: Trinity Church is reflected in the mirrored side of the Hancock Tower, a clichéd but perfect example of Boston's mix of old and new.)

The observation deck on the 60th floor, originally opened to the public in response to community feedback, was permanently closed for security reasons after the events of September 11, 2001. Height junkies must now head over to the nearby Prudential Center for a what-a-view fix.

How to Get There—Driving

From the south, take I-93 N to Exit 18 (Massachusetts Avenue/Roxbury). Follow signs to Massachusetts Avenue and turn right. Turn right on Huntington Avenue, then left onto Dartmouth Street. From the north, take I-93 S to Exit 26 (Storrow Drive). Follow Storrow Drive west to the Copley Square exit. Follow Storrow Drive west to the Copley Square exit and, after two blocks, turn left onto Beacon Street and, after two blocks, turn left onto Clarendon Street. After five blocks, turn right onto St. James Avenue. This is one of two examples in the city (the other being the Pru) where the "look up, locate the giant building, and drive towards it" method of navigation works well.

How to Get There—Mass Transit

Take the Green Line to the Copley stop. Alternatively, take the Orange Line to the Back Bay stop, exit, and head to your right along Dartmouth Street. Again, if you're not sure which way to go, look for the giant glass building.

General Information

NFT Map:	6
Address:	700 Boylston St,
	Boston, MA 02116
Phone:	617-536-5400
Website:	www.bpl.org
Hours:	Mon–Thurs: 9 am–9 pm, Fri–Sat:
	9 am–5 pm, Sun: 1 pm–5 pm
	(Oct–May)

Overview

The Boston Public Library, founded in 1848, was the country's first publicly-supported municipal library. The BPL was also the first public library to lend a book and the first to institute a children's room. Furthermore, if you don't like reading in English then don't miss the library's large collection of books in dozens of other languages. Today, its circulating collection and the Norman B. Leventhal Map Center (home to a whopping 350,000 maps), Rare Books and Manuscripts Department (M–F 9 am–5 pm), and many other research-oriented nooks and crannies continue to attract scholars and tourists alike. Additionally, the BPL's ever-changing exhibits are always good for a rainy-day, freebie activity, as are the frequent talks by bestselling authors.

The BPL's main branch is the Central Library, composed of two august buildings adjacent to Copley Square that hold a lot more than just books. Facing Dartmouth Street, the McKim Building (the "old wing") was designed by noted 19th-century architect Charles Follen McKim and opened in 1895. The old wing, which houses the Research Library, is built around a delightful Italianate courtyard that offers readers a most un-library-like place to relax with a book. A set of murals painted by John Singer Sargent hangs inside. Sargent, better known for his portraits than for large installations, intended for these mammoth murals to be his masterpiece. There's also a set of allegorical murals by Pierre Puvis de Chavannes and the architecturally significant Bates Hall.

Opened to the public in 1972, the Johnson Building was designed by legendary architect Philip Johnson. The building, which houses the General Library, faces Boylston Street and is still referred to as the "new wing." (Granted, a better nickname might be the "ugly wing.") The Johnson Building has less knock-out art than the McKim Building, but it does have the tiled architectural frieze *The Goose Girl*, which is worth seeking out if you're wandering through the building. The BPL offers guided tours of both the old and new wings.

Internet

If you're ever stuck without Internet access, head over to the Central Library. Both the old and new wings have PCs available for use by the general public. (All computers have Internet connections and Microsoft Office software.) The first floor of the new wing also has "express" PCs that limit use to 15 minutes—handy for a quick e-mail hit. Both buildings are also equipped with Wi-Fi access.

For the Kids

Besides the weekly and seasonal programs it offers for everyone small from infants to teens, the Central Library has an outstanding collection of materials for even the youngest readers. Most of these materials can be found in the Margret and H.A. Rey Children's Room, named for the creators of that beloved, inquisitive simian, Curious George. The Children's Room also offers access to computers with Internet filtering software, which is helpful for protecting fragile little minds. For more information, check the website or call 617-859-2328.

Restaurants

The Central Library now has two restaurants to sate you during long hours of research. Novel, the fancier of the two restaurants, is set in a spacious room overlooking the courtyard in the center of the McKim Building. (Tip: Nip in for afternoon tea, served 2:30 pm to 4 pm on weekdays.) Next door to Novel, Sebastian's Map Room Café serves breakfast, lunch, and snacks. For reservations at Novel, or for additional information, call 617-385-5660. Note that food and drink are generally prohibited from the public areas of the Central Library, so chug your coffee before entering.

How to Get There—Driving

From the north or the south, take I-93 to Exit 26 (Storrow Drive). From Storrow Drive, take the Copley Square exit. The exit dead-ends at Beacon Street. Turn right on Beacon Street, drive four blocks to Exeter Street, and make a left. Drive along Exeter Street until you reach Boylston Street. The Central Library is on the corner of Boylston Street and Exeter Street.

From the west, take the Mass Pike (I-90 E) to Exit 22 (Prudential Center/Copley Square). Move to the right lane and follow the road in the tunnel toward Copley Square. The tunnel exits onto Stuart Street. Quickly move to the far left lane of Stuart Street and make a left at the next light onto Dartmouth Street. Drive through the next set of lights. The Central Library will be on the left.

Parking

The Central Library's location near Copley Square doesn't offer much in the way of easy street parking. If you're feeling unlucky, try the parking garage on Stuart Street between Dartmouth Street and Exeter Street.

How to Get There—Mass Transit

Take the T's Green Line to the Copley stop or the Orange Line to the Back Bay stop. From there, it should be pretty obvious: Look for the biggest, oldest, and grayest building around.

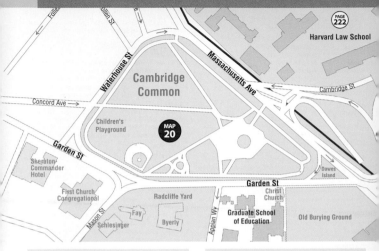

PAGE 222

Overview

Cambridge Common was the center of rebel activity in the early years of the Revolution and has been a hub of political and social activity ever since. George Washington rallied the 16,000-man Continental Army under an elm tree on the green on July 3, 1775, and the area became the primary training ground for the troops.

William Dawes, along with Paul Revere and Dr. Samuel Prescott, rode his horse across the Common on his way to warn those in Lexington and Concord that "the regulars are coming" (not that "the British are coming"). While Revere inspired a famous poem and became the namesake of many American cities, Dawes was commemorated with some lousy bronze hoof prints in the pavement of the Common.

Three cannon that the colonists seized from the Lobsterbacks still sit by the flagpole. There's also a memorial to victims of the Irish Potato Famine.

Even with the addition of a playground and a softball field, this historical urban oasis remains an important place to voice ideas and protests. Just steps away from Harvard University, the Common's corner on Mass Ave has been used by activists protesting everything from the occupation of Iraq to the existence of SUVs.

Attractions

Relaxing and people-watching are, by far, the two best activities to undertake on the Common. With its prime location next to Harvard Square, you can feel like a Harvard student, without the excessive course fees and mandatory high IQ, though tree-shaded benches are available for reading if you want to play the part.

The park has a fenced-in playground, located on the corner of Garden and Waterhouse Streets, where kids can frolic safely. The playground was last renovated in 1990 (including the addition of a wooden climbing structure, swings, bridges, slides, and benches/picnic tables) and is recommended for parents with children aged one to ten.

Sports

There's a softball field, soccer fields, and designated areas for other light recreation along with bike paths for cyclists, skaters, joggers, and walkers. Despite the close link between afternoon softball games and booze, the rules forbid alcoholic beverages on the ball field.

Parks & Places • **Charlestown Navy Yard**

General Information

NFT Map: 8
Address: 1st Ave, Charlestown, MA 02129
Phone: 617-242-5601 (Visitor Center);
617-242-5671 (USS Constitution)
Websites: www.nps.gov/bost/Visiting_Navy_Yard.htm
www.cityofboston.gov/freedomtrail/
ussconstitution.asp
www.charlestownonline.net/navyyard.htm
Hours: 10 am–4 pm daily (Winter); 9 am–6 pm
(Summer); 9 am–5 pm (Fall); free admission

Practicalities

The Charlestown Navy Yard is a must-see for anyone who likes big ships or US naval history. The two main attractions are the USS Cassin Young and "Old Ironsides" herself, the USS Constitution. The yard was established in 1800 as one of the first naval shipyards in the country, and the Constitution is almost as old as the country itself. When the Navy retired the yard in 1974, the yard became part of the Boston National Historic Park.

Attractions

Typical Fourth of July celebrations in Boston range from backyard barbecues to beach sunbathing, but the Navy Yard has its own unique tradition. Independence Day is celebrated with the customary turning of the Constitution—an annual practice in which the great vessel is tugged out of the dock and rotated to ensure uniform weathering. The Cassin Young has battle scars from its service in both World War II and the Korean War. The nearby Commandant's House, the oldest building in the Navy Yard, is no longer a private home, but an elegant museum, which is open to the public. The Navy Yard

Visitor Center/Bunker Hill Pavillion also serves those visiting the nearby Bunker Hill Monument.

How to Get There—Driving

From the north, take I-93 S to Exit 28 (Sullivan Square/Charlestown), go under I-93, and follow signs to Sullivan Square. Bear left at the first traffic light and drive into the Sullivan Square rotary; take the second right onto Bunker Hill Street, turn right onto Chelsea Street, and make an immediate left onto Fifth Street. Drive one block (Fifth Street dead-ends) and turn left onto First Avenue.

From the south, take I-93 N to Exit 26 (Storrow Drive) and aim for the "North Station, USS Constitution" signs. Turn left onto Martha Road (which becomes Lomasney Way), left on Causeway Street, then left at N Washington Street, and get into the right lane as quickly as possible. At the end of the bridge, turn right onto Chelsea Street.

From the west, take the Mass Pike (I-90 E) to I-93 N, and follow the directions above.

Parking

Though public transportation is strongly recommended for this area, discounted parking with Boston National Historical Park validation is available from the Nautica Parking Garage across from the park's Visitor Center on Constitution Road.

How to Get There—Mass Transit

Visitors can take the MBTA Water Shuttle to Pier 4 at the Navy Yard from Long Wharf for $1.70. For more information, see page 258.

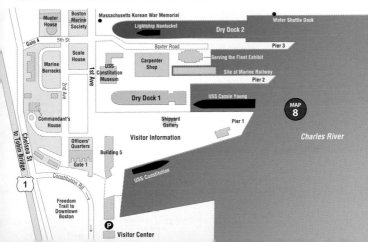

General Information

NFT Map: 3
Address: 147 Tremont St (b/w Temple Pl & West St)
Phone: 617-426-3115
Websites: www.bostonusa.com
www.cityofboston.gov/freedomtrail/
bostoncommon.asp
www.cityofboston.gov/parks/streettrees/
inventories.asp

Overview

One of the nation's oldest public parks, Boston Common was purchased by the Commonwealth of Massachusetts in 1634 to serve as livestock grazing ground. The city charged each household six shillings to pay for "the Commonage." (It was Tax-achusetts even back then!) People also used the Common to watch others being hanged at the gallows (like them cursed Quakers), for public meetings, and for military drills. The gallows were removed in 1817 and cow grazing was officially banned in 1830, around the time that urban cow ownership began falling out of fashion. In 1910, the Olmsted brothers oversaw a massive landscape renovation, designating Boston Common as the anchor of the "Emerald Necklace," a system of connected parks that winds through many of Boston's neighborhoods. Boston Common is the beginning of the Freedom Trail and the Black Heritage Trail.

Situated across from the State House, Boston Common embodies the spirit of the city around it. Tourists, students, lunching suits, homeless Bostonians, and strolling older folks all share the park. On the lawn, squirrels and pigeons fight the latest chapter in their centuries-old gang war, while ducks enjoy free bread from park-goers. It is home to America's first and second subway stations (Park St and Boylston St), the Central Burying Ground, and the Robert Gould Shaw Civil War Memorial (a.k.a. the dudes from *Glory*).

Adjacent to the park is the Public Garden, former swampland that was filled in 1837. The nation's first botanical garden, the Public Garden's French style of ornamental beds and paths stand in sharp contrast to the Common's informal, pastoral English layout. This is where you can ride the famous Swan Boats and admire the *Make Way for Ducklings* sculpture.

Activities

The Freedom Trail is a 2.5-mile path through central Boston that passes by 16 of the city's historic landmarks. You'll find detailed route maps and information at the Visitor Center on Boston Common. Many of the sites along the red-painted line offer free admission, others "recommend" a donation, and some actually charge.

Frog Pond serves as a part-time ice-skating rink in winter and a splashing pool for children in summer. The smooth, paved paths that traverse the Common make it ideal for cyclists, rollerbladers, scooters, joggers, and walkers. Throughout the year the park hosts concerts, plays, political rallies, and other formal and informal gatherings.

How to Get There

Tremont, Beacon, Charles, Park, and Boylston Streets bound Boston Common. Parking is available, believe it or not, under the Common on Charles Street. By car, take the Mass Pike (I-90) to the Copley Square exit. Go straight at the off ramp onto Stuart Street. Take a left onto Charles Street by the Radisson Hotel.

By mass transit, take the Green Line or the Silver Line bus to the Boylston T stop at the corner of Boylston Street and Tremont Street. This stop is heavily used by tourists and locals, so expect crowds. Another equally bustling option is to take the Red Line or Green Line to the Park Street T stop at the northeastern edge of the Common.

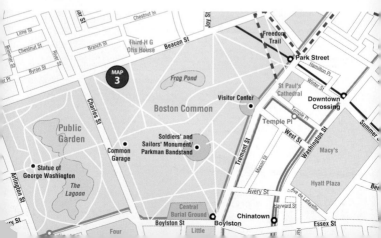

Freedom Trail & Black Heritage Trail

General Information

NFT Maps:	1, 2, 3, 4, 8
Address:	Visitor Center, 147 Tremont St, Boston, MA 02111
Freedom Trail:	www.thefreedomtrail.org
Black Heritage Trail:	www.afroammuseum.org/trail.htm
Walking Tours:	Available daily during spring/summer/fall, from Boston Common to Faneuil Hall, daily: 11 am, 12 pm, 1 pm, & 3:30 pm; Mon–Fri: 10 am, 1:30 pm, & 4:45 pm. From Faneuil Hall to Boston Common, daily: 10:30 am & 1 pm. ($12 adults, $6 children, cash only)
Audio Tours:	Available at the Visitor Center $15 rental; 617-357-8300

Freedom Trail Overview

The Freedom Trail conveniently links several important colonial and post-colonial historical sites. Marked by a thick red path on the sidewalks, either painted or made of inlaid brick, the trail leads sightseers from the Visitor Center on Boston Common to the Charlestown Navy Yard on the opposite side of the Charles River. The 2.5-mile trek passes by 16 different sites, including the location of the Boston Massacre, Paul Revere's house, a couple of old cemeteries, and Bunker Hill. Walking tours led by costumed guides leave the Visitor Center or Faneuil Hall, and a complete trail walk usually lasts about 90 minutes. Audio tours are also available.

Trail Head: The Boston Common—America's oldest public park, 44-acre Boston Common is home to well-fed squirrels, pigeons, walkers, joggers, bikers, fat squirrels, pigeons, dogs, ducks, and pigeons.

1. **The State House**—The Massachusetts state government sits here in this gold-domed building, the oldest on Beacon Hill, in fact. Tour Hours: Mon–Fri 10 am–4 pm; 617-727-3676.

2. **Park Street Church**—The Evangelical Church was constructed in 1809 and has since stood as a testament to Bostonian faith. Lucky passersby may even be treated to a tirade being given from the outdoor pulpit. 617-523-3383. Traditional worship: 8:30 am and 11 am. Contemporary worship: 4 pm and 6 pm.

3. **Granary Burying Ground**—An epitaph here reads "Revere's Tomb" near the resting places of both John Hancock and Samuel Adams, along with a giant monolith paying tribute to the family of Boston-born Ben Franklin. This is the city's third-oldest burial ground, the resting place of the victims of the Boston Massacre. Open daily 9 am–5 pm; 617-635-4505.

4. **King's Chapel**—The chapel date dates from 1688, and the current chapel was built in 1754 with the objective that it "would be the equal of any in England." The bell was made by Paul Revere. Summer hours: Sun 1:30 pm–4 pm, Mon-Sat 10 am–4 pm; winter hours: Sat 10 am–4 pm, Sun 1:30–4 pm. Entry is free but there's a $2 "suggested" donation. Concerts on Tuesdays at 12:15 pm and Sundays at 5 pm. Services are held Wednesdays 12:15 pm and Sundays 9:45 am and 11 am; 617-227-2155.

   King's Chapel Burying Ground—Older than the Granary and the final resting place of some of Boston's first settlers. Open daily, 9 am–5 pm.

5. **Benjamin Franklin's Statue/Site of the First Public School**—Boston Latin School, founded in 1635, is still open (but it's since moved to the Fenway). The old high school is considered the top public school in Boston. A mosaic in the sidewalk marks its original site nearby to a statue of one of its famous students, Ben Franklin. Both are in the courtyard of Old City Hall, also worth a look.

6. **Old Corner Bookstore Building**—Built in 1718, this is one of Boston's oldest surviving structures. Once an apothecary, during the 19th century the building housed the publisher of classic New England titles *Walden* and *The Scarlet Letter*.

7. **Old South Meeting House**—"Voices of Protest," a permanent exhibit in the house, speaks of generations who made history under one roof, including the instigators of the Boston Tea Party. Nov–Mar, 10 am–4 pm. Apr–Oct, 9:30 am–5 pm. Adults $5, students and seniors $4, children (6-18) $1, children under six free; 617-482-6439.

8. **Old State House**—The oldest surviving public building in Boston, its lush exterior will draw you inside where the Bostonian Society houses a library along with its museum of Boston's past.

   Library: Tues, Wed, and Thurs 10 am–3:30 pm, closed weekends and holidays. Daily use fee: non-members $10, college students $7.

   Museum: 9 am–5 pm, extended hours in summer, closed New Year's Day, Thanksgiving, and Christmas Day. Adults $5, older adults (62+) $4, students (over 18) $4, children (6–18) $1; 617-720-1713.

9. **Site of the Boston Massacre**—Cobblestones now mark this historic site outside the Old State House.

10. **Faneuil Hall**—Shopping mixed with history, with some eateries to boot. If you like touristy knick-knacks, this is the place to shop. The actual hall still holds public meetings and houses an armory museum. Open daily 10 am–9 pm. Historical talks every thirty minutes, 9:30 am–4:30 pm. See page 196.

11. **Paul Revere House**—See how Boston's favorite patriot once lived. Keep in mind that when he lived there, the area wasn't filled with Italian restaurants. Apr 15–Oct 31, 9:30 am–5:15 pm, Nov 1–Apr 14, 9:30 am–4:15 pm. Closed Mondays in Jan–Mar and on Thanksgiving, Christmas Day, and New Year's Day. Adults $3, seniors and college students $2.50, children (5–17) $1; 617-523-2338.

12. **Old North Church**—"One if by land, two if by sea," goes the poem. And so two lanterns were placed in the Old North Church, the oldest church building in Boston, warning that the British were making their way across the Charles towards Lexington and Concord. The church has held services since 1723 and is the most visited historical site in Boston. Winter hours: 9 am–5 pm daily. Summer hours: 9 am–6 pm daily; 617-523-6676.

13. **Copp's Hill Burying Ground**—The site began as a cemetery in the 1660s and was later used by the British as a strategic vantage point in the Battle of Bunker Hill. Open daily 9 am–5 pm.

14. **Bunker Hill Monument**—A 221-foot granite obelisk commemorates the Battle of Bunker Hill—the first major battle of the American Revolution. The monument sits atop Breed's Hill, where the misnamed battle actually took place. Exhibitions at the visitor's center explain how the battle came to be and how it was won. Hours: 9 am–4:30 pm; 617-242-5641.

15. **USS Constitution**—a.k.a. "Old Ironsides," America's oldest commissioned warship, with daily flag-raising and lowering ceremonies accompanied by cannon fire. Winter hours: Thurs-Sun, 10 am–4 pm. Summer hours: Tues–Sun: 10 am–6 pm. Tours depart every half hour; 617-242-5670. See Charlestown Navy Yard, page 189.

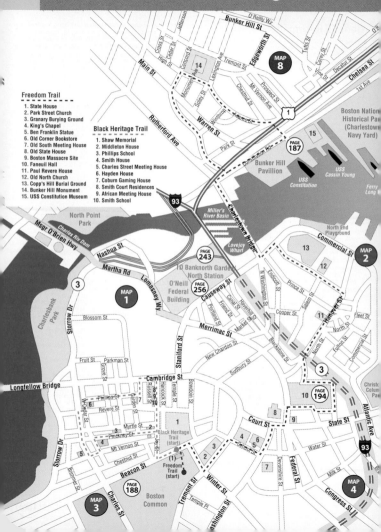

Freedom Trail & Black Heritage Trail

Freedom Trail
1. State House
2. Park Street Church
3. Granary Burying Ground
4. King's Chapel
5. Ben Franklin Statue
6. Old Corner Bookstore
7. Old South Meeting House
8. Old State House
9. Boston Massacre Site
10. Faneuil Hall
11. Paul Revere House
12. Old North Church
13. Copp's Hill Burial Ground
14. Bunker Hill Monument
15. USS Constitution Museum

Black Heritage Trail
1. Shaw Memorial
2. Middleton House
3. Phillips School
4. Smith House
5. Charles Street Meeting House
6. Hayden House
7. Coburn Gaming House
8. Smith Court Residences
9. African Meeting House
10. Smith School

MAP 8
Boston National Historical Park (Charlestown Navy Yard)
PAGE 187
MAP 2
PAGE 243
PAGE 256
MAP 1
MAP 3
PAGE 188
PAGE 194
MAP 4

Bunker Hill Pavillion

USS Constitution
USS Cassin Young

North End Playground

10 Banknorth Garden
North Station

O'Neill Federal Building

Black Heritage Trail (start)

Freedom Trail (start)

Boston Common

Longfellow Bridge

Black Heritage Trail Overview

Running north from the State House, this trail recognizes the historical significance of Boston's post-Revolution African-American community. Before being forced into the South End and Roxbury in the 20th Century, the first community of free African-Americans actually lived in Beacon Hill after the American Revolution, in what is now known as the North Slope. According to the first federal census in 1790, Massachusetts was the only state in the country without slaves. The Museum of African-American History is housed in two of the buildings on the trail, the African Meeting House and the Abiel Smith School, which are open to visitors. Most of the historic homes on the Trail are private residences, closed to the public.

1. **Robert Gould Shaw and the 54th Regiment Memorial**—Located on Boston Common across from the State House, this monument was built in 1897 in honor of the first all-black regiment that fought for the Union Army during the Civil War.

2. **George Middleton House**—(5–7 Pinckney St) George Middleton was the commander of an all-black military company during the Revolutionary War called the Bucks of America. His house, erected in 1797, is the oldest standing wooden structure on Beacon Hill. It is a private residence.

3. **The Phillips School** (Anderson & Pinckney Sts) One of the first Boston public schools to be integrated (in 1855) as a result of the historic court case *Roberts v. The City of Boston*, which opposed the racial segregation of the city's schools.

4. **John J. Smith House**—(86 Pinckney St) John J. Smith was born free in Virginia in 1820 and eventually moved to Boston where he opened a successful barbershop that catered to many wealthy white customers from all over the city. His shop served as a haven for anti-slavery debates, fugitive slaves, and advocates for equal education rights.

5. **Charles Street Meeting House**—(Mt Vernon & Charles Sts) Built in 1807, the Charles Street Meeting House was originally the site of the segregated Third Baptist Church. After a failed attempt to desegregate the church, Timothy Gilbert and several other abolitionist sympathizers left to form the Free Baptist Church (now the Tremont Temple), the first integrated church in America. In 1876, the Meeting House was sold to the African Methodist Episcopal Church, which eventually left Beacon Hill for Roxbury in 1939, due to changing economic conditions in the area.

6. **Lewis and Harriet Hayden House**—(66 Phillips St) Lewis and Harriet Hayden ran a boarding house out of their home, which was also a stop on the Underground Railroad. Lewis Hayden was an ardent African-American abolitionist and community leader who served as a delegate for the Republican Convention, fought for women's rights, and helped found the Museum of Fine Arts.

7. **John Coburn Gaming House**—(2 Phillips St) Home to one of Boston's wealthiest African-Americans, clothier James Coburn, the gaming house was built in 1843. Serving Boston's white elite, it became one of the most successful black-owned businesses in the city. Coburn used the profits to finance several abolitionist groups in the community, including the Massasoit Guards. Founded as an all-black military company to support the state's troops in case of war, the Guards also patrolled Beacon Hill to protect African-Americans from slave catchers.

8. **Smith Court Residences**—(3, 5, 7, 7A, & 10 Smith Ct) Five remaining wooden houses located on Beacon Hill's north slope were all purchased by free African-Americans from white landowners in the mid-1800s.

9. **The African Meeting House**—(8 Smith Ct) Founded as a response to racial discrimination in Boston's religious communities, the African Meeting House remains the oldest standing black church building in the country. The structure was built using labor and donations from the African-American community. It was used for religious services, as a safe haven for political discussion, and as a makeshift school for black children until the Abiel Smith School came into existence. It is currently being restored to its original appearance. With the Abiel Smith School, it houses the Museum of African-American History.

10. **Abiel Smith School**—(46 Joy St) Built in 1834 as the first schoolhouse in America to educate black school children, the Abiel Smith School was consistently overcrowded and neglected by the city. Substandard conditions led to *Roberts v. Massachusetts* and the desegregation of schools in 1855. Hours: 10 am–4 pm, Mon–Sat. Extended summer hours, Thurs 10 am–8 pm. Closed Thanksgiving, Christmas, and New Year's Day. Admission is free. 617-725-0022.

General Information

NFT Maps: 14, 15, 16, 17, 30, & 31
Address: Two Brookline Pl, Brookline, MA 02445
Phone: 617-232-5374
Websites: www.emeraldnecklace.org
www.cityofboston.gov/parks/necklace.asp

Overview

Known primarily for his work designing New York's Central Park, celebrated landscape architect Frederick Law Olmsted also created a beautiful string of Boston parks when he moved to Brookline in 1883. Olmsted's Necklace was designed as an uninterrupted five-mile walkway from Back Bay to Franklin Park, where Bostonians could stroll barefoot and without worry. The Necklace has been broken up over the years, both by the construction of the Casey Overpass near Franklin Park and by the conversion of the Riverway, Jamaicaway, and Arborway from pleasant carriage paths to major roads carrying highway-amounts of traffic. The city and conservation groups are putting together a "master plan" for the severed sections of the Necklace and together are trying to balance path restoration with traffic concerns. With the future construction of the Rose Kennedy Greenway where the Central Artery once stood, the idea is to link all of Boston's parks into an actual necklace.

Franklin Park

Occupying 500 acres, Franklin Park is the Necklace's largest park and was originally designed as a country retreat in the vein of Central Park in New York. Named after Benjamin Franklin, the park encompasses the Zoo (617-541-LION), one of the first public golf courses in the country (617-265-4084), 100 acres of woodland, and the seven-acre Scarboro Pond. The Franklin Park Zoo (not part of Olmsted's original plan), which opened in 1911, is home to the "Butterfly Landing," a butterfly enclosure open seasonally from June through September. The zoo made headlines in 2003 when adolescent gorilla "Little Joe" escaped from his enclosure—twice. The first time, he stayed on site. The second time, he ended up at a bus stop in Roxbury. Zoo entry: Adults $11, children $6, seniors $9.50, half price the first Sat of each month, 10 am–12 pm; winter hours (Oct 1–Mar 31), 10 am–4 pm; summer hours, 10 am–5 pm weekdays, and 6 pm weekends and holidays, admission is free the Friday after Thanksgiving; www.zoonewengland.com.

Arnold Arboretum

The oldest arboretum in the country, Arnold Arboretum is named after its financier, whaling tycoon and horticulturalist James Arnold. Visitors come primarily to stroll amongst the exotic greenery, which includes bonsai and lilac trees. Because Arnold left most of his estate to Harvard and the school uses the arboretum as a nature museum, it seems only fair for the city to allow the grand university to rent the land for just a dollar a year. Open every day until dusk, the visitor center is open 9 am–4pm weekdays, 10 am–4 pm Sat, 12 pm–4 pm Sun, and closed holidays. Entry is free!

Jamaica Park

Wealthy Bostonians of yesteryear built their summer homes in this spot, called "the jewel in the Emerald Necklace" because of the 60-acre sparkling Jamaica Pond. The largest and purest body of water in Boston, the glacier-formed pond is fed by natural springs and is 90 feet deep in some places. The pond is so clean that it serves as a back-up city reservoir. What looks like a haunted house is actually Pinebank, the only building within the Emerald Necklace that pre-dates the park's creation. It sits in a state of disrepair and neglect, despite Boston Parks Department plans to protect the Victorian Gothic site from further deterioration. Joggers and dog-walkers share the 1.5 mile paved trail around the pond. Fishing is one of the most popular activities, and every year the City of Boston stocks the pond with trout, salmon, and indigenous pickerel, bass, hornpout, and perch. The boathouse rents canoes, sailboats, and rowboats, and, in winter, has a fireplace going. Around Halloween, the community organization Spontaneous Celebrations sponsors a lantern walk around the pond.

Olmsted Park

A joint project between the City of Boston and the Town of Brookline to link the two cities together, Olmsted Park showcases the landscape architect's unique design philosophy with a series of ponds and wooded paths that open onto expansive views that help you understand why Olmsted is the Boston Brahmin equivalent of a rock star. (The city boasts at least one Olmsted impersonator.) A great feature of the park is the human-made Muddy River, currently the site of a major dredging project. Leverett, Willow, and Ward's Ponds are more secluded and less crowded than nearby Jamaica Pond. A new bike/pedestrian path system on the Brookline side from Jamaica Pond to Boylston Street (Route 9) was completed in 1997.

Riverway Park

Hidden below the busy street level is the narrowest park in the system and also the only one that is completely human-made. Riverway lies in the valley of the Muddy River (the boundary between Boston and Brookline) and features several small islands, wooded paths, and pretty footbridges. Its steep tree-lined banks protect visitors from the city bustle above. Footbridges connect the Boston and Brookline sides, but these are poorly lit at night.

Back Bay Fens

Olmsted's first phase of the Necklace in 1878, the Back Bay Fens was a sewage-infested saltwater marsh on the verge of extinction when he stepped in, transforming the swampy area into a meandering brackish creek. The creation of the Charles River Dam in 1910 turned the Fens into a freshwater marsh. Today, the Fens has quite a few notable attractions, including recreational facilities, the Kelleher Rose Garden, War Memorials, and the Victory Garden. The Victory Garden was created in 1941, in an effort to grow extra food for troops, and is currently tended to by local green thumbs who shell out $20 per year to maintain personal plots. A former parking lot, the western end of the Fens was recently converted into green space. But it's a notorious local fact that more than mere gardening takes place on the grounds—think George Michael.

General Information

NFT Map:	2
Phone:	617-523-1300
Websites:	www.faneuilhallmarketplace.com
	www.faneuilhall.com
	www.cityofboston.gov/freedomtrail/
	faneuilhall.asp
	www.nps.gov/bost/Faneuil_Hall.htm

Faneuil Hall

Faneuil Hall was built as a food and produce market/ meeting hall by Boston's wealthiest merchant, Peter Faneuil, in 1742. It's a historically poignant section of commercial property: At this location, Samuel Adams rallied for independence (prior to his interest in brewing beer), the doctrine of "no taxation without representation" was established, and George Washington and company celebrated our country's freedom. In later years it was the site of abolitionist rallies. It's still both a commercial spot and a meeting place used by campaigning politicians, with shops in the basement and the first floor, the Great Hall on the second, and a museum on the third.

Since its inception, the Faneuil Hall Marketplace has been a major shopping arena, and it's now stocked with more than 100 stores and pushcarts and 17 sit-down restaurants as well as a gastronomic orgy of a food hall. The marketplace alone attracts more than 12 million visitors a year and hosts numerous events and festivals. Local talent includes jugglers, mimes (yes, those, too), magicians, bands, and the occasional strolling Ben Franklin. If you're looking to be entertained while you shop, Faneuil Hall is your place.

Four buildings make up the marketplace: Faneuil Hall, Quincy Market, North Market, and South Market. Touristy and crowded at times, it's still one of the best and most visually pleasing places to buy souvenirs, shop in a mall-like environment, and try any number of local dishes. Standard mall stores occupy most of North and South Market, while local vendors and souvenir slingers can be found in the Hall or at pushcarts in Quincy Market. The Hall and all pushcarts are open Monday through Saturday from 10 am to 9 pm, and from noon to 6 pm on Sundays. Shopping hours in the other marketplaces vary by vendor. The Hall and all shops are closed on Christmas.

Quincy Market

Located directly behind Faneuil Hall, Quincy Market is where you go to chow down. The food court runs the length of the building and far exceeds a typical food court in both variety and quality of offerings. Whatever you crave, it's hard to go away disappointed. It is usually crowded at lunch, especially during the field trip and leaf-peeping seasons, so avoid peak hours if you're in a rush. Various sit-down bars and restaurants and pushcarts encircle the food court around the perimeter. The North Market and South Market, which stand on either side

of Quincy Market, have other places to sit for a meal, including the still-there Durgin Park.

Like many places in Boston, Quincy Market is built on landfill in what used to be Boston Harbor. Unlike other sections, when you're in Quincy Market, you're standing on bones. The butchers who used to occupy the wharves behind Faneuil Hall would let their unusable animal parts pile up, creating a sanitation nightmare. Then, someone had the bright idea of throwing the bones in the water, which eventually helped fill the wharf area and allowed for the construction of Quincy Market.

Museum

Ancient and Honorable Artillery Company Museum; 617-227-1638; www.ahacsite.org

Located on Faneuil Hall's third floor, the museum and library showcase the history of the Ancient and Honorable Artillery Company. The oldest military organization in the US (and third-oldest in the world), this august body was established as the Military Company of Boston in 1637 and still holds military drills and participates in various ceremonial events. The museum proudly displays the company's artifacts. It is a unique collection that is well worth a visit for military and history buffs. The museum is open Monday–Friday; 9 am–3:30 pm.

How to Get There—Driving

From the south, take I-93 N to Exit 23 ("Government Center"). Upon exiting, follow the signs to the Aquarium. At Surface Road, turn left. Faneuil Hall will be on the right-hand side.

From the west, take the Mass Pike (I-90) to Exit 24B (I-93 N). From I-93, take Exit 23 ("Government Center") and follow the directions above.

From the north, take I-93 S to Exit 24A toward Government Center. Stay to the right, and follow the signs for Faneuil Hall. Immediately off the exit, turn right. Faneuil Hall will be directly in front of you.

Parking

There are over 10,000 parking spaces within a two-mile radius of Faneuil Hall. The 75 State Street garage near the intersection of State Street and Broad Street offers a $2 discount on weekdays with store validation, and $10 parking after 5 pm daily and on selected holidays with store validation.

How to Get There—Mass Transit

To get to Faneuil Hall Marketplace, take the T's Green Line to Government Center or Haymarket, the Blue Line to State or Aquarium, or the Orange Line to State or Haymarket.

Shopping

A Hat for Every Head (pushcart)
Ann Taylor
Bill Rodgers Running Center
Boston Logos (pushcart)
Boxers To Go (pushcart)
Celtic Weavers
Coach
Cuoio
Fantasy Island (pushcart)
Harvest Fare (pushcart)
Head Games
La Cloche (pushcart)
Life is a Highway (pushcart)
Merry Trading Company (pushcart)
Nightshirts To Go (pushcart)
Nine West
Ocean Man (pushcart)
Orient Express (pushcart)
Orvis
Sacs (pushcart)
Sea Boston USA (pushcart)
Sock It To Me
Trenz (pushcart)
Ulyssian Imports (pushcart)
Urban Outfitters
Victoria's Secret

Goods & Gifts

African Collections (pushcart)
Arman Time Company (pushcart)
Art for 'Em (pushcart)
Artists See Boston (pushcart)
Batik Adventure (pushcart)
Best of Boston
Boston Campus Gear
Boston Pewter Company
The Boston Sun Spot
Bostonian Society Museum Shop
Build-A-Bear Workshop
Camera Center
Cheers Gift Shop
The Christmas Dove
Conversations (pushcart)
Crabtree & Evelyn
Crate & Barrel
Destination Boston
Discovery Channel Store
Every Bead of My Heart (pushcart)
Exotic Flowers
Friends 2B Made
Funusual
Gateway News
Geoclassics
Godiva Chocolatier
Happy Hangups (pushcart)
Harley Davidson-Boston (pushcart)
Headlines of America (pushcart)
Henri's Glassworks
Illusions (pushcart)
Irish Eyes (pushcart)

Local Charm
Magnetic Chef (pushcart)
Museum of Fine Arts Store
Musically Yours (pushcart)
On the Edge
Origins
Sluggers Upper Deck Kiosk (pushcart)
Stuck on Stickpins (pushcart)
Sunglass Hut & Watch Station
Swatch
Teeny Billboards (pushcart)
Wit Crafts (pushcart)
Yankee Candle Company

Food

A La Carte
Al Mercantino
Ames Plow Tavern
Aris Barbeque
Bangkok Express
Beard Papa Sweets Cafe
Bistany International
Bombay Club
Boston & Maine Fish Co
Boston Chipyard
Boston Chowda
Boston Pretzel
Boston Rocks
Brown Derby Deli
Carol Ann's Bake Shop
Columbo Frozen Yogurt Shoppe
Dick's Last Resort
The Dog House
Durgin Park Restaurant
El Paso Enchilada
Fisherman's Net
Jen Lai Rice & Noodle Company
Joey's Gelateria
Kilvert & Forbes
Kingfish Hall
La Pastaria
McCormick & Schmick's
Megumi
North End Bakery
Philadelphia Steak & Hoagie
Piccolo Panini
Pizzeria Regina
Plaza III, the Kansas City Steak House
Salty Dog Seafood Grill & Bar
Sam's Café at Cheers
Slugger's Dugout
Sprinkles Ice Cream
Starbucks
Steve's Greek Cuisine
Ueno Sushi
Wagamama
Walrus and the Carpenter
West End Strollers
Zuma's Tex Mex Café

Bars & Entertainment

Cheers
Comedy Connection
Coogan's
Hard Rock Cafe
Jose MacIntyre's
Ned Devine's Irish Pub
Parris
The Monkey Bar
Trinity

Services

BosTix Ticket Booth
Faneuil Hall Marketplace Information
City View Trolley Tours

Nearby Bars

The Atrium Lounge
Bell in Hand Tavern
Black Rose
Dockside Restaurant & Bar
Hennessey's
McFadden's
Kitty O'Shea's
The Rack
The Place
Purple Shamrock
Sissy K's
Union Oyster House
Vertigo

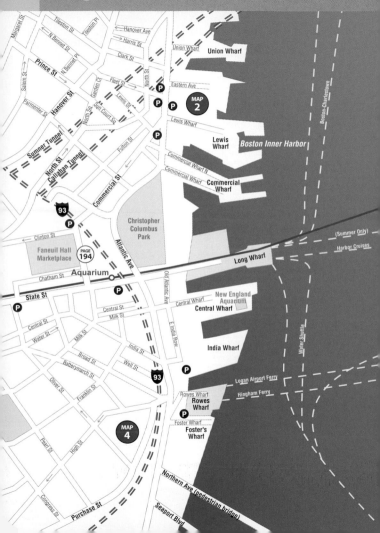

Overview

Originally named Boston Pier, Long Wharf juts into Boston Harbor at the bottom of State Street, while Rowes Wharf is farther south, near Broad Street. In the 1700s, Long Wharf extended more than one-third of a mile into Boston Harbor, but the dumping of urban landfill has resulted in a significant portion of the pier being surrounded by land rather than water. Purportedly the oldest continually operating wharf in the US, Long Wharf is the site of the Chart House. It has operated as a restaurant since 1961, and is the oldest existing pre-Revolutionary War warehouse in Boston.

Attractions

During the warmer months, stop by the Landing Bar on Long Wharf for a drink in the sunshine. It's the perfect place to hang out and catch a Red Sox game on television after work or when you're waiting to board a ferry.

The New England Aquarium is located at nearby Central Wharf and operates an IMAX Theatre next door. The Aquarium allows scientists and researchers to study marine and aquatic habitats and to educate visitors about conservation issues. One of the most exciting events to participate in is a "release party," when an animal is returned to its natural habitat. Hours: 9 am–5 pm weekdays (6 pm summer), 9 am–6 pm weekends (7 pm summer). Closed Thanksgiving and Christmas Day. Adults $18.95, children (3–11) $10.95. www.neaq.org; 617-973-5200.

There are several whale-watching excursions that leave from the wharves. Whale-watching season starts in April and ends in the fall.

• **Voyager III** • Central Wharf • 617-973-5281
• **Boston Harbor Cruises** • 1 Long Wharf • 617-227-4321
• **Massachusetts Bay Lines Whale Watch** •
  60 Rowes Wharf • 617-542-8000

Long Wharf is also where you catch the Harbor Express boat to the Boston Harbor Islands. There are 34 islands in all, six of which are staffed and serviced by a free boat shuttle from the headquarters on Georges Island. These islands are still underutilized by locals and unfrequented by tourists. They vary in size, but most offer trails, old forts, diverse flora and fauna, camping (on Grape, Lovells, and Bumpkin), and great views of Boston and the harbor. Spectacle Island's past as a former quarantine island, glue factory, and garbage dump has been covered with rubble from the Big Dig and transformed into an eco-friendly recreation spot. The island is now open to the public and features a visitor center and a café. The islands open seasonally, so check the website, www.bostonislands.com, or call 617-223-8666.

If you're prone to seasickness, or if watching whales isn't your bag, the newly-renovated Christopher Columbus Park is a short walk from Long Wharf. The playground for the little ones is top-notch, and its famous rose garden is dedicated to Rose Fitzgerald Kennedy. It's also a good viewing spot for the fireworks on First Night. Next door is Tia's, a popular after-work, meat market bar in the summer.

Architecture

Rowes Wharf features a commanding arch that looks out onto Boston Harbor. The Wharf is a mixed-use complex that has won numerous design awards, including the Urban Land Institute's "Award for Excellence." The complex is shared by the Boston Harbor Hotel, 100 luxury condominiums, and offices. There is a little-known observation deck on the ninth floor named the Forester Rotunda, offering views of both the city and harbor. Though not advertised, you can go through the hotel to gain access. In the summertime, a floating dock hosts outdoor concerts and movies under the stars.

Ferries

Both Long Wharf and Rowes Wharf serve as ferry terminals for the MBTA. F1 transports people to and from Rowes Wharf and Hingham Shipyard. F2 and F2H stop at Long Wharf, Logan Airport, and the Fore River Shipyard in Quincy. F2H also has limited service to Pemberton Point in Hull. F4, which travels to the Charlestown Navy Yard, also uses the Long Wharf terminus. The Harbor Express to Georges Island also leaves from Long Wharf. For more information on ferries, see page 254. For schedules and maps, go to www.mbta.com/schedules_and_maps/boats, or call 617-222-5000. You can also catch the high-speed catamaran ferry to Provincetown from Long Wharf. For schedules, rates, and area information visit www.bostonharborcruises.com/ptown_main.html.

How to Get There—Driving

To Long Wharf from the north, take I-93 S, and get off at Exit 24A (Government Center/Aquarium). Follow signs to the Aquarium. From the south, take Exit 23 (Government Center) and follow signs to the Aquarium.

To Rowes Wharf from the north, take I-93 S and get off at Exit 23 (aim for South Station). Turn left onto Congress Street and immediately left onto Atlantic Avenue. The wharf is on the right, two blocks past the intersection of Congress Street and Atlantic Avenue.

From the south, take I-93 N to Exit 20, and follow signs to South Station. Once you drop onto Atlantic Avenue, proceed through the Congress Street intersection and drive two blocks. The wharf will be on your right.

Parking

There is very limited street parking in the area, so if you want to forego driving around to find a free spot, you should try one of the many parking garages that are all within walking distance of the various wharves. Parking fees can cost $25 or more, depending on how long you stay, though there are usually discounted rates on weekends and after 5 pm on weekdays. If you're willing to shell out the cash, here are a few nearby garages:

• **The Rowes Wharf building** features an underground discounted parking garage with an entrance on Atlantic Avenue.
• **Harbor Garage at the Aquarium,** 70 East India Row; 617-367-3847
• **Dock Square Garage,** 200 State St; 617-367-4373
• **Laz Parking,** 290 Commercial St; 617-367-6412
• **Fitz-Inn Parking,** 269 Commercial St, 617-367-1681
• **Central Parking,** 2 Atlantic Ave; 617-854-3365

How to Get There—Mass Transit

To Long Wharf, take the T's Blue Line to the Aquarium stop. To Rowes Wharf, take either the Blue Line to Aquarium or the Red or Silver Line to South Station.

Stores

1 PF Chang's China Bistro	46 Travel 2000
5 US Post Office	47 Truffles Fine Confections
11 Ann Taylor Loft	103 Legal Sea Foods
17 Au Bon Pain	107 Sephora
19 Best of Boston	111 F Carriere
21 St Francis Chapel	113 Talbots Collection/Talbots Kids/Talbots Mens
23 Dunkin' Donuts	123 Olympia Sports
27 Ann Taylor	125 Chico's
39 Jasmine Sola	127 The Body Shop
41 Free People	131 Alpha Omega
43 GameStop	133 Johnston & Murphy
45 Florsheim Shoes	

135 Aldo	173 J Jill—The Store
139 Sunglass Hut	175 Club Monaco
141 Teavana	175A Charles David
143 Papyrus	177 Franklin Covey
145 Landau Collections	181 The Sharper Image
147 Optical Shop of Aspen	183 Sovereign Bank
153 L'Occitane	187 Cold Stone Creamery
155 California Pizza Kitchen	189 The Cheesecake Factory
159 Crane & Co	193 Applebee's
163 Lacoste	197 FitCorp
165 Yankee Candle	
167 Swarovski	
169 Arden B	
171 Levenger	

Food Court

FC1 Qdoba Mexican Grill
FC2 Panda Express
FC3 Pizzeria Regina
FC4 Poulet Rotisserie Chicken
FC5 Boston Chowda
FC6 Flamers
FC7 Gourmet India
FC8 Sakkio Japan
FC9 Ben & Jerry's
FC10 Paradise Bakery & Café
FC11 Louis Barry Florist

General Information

NFT Maps: 5 & 6
Address: 800 Boylston St, Boston, MA 02199
Phone: 1-800-SHOP-PRU or 617-236-3100
Website: www.prudentialcenter.com

Overview

The Prudential Center opened in 1965 and, at 52 stories, reigned as the city's tallest building until the 60-story John Hancock Tower was completed eleven years later. With the exception of the top two floors, which house an observation deck and a restaurant, the Prudential Tower is used mainly as office space. The Prudential Mall (not be confused with the more highbrow Copley Place mall, attached to the Prudential Mall by a natty skywalk) was opened in the 1990s on the lower floors and houses almost 50 shops, including Saks Fifth Avenue and numerous restaurants and services. The "Pru" is also home to several apartment buildings and is connected to the Hynes Convention Center and the Sheraton Boston Hotel. If you're not in the mood for the maddening crowd, avoid the mall, which is always teeming with tourists, hardcore browsers, and convention attendees.

Skywalk and Top of the Hub

Other than shopping, the Prudential Center's main attractions are its Skywalk Observatory and Top of the Hub restaurant (both located in the Prudential Tower). The Skywalk is open daily from 10 am until 9:30 pm (8 pm in the winter). It offers spectacular views of Boston and its suburbs, as well as the harbor, Blue Hill, and—way off in the distance—Cape Cod. (By default, the Skywalk became the best place to see Boston from on high after the observatory at the John Hancock Tower closed following September 11.) The Skywalk costs $11 adults, $9 seniors and students, and $7.50 children under 12. As you walk around the Skywalk, focus on the huge windows, which are marked to help you locate some of the more well-known features of the Boston skyline.

For a less informative, slightly more expensive, but extremely relaxing city view, walk two floors up from the Skywalk to the Top of the Hub restaurant and cocktail lounge. Entrees are pricey, but juice and cocktails from the bar are fairly priced and served with a spectacular view. For about $5 apiece—cheaper than the Skywalk—you can peer down at the city or across at the top of the John Hancock Tower with beverage in hand. The restaurant and lounge get busy at night, especially when the jazz band is playing. A semi-casual but "anti-slob" dress code is in effect.

How to Get There—Driving

From the north, take I-93 S to Exit 26 (Storrow Drive) and follow it to the Copley Square exit on the left. Take a right onto Beacon Street and follow it to Exeter Street. Make a left onto Exeter Street and the Prudential Center Garage will be four blocks down on the right.

From the west, follow the Mass Pike (I-90 E) into Boston. Get off at Exit 22 (Copley Square/Prudential Center) and follow the signs for Prudential Center. This will take you directly to the Prudential Center Garage entrance on your right.

From the south, take I-93 N to Exit 26 (Storrow Drive) and follow to the Copley Square exit on the left. Take a right onto Beacon Street and follow it to Exeter Street. Take a left onto Exeter Street. The Prudential Center Garage will be four blocks down on the right.

If you get lost, try this: Look up. Find the giant building that says "Prudential" on top. Drive towards it.

How to Get There—Mass Transit

The Green Line will take you to the Prudential T stop on Huntington Avenue (E train only; FYI: Only the doors of the first car open for this stop), the Copley stop on Boylston Street at Dartmouth Street, and the Hynes/ICA stop on Newbury Street at Mass Ave. The Orange Line and the MBTA Commuter Rail both stop at Back Bay Station, just across the street from Copley Place and a short walk away.

Overview

Originally one of the least fashionable streets of Back Bay, Newbury Street has undergone quite a transformation, morphing into Boston's most popular shopping area and an excellent place to hang out and strut your stuff.

A beautiful stretch of real estate featuring late 19th- and early 20th-Century architecture, Newbury Street runs eight blocks from the Public Garden west to Massachusetts Avenue. The cross streets run alphabetically from east to west, starting with Arlington, then Berkeley, Clarendon, etc. Stores pack the buildings along Newbury, which were originally designed for residential use, making for a lot of oddly shaped, quirky boutiques. The good shopping extends to either side of Newbury St with trendy stores and big name designers lining Boylston Street and many of the cross roads. Though the area features shops for all ages and tax brackets, the ambiance of Boston's most famed street may make an indulgence in $300 shoes or a $15 martini seem perfectly sensible.

In the summertime, the cafés spill out onto the sidewalk, providing a perfect spot from which to partake in unparalleled people-watching. The street is a veritable human car crash; the "hippest" elements of every age group, from 80-year-olds to eight-year-olds, interact and fight for space (and attention) on the same small sidewalk.

For an updated list of shops, see www.newbury-st.com.

History

The whole of Back Bay was swampland until about 1870, when workers completed a massive filling project. As a result, Back Bay is the only neighborhood in Boston to benefit from a modern urban planning. Streets actually cross each other at 90-degree angles, and at no point is there a rotary or an eight-way intersection. Fluctuations in the water table, however, are rotting the wooden planks on which most of the area's structures sit. The result: Back Bay is sinking.

The architecture on Newbury Street is fairly uniform, since most of the development occurred during the same half-century. Emmanuel Church, designed by Alexander Estey in 1862, was the first building completed on Newbury Street. The Church of the Covenant, built in 1865, houses some spectacular stained glass windows and was once described by Oliver Wendell Holmes as "absolutely perfect." Its Emmaus Window shines even in the dimmest of lights.

How to Get There—Driving

Newbury Street is easy to get to. From I-93 take Exit 26 to Storrow Drive. Take the exit for Arlington Street, and proceed up Arlington until you hit Newbury Street (right turn only, one-way). Newbury Street lies between Boylston Street and Commonwealth Avenue, so if you get twisted around use these larger streets as landmarks.

How to Get There—Mass Transit

From the T's Green Line you can get off at the Arlington stop, the Copley stop, or the Hynes/ICA stop. Note that the Green Line's E train breaks off the main track at Copley, so use the B, C, or D train to get to Hynes/ICA.

All addresses are on Newbury Street

Clothing

9 Months · 286 · maternity wear
A Pea in the Pod · 10 · maternity wear
AG Adriano Goldschmied · 201 ·
men's and women's clothing
Agnes b · 172 ·
French clothing for men and women
Akris Boutique · 16 · shoe store
Alan Bilzerian · 34 · designer clothes
Alan Rouleau Couture · 73 ·
custom tailoring
Aldo · 180 · shoes and leather goods
Allen Edmonds · 36 ·
shoes and cedar products
American Apparel · 138 ·
men's and women's clothing
American Eagle Outfitters · 201 ·
youth clothing
Ana Hernandez Bridal · 165 ·
bridal boutique
Ann Taylor · 18 · women's clothes
Anneke Thio · 316 · bridal, children's
clothing, tailoring and alterations
Aria Bridesmaids · 39 ·
custom dresses
Army Barracks · 328 · military duds
Banana Republic · 28 ·
men's and women's clothing
Barbour by Peter Elliot · 134 ·
men's and women's clothing
BCBG Max Azaria · 71 ·
women's designer clothing
Bebe · 349 ·
women's clothing, accessories
Bella Bridesmaid · 163 ·
wedding clothing
Best of Scotland · 115 ·
sweaters at mill prices
Betsey Johnson · 201 ·
designer clothes
Betsy Jenney of Boston · 114 ·
women's unusual designer clothes
Borelli · 73 · high-end fashion

The Boston Baked Bean · 291 ·
keychains and more
Boutique Giorgio Armani · 22 · clothes
Boutique Longchamp · 139A ·
French handbags
Brooks Brothers · 46 ·
classy clothing for men and women
Burberry Limited · 2 ·
clothes for men and women
Calypso · 114 · women's clothing
Camper Shoes · 139 · shoes
Ceri · 31 · women's clothing
Chanel · 5 · clothing and accessories
Classic Tuxedo · 223 · ummm…?
The Closet · 175 · consignment;
men's and women's clothing
Cole-Haan · 109 ·
men's and women's clothing
Cuoio · 115 ·
European shoes for women
Daniela Corte Fashion · 91 ·
women's fashion
Designer Shoes · 125 · designer shoes
Diesel · 339 · clothing
DKNY · 37 · clothing
Dress · 221 · women's clothing
Easter Wings · 244 · women's clothing
Ecco Newbury Street · 216 · shoes
Emporio Armani · 210-214 ·
men's and women's clothing
Envi-Eco Fashion Boutique · 164 ·
womens fashion accessories
Ermengildo Zegna · 39 · clothes
Fiandaca · 73 · couture clothing
Flair Bridesmaid Boutique · 129 ·
wedding clothing
Footstock · 133 · shoes
French Connection · 208 ·
men's and women's clothing
G-Star Raw · 348 ·
men's and women's clothing
Gap · 201 · clothing
GapKids · 201 · children's clothing
Guess? · 80 · clothing

H&M · 100 ·
men's and women's clothing
Hempest · 207 · hemp clothing
I Boutique · 251 ·
men's and women's clothing
In the Pink · 133 · women's clothing
Intermix · 186 · women's clothing
Jasmine Sola Shoes · 329 · shoes
Jessica McClintock · 201 ·
women's cocktail attire
John Fluevog Shoes · 302 · shoes
Johnny Cupcakes · 279 ·
men's and women's clothing
Juicy Couture · 12 · women's clothing
Karmaloop Boston · 160 ·
men's and women's clothing
Kate Spade Shoes · 117 ·
shoes, purses, etc.
Kenneth Cole Productions · 128 · shoes
L'Elite · 276 · bridal boutique
Lester Harry's · 115 · bedding,
children's and infant's clothing
Life is Good · 285 ·
men's and women's clothing
Lingerie Studio · 264 · lingerie
LF Stores · 353 · women's clothing
Loro Piana · 43 ·
men's and women's clothing,
accessories, tailoring and alteration
Lucky Brand · 229 · denim
Luna Boston · 286 ·
accessories and handbags
Maha Barson · 127 · women's clothing
Marc Jacobs · 81 · fashion
Matsu · 259 · handbags
Max Mara · 69 · designer clothing
Mudo · 205 · clothing
Nanette Lepore · 119 ·
women's clothing
Niketown · 200 · everything Nike
Oilily · 31 ·
Dutch clothing for women and children
Oilily Women's · 32 · women's clothes
Patagonia · 346 · clothing for the great
outdoors

Clothing–continued

Pavo Real Boutique • 115 • women's clothing and accessories
Petit Bateau • 171 • women's clothing
Players of Newbury • 250 • women's clothing
Puma • 333 • wildlife
Queen Bee • 85 • women's clothing
Ralph Lauren • 95 • clothing
Reiss • 132 • men's and women's clothing
Relic • 116 • men's and women's clothing
Riccardi Boutique • 116 • clothing
Rockport • 83 • shoes
Rugby Ralph Lauren • 342 • men's clothing
Sean Store • 154 • men's clothing
Second Time Around Collections • 176 & 219 • new and consignment clothes
Serenella • 134 • European women's clothes
Sigrid Olsen • 141B • women's clothing
Soudee • 293 • fashion
Stel's • 334 • men's and women's clothing, accessories, and jewelry
Steve Madden • 324A • shoes and handbags
Stil • 170 • women's clothing
Technical • 230 • skate style and art
Tess & Carlos • 141A • women's clothing
Thom Brown of Boston • 337 & 331 • shoes
United Colors of Benetton • 140 • women's clothing
Urban Outfitters • 361 • clothing
Valentino • 47 • men's and women's clothing
Vera Wang • 253 • wedding clothing
Victoria's Secret • 82 • fig leaves
Whim Boutique • 253 • men's and women's clothing

Restaurants

29 Newbury • 29 • new American food
Ben & Jerry's • 174 • ice cream
Boloco Inspired Burritos • 247 • burritos
Boston Baked Bean • 291 • gourmet gifts
Bouchee • 159 • American and French food
Bostone Pizza • 225 • pizza
The Capital Grille • 359 • steak house
Charley's Eating & Drinking Saloon • 284 • American food
Ciao Bella • 240 • Italian food
Croma • 269 • pizza
Daisy Buchanan's • 240 • bar
Dunkin' Donuts • 335 • donuts
Emack & Bolio's Ice Cream • 290 • ice cream
Emporio Armani Café • 214 • Italian cuisine
Espresso Royale Café • 286 • coffee house
The Jewel of Newbury • 254 • Italian food

JP Licks Ice Cream • 352 • local ice cream shop
Kashmir • 279 • Indian food
L'Aroma Café • 85 • coffee shop
Marcello's Restaurant • 272 • Persian, Italian
Piattini Wine Café • 226 • Italian food
Scoozi • 237 • pizza and sandwiches
Shino Express Sushi • 144 • Japanese food
Sonsie • 327 • international cuisine
Starbucks • 350 & 165 • coffee shop
Stephanie's on Newbury • 190 • American food
Steve's • 316 • Greek-American food
Tapeo • 268 • Spanish food
Tealuxe • 108 • tea bar
Thai Basil • 132 • Thai food
The Upper Crust • 222 • pizza
Wisteria House • 264 • Chinese-American cuisine

Services

30 Newbury Spa • 30 • skin care, hair removal, hair salon
350 Newbury Tan • 350 • tanning
Acru Salon • 167 • beauty salon
Alexander's Salon • 163 • beauty salon
Anthony Pino Salon • 299 • hair salon
Avanti Salon • 11 • hair and skin care
Back Bay Framery and Photo • 303 • framing and photo finishing
Back Bay Hair Designs • 291 • hair salon
Bang & Olufsen • 30 • home audio/video systems
Beaucage Salon • 71 • salon for men and women
Beauty Rules • 274 • hair salon
BeBe Nail and Skin Salon • 154 • skin care, nail care
Bella Sante • 38 • day spa
Best Fit Tailoring • 268 • tailor
BLU Salon on Newbury • 118 • hair salon
Cherry Mart • 349 • grocer
Christopher J Hawes Color Design Group • 36 • hair colorists
Cititan Baron's of Boston • 316 • tanning
Condom World • 332 • sexual novelties
CVS • 240 • pharmacy
Daryl Christopher Limited • 37 • beauty salon
Dekwa Elements of Hair • 132 • feng shui-inspired hair salon
DeLuca's Market • 243 • grocery store
Deuxieme Salon • 235 • hair salon
Diego • 143 • hair and nail services
Dreams Beauty • 350 • day spa and hair services
Eclipse Salon Gallery • 164 • beauty salon
Elizabeth Grady Skin Care Salon • 11 • skin care
Emerge Spa and Salon • 275 • day spa
Enzo & Company • 135 • hair salon, skin care, nail care
Everbare Laser Hair Removal • 10 • laser hair removal
Executive II Haircutting • 333 • barber

Fenway Sportszone • 306 • sports memorabilia
For Eyes Optical Co. • 222A • eyeglass store
G Spa Inc • 35 • day spa, hair salon
g20 Spa and Salon by Giuliano • 338 • spa
Highlights Hair Salon • 286 • hair salon
Hollywood Nail and Skin Salon • 253 • day spa, skin care, nail care, hair removal
Hot Gossip • 207 • salon
Isoci Salon • 8 • beauty salon
James Joseph Studio • 168 • salon
James Joseph Salon • 30 • hair salon
James Patrick Salon • 121 • salon
Jean-Pierre Salon • 116 • salon
Jennifer's Nail & Skin Care • 224 • nail care, hair removal
Jerel Hair Studio • 119 • hair coloring and styling
John Lewis • 97 • gold and silver craftsmen
Johnson Paint Company • 355 • art supplies
Jordan the Tailor • 271 • tailor
Kang's Corner Newbury Street • 314 • smoke shop, etc
Katrina Hess Makeup Studio • 101 • makeup and bridal
Kosmetika European Skin Care • 77 • skin care
L'Atelier Haute CoiffureSalon • 174 • salon
L'Elegance Coiffure • 104 • salon
La Tete • 221 • salon
Laser Skin Center Medical Spa • 119 • skin care, hair removal
Laura's Nails & Spa • 215 • day spa, skin care, nail care, hair removal
Lauren's Nail and Skin Salon • 164 • nail and skin salon
Les Amis • 91 • salon
Lux Lash • 232 • make-up, skin care
Mario Russo Salon • 9 • salon
Mechanique • 115 • salon
Mia's Nail Salon • 168 • manicures
Michaud Cosmetics • 69 • eyebrow shaping and cosmetics
New England Genealogical Society • 101 • genealogical research
Newbury Electrology • 271 • permanent hair removal
Newbury Natural Nails • 247 • nail salon
Newbury Tailoring Company • 91 • tailoring and alterations
Nora's Convenience Store • 303 • convenience store
The North Face • 326 • outdoor apparel and gear
Oasis Hair Salon • 9 • salon and spa
Parks True Value Hardware • 233 • hardware store
Persona Hair Salon • 331 • salon
Pierre Deux • 109 • French interior design
Pini Swissa Salon • 18 • hair salon
Pour Moi Skin & Body Salon • 105 • day spa
Rachel's Makeup & Eyebrow Studio • 176 • make-up, hair removal

Richard-Joseph Hair · 164 · salon
Roffi · 134 · day spa
Roger E Lussier · 168 · framing
Safar Coiffures · 235 · salon
Sabon · 129 · beauty products
The Salon at 10 Newbury · 10 · salon
Salon 350 · hair salon
Salon Acote · 132 ·
men's and women's hairstyling
Salon Luiz · 115 · salon
Salon Marc Harris · 30 · hair salon
Salon Monet · 176 · hair salon
Salon Nordic Skin Care · 221 ·
skin care
Salon Red & Spa · 144A ·
hair salon, skin care, nail care
Salon Trio · 115 · nail care, hair removal
Secret Garden · 338 · florist
See · 125 · eyeglass store
Skin Health Medical Spa · 73 ·
skin care
Skin SpaClinic · 205 ·
skin care, hair removal
Sleek Medspa · 228 ·
skin care, hair removal
Spa Newbury · 115 · salon
Sprint-PCS Wireless · 330 ·
mobile phone communications
Starr Hair Studio · 114 · salon
Stilisti · 138 · hair salon
T-Mobile · 118 ·
mobile phone communications
Tanorama · 226 · tanning
Tech Superpowers · 252 · computers
Thy's Nail & Skin Care Salon · 173 ·
nail care, hair removal
Town's Nails · 336 · nail care
UMI · 75 · salon
Verizon Wireless/Wireless City · 225 ·
mobile phone communications
Vidal Sassoon · 14 · salon
Violet Skin Boutique · 257 ·
day spa, skin care, nail care
Wellesley Optical · 74 · eyeglass shop
Winston Flowers · 131 · florist
Yuri's Watches · 142 · watches

Gifts & Miscellaneous

1154 Lill Studio · 220 · handbags
A Touch of France Gallery · 173 ·
art gallery
Acme Fine Art · 38 ·
bought and sold modern American art
Aldo Accessories · 184 ·
accessories, handbags, jewelry
Alfred J. Walker Fine Art · 162 ·
art gallery
Alpha Gallery Inc · 38 · art gallery
Andrea Marquit Fine Arts · 38 ·
art gallery
Arden Gallery · 129 · art gallery
Atelier Janiye · 165 · jewelry
Aurum · 293 · jewelry
Axelle Fine Arts · 91 · art gallery
Back Bay Oriental Rugs · 154 · rugs
Barbara Krakow Gallery · 10 ·
art gallery
Bauer Wines Spirits · 330 · liquor store
Beadworks · 167 ·
make your own jewelry

Beth Urdang Gallery · 14 · art gallery
Bliss · 121 · home furnishings, cooking
and dining
Brodney Antiques & Jewelry · 145 ·
antiques and jewelry
Cartier · 40 · jewelry
CD Spins · 324 · music and records
Chase Gallery · 129 · art gallery
Childs Gallery · 169 · art gallery
Cohen's Fashion Optical · 179 ·
sunglasses and glasses
Comenos Fine Arts · 9 · art gallery
Commonwealth Fine Art · 236 ·
art gallery
Comptoir de Famille · 127 ·
home accessories, furniture, bedding
CoSo Artist's Gallery · 158 · art gallery
Dajuli Sparkles · 304 · jewelry
Diptyque · 123 · French perfumery
Domain Home Fashions · 7 · furniture
Dona Flor · 246 · home ceramics
Dorfman Jewelers · 24 · jewelry
Down to Basics · 249 · bedding
DTR Modern Galleries · 167 ·
art gallery
Erwin Pearl · 4 · jewelry
European Watch Co · 232 ·
watch repair and shop
Fairy Shop · 302 · Fairies, bubbles,
incense, jewelry, you name it
Family Treasures Bookstore · books
and magazines
Felicia's Cosmetics · 314 · cosmetics
Fiddlehead · 292 · jewelry and more
Firefly Jewelry and Gifts · 270 ·
jewelry and gift shop
Firestone and Parson · 8 ·
antique jewelry
Fresh · 121 · bath products
Galerie d'Orsay · 33 · art gallery
Gallery NAGA · 67 · art gallery
Guido Frame Studio · 118 ·
ready-to-frame prints
The Guild of Boston Artists · 162 ·
art gallery
Hope · 302 · unique gift shop
Howard Yezerski Gallery · 14 ·
art gallery
International Poster Gallery · 205 ·
poster art gallery
Inviting Company · 213 · stationery
Judi Rotenberg Gallery · 130 ·
art gallery
Judy Ann Goldman Fine Art · 14 ·
art gallery
Kidder Smith Gallery · 131 · art gallery
Kiehl's · 112 · beauty products
Kitchen Arts · 161 · kitchen tools
Kitty World · 279 · Hello Kitty heaven
Knit and Needlepoint · 11 ·
crafts and sewing supplies
L'Attitude Gallery Sculpture Garden ·
218 · art gallery
Lalo Treasures · 255 · jewelry
Lanoue Fine Art · 160 · art gallery
Lavender Home & Table · 173 · home
and garden, bedding, antiques
Lush Cosmetics · 166 ·
beauty products
M-A-C Newbury · 112 ·
beauty products
Madura Company · 144 ·
home furnishings, bedding

Marcoz Antiques · 177 · Antiques
Martin Lawrence Gallery · 77 ·
art gallery
Mayan Weavers · 268 ·
Native American crafts
Mercury Gallery · 8 · art gallery
Miller Block Gallery · 14 · art gallery
Needlepoint of Back Bay · 125 ·
crafts and sewing
Newbury Comics · 332 ·
music and video store
Newbury Fine Arts Gallery · 29 ·
art gallery
Newbury Visions · 215 ·
sunglasses and glasses
Newbury Yarns · 164 ·
crafts and sewing supplies
Nielsen Gallery · 179 · art gallery
O & Company · 161 · olive oil store
O'Brien Stephen B · 268 · art gallery
Pageo · 33 · Jewelry
Pepper Gallery · 38 · art gallery
Pierre Deux · 109 ·
gourmet gifts and home accessories
Poggenpohl Boston Showroom · 135 ·
designer kitchens
Pottery Barn · 122 · home décor
Pratesi Linens · 110 ·
bed and bath linens
Prem-La · 211 · home and garden
Pucker Gallery · 171 · art gallery
Q Optical · 287 · glasses and sunglasses
Richardson-Clarke Gallery · 38 ·
art gallery
Robert Klein Gallery · 38 · art gallery
Robert Marc Newbury Street · 35 ·
glasses and sunglasses
Royka's Fine Arts Antiques Gallery ·
213 · antiques
SAC Gallery · 175 · art gallery
Sarkis Sajonian · 273 · jewelry
Shu Uemura · 130 · beauty products
Simon Pearce Glass · 115 · glassware
Small Pleasures · 142 · jewelry
So Good Jewelry · 349 · jewelry
Solstice · 168 · glasses and sunglasses
St George Gallery · 245 · art gallery
Sugar Heaven · 218 · candy
Sunglass Hut International · 182 & 86 ·
sunglasses store
Swiss Watch Boston · 217 · timepieces
Teuscher Chocolates of Switzerland ·
230 · chocolates
Time & Time Again · 249 · watch store
Timeless Teas · 85 · tea
Trident Booksellers and Café · 338 ·
bookstore and café
Victoria Munroe Fine Art · 179 ·
art gallery
VOSE Galleries of Boston Inc. · 238 ·
art gallery
Waterworks · 103 ·
bathroom accessories

Parking Garages

Danker Donohue Garage · 347
Fitz Inn Auto Parks · 149
Interpark · 4

203

Boston Convention & Exhibition Center

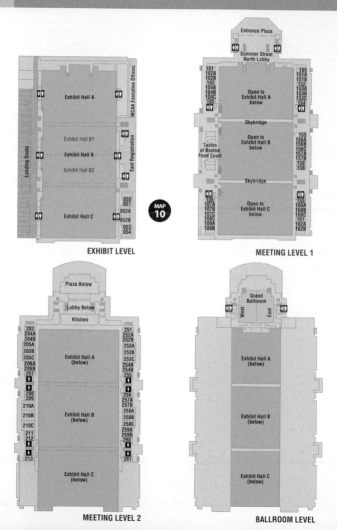

EXHIBIT LEVEL

Exhibit Hall A

Exhibit Hall B1

Exhibit Hall B

Exhibit Hall B2

Exhibit Hall C

MCAA Executive Offices

East Registration

Loading Docks

050
051
052A
052B
053
054

MAP 10

MEETING LEVEL 1

Entrance Plaza

Summer Street
North Lobby

101
102A
102B
103
104A
104B
104C
105

Open to
Exhibit Hall A
below

Skybridge

Tastes
of Boston
Food Court

Open to
Exhibit Hall B
below

Skybridge

106
107A
107B
107C
108A
108C
109A
109B

Open to
Exhibit Hall C
below

105
151A
151B
152
153A
153B
153C
154

155
156A
156B
156C
157A
157B
158
158.1

159
160A
160B
160C
161
162A
162B

MEETING LEVEL 2

Plaza Below

Lobby Below

Kitchen

203
204A
204B
205A
205B
205C
206A
206B
207
208
209
210A
210B
210C
211
212
213

Exhibit Hall A
(below)

Exhibit Hall B
(below)

Exhibit Hall C
(below)

251
252A
252B
253A
253B
253C
254A
254B
255
256
257A
257B
258A
258B
258C
259A
259B
260
261

BALLROOM LEVEL

Grand
Ballroom

West   East

Exhibit Hall A
(below)

Exhibit Hall B
(below)

Exhibit Hall C
(below)

Boston Convention & Exhibition Center

General Information

NFT Map: 10
Address: 415 Summer St,
Boston, MA 02210
Phone: 617-954-2000
Fax: 617-954-2299
Websites: www.mccahome.com
www.advantageboston.com

Overview

It took longer than expected to complete (what doesn't in this town?) and was plagued by cost overruns and contractor squabbling, but the Boston Convention & Exhibition Center finally opened in June 2004. In our humble opinion, it was worth the wait. Designed by noted architect Rafael Viñoly, the BCEC, which stands near Fort Point Channel on Summer Street (about a half-mile from South Station), is a stunning addition to the South Boston waterfront landscape.

Put simply, the BCEC is gargantuan. With 516,000 square feet of contiguous exhibition space, 160,000 square feet of flexible meeting space, more than 80 meeting rooms, and a 40,000-square-foot grand ballroom, the building covers an overall area of 1.7 million square feet. The BCEC now holds the coveted title of New England's Largest Man-Made Space and is big enough to hold 16 football fields.

The new complex is the centerpiece of the city's initiative to attract more convention business to Boston. As the old real estate mantra goes, it's all about "location, location, location," and a prime selling point for the BCEC is its proximity to both South Station and Logan Airport. Only two miles from Logan, the BCEC is closer to its city airport than the convention center of any other American city.

Services

The BCEC is used for large-scale conferences, meetings, and exhibitions. To schedule an event and be assigned a personal coordinator, contact the sales department at 617-954-2411 or sales@massconvention.com.

Catering services at the BCEC are provided by Aramark. If you are planning a catered event, contact Aramark at 617-954-2211.

How to Get There—Driving

The BCEC is easy to reach from the Mass Pike (I-90). From the Pike, take Exit 25 (South Boston). Turn right onto Congress Street, then right onto D Street, then the second right onto Summer Street. The BCEC will be immediately on the left. It's hard to miss.

From the south, take I-93 N, get off at Exit 20, follow the signs to I-90 E and Exit 25. Follow the directions above.

From the north, take I-93 S, get off at Exit 23 (Purchase Street/South Station), proceed straight onto Purchase Street at the end of the exit ramp, and take a left onto Summer Street at South Station. Drive about a mile down the road to D Street and make a right.

Parking

If you must drive, you'll probably be dropping your car in a garage or fenced parking lot. The establishments listed below are the closest to the BCEC.

LAZ Parking· 10 Necco St, 617-426-1556
Fitz-Inn Auto Parks · 30-60 Necco St, 617-426-1556
Farnsworth Parking Garage · 17-31 Farnsworth St, 617-737-8161
Stanhope Garage · 338 Congress St, 617-338-5657
Stanhope Garage · 381 Congress St, 617-426-5326
Fanpier Parking Lots · 28 Northern Ave, 617-737-0910
Transpark · 390 Congress St, 617-737-3363
Transpark · 25 Northern Ave, 617-451-7732

How to Get There—Mass Transit

The Silver Line stops at the BCEC (alight at the World Trade Center stop, escalate to the top entrance, and traverse the bridge). To connect to the Silver Line from points other than Logan Airport, take the T's Red Line to South Station. The BCEC is only a few hundred yards away from South Station, so if you want to stretch your legs take a stroll across Fort Point Channel instead of transferring to the Silver Line.

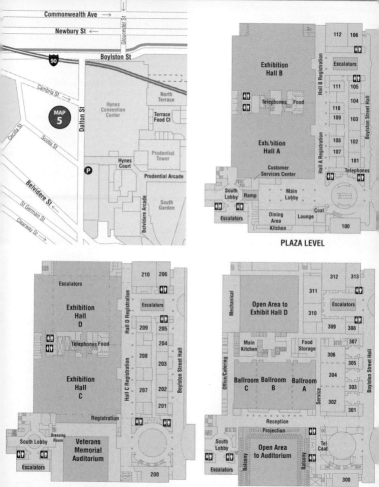

PLAZA LEVEL

SECOND LEVEL

THIRD LEVEL

General Information

NFT Map: 5
Address: 900 Boylston St, Boston, MA 02115
Phone: 617-954-2000
Websites: www.mccahome.com
www.advantageboston.com

Overview

The John B. Hynes Veterans Memorial Convention Center is a relatively small center, with just 193,000 square feet of exhibit space, a 25,000-square-foot ballroom, and 41 meeting rooms. The Hynes is conveniently located in Back Bay with many hotels, historical sites, and tourist attractions within close proximity. Only a short walk from the Green Line's Hynes Convention Center/ICA stop, it is easily accessible by public transportation.

Once the big name in town for would-be conventioneers, the Hynes Convention Center now plays second fiddle to the Boston Convention and Exhibition Center (see page 204). Because the Hynes adjoins the Prudential complex and sits in the midst of a few thousand hotel rooms, it continues to attract convention business, focusing on mid-size meetings (think the American Association of Immunologists and the National Council of Teachers of Mathematics) and letting the biggest fish (like the International Boston Seafood Show) swim to the Southie Starship. A state commission was convened in 2004 to determine whether the Hynes should continue to operate as a convention center, be converted into retail, sold to the highest bidder, etc., but as of press time, no decisions have been made.

Services

The Hynes is used for conferences, meetings, exhibitions, and most other events where groups of people gather. (Word to the wise: Stay far, far away during CollegeFest.) To schedule an event and be assigned a personal coordinator, contact the sales department by phone at 617-954-2411, or by email at sales@massconvention.com.

Like every other big building in the universe, catering services at the Hynes are provided by Aramark. If you are considering planning a catered event, contact Aramark at 617-954-2330.

How to Get There—Driving

The Hynes is only four miles from Logan Airport. Two major roadways, I-93 and the Mass Pike (I-90), will deliver you close to the venue. From I-93, take Exit 26 B (Storrow Drive). Follow Storrow Drive for about two miles to the Fenway/Kenmore exit and head towards Fenway. Continue to the first set of lights and merge left onto Boylston Street.

From the Mass Pike, take Exit 22 (Prudential/Copley Place), stay left as you exit, and turn onto Huntington Avenue. At the next set of lights (Belvidere Street), take a right, follow the curve, and bear right onto Dalton Street. At the lights, turn right onto Boylston Street.

The main entrance to the Hynes is at 900 Boylston Street and is easily accessible to taxis and buses via an access lane, which is set apart from Boylston Street.

Parking

There are numerous parking garages within a three-block walk of the Hynes, totaling more than 4,400 spaces. There is metered parking available around the Hynes and adjacent streets, but these spots are hard to come by.

- **Prudential Center Parking Garage**,
  800 Boylston St, 2–10 hours for $34, and the daily maximum is $39. 617-236-3060.
- **Copley Place Parking Garage**,
  100 Huntington Ave (corner of Huntington Ave & Dartmouth St), $6 for the first half hour with an increase of $4 for every additional half hour, $26 for 3–10 hours, but only $7 for three hours with validation. Maximum day rate is $32. 617-369-5025.
- **Boston Marriott Hotel Copley Place**,
  100 Huntington Ave, self-parking $32 per day, valet parking, $41 per day. 617-236-5800.
- **Westin Copley Place Parking Garage**,
  10 Huntington Ave, $21 for up to 2 hours, $27 for 2–4 hours, $32 for 4–6 hours, $35 for 6–8 hours, and $40 per night (with unlimited in-and-out access). 617-262-9600.
- **Colonnade Hotel Parking Garage**,
  120 Huntington Ave, $12 for the first hour, with a $4 increase every additional hour; $24 for 3–12 hours. $36 for overnight parking. 617-424-7000.
- **Back Bay Hilton Hotel Parking Garage**,
  40 Dalton St, $5 for 1/2 hour, $12 for 1 hour, $20 for 1–2 hours. $22 for 2–3 hours, $24 for 3–12 hours, $35 for overnight parking, $39 for overnight parking with valet service. 617-236-1100.

How to Get There—Mass Transit

The subway stops just two blocks away from the Hynes. Take the Green Line (B, C, or D train) to the Hynes Convention Center/ICA stop. Once you get off the subway, exit at any entrance and follow signs to the Hynes.

Bayside Expo & Conference Center

General Information

NFT Map: 32
Address: 200 Mt Vernon St, Columbia Point
Boston, MA 02125
Phone: 617-474-6000
Website: www.baysideexpo.com

Overview

Located three miles from downtown Boston, the Expo Center was once "New England's largest conference center and hotel complex," but has now ceded that crown to the much larger Boston Convention and Exhibition Center in Southie. Built on the site of a bankrupt mall and ringed by parking lots, the stark white, square Expo Center didn't win any design awards, but the building is functional, allowing visitors to focus on the boat, auto, RV, trade, or flower show that attracted them there in the first place.

The center's single-level exhibit space includes 12 meeting rooms, a full-service restaurant, lounge, cafeteria, and concessions. While they are convenient, on-site vendors' price-to-quality ratios are not the best. A small cup of coffee costs more than $2—and that's for the standard stuff, not a chic, unpronounceable foreign blend. An alternative would be to tailgate in the Expo Center's immense parking lot, but that will cost you, too ($12, to be precise), making the T the best choice for thrifty show-goers.

Adjacent to the exhibit space, the Executive Conference Center has everything an executive could wish for (well, almost everything), such as T-1 Internet access, wireless LAN, and wireless phone and video conferencing.

On nice days, be sure to take a drive around the back to the center's "bayside," where there are pleasant views of grassy Old Harbor, South Boston, and planes landing at Logan Airport.

The Doubletree Hotel (240 Mt Vernon St; 617-822-3600) markets itself to business travelers and vacationing tourists alike. This 197-room hotel's loftier rooms offer both city and ocean views. In addition to standard hotel amenities such as a fitness room, lounge, and a tour/recreation desk, the Doubletree Club offers free chocolate chip cookies at check-in.

How to Get There—Driving

From the south, take I-93 N to Exit 14. Stay in the right lane and follow Morrissey Boulevard. At the third set of lights, take a right onto Mt Vernon Street. Follow the signs and take the third left into the Bayside Expo main entrance.

From the north and west, take the Mass Pike (I-90) E to I-93 S. Get off I-93 at Exit 15 (Columbia Road). Stay in the left lane and take a left off the ramp. Go three-quarters of the way around the rotary and bear right onto Day Boulevard. Proceed past the Massachusetts State Police barracks and take the first right into the Bayside Expo north entrance.

Parking

Don't be fooled into off-site parking by the shifty folks at the Sovereign Bank parking lot across the street from the Expo Center. If you do, you'll have to lug your stuff across the street, only to walk by dozens of available spaces in the Expo Center lot. Make sure you follow the signs for on-site parking at Bayside Expo Center. Parking costs $12 on show days.

How to Get There—Mass Transit

Take the Red Line T or MBTA Commuter Rail to the JFK/UMass station. The Expo Center is directly across the street. The red "Beantown Trolley" runs from the T stop to the front entrance of the Expo Center, a distance of about a half-mile.

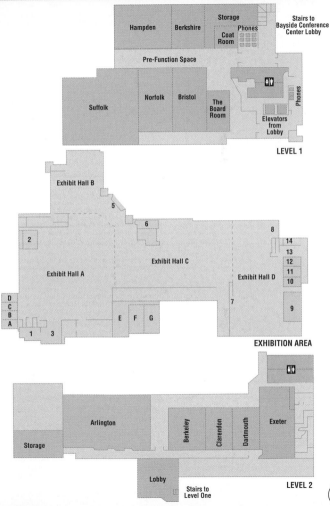

Bayside Expo & Conference Center

LEVEL 1

- Hampden
- Berkshire
- Storage
- Coat Room
- Phones
- Stairs to Bayside Conference Center Lobby
- Pre-Function Space
- Suffolk
- Norfolk
- Bristol
- The Board Room
- Phones
- Elevators from Lobby

EXHIBITION AREA

- Exhibit Hall B
- Exhibit Hall A
- Exhibit Hall C
- Exhibit Hall D
- 5
- 6
- 8
- 2
- 14
- 13
- 12
- 11
- 10
- 7
- 9
- D
- C
- B
- A
- 1
- 3
- E
- F
- G

LEVEL 2

- Storage
- Arlington
- Berkeley
- Clarendon
- Dartmouth
- Exeter
- Lobby
- Stairs to Level One

The library, which overlooks Boston Harbor from windswept Columbia Point, was designed by architect I.M. Pei (who also designed the Christian Science Center next to the Pru and the Hancock Tower). The centerpiece of the complex is a nine-story concrete tower fronted by a glass-enclosed pavilion. The adjacent Stephen E. Smith Center, used for educational programs and conferences, opened in 1991. Outside on the lawn sits *Victura*, JFK's 26-foot sloop.

What's Inside

The JFK Library holds 8.4 million pages of presidential papers, 180,000 still photographs, six million feet of film and videotape, and 15,000 catalogued museum objects. The library also houses the world's most comprehensive collection of the papers and mementos of Ernest Hemingway, but they are available to professional researchers only. If you are a scholar who seeks access to Papa's papers, check the library's website to review the restrictive rules.

The library's Centennial Room displays rotating exhibits showcasing the Kennedy White House's embrace of cultural values and the arts. Visitors can watch a 17-minute film about the Kennedy administration before entering the main exhibit space. On weekends, the 2 pm showing of the introductory film is replaced by a 30-minute film about JFK's brother/attorney general, Robert F. Kennedy. Visitors can also watch a 20-minute film about the Cuban Missile Crisis.

A museum café serves light meals and snacks from 9 am to 5 pm, and the gift shop is open during visiting hours.

How to Get There—Driving

The JFK Library is off Morrissey Boulevard next to the UMass Boston campus. From the north or the south, take I-93 to Exit 14 (Morrissey Boulevard) and follow the signs. From the west, take the Mass Pike (I-90) east to the intersection with I-93. Take the exit toward I-93 S, get off I-93 at Exit 14, and follow the signs. The library provides free on-site parking.

How to Get There–Mass Transit

Take the T's Red Line to the JFK/UMass stop. A free shuttle bus runs between the T stop and the library. Shuttle buses run every 20 minutes between 8 am and 5 pm.

General Information

NFT Map: 32
Address: Columbia Point
Boston, MA 02125
Phone: 617-514-1600
Website: www.jfklibrary.org
Hours: 9 am–5 pm daily except Thanksgiving,
Christmas, and New Year's Day
Research Library is open M–F 8:30–
4:30 by appointment
Admission: Adults $10, seniors and students
$8, children $7, free for children 12 and
under

Overview

The John F. Kennedy Library and Museum, dedicated to our 35th president on October 20, 1979, houses 25 multimedia exhibits examining the life and work of JFK, his administration, his family, and his legacy. The library is one of eleven presidential libraries administered by the National Archives and Records Administration, a federal government agency. The library draws approximately 200,000 visitors each year.

General Information

Cape Cod Chamber of Commerce:
508-362-3225; www.capecodchamber.org
Wellfleet Bay Wildlife Sanctuary:
508-349-2615; www.wellfleetbay.org
Cape Cod National Seashore Salt Pond Visitor Center:
508-349-3785; www.nps.gov/caco

Overview

Thanks to the eternal appeal of picturesque beaches, fried seafood, and miniature golf, Cape Cod is one of New England's most popular getaway destinations. Separated from mainland Massachusetts by the Cape Cod Canal, the region is located on the portion of the state that looks like a strong, flexing arm. There are only two roads that cross the canal, both via bridge; those Cape Cod Canal Tunnel stickers on locals' cars are just a mind game played on the out-of-towners.

The Cape is composed of 15 towns, with a permanent population of roughly 230,000 that swells to over 550,000 in the summer months. The islands of Martha's Vineyard and Nantucket are not officially part of Cape Cod, but are generally considered the same destination region. Each town has its own character: Bustling and bawdy Provincetown is home to a large and proud gay community, while Falmouth is a more tranquil, wooded locale.

Highlights and essentials:

• Beaches—With a total of 559.6 miles of coastline, the Cape is perhaps most well-known for its beaches, many of which are open to the public for a modest daily parking fee. The northern ocean water resists warming though, so swimming is generally, let's say, refreshing.

• Seafood—Fried clams, twin lobsters, steamers, baked stuffed quahogs…need we say more?

• Christmas Tree Shops—The merchandise sold at this thriving retail chain can be best described as discount "stuff." The company has expanded beyond its Cape Cod origins, but there is no better place to go when you need picture frames, beach toys, or souvenir tchotchkes.

• Miniature Golf—The Cape has elevated mini-golf landscaping to a fine art. Whether you prefer putting in a serene garden setting or braving darkened caves in a pirate-inspired golf adventure, Cape Cod has something for you.

• Lighthouses—If you have time to visit a lighthouse or two, we recommend the Nobska Point Lighthouse at Woods Hole, an oft-photographed white tower at the southwestern tip of Cape Cod, the Cape Cod (Highland) Lighthouse in North Truro, or the Chatham Lighthouse on the southeastern corner of the Cape.

• Whale Watches—Hop aboard a whale watch voyage out of Wood's Hole, Hyannis, or Provincetown to experience the truly breathtaking phenomenon of cruising alongside some of the world's largest and most powerful creatures.

The Towns

The Cape, about 70 miles in length, is often divided into three regions:

The Upper Cape—The first area you reach after crossing the canal, the Upper Cape includes the towns of Falmouth, Mashpee, Sandwich, and Bourne. For the best views and smoothest journey, avoid the highways and take surface routes, such as 28A, that take you close to the water. Film buffs might consider a visit to Woods Hole, where part of the movie *Jaws* was filmed.

The Mid Cape—Continuing eastward, the next area you will reach includes Dennis, Yarmouth, and Barnstable, a town containing seven villages: Hyannis, Osterville, Centerville, Cotuit, West Barnstable, Barnstable Village, and Marstons Mills. Almost 70% of the Cape's permanent population resides in the Hyannis area, so the downtown remains busy throughout the year, and it is about the only place in the area to find such national chains as Barnes and Noble or Old Navy. If such conventional commercialism isn't on your vacation itinerary, take the Old King's Highway (Route 6A) to stay in the Cape mood.

The Outer Cape—Home of the peaceful Cape Cod National Seashore, Nickerson State Park, and the quiet towns of Brewster, Orleans, Eastham, Wellfleet, Chatham, Harwich, and Truro, it's difficult to imagine the spectacle sitting at the tip of the Outer Cape: Provincetown. At land's end sits one of the most "out" towns, where gay couples are as plentiful as seagulls, and the prevailing aesthetic can best be described as "flamboyant." After a day in the sun, cruise into P-town for a night of revelry. Gay or straight, the town knows how to party. For full effect, visit during Carnival in August. More information is available at www.provincetown.com.

The Islands—Martha's Vineyard and Nantucket each possess a distinct feel. Martha's Vineyard is well known for great beaches, ocean vistas, and the annual (and controversial) Monster Shark Tournament. It's even better known for its well-heeled rich folk and the Kennedy Compound. Nantucket, only three and a half by fourteen miles, is a quaint New England destination where tourists roam the cobble-stoned streets year-round. In addition to shops and galleries, the downtown is home to the Nantucket Whaling Museum. The natural beauty of Nantucket is stunning, as are the real estate prices—the median home price is the $2 million range. The best way around the island is to rent a moped or a bicycle but remember to pack a lunch if you head the beaches because there are no restaurants or snack bars

The Outdoors

Sculpted dunes, haunting marshlands, and miles of hiking trails make the Cape an ideal area for outdoor exploration. If the water calls, you can splash about at one of the Cape's many bay or ocean beaches, take a boat out to sea, dive or snorkel in the bay, canoe or kayak, parasail, kiteboard, or enjoy one of the whale- or seal-watching excursions offered.

Flora and fauna enthusiasts come here to explore the lush plant and animal life at the Cape's many sanctuaries. The Audubon Society's Wellfleet Bay Wildlife Sanctuary is the

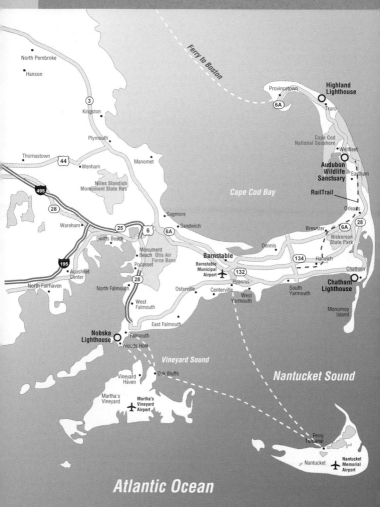

Parks & Places • Cape Cod

only sanctuary with a visitor's center. It boasts 1,000 acres of woodlands, wetlands, and grasslands that attract an exciting variety of wildlife, including songbirds and shorebirds. Five miles of scenic trails wind through the various habitats, while the newly renovated Nature Center uses "green" elements such as solar heating and composting toilets. Inside the nature center, you'll find two 700-gallon aquariums that feature the underwater worlds of the salt marsh and tidal flats. Other sanctuaries on the Cape include Long Pasture near Barnstable, Skunknett River near Osterville, Sampson's Island (accessible only by private boat from local marinas and town landings), and Ashumet Holly near Falmouth. The Cape Cod National Seashore Salt Pond visitor center in Eastham offers guided tours and nature walks through the salt marshes.

Monomoy Island, established in 1944 as a National Wildlife Refuge, is a barrier island that sits ten miles south of Chatham. It is prime habitat for migratory birds and a seal population that has grown in recent years. It is not uncommon to sit on Nauset beach to the north and see seals swimming regularly along the shoreline, which wasn't the case ten years ago. Monomoy has hiking trails and bird watching opportunities as well as commercial boat tours for seal-watching. Check out www.fws.gov/northeast/monomoy.

Sports

Cape Cod is an ideal location for sport fishing. Charters and tours are available and, for those looking to have a little fun on the water, ships such as the Yankee offer party cruises, perfect for those who hate lugging around a heavy cooler. Be warned: Drinking and waves are not always the best combo.

Golf is also popular here. There are a dozen or so courses on the Cape, varying in price, size, and level of difficulty. Dennis Pines and Dennis Highlands are two highly-respected municipal courses where a challenging game can be had for a reasonable price, and Highland Links in Truro is perched atop sheer bluffs that overlook the ocean.

Biking is another favorite pastime in the area, with free trails including the epic 22-mile RailTrail at Cape Cod National Park. The trail runs along the bed of a defunct railroad (hence the name) from Dennis (get on at Route 134 just south of Exit 9 from Route 6) to the South Wellfleet General Store.

Diehard baseball fans shouldn't miss the 104-year-old Cape Cod League, where top college athletes are recruited to play in the summer, many of whom go on to the majors. Thurman Munson, "Nomah" Garciaparra, Jason Varitek, and other stars once played for one of the league's ten teams. Attending one of their early evening games is what summer is all about. Bring your beach chair, grab a hot dog, and watch the little kids scramble for foul balls.

Arts and Culture

Though better-known for its natural splendor, Cape Cod also boasts a thriving arts community. Every summer, the Cape Cod Melody Tent in Hyannis hosts popular music and comedy acts ranging from Willie Nelson to Lewis Black. In Dennis, the Cape Playhouse hosts theatrical productions such as Guys and Dolls and Thoroughly Modern Millie.

Galleries, studios, specialty museums, and whimsical artisan shops are to be found on almost every corner. For help

navigating, drop $9.95 on Amazon.com or at the Cape Cod Chamber of Commerce for a copy of Arts and Artisans Trails, a book featuring self-guided tours of the Cape and Islands that highlight the best of the area's arts scene.

Ever since Henry David Thoreau penned Cape Cod, the region has also been the full-time or summer home of a number of notable authors. Norman Mailer, the late Kurt Vonnegut, and mystery maven Mary Higgins Clark are among the Cape's more prominent literary names.

If you aspire to join this tradition, check out the Fine Arts Work Center in Provincetown, where summer workshops in painting, drawing, and writing could help you find your hidden muse.

How to Get There

By Car: The only two driving routes onto Cape Cod are via the overburdened Bourne and Sagamore bridges. This limited access has traditionally resulted in multi-mile gridlock on Friday evenings and Saturday mornings. The Sagamore Rotary has recently been replaced with a direct ramp known as the flyover, intended to tame the traffic. Plan to travel outside of the peak times and slowdowns should be minimal. Once on the Cape, most places are pretty drivable, though downtown areas such as Hyannis and Provincetown can get a bit tangled up.

By Ferry: Avoid traffic and cut down on gas expenditures by hopping a ferry to the Cape or Islands. Bringing along a car or bike generally increases the fare, but the price may be a bargain if you have limited patience for the traffic that driving across the Canal can entail.

Bay State Cruise Company • 617-748-1428 • www.boston-ptown.com
Boston-Provincetown. May–October.
Round-trip fare: $33 on weekend excursion ferry, $50–$71 on daily fast ferry. $10 for bikes.

Boston Harbor Cruises Provincetown Fast Ferry • 617-227-4321 • www.bostonharborcruises.com
Boston-Provincetown. May–October.
Round-trip fare: $60–$71. $10 for bikes.

Hy-Line Cruises • 800-492-8082 • www.hy-linecruises.com
Hyannis-Martha's Vineyard. High-speed ferry, April–October. Standard ferry, May–October.
Hyannis-Nantucket, High-speed ferry year-round. Standard ferry, May–October.
Martha's Vineyard-Nantucket. June–September
Round-trip fare: $25–$71. $12 for bikes.

Island Queen Ferry • 508-548-4800 • www.islandqueen.com
Falmouth Harbor- Martha's Vineyard. June–September.
Round-trip fare: $7–$15. $6 for bikes.

Steamship Authority • 508-693-9130 • http://steamshipauthority.com
Woods Hole-Martha's Vineyard. Year-round.
Hyannis-Nantucket, Year-round.
Woods Hole-Martha's Vineyard round-trip fare: $7.50–$14. $6 for a bike. $80–$150 for a car.
Hyannis-Nantucket round-trip fare: $15.50–$61. $12 for a bike. $250–$420 for a car.

Berklee College of Music

1. 130 Massachusetts Avenue
2. Berklee Performance Center
3. 150 Massachusetts Avenue
4. 155 Massachusetts Avenue
5. 171 Massachusetts Avenue
6. The Berklee Bookstore
7. 120 Belvidere Street
8. 19 Belvidere Street
9. 1140 Boylston Street
10. 22 The Fenway
11. 198 Hemingway Street
12. Boston Architectural Center
13. 921 Boylston Street
14. 264-270 Commonwealth Avenue
15. 100 Massachusetts Avenue
16. 168 Massachusetts Avenue
17. 899 Boylan Street
18. 867 Boylan Street
19. 855 Boylan Street

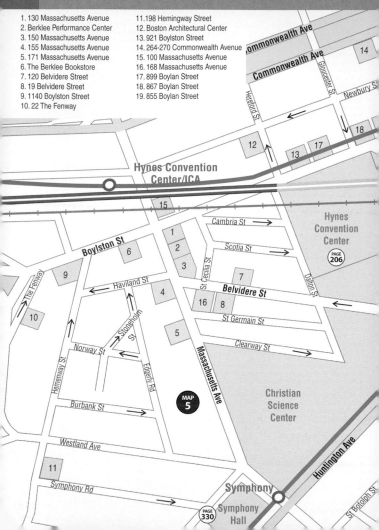

Berklee College of Music

General Information

NFT Map: 5
Address: 1140 Boylston St, Boston, MA 02215
Phone: 617-266-1400
Website: www.berklee.edu

Overview

Berklee is the largest independent music college in the world and calls itself the "premier institution for the study of contemporary music." Founded in 1945 by pianist and MIT-trained engineer Lawrence Berk, the school became accredited in 1973. Berklee offers four-year degrees as well as diploma programs that allow students to forego the liberal arts and focus exclusively on music. Facilities include more than 250 private practice rooms. In addition to performance, students study Music Business/Management, Music Education, and Music Therapy. During the summer, the school offers specialized programs including Berklee in Los Angeles.

The college enrolls close to 4,000 students, with the highest percentage (about 26%) of international students of any college in the United States from more than 70 different countries. The student body is a funky, diverse lot, with many musicians from Japan, Korea, Germany, Switzerland, and Brazil. They tend to congregate on Mass Ave, particularly outside the Berklee Performance Center where bedraggled musical geniuses stand around with their instruments. Tracy Bonham, Melissa Etheridge, Patty Larkin, Branford Marsalis, Howard Shore, and Aimee Mann are among Berklee's notable alumni. Furthermore, Berklee was the first college to recognize the guitar as a principal instrument and develop a curriculum for it back in the '60s.

Tuition

For the 2007–2008 academic year, tuition fees will amount to $33,180 and housing will be an additional $13,550 per year. However, costs vary between degree and diploma programs, and additional fees may apply. Fourteen million dollars in scholarship funds are available to Berklee students each year.

Sports

There are no college-level athletics at Berklee, but student clubs do offer soccer, basketball, softball, and yoga, among others. Nearby fitness facilities, including the YMCA, the Tennis and Racquet Club, and Boston Kung-Fu Tai-Chi Institute offer discounted rates for students. Much more popular than sports are the 350-plus student music ensembles in an impressive range of styles.

Culture on Campus

Housed in the historic Fenway Theater, the 1,220-seat Berklee Performance Center (BPC) stands as one of the finest concert halls on the East Coast. Located at 136 Massachusetts Avenue near the intersection with Boylston Street, the BPC offers numerous performances by major concert promoters as well as faculty and student concerts throughout the year. To attend a performance, check out the Event Calendar at www.berkleebpc.com or call the box office at 617-747-2261.

Departments

Admissions 617-747-2047
Financial Aid . . . . 617-747-2274 or 800-538-3844
Registrar. 617-747-2240
Housing 617-747-2292
Alumni Relations. 617-747-2236
Berklee Performance Center. 617-747-2474
Library. 617-747-2258

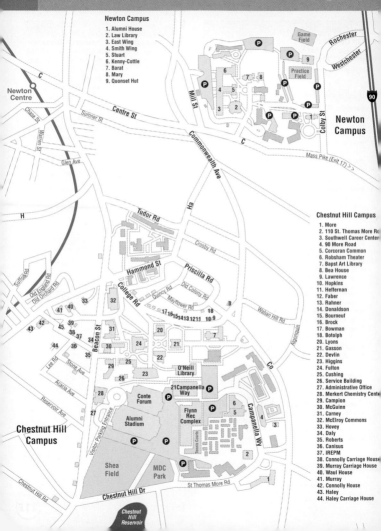

Newton Campus

1. Alumni House
2. Law Library
3. East Wing
4. Smith Wing
5. Stuart
6. Kenny-Cottle
7. Barat
8. Mary
9. Quonset Hut

Chestnut Hill Campus

1. More
2. 110 St. Thomas More Rd
3. Southwell Career Center
4. 90 More Road
5. Corcoran Common
6. Robsham Theater
7. Bapst Art Library
8. Bea House
9. Lawrence
10. Hopkins
11. Heffernan
12. Faber
13. Rahner
14. Donaldson
15. Bourneuf
16. Brock
17. Bowman
18. Botolph
19. Lyons
20. Gasson
21. Devlin
22. Higgins
23. Fulton
24. Cushing
25. Service Building
26. Administrative Office
27. Merkert Chemistry Center
28. Campion
29. McGuinn
30. Carney
31. McElroy Commons
32. Hovey
33. Daly
34. Roberts
35. Canisius
36. IREPM
37. Connolly Carriage House
38. Murray Carriage House
39. Waul House
40. Murray
41. Connolly House
42. Haley
43. Haley Carriage House

General Information

Main Campus: 140 Commonwealth Ave,
                  Chestnut Hill, MA 02467
Newton Campus: 885 Centre St,
                  Newton Center, MA 02459
Phone: 617-552-8000
Website: www.bc.edu

Overview

It all began one day in Paris in 1534, when a group of students at the University of Paris got together and decided to combine their devotion to God with their commitment to bettering society. They called themselves the Society of Jesus, or the Jesuits. A few centuries later, in 1863, three Jesuits opened a college in the South End and cleverly named it Boston College. The college began with just 22 students, but even then the Jesuit profs envisioned a grander institution that would integrate intellectual development with religious and ethical growth.

Over the past century-and-a-half, the school has drifted a bit, both geographically and ethically. Once located in Boston proper, the school now sits six miles to the west, sprawling over 117 acres in Chestnut Hill and another 40 in Newton. And while the college is still officially Jesuit through and through, today's BC students aren't known for being particularly pious or devout.

BC's 9,000 undergraduates and 4,700 graduate students have a bit of a bad reputation among locals and students at other area colleges—the stereotype pegs all BC guys as binge-drinking jock wannabees sporting backwards baseball caps, more likely to be looking for a fight than searching for knowledge. It is widely rumored that the girls' appetite for Abercrombie & Fitch is matched only by their thirst for peach schnapps. Overlooked by naysayers is BC's excellent academic reputation. Its 8 colleges and schools offer degree programs in more than fifty fields of study, and *U.S. News & World Report* rated BC the 34th best college in the country. In 2003, two BC students were selected as Rhodes Scholars and a school-record of 14 Fulbright Grants were awarded to graduating seniors.

Tuition

For the 2007–2008 academic year, undergraduate tuition will amount to $37,690 with room and board an additional $1200 or so. Add on books, lab fees, and personal expenses. Graduate student tuition, fees, and expenses vary by college. However, approximately 65% of students receive financial aid.

Sports

Boston College has been hailed by *U.S. News & World Report* as having one of the top 20 overall college sports programs. Supporting 31 varsity and 38 club and intramural sports, the college boasts a diverse and strong athletic department. The varsity teams all compete at the NCAA Division I level. In 2007, the football team won the Meineke Car Care Bowl, making it BC's seventh consecutive bowl win. The biggest game every year is against Notre Dame. The men's hockey team has been perennially successful, winning the national championship in 2001 and losing in the semifinals of the Frozen Four in 2004. In 2008, however, Boston College won, much to the BU's chagrin. In 2008 Boston College won the Beanpot, which is a hockey tournament amongst Boston colleges.

Culture on Campus

The Robsham Theater Arts Center is Boston College's creative center. Built in 1981, the theater seats 591 people. The building also includes a black box theater that seats 150–200 people. The three main departments housed in the facility are the Department of Theater Arts, the Robsham Dance and Theater Company, and the Boston Liturgical Dance Ensemble. The university presents four faculty-directed and two student directed productions each year, and 20 musical and dance groups perform throughout the year. BC also has its share of improv and sketch comedy troupes including one that puts on comedic, part-improv murder mysteries once per semester. Worth checking out to get a better sense of the school's culture is the Web site for "The BC" (www.bc.edu/clubs/thebc/) a send-up of "The OC" that is set at the Heights (local-speak for BC's Chestnut Hill campus). Download one of the show's commercials such as "Jon Bon Jesuits" for an hysterical, rocking-good time.

Another source of culture at Boston College is the McMullen Museum of Art. Located on the first floor of Devlin Hall, the museum is housed in one of the many Neo-Gothic buildings on the main campus. Aside from its notable permanent collection, the museum has frequent exhibitions of international and scholarly importance from all periods and cultures. The museum is free and open to the public. Hours: Mon–Fri 11 am–4 pm and Sat–Sun 12 pm–5 pm.

Departments

Undergraduate Admissions 617-552-3100
A&S Graduate Admissions 617-552-3265
Carroll Graduate School of Management . . . 617-552-3920
Connell School of Nursing 617-552-4928
Law School Admissions 617-552-4350
Lynch School of Education 617-552-4214
Graduate School of Social Work 617-552-4024
Student Services 617-552-3300
. . . . 800-294-0294
Athletic Departments and Tickets 617-552-GoBC
O'Neill Library 617-552-4470

General Information

NFT Map: 16
Address: One Sherborn St, Boston, MA 02215
Phone: 617-353-2000
Website: www.bu.edu

Overview

If you really want to go to school *in* Boston, BU is the school for you. Consisting of a strip of buildings along Commonwealth Avenue, BU's campus doesn't win any points for style, beauty, or landscape architecture (since that would require having a clearly defined landscape). Aside from several thousand red banners on the lampposts that say "Boston University," and a larger than usual concentration of jaywalking young folk along Comm Ave, there's little indication that you've even entered BU's domain.

The fourth-largest private university in the country, the school's "campus" is the learning center for all students and the residence of many of its 30,000 undergraduates and grad students. The upshot of the ill-defined BU campus is that its students are truly living in the city. BU students make the best of the little green space they have. "The Beach," a strip of greenery on the inbound side of Storrow Drive (which runs along the Charles), is a springtime hotspot for socializing and sunbathing.

When the university was founded in 1839, it was intended to be a theological school for ministers of the Methodist Episcopal Church. As the years went by, the university expanded its curriculum in order to accommodate the needs and interests of its growing student population. Today, there are 11 schools and colleges and over 250 different degree programs. Boston University students represent all 50 states, as well as 140 countries. BU also holds the distinction of having the most property owned by a non-government institution in the City of Boston. The university also boasts a bevy of outspoken alumni including Howard Stern, Bill O'Reilly, and Rosie O'Donnell (who didn't graduate).

Longtime president and infamous curmudgeon John Silber stepped down in 1996 after more than thirty years of leading the school to wherever he pleased. His replacement, former NASA chief Daniel Goldin, was called off the job even before he began his first day due to conflicting ideas about how the university should be run. Goldin said he took the job on the condition that Silber would not occupy a seat on the board of trustees. The Executive Committee balked at this stipulation and, after a little mud was slung, Goldin's termination was signed, thereby embarrassing the university in national headlines. Following the reign of an interim president since the resignation of Jon Westling in 2002, BU's tenth and current president, Robert A. Brown, was inaugurated to the post in April 2006.

Tuition

Undergraduate tuition costs run at about $35,418 per year with room and board an additional $10,950. Add on books, lab fees, and personal expenses. Graduate student tuition, fees, and expenses vary by college.

Sports

Notwithstanding the termination of the university's football program in 1997, the Terriers have quite an impressive athletics department. With 24 NCAA Division I varsity sports, Boston University provides a rich environment for sports lovers. The department prides itself on its equal emphasis on women's and men's varsity sports. The men's varsity ice hockey team is, by far, the most popular sports team at BU, with the most enthusiastic community support. There is fierce competition every year for the Beanpot—the "New England Invitational" tournament. In the past 53 years, BU has won the Beanpot 28 times, with Boston College being their biggest rival for the title. The university's hockey and basketball teams play in the Agganis Arena, a spiffy new facility that also hosts other sporting and entertainment events.

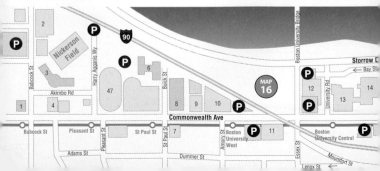

Culture on Campus

The first university to have a music program, BU remains committed to the arts. The Boston University Art Gallery is located at 855 Commonwealth Avenue. Although the gallery has no permanent collection, the architecture of the building is like an exhibit unto itself. Alluding to both the Classical and the Medieval, the columns that adorn the façade are a rare beauty and have attracted many people on that basis alone. You would never guess that the building is actually a converted Buick dealership. If this piques your interest, you'll be happy to learn that the gallery is open and free to the public, but only during the academic school year: Tues–Fri 10 am–5 pm and Sat–Sun 1 pm–5 pm.

Departments

Undergraduate Admissions	617-353-2300
Graduate Admissions	617-353-2696
Graduate School of Management	617-353-9720
School of Medicine	617-638-4630
School of Law	617-353-3100
School of Education	617-353-4237
School of Public Health	617-638-4610
School of Social Work	617-353-3765
Athletic Department and Ticket Office	617-353-GoBU
Mugar Memorial Library	617-353-3732

Building Legend

1. 1019 Commonwealth Ave (major residence)
2. Case Athletic Center
3. West Campus (major residence)
4. Office of Housing
5. Fitness and Recreation Center
6. 10 Buick St (major residence)
7. Center for English Language and Orientation Programs
8. Comptroller; Financial Assistance; Registrar; Student Health Services
9. College of General Studies
10. College of Fine Arts; University Art Gallery
11. School of Hospitality Administration; Metropolitan College Academic departments and other programs
12. Boston University Academy
13. George Sherman Union; Dean of Students; Student Activities Center; Howard Thurman Center
14. Mugar Memorial Library;University Information Center
15. School of Law
16. Metropolitan College; Summer Term
17. School of Theology; University Professors Program
18. Marsh Chapel
19. Photonics Center
20. College of Arts and Sciences
21. School of Social Work
22. Graduate School of Arts and Sciences
23. The Tsai Performance Art Center
24. The Castle
25. Warren Towers (major residence)
26. Office of Information Technology
27. College of Engineering
28. Sargent College of Health and Rehabilitation Sciences
29. College of Communication
30. School of Education
31. Morse Auditorium
32. Biological and Physics Research Buildings
33. The Towers (major residence)
34. Chancellor's Office; President's Office; Provost's Office; Development and Alumni Relations
35. School of Management
36. 575 Commonwealth Ave (major residence)
37. Metcalf Science Center
38. Admissions Reception Center
39. Kenmore Classroom Building
40. Shelton Hall (major residence)
41. International Students and Scholars Office; Career Services; Disability Services; Judicial Affairs & Student Safety
42. University Computers
43. Barnes & Noble at BU; Asian Archeology & Cultural History
44. Hotel Commonwealth
45. Miles Standish Hall (major residence)
46. Danielsen Hall (major residence) (off map)
47. Agganis Arena

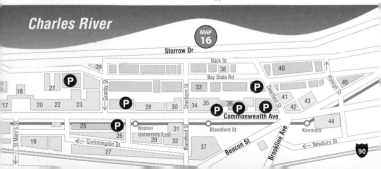

1. Ansin Building
2. Cutler Majestic Theatre
3. Little Building
4. Walker Building
5. Tufte Performance and Production Center
6. Student Campus Center
7. Student Residence
8. Student Union
9. Student Residence
10. Student Residence
11. Piano Row Residence

General Information

NFT Maps:	3 & 6
Address:	120 Boylston St, Boston, MA 02116
Phone:	617-824-8500
Website:	www.emerson.edu

Overview

Emerson College is the country's only comprehensive college or university dedicated solely to communication and the arts in a liberal arts context. In close proximity to Boston's Theater District, Emerson is near all of the city's major media interests. Founded as a small oratory school in 1880, Emerson has expanded its curriculum over the years to include other forms of communication. Today, Emerson specializes in communications, marketing, communication sciences and disorders, journalism, the performing arts, the visual and media arts, and writing, literature, and publishing. Emerson also operates semester-study programs in Los Angeles and the Netherlands. There is also a thriving continuing education department, recently renamed the Department of Professional Studies and Special Programs, which offers—besides communications classes—certificate programs in media, publishing, and screenwriting.

The college enrolls about 3,000 full-time undergraduates and 1,000 graduate students, many of whom can be found sporting funky haircuts and smoking outside Emerson buildings between classes. Students take pride in their award-winning radio station, WERS (88.9 FM). Most alumni go on to pursue careers in the communications and entertainment fields. Notable alumni include talk show host Jay Leno, actor Denis Leary, and entrepreneur and make-up artist Bobbi Brown.

Tuition

In the 2007–2008 academic year, undergraduate tuition fees were $26,880. Room and board costs about $11,376. Add on books, service fees, activity fees, and personal expenses. Graduate student tuition, fees, and expenses vary by the number of credits taken.

Sports

Although Emerson does have an athletic department, it has never been one of the school's top priorities. Since most of the students attending Emerson College are interested primarily in the fields of communications and performing arts, sports are considered nothing more than a lighthearted diversion. Still, Emerson College sponsors 13 men's and women's varsity teams that compete in the NCAA's Division III.

Culture on Campus

Because Emerson considers itself an arts school, it takes great pride in its theater. The aptly named Majestic Theatre was built in 1903 as an opera house. In 2001, the college closed the theater temporarily for renovation and reopened its doors in 2003. Today, the historic venue seats 1,200 people and has become an integral part of the campus. Not only does it provide a venue for all types of productions by Emerson students, it also serves the greater New England community. It hosts more operas than any other theater in New England and is the top stop for most touring dance companies. To visit the theater or check out a performance, go to the theater box office located at 219 Tremont Street in Boston or call 617-824-8000.

Departments

Undergraduate Admissions Office	617-824-8600
Graduate Admissions Office	617-824-8610
Majestic Theatre	617-824-8000
	or 800-233-3123
Athletics Department	617-824-8690
Fitness Center	617-824-8692
Library	617-824-8668

Mt Vernon St

Dorchester Bay

MAP 32

UMass-Boston

JFK Library

PAGE 210

To Morrissey Blvd
JFK/UMass
T Stop

University Dr W

University Dr N

Columbia Pl

Clark Athletic Center

Quinn Admin

Massachusetts State Archives/ Commonwealth Museum

Healey Library

Science Center

Site of Student Center

University Dr S

McCormack

University Dr E

Wheatley (CCDE Office)

General Information

NFT Map: 32
Address: 100 Morrissey Blvd, Boston, MA 02125
Phone: 617-287-5000
Website: www.umb.edu

Overview

The University of Massachusetts Boston is one of five UMass campuses. The campus opened in 1982 when UMass acquired Boston State College. The university has been described as a sensibly priced, high-quality college that provides excellent academic programs to people from all walks of life. UMass Boston aims "to bring technical, intellectual, and human resources to the community."

The school's most famous alum is Boston Mayor Thomas M. Menino. Not exactly renowned for his oratory skills, he is nevertheless a well respected champion of the low-income neighborhoods. Menino graduated from UMass Boston at the age of 45 in 1988 with a degree in community planning. UMass Boston's campus, which has been described as a "concrete jungle," is only three miles from downtown Boston and is pretty easy to reach by public transportation. (Take the Red Line to JFK/UMass Station, then jump on the shuttle buses, which run almost constantly.)

While on campus, be sure to check out the Campus Center—simply look for the most modern-looking (and attractive) building on campus. A graceful building featuring huge windows that overlook magnificent Boston Harbor, the Center makes it easy to forget that the rest of the campus is pockmarked by bomb-shelteresque architecture. Also, a trip to campus should always include a quick walk or drive over to the JFK Presidential Library, which shares Columbia Point Peninsula with UMASS Boston.

Tuition

Recent controversial tuition hikes have put undergraduate tuition costs at about $22,068 per year for out-of-towners and $10,249 for in-state residents. Graduate tuition costs run at about $22,081 per year for out-of-towners and $11,574 for in-state residents.

Sports

The University of Massachusetts Boston offers 14 varsity sports, including basketball, soccer, lacrosse, and ice hockey. All teams compete in the NCAA's Division III. The Beacon Fitness Center is open to all students and staff free of charge. The UMass teams are called the Beacons, carry the slogan "Follow the Light," and have been named All-Americans 64 times in seven sports. UMass Boston provides a community service program which offers, for free or at very low cost, the use of all athletic facilities and coaches to the general public.

Culture on Campus

Often considered a commuter-centric school, UMass Boston is nonetheless a mini-mecca of culture, offering everything from rampant community-service opportunities to myriad student-run publications. The current Performing Arts Department is actually a conglomerate of three previously separate theater arts, music, and dance departments. Music courses provide grounding in music theory, history, and performance. Private music lessons are also available for one credit. The college Jazz Band, Chamber Orchestra, and Chamber Singers all give public performances at the end of each semester.

Departments

Undergraduate Admissions........................ 617-287-6100
Graduate Admissions 617-287-5700
Graduate College of Education 617-287-7600
College of Nursing & Health Sciences 617-287-7500
Performing Arts Department 617-287-5640
Athletic Department 617-287-7801
Healey Library 617-287-5900
Honors Program 617-287-5520
Campus Center 617-287-4800

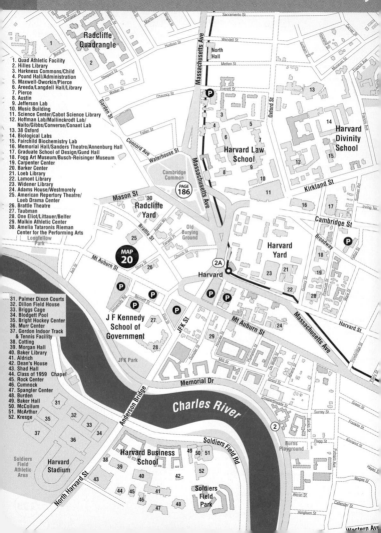

1. Quad Athletic Facility
2. Hilles Library
3. Harkness Commons/Child
4. Pound Hall/Administration
5. Maxwell-Dworkin/Pierce
6. Areeda/Langdell Hall/Library
7. Pierce
8. Austin
9. Jefferson Lab
10. Music Building
11. Science Center/Cabot Science Library
12. Hoffman Lab/Mallinckrodt Lab/
    Naito/Gibbs/Converse/Conant Lab
13. 38 Oxford
14. Biological Labs
15. Fairchild Biochemistry Lab
16. Memorial Hall/Sanders Theatre/Annenburg Hall
17. Graduate School of Design/Gund Hall
18. Fogg Art Museum/Busch-Reisinger Museum
19. Carpenter Center
20. Barker Center
21. Loeb Library
22. Lamont Library
23. Widener Library
24. Adams House/Westmorely
25. American Repertory Theatre/
    Loeb Drama Center
26. Brattle Theatre
27. Taubman
28. One Eliot/Littauer/Belfer
29. Malkin Athletic Center
30. Amelia Tataronis Rieman
    Center for the Performing Arts

31. Palmer Dixon Courts
32. Dillon Field House
33. Briggs Cage
34. Blodgett Pool
35. Bright Hockey Center
36. Murr Center
37. Gordon Indoor Track
    & Tennis Facility
38. Cotting
39. Morgan Hall
40. Baker Library
41. Aldrich
42. Dean's House
43. Shad Hall
44. Class of 1959 Chapel
45. Rock Center
46. Cumnock
47. Spangler Center
48. Burden
49. Baker Hall
50. McCollum
51. McArthur
52. Kresge

Radcliffe Quadrangle

Radcliffe Yard

Harvard Law School

Harvard Divinity School

Harvard Yard

J F Kennedy School of Government

Harvard Business School

Harvard Stadium

Soldiers Field Athletic Area

Soldiers Field Park

Burns Playground

Charles River

Longfellow Park

Cambridge Common

Old Burying Ground

JFK Park

PAGE 186

MAP 20

General Information

NFT Map: 20
Address: University Hall, Cambridge, MA 02138
Phone: 617-495-1000
Website: www.harvard.edu

Overview

You've probably heard quite a bit about Harvard. Chances are, you associate it with academic excellence, cutting-edge research, red brick, and students with at least two roman numerals after their names.

That stereotype hits the nail at least partly on the head. Founded in 1636, Harvard remains the richest and most revered university in the country (and perhaps even the world). True to myth, its pool of 19,000+ undergrads and grad students include children of royalty, famous actors, heirs, heiresses, and an assortment of other fortunate sons and daughters. But the truth is that these folks are more the exception than the rule. Harvard's deep pockets have allowed it to offer generous scholarships and increase the cultural and financial diversity of its student population (and to allow such great intellectuals like Conan O'Brien to attend). The same loot also helps them net world-class professors in each of its 11 schools and colleges.

With the goal of properly housing and educating "the best of the best" in all fields from arts and humanities to business and technology, Harvard is hungry for more than just talented minds. The university continues to gobble up land in Cambridge and across the river in Allston, disgruntling some locals.

Perhaps Harvard needs more space for its livestock. A phrase coined to mock the local accent states that you cannot "pahk the cah in Havahd Yahd," since automobile traffic is prohibited there. However, an old contract clause allows each full professor to pasture one cow in the Yard. Assistant faculty members are allowed a sheep. Luckily for Harvard, no professor in recent memory has taken advantage of this opportunity.

In early 2007, Harvard made news yet again by naming its first female president, historian Drew G. Faust.

Tuition

For the 2007–2008 academic year, undergraduate tuition, room, board, and college fees amounted to $45,620. Graduate school tuition varies depending on the program.

Sports

Athletics at Harvard began around 1780, when a small group of students began challenging each other to wrestling matches, thereby starting an early version of *Fight Club*. Since then, the spirit of athletic competition has remained integral to the Harvard experience. Harvard introduced its crew team in 1844, and won its first championship just two years later. Since then, the men's heavyweight and lightweight crew teams have won 15 championships between them and the women's lightweight crew team has won five championships. Years ago, Harvard was a football powerhouse, always ranked among the top ten in the nation. Harvard still consistently tops the Ivy League, and games against the likes of Yale continue to fill century-old Harvard Stadium on fall afternoons. The men's tennis team has also been a source of pride in the athletic department, consistently producing top-class players, many of whom have gone on to play professionally. In the fall of 2004, the team captured their second consecutive Eastern College Athletic Conference title.

Not all jocks are dumb: Since 1920, Harvard athletes have netted 45 Rhodes Scholarships.

Not all nerds suck at sports: More than 100 Harvard athletes have participated in the Olympics.

Culture on Campus

Harvard boasts four art museums (free every day after 4:30 pm and from 10 am until noon on Saturdays), each showcasing art from different parts of the world. The university also runs an extensive music and theater program. Music department performances are held in the prestigious Sanders Theater, renowned for its acoustics and design. Aside from hosting most of the orchestral and choral performances by Harvard groups, Sanders Theatre is also a popular venue for professional groups such as the Boston Philharmonic, the Boston Chamber Music Society, and the Boston Baroque.

Harvard's various dance troupes perform at the Amelia Tataronis Rieman Center for the Performing Arts.

The country's only not-for-profit theater company housing a resident acting company and an international training conservatory, the American Repertory Theater (A.R.T.) operates out of the Harvard University campus.

A building shaped suspiciously like "Linguo, the Grammar Robot" of *Simpsons* fame houses the offices of the Harvard Lampoon on Mt Auburn Street. Graduates of this famed humor publication have gone on to work for *Saturday Night Live*, *The Simpsons*, and *The Office*.

Departments

Undergraduate Admissions 617-495-1551
Graduate School of Arts and Sciences 617-495-1814
Graduate School of Education 617-495-0740
Kennedy School of Government 617-495-1100
Harvard Crimson 617-576-6565
Harvard Law School 617-495-3100
Harvard Medical School 617-432-1000
Harvard Business School 617-495-6000
Athletics Department Ticket Office 877-GO-HARVARD
or 617-495-2211
Sanders Theatre 617-496-2222

General Information

NFT Maps: 26 & 27
Address: 77 Massachusetts Ave, Cambridge, MA 02139
Phone: 617-253-1000
Website: www.mit.edu

Overview

Just down the Chuck River from Harvard, MIT is one of the top tech schools in the world. The school's 998 faculty and over 10,000 slide-rule-bearing graduate and undergraduate students inhabit a 168-acre "factory of learning" that features both neoclassical domes and some of the most aggressively modernist buildings in Boston (including the Stata Center, designed by world-renowned architect Frank Gehry).

MIT profs are infamous for assigning massive amounts of work, but some students can't seem to get enough of engineering, spending their downtime planning and executing "hacks,"

technically elaborate pranks. A frequent target of hackers is MIT's Great Dome. In 1994, a replica of an MIT police cruiser appeared atop the dome. In 1996, it was adorned with a gigantic beanie cap complete with a fully functioning propeller. Just before the release of Star Wars Episode One: The Phantom Menace, students decorated the dome to look like the robot R2-D2. Harvard is another frequent target of hackers. During a 1990 Harvard-Yale football game, players and spectators alike were surprised when an 8.5' x 3.5' rocket-propelled banner with the letters MIT sprang up from under the end zone as Yale lined up to kick a field goal.

Tuition

In the 2007–08 academic year, undergraduate tuition fees cost $34,986. Room and board totaled $10,400.

Sports

Whoever said science nerds can't play sports was totally right. Nevertheless, they keep trying, posting moderate success in both

1. Pierce Laboratory
2. Fluid Dynamic Laboratory/ Dept of Mathematics
3. Maclaurin Buildings
4. Maclaurin Buildings
5. Pratt School
6. Eastman Laboratories
6B. Solvent Storage
7. Rogers Building
8. 21 Ames Street
9. Center for Advanced Educational Services
10. Maclaurin Building/Alumni Center
11. Homberg Building
12. 60 Vassar Street
12A. Waste Chemical Storage
13. Bush Building
15. Hayden Memorial Library
16. Dorrance Building
17. Wright Brothers Wind Tunnel
18. Dreyfus Building
24. CANES/Center for Nanofluids Technology ESG/Dept of Nuclear Science and Engineering
26. Compton Laboratories
31. Sloan Laboratories
32. State Center
33. Guggenheim Laboratory
34. EG & G Education Center
35. Sloan Laboratory
36. Fairchild Building

37. McNair Building
38. Fairchild Building
39. Brown Building
41. Lean Aerospace Initiative/ Fuel Cell Lab
42. Power Plant
43. Power Plant Annex
44. Cyclotron
46. Brain and Cognitive Sciences
48. Parsons Laboratory
50. Walker Memorial
51. Wood Sailing Pavilion
54. Green Building
56. Whitaker Building
57. MIT Alumni Pool
63. Alumni Houses: Munroe Hayden Wood
64. Alumni Houses: Walcott Bemis Goodale

66. Landau Building
68. Koch Biology Building
E1. Gray House
E2. Senior House
E15. Wiesner Building
E17. Mudd Building
E18. Ford Building
E19. Ford Building
E23. Health Services
E25. Whitaker College
E28. Publishing Services Bureau (PSB)/Reference Publications Office (RPO)
E33. Rinaldi Tile

E34. Earth Resources Li
E38. Suffolk Building
E39. MIT Press
E40. Muckley Building
E48. MIT Investment Ma Company
E51. Tang Center
E52. Sloan Building
E53. Hermann Building

Division II and III. Believe it or not, MIT actually boasts the largest number of NCAA-sponsored programs in the nation, and the coaches and students have received numerous awards for sports excellence. The heavyweight crew squads and the men's cross-country and track teams have garnered accolades for the university.

Culture on Campus

In a time when art and technology are often indistinguishable, it's not hard to believe that MIT has a happening arts program, too. We highly recommend a visit to the MIT Museum. Holographic images, scientific photographs, and mechanical sculptures with names like "Untitled Fragile Machine" show just how beautiful math-type stuff can be.

The Weisner Building (designed by I.M. Pei and housing the Media Laboratory) opened in 1985 and was used, for much of its first decade, to explore digital video and multimedia. The Media Lab allows for interdisciplinary research, and the developing focus of study is on how electronic information affects our daily lives—how we use it to think, express, and communicate ideas.

Many of the Media Lab's research projects are made possible through corporate sponsorship, and the lab fosters a positive relationship between academia and industry.

According to the MIT website, the Media Lab "houses a gigabit fiber-optic plant that connects a heterogeneous network of computers, ranging from fine-grained, embedded processors to supercomputers." Unfortunately, in its role as an academic research laboratory, the Media Lab is not able to accommodate visits from the general public.

Departments

Undergraduate Admissions	617-253-4791
Graduate Admissions	617-253-2917
School of Humanities, Arts, and Social Sciences	617-253-3450
School of Engineering	617-253-3291
School of Science	617-253-8900
Sloan School of Management	617-253-2659
Office of the Arts	617-253-4003
Athletic Department	617-253-4498

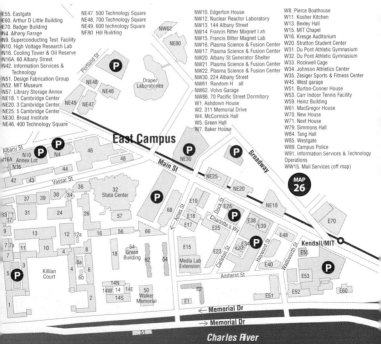

NE55. Eastgate
NE60. Arthur D Little Building
NE70. Badger Building
N9. Superconducting Test Facility
N10. High Voltage Research Lab
N16. Cooling Tower & Oil Reserve
N16A. 60 Albany Street
N42. Information Services & Technology
NE18. 1 Cambridge Center
NE20. 3 Cambridge Center
NE25. 5 Cambridge Center
NE30. Broad Institute
NE46. 400 Technology Square
NE47. 500 Technology Square
NE48. 700 Technology Square
NE49. 600 technology Square
NE80. Hill Building

NW10. Edgerton House
NW12. Nuclear Reactor Laboratory
NW13. 144 Albany Street
NW14. Francis Bitter Magnet Lab
NW15. Francis Bitter Magnet Lab
NW16. Plasma Science & Fusion Center
NW17. Plasma Science & Fusion Center
NW20. Albany St Generator Shelter
NW21. Plasma Science & Fusion Center
NW22. Plasma Science & Fusion Center
NW30. 224 Albany Street
NW61. Random H all
NW62. Volvo Garage
NW86. 70 Pacific Street Dormitory
W1. Ashdown House
W2. 311 Memorial Drive
W4. McCormick Hall
W5. Green Hall
W7. Baker House

W8. Pierce Boathouse
W11. Kosher Kitchen
W13. Bexley Hall
W15. MIT Chapel
W16. Kresge Auditorium
W20. Stratton Student Center
W31. Du Pont Athletic Gymnasium
W32. Du Pont Athletic Gymnasium
W33. Rockwell Cage
W34. Johnson Athletics Center
W35. Zesiger Sports & Fitness Center
W45. West garage
W51. Burton-Conner House
W53. Carr Indoor Tennis Facility
W59. Heinz Building
W61. MacGregor House
W70. New House
W71. Next House
W79. Simmons Hall
W84. Tang Hall
W85. Westgate
W89. Campus Police
W91. Information Services & Technology Operations
WW15. Mail Services (off map)

Northeastern University

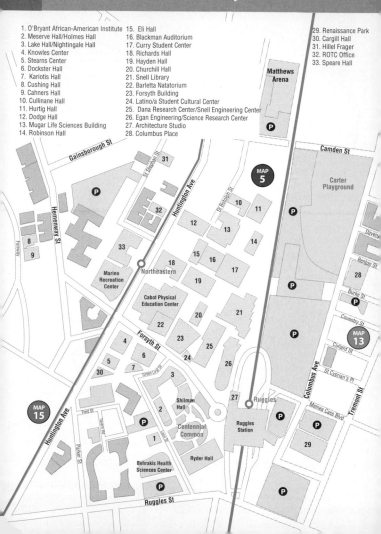

1. O'Bryant African-American Institute
2. Meserve Hall/Holmes Hall
3. Lake Hall/Nightingale Hall
4. Knowles Center
5. Stearns Center
6. Dockster Hall
7. Kariotis Hall
8. Cushing Hall
9. Cahners Hall
10. Cullinane Hall
11. Hurtig Hall
12. Dodge Hall
13. Mugar Life Sciences Building
14. Robinson Hall
15. Eli Hall
16. Blackman Auditorium
17. Curry Student Center
18. Richards Hall
19. Hayden Hall
20. Churchill Hall
21. Snell Library
22. Barletta Natatorium
23. Forsyth Building
24. Latino/a Student Cultural Center
25. Dana Research Center/Snell Engineering Center
26. Egan Engineering/Science Research Center
27. Architecture Studio
28. Columbus Place
29. Renaissance Park
30. Cargill Hall
31. Hillel Frager
32. ROTC Office
33. Speare Hall

General Information

NFT Maps: 5, 13 & 15
Address: 360 Huntington Ave, Boston, MA 02115
Phone: 617-373-2000
Website: www.northeastern.edu

Overview

Northeastern University has come a long way from being a commuter school with a fairly unimpressive urban campus. In recent years, the university has emerged as an important national research institution with sparkly new academic, athletic, and residential facilities. NU originally began as a five-year school with an academic model called "Practice-Oriented Education," a program that combines education and internships (co-op) and is alternatively dubbed "real-life learning" by school officials. The school added more four- and five-year options, along with online study for a number of degrees. Northeastern University is ranked 98th among the nation's top 500 universities by *U.S. News & World Report.*

Founded in 1898 as a part-time night school, Northeastern is located on more than 67 acres along Huntington Avenue and served by three Green Line E train stops. The current enrollment at NU is approximately 15,000 full-time undergraduate students and around 4,800 graduate students with a male-to-female ratio that is pretty evenly matched. However, cultural diversity isn't something for which the university is known. The most popular degree programs on offer are in Business, Health, and Engineering/Technology. The now 20-year-old University Honors Program is also a big draw for potential undergrads.

Tuition

Undergraduate tuition costs run at about $31,500 per year with room and board adding up to an additional $11,010. Books, lab fees, and personal expenses are, as always, extra. Graduate student tuition and fees vary by college, as do individual online courses.

Sports

The Northeastern Huskies compete in Division I with varsity teams in nine men's and ten women's sports. The school's various teams had their finest collective performance ever in the 2002-03 season. The Huskies sent four teams to the NCAA playoffs and won a total of seven conference titles—Northeastern's most ever in both categories.

Culture on Campus

While Northeastern University doesn't offer much in the way of the arts, it is located in a prime spot for cultural enrichment. Huntington Avenue, also known as "Avenue of the Arts," runs through the urban campus, making it easy to visit the neighborhood museums. Among the most notable are the Isabella Stewart Gardner Museum, a ten-minute walk from the center of campus, and the Museum of Fine Arts (page 326), a four-minute walk from the main quad. Massachusetts College of Art is also located just a few T stops away and Symphony Hall (Boston Pops, anyone?) is next door. Thai, soul food, and pizza abound—whether you walk or T it, you can hit anywhere from five to infinite restaurants with one stone.

For on-campus entertainment, AfterHOURS, the campus's late-night club, welcomes various musical acts, ranging from local unknowns to bigger names like Gavin DeGraw. Additionally, the Curry Student Center is a magnet for Huskies in search of a bite (the Food Court includes everything from a salad bar to a Taco Bell) or an e-mail fix.

Departments

Admissions 617-373-2200
(TTY) 617-373-3768
Library. 617-373-2350
Registrar. 617-373-2300
Athletics Department 617-373-2672
Athletics Ticket Office 617-373-4700

Undergraduate:
Admissions 617-373-2200
College of Arts & Sciences 617-373-3980
Bouvé College of Health Sciences. 617-373-3321
College of Business Administration . . . 617-373-3270
College of Computer & 617-373-2462
Information Science
College of Criminal Justice 617-373-3327
College of Engineering 617-373-2152
School of Engineering Technology. . . . 617-373-7777
School of Nursing 617-373-3649

Graduate:
Bouvé College of Health Sciences. . .617-373-2708
College of Arts & Sciences 617-373-3982
College of Business Administration .617-373-5992
College of Computer & 617-373-2464
Information Science
College of Criminal Justice 617-373-3327
College of Engineering 617-373-2711
Law School 617-373-2395
School of Professional & 617-373-2400
Continuing Studies

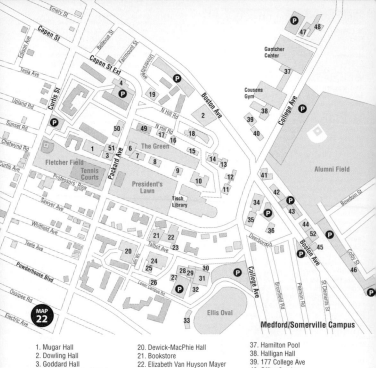

1. Mugar Hall
2. Dowling Hall
3. Goddard Hall
4. Granhoff Family Hillel Center
5. Dana Lab
7. Barnum Hall
8. Ballou Hall
9. Goddard Chapel
10. Eaton Hall
11. Miner Hall
12. Paige Hall
13. Lincoln-Filene Center
14. Braker Hall
15. East Hall
16. Packard Hall
17. Bendelson Hall
18. Central Heating Plant
19. Lane Hall

20. Dewick-MacPhie Hall
21. Bookstore
22. Elizabeth Van Huyson Mayer Campus Center
23. 55 Talbot Ave
24. Pearson Chemical Laboratory
25. Michael Lab
26. Academic Computing Building
27. Costume Shop
28. Jackson Gym
29. Baltch Arena Theatre
30. Remis Sculpture/ Leir Hall
31. Cohen Auditorium
32. Aidekman Arts Center
33. Baronian Field House
34. Anderson Hall
35. Robinson Hall
36. Bromfield-Pearson

37. Hamilton Pool
38. Halligan Hall
39. 177 College Ave
40. Office Services
41. Curtis Hall
42. Psychology Building
43. Bray Laboratory
44. Central Services
45. Bacon Hall
46. Science and Technology Center
47. Eliot-Pearson Child Development Center
48. Eliot-Pearson Children's School
49. West Hall
50. Olin Center
51. Cabot Center
52. Scene Shop

General Information

NFT Map:	22
Tufts Admin Building:	169 Holland St, Somerville, MA 02144
Medford/Somerville Campus:	Medford, MA 02155
Boston Campus:	136 Harrison Ave, Boston, MA 02111
North Grafton Campus:	200 Westboro Rd, North Grafton, MA 01536
Tufts General Phone:	617-628-5000
Website:	www.tufts.edu

Overview

There's a perception that Tufts is a school for kids who didn't get into Harvard, just two Red Line stops away. This is (mostly) not true. Tufts possesses academic prowess in its own right, especially in its engineering, veterinary, international relations, and science departments. The Fletcher School is the country's oldest graduate school of international affairs, and its prestige and strong curriculum draw students from across the globe. To boot, Tufts boasts a kick-ass study-abroad program (pick a continent, any continent) and a laudable community-service focus.

The university has three campuses. The main Medford/Somerville campus is where approximately 5,500 students, mostly liberal arts undergrads, live and learn. The Medford/Somerville campus also houses the School of Engineering, the Graduate School of Arts and Sciences, and the School of Special Studies. Tufts prides itself on diversity: A whole center is devoted to lesbian, gay, bisexual, and transgender students, and on any given day the "viewpoints" section of The Tufts Daily—the school's impressive and professional-looking student newspaper—will have several pieces about the LGBT community. As touchy-feely as campus politics may be, though, academics remain pretty hardcore.

The centrally located Boston campus houses the School of Medicine, School of Dental Medicine, Sackler School of Graduate Biomedical Sciences, Jean Mayer USDA Human Nutrition Research Center on Aging, and The Gerald J. and Dorothy R. Friedman School of Nutrition Science and Policy.

Tuition

In the 2007–2008 academic year, undergraduate tuition fees totaled $36,700. Room and board cost an additional $10,160. Books, service fees, activity fees, and personal expenses are extra. Graduate student tuition, fees, and expenses vary by college.

Sports

If you ever find yourself at Tufts University and, more specifically, in the office of the Athletic Director, you might notice a peanut butter jar with ashes in it. Don't be frightened; it's only Jumbo. Jumbo is the elephant mascot of Tufts University. P.T. Barnum, of the Barnum and Bailey Circus, was one of the University's original trustees. His prize act was an elephant named Jumbo, who was hit by a train and killed in 1885. His stuffed body was donated to Tufts, where it was stored in a museum on campus that eventually became a student lounge. Sadly, however, the museum burned in 1975 and Jumbo went up with it. The ashes in the jar are said to be those of Jumbo, though university officials say they have no evidence that is the case. Luckily, they have his tail in a cardboard folder in their archives. (Extra trivia fun: Jumbo also has the honor of being the only mascot mentioned in Webster's. Take that, Ivy Leaguers.)

If that isn't enough to attract you to the sports, then maybe the recent successes of the golf and women's sailing teams will pique your interest.

There's also an old campus joke: "What's Brown and Blue and loses every weekend?" Answer: "The Tufts football team." It's not really funny, but often accurate.

Culture on Campus

If sports aren't your thing, cultural activities are plentiful at Tufts. In the Aidekman Arts Center on the Medford/Somerville campus, you'll find the Tufts University Art Gallery. Again, the mantra seems to be diversity, diversity, and more diversity. The Gallery's mission is to explore art through all of its cultural complexities.

Over 70 students make up the Tufts Symphony Orchestra, which performs regularly throughout the school year. A capella groups abound, ranging from all-male to all-Jewish. The Department of Drama and Dance is where all of the performing artists can be found. Its students—a tight-knit, talented group— perform regularly at the Balch Arena Theater. Lately, though, music has been taking center stage on the Medford Campus: In February 2007, the $27-million, 55,000-square-foot Granoff Music Center opened to campus-wide accolades.

Departments

Undergraduate Admissions	617-627-3170
Graduate and Professional Studies	617-627-3395
The Fletcher School	617-627-3040
School of Medicine	617-636-7000
School of Dental Medicine	617-636-6828
Sackler School of Graduate Biomedical Sciences	617-636-6767
School of Nutrition Science and Policy	617-636-3737
School of Veterinary Medicine	508-839-5302
School of Engineering	617-627-3237
Athletics Department and Ticket Office	617-627-3232
Balch Arena Theater	617-627-3524
Tufts Symphony Orchestra	617-627-4042
Tisch Library	617-627-3460

Continuing Education in Boston

Harvard, MIT, Boston College…the city of Boston has long been associated with academic achievement. But even if you're not ready to matriculate at one of the city's famed institutions of higher learning, Boston is a great place to learn everything and anything from basic Arabic to authentic Italian cooking.

For those looking to change careers—or simply get ahead in a current position—many of the area's renowned schools offer continuing education or professional development classes. Tuition at Harvard Extension School is very reasonable and comes with unbeatable name recognition. Even community colleges like North Shore Community College, Bunker Hill, and Quincy College (Red line accessible) offer credited and non-credited courses from everything like computers to feng shui

Those who are feeling less cerebral can try gymnastics at Cambridge's Jam'nastics or take a golf lesson at CityGolf. Got an urge to indulge your creative side? Explore painting or sculpture with a studio art class at the MFA or learn the craft of glass-blowing at Diablo Glass and Metal.

Adrenaline junkies can hop the commuter rail and head out to Trapeze School, hidden in the Jordan's Furniture complex in suburban Reading.

Continuing Education and Professional Development

Boston College Woods College of Advancing Studies, www.bc.edu, 617-552-3900, 140 Commonwealth Ave, Chestnut Hill

Boston Language Institute, www.bostonlanguage.com, 617-262-3500, 648 Beacon St, Boston

Boston University Metropolitan College, www.bu.edu/met, 617-353-6000, 755 Commonwealth Ave, Boston

Bunker Hill Community College, www.bhcc.mass.edu/, 617-228-2000, 250 New Rutherford Ave, Boston

Harvard Extension, www.dce.harvard.edu/extension, 617-495-4024, 51 Brattle St, Cambridge

MIT, www.mit.edu/education/professional, 617-253-1000, 77 Massachusetts Ave, Cambridge

North Shore Community College, www.northshore.edu/, 978-762-4000, 1 Ferncroft Rd, Danvers

Northeastern University, www.ace.neu.edu, 617-373-2000, 360 Huntington Ave, Boston

Quincy College, www.quincycollege.edu/, 617-984-1700, 150 Newport Ave, Quincy

Little Bit of Everything

Boston Center for Adult Education, www.bcae.org, 617-267-4430, 5 Commonwealth Ave, Boston

Cambridge Center for Adult Education, www.ccae.org, 617-547-6789, 42 Brattle St, Cambridge

Arts and Lifestyle

Beadworks, www.beadworksboston.com, 617-247-7227, 167 Newbury St, Boston and 617-868-9777, 23 Church St, Cambridge

Boston Wine Tasting Classes, www.invinoveritas.com, 617-784-7150, 1354 Commonwealth Ave, Allston

Cambridge School of Culinary Arts, www.cambridgeculinary.com, 617-354-2020, 2020 Massachusetts Ave, Cambridge

Diablo Glass and Metal, www.diablo glassandmetal.com, 617-442-7444, 123 Terrace St, Boston

Grub Street Writing Center, www.grubstreet.org, 617-695-0075, 160 Boylston St, Boston

Massachusetts College of Art, www.massart.edu, 617-879-7000, 621 Huntington Ave, Boston

Mudville Pottery Classes, www.nanhamilton.com/mudville/mudville/, 617-623-9191, 181 Pearl St, Somerville

Museum of Fine Arts, www.mfa.org, 617-267-9300, 465 Huntington Ave, Boston

Spark Craft Studios, www.sparkcrafts.com, 617-718-9132, 50 Grove St, Somerville

Athletics and Dance

Boston Sailing Center, www.bostonsailingcenter.com, Lewis Wharf, Boston

CityGolf Boston, www.citygolfboston.com, 617-357-4653, 38 Bromfield St, Boston

Fred Astaire Dance Studios, www.fadsboston.com, 617-247-2435, 179 South St, Boston

GottaDance Cambridge, www.gottadance.org, 617-864-8675, 11 Garden St, Cambridge and 7 Temple St, Cambridge

Green Street Studios, www.greenstreetstudios.org, 617-864-3191, 185 Green St, Cambridge

Jam'nastics, www.jamnastics.org, 617-354-5780, 199 Columbia St, Cambridge

Trapeze School, http://boston.trapezeschool.com, 781-942-7800, 50 Walkers Brook Dr, Reading

Overview

Bostonians love that dirty water, but we like clean water even better. This fact is best reflected by the Boston Harbor Project. Thanks to over $3 billion spent cleaning it up, the Hub's harbor is no longer on that shameful list of the country's dirtiest waterways, but it's still a work in progress. So while you may still hear that damn Standells' song coming from every bar on Lansdowne Street, you no longer need to worry about your genetic makeup should you go for a swim in the Charles. However, NFT does not recommend donning those speedos and goggles just yet. Instead, consider more appropriate activities as reflected in the slew of yacht clubs and boating centers that decorate the coastline and upriver all the way to Watertown.

A perfect place to start is at one of Boston Harbor's 34 beautiful islands, which have been collectively designated a National Recreation Area. Nine of the islands are fully or partially accessible to the public and are a great, affordable getaway within 10-miles of downtown Boston. For the most part, amenities consist of composting toilets, but if you come prepared, the islands are great for a picnic or a camping excursion (www.bostonislands.com). On George's Island (Boston Harbor Cruises) you will find historic Fort Warren, a former Civil War prison replete with ghost—the wife of a Civil War inmate nicknamed "Lady in Black." The trails across 48-acre Lovell's Island pass through dunes, forests, and the ruins of Fort Standish. There's a supervised swimming beach, some picnic areas, and 11 campsites. Little Brewster Island is the home of Boston Light, the oldest continually used lighthouse site in America (1716). While not open to casual visitors, private boaters and tours are welcomed; call for specifics (617-223-8666). If your boss is scheduling a Survivor-style teamwork safari or if your kids are looking for that Kevin Bacon, White Water Summer role model, chances are you're heading to

privately owned Thompson Island. If you want to venture a bit farther out, consider Buzzards Bay to the south. Touching more than 280 miles of the Massachusetts coastline, the bay stretches from Rhode Island Sound to the Cape Cod Canal. Calmer waters inside the bay make for good sailing conditions.

Back on the Charles (don't even think about pronouncing the "r"), crew is a popular sport, particularly among the local colleges and universities. Many of the clubs and organizations offer instruction to the general public. The Head of the Charles Regatta, held every fall, is the world's largest two-day rowing event. The race schedule includes single and team events and draws competitors from around the world. Check out www.hocr.org for more information.

The nonprofit Community Boating Inc. (located between the Charles/MGH Red Line stop and the Hatch Shell) offers summer kayaking, windsurfing, and sailing lessons for kids aged 10–18 for just $1. (Participants must be able to swim 75 yards.) Visit www.community-boating.org for more information.

If you're looking for waves but find the Harbor a bit intimidating, check out the Jamaica Pond Boat House (617-522-5061) for mini-sailboat and rowboat rentals. At around 68-acres, the pond is the purest and largest body of water within city limits and the only date-friendly glacial-kettlehole in town. It's also a great place to watch kamikaze drivers on the Jamaicaway. As they scream expletives and give each other the finger, you can fish in the liberally stocked pond and gloat. If that isn't relaxing, what is? Visit www.jamaicapond.com for further information.

Boston is also home to the CRASH—B World Indoor Rowing Championships, held annually in February at Agganis Arena at Boston University. More information is available at www.crash-b.org.

Sailing/Boating Centers

	Address	Phone	Website
Boston Harbor Cruises	1 Long Wharf, Boston	617-227-4321	www.bostonharborcruises.com
Boston Harbor Sailing Club	58 Batterymarch St, Boston	617-720-0049	www.bostonharborsailing.com; moorings/hire/lessons racing/clothing
Boston Harbor Shipyard & Marina	256 Marginal St, East Boston	617-561-1400	www.bhsmarina.com; moorings/lessons
Boston Sailing Center	The Riverboat at Lewis Wharf	617-227-4198	www.bostonsailingcenter.com; hire/courses/lessons/racing
Community Boating	21 David Mugar Way, Boston	617-523-1038	www.community-boating.org; sailing lessons
Courageous Sailing Center	One 1st Ave, Charlestown	617-242-3821	www.courageoussailing.org; lessons/racing
Jamaica Pond Boat House	Jamaicaway at Pond St, Jamaica Plain	617-522-5061	www.jamaicapond.com; sailing/rowing
Lincoln Sailing Center	PO Box 492, Hingham	781-741-5225	www.lincolnsailing.org; non-profit/lessons/sailing/rowing
MIT Sailing	134 Memorial Dr, Cambridge	617-253-4884	http://sailing.mit.edu; lessons/racing
Piers Park Sailing	95 Marginal St, East Boston	617-561-6677	www.piersparksailing.org; hire/lessons/racing/sale

Yacht Clubs

	Address	Phone	Website
Bass Haven Yacht Club	10 McPherson Dr, Beverly	978-922-9712	www.basshavenyachtclub.com
Boston Yacht Club	1 Front St, Marblehead	781-631-3100	www.bostonyc.org
Braintree Yacht Club	9 Gordon Rd, Braintree	781-843-9730	
Corinthian Yacht Club	1 Nahant St, Marblehead	781-631-0005	www.corinthianyc.org
Danversport Yacht Club	161 Elliott St, Danvers	978-774-8620	www.danversport.com
Eastern Yacht Club	47 Foster St, Marblehead	781-631-1400	www.easternyc.org
Hull Yacht Club	5 Fitzpatrick Wy, Hull	781-925-9739	www.hullyc.org
Jeffries Yacht Club	565 Sumner St, East Boston	617-567-9656	www.jeffriesyachtclub.com
Jubilee Yacht Club	126 Water St, Beverly	978-922-9611	www.jubileeyc.net
Metropolitan Yacht Club	39 Vinedale Rd, Braintree	781-843-9882	www.metyc.com
New Bedford Yacht Club	208 Elm St, South Dartmouth	508-997-0762	www.nbyc.com
Old Colony Yacht Club	235 Victory Rd, Dorchester	617-436-0513	
Peninsula Yacht Club	671 Summer St, Boston	617-464-7901	www.pycboston.org
Plymouth Yacht Club	34 Union St, Plymouth	508-746-7707	www.plymouthyachtclub.org
Sandy Bay Yacht Club	5 T Wharf, Rockport	978-546-9433	www.sandybay.org
South Boston Yacht Club	1849 Columbia Rd, South Boston	617-268-6132	www.southbostonyc.com
Squantum Yacht Club	646 Quincy Shore Dr, Quincy	617-770-4811	www.squantumyc.org
Wianno Yacht Club	101 Bridge St, Osterville	508-428-2232	www.vsb.cape.com/~wianno
Winthrop Yacht Club	649 Shirley St, Winthrop	617-846-9774	www.win-yc.org

Rowing Clubs

	Address	Phone	Website
Community Rowing (Apr–Oct)	600 Pleasant St, Watertown	617-923-7557	www.communityrowing.org
Whaling City Rowing Club	5 Dover St, New Bedford	508-517-1251	www.whalingcityrowing.com

Sports · Biking

General Information

City of Boston Bicycling:	www.ci.boston.ma.us/transportation/bike.asp
City of Cambridge Bicycling:	www.ci.cambridge.ma.us/CDD/et/bike/index.html
MassBike:	www.massbike.org
Charles River Wheelmen:	www.crw.org
Rubel BikeMaps:	www.bikemaps.com
Bike to Bridge Boston:	www.hubonwheels.org

Overview

The city's streets are narrow, congested, and short-tempered, bike-hating drivers abound. Make no mistake, Boston is tough for cyclists.

That said, Boston and the surrounding cities are making efforts to increase the accessibility and safety of bike transportation, and it's a great way to explore the city. Relatively flat and compact, it's generally quicker to get around on a bike, and you'll find, even in the middle of winter, hardy cyclists trekking through the city, delivering packages, and heading to class. Bike-only or mixed-use bike/pedestrian paths run through most of the area's parks, paralleling major roads such as the Riverway, Storrow Drive, and Memorial Drive. While getting "doored" is a serious threat in Central Square, a much-needed repaving of Mass Ave has smoothed the bike lane connecting Boston to Harvard.

Danger lurks around every non-perpendicular corner. To avoid catastrophe, have your best cycling wits about you and be especially wary of:

- **Drivers**—Boston drivers reserve some of their most venomous roadrage for cyclists. They're also notoriously self-centered, erratic, prone to underestimate your speed, and quick to double-park to dash in for liquor or donuts.

- **Potholes**—They can sneak up on you, especially at night. The bigger ones will swallow you whole, while bumping over the little ones lead to nasty bruises in the nether regions.

- **Trolley Tracks**—Green Line tracks will flip you over and buckle your wheel, especially in parts of Mission Hill, Jamaica Plain, and in Cleveland Circle. If you're going to cross the tracks, take them at a 90-degree angle.

- **Bridges**—All the bridges across the Charles are narrow and heavily trafficked.

- **Pedestrians**—If they aren't darting across the street, they're on the paths listening to their iPods and ignoring everybody and everything.

If you plan on biking in Boston and you have a brain that you'd like to keep, invest in a helmet and a battery-powered red light to place below your seat or on your back. Front lights and rear reflectors are the law after dark.

The city offers many options for recreational riding, including the popular 11-mile Minuteman Bikeway through Lexington and the 17-mile Charles River Bikeway growing past Watertown. Shorter but handy for commuting, the Southwest Corridor sends you from Northeastern along the Orange Line to Forest Hills. Recent funding should improve one of the serious flaws of the Boston bike system: a lack of cross-trail connections, crossing lights, or route markings. This makes them less than ideal for outing with small children. Of particular danger to families are the many bridge intersections along the south Charles River Bikeway.

For something a little longer and farther away, the Bay Circuit Trail winds its way 150 miles from Newburyport on the North Shore to Duxbury on the South Shore, creating a "C" shape around Boston. Cycling enthusiasts refer to it as "Boston's outer Emerald Necklace." You'll find the boy racers skipping the summer crowds on the Minuteman for spins around Concord and many of the cycle shops sponsor club teams. The Charles River Wheelmen is one of the nation's oldest bicycle clubs with a year round calendar of rides and still full of cue sheets. For the distance riders, the BMB (Boston-Montreal-Boston) ride draws randonneurs from across the country for the grueling 90 hour, 1,200K ride.

Rubel BikeMaps produces maps of riding paths and trails throughout the Greater Boston area and is well worth five bucks. You'll likely want both the Boston map and the Eastern Mass map. They can be purchased at most bike shops, bookstores, or on the Rubel website. Take it to the State House with MassBike, the primary lobbying and bicycle advocacy group in the state. They maintain an extensive website of all things pedal-powered in Massachusetts. Bike to Bridge Boston is a new addition to the city and organizes free tours to offbeat Boston during the summer. DIY guides to biking Jewish Boston, the Underground Railroad, and other routes are on their web site, and they organize a city bike rally and ride in early October.

Bikes and Mass Transit

Bikes are allowed on the Red, Orange, and Blue Lines, on the MBTA Commuter Rail with some limitations, on all busses equipped with bike racks, and on the MBTA ferries at all times. Bikes (with the exception of folding bikes) are not permitted on the Green Line, the Mattapan Trolley, or the Silver Line. On the subway and commuter rail, bikes are permitted during non-rush hours (roughly 10 am–2 pm and after 7pm). Bikes are allowed at all subway stations except Park Street, Downtown Crossing (except to transfer), and Government Center. Crosstown buses are equipped with bike racks and can be used at any time. Other bus services do not provide racks and bikes are not permitted on board.

If you're traveling on commuter rail, wait for the conductor's instructions before entering or exiting the train. On subways, head for the rear of the train. You're only allowed to enter the last carriage and, even then, there's a two-bikes-per carriage limit. There is no additional fee for bikes on any public transportation. See the MBTA website for (www. mbta.com) for schedules.

Bike Shops and Makers

Boston's got a great variety of shops. While most will have a low-end city cruiser or two, it's worth getting to know your local shops for their specialties, whether the high-end racing bikes at ATA or fixies at Beacon Street. Oddly enough, Boston's most famous shop and mechanic, Sheldon Brown, are way out in West Newton at Harris Cyclery. However, if you don't mind getting your hands dirty, we applaud the rent-by-the-hour stands and geniuses at Broadway Bicycle School.

· **Ace Wheelworks** ·
145 Elm St, Somerville · 617-776-2100

· **ATA Cycle** ·
1773 Massachusetts Ave, Cambridge · 617-354-0907

· **Back Bay Bicycles** ·
366 Commonwealth Ave, Boston · 617-247-2336

· **Bicycle Bill's** ·
253 North Harvard St, Allston · 617-783-5636

· **Bicycle Exchange** ·
2067 Massachusetts Ave, Cambridge · 617-864-1300

· **Bikes Not Bombs** ·
18 Bartlett Sq, Jamaica Plain · 617-442-0004

· **Broadway Bicycle School** ·
351 Broadway, Cambridge · 617-868-3392

· **Cambridge Bicycle** ·
259 Massachusetts Ave, Cambridge · 617-876-6555

· **Community Bike Supply** ·
496 Tremont St, Boston · 617-542-8623

· **Federico's Bike Shop** ·
126 Emerson St, Boston · 617-269-1309

· **Ferris Wheels Bicycle Shop** ·
66 South St, Jamaica Plain · 617-522-7082

· **Harris Cyclery** ·
1353 Washington St, West Newton · 617-244-1040

· **International Bicycle Center** ·
89 Brighton Ave, Brighton · 617-783-5804

· **Jamaica Cycle** ·
667 Centre St, Jamaica Plain · 617-524-9610

· **Paramount Bicycle Repair** ·
860 Broadway, Somerville · 617-666-6072

· **Park Sales & Service** ·
510 Somerville Ave, Somerville · 617-666-3647

· **Revolution Bicycle Repair** ·
753 Atlantic Ave, Boston · 617-542-4327

· **Ski Market** ·
860 Commonwealth Ave, Boston · 617-731-6100

When out on the road, what's better than showing off some Yankee ingenuity? Boston's been a center of bike fabrication since Columbia popularized the ready-made bike in 1877. Here are some sweet hand-crafted builders welding new traditions:

· **A.N.T.** ·
24 Water St, Holliston · 508-429-3350

· **Independent Fabrication** ·
86 Joy St, Somerville · 617-666-3609

· **Seven Cycles** ·
125 Walnut St, Watertown · 617-923-777

Sports · **Skating**

Overview

If you like the idea of lowering your center of gravity and darting around at high speeds on tiny wheels or thin blades, then Boston is the place for you. The city is jam-packed with parks and rinks that accommodate inline skaters in the summer and ice skaters in the winter.

Inline Skating

Boston drivers are no more sympathetic to skaters than they are to bikers. If you're skating for recreation, it is probably best to stick to the numerous places designated for outdoor activities. A favorite haunt of Boston skaters is Harvard's Arnold Arboretum (125 Arborway, Jamaica Plain, 617-524-1718), which offers one of the most scenic (and hilly) skates in the area. The best thing about this place is that skaters are welcome everywhere. There are two or three miles of paved paths and you don't have to worry about cars (although you might find yourself dodging strollers, cyclists, and fellow skaters, particularly on sunny weekends).

Boston Common (see page 188) is another popular skating destination, but the pedestrian traffic on the Common makes skating quite challenging. The Common is usually crowded with meandering tourists and fast-walking business folk who don't take too kindly to being mowed down by skaters. The upside, though, is that you can take in some impressive cityscapes as you zip around. The best way to get there is to take the T to Park Street. Note: Wearing skates on the T is prohibited.

For a great view of the bridges that stretch over the Charles River, try the Charles River Bike Path. The trail runs along both sides of the river between the Galen Street Bridge in Watertown and River Street Bridge in Boston, and from the Science Museum to Watertown Square. The path is about 8.5 miles each way.

Beacon Hill Skate Shop (135 Charles St S, 617-482-7400) rents top-of-the-line inline skates, roller skates, and ice skates. Rentals cost $10/hour, $15/day, and $20 overnight. Beacon Hill Skate Shop accepts cash only and requires you to leave a credit card as a deposit. All rentals come with safety equipment.

Ice Skating

Even on crisp winter days, when the cold makes it almost unbearable to be outside, Boston Common's famous Frog Pond entices many Bostonians to bundle up and head out for some good, old-fashioned ice skating—either that or some good, old-fashioned heckling from the sidelines. Skating is free for children 13 and under and $4 for everyone else. Skate rental is $5 for children and $8 for everyone else. Lockers are available for a dollar. Regulars might consider buying individual season passes for $100 or a family pass for $150. Lunchtime passes are valid Mon–Fri, 11 am to 3 pm (holidays excluded), and cost $60. Frog Pond is open Sun–Thurs 10 am-9 pm (except Mon when the rink closes at 5 pm) and Fri–Sat 10 am–10 pm. For more information, call 617-635-2120.

The Larz Anderson Park in Brookline is a great back-up option when Frog Pond gets too crowded (and it will). Larz Anderson Park is located on a former 64-acre estate and is the largest park in Brookline. In addition to the outdoor skate rink, the park has picnic areas, ball fields, and an incredible view of Boston. The only downside is that the skating rink is only open a few months every year, from December to

February. Skating fees cost $4 for adults and $3 for kids ($7 and $4, respectively, for non-residents). The rink is open Tues and Thurs 10 am–12 pm, Fri 7:30 pm–9:30 pm, Sat–Sun 12 pm–5 pm. For more information, call 617-739-7518.

Ice Skating Rinks

If you have your own skates, you might opt for one of the following rinks run by the Department of Conservation and Recreation, where skating in the winter is free. Call rinks for hours of operation:

Bajko Memorial Rink,
75 Turtle Pond Pkwy, Hyde Park, 617-364-9188
Jim Roche Community Ice Arena,
1275 VFW Pkwy, West Roxbury, 617-323-9532
Daly Memorial Rink,
1 Nonantum Rd, Brighton, 617-527-1741
Devine Memorial Rink,
995 Morrissey Blvd, Dorchester, 617-436-4356
Emmons Horrigan O'Neill Memorial Rink,
150 Rutherford Ave, Charlestown, 617-242-9728
Flynn Skating Rink,
2 Woodland Rd, Medford, 781-395-8492
Kelly Outdoor Skating Rink,
1 Marbury Ter, Jamaica Plain, 617-727-7000
LoConte Memorial Rink,
3449 Veterans Pkwy, Medford, 781-395-9594
Murphy Memorial Rink,
1880 William J Day Blvd, South Boston, 617-269-7060
Porazzo Memorial Rink,
20 Coleridge St, East Boston, 617-567-9571
Reilly Skating Rink,
355 Chestnut Hill Ave, Brighton, 617-277-7822
Skating Club of Boston,
1240 Soldiers Field Rd, Brighton, 617-782-5900
Simoni Memorial Rink,
155 Gore St, Cambridge, 781-982-8166
Steriti Memorial Rink,
561 Commercial St, Boston, 617-523-9327
Veterans Memorial Rink,
570 Somerville Ave, Somerville, 617- 623-3523

Skateboarding

The Charles River Skatepark, 40,000 square feet of pipes, ramps, and rails, will be constructed at North Point Park along the Charles River where Cambridge meets Charlestown. Scheduled to break ground in Spring of 2008, it's expected to be open to the public by the end of the year, it will be one of the largest skateparks in the country, perfect for catching air like Tony Hawk or busting backside lipslides like Ryan Sheckler. For info, go to www.charlesriverskatepark.com. Until then, you can thrash all year long on the indoor mini ramp at Underground Snowboard (860 Commonwealth Ave, Boston, 617-232-8680).

Gear

Beacon Hill Skate Shop,
135 Charles St S, Boston, 617-482-7400
Coliseum Skateboard,
150 Huntington Ave, Boston, 617-399-9900
True East Skate Shop,
32 Province St, Boston, 617-451-8999
Underground Snowboard,
860 Commonwealth Ave, Boston, 617-232-8680

General Information

Boston Parks and Recreation Office
Phone: 617-635-4505
Hotline: 617-635-PARK
Website: www.cityofboston.gov/parks

Brookline Recreation Department
Phone: 617-730-2083
Website: www.townofbrooklinemass.com/
                recreation/Tennis.html

Cambridge Recreation Department
Phone: 617-349-6200
Website: www.cambridgema.gov

Department of Conservation and Recreation
(Division of Urban Parks)
Phone: 617-626-1250
Website: www.mass.gov/dcr/recreate/tennis.htm

Outdoor Courts—Open to the Public

These public courts operate on a first-come, first-served basis. Most courts are not equipped with lights, so get there early to get your game in. Although many courts are in good condition, some have pretty major divots, à la the Boston Garden's parquet floor, making the ball spin in unexpected directions. Courts are managed by the city or the town recreation department, or by the Commonwealth's Department of Conservation and Recreation's Division of Urban Parks (DCR). Until recently, the DCR was the Metropolitan District Commission (MDC), so the courts might still be labeled with the wrong acronym. Don't let it affect your game! Many locals also use the well-maintained school courts in the university-rich area. Each school has a different policy regarding outsiders depending on season, location, and the mood of the athletic director on a particular day. Contact the schools or just take your chances.

Tennis Courts	Address	Type	# of Courts	Map
Charlesbank Park (DCR)	Charles St	Public	4	1
North End Park (DCR)	Commercial St	Public	2	2
Boston Common	Boylston St & Charles St	Public	2	3
Pagoda Park	Kneeland St	Public	1	4
Cook Street Play Area	Hill St & Cook St	Public	1	8
Porzio Park	Maverick Sq	Public	2	9
Boston Athletic Club	653 Summer St	Private		11
Marine Park (DCR)	Day Blvd	Public	1	11
Clifford Playground	Norfolk Ave & Proctor St	Public	1	12
Carter Playground	Columbus Ave & Camden St	Public	5	13
Jeep Jones Park	King St	Public	1	13
Malcolm X Park	Dale St & Bainbridge St	Public	2	13
Trotter School Playground	Humboldt Ave & Waumbeck St	Public	1	13
Mission Hill Deck (DCR)	Southwest Corridor Park	Public	2	14
South Street Mall	South St & Carolina Ave	Public	2	14
Stony Brook Deck (DCR)	Southwest Corridor Park	Public	2	14
Amory Clay Tennis Courts	Amory St	Public		16
Longwood Playground Park	Newall Rd off Kent St	Public	3	16
Waldstein Playground	37 Dean Rd	Public	8	17
Rogers Park	Lake St & Foster St	Public	2	18
Coolidge Playground	Kenwood St b/w Harvard St & Columbia St	Public	1	19
Devotion Playground	Steadman St off Harvard St	Public	3	19
Driscoll School	Washington St	Public	2	19
Ringer Playground	Allston St & Griggs Pl	Public	2	19
Anderson Courts	Pemberton St & Haskell St	Public		22
George Dilboy Field (DCR)	Alewife Brook Pkwy	Public	2	22
Saxton J Foss Park (DCR)	McGrath Hwy & Broadway	Public	2	24
Hoyt Field	Western Ave & Howard St	Public		27
Riverside Press Park	River St & Memorial Dr	Public		27
Harvard Street Park	Harvard St & Clark St	Public		28
Joan Lorentz Park at Cambridge Public Library	Broadway & Ellery St	Public		28

Public Courses

Public Courses	Address	Phone	Par	Fees (WD/WE)	Map
Franklin Park Golf Course	1 Circuit Dr, Dorchester	617-265-4084	70	$23–26 weekday / $29–34 weekend	n/a
Fresh Pond Golf Course	691 Huron Ave	617-349-6282	35/70	$30 weekday / $36 weekend	n/a
Presidents Golf Course	357 W Squantum St, Quincy	617-328-3444	70	$35 weekday / $44 weekend	n/a
Putterham Meadows Golf Club	1281 W Roxbury Pkwy, Chestnut Hill	617-730-2078	71	$35 weekday / $38 weekend	n/a

Driving Ranges

Driving Ranges	Address	Phone	Fees (WD/WE)	Map
Boston Golf Academy	200 Stuart St	617-457-2699	$10/bucket	3
City Golf Boston	38 Bromfield St	617-357-4653	$10/bucket	3

Bowling

First and foremost, if you prefer tenpin over candlepin bowling than you are clearly not from Boston. If you are trying to fit in with the cutters or if want your girlfriend to think you're the real life Will Hunting, then you better learn how to hit those skinny sticks. On the other hand, if you are comfortable admitting that you were born in upstate New York and that you collected Don Mattingly cards when you were a kid, then embrace the tenpin, no one will think less of you for it (yeah, right).

All kidding aside, bowling has become hip and bowling has become expensive. Take **Kings (Map 16)**, for instance. Go there on a Friday night and it's filled with people who wouldn't have been caught dead bowling on a Friday night back in high school. Then there's **Lucky Strike Lanes (Map 16)** with a friggin' dress code. If that's your idea of bowling, by all means, have at it. If you straddle the line between hip bowling and down-home bowling, check out the **Milky Way Lounge (Map 14)**. There's usually a cover and live music, but the atmosphere is booze-induced and friendly, and if you really want to, you can get a frou-frou cocktail. If you're an old-school bowler, the kind that embraces leagues and finds no kitsch value in a button up short sleeve with your name in cursive on it (your real name), then you must head straight to **Lanes & Games,** order yourself a Bud and some steak tips, and get out your lucky glove. Another similar option is **Sacco's Bowl Haven (Map 22)** in Somerville (candlepin only). And here's one of those moments that remind you why you bought this little awesome book in the first place—**Boston Bowl Family Fun Center (Map 32)** on Morrissey Boulevard is open all night! You read correctly: In the squarest late-night town in America, where your options are your buddy's stained futon or the South Street Diner, Boston Bowl has you covered 24 hours a day.

Bowling Lanes

Bowling Lanes	Address	Phone	Fees	Map
King's Boston	50 Dalton St	617-266-2695	$5.50/game, $4/shoes	5
Central Park Lanes	10 Saratoga St	617-567-7073	$2.50/game, $1/shoes	9
South Boston Candlepin	543 E Broadway	617-464-4858	$3.50 per person/ per game; $1.50 shoes	11
Milky Way Lounge & Lanes	403 Centre St	617-524-3740	$25 per lane (shoes included)	14
Lucky Strike Lanes	145 Ipswich St	617-437-0300	$4/game, $3/shoes	16
Sacco's Bowl Haven	45 Day St	617-776-0552	$3/game, $2/shoes	22
Boston Bowl (open 24 hours)	820 Morrissey Blvd,	617-825-3800	$4.95/game, $4.25/shoes	32
Lanes & Games	195 Concord Tpke, Cambridge	617-876-5533	$4.75/game, $2.75/shoes	n/a

Yoga

Yoga	Address	Phone	Website	Map
Dahn Yoga	122 Cambridge St	617-742-9642	www.dahnyoga.com	1
Exhale Mind Body Spa	28 Arlington St	617-532-7000	www.exhalespa.com	3
Bikram Yoga Boston	108 Lincoln St	617-556-9976	www.bikramyogaboston.com	4
Back Bay Yoga Studio	1112 Boylston St	617-375-0785	www.backbayyoga.com	5
Dahn Yoga	551 Boylston St	617-262-9642	www.dahnyoga.com	6
Charlestown Yoga	191 Main St	617-241-0824	www.charlestownyoga.com	8
South Boston Yoga	141 Dorchester Ave	617-548-2694	southbostonyoga.net	12
Blissful Monkey Yoga Studio	663 Centre St	617-522-4411	www.blissfulmonkey.com	14
Dahn Yoga	10B Green St	617-983-9642	www.dahnyoga.com	14
Inner Space	17 Station St	617-730-5757	www.yogainthevillage.com	16
Dahn Yoga	235 Harvard St	617-264-4851	www.dahnyoga.com	17
The Yoga Studio	29 Harvard St, 2nd Fl	617-566-1489	www.yogastudio.org	17
Ayurvedic Rehabilitation Center	103 Bennett St	617-782-1727	www.ayurvedicrehabilitationcenter.com	18
Rock City Body	14 Harvard Ave	617-782-4410		19
Zen Athletica	1065 Commonwealth Ave	617-789-3733	www.zenathletica.com	19
Baptiste Power Yoga	2000 Massachusetts Ave	617-661-9642	www.baronbaptiste.com	23
Baptiste Power Yoga	25 Harvard St	617-661-9642	www.baronbaptiste.com	23
O2 Yoga	288 Highland Ave	617-625-0267	www.o2yoga.com	23
Cambridge Racquet & Fitness Club	215 First St	617-491-8989	www.cambridgefitness.com	26
Dahn Yoga	1110 Massachusetts Ave	617-576-9642	www.dahnyoga.com	27
Karma Yoga Studio	1120 Massachusetts Ave	617-547-9642	www.karmayogastudio.com	27
Mystic River Yoga	196 Boston Ave	781-396-0808	www.mysticriveryoga.com	n/a

Billiards

Billiards	Address	Phone	Fees	Map
Boston Beer Works	112 Canal St	617-896-2337	$10/hr	2
Felt	533 Washington St	617-350-5555	$14/hr	3
King's Boston	50 Dalton St	617-266-2695	$14/hr	5
4 X 4 Billiards	1260 Boylston St	617-424-6326	$12/hr	15
Boston Billiard Club	126 Brookline Ave	617-536-7665	$10/hr	16
Lucky Strike Lanes	145 Ipswich St	617-437-0300	$14/hr weekends; $10/hr weekdays	16
Big City	138 Brighton Ave	617-782-2020	$10/hr	19
Sacco's Bowl Haven	45 Day St	617-776-0552	$7.50/hr	22
Good Time Emporium	30 Assembly Square Dr	617-628-5559	$11/hr	25
Flat Top Johnny's	One Kendall Sq, Bldg 200	617-494-9565	$12/hr	26
Boston Bowl (open 24 hours)	820 Morrissey Blvd	617-825-3800	$13/hr	32

Hiking in Boston

While it may not be the greatest city for driving, Boston is a great walking city. Whether you're in the mood for a casual stroll or a major trek, the city offers a surprisingly wide array of hikes and walks from which to choose. The trails closest to the city tend to be more scenic walks than hikes—appropriate for strolling students or families who want to get out and about in the city. If you're hungering for some real hiking, you'll need to be prepared for a drive. Boston's outskirts offer plenty of rigorous hiking trails with breathtaking views of the city and a taste of Massachusetts nature. If none of that is hardcore enough for you, the White Mountains of New Hampshire are just a Zipcar (see page 261) away.

A great source for information about various Boston trails is *Exploring in and Around Boston on Bike and Foot* by Lee Sinai (Appalachian Mountain Club Books).

Boston Harbor Islands

Seven miles from downtown Boston, this cluster of pretty much undiscovered islands is a great day trip to walk among historical forts and bucolic landscapes, birdwatch, or do some beachcombing. The inexpensive ferry from Long Wharf drops you off at Georges Island, where you can explore Fort Warren, a former Civil War prison that supposedly has its own ghost, "The Lady in Black." From there you can take free shuttles to the other islands. Peddocks Island has the longest coastline of all the islands and the most diverse set of trails. Grape Island takes you through forests, orchards, and rocky shoreline. Lovells has nine sand dunes and swimming beaches. Ferry service runs six times a day to Spectacle Island, a former dump site, which has been refurbished with excavated dirt from the Big Dig. It features a renewable energy visitor center, electric cars, a marina, beaches, and five miles of trails. There is camping on Peddocks, Grape, Lovells, and Bumpkin, but you must pack in and pack out everything yourself. Ferries to Spectacle Island and Georges Island operate from 9 am until sunset in the summer. Round-trip tickets cost $10–$12, $7–$9 seniors, and anywhere from free to $7 for children, depending on their age. For more information, go to www.bostonislands.com or call 617-223-8666 for schedules.

HarborWalk

With the cleaning up of Boston Harbor (though we still wouldn't swim in it) and the removal of the Central Artery, the waterfront has become more beautiful and accessible to pedestrian traffic. Finally realizing that people are attracted to a picturesque waterfront, Boston decided to capitalize on its coastal setting and incorporate it into the life of the city. The HarborWalk is a multi-use attraction consisting of walkways, parks, benches, artwork, restaurants, and swimming spots extending from Chelsea to Neponset. Currently 38 miles long, it is 80% complete and meanders through diverse waterfront neighborhoods with views of the Harbor Islands and Boston skyline. A don't miss highlight is the Institute of Contemporary Art (ICA), which recently relocated here in a glass building perched over the waterfront. It is really quite pleasant on warm summer nights to wander among the boats and the lights of the city and revisit neighborhoods from a whole new perspective. Plans are to eventually link it to the city's inland parks and the future Rose Kennedy Greenway.

Arnold Arboretum

Harvard's Arnold Arboretum, located in Jamaica Plain, occupies 265 acres and boasts a dizzying array of woody plants, more than 700 of which are over 100 years old. You can take a free guided tour of the grounds (call 617-524-1718 for tour schedules) or amble along the three-mile trail at your own pace. The arboretum welcomes dogs as long as they're kept on a leash. The botanical haven is just two blocks away from the Forest Hills T stop (Orange Line) and parking is available outside the main gate. Restrooms are located next to the entrance gate in the Hunnewell Visitor Center. The grounds are open every day of the year during daylight hours. For more information, visit www.arboretum.harvard.edu.

Fresh Pond Reservation

This is a favorite of local residents and Harvard students. Located just one mile from the university and six miles from downtown Boston, the Fresh Pond Reservation offers a rather easy 2.25-mile paved trail around comely Fresh Pond, the 155-acre reservoir. The trail has become a hot spot for joggers, cyclists, and skaters. If you take your dog, be sure to check out the pooper-scooper dispensers! But it's not just the athletic types that reap the benefits of the reservation—the reservoir provides drinking water to many residents and businesses in Cambridge. To reach the reservation by train, take the Red Line to Alewife (last stop). By car, follow Route 2 east or west to Fresh Pond Parkway. The reservation lies on the corner of Huron Avenue and Fresh Pond Parkway. You'll find the best entrance to the reservation directly across from Wheeler Street. Parking in the reservation is reserved for cars with a Cambridge permit. There is parking after hours at the Tobin School, or take bus #72, #74, #75, or #78. For more information, visit www.friendsoffreshpond.org or call 617-349-6319.

Mount Auburn Cemetery

Hailed as America's first landscaped cemetery and a National Historic Landmark, Mount Auburn provides two miles of leisurely walking, alternating between paved walkways and unpaved footpaths, and is considered one of the best birding spots in the state. Aside from the 86,000 graves, the cemetery is home to over 5,000 native and foreign trees. Located just 1.5 miles west of Harvard Square, the cemetery can be reached via Route 2 or 3 to Route 16 at the Mount Auburn/Brattle Street intersection on Fresh Pond Parkway. If you follow Mount Auburn Street (Rte 16) for two blocks, you will reach the entrance. Contact the Friends of Mount Auburn Cemetery (617-547-7105) for information about guided tours and lectures or visit their website at www.mountauburn.org. No dogs allowed.

Forest Hills Cemetery

Jamaica Plain's Forest Hills Cemetery is overshadowed in popularity (perhaps unfairly) by Mount Auburn Cemetery. Established in 1848, it's one of the country's oldest burial grounds, featuring 275 acres of beautifully sculpted landscape. The cemetery offers guided tours ($5–$8) or brochures and maps to help visitors create their own (free) tours of the grounds and its famous residents, including Eugene O'Neill and e.e. cummings. One of its most impressive features is Lake Hibiscus, which hosts the Buddhist-inspired lantern lighting festival held annually in the summer season. Another highlight is the Sculpture Path, a revolving exhibit of work by contemporary local and national artists. The cemetery is located conveniently next to the Forest Hills T stop. If you're driving, take the Arborway east over the Casey Overpass and follow signs for the cemetery exit, located on the right on Shea Circle. The grounds are open year-round during daylight hours. For more information, visit www.foresthillscemetery.com or call 617-524-0128.

Hammond Pond Reservation

Hammond Pond is located behind a suburban mall in Chestnut Hill—an unlikely place to find a reservation. You can see the department stores as you hike through the 114 acres of woodlands. It's also one of the few outdoor places in Boston where you can rock climb. The best place to start is at the entrance to the reservation, located on the left of Hammond Pond at the north side of the parking lot. Walk through the metal gate and remain on the wide main path through the woods. If you're interested in rock climbing, you'll see rocks to your left a little way along the path. If climbing rocks is not your thing, continue on for two miles of easy walking or try fishing in the pond. Hammond Pond Reservation can be reached by foot from the Chestnut Hill T stop. Hammond Pond Reservation is open year round during daylight hours. For more information, call 617-698-1802.

Breakheart Reservation

Hidden amidst strip malls and fast-food joints along Route 1, this 640-acre hardwood forest is a treasure for hikers lucky enough to stumble across it. The reservation offers many miles of scenic views and plenty of strenuous trails to get your heart pumping. Fishing, bird watching, cross-country skiing, swimming, and biking are other attractions that lure nature lovers out to Breakheart. As there's really no way to get to there by mass transit, you'll have to drive. Take Route 1 to the Lynn Fells Parkway exit towards Melrose and Stoneham. Turn right onto Forest Street, and follow the signs to Breakheart Reservation. A good place to begin your hike is on the paved Pine Tops Road, located next to the parking lot adjacent to the headquarters building. For more information, call 781-233-0834.

Skyline Trail

This seven-mile trail is located in Blue Hills Reservation (near Milton), the largest open space within 35 miles of Boston. The Skyline Trail winds through rocky hills and provides scenic views of the city. With an elevation gain of 2,500 feet, this hike is not for the faint of heart. But don't fret! If you're not up for a real workout, there are plenty of less challenging trails in the park and the color-coded trail map available at the headquarters building will help you find your way around. To get there, take Route 138 to Exit 3 towards Houghton's Pond. After exiting, turn right at the stop sign onto Hillside Street and travel about a mile until you reach Houghton's Pond. The trail is open year-round from sunrise until sunset. Also in the Reservation is the Ponkapoag Pond trail, a four-mile loop around the pond, the highlight of which is a boardwalk trail (two miles roundtrip) through a rare Atlantic white cedar swamp. It's fun and different, but be warned: Wear waterproof shoes. Seriously. The boardwalk is made up of half submerged logs.

Middlesex Fells Reservation Eastern Section

Located seven miles north of Boston, Middlesex Fells is a 2,060-acre reservation where you'll find some of the area's most challenging hikes, many of which are considered some of the Boston area's best kept secrets. (If anyone asks, you didn't hear about it from us.) Middlesex Fells is off I-93 past the Stone Zoo. Parking is available on Pond Street. The beginning of the trail is located on the south side of Pond Street and begins behind a Virginia Wood sign near Gate 42. The trail is approximately 5.5 miles long, but can be extended to 16 miles if you connect trails. All of the hikes in this area are fairly strenuous and involve climbing and descending rocky slopes.

Moose Hill Wildlife Sanctuary

This is the oldest and second-largest Massachusetts Audubon (MAS) sanctuary. Moose Hill covers 1,984 acres that teem with wildlife and offers more than 25 miles of well-marked trails. One trail in particular, the Warner Trail, provides an exceptional view of the surrounding area from 491 feet. (You have to earn the view by climbing up Bluff Head.) Admission is $4 for adults, $3 for seniors and children aged 3–12. Members enter for free. Trails are open daily from dawn to dusk. The best way to get to Moose Hill is off of Route 128/I-95 S. Take Exit 10. At the end of the ramp, make a left towards Sharon Street; then travel a quarter-mile and turn right onto Route 27 towards Walpole. After half a mile, turn left onto Moose Hill Street. Follow the MAS signs to the parking lot on the left. Find your way to the Visitor Center. All of the trails stem from there. For more information call 781-784-5691.

Walden Woods

Henry David Thoreau's account of his two-year stay in Walden is credited with sparking the conservation movement. Though nestled between railroad tracks and busy Route 2, Walden Pond is still a peaceful and pleasant setting for an afternoon walk no matter what season. The 102-foot deep Walden Pond is just one part of the 2680-acre Walden Woods. There is an easy loop trail around the pond, which passes by the site of Thoreau's house (a replica sits in the parking lot). If you get too hot, you can always stop for a quick dip. Easy interconnecting trails link up with the neighboring Walden Woods and Lincoln Conservation Trust. The main parking area is on Route 126 off of Route 2. Parking ($5) is limited to 350 spaces and fills up quickly on hot summer days. If there is no ranger at the gate, you will need exact change for the annoying automated ticket machine, inevitably causing longer delays than dealing with a live person. On crowded days, there are designated times of the day when they let people in. Call ahead at 781-259-4700, and visit www.walden.org for more information.

Sports · **Swimming**

General Information

City of Boston Swimming:	www.cityofboston.gov/bcyf/facilities.asp
Department of Conservation Resources:	www.mass.gov/dcr/recreate/swimming.htm
MIT Zesiger Center:	http://web.mit.edu/zcenter/aquatics/index.html
YMCA of Greater Boston:	www.ymcaboston.org
New England Masters Swimming:	www.swimnem.org

Overview

With your swimming options including universities, the oldest Y in the country, and few local gyms, it's easier to skip the many poorly maintained pools of the city with their odd hours. While the city's pools are the cheapest option (meaning free), they're only open from mid-June to mid-August. You'll find the city's website little help in locating pools and the only way to get schedules is to call each pool directly. For serious lap swimmers, the largest indoor pool in Boston is at **MIT's Zesiger Center (Map 27)**, running short course all winter and changing lanes to a 50 m for summer. Day passes are available. New England Masters maintains a comprehensive listing on swimming clubs, workout locations, and stroke clinics. There are also YMCAs scattered around the metro area.

In the summer, the DCR operates many outdoor swimming and wading pools and public beaches along the Bay and at local ponds. Their Website lists the hours and locations. The most famous wading pool is the Frog Pond in Boston Common. If fighting for pool space amongst hordes of screaming children is not your thing, favorite alternatives include taking a dip in Walden Pond in Concord (get there early, as the parking lot fills up fast) and strolling the busy beaches at Revere and Wollaston, which can be accessed by the Blue and Red Lines respectively. The Standells might "love that dirty water," but ongoing efforts to improve the once dangerous water quality of the Charles River continue, and the Charles River Swimming Club held its first ever one-mile swim in 2007 to demonstrate its safety (toxic algae postponed it in 2006), but recreational swimming is not encouraged, especially after a heavy rain.

Where to Swim

	Address	Phone	Fees	Map
Boston Harbor Island National Park Beach	ferry leaves from Long Wharf outside Marriott Hotel, 296 State St	617-223-8666	Free (but unavoidable $10–12 ferry ticket)	2
Mirabella Pool	585 Commercial St	617-635-5235	$10 adults, kids under 5 free	2
Central Branch YMCA Pool	316 Huntington Ave	617-536-6950	Membership $55.60 per month. Plus $100 joining fee	5
Blackstone Community Center	50 W Brookline St	617-635-5162	$25 per year, children $5	7
Charlestown Community Center	255 Medford St	617-635-5169	$25 per year adults, $5 children	8
Harborside Community Center	312 Border St	617-635-5114	$25 per year adults, $5 children	9
Paris Street Pool	113 Paris St	617-635-5122	$20 per year adults, $5 children	9
Condon Community Center	200 D St	617-635-5100	$5 adults, $3 youth	10
Curley Community Center	1663 Columbia Rd	617-635-5104	$25 per year	11
Madison Park Community Center	55 New Dudley St	617-635-5206	$10 per year adults, $4 children	13
Curtis Hall Community Center	20 South St	617-635-5193	$25 per year adults, $5 children	14
Hennigan Community Center	200 Heath St	617-635-5198	$25 per year adults, $5 children	15
Clougherty Pool	Bunker Hill St	617-635-5173	Free	16
Dealtry Memorial Pool	114 Pleasant St	617-923-0073	Free	16
Brookline Swimming Pool	60 Tappan St	617-713-5435	$5 adults, $3 students	17
Brighton/Allston Pool	380 N Beacon St	617-254-2965	Free	18
Oak Square YMCA	615 Washington St	617-782-3535	$58/month	18
McCrehan Memorial	356 Rindge Ave	617-354-9154	Free	22
Cambridge Family YMCA	820 Massachusetts Ave	617-661-9622	$48 per month & $50 joining fee	27
Veterans Memorial Pool	719 Memorial Dr	617-354-9381	Free	27
Zesiger Sports and Fitness Center	120 Vassar St	617-452-3690	$12 per day adults, $7 children	27
Mason Pool	159 Norfolk Ave	617-635-5241	$10 per year (adult), $5 (under 18)	28
Boston Chinatown Neighborhood Center Pool	885 Washington St	617-635-5129	$32 per year adults, $12 children	31
Constitution Beach	Orient Heights, E Boston	617-626-4973	Free	n/a
Crane Beach	Argilla Rd, Ipswich	978-356-4354	$2 per car for members / $7 per car for non-members	n/a
Nantasket Beach	Nantasket Ave, Hull	617-727-8856	Free	n/a
Revere Beach	Revere Beach Blvd, Revere	617-727-8856	Free	n/a

General Information

NFT Map: 16
Address: 4 Yawkey Wy
                Boston, MA 02215
Phone: 617-267-9440
Website: www.redsox.com

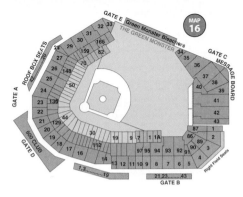

Overview

It would be only the slightest of exaggerations to say that, in Boston, the Red Sox are a religion and Fenway Park is a house of worship. Situated just outside Kenmore Square, Fenway Park is a place where the reputedly unfriendly locals find fellowship in their deep love of the Sox and an even deeper hatred of the Yankees. In fact, Red Sox Nation is still (and will forever be) gloating over the historic 2004 comeback win against the evil men in pinstripes. Yet, our gloating increased quite a bit in 2007, as the Sox once again brought home the World Series Trophy with a four game sweep of the Colorado Rockies, while the Yankees were at home washing their uniforms. That's two World Series wins in four seasons, after an 86-year drought. Boston is truly in its baseball renaissance.

Despite this devotion, even the most die-hard fan cannot deny two basic truths: Fenway is old and Fenway is small. The first game at Fenway Park, played on April 20, 1912, got bumped off the front page of the newspapers by the breaking news of the Titanic sinking a few days earlier. With only 39,928 seats, it's the smallest park in the majors, though management has recently added a few thousand more seats in some very creative locations to expand capacity.

With age, however, comes a rich sense of history, and the dusty corners of Fenway have more personality than perhaps any other park in the game. The best-known of these character traits is the towering Green Monster, the 37-foot left field wall whose odd location can turn pop flies into homers and homers into singles. Marking the right field foul line is Pesky's Pole, named for Sox legend Johnny Pesky. On the manually operated scoreboard in left field, Morse Code dots and dashes spell out the initials of Red Sox owner Tom Yawkey and his wife.

Truly patriotic citizens of Red Sox Nation should take the Fenway Park tour. A tour leaves from Yawkey Way every hour Mon–Sun 9 am–4 pm. To get more information (recommended), call the Tours Hotline on 617-226-6666 or email tours@redsox.com.

How to Get There—Driving

Driving isn't the best idea—parking is tight and traffic gets bad on game days. If you must drive, take I-93 to Exit 26 (Storrow Drive). Take the Fenway exit off Storrow Drive and turn right onto Boylston Street for parking.

Parking

Fenway does not provide parking. Area garages and lots charge between $10–$30, but they tend to fill up quickly and empty VERY slowly after the game, often trapping the uninitiated for hours. To grab some of the limited street parking, arrive at least two hours before game time.

How to Get There—Mass Transit

Take the Green Line to Kenmore and follow the crowd to the ballpark. If you're on the D train of the Green Line, use the Fenway stop. The MBTA Commuter Rail's Worcester/Framingham line also goes to Yawkey, a short walk from Fenway Park. There's also a free game-day-only shuttle that connects Gate B at Fenway Park with the Ruggles stop, served by the T's Orange Line and the MBTA Commuter Rail's Attleboro/Stoughton, Needham, and Franklin lines. Subway fare is $1.70; commuter rail fares range from $1.70 to $7.75.

How to Get Tickets

Always difficult to score, Red Sox tickets have become even more precious commodities since the team's curse-shattering World Series win. The first places to try for individual game and season ticket information, are the Red Sox box office at 877-REDSOX9 and the team's website. Ticket prices range from $12 bleacher seats to $312 dugout box seats. For a unique Fenway experience, try to get tickets on the Green Monster: $30 for standing room only and $140 for actual, you know, seats. If the conventional route fails, you will need a combination of money and luck. Check StubHub.com, eBay, or craigslist, but beware of scams. And there are always scalpers trawling Kenmore Square on game day, usually peddling tickets at a substantial mark-up, especially during the playoffs and games against the hated Yankees.

General Information

Address: One Patriot Pl
Foxborough, MA 02035
Phone: 508-543-8200
Websites: www.gillettestadium.com
www.patriots.com
www.revolutionsoccer.net

Upper Level, Corner/End Zone
Upper Level, Sideline
Mezzanine Level, Corner/End Zone
Lower Level, Corner/End Zone
Lower Level, Sideline
* N/A=Non-Alcoholic Section

Overview

As far as NFL franchises go, the New England Patriots were a joke until Bill Parcells took over as head coach in 1993 and Robert Kraft bought the team in 1994. The team continued to play in a mediocre stadium until 2002. Old Schaefer/Sullivan/Foxboro Stadium was an unsightly, obsolete, charmless concrete slab, but the Pats sent it packing in style. The last game at Foxboro Stadium was the hotly debated "Snow Bowl" vs. the Oakland Raiders. Depending on your loyalties, QB Tom Brady either fumbled or "tucked" the ball during a key late-game possession. (It was a tuck.) The Pats won, propelling them to victory in the 2002 Super Bowl.

The 2002 season was ushered in by the opening of Gillette Stadium, where the Patriots proved that their first championship season was no fluke, winning two more Super Bowls over the next three years. Unfortunately they couldn't cap off a perfect season in 2008. The stadium has been accessorized with a 12-story lighthouse and a replica of the Longfellow Bridge at one end of the field. Game attendees who enjoy a snack may be paralyzed by the selection of 106 different concession stands, some of which now sell Patriot-brand meat products such as the First Down Beef Frank and the Sack Attack Mild Italian Sausage. A high definition screen, nearly 1,300 square feet in size, hangs over each end zone.

With a seating capacity of over 68,000, Gillette Stadium does triple duty, also acting as the home of Major League Soccer's New England Revolution and a major concert venue. It can be a good place to catch big names like the Rolling Stones or U2 but, given the size of the stadium, make sure to bring a pair of binoculars if you have anything but the best seats.

The first phase of Patriot Place, a one-million-square-foot entertainment, shopping, and commercial complex on land around the stadium opened in 2007. In other words, it will be a wicked huge mall. Look for more shops and attractions to open in the coming years.

How to Get There—Driving

From Boston, take I-93 S to I-95 S; take I-95 S to Exit 9 (Wrentham) onto Route 1 S. Follow Route 1 S approximately three miles to Gillette Stadium (on the left).

Parking

The lots open four hours before Pats games and three hours before concerts and other events and two hours before Revolution games, leaving plenty of time for tailgating—an opportunity fans use to the fullest. General Seating ticket holders should enter lot P2, P5, or P10 from Route 1. Follow signs for "General Stadium Parking." Disabled parkers and limos should head for P2, buses for P5, and RVs for P10. For Patriots games, car parking costs $35, RV and limo parking costs $125, and bus parking costs $200. Prices vary for other Gillette events.

How to Get There— Mass Transit

MBTA commuter rail trains leave South Station for Foxboro Station on game days. A round-trip ticket costs $10. The train departs from the stadium 30 minutes after the game.

How to Get Tickets

With the Pats' status as a dynasty now official (including an NFL-record 21-game winning streak), tickets get snapped up. To get on the season ticket waiting list, visit the Patriots' website and have $100 a seat on hand for a deposit. For regular tickets (or concert tickets), call Ticketmaster at 617-931-2222. Game tickets range from $59 to $125. The ubiquitous scalpers can be found roaming the parking lots and approaches to the stadium. StubHub.com, eBay, and Craiglist also accommodate folks who are selling and buying tickets, but be careful—season ticket holders have been known to lose their seats after being caught selling extra tickets online.

General Information

NFT Map: 1
Address: 150 Causeway St
Boston, MA 02114
Phone: 617-624-1805
Celtics: 617-854-8000
Bruins: 617-624-1900
Websites: www.tdbanknorthgarden.com
www.bostonceltics.com
www.bostonbruins.com

Overview

Greater Boston's long regional sports nightmare is over. Once again Celtics and Bruins fans can accurately say that their teams compete in "the Garden." The original Boston Garden, which opened in 1928, earned the adoration of Bostonians as the arena in which Bird, McHale, and Parish propelled the Celts to dynasty status. In footage of the team's 1984 NBA finals victory over the Lakers, fans crowd the sidelines and rush the court with time left on the clock. Bruins games could be even less civil and, correspondingly, even more fun.

As the 1980s drew to a close, however, both the Celtics and the Garden lost a bit of their luster. The team began a slow decline from glory and the venue grew more and more decrepit. Finally in 1995, the FleetCenter was constructed next door and both the Celtics and the Bruins said goodbye to their old stomping grounds. The new name took years to catch on among the area's stubborn traditionalists. When Fleet was acquired by Bank of America, the new parent company sold the naming rights—for $6 million a year—to TD Banknorth, who promptly reinstated the proper name. The 19,580-seat TD Banknorth Garden has all that you would expect from a modern arena—rocket-launched t-shirts, overpriced food and beer, luxury box TVs, and airline and casino promotions during timeouts—but still holds on to touches of tradition, including the Celts' legendary parquet floor. Nonetheless, even with the relative success of the Celts and Bs in recent years, the new venue just doesn't seem to inspire the same sort of love as did its dilapidated predecessor. That's beginning to change as the unstoppable trio of Paul Pierce, Ray Allen, and Kevin Garnett are winning games, pumping up the home crowd, and making the hardcore Celtics fans start to wonder if they might be adding a 17th Championship banner to the rafters in the near future.

In addition to sporting events, the TD Banknorth Garden hosts the circus and concerts by artists ranging from Beyonce to U2.

How to Get There—Driving

Driving to the Garden is no more difficult than getting any place else in Boston by car—which is to say that it is quite difficult. From the north, take I-93 S to Exit 26A (Leverett Circle/Cambridge). Follow the signs (if construction hasn't relocated them) towards North Station/TD Banknorth

| | Loge | | Club | | Balcony |

Garden. Take a right at the end of the ramp; the arena will be on your left. From the south, take I-93 N to Exit 26 (Storrow Drive). After the exit, keep left and follow the signs (see above warning) for TD Banknorth Garden. Watch out, it's a left-hand exit. The Garden will be on your left.

Parking

Reason number two not to drive: The TD Banknorth Garden doesn't have its own parking facilities, but there are several nearby garages ready and willing to gouge you, including a parking facility underneath the arena.

How to Get There— Mass Transit

The TD Banknorth Garden sits atop the North Station commuter rail station, which services the northern suburbs. Directly underneath is a new "superstation" that finally puts North Station's Green Line and Orange Line T stops in the same location. The Charles/MGH Red Line stop and the Bowdoin Blue Line stop are less than a two-minute walk away. Commuter rail fares range from $1.70 to $7.75.

How to Get Tickets

To get Celtics season tickets, call 866-4CELTIX or visit the Celtics' website. They offer full-season, half-season, and multi-game packages. Individual ticket prices range from $25 nosebleed seats to $275 courtside seats. The mid-range $55 end-court seats offer an excellent value.

To get Bruins season tickets call 617-624-BEAR or visit the Bruins' website. The Bs offer full-season, half-season, and ten-game packages, with individual ticket prices ranging from $26 to $101, topping out with the mysteriously un-priced Premium Club. (If you have to ask, you can't afford them.)

If you don't have tickets but have cash to burn, scalpers can be found on Causeway Street on game days.

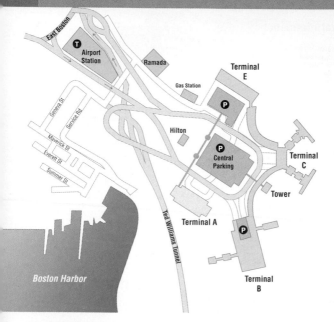

Airline	Terminal	Phone Number
Aer Lingus	E	800-474-7424
Air Canada/ Air Canada Jazz	B	888-247-2262
Air France	E	800-237-2747
AirTran	C	800-247-8726
Alaska Airlines	B	800-252-7522
Alitalia	E	800-223-5730
American (except int'l arrivals)	B	800-433-7300
American (int'l arrivals only)	E	800-433-7300
American Eagle	B	800-433-7300
British Airways	E	800-247-9297
Cape Air	C	800-352-0714
Continental	A	800-525-0280
Delta Air Lines	A	800-221-1212
Delta Connection/Com Air	A	800-354-9822
Delta Shuttle	A	800-221-1212
Finnair	E	800-950-5000
Iberia	E	800-772-4642

Airline	Terminal	Phone Number
Icelandair	E	800-223-5500
JetBlue (except int'l arrivals)	C	800-538-2583
JetBlue (int'l arrivals only)	E	800-538-2583
Lufthansa	E	800-645-3880
Midwest	C	800-452-2022
Northwest/ KLM	E	800-225-2525
SATA	E	800-762-9995
Spirit Airlines	B	800-772-7117
Swiss	E	877-359-7947
TACV	E	866-359-8228
United	C	800-241-6522
United Express	C	800-241-6522
US Airways	B	800-428-4322
US Airways Express	B	800-428-4322
US Airways Shuttle	B	800-428-4322
Virgin Atlantic	E	800-862-8621

General Information

Website:	www.massport.com/logan
Customer Service:	617-561-1800
Ground Transportation Info:	800-23-LOGAN
Logan Lost and Found:	617-561-1714
Parking Office:	617-561-1673

Overview

The 120th-busiest airport in the United States, Logan International Airport features all the serpentine security lines and two-mile gate runs of most major airports and is located in an area of the country where weather can ground planes at any time of the year. Nonetheless, it was ranked seventh in traveler satisfaction in a 2007 survey by J.D. Power and Associates. And, thanks to the completion of the Big Dig and the extension of the Silver Line, getting to Logan is easier now than ever.

Jutting into the harbor from East Boston, Logan opened in 1923 as the "temporary occupant" on landfill originally intended to be a port. By 1939, flying contraptions had proven their worth and the site was made permanent. The airport is named after Lt. General Edward Lawrence Logan, a local and a Harvard grad who served in the Spanish-American War, the Massachusetts House of Representatives, and the Senate.

The decade-long Logan Modernization Project, now moving into its later stages, has been taking the airport through a bewildering maze of construction and renovation. Within the past few years, the airport opened a completely overhauled Terminal A, a new T station, an extended Silver Line, a new arrivals hall in international-serving Terminal E, and improved access to the Central Parking Garage. The final piece of the project, a two-year, $14 million initiative to standardize and improve the airport's signage, is under way.

If good planning or bad weather leaves you with time to kill before your flight, you can get your hair coiffed at the salon, grab a gourmet snack at Jasper White's Summer Shack or one of the three Legal Seafood locations, or just spend an hour letting yourself be hypnotized by the rhythmic movements of billiard balls through the kinetic sculpture in Terminal C.

How to Get There—Driving

To get to Logan from the west, take the Mass Pike (I-90) E through the Ted Williams Tunnel until the highway ends. From the south, use I-93 N and take Exit 20 to I-90 E. From the north, take I-93 S and follow the signs to the Callahan Tunnel. Check www.massport.com for traffic and construction updates.

Parking

Hourly and daily parking are available at Central Parking Garage, Terminal B Garage, and Terminal E Parking Lots 1 and 2. Rates range from $3 to $24 during the day and $36 to $48 a day for overnight parking. The Economy Parking lot charges a daily rate of $27 and a weekly rate of $108.

How to Get There—Mass Transit

Seriously, take the T. It's a quick ride on the Blue Line from downtown to the Airport stop. A free shuttle bus that runs 4am–1am, will take you from the T stop to your terminal. Or take the Red Line to South Station and transfer to the Silver Line bus, which stops at each airport terminal. If you're coming in from the 'burbs, check out the Logan Express buses that service Braintree, Framingham, Peabody, and Woburn. A Park-and-Ride system is in place, and although the prices for parking and buses vary, they will always be cheaper than taking a cab. If you're downtown near the water, the MBTA's Harbor Express water taxi can get you from Long Wharf to the airport in less than ten minutes.

How to Get There—Taxi

It's hard to get to Logan from anywhere except Eastie for less than $20. Boston Cab: 617-536-5010; Checker Taxi: 617-536-7000; City Cab: 617-536-5100; Green Cab (Somerville): 617-623-6000; Cambridge Cab: 617-776-5000.

Rental Cars

Alamo	800-327-9633
Avis	800-831-2847
Budget	800-527-0700
Dollar	800-800-4000
Hertz	800-654-3131
National	800-227-7368
Enterprise	800-325-8007 (off-airport)
Thrifty	800-367-2277 (off-airport)

Hotels

Courtyard Boston Tremont • 275 Tremont St • 617-426-1400
Embassy Suites • 207 Porter St • 617-567-5000
Hampton Inn • 230 Lee Burbank Hwy • 781-286-5665
Hilton • 85 Terminal Rd • 617-568-6700
Holiday Inn • 225 McClellan Hwy • 617-569-5250
Hyatt • 101 Harborside Dr • 617-568-1234 • 800-633-7313
Marriott Long Wharf • 296 State St • 617-227-0800
Omni Parker House • 60 School St • 617-227-8600
Hilton Boston Downtown • 89 Broad St • 617-556-0006

History

The story begins just after World War II. When the good people at the Massachusetts Department of Public Works noticed the increasing popularity of automobiles and the stream of people leaving the city for the suburbs, they decided to make plans to build some major highways. The first highway to be completed was I-93, the Central Artery, hailed at the time as "a futuristic highway in the sky."

It soon became apparent that I-93 totally sucked. It was ugly, disruptive to neighborhoods, and boasted a high accident rate due to the excessive number of entry and exit ramps along the 1.5-mile stretch through the city. Recognizing that the Central Artery was a disaster, community groups fought successfully to stop other major highway projects. Two plans that never came to fruition were the Inner Belt (unbuilt I-695), which would have taken traffic around I-93 via a new, ten-lane BU bridge, and the Southwest Corridor Highway (unbuilt I-95), which would have run from the 93/128 split up through Hyde Park and JP to central Boston.

While averting construction of two new highways was a small victory for city dwellers, I-93 was still operating at triple its capacity, resulting in traffic jams more than hours of the day. The solution to the congestion was to dig a highway under the city—a solution that rather resembled performing open-heart surgery on a fully awake patient. Planning the project took the entirety of the 1980s and construction finally began in September 1991. After fifteen years and almost fifteen billion dollars, the project is officially finished. Hallelujah!

What is the Big Dig?

As most Bostonians know, the substantially completed "Central Artery/Tunnel Project" was, as the Massachusetts Turnpike Authority puts it, "the largest, most complex and technologically challenging highway project ever." The most important element of the Big Dig is the routing of I-93 from the Central Artery to a new (and leaky) tunnel. Other major aspects of the Dig include the extension of the Mass Pike to Logan Airport through the Ted Williams Tunnel, the construction of the beautiful Leonard P. Zakim Bunker Hill Bridge (yeah, it's a ridiculously long name), the erection of the Leverett Circle Connector Bridge, and a complete overhaul of the roads and traffic patterns around Logan Airport. The 2006 opening of the Albany Street off-ramp from I-93 S marked the point when all of the Dig's tunnels and bridges and their connection and ramps to surface roads were open to general traffic.

But when exactly does a civil engineering project of this magnitude "end"? Is it when the last orange pylon is removed from the road, or when the litigation finally wraps up? The I-93 tunnel (O'Neill Tunnel) sprouted a leak in 2004 shortly after opening to traffic. In its design for the tunnel, contractor Bechtel/Parsons Brinckerhoff recommended an approach that had never been used for another highway tunnel in the US, rejecting the more conventional design of lining the huge slurry walls with a concrete "tunnel box" in favor of making the slurry walls the tunnel's *only* walls. When the tunnel construction later necessitated waterproofing, the lack of interior walls caused some major problems. While the leaky walls and the endless construction are causes of concern and ennui for the daily commuters, the faulty bolts that fasten the concrete ceiling tiles are another issue all together. In July 2006, a woman was killed by one such tile falling on her car in the I-90 connector on her way to Logan Airport, a tragic event that lead to comprehensive inspections within the tunnels and the discovery of dangerous structural flaws and evidence of negligence. After extensive closings and traffic rerouting, the tunnel ceiling tiles have all reportedly been reinforced, though, and we are told that travel is once again wet and safe, but the loss of human life has added an unfortunate and serious undertone to Big Dig's already infamous story.

Development Plans

As of December 31, 2007, the Big Dig is officially finished, with the final price tag ringing up at $14.8 billion (ouch). The old elevated 93 has finally come down, leading to a great deal more walking traffic from Faneuil Hall to the North End, and requiring facelifts on the sides of the buildings that now face the lovely Rose Kennedy Greenway, a 27-acre green space extending from Chinatown to the North End. Post-Dig developers also hope to incorporate the construction of parks and other pedestrian-friendly spots along the Fort Point Channel, along the Charles River between the Museum of Science and the North End, and in East Boston.

For updates on all the exciting plans, check out www.rosekennedygreenway.org.

General Information

Mass Highway Department: www.mhd.state.ma.us
Massport: www.massport.com
Big Dig: www.masspike.com/bigdig

Overview

The first bridge built in the American colonies (a pile bridge, incidentally) was completed in 1662, connecting Cambridge and Brighton. It stood where the Larz Anderson Bridge stands today. Fast-forward 350 years and you'll find no fewer than ten bridges spanning the Charles River from the Inner Harbor to Brighton, including the Boston University Bridge, the Harvard Bridge (a.k.a. the Mass Ave Bridge), and the Longfellow Bridge (with its salt-and-pepper-shaker towers), all of which offer great views of the skyline. (The view from the BU Bridge is our favorite.) Other bridges further upstream cross the river at River Street, Western Avenue, JFK Street/North Harvard Street (the Larz Anderson Bridge), and Gerry's Landing Road/Soldiers Field Road (the Eliot Bridge).

The Hub's new pet landmark is the Leonard P. Zakim Bunker Hill Bridge. No postcard of the Boston skyline seems complete without the Zakim, which connects downtown Boston with Charlestown. Perhaps the only Big Dig undertaking worth its salt, the Zakim is the widest cable-stayed bridge in the world, with soaring towers designed to reflect nearby Bunker Hill Monument. The bridge gives off a luminous glow at night, adding to its impressive appearance. According to the *Portsmouth Herald*, some call it the "Bill Buckner Bridge" as traffic passes through an inverted Y-shaped structure like the ball that passed through the legs of the Red Sox first baseman during the 1986 World Series. Poor Bill Buckner. Unlike the other bridges crossing the Charles, the Zakim is unfortunately not open to pedestrians. The Charlestown Bridge, now somewhat overshadowed by the Zakim, connects the North End and Charlestown and was once the scene of many Irish/Italian gang fights.

The old green lady crossing the Mystic River and connecting Charlestown with Chelsea is the Tobin Bridge. The three lanes on the lower level of the Tobin run northbound; the three lanes on the upper level run southbound. Drivers heading south on the Tobin must pay a toll (30 cents with a resident commuter permit and $3 for everyone else).

The Evelyn Moakley Bridge, built in the mid-1990s over the Fort Point Channel to divert traffic from the historic-but-decaying Northern Avenue Bridge, is itself decaying at an alarmingly fast pace. Be careful walking across the bridge at high tide.

And remember: The Callahan Tunnel takes you to the airport (no toll) and the Sumner Tunnel takes you from the airport (yes, toll).

Bridge	Engineer (E); Architect (A)	Length	Opened
Boston University Bridge	Desmond and Lord (A) John Rablin (E)		1928
Charlestown (N Washington St) Bridge			1901
Congress Street Bridge			1930
Eliot Bridge	Maurice Witner (A) Burns & Kennerson (E)		1950
Evelyn Moakley Bridge	Ammann & Whitney (A) Modern Continental (E)	800'	1996
Harvard Bridge	William Jackson (E)	364.4 smoots, one ear	1891
Larz Anderson Bridge	Wheelright, Haven, and Hoyt (A) John Rablin (E)		1915
Leverett Circle Connector Bridge	HNTB Corporation (E)	830'	1999
Longfellow Bridge	Edmund M. Wheelwright (A) William Jackson (E)	1,768'	1906
Malden (Alford St) Bridge		2420'	
Northern Avenue Bridge		636'	1908
River Street Bridge	Robert Bellows (A) John Rablin (E)	330'	1926
Summer Street Bridge	John Cheney (A) William Jackson (E)		1899
Tobin Memorial Bridge	JE Grenier Co (A)	1,525'	1950
Weeks Footbridge	McKim, Mead, and White (A) John Rablin (E)		1924
Western Avenue Bridge	John Rablin (E)	328'	1924
Leonard P. Zakim Bunker Hill Bridge	Christian Menn (designer) Miguel Rosales (A) HNTB Corporation (E)	1,457'	2002

Tunnel	Engineer	Length	Opened
Callahan Tunnel			1961
O'Neill Tunnel	Bechtel/Parsons Brinckerhoff (E)		2003
Sumner Tunnel			1934
Ted Williams Tunnel	Jacobs Engineering Group (designer) Bechtel/Parsons Brinckerhoff (E)	8,500'	1995

Transit · **Driving**

General Information

Websites:
Boston: www.cityofboston.gov/transportation/
parking.asp
Brookline: www.town.brookline.ma.us/
transportation
Cambridge: www.cambridgema.gov/traffic
Somerville: www.ci.somerville.ma.us
Mass. RMV: www.state.ma.us/rmv

Phones:
Boston: 617-635-4680
Brookline: 617-730-2177
Cambridge: 617-349-4700
Somerville: 617-666-3311

Overview

Boston driving is a sport in which locals claim a distinct home-field advantage. We intentionally put up very few signs, have roadways that are labeled as both North and South at the same time, and claim, with pride mind you, the most aggressive road-ragers in the entire Northeast. Driving in the city itself is done more by "feel" than by specific directions, as traffic, Sox games, and construction projects make every trip an adventure in side streets and wrong turns.

The road system in Boston grew organically as the city expanded and merged with small farming villages such as Brighton, Dorchester, and Roxbury. Little, if any, urban planning took place. The result is the chaos of today, an exasperating, exhilarating tangle of streets that are a source of pride to those who master them.

Depending on who you ask, Boston drivers are either the best in the country or the most frightening. As a rule, however, they are both aggressive and competent. Years of experience have taught them precisely how far they can push the envelope on sudden lane changes and risky passing maneuvers.

For the novice, it may be intimidating, but the initial challenge makes the eventual mastery that much more satisfying.

Survival Tips

Learn the Vocabulary: In driving, as in other areas, Bostonians have their own distinct vocabulary. Therefore, it is wicked important to know the following terms:

- Rotary- Known in other parts of the country as a roundabout or traffic circle. Poor rotary skills are near the top of most Bostonians driving pet peeve lists, so it is important to remember that vehicles already in the rotary have right-of-way.

- Square- A location at which several feeder streets connect in odd formations and strange angles (e.g. Harvard or Davis). Squares are rarely, if ever, square.

- Masshole- From the mouths of out-of-staters, a derogatory term. For a true Boston driver, a label worn with pride.

- The Expressway- Refers to the Southeast Expressway, the southern half of the length of I-93 that runs through the city. Common usage: "The Expressway is a parking lot."

- *@%$ you- A helpful driving tip frequently offered by fellow motorists.

Be aggressive: Drive the streets of Boston, don't let the streets drive you. Other drivers express their displeasure with such assertiveness, but, secretly, they respect it.

Be color blind: A yellow light (and the first ten seconds of a red light) are generally considered the functional equivalent of a green light. This goes both ways though, so make sure to pay close attention when you move through a new green light, as you might meet one of the color blind drivers head on.

Plan Very Carefully: Once you deviate from your planned route, one-way streets and unexpected turns may make it hard to get back on track. And once your route is in place…

Triple-check your directions: Because of the paucity of road signs in Boston, driving directions are likely to be heavily landmark-based. Be wary of landmarks like "that bridge with the construction on it" or "that Dunkin' Donuts on the corner," since that could be any block in the city. If someone tells you to take a right or a left, ask *how much* of a right or a left.

Get lost anyway: There's really no good way of preparing for what's in store. Just do it. Leave yourself some extra time and learn to enjoy being lost. We promise, one day it will start making sense.

General Information

Websites:
Boston: www.cityofboston.gov/transportation/
             parking.asp
Brookline: www.town.brookline.ma.us/
             transportation/parking/parking.html
Cambridge: www.cambridgema.gov/Traffic/
             index.cfm
Somerville: www.ci.somerville.ma.us

Phones:
Boston: 617-635-4680
Brookline: 617-730-2230
Cambridge: 617-349-4700
Somerville: 617-625-6600

Overview

When parking within the city, you'll need time, patience, and a sixth sense for parking spots that are *about* to open up. With a few notable exceptions (near Fenway during Sox games comes to mind), careful circling of a target area will eventually yield results. If patience fails, a willingness to pay the outrageous fees at a parking garage is also helpful. There are, however, bargains to be found; the rates at the Post Office Square garage are amazing considering its location and the Cambridgeside Galleria charges only $1 per hour.

Depending on where you live, and whether parking in Boston causes you to regularly lose your temper, you might want to reconsider even owning a car. The North End and Allston are crowded neighborhoods with narrow streets jam-packed with parked cars. As it becomes colder and snowier, Boston residents become fiercely protective of their parking spots, using traffic cones, lawn chairs, and other assorted paraphernalia to claim their freshly shoveled out spaces. Fisticuffs over disputed parking spots are not unheard of. Somerville, Cambridge, and Brookline, however, aren't quite as bad for parking, in part due to vast "resident-only parking" zones (generally resented by non-residents).

Ultimately, if you live in Boston and own a car, you will receive *at least* one ticket a month. Maybe there was street cleaning the night before. Maybe there was a parking ban because of snow. Or maybe you got towed because there's a construction project and you missed the half-hidden "Tow Zone" sign that workers positioned conveniently on the sidewalk under a discarded pizza box. It doesn't matter what you do and how careful you are—*they will get you*—so just add it to the monthly budget.

How to Get Permits

In Somerville, take a lease or a current bill with your address and your registration to 133 Holland Street. In Boston, take your registration and a current bill with your address to City Hall, Room 224, at Government Center. All Brookline wants is $15 and, apparently, they don't care where you live. Brookline Town Hall is at 333 Washington Street. In the People's Republic of Cambridge, you need your registration saying that either you or your car (it's not clear which) weighs less than 2.5 tons and proof of residency. You can visit the website and download the form and send copies of the above with a check for $8 (bargain!) to Cambridge Traffic, Parking & Transportation, Resident Parking, 238 Broadway, Cambridge, MA 02139.

Towing

Cars get towed for snow emergencies, street cleaning, and other emergency violations, so keep an eye out for Nor'easters, third Thursdays, and massive construction. If your car gets towed, it'll cost you at least $100 to get it back.

The Boston BTD Tow Lot is located at 200 Frontage Road, near the Andrew T stop in Dorchester/Southie. The City of Boston website says that "walking is not encouraged" due, obviously, to the Big Dig. Cabs can be hailed at the Andrew T stop.

Brookline, Somerville, and Cambridge use private, commercial lots to store your newly towed car. Call one of the numbers above, and they'll (hopefully) be able to tell you where your car is.

The Somerville tow lot is, for reasons unknown, Pat's Auto Body on McGrath Highway near Union Square.

Cambridge either has a top-secret tow lot, or it rotates. If your car gets towed, they ask you to call the police (617-349-3300), who will presumably then tell you where your car is.

Brookline has a similarly clandestine car imprisonment system. A call to their transportation/parking office should unearth your car.

Tickets

Because it allows them to take your money immediately, all four places offer online ticket payment. Tickets are dispensed for offenses such as double-parking, expired meters, non-resident parking on a resident-only street, street cleaning violations, and the city/town needing money. Regardless of the city, you're looking at about 50 bucks per infringement.

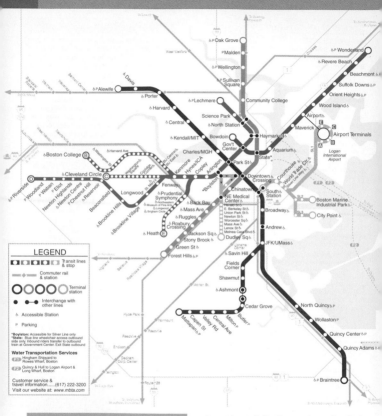

General Information

Website:	www.mbta.com
Phone:	617-222-5000

Overview

Maps of the T show its four subway lines (Red, Orange, Blue, and Green) and the Silver Line (the T's mash-up of a subway line and a bus). All of the T lines except the Green Line's B train move you across the city at a decent clip. But if you need to get from Davis Square (Somerville) to Cleveland Circle (Brighton), well…it's not easy. Despite the proximity of the two places, you have to go downtown on one line (Red) and back out on another (Green)—an 11-mile trip connecting destinations that are 6.5 miles apart. Another T peeve is that the last trains depart from stations between midnight and 1 am, even though last call at Boston bars is between 1 and 2 am. (Some Redcoat traditions live on.) Late-night revelers are left to shell out for cabs.

The Red Line: The T's flagship line, the Red Line runs from Alewife in Cambridge through Davis Square, Harvard Square, MIT, the Esplanade (where you can admire the sparkling new Charles/MGH station,) the Common, Southie, and Dorchester. At the JFK/UMass stop, the line splits in two: The Ashmont train goes to Dorchester (with a connecting trolley to Mattapan), and the Braintree train runs through Quincy. A fun game to play on the Red Line: Bet with your friends about which student riders and professorial-looking types will get off at which university stops.

The Green Line: This is the oldest operational subway in the country, and it shows. Not a grown-up subway like the Red, Orange, and Blue Lines, the Green Line features light-rail "trolleys"—130-foot-long green Twinkies—that shoot you beneath the city of Boston before emerging onto streets and getting stuck in traffic.

The Green Line runs from Lechmere in Cambridge as far as Kenmore in Boston. Stops along the way include the Museum of Science, TD Banknorth Garden, Faneuil Hall, the Common, Back Bay, and Fenway Park. At Kenmore, the B (Boston College), C (Cleveland Circle), and D (Riverside) trains diverge and emerge from the ground as trolleys. The E train parts ways two stops back at Copley. The B is the slowest train because you forbid the Boston University kids walk anywhere. Lots of stops + lots of red lights = long rides. The B takes you through BU, Allston, Brighton, and as far as Boston College. The C runs along Beacon Street through Coolidge Corner (in Brookline) to Cleveland Circle (in Brighton). When getting off the train at Cleveland Circle, note the trolley making a wide circular turn through four-way traffic which, inexplicably, leads to a lot of accidents. The D runs through Fenway and Brookline Village to Chestnut Hill before hitting several Newton neighborhoods. The E (Heath Street) train splits before Kenmore at Copley and services Symphony Hall, Mission Hill, Northeastern University, the Museum of Fine Arts, and Longwood Medical Area. Don't believe the maps that tell you E trains terminate at Forest Hills. This service was "temporarily" suspended in 1986—meanwhile, the 39 bus will take you from Heath Street to Forest Hills.

Somerville residents have been patiently waiting for the arrival of a long-promised, but controversial, extension of the Green Line. This extension, which would take the Green Line from Lechmere through exhaust-clogged Union Square to West Medford, is now expected to open no sooner than 2011, and even that delayed date could be pushed back.

The Orange Line: The Orange Line worked as an elevated trolley running above Washington Street until the 1980s. Today, it's a legitimate train that runs below the Southwest Corridor Park. The park and the Orange Line follow a path originally designed for the extension of I-95 through Boston. Community groups defeated the proposal in 1979, convincing officials to put a subway and park on the land instead. The Orange Line runs from Oak Grove in Malden to Forest Hills in Jamaica Plain. Stops along the way include Sullivan Square, Bunker Hill Community College, TD Banknorth Garden, Faneuil Hall, Downtown Crossing, Chinatown, New England Medical Center, Back Bay/South End, as well as a few stops in Roxbury and Jamaica Plain.

The Blue Line: Who rides the Blue Line? MBTA ridership figures show a little over 55,000 daily boardings on the Blue Line, compared to 154,000 on the Orange, 210,500 on the Red, and about 205,000 on the Green. Running from Bowdoin Street downtown to Wonderland in Revere, this is the line you want to ride if you're going fishing, flying, or betting on horses and dogs. On your way east, you'll pass the Aquarium, Logan Airport, Suffolk Downs, and Revere Beach before winding up at Wonderland and its dog track. The stations at Aquarium and Logan have been renovated and made more accessible; other stations on the Blue Line are due to get the same treatment over the next couple of years.

The Silver Line: Now the most convenient way to the airport, this is actually a high-speed bus line. See page 252 for all the salacious details.

Parking

Your chances of finding parking increase as you move further away from downtown, but generally only end cap stations and suburban stations provide day parking. Garages and lots fill up quickly on weekdays. Prices vary. Parking in resident-only spots will result in a ticket and, in some areas, a keying.

Fares and Passes

In 2007, the MBTA replaced subway tokens with the magnetic-stripe CharlieCard and the paper CharlieTicket. (The "Charlie" moniker was taken from the Kingston Trio's 1959 hit, "Charlie on the MTA.") A subway ride costs $1.70 using the CharlieCard, and $2 with the paper CharlieTicket. The monthly subway/bus "Linkpass" costs $59, and reduced fares are available for seniors, people with disabilities, and junior-high and high school students. Children under 11 ride free when accompanied by an adult. Passes are sold at certain T stops and in some stores, however—the T has stated that it will no longer give away the rechargeable plastic CharlieCard, and will instead charge a fee for new and replacement cards. To find out where to buy a pass or to purchase one online, visit www.mbta.com.

MBTA Buses

Website: www.mbta.com
Phone: 617-222-3200

Every day, intrepid T bus drivers pilot their behemoth vehicles down too-narrow streets filled with angry drivers, errant pedestrians, unfortunate bikers, and, in the winter, ice and snow. (A simple "thank you" to the driver as you get off the bus isn't too much to ask.) MBTA buses run everywhere the subway doesn't, and some places it does. Usually at least one of any bus route's end points is a subway station. The T also runs several popular express buses from outlying neighborhoods to downtown along the Mass Pike and other highways.

The T is in the process of replacing the bulk of its aging diesel fleet with new Compressed Natural Gas (CNG) buses. Identifiable by their blue strip and the low roar of their engines, the new buses reduce emissions by up to 90 percent and, so far, are cleaner on the inside as well (just give them a few years). Some buses on busy routes feature low floors and articulated midsections, such as those used along the Silver Line and JP's 39 bus.

The MBTA has discontinued its popular but unprofitable Night Owl service (is a public service supposed to be profitable, anyway?). The Night Owl used to run buses along the subway routes until 2:30 am on Friday and Saturday nights, helping late-night partiers with a lift home. No word from the MBTA on whether this service will ever re-appear.

With the fare increase in January 2007 and the updating of the T's fare payment system, buses cost $1.50 if you use the paper Charlie Ticket or $1.25 if you use the plastic Charlie Card. The fares on the express buses are also different depending on if you use the ticket ($3.50 for inner express buses $5 for outer express) or card ($2.80 for inner express and $4 for outer express). Monthly bus passes are $40 and subway/bus combos cost as little as $59 for a subway/local bus packages, while express bus combos are either $89 or $129. Students, seniors, and disabled persons can purchase monthly passes at reduced rates. Bus passes can be bought at several T stations or online at www.mbta.com. And you should be able to pick up a Charlie Card at customer service booths in T stations or buy a pre-loaded one at the T's Web site.

Silver Line

Website: www.allaboutsilverline.com
Phone: 617-222-3200

Although the Silver Line appears on the MBTA's subway map, it is actually a high-speed bus line (a "state-of-the-art Bus Rapid Transit system," no less) that, according to the MBTA, "combines the quality of rail transit with the flexibility of buses." The MBTA's public relations materials may be as gassy as the CNG used by some of the new buses, but in fact the new system provides much-needed additional public transport options for Roxbury residents, and is proving handy to airport travelers, Moakley Courthouse staff, and people working at construction sites downtown the waterfront. It's also a convenient way to get to the Bank of America Pavilion for concerts or to one of the many Seaport district restaurants, like the Legal Test Kitchen or Anthony's Pier Four, for dinner and drinks.

The Silver Line is being constructed in three phases. Completed Phase I runs between Downtown Crossing and Dudley Square in Roxbury. Phase II, also completed, runs from South Station to Logan Airport, Boston Marine Industrial Park, and City Point. (The MBTA is waffling on its original plan to extend the Silver Line to the Andrew T stop in South Boston/Dorchester.)

Phase III will make it possible to use the Silver Line to travel all the way from Dudley Square to Logan Airport. Phase III will link Phase I and Phase II with a mile-long underground tunnel, which will run beneath Essex Street and Boylston Street and make new connections to the Orange Line (at the Chinatown T stop) and the Green line (at the Boylston T stop). Phase III is scheduled to be completed in 2010, but because there hasn't yet been a decision taken on how the buses will actually *get into* the tunnel, it's anyone's guess when Phase III will go on-line.

The Silver Line Waterfront fare follows the above fare structure for the subway (subway passes are valid) and the Silver Line Washington Street follows that of the bus (bus passes are valid), with Charlie Tickets and Cards in effect for both.

Cambridge EZRide

Website: www.masscommute.com/tmas/crtma/ ezride.html
Phone: 617-839-4636

Cantabridgians who traverse the Charles each morning on their daily commute should check out the EZRide bus service, whose cheery sky-blue coaches run through Cambridge to North Station. The EZRide route begins in Cambridgeport and passes through University Park, Kendall Square, and East Cambridge, making a dozen or so stops along the way.

EZRide operates Monday through Friday only, and does not run on holidays. Service in the morning runs from approximately 6:15 am to 10 am; afternoon service runs from approximately 3:30 pm to 7:30 pm.

A trip on EZRide costs $1. Students, seniors, disabled persons, and children aged 5–11 traveling with an adult pay 50 cents. Flashing an MIT ID lets you ride for free.

Transit · Greyhound / Chinatown Buses

Greyhound

NFT Map: 4
Website: www.greyhound.com
Phone: 800-231-2222

Greyhound buses leave from the South Station bus terminal and they'll take you *anywhere*. It ain't the Concorde, but it'll eventually get you to one of its 3,700 stations across North America. Round-trip tickets to New York usually cost $55–$65 round-trip to Washington DC is $132–$142, and Boston to Philadelphia is $92–$118 round-trip.

South Station is on Atlantic Avenue, one block down from Summer Street. The bus terminal is the taller building behind the rail building.

To get to South Station from the Mass Pike (I-90), take Exit 24A. This exit drops you onto Atlantic Avenue—the bus terminal is on the right side. From I-93 N, take Exit 20 and follow signs for Downtown and South Station. At the lights, continue straight onto Atlantic Avenue.

From I-93 S, take Exit 23 onto Purchase Street, make a left on Kneeland Street, continue to the end of the street, and then take a left onto Atlantic Avenue. On-street parking is scarce. If you're pinched, try the bus terminal's parking garage. The entrance is on Kneeland Street.

The Red Line T line has a stop at South Station, also the end point for the southern routes of the commuter rail. Walk through the train station and past the tracks to reach the bus station entrance.

Chinatown Buses

If you want to get to New York City for *really* cheap, take a Chinatown bus. A round-trip ticket will only cost you $30 on Boston Deluxe, Fung Wah, Lucky Star, or Sunshine. Chinatown buses range from small coaches to full-blown buses with stinky bathrooms and non-functional TVs. We strongly recommend using the bathrooms only in emergency situations, and even then we're not so sure. Fung Wah is the best known, most recently because its notoriously speedy drivers have been involved in several accidents and bus fires. The other carriers are likely to be less crowded and chaotic. Watch out—you don't get left behind in Connecticut during the bathroom break at the Roy Rogers or the buffet at the strip mall.

If you take a late Chinatown bus from NYC, you will get into Boston after the T closes, meaning you'll have to pay for a cab that will cost more than the 200-plus-mile journey from New York.

Boston Deluxe

www.gotobus.com/bostondeluxe/; 617-354-2101
Christian Science Plaza, 175 Huntington Ave (Map 5)
Pick up the Boston Deluxe near the Prudential Center for trips to New York City and Hartford. New York-bound buses depart Friday through Sunday at 8:30 am, 11 am, 1 pm, 4:30 pm, 6 pm, and 10:30 pm and drop off at Broadway and 32nd Street as well as E 86th Street and Second Avenue. Buses to Hartford depart Friday to Sunday at 8:30 am, 11 am, 1 pm, 6 pm, and 10:30 pm and drop off at 365 Capitol Avenue (Charter Oak Supermarket). Both routes cost $30 round-trip.

Fung Wah Bus

www.fungwahbus.com; 617-345-8000
South Station, 700 Atlantic Ave (Map 4)
Buses to New York depart every hour on the hour, from 7 am until 10 pm, with an additional trip at 11:30 pm. Round-trip tickets cost $30. Buses leave from Gate 25 at South Station (left side) and drop off at 139 Canal Street in New York's Chinatown.

Lucky Star Bus

www.luckystarbus.com; 617-426-8802
South Station, 700 Atlantic Ave (Map 4)
Buses to New York depart every hour on the hour, from 7 am until 8 pm. There are also departures at 11:30 pm and 2 am. Round-trip tickets cost $30 (add $10 for the 2 am trip). Buses leave from Gate 13 at South Station and drop off at Christie and Hester Streets in New York's Chinatown.

Sunshine Travel

www.sunshineboston.com;
617-328-0862 or 617-695-1989
31 Harrison Ave, Boston (Map 4);
McDonald's Plaza, Fields Corner, Dorchester (Map 32)
Along with buses departing hourly for NYC ($15 each way, $25 for the 2 am bus), Sunshine Travel offers two-, three-, and four-day tours to places like Tennessee (four days, $178), Chicago (four days, $269), Washington DC (three days, $118), Niagara Falls (two days, $105), and destinations in eastern Canada ($128–$278). Buses to the Mohegan Sun casino in Connecticut depart five times daily, picking up in Dorchester, Boston, and Quincy. Round-trip tickets cost $10, and you'll receive a $20 gambling voucher and a $15 dining voucher if you're 21 years of age or older.

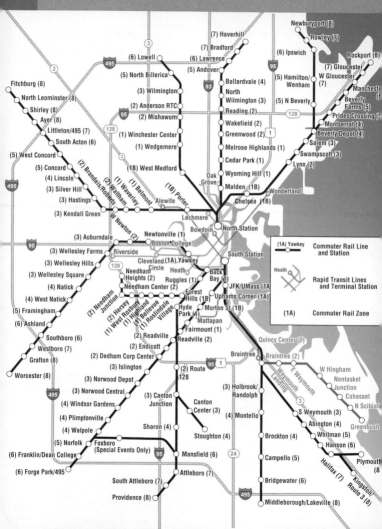

General Information

Website: www.mbta.com
Phone: 617-222-3200 or 800-392-6100

Overview

The commuter rail is a series of train lines that service the outer limits of Greater Boston, the suburbs, and points as far out as Worcester and Providence, Rhode Island. Northbound routes leave from North Station, and southbound routes depart from South Station. Compared to the commuter rail systems of other East Coast cities, Boston's trains make for a relatively pleasant experience. Massachusetts is working to renovate all of the stations, outfitting them with new platforms, electronic signaling, and new ramps and elevators to make them handicapped accessible. As with any major transit network, there are occasional (read: daily) delays on the commuter rail. Still, a ride on the rails is 1,000 percent less stressful than driving in and out of the city every day.

The commuter rail is also a great option for day-trippers going in either direction. Taking the train allows inbound visitors to enjoy, rather than just get lost in, the city. City-dwellers who want to escape the familiar urban landscape can head up to Gloucester for a day at the beach, venture to Plymouth for a history lesson, or just explore a new city down in Providence.

If you're looking at the commuter rail map for the first time, you might think that the lack of a connection between North Station and South Station is a mistake. Well, it may be a mistake, but not on the part of the mapmakers. To get from one station to another, you'll have to use the T (and transfer to a second T), take a cab, or walk. Seriously. For additional information about North Station and South Station, see the next page.

Two projects are extending the commuter rail's reach into the southern part of the state. The MBTA has decided to restore long suspended commuter rail service to the South Shore towns of Braintree, Weymouth, Hingham, Cohasset, and Scituate on what is known as the Greenbush Line. Service was expected to begin mid-2007. In the longer term, Gov. Deval Patrick has pledged to bring commuter rail service back to the cities of New Bedford and Fall River by 2016.

Parking

Parking is available at every commuter rail station except Back Bay, Belmont Center, Chelsea, JFK/UMass, Morton Street, Porter Square, River Works, Ruggles, Silver Hill, Uphams Corner, Waverley, Windsor Gardens, and Yawkey. Rates vary, with some as low as $1 per day.

Fares and Passes

Commuter rail tickets range in price from $1.70 to $7.75. Tickets can be purchased on the train, but depending on how busy the train is and the ticket-taker's mood, a surcharge may be added to the price. Kids 5–11, high school students, seniors, and disabled persons ride for half-price. Children under five and blind people ride free. The cost of monthly passes ranges from $59 to $250, depending on the zone. Some monthly passes offer varying perks like free subway, bus, and ferry use. Passes are sold at certain T stops and other locations (usually a local shop close to the station), as well as online at www.mbta.com.

General Information

NFT Maps: 1 & 4
Websites: www.amtrak.com (Amtrak)
www.mbta.com (MBTA)
Amtrak: 800-872-7245 (800-USA-RAIL)
MBTA: 617-222-5215

Overview

North Station and South Station are the main Amtrak and MBTA Commuter Rail depots in Boston. North Station, near the North End and underneath TD Banknorth Garden, sits above the T's new "superstation" that (finally) connects the Green Line and Orange Line. South Station, on Atlantic Avenue and Summer Street at the gateway to South Boston, is served by MBTA and Amtrak and also has a bus terminal, a food court in the domed arrival hall, a bar, a newsstand, and a bookstore.

Traveling between Stations

There is a one-mile gap between the two Amtrak stations. The North Station stop is on the Orange and Green Lines of the MBTA subway, and the South Station stop is on the Red Line. Yes, it *is* crazy that the stations aren't on the same line and don't directly connect to each other. No, they're *not* going to do anything to correct the problem in the near future. Yes, they *could* have rolled it into the Big Dig project, since they were digging under the city anyway. No, we *don't* know why they didn't. And yes, it *does* seem odd that they spent billions to improve automobile transportation while ignoring public transportation. As it stands, travelers going from New York to Maine have to get off the train at South Station and either take a cab, take two subway trains, or walk to get to North Station to continue their journey.

How to Get There—Driving

Both stations are located off I-93 in downtown Boston. For North Station, take Exit 26 (Storrow Drive), and for South Station, take Exit 23 (Purchase Street/South Station). To get to South Station from the Mass Pike (I-90), take Exit 24B to Atlantic Avenue.

Parking

The MBTA says there's no parking at either station, but "street or private parking may exist." Helpful, huh? In fact, both North Station and South Station are served by nearby, expensive parking garages, and neither station offers much in the way of street parking. Lovely.

How to Get There—Mass Transit

North Station is on the T's Green and Orange Lines. South Station is on the Red Line.

Amtrak

Amtrak trains leave out of North Station and South Station going north to Portland, Maine and south to NYC and beyond. When you go north, they call it the Downeaster (that's Mainer for "near Canada"). When you go south, they call it a bunch of things, including "the Federal," "the Acela," and the mundanely titled "Regional." The Acela is Amtrak's flagship route, offering "high-speed" service from South Station to NYC, Philly, and DC, with stops along the way. On a good day, the Acela chugs from Boston to New York in 3.5 hours, which is still only slightly faster than a bus and, at $100 a ticket, costs much more than taking one of the Chinatown buses or Greyhound (see page 253).

Baggage Check

Three items of baggage weighing up to 50 lbs each may be checked up to 30 minutes prior to train departure. For an additional fee of $10 per bag, three additional pieces can be checked. Each passenger is allowed two carry-on items on board. No dangerous, fragile, valuable items, animals, or household goods can be checked. Bikes, skis, and other odd-shaped equipment usually count as one checked bag and should not be carried aboard the train. With the exception of service animals, all pets are prohibited on Amtrak trains.

How to Get Tickets

To purchase train tickets, call Amtrak or visit their website. The website sometimes offers discounts for purchasing on-line, so it's worth checking the website before heading to the station.

Going to New York

One-way fares start at $59 and the journey takes about 4.5 hours from South Station. You could cut an hour off your commute by riding express on the Acela, but the comfort and convenience will cost ya ($100 or more).

Going to Philadelphia

One-way fares start at $76 and the ride takes about six hours. Fares on the speedier Acela Express start at $173 and cut about an hour off the journey.

Going to Washington DC

A trip to Washington on the regular Amtrak train will cost you at least $83 and will take you between eight and nine hours. Acela Express tickets start at $187 and the trip takes between six and seven hours.

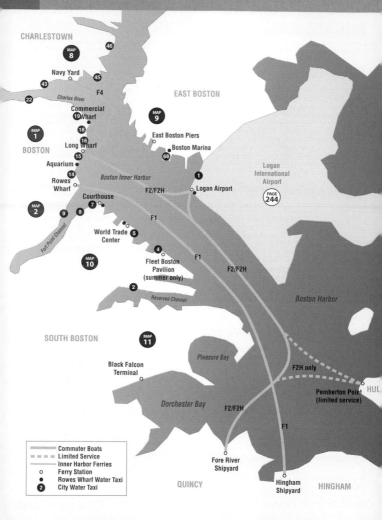

General Information (Ferries)

MBTA: www.mbta.com/schedules_and_maps/boats/; 617-222-5215

Harbor Express: www.harborexpress.com; 617-222-6999

Overview

The MBTA Commuter and Excursion Boat Service connects Boston to Logan Airport and is one of the best routes in and out of Charlestown and other shore side communities. One thing that makes the T boat better than any other form of Boston transportation is the fun factor. On a nice day, paying a buck and a half for a quick jaunt across the harbor feels like a steal. And on any day, not having to deal with Boston traffic is priceless. The views of the city from the water are gorgeous, and since the routes are in the Inner Harbor, the ride remains relatively smooth even in bad weather. There is also that delicious old-time feeling that comes with ferrying across the harbor. You'll want to keep in mind that boat schedules are more limited than bus schedules (particularly on weekends) and are more susceptible to disruptions due to inclement weather.

Most ferries operated by the MBTA leave from Long Wharf and travel to the Charlestown Navy Yard (F4), the Fore River Shipyard in Quincy (F2), and Pemberton Point in Hull (F2H). The F1 boat travels between Rowes Wharf and Hingham Shipyard.

The F2 and the F2H boats, catamarans operated by Harbor Express, stop at Logan Airport, but not at all times of the day—check the MBTA website for timetables. During rush hour (and decent weather) the Harbor Express is a sensible choice for getting to the airport. It takes a mere seven minutes to get to the airport dock from Long Wharf and about 25 minutes from Quincy and Hull. From the airport dock, take the free Water Shuttle bus 66 to the terminals. The 66 bus takes about 15 minutes to visit all terminals and return to the dock.

All ferry stops are accessible to wheelchair users. Bicycles can also be taken on board for free.

Parking

Parking for commuter ferry stops in the Inner Harbor is available only on the street or in a garage. Parking in Quincy costs $1 for a day and $6 overnight. In Hingham, parking costs $1 for a day and $1.75 overnight. Free parking is available at Hull High School.

Fares

A trip on a boat between destinations in the Inner Harbor costs $1.70 (pay a crewmember when boarding the boat). Trips from Hull, Quincy, and Hingham to the Inner Harbor (Rowes Wharf or Long Wharf) cost $6 ($3 for kids, seniors, and disabled persons). Trips from Quincy and Hull to Logan Airport on the Harbor Express are $12 ($10 for seniors, $3 for kids 5–11). Pay a crewmember when boarding the boat.

General Information (Water Taxis)

City Water Taxi: www.citywatertaxi.com; 617-422-0392

Rowes WharfWater Taxi: www.roweswharfwatertaxi.com/ 617-406-8584

Massport: www.massport.com/logan/getti_typeo_water.html; 800-23-LOGAN

Overview

On the charmed waters of the Inner Harbor, two water taxi companies ply their trade. During the warmer months, water taxis provide an enjoyable way to cross the Inner Harbor. Both water taxi companies stop at the Logan Airport dock.

City Water Taxi

City Water Taxi offers direct service to the entire Boston waterfront, year-round, with enclosed boats that are heated when the weather is bad. (Mon–Sat 7 am–10 pm; Sun 7 am–8 pm). In addition to the airport dock, City Water Taxi serves 16 other points, including Bank of America Pavilion, Fan Pier, Charlestown Navy Yard, Black Falcon Terminal, and all the major wharves in the Inner Harbor. (To get to the Boston Convention and Exhibition Center, aim for the World Trade Center.) To catch a City Water Taxi from the airport, take Massport's 66 bus to the airport dock. Use the call box at the dock to call for a boat if there isn't one already there. From other destinations, call City Water Taxi to arrange a pick-up.

Tickets are sold on board the boat. Fares to downtown points and Logan Airport cost $10 one-way and $17 round-trip. There is a $20 minimum to Charlestown, North Station, and Black Falcon Terminal, but if you have a traveling companion, the fare is $15 each.

Rowes Wharf Water Taxi

Also operating year-round, Rowes Wharf Water Taxi provides on-call service to 31 points in the Inner Harbor (from Nov 2–April 1, service runs 7 am–7 pm; from April 2–Nov 1, service runs from 7 am–10 pm Mon–Sat and 7 am–8 pm on Sun). After-hours service is available upon request. Rowes Wharf Water Taxi serves 17 different docks and now operates a Seaport Express providing weekday service between Rowes Wharf, Central Wharf, and the Seaport World Trade Center for $1.70. For the complete schedule, look online. To hail a boat from the airport dock, use the company's call box; from other destinations, give them a call from your own phone.

Tickets are sold on board. The fare costs $10 one-way and $17 round-trip.

Car Rental

Map 1 • Beacon Hill / West End

Avis	3 Center Plz	617-534-1400
Dollar	209 Cambridge St	617-723-8312

Map 2 • North End / Faneuil Hall

Enterprise	1 Congress St	617-723-8077

Map 3 • Downtown Crossing / Park Square / Bay Village

Budget	28 Park Plz	617-497-3669
Hertz	30 Park Plz	617-338-1500

Map 4 • Financial District / Chinatown

Alamo	270 Atlantic Ave	617-557-7179
Dollar	30 Rowes Wharf	617-367-2654
Hertz	2 International Pl	617-204-1165
Hertz	Summer St & Atlantic Ave	617-338-1503
National	270 Atlantic Ave	617-557-7179

Map 5 • Back Bay (West) / Fenway (East)

Enterprise	800 Boylston St	617-262-8222
Select	39 Dalton St	617-236-6088

Map 6 • Back Bay (East) / South End (Upper)

Avis	100 Clarendon St	617-534-1404
Dollar	110 Huntington Ave	617-578-0025
Hertz	10 Huntington Ave	617-338-1506
Hertz	145 Dartmouth St	617-338-1500

Map 9 • East Boston

Affordable	84 Condor St	617-561-7000
Alamo	2 Tomahawk Dr	617-561-4100

Map 10 • South Boston (West) / Fort Point

Select	1 Seaport Ln	617-345-0203

Map 12 • Newmarket / Andrew Square

Enterprise	230 Dorchester Ave	617-268-1411

Map 13 • Roxbury

Enterprise	17 Melnea Cass Blvd	617-442-7500

Map 16 • Kenmore Square / Brookline (East)

Select	500 Commonwealth Ave	617-532-5060

Map 18 • Brighton

Rent A Wreck	2022 Commonwealth Ave	617-254-9540

Map 19 • Allston (South) / Brookline (North)

Adventure	226 Harvard Ave	617-566-1018
Adventure	27 Harvard Ave	617-783-3000
Budget	95 Brighton Ave	617-497-3608
Enterprise	292 Western Ave	617-783-2240
Enterprise	996 Commonwealth Ave	617-738-6003
Hertz	414 Cambridge St	617-787-2894
U-Save	25 Harvard Ave	617-254-1000

Map 20 • Harvard Square / Allston (North)

Alamo	1663 Massachusetts Ave	617-661-8747
Avis	1 Bennett St	617-534-1430
Hertz	24 Eliot St	617-338-1520
National	1663 Massachusetts Ave	617-661-8747
Thrifty	110 Mt Auburn St	617-876-2758

Map 23 • Central Somerville / Porter Square

Hertz	646 Somerville Av	617-625-7958

Map 24 • Winter Hill / Union Square

Americar	190 Highland Ave	617-776-4640l

Map 25 • East Somerville / Sullivan Square

Enterprise	37 Mystic Ave	617-625-1766

Map 26 • East Cambridge / Kendall Square / MIT

Enterprise	1 Broadway	617-577-0404

Map 27 • Central Square / Cambridgeport

Budget	20 Sidney St	617-577-7606
Enterprise	25 River St	617-547-7400

Map 28 • Inman Square

U-Save	70 Prospect St	617-628-8800

Zipcar General Information

Website: www.zipcar.com
Phone: 617-933-5070

Background

Zipcar rents out cars by the hour. The company, which now runs similar services in DC, New Jersey, New York, and elsewhere, was founded at MIT: "People would achieve transportation nirvana by having a transit pass and a Zipcard in their pockets. The result would be reduced congestion, fewer auto emissions, more green space, and a revolution in urban planning." That's Cantabridgian for "Give us $9/hr, we'll give you a Jetta." This seems like the smartest idea on wheels if you live in congested areas like the North End, Allston, or Harvard Square and you need to get somewhere the T can't take you. For infrequent drivers, the $25 application fee and minimum annual fee of $50 still make Zipcar service cheaper than owning a car.

How It Works

If you're 21 or older, in possession of a valid driver's license, and you've completed the online application, all you need to do is call or go online to reserve one of the hundreds of cars available at zipcar.com. (You get to choose from a fleet of BMWs, Minis, pick-ups, and others.) Your Zipcard unlocks the car that has been reserved for you, which you pick up at the most convenient of their many locations. Cars must be returned to the same spot where they were picked up. The car unlocks when a valid Zipcard is held to the windshield; your card will only open the car during the time you have reserved it.

Costs

The cost of Zipcar varies depending on the pick-up location, but rates start at $9 an hour. A reservation for 24 hours, the maximum amount of time that a car can be reserved, starts at about $68. The first 125 miles are free; each additional mile costs about 35 cents. Membership costs are additional. Make sure to return your car on time, as Zipcar charges exorbitant hourly late fees on unreturned cars.

If you've just moved to Boston and need a crash course on the "sights," you must check out the **Freedom Trail** (see page 189). Yes, it's touristy, but it's the best self-guided tour of Revolution-era Boston and gives you the skinny on aspects of Boston colonial history that every resident should know. To gain a better appreciation of just where it is you live, hit the top of the **Prudential Tower (Map 5)** for a bird's eye view, which will show you that Boston has a lot more hills and water than you might have suspected. For a more human perspective, get familiar with the Charles River with a stroll along the **Esplanade (Map 6)**, or, for a walk with an impressive view of Beacon Hill and Back Bay, cross the **Harvard Bridge (Map 26)** and take a stroll along Memorial Drive in Cambridge. For a nice rest, grab a snack in Harvard Square, and find a tree in **Harvard Yard (Map 20)** under which to chill.

If winter keeps you from strolls outside, there's plenty to see indoors. The **Museum of Fine Arts (Map 15)** (see page 326) is world-class. Across the street, the **Isabella Stewart Gardner Museum (Map 15)** has a first-rate collection, and the setting (inspired by a 15th-century Venetian palace) is stunning. The ornate interior of **Trinity Church (Map 6)** and the Sargent Murals of the **Boston Public Library (Map 6)** (see page 185) are also impressive. Boston's best concert halls are in the neighborhood,

so why not catch a show at internationally acclaimed **Boston Symphony Hall (Map 5)** or one of the many free shows at the New England Conservatory's **Jordan Hall (Map 5)**. You'll also not want to overlook the many museums of Harvard, notably the **Fogg Art Museum (Map 20)** (focusing on Western art) and the **Natural History Museum (Map 20)** (with its brilliant glass flowers).

If you've already checked out Boston's big hits, there are plenty of quirky spots to fill your time. See the skull of Phineas Gage, the 19th century medical oddity who survived a thirteen-pound rod of steel shot through his brain at the **Warren Anatomical Museum (Map 15)**. The **Boston Athenaeum (Map 1)** has a true crime account bound with the skin of it's author. If that's not to your sense of everlasting life, you could sip coffee in the North End and wander over to see if Peter Baldassari is home and his folksy **All Saints Way (Map 2)** is open. Roxbury has the only scale Nubian tomb at the **Museum of the National Center for Afro-American Artists (Map 13)**. The Mapparium at the **Christian Science Center(Map5)** highlights the ambitions of Mary Baker Eddy and her clean-living movement. Those with a more criminal bent can find mobster haunts like "Whitey" Bulger's old Southie **liquor store (Map 10)** or the garage of the **Brink's Job (Map 2)** in the North End.

Map 1 · Beacon Hill / West End

Abiel Smith School	46 Joy St	Center of 19th-century African-American Boston.
Acorn Street	b/w West Cedar St & Willow St, running parallel to Chestnut St	The most photographed street in America.
Boston Athenaeum	10 1/2 Beacon St · 617-227-0270	Old books, including one true crime account bound in the author's skin.
Leonard P Zakim Bunker Hill Bridge	I-93 & Charles River	World's widest cable-stayed bridge. Boston's newest landmark.
Longfellow Bridge	Cambridge St & Charles St	The "salt and pepper shaker bridge."
Louisburg Square	b/w Mt Vernon St & Pinckney St	Charming square with elegant homes, including John Kerry's.
Make Way for Ducklings	Charles St & Beacon St	Inspired by the Robert McCloskey children's book.
Massachusetts General Hospital	55 Fruit St · 617-726-2000	The Ether dome, site of first the use of ether; contains an antique surgical museum.
TD Banknorth Garden	150 Causeway St · 617-624-1050	Looking for the FleetCenter? This is it. Used to be historic Boston Garden.
Vilna Shul	18 Phillips St · 617-523-2324	Recently revived Beacon Hill synagogue.

Map 2 · North End / Faneuil Hall

All Saints Way	Battery St & Hanover St	Peter Baldassari's folksy, handcrafted devotional alley.
The Boston Stone	Marshall St	Centre of ye olde city.
Boston Tea Kettle	63 Court St	Long before Starbucks, this gigantic 1873 copper kettle was steaming.
The Brink's Job	165 Prince St	Where Brink's Gang robbery occurred in 1950; now used for TD Banknorth Center parking.
Christopher Columbus Park	Atlantic Ave	Destruction of the Artery gives this park new breath.
City Hall	1 City Hall Plz · 617-635-4000	The box Faneuil Hall came in.
Faneuil Hall	Congress St & North St · 617-523-1779	Faneuil Hall (that is, the building) dates from 1742.
Holocaust Memorial	Congress St at Union St · 617-457-8755	Six glass towers, with victims' numbers representing six camps.
New England Aquarium	Central Wharf · 617-973-5200	Check out penguin snack-time.
North End Playground	Commercial St & Foster St	
Old North Church	193 Salem St · 617-523-6676	One if by land, two if by sea.
Paul Revere House	19 North Sq · 617-523-2338	Where Paul was born and raised.
Union Oyster House	41 Union St · 617-227-2750	Oldest restaurant in America, saddle up to oyster bar.

Map 3 · Downtown Crossing / Park Square / Bay Village

Arlington Street Church	351 Boylston St · 617-536-7050	Congregation dates from 1729, building from 1861.
Boston Irish Famine Memorial	School St & Washington St	Statue commemorating the Great Hunger of the 1840s.
Boston Opera House	539 Washington St · 617-259-3400	Beaux-Arts landmark open again after many years.
Colonial Theatre	106 Boylston St · 617-426-9366	Boston's oldest continuously operating theater, since 1900.
Four Seasons Hotel	200 Boylston St · 617-338-4400	The preferred local home of the Rolling Stones.
Frog Pond	Boston Common	Cool statues. Ribbit.
Granary Burying Ground	Tremont St & Park St · 617-635-4505	Featuring John Hancock, Mother Goose, many others.
Harpoon Brewery	306 Northern Ave · 617-574-9551	Brewery tours, seasonal special events.

Harriet Tubman Square	Columbus Sq	Statue, park, and timeline tablet honoring Tubman and her work.
Hub of the Universe Bronze Marker	Washington St & Summer St	Um, located in the floor of a fruit and vegetable stand.
John Hancock's Phallic Gravestone	Tremont St & Park St	Size matters.
Old South Meeting House	310 Washington St • 617-482-6439	Where Sam Adams gave the order for the Boston Tea Party.
Old State House	206 Washington St • 617-720-1713	Oldest surviving public building in Boston.
Omni Parker House	60 School St • 617-227-8600	One-time employees include Ho Chi Minh and Malcolm X.
State House	Beacon St & Park St • 617-727-3679	Finished in 1797. Gold dome added later.
Swan Boats	Arlington St & Boylston St • 617-522-1966	Since 1877. Ideal for wee ones.
Wang Theatre	270 Tremont St • 617-482-9393	Eye-popping, opulent interior. A must see.

Map 4 • Financial District / Chinatown

Boston Harbor Hotel	70 Rowes Wharf • 617-439-7000	The "building with a hole in the middle."
Chinatown Gate	Beach St & Hudson St	Everything under the sky is for the people.
Custom House Tower	3 McKinley Sq	Boston's first "skyscraper," completed in 1915.
Federal Reserve	600 Atlantic Ave • 617-973-3463	Easy-to-spot concrete monolith, built in 1983.
South Station	Atlantic Ave & Summer St	Busier train station, with the new Silver Line and bus terminal.

Map 5 • Back Bay (West) / Fenway (East)

Burrage House	314 Commonwealth Ave	19th-century French-Renaissance mansion. Private.
Christian Science Center	175 Huntington Ave • 617-450-3790	Mother Church, Mapparium, reflecting pool. Quite nice.
Hynes Convention Center	900 Boylston St • 617-954-2000	Still a convention center, for now.
Jordan Hall	30 Gainsborough St	Hundred-year-old theater seats over 1,000 and has remarkable acoustics.
Prudential Tower	800 Boylston St • 617-236-3100	The other tall building. Equally loved and reviled.
Symphony Hall	301 Massachusetts Ave • 617-266-1492	Home of the Boston Symphony Orchestra.

Map 6 • Back Bay (East) / South End (Upper)

Boston Public Library	700 Boylston St • 617-536-5400	Impressive. Enjoy a respite in the beautiful courtyard.
Charles River Esplanade	n/a	Great place to run or read a book.
Church of the Covenant	67 Newbury St	Gothic revival church called "absolutely perfect" by Oliver Wendell Holmes.
Commonwealth Ave	Arlington St to Mass Ave	Boston's most distinguished promenade with oddest collection of statues.
Copley Square	Boylston St & Dartmouth St	Back Bay's living room.
First Church in Boston	66 Marlborough St • 617-267-6730	Founded 375 years ago.
French Library and Cultural Center	53 Marlborough St • 617-912-0400	Classes, food, and movies, tous en francais.
Hatch Shell	Esplanade	Where the Pops play each July 4.
John Hancock Tower	200 Clarendon St	New England's tallest building, designed by I.M. Pei.
New England Historic Genealogical Library	101 Newbury St • 617-536-5740	Trace your roots back to the Mayflower.
Old South Church	645 Boylston St • 617-536-1970	Northern Italian Gothic, finished in 1875.
Trinity Church	206 Clarendon St • 617-536-0944	Romanesque, with massive open interior. Completed in 1877.

Map 7 • South End (Lower)

| Cathedral of the Holy Cross | 1400 Washington St • 617-542-5682 | Mother church of the Archdiocese of Boston. |
| SoWa Building | 450 Harrison Ave | A converted warehouse, now home to several galleries. |

Map 8 • Charlestown

Bunker Hill Monument	Monument Ave • 617-242-5641	Battle actually took place on nearby Breed's Hill.
Charlestown Navy Yard	Constitution Rd & Warren St • 617-242-5601	Home of the USS Constitution ("Old Ironsides")
Tobin Memorial Bridge	US-1	Lovingly photographed in Mystic River.
Warren Tavern	2 Pleasant St • 617-241-8142	One of Paul Revere's favorite watering holes.

Map 9 • East Boston

| LoPresti Park | Summer St & Jeffries St | Best view of the Boston skyline and harbor for landlubbers. |

Map 10 • South Boston (West) / Fort Point

Boston Children's Museum	300 Congress St • 617-426-8855	Featuring the giant Hood milk bottle.
Boston Convention & Exhibition Center	415 Summer St • 617-954-2100	The Southie Starship.
Institute of Contemporary Art	100 Northern Ave • 617-478-3100	Stunning new building. Oh, and the art's pretty good too.
South Boston Liquor Mart	295 Old Colony Ave • 617-269-3600	Whitey Bulger's HQ.

General Information · **Landmarks**

Map 11 · South Boston (East)

Bank of America Pavilion	290 Northern Ave · 617-728-1690	Music venue.
Black Falcon Terminal	1 Black Falcon Ave · 617-330-1500	Heavily trafficked cruise boat terminal.
Boston Design Center	1 Design Center Pl · 617-338-6610	For interior design junkies; several dozen showrooms.
Boston Fish Pier	212 Northern Ave	Opened in 1914, the oldest working fish port.
L Street Bathhouse	William J Day Blvd & L St	Old-timey bathhouse, home of the L Street Brownies.
L Street Tavern	658 E 8th St · 617-268-4335	Matt & Ben's pub in that movie.
World Trade Center Boston	200 Seaport Blvd · 617-385-5090	Event space that's part of "The Seaport Experience."

Map 12 · Newmarket / Andrew Square

Suffolk County House of Correction	20 Bradston St · 617-635-1000	Just so you know.

Map 13 · Roxbury

Highland Park	Fort Ave & Beech Glen St	Little visited Fort Hill monument with great views
Islamic Cultural Center	1 Malcolm X Blvd	Largest mosque in the Northeast.
Malcolm X and Ella Little-Collins House	72 Dale St	Malcolm X lived here with his sister during formative years.
National Center for Afro-American Artists	300 Walnut Ave · 617-442-8614	Puddingstone mansion holds Nubian tomb model.
Roxbury Center for Arts	182 Dudley St · 617-541-3900	Located in the recently renovated Hibernia Hall.
Shirley-Eustis House	33 Shirley St · 617-442-2275	18th-century royal governor's country estate.

Map 14 · Jamaica Plain

Arnold Arboretum	125 Arborway · 617-524-1718	The most famous collection of trees in America, an oasis.
Doyle's Café	3484 Washington St · 617-524-2345	A century's worth of pols have slapped backs here.
First Church, Unitarian Universalist	6 Eliot St · 617-524-1634	The first church in Jamaica Plain, ca. 1853. Impressive stone façade, creepy graveyard.
The Footlight Club	7A Eliot St · 617-524-3200	Oldest running theatre in the US.
The Loring-Greenough House	12 South St · 617-524-3158	Built as a country estate in 1760. Open for tours.
Samuel Adams Brewery	30 Germania St · 617-368-5080	Love the product, but not much of an experience.
Spontaneous Celebrations	75 Danforth St · 617-524-6373	JP community arts organization.

Map 15 · Fenway (West) / Mission Hill

Isabella Stewart Gardner Museum	280 The Fenway · 617-278-5180	Eccentric collection highlighting the Renaissance and the pleasures of having money. A gem.
Mission Church Basilica	1545 Tremont St · 617-445-2600	Mission Hill beautiful. Recently renovated.
Museum of Fine Arts	465 Huntington Ave · 617-267-9300	Arguably one of the top museums in the country. Go for the Copleys.
Warren Anatomical Museum	10 Shattuck St · 617-432-6196	Phineas Gage's skull and other medical oddities.

Map 16 · Kenmore Square / Brookline (East)

BU Bridge	Essex St & Mountfort St	Arguably Boston's best river/skyline view.
Citgo Sign	Commonwealth Ave & Beacon St	Beloved Kenmore Square landmark.
Fenway Park	4 Yawkey Wy · 617-267-9440	Home to the Sox since 1912.

Map 17 · Coolidge Corner / Brookline Hills

Frederick Olmstead Home	99 Warren St	Genius of American landscapes, the ultimate home office.

Map 19 · Allston (South) / Brookline (North)

JFK National Historic Site	83 Beals St · 617-566-7937	Understated residential home, open only in summer.
The Publick Theatre	1400 Soldiers Field Rd · 617-782-5425	Outdoor theater along the Charles.

Map 20 · Harvard Square / Allston (North)

Brattle Theatre	40 Brattle St · 617-876-6837	Oldest repertory cinema in Boston, since 1953 and still projecting.
Fogg Art Museum	32 Quincy St · 617-495-9400	Fine collection, more humane scale than the MFA.
Harvard Museum of Natural History	26 Oxford St · 617-495-3045	The public face of the botanical, zoological, and geological museums.
Harvard Stadium	N Harvard St & Soldiers Field Rd	The nation's oldest stadium.
Harvard Yard	b/w Broadway, Quincy St, Peabody St, & Massachusetts Ave	The core of the campus–full of historical landmarks.
John Harvard Statue	Harvard Yard	The "statue of the three lies."
Out of Town News	0 Harvard Sq · 617-354-7777	The sensible Harvard Square rendezvous spot.
The Pit	0 Harvard Sq	Favorite hang-out for the counter-culture kids.
Weeks Footbridge	Memorial Dr & DeWolfe St	Most beautiful bridge on the Charles, hosts full moon tangos.

Map 22 · North Cambridge / West Somerville

Somerville Theatre	55 Davis Sq · 617-625-5700	Movies, concerts, and more.

Map 23 · Central Somerville / Porter Square

Art at Porter Square	Somerville Ave & Massachusetts Ave	The T's best public art display.
Milk Row Cemetery	439 Somerville Ave	Historic 1804 boneyard. Next to a supermarket.
Powderhouse	College Ave & Broadway	Revolutionary War-era gunpowder store, park centerpiece.
The Round House	36 Atherton St	Round since 1856. Not open to the public.
Somerville Museum	1 Westwood Rd · 617-666-9810	Great exhibits of Somerville history.

Map 24 · Winter Hill / Union Square

Prospect Hill Monument	Munroe St b/w Prospect Hill Ave & Walnut St	Excellent view of Boston from Somerville.
Somerville City Hall	93 Highland Ave · 617-625-6600	A classic New England municipal building.

Map 25 · East Somerville / Sullivan Square

Schrafft's Building	529 Main St	Once the country's largest candy factory.

Map 26 · East Cambridge / Kendall Square / MIT

Harvard Bridge	Massachusetts Ave	364 smoots and an ear, the Harvard Bridge leads to MIT.
Kendall / MIT T Station	Main St	Every T-Stop should have musical instruments by MIT students.
Stata Center	32 Vassar St	Frank Gehry's curvy and colorful MIT building.

Map 27 · Central Square / Cambridgeport

Cambridge City Hall	795 Massachusetts Ave · 617-349-4000	Recently got a needed facelift.
Edgerton Center & Strobe Alley	77 Massachusetts Ave, MIT · 617-253-4629	4th floor of Building 4 displays of slow-mo destructive photography and tech.
Necco Building/Novartis	250 Massachusetts Ave	Yet another candy company leaves Cambridge.
Polaroid Bldg	784 Memorial Dr	Distinctive Art Deco ex-headquarters of Polaroid.
Shell Oil Sign	187 Magazine St	Can't miss it. Logo designed by Raymond Loewy.
Simmons Hall	229 Vassar St · 617-253-5107	Agressively modernist MIT dorm by Stephen Holl.
University Park	Massachusetts Ave & Sidney St	Complex of cool structural and landscape architecture.

Map 28 · Inman Square

Julia Child's Home	103 Irving St	The kitchen was dismantled and moved to the Smithsonian.

Map 29 · West Roxbury

Millennium Park	VFW Pkwy & Gardner St	Clear your head by flying a kite.

Map 30 · Roslindale

Forest Hills Cemetery	95 Forest Hills Ave · 617-524-0128	This 250-acre beautiful cemetery is not only home to such literary greats as e.e. cummings but is also great spot to picnic and bike ride.
Roslindale Square	Washington St & Belgrade Ave	Or, Roslindale Village.

Map 31 · Mattapan / Dorchester (West)

Franklin Park Zoo Bear Cages	1 Franklin Park Rd	The abandoned bear cages outside the zoo's fences make for a creepy outing.
United House of Prayer	206 Seaver St · 617-445-3246	Impressive Mishkan Tefila synagogue, now church and soul food kitchen.

Map 32 · Dorchester (East)

All Saints' Church	209 Ashmont St · 617-436-6370	Founded in 1867. Beautiful stained glass.
Commonwealth Museum	220 Morrissey Blvd · 617-727-9268	Operated by the Massachusetts Historical Society.
Dorchester North Burying Ground	Columbia Rd & Stoughton St	Interesting and eerie gravestones spanning 4 centuries.
The James Blake House	735 Columbia Rd	Built in 1648, Boston's oldest house.
John F Kennedy Library and Museum	Morrissey Blvd & Columbia Pt · 617-514-1600	Houses 21 permanent exhibits examining JFK's life and work.
Strand Theatre	543 Columbia Rd	Vaudeville, movie house time capsule. Under renovation.

Map 33 · Hyde Park

Stony Brook Reservation	Washington St & Turtle Pond Pkwy	Great option for biking and hiking.

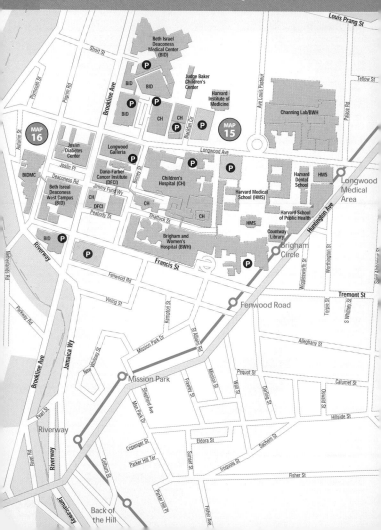

Louis Prang St

Short St

Brookline Ave

Beth Israel
Deaconess
Medical Center
(BID)

Judge Baker
Children's
Center

Harvard
Institute of
Medicine

Tetlow St

Ave Louis Pasteur

Palace Rd

Channing Lab/BWH

Plimpton St

Pilgrim Rd

BID

BID

BID

CH

CH

Blackfan Cr

CH

MAP
15

Longwood Ave

Autumn St

MAP
16

Joslin
Diabetes
Center

Longwood
Galleria

Bickney St

Children's
Hospital (CH)

Harvard Medical
School (HMS)

Harvard
Dental
School

HMS

Longwood
Medical
Area

Joslin Pl

BIDMC

Deaconess Rd

Dana-Farber
Cancer Institute
(DFCI)

Jimmy Fund Wy

Harvard School
of Public Health

HMS

Beth Isreal
Deaconess
West Campus
(BID)

DFCI

DFCI

CH

Huntington Ave

Peabody St

Shattuck St

CH

Countway
Library

BID

Riverway

Brigham and
Women's
Hospital (BWH)

Brigham
Circle

Wigglesworth St

Worthington St

Saint Alphonsus St

Francis St

Fenwood Rd

Tremont St

Netherlands Rd

Vining St

Fenwood Road

Topliff St

S Whitney St

Parkway Rd

Kempton St

St Albans Rd

Alleghany St

Brookline Ave

Jamaica Wy

New Whitney St

Mission Park Dr

Mission Park

Shepherd Ave

Frawley St

Mission St

Pequot St

Wait St

Calumet St

Oswald St

Darling St

Pearl St

River St

Riverway

Shepherd Ave

Mssn Park Dr

Copenger St

Parker Hill Ter

Sunset St

Eldora St

Iroquois St

Hillside St

Jamaicaway

Colburn St

Parker Hill Pl

Parker Hill Ave

Fisher St

Fisher Ave

Back of
the Hill

Hospitals

Boston's medical facilities rank among the best in the world. Many medical firsts happened in Boston, including the:

- First public demonstration of anesthesia during surgery, at Massachusetts General Hospital (1846).
- First identification and analysis of appendicitis, at Massachusetts General Hospital (1886).
- First surgical procedure to correct a congenital cardiovascular defect, performed by Dr. Robert Gross (1938).
- First successful fertilization of a human ovum in a test tube, by researchers at Peter Bent Brigham Hospital (1944).
- First successful pediatric remission of acute leukemia, achieved by Dr. Sidney Farber (1947).
- First isolation of the polio virus, at Children's Hospital (1948).
- First successful kidney transplant, at Peter Bent Brigham Hospital (1954).
- First demonstration of the effectiveness of an oral contraceptive, by Dr. John C. Rock (1959).

The Longwood Medical Area (see map on the facing page) compresses a dozen medical institutions into a handful of blocks below Mission Hill. These institutions, including **Brigham and Women's Hospital (Map 15)**, **Beth Israel Deaconess Medical Center (Map 16)**, **Children's Hospital (Map 15)**, **Dana-Farber Cancer Institute (Map 15)**, **Joslin Diabetes Center (Map 16)**, the **CBR Institute for Biomedical Research (Map 16)**, and Harvard's medical, dental, and public health schools, comprise what is probably the world's leading center for health care and medicine.

Massachusetts General Hospital (Map 1), which opened in 1811, is the oldest and largest hospital in New England. Each year MGH admits over 45,000 in-patients, processes over 76,000 emergency visits, and, at its West End main campus and four satellite facilities, handles more than 1.5 million outpatient visits.

Mount Auburn Hospital (Map 21) is a Harvard Medical School teaching hospital and the most prominent hospital in Cambridge.

Emergency Rooms	Address	Phone	Map
Massachusetts Eye and Ear Infirmary	243 Charles St	617-523-7900	1
Massachusetts General Hospital	55 Fruit St	617-726-2000	1
Tufts-New England Medical Center	750 Washington St	617-636-5000	3
Boston Medical Center	1 Boston Medical Ctr Pl	617-638-8000	7
Brigham and Women's Hospital	75 Francis St	617-732-5500	15
Children's Hospital	300 Longwood Ave	617-355-6000	15
Beth Israel Deaconess Medical Center	330 Brookline Ave	617-667-7000	16
Mount Auburn	330 Mt Auburn St	617-492-3500	21
Somerville Hospital	230 Highland Ave	617-591-4500	23
The Cambridge Hospital	1493 Cambridge St	617-665-1000	28

Other Hospitals	Address	Phone	Map
Boston Shriners Hospital	51 Blossom St	617-722-3000	1
Spaulding Rehabilitation Hospital	125 Nashua St	617-573-7000	1
Jewish Memorial Hospital & Rehabilitation Center	59 Townsend St	617-989-8315	13
Arbour Hospital	49 Robinwood Ave	617-522-4400	14
CBR Institute for Biomedical Research	220 Longwood Ave	617-734-9500	15
Dana-Farber Cancer Institute	44 Binney St	866-408-3324	15
New England Baptist Hospital	125 Parker Hill Ave	617-754-5800	15
VA Boston-Jamaica Plain Campus	150 S Huntington Ave	617-232-9500	15
Joslin Diabetes Center	1 Joslin Pl	617-732-2400	16
Franciscan Hospital for Children	30 Warren St	617-254-3800	18
St Elizabeth's Medical Center	736 Cambridge St	617-789-3000	18
The Boston Center	14 Fordham Rd	617-783-9676	19
Youville Hospital & Rehabilitation Center	1575 Cambridge St	617-876-4344	28

Post Offices & Zip Codes

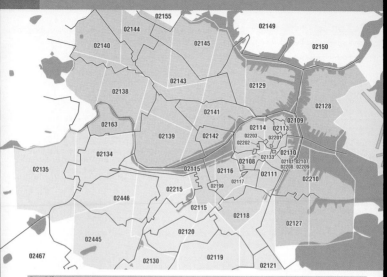

Post Offices	Address	Phone	Zip Code	Map
Charles Street Station	136 Charles St	617-723-7434	02114	1
John F Kennedy Station	25 New Chardon St	617-523-6566	02114	1
State House Station	24 Beacon St	617-742-0012	02133	1
Hanover Street Station	217 Hanover St	617-723-6397	02113	2
Post Offices	1 Faneuil Hall Sq	800-275-8777	02109	2
Fort Point Station	25 Dorchester Ave	617-654-5302	02205	4
Lafayette Station	7 Ave de Lafayette	617-423-7822	02111	4
Milk Street	31 Milk St	617-482-1956	02109	4
Astor Station	207 Massachusetts Ave	617-247-2429	02115	5
Prudential Center Post Office	800 Boylston St	617-267-4164	02199	5
Back Bay Annex Station	390 Stuart St	617-236-7800	02117	6
Post Offices	31 St James Ave	800-275-8777	02116	6
Cathedral Station	59 W Dedham St	617-266-0989	02118	7
Charlestown	23 Austin St	617-241-5322	02129	8
East Boston Station	50 Meridian St	617-561-3900	02128	9
South Boston Station	444 E 3rd St	617-269-9948	02127	10
Roxbury Station	55 Roxbury St	617-427-4898	02119	13
Jamaica Plain Station	655 Centre St	617-524-3620	02130	14
Mission Hill Station	1575 Tremont St	617-566-2040	02120	15
Boston University	775 Commonwealth Ave	617-266-0665	02215	16
Kenmore Station	11 Deerfield St	617-437-1113	02215	16
Brookline Branch	1295 Beacon St	617-738-1649	02446	17
Brookline Village Branch	207 Washington St	617-566-1557	02445	17
Brighton	424 Washington St	617-254-5026	02135	18
Allston Station	47 Harvard Ave	617-789-3769	02134	19
Soldiers Field Station	117 Western Ave	617-354-0131	02163	19
Harvard Square Station	125 Mt Auburn St	617-876-3883	02138	20
West Somerville	58 Day St	617-666-2255	02144	22
Porter Square	1953 Massachusetts Ave	617-876-5599	02140	23
Somerville Branch	237 Washington St	617-666-2332	02143	24
Winter Hill Branch	320 Broadway	617-666-5225	02145	24
East Cambridge Station	303 Cambridge St	617-876-8558	02141	26
Kendall Square Station	250 Main St	617-876-5155	02142	26
MIT	84 Massachusetts Ave	617-494-5511	02139	26
Cambridge	770 Massachusetts Ave	617-575-8700	02139	27
Inman Square Station	1311 Cambridge St	617-864-4344	02139	28

General Information

All Emergencies: 911
Crime Stoppers: 800-494-TIPS
Boston Area Rape Crisis Center (BARCC): 617-492-RAPE
State Police: 617-727-7775
Boston: www.ci.boston.ma.us/police
Brookline: www.brooklinepolice.com
Cambridge: www.ci.cambridge.ma.us/~CPD/
Somerville: www.ci.somerville.ma.us

Statistics

	2007	2006	2005	2004	2003	2002
Murder	53	55	75	73	61	39
Rape & Attempted	216	234	297	268	269	263
Robbery & Attempted	1,712	2,071	2,678	2,649	2,428	2,759
Aggravated Assault	3,379	3,510	4,358	4,113	4,159	4,113
Burglary & Attempted	2,892	3,041	4,007	4,531	4,545	4,344
Larceny & Attempted	13,235	12,824	16,372	15,957	17,526	17,069
Vehicle Theft & Attempted	2,740	3,199	4,076	4,717	5,545	6,483

Police Stations

	Address	Phone	Map
District A-1	40 New Sudbury St	617-343-4240	1
Temporarily relocated to 152 North End St			
District D-4	650 Harrison Ave	617-343-4250	7
District A-7	69 Paris St	617-343-4220	9
District C-6	101 W Broadway	617-343-4730	10
District B-2	135 Dudley St	617-343-4270	13
District E-13	3345 Washington St	617-343-5630	14
Brookline Police Department	350 Washington St	617-730-2222	17
District D-14	301 Washington St	617-343-4260	18
Somerville Police Department	220 Washington St	617-625-1600	24
Cambridge Police Department	5 Western Ave	617-349-3300	27

Map 1 • Beacon Hill / West End

		last pick-up
Self-Service	170 Canal St	7:45 pm
Self-Service	55 Fruit St	7 pm
Self-Service	7 Bulfinch Pl	6:30 pm
Self-Service	25 New Chardon St	6:30 pm
Self-Service	165 Cambridge St	6:30 pm
Self-Service	101 Merrimac St	6:30 pm
Self-Service	50 Staniford St	6 pm
Self-Service	185 Cambridge St	6 pm
Self-Service	1 Bowdoin Sq	4:30 pm
FedEx Kinko's	2 Center Plz	4:30 pm
Self-Service	15 New Sudbury St	4 pm

Map 2 • North End / Faneuil Hall

Self-Service	200 State St	7:45 pm
Self-Service	343 Commercial St	7:30 pm
Self-Service	28 State St	7:30 pm
Self-Service	240 Commercial St	7:30 pm
Self-Service	98 N Washington St	7 pm
Self-Service	77 N Washington St	7 pm
Self-Service	1 Boston Pl	7 pm
Self-Service	66 Long Wharf	6:30 pm
Prince Postale	71 Prince St	6 pm
FedEx Kinko's	60 State St	6 pm
Self-Service	1 Congress St	5:30 pm

Map 3 • Downtown Crossing / Park Square / Bay Village

Jewelers Bldg	333 Washington St	8 pm
Self-Service	75 Arlington St	7:45 pm
Self-Service	821 Washington St	7:30 pm
Self-Service	750 Washington St	7 pm
Self-Service	73 Tremont St	7 pm
Self-Service	80 Boylston St	6:30 pm
Self-Service	1 Beacon St	6:30 pm
Self-Service	252 Washington St	6 pm
Self-Service	141 Tremont St	6 pm
Self-Service	10 Park Plz	6 pm
FedEx Kinko's	252 Washington St	6 pm
FedEx Kinko's	125 Tremont St	6 pm
Self-Service	260 Tremont St	5 pm
Mail Boxes Etc	276 Washington St	5 pm
Self-Service	45 School St	4:30 pm

Map 4 • Financial District / Chinatown

Self-Service	75 Federal St	8 pm
Self-Service	225 Franklin St	8 pm
Self-Service	150 Federal St	8 pm
Self-Service	101 Arch St	8 pm
Self-Service	100 Summer St	8 pm
Self-Service	1 International Pl	8 pm
Self-Service	1 Financial Ctr	8 pm
Self-Service	745 Atlantic Ave	7:30 pm
Self-Service	600 Atlantic Ave	7:30 pm
Self-Service	45 Batterymarch St	7:30 pm
Self-Service	25 Dorchester Ave	7:30 pm
Self-Service	155 Federal St	7:30 pm
Self-Service	125 Summer St	7:30 pm
Self-Service	265 Franklin St	7:15 pm
Self-Service	1 Federal St	7:15 pm
Self-Service	99 High St	7 pm
Self-Service	33 Arch St	7 pm
Self-Service	260 Franklin St	7 pm
Self-Service	21 Custom House St	7 pm
Self-Service	136 Harrison Ave	7 pm
Self-Service	100 Federal St	7 pm
Penfield's	250 Franklin St	7 pm
Self-Service	99 Summer St	6:30 pm
Self-Service	88 Broad St	6:30 pm
Self-Service	470 Atlantic Ave	6:30 pm
Self-Service	31 Milk St	6:30 pm
Self-Service	50 Milk St	6 pm
Self-Service	211 Congress St	6 pm
Self-Service	175 Federal St	6 pm
FedEx Kinko's	211 Congress St	6 pm
FedEx Kinko's	10 Post Office Sq	6 pm
Self-Service	1 Lincoln St	5:30 pm
Self-Service	35 Kneeland St	4:30 pm
Self-Service	7 Ave De Lafayette	4 pm

Map 5 • Back Bay (West) / Fenway (East)

Self-Service	800 Boylston St	8 pm
Self-Service	346 Huntington Ave	6 pm
Penfields	39 Dalton St	6 pm
Self-Service	900 Boylston St	4 pm
Self-Service	800 Boylston St	4 pm
Self-Service	380 Massachusetts Ave	4 pm

Map 6 • Back Bay (East) / South End (Upper)

Self-Service	500 Boylston St	8 pm
Self-Service	197 Clarendon St	8 pm
Self-Service	699 Boylston St	7:30 pm
Self-Service	399 Boylston St	7:30 pm
Self-Service	31 St James Ave	7:30 pm
Self-Service	187 Dartmouth St	7:30 pm
Self-Service	142 Berkeley St	7:30 pm
Self-Service	162 Columbus Ave	7:15 pm
Self-Service	116 Huntington Ave	7:15 pm
Self-Service	200 Clarendon St	7 pm
Self-Service	101 Huntington Ave	7 pm
Self-Service	380 Stuart St	6 pm
Self-Service	100 Huntington Ave	6 pm
Self-Service	10 St James Ave	6 pm
Penfields	6 Huntington Ave	6 pm
FedEx Kinko's	575 Boylston St	6 pm
FedEx Kinko's	187 Dartmouth St	6 pm
Self-Service	95 Berkeley St	5 pm
Self-Service	745 Boylston St	5 pm
Self-Service	200 Berkeley St	5 pm

Map 7 • South End (Lower)

Self-Service	88 E Newton St	8:15 pm
Self-Service	80 E Concord St	8 pm
Self-Service	818 Harrison Ave	7:45 pm
Self-Service	715 Albany St	6 pm
FedEx Kinko's	715 Albany St	6 pm
Self-Service	700 Albany St	5 pm
Self-Service	85 E Concord St	4 pm

Map 8 • Charlestown

Self-Service	Charlestown Navy Yard	7 pm
Self-Service	20 City Sq	7 pm
Self-Service	149 13th St	7 pm

Map 9 • East Boston

Self-Service	50 Meridian St	6:30 pm
Self-Service	256 Marginal St	6:30 pm
Self-Service	580 Chelsea St	6 pm

Map 10 • South Boston (West) / Fort Point

Self-Service	68 Fargo St	8 pm
Self-Service	313 Congress St	7:30 pm
Self-Service	25 Thomson Pl	7:30 pm
Self-Service	2 Seaport Ln	7:30 pm
Self-Service	430 W Broadway	7 pm
Self-Service	280 Summer St	7 pm
Self-Service	1 Gillette Park	7 pm
Self-Service	415 Summer St	4 pm
FedEx Kinko's	415 Summer St	4 pm

Map 11 • South Boston (East)

Self-Service	775 Summer St	9 pm
Federal Express	775 Summer St	9 pm
Self-Service	212 Northern Ave	7:15 pm
Self-Service	88 Black Falcon Ave	7 pm
Self-Service	1 Design Center Pl	7 pm
Self-Service	1 Harbor St	5 pm

Map 12 • Newmarket / Andrew Square

Self-Service	8c Allstate Rd	6 pm
Self-Service	1 Widett Cir	6 pm
Self-Service	1010 Massachusetts Ave	5 pm
Self-Service	100 Newmarket Sq	5 pm

Map 13 • Roxbury

Self-Service	716 Columbus Ave	7 pm
Self-Service	1135 Tremont St	6 pm
Self-Service	55 Roxbury St	4 pm

Map 14 • Jamaica Plain

Self-Service	670 Centre St	6 pm
Self-Service	64 South St	4 pm

Map 15 • Fenway (West) / Mission Hill

Self-Service	44 Binney St	8 pm
Self-Service	300 Longwood Ave	8 pm
Self-Service	4 Blackfan Cir	7:30 pm
Self-Service	75 Francis St	7 pm
Self-Service	370 Huntington Ave	7 pm
Self-Service	300 Fenway	7 pm
Self-Service	200 Longwood Ave	7 pm
Self-Service	188 Longwood Ave	7 pm
Self-Service	180 Longwood Ave	7 pm
Mobile Unit	44 Binney St	7 pm
Self-Service	677 Huntington Ave	6:30 pm
Self-Service	150 S Huntington Ave	6:30 pm

Self-Service	125 Parker Hill Ave	6:30 pm
Self-Service	550 Huntington Ave	6 pm
Self-Service	43 Leon St	6 pm
Self-Service	11 Leon St	6 pm
Self-Service	1 Blackfan Cir	6 pm
Self-Service	20 Shattuck St	5:30 pm
UPS Store	360 Huntington Ave	5 pm
Self-Service	221 Longwood Ave	5 pm
Self-Service	1620 Tremont St	5 pm

Map 16 • Kenmore Square / Brookline (East)

Self-Service	375 Longwood Ave	7:30 pm
Self-Service	890 Commonwealth Ave	7 pm
Self-Service	771 Commonwealth Ave	7 pm
Self-Service	675 Commonwealth Ave	7 pm
Self-Service	330 Brookline Ave	7 pm
Self-Service	364 Brookline Ave	6:45 pm
Self-Service	590 Commonwealth Ave	6:30 pm
Self-Service	44 Cummington St	6:30 pm
Self-Service	110 Francis St	6:30 pm
Self-Service	1 Overland St	6:30 pm
Self-Service	1 Deaconess Rd	6:30 pm
Self-Service	1 Brookline Pl	6:30 pm
Self-Service	1 Joslin Pl	6:15 pm
Self-Service	401 Park Dr	6 pm
Self-Service	330 Brookline Ave	6 pm
Self-Service	1 Autumn St	6 pm
FedEx Kinko's	115 Cummington St	6 pm
Self-Service	15 Deerfield St	6 pm

Map 17 • Coolidge Corner / Brookline Hills

Self-Service	235 Cypress St	6 pm
Self-Service	207 Washington St	6 pm
Self-Service	138 Harvard St	6 pm
Self-Service	1295 Beacon St	6 pm
Mail Boxes Etc	258 Harvard St	6 pm
FedEx Kinko's	1295 Beacon St	6 pm
Self-Service	1295 Beacon St	4 pm

Map 18 • Brighton

Self-Service	736 Cambridge St	7 pm
elf-Service	736 Cambridge St	7 pm
Self-Service	20 Guest St	7 pm
Self-Service	424 Washington St	6:45 pm
Self-Service	1660 Soldiers Field Rd	6:30 pm

Map 19 • Allston (South) / Brookline (North)

Self-Service	214 Lincoln St	7:30 pm
Self-Service	881 Commonwealth Ave	7 pm
Self-Service	1505 Commonwealth Ave	7 pm
Self-Service	119 Braintree St	6:45 pm
Self-Service	300 Western Ave	6 pm
Signal Graphics	450 Cambridge St	3 pm

Map 20 • Harvard Square / Allston (North)

Self-Service	1 Mifflin Pl	8 pm
Self-Service	79 JFK St	7 pm
Self-Service	50 Church St	7 pm
Self-Service	48 Quincy St	7 pm
Self-Service	33 Kirkland St	7 pm
Self-Service	20 University Rd	7 pm
Self-Service	1563 Massachusetts Ave	7 pm
Self-Service	124 Mt Auburn St	7 pm
Self-Service	35 Oxford St	6:30 pm
Self-Service	12 Oxford St	6:30 pm
Self-Service	60 Garden St	6 pm
Self-Service	230 Western Ave	6 pm
Self-Service	1350 Massachusetts Ave	6 pm
FedEx Kinko's	1 Mifflin Pl	6 pm

Map 21 • West Cambridge

Self-Service	36 Bay State Rd	6:30 pm

Map 22 • North Cambridge / West Somerville

Self-Service	62 Whittemore Ave	7 pm
Self-Service	5 Cameron Ave	7 pm
Self-Service	199 Alewife Brook Pkwy	7 pm
Self-Service	2067 Massachusetts Ave	6:30 pm
Self-Service	167 Holland St	6:30 pm
Self-Service	406 Highland Ave	6 pm
Self-Service	186 Alewife Brook Pkwy	6 pm
Self-Service	147 Sherman St	5:30 pm
Self-Service	90 Sherman St	5 pm

Map 23 • Central Somerville / Porter Square

Self-Service	48 Grove St	7 pm
Self-Service	1972 Massachusetts Ave	7 pm
Self-Service	1815 Massachusetts Ave	7 pm
Self-Service	815 Somerville Ave	6 pm

Map 24 • Winter Hill / Union Square

Self-Service	100 Fellsway W	7 pm
Self-Service	237 Washington St	6 pm

Map 25 • East Somerville / Sullivan Square

Self-Service	529 Main St	7 pm
Self-Service	500 Rutherford Ave	7 pm
Self-Service	52 Roland St	5:45 pm

Map 26 • East Cambridge / Kendall Square / MIT

Self-Service	1 Broadway	M-Th 6 pm
Self-Service	400 Technology Square	7:30 pm
Self-Service	600 Technology Sq	7 pm
Self-Service	5 Cambridge Ctr	7 pm
Self-Service	43 Thorndike St	7 pm
Self-Service	25 1st St	7 pm
Self-Service	101 Main St	7 pm
Self-Service	1 Memorial Dr	7 pm
Self-Service	1 Main St	7 pm
Self-Service	1 Kendall Sq	7 pm
Self-Service	4 Cambridge Ctr	6:30 pm
Self-Service	245 1st St	6:30 pm
Self-Service	55 Cambridge Pkwy	6 pm
Self-Service	31 Ames St	6 pm
FedEx Kinko's	600 Technology Sq	6 pm
Self-Service	300 3rd St	5:30 pm
Self-Service	222 3rd St	5 pm

Map 27 • Central Square / Cambridgeport

Self-Service	350 Massachusetts Ave	7:15 pm
Self-Service	675 Massachusetts Ave	7 pm
Self-Service	64 Sidney St	7 pm
Self-Service	38 Sidney St	7 pm
Self-Service	359 Green St	7 pm
Self-Service	26 Landsdowne St	7 pm
Self-Service	21 Erie St	7 pm
Self-Service	1033 Massachusetts Ave	7 pm
Self-Service	875 Massachusetts Ave	6 pm
Self-Service	840 Memorial Dr	6 pm
Self-Service	790 Memorial Dr	6 pm
Self-Service	2 Central Sq	6 pm
Self-Service	955 Massachusetts Ave	4:30 pm

Map 28 • Inman Square

Self-Service	950 Cambridge St	6:30 pm
Self-Service	432 Columbia St	6:30 pm
Self-Service	120 Beacon St	6:30 pm
Self-Service	201 Broadway	6 pm
Self-Service	141 Portland St	6 pm

Though Boston is chiefly known for its college-town feel, there is plenty for the younger set to enjoy. There's bound to find something to hold the attention of your little ones among the many, MANY museums and parks.

The Best of the Best

- **Best Kid-Friendly Restaurant:** Full Moon (344 Huron Ave, Cambridge, 617-354-6699). Full Moon is the brainchild of two restaurateurs who also happen to be moms. The result is a restaurant that features a sophisticated menu with an extensive wine list for adults and a tasty assortment of kids' tried-and-true favorites. With sippy cups, toy buckets at every table, and a play area stocked with pretty much every toy imaginable, Full Moon gives you "grown-up dining with a kid-friendly twist."
- **Quaintest Activity:** Swan Boats in the Public Garden (Public Garden, Boston, 617-522-1966). Owned and operated by the same family for over 120 years, the swan boats have directly inspired two children's classics: Robert McCloskey's *Make Way for Ducklings* and E.B. White's *The Trumpet of the Swan*. The people-paddled boats can hold up to 20 passengers during the 15-minute cruise around the lagoon and under the world's smallest suspension bridge. An inexpensive and adorable treat for all. Open April–Sept.
- **Funnest Park:** Rafferty Park (799 Concord Ave, Cambridge). One of the area's best-hidden playgrounds, this wooded park provides tons of fun stuff for older children, including a new metal climbing structure with a twisty slide, wobbly bridge, boat-shaped sand box, and a mini schoolhouse with a chalkboard roof. Basketball hoops, tennis courts, and a baseball field reside next door.
- **Coolest Bookstore:** Curious George Goes to Wordsworth (1 JFK St, Harvard Square, Cambridge, 617-498-0062). With floor-to-ceiling shelves packed with books for children of all ages, there's something for everyone in this charming jungle-themed bookstore. And if you're tired of reading, they've got TOYS.
- **Best Rainy Day Activity:** Children's Museum (300 Congress St, Boston, 617-426-8855). This world-renowned museum—reopened in spring 2007 after a pricey and well-received renovation and expansion—has designed early learning experiences for kids of all ages with its inventive hands-on exhibits. Permanent exhibits include the Japanese House, where children experience the culture of Kyoto, Japan through a replica of a silk merchant's house, as well as a Hall of Toys, in which children can look at toys of the past, but not touch.
- **Cutest Event:** The Annual Ducklings Day Parade (Boston Common). Held every year on Mother's Day, the parade commemorates Robert McCloskey's book *Make Way for Ducklings* set on Boston Common. Children come dressed as their favorite duckling character and ready to parade.
- **Neatest Store:** Irving's Toy and Card Shop (371 Harvard St, Brookline, 617-566-9327). Since 1939, Irving's has been a favorite neighborhood source for ice cream, candy, and little nostalgic toys galore. This small store is packed with everything you never knew you needed from kazoos, to jacks, to tiny plastic farm animals.

Shopping Essentials

- **Nine Months Maternity and Infant Wear** (mom & baby clothes) 272 Newbury St, Boston, 617-236-5523
- **Barefoot Books Store** (kids' books) 1771 Massachusetts Ave, Cambridge, 617-349-1610
- **Barnes & Noble:**
  325 Harvard St, Brookline, 617-232-0594
  660 Beacon St, Boston University, 617-638-5496
  800 Boylston St, Prudential Center, 617-247-6959
- **Black Ink** (stamps):
  101 Charles St, Boston, 617-723-3883
  5 Brattle St, Cambridge, 617-497-1221
- **Boing!** (toys) 729 Centre St, Jamaica Plain, 617-522-7800
- **Borders Books & Music:**
  100 Cambridgeside Pl, Cambridgeside Galleria, Cambridge, 617-679-0887
- **Calliope** (toys & kids' clothes) 33 Brattle St, Cambridge, 617-876-4149
- **The Children's Book Shop** (kids' books) 237 Washington St, Brookline, 617-734-7323
- **Co-op for Kids at the Harvard Co-op** (kids' books) 1400 Massachusetts Ave, Harvard Square, Cambridge, 617-499-2000
- **Curious George Goes to Wordsworth** (kids' books & toys) 1 JFK St, Harvard Square, Cambridge, 617-498-0062
- **Discovery Channel Store** (educational gifts) 40 South Market Building, Faneuil Hall, 617-227-5005
- **Fish Kids** (kids' clothes) 1378A Beacon St, Coolidge Corner, Brookline, 617-738-1006
- **Henry Bear's Park** (kids' books & toys) 361 Huron Ave, Cambridge, 617-547-8424
- **KB Toys** (toys) 100 Cambridgeside Pl, Cambridgeside Galleria, Cambridge, 617-494-8519
- **Oilily** (up-scale kids' clothes) 32 Newbury St, Boston, 617-247-9299
- **The Red Wagon** (kids' toys & clothes) 69 Charles St, Boston, 617-523-9402
- **Sloane's Children's Shoes** (kids' shoes) 1349 Beacon St, Coolidge Corner, Brookline, 617-739-0582
- **Stellabella Toys** (toys)
  1360 Cambridge St, Inman Square, Cambridge, 617-491-6290
  1967 Massachusetts Ave, Porter Square, Cambridge, 617-864-6290

Parks for Playing

Kids need fresh air. And singing into the rotating fan doesn't count. Take them out for a swing. In addition to the roomy Boston Common and Cambridge Common, Boston boasts many smaller neighborhood parks:

- **Alden Playground** (Oxford St and Sacramento St, Cambridge). A great neighborhood playground located in the shadow of Baldwin School and Lesley University, this toddler and big-kid-friendly park includes a mini-track, jaw-dropping climbing equipment, and what may be the World's Coolest Slide.
- **Charlesbank/Esplanade Playground** (Charles St at Longfellow Bridge). This large play area features several climbing structures, slides, and swings for all ages with a nearby snack bar, open during the summer months.
- **Christopher Columbus Park** (Atlantic Ave & Commercial Wharf, Boston). One large climbing structure dominates this playground that is mostly geared towards the six-and-under set.
- **Clarendon Street Playground** (Clarendon St & Commonwealth Ave, Boston). This fenced and gated area provides ample scope for the imagination of children of all ages. The park features several climbing structures, slides, swings, and a sand area, along with a larger, open area for games of tag and soccer.
- **Constitution Beach** (Orient Heights, East Boston). Lifeguarded swimming areas, a bathhouse with a snack bar, tennis courts, and a playground with lots of climbing and sliding prospects make this a great destination to take the kids.
- **Emerson Park** (Davis Ave & Emerson St, Brookline). The Park boasts one of the town's oldest spray pools, with lots of trees for shade and a casual open space for tag.
- **Green Street Playground** (Green St, Jamaica Plain). On summer days, the city turns on the water, and kids in bathing suits splash around in the fountains. Families set up picnics around the periphery, and there is a sandy jungle gym and swingset area nearby.
- **Huron Avenue Playground** (Huron Ave, Cambridge). This newly renovated play area has two climbing structures for

children of all ages, as well as a play train and spray fountain for the summer months. The lack of tree shade may bother some parents.

- **Langone Park** (Commercial St, Boston). The park features a brand-new playground with multi-age, multi level climbing structures, and a swing set hovering on the edge of the harbor, great for that flying-across-water feeling. There are also three bocce courts and a baseball field.
- **Larz Anderson Park** (Newton, Avon, & Goddard Sts, Brookline). The largest park in Brookline holds an enclosed playground, picnic areas, ball fields, and an outdoor skating rink open December through February.
- **Millennium Park** (VFW Pkwy & Gardner St, West Roxbury). This park is larger than the Boston Common and TD Banknorth Garden combined and located on the site of the former Gardner Street landfill. The park provides picnic areas, play structures, and hiking and walking trails, as well as access to the river for boating and fishing.
- **Myrtle Street Playground** (Myrtle St & Irving St, Boston). Situated at the top of Beacon Hill, this playground features several climbing structures, a glider, a fire pole, swings, and a crazy daisy.
- **Public Garden** (Between Arlington St & Charles St, Boston). The first public botanical garden in the US, the Public Garden has 24 acres of flowers and green in the middle of the bustling city. Among the park's winding pathways and tranquil lagoon are the prized bronze statues of a mama duck and her brood commemorating Robert McClosky's famous children's book, *Make Way for Ducklings*.
- **Rafferty Park** (799 Concord Ave, Cambridge). One of the area's best-hidden playgrounds, this wooded park provides tons of fun activities for older children, including a new metal climbing structure with a twisty slide, wobbly bridge, boat-shaped sand box, and a mini-schoolhouse with a chalkboard roof. Basketball hoops, tennis courts, and a baseball field reside next door.
- **Raymond Street Park** (Walden St & Raymond St, Cambridge). Located on the shady side of the field, this playground is split up into two sections: one sandy, sunken area for the younger toddlers and one area for older children, equipped with a large climbing structure. Play gear ranges from a bridge to swing sets, including one handicapped swing seat.
- **Stoneman Playground** (Fairfield Ave & Massachusetts Ave, Cambridge). This playground is divided into a toddler area and an older children's space, with entertaining activities for both groups. Supervised model sailboat racing and fishing takes place on Sundays in the summer months.

Rainy Day Activities

It rains in Boston. A lot. It's also one of the windiest cities in the country. Foul weather can drench even the highest aspirations for outdoor fun. Here are some dry alternatives:

Museums with Kid Appeal

- **Museum of Afro-American History** (46 Joy St, Boston, 617-725-0022). The first publicly funded grammar school built for African-Americans now has interactive exhibits for kids. www.afroammuseum.org
- **Children's Museum** (300 Congress St, Boston, 617-426-8855). This world-renowned museum, freshly renovated, has designed early learning experiences for children of all ages with its inventive hands-on exhibits. Permanent exhibits include the Japanese House, where children get to experience the culture of Kyoto, Japan through a replica of a silk merchant's house, as well as a Hall of Toys where children can look at toys of the past,

but not touch. www.bostonkids.org
- **New England Aquarium** (Central Wharf, 617-973-5200). Among the many exhibits you'll find here are the sea lion show and a supervised hands-on demonstration that allows children to touch sea stars, snails, and mussels. Whale-watching trips and summer classes are also offered through the aquarium. www.neaq.org
- **Larz Anderson Auto Museum** (Larz Anderson Park, 15 Newton St, Brookline, 617-522-6547). Located in the grand Carriage House, the museum features an extensive exhibit on the history of the automobile, as well as America's oldest car collection. www.mot.org
- **Museum of Science** (Science Park, 617-723-2500). This award-winning interactive science museum features permanent and changing exhibits, including a Virtual Fish Tank, where children see life through the eyes of a fish. The museum also houses the Charles Hayden Planetarium, featuring sky and laser shows, and the five-story IMAX Mugar Omni Theater. Various science classes are also available. www.mos.org
- **Harvard Museum of Natural History** (26 Oxford St, Cambridge, 617-495-3045). This museum has great educational programs and exhibits for little explorers interested in botany, zoology, and geology. The Sunday afternoon programs and lectures are highly recommended for families with middle school children. www.hmnh.harvard.edu

Other Indoor Distractions

- **The Clayroom** (1408 Beacon St, Brookline, 617-566-7575). Paint your own pottery place. Great for parties. www.clayroom.com
- **Lanes and Games** (195 Concord Tpke, Rte 2, Cambridge, 617-876-5533). Candlepin bowling and ten-pin lanes for the whole family. www.lanesgames.com
- **Puppet Showplace Theater** (32 Station St, Brookline, 617-731-6400). This 100-seat theater has staging shows for Boston's young brood for over 30 years. The company stages classic puppet shows, as well as many original productions. Shows are recommended for children five and older. Great for parties. www.puppetshowplace.org

Outdoor *and* Educational

For when you've come to realize your children are a little too pale from sitting inside and playing video games all day.

- **Boston Duck Tours** (departure points: Prudential Center and Museum of Science, information: 617-267-DUCK). The Boston Duck is an original WWII amphibious landing vehicle that takes guests on an 80-minute tour (rain or shine) around the city by land and by sea. Kids are encouraged to quack at passersby. Tickets are sold inside the Prudential Center and Museum of Science beginning at 8:30 am. An additional ticketing location is at Faneuil Hall. Operating season: March 27th–Nov 26th. www.bostonducktours.com
- **Zoo New England** (1 Franklin Park Rd, Boston, 617-541-LION). The zoo holds all the standard zoo fare, plus the Butterfly Landing exhibit, a tented outdoor area where you can walk among more than 1,000 butterflies in free flight. (Smaller but still fun is the other Zoo New England site, Stone Zoo, in suburban Stoneham.) Adults: $9.50, seniors: $7.00, children (2–12): $5.50, under 2: free, and half-price tickets the first Sat of each month 10 am–12 pm. www.zoonewengland.com

Classes

Boston kids can participate in any number of structured activities that could help to mold and shape them like the blobs of clay that they are.
- **Boston Ballet School** (19 Clarendon St, Boston, 617-695-6950). Ballet classes for kids ages three and up. www.bostonballet.org
- **Boston Casting** (129 Braintree St, Suite 107, Allston, 617-254-1001). Acting classes for kids ages five and up. www.bostoncasting.com
- **Boston Children's Theatre** (321 Columbus Ave (Studio/Office), Boston, 617-424-6634). "Theatre for children by children," this theatre group has children involved in all phases of production. The theatre also offers acting classes and a summer creative arts program, in which kids learn stage combat, clowning, and juggling. www.bostonchildrenstheatre.org
- **Brookline Arts Center** (86 Monmouth St, Brookline, 617-566-5715). A non-degree school for the visual arts, the Brookline Arts Center offers classes for children ages two to teen in subjects ranging from jewelry-making to sculpture. www.brooklineartscenter.com
- **Cambridge Multicultural Arts Center** (41 Second St, Cambridge, 617-577-1400). A program designed for Cambridge residents to promote cross-cultural interchange using dance, music, writing, theater, and the visual arts. www.cmcusa.org
- **Community Music Center of Boston** (34 Warren St, Boston, 617-482-7494). A music program designed to promote musical development through experimental learning for kids of all ages. The center also offers visual arts classes, summer programs, and individual instruction. www.cmcb.org
- **French Library and Cultural Center** (53 Marlborough St, Boston, 617-912-0400). French classes for children ages three to ten. www.frenchlib.org
- **Full Moon** (344 Huron Ave, Cambridge, 617-354-6699). This kid-friendly restaurant offers cooking classes for parents and children ages three and up. www.fullmoonrestaurant.com
- **Grace Arts Project** (Grace United Methodist Church, 56 Magazine St, Cambridge, 617-864-1123). The program offers non-sectarian classes in music.
- **Grub Street Writers, Inc.** (160 Boylston St, Boston, 617-695-0075). Boston's only private writing school offers workshops and summer courses for young adults. www.grubstreet.org
- **Happily Ever After** (799 Concord Ave, Cambridge, 617-492-0090). The classes use fitness with creative stories and games for children aged three to six. Great for birthday parties. www.evergreendayschool.org
- **Hill House** (127 Mt. Vernon St, Boston, 617-227-5838). A non-profit community center that offers activities such as inline skating, karate, and youth soccer teams to downtown residents. www.hillhouseboston.org
- **Isis Maternity** (Two Brookline Pl, Brookline, 781-429-1599; 397 Massachusetts Ave, Arlington, 781-429-1598; 110 2nd Ave, Needham, 781-429-1597). The brainchild of Boston-area moms and health professionals, each Isis Center offers classes to stimulate everyone from the newly born to those about to bop into kindergarten. Infant massage, anyone? www.isismaternity.com
- **Jeanette Neill Children's Dance Studio** (261 Friend St, Boston, 617-523-1355). Since 1979, the program has offered children ages three to 12 an "intelligent dance alternative" with its focus on education, not preparation. www.jndance.com

- **Jose Mateo's Ballet Theatre** (Old Cambridge Baptist Church, 400 Harvard St, Cambridge, 617-354-7467). A professional performance company that provides ballet instruction for children ages three through 18. www.ballettheatre.org
- **Longy School of Music** (1 Follen St, Cambridge, 617-876-0956). Music instruction for children ages 1 to 18. www.longy.edu
- **Made By Me in Harvard Square** (1685 Massachusetts Ave, Cambridge, 617-354-8111). A paint-your-own-pottery studio. Great for birthday parties. www.made-by-me.com
- **Make Art Studio** (44 N Bennett St, Boston, 617-227-0775). Children ages four to 13 are encouraged to "choose their own medium" with guidance and instruction in small, age-appropriate classes.
- **Mudflat Studio** (149 Broadway, Somerville, 617-628-0589). For the past 30 years, the studio has offered hand-building, pot throwing, and individual workshops for children ages four and up. www.mudflat.org
- **Museum of Fine Arts** (465 Huntington Ave, Boston, 617-267-9300). The museum offers weekday and Saturday instruction that combines gallery study and creative expression for children ages five to 18. www.mfa.org/learn/index.asp?key=3117
- **New School of Music** (25 Lowell St, Cambridge, 617-492-8105). Newborns and up are provided with musical instruction for all levels of interest and skill, as well as musical theater classes for the older kids. www.cambridgemusic.org
- **North Cambridge Family Opera** (23 North St, Cambridge, 617-492-4095). Adults and children ages seven to 14 can participate in theatrical and operatic production. www.familyopera.com
- **North End Music and Performing Arts Center** (Paul Revere Mall, between Hanover St and Unity St, Boston, 617-227-2270). The center offers classes in music, language, and the performing arts to North End residents. www.nempac.org
- **New England Conservatory** (290 Huntington Ave, Boston, 617-585-1130). Music lessons for kids ages four and up at the oldest independent school of music in the US. www.newenglandconservatory.edu
- **Oak Square YMCA** (615 Washington St, Brighton, 617-782-3535). The center offers instruction in swimming, gymnastics, basketball, and art as well as after school programs for kids of all ages. www.ymcaboston.org
- **The Skating Club of Boston** (1240 Soldiers Field Rd, Brighton, 617-782-5900). Classes for skaters and hockey players of all levels. www.scboston.org
- **Topf Center for Dance Education** (551 Tremont St, Boston, 617-482-0351). The center provides underserved youth access to classes in jazz, tap, ballet, hip hop, and African dancing. www.topfcenter.org
- **Upon a Star** (441 Stuart St, Studio 4, Boston, 617-797-5562). Music and movement classes for children ages 14 months to three. www.uponastar.net
- **Wang YMCA of Chinatown** (8 Oak St W, Boston, 617-426-2237). Activities ranging from swimming instruction to music and art classes for children of all ages. www.ymcaboston.org
- **Wheelock Family Theatre** (180 The Riverway, Boston, 617-879-2147). The Theatre offers classes for kids ages four to 17. www.wheelock.edu/wft

For more information, visit www.gocitykids.com

Overview

The Boston Public Library, founded in 1848, was the first publicly supported municipal library in the United States, and is the only public library in the United States that is also a Presidential library, that of John Adams. It is also the first library to open and operate neighborhood branches. By far the coolest looking branch, the **Honan-Allston (Map 19)**, was designed by Machado & Silvetti Associates, Inc. and features tree guards and bike racks created by artist Rich Duca. The BPL now operates 27 branch libraries, each of which offers free wireless internet access. Check out the details on the BPL's website. If you're looking for a getaway in Copley Square, the Italian courtyard is the perfect place to sit down with a book or a bagged lunch. For more information on the BPL's main branch and just how much cultural heat it's packing (**see page 185**).

Brookline, Cambridge, and Somerville have their own public libraries, which are part of the Minuteman System. The Brookline Public Library houses government documents, Russian and Chinese materials, Brookline high school yearbooks and newspapers, DVDs, videos, new books, and local newspapers. The **Cambridge Public Library's Main Library (Map 28)** has occupied the same building since 1889, and is currently undergoing renovations and expansion slated for completion in 2008. It is temporarily located in the old Longfellow School at 359 Broadway. The Cambridge History and Local History Collections will be made available to the general public within the next two years, when the Main Library renovations are complete. The 93-year-old **Somerville Public Library (Map 24)** is also considering new construction in the future. Both Cambridge and Somerville libraries offer residents free passes to visit the Children's Museum, Harvard University Museum of Natural History, the JFK Library and Museum, the Museum of Fine Arts, the New England Aquarium, the Roger Williams Park Zoo, and others. To reserve FREE tickets, call 617-623-5000 (Somerville) or 617-349-4040 (Cambridge). For more information about hours, collections, and special events, check the library websites.

Library	Address	Phone	Map
West End	151 Cambridge St	617-523-3957	1
North End	25 Parmenter St	617-227-8135	2
Kirstein Business	20 City Hall Ave	617-523-0860	3
The Mary Baker Eddy Library	200 Massachusetts Ave	617-450-7000	5
Boston Public Library	700 Boylston St	617-536-5400	6
South End	685 Tremont St	617-536-8241	7
Charlestown	179 Main St	617-242-1248	8
East Boston	276 Meridian St	617-569-0271	9
Washington Village	1226 Columbia Rd	617-269-7239	10
South Boston	646 E Broadway	617-268-0180	11
Dudley	65 Warren St	617-442-6186	13
Connolly	433 Centre St	617-522-1960	14
Jamaica Plain	12 Sedgwick St	617-524-2053	14
Parker Hill	1497 Tremont St	617-427-3820	15
Brookline Main Library	361 Washington St	617-730-2370	17
Brighton	40 Academy Hill Rd	617-782-6032	18
Faneuil	419 Faneuil St	617-782-6705	18
Coolidge Corner	31 Pleasant St	617-730-2380	19
Honan-Allston	300 N Harvard St	617-787-6313	19
Boudreau Public Library	245 Concord Ave	617-349-4017	21
O'Neill Public Library	70 Rindge Ave	617-349-4023	22
Somerville West	40 College Ave	617-623-5000	22
Somerville East	115 Broadway	617-623-5000	24
Somerville Main Library	79 Highland Ave	617-623-5000	24
O'Connell Public Library	48 Sixth St	617-349-4019	26
Central Square Public Library	45 Pearl St	617-349-4010	27
Cambridge Main Library	359 Broadway	617-349-4030	28
Valente Public Library	826 Cambridge St	617-349-4015	28

Websites

Boston Gay Men's Chorus · www.bgmc.org
Now in its 24th year, the BGMC, through its collaboration with The Boston Pops, was the first gay chorus in the world to be recorded with a major orchestra on a major label.

craigslist · http://boston.craigslist.org
General community site (for straights, gays, and everyone else) that offers heavily trafficked "men seeking men" and "women seeking women" sections, as well as other community-related listings and information.

EDGE Boston · www.edgeboston.com
Gay Boston news and entertainment.

Gay & Lesbian Advocates & Defenders (GLAD) · www.glad.org
New England's leading legal rights organization dedicated to ending discrimination based on sexual orientation.

Greater Boston Business Council · www.gbbc.org
Promotes the vitality of Boston's LGBT business and professional community.

Out In Boston · www.outinboston.com
Local news and events, personal ads, business ads, chat, and community message boards.

PinkWeb · www.pinkweb.com
The LGBT yellow pages for New England and beyond.

Provincetown Business Guild · www.ptown.org
A gay and lesbian guide to P'town.

Publications

Bay Windows—New England's largest gay and lesbian newspaper is a weekly publication that prints local, national, and international news as well as community events and guides. www.baywindows.com.

In Newsweekly—News and entertainment weekly, including a calendar of events and a club guide. www.innewsweekly.com.

Bookstores

Calamus Bookstore · 92B South St, Boston · 617-338-1931 · www.calamusbooks.com

Sports

Beantown Softball League · www.beantownsoftball.com
LGBT softball since 1978.

Boston Bay Blades · www.bayblades.org/boston
For rowers and scullers.

Boston Boasts Squash League · www.bostonboasts.com
The country's oldest and largest gay and lesbian squash league.

Boston Gay Basketball League · www.bgbl.com
The country's largest LGBT basketball league.

Boston Strikers · www.bostonstrikers.com
Indoor and outdoor soccer league for gay and straight players of all levels.

Cambridge-Boston Volleyball Association · www.gayvolleyball.net
Indoor league with three levels of play.

Chiltern Mountain Club · www.chiltern.org
New England's largest LGBT outdoor recreation club.

East Coast Wrestling Club · www.eastcoastwrestlingclub.org
Gay men's wrestling group for athletes of all abilities.

FLAG Flag Football · http://flagflagfootball.tripod.com/flagflagfootballonline
Plays a full fall season and an abbreviated spring season.

FrontRunners Boston · www.mindspring.com/~frontrunners/index.htm
Welcomes joggers, walkers, and runners of all experience levels.

PrideSports Boston · 617-937-5858 · www.geocities.com/pridesportsboston
Gay & lesbian athletic alliance with more than 20 sports clubs.

Health Centers & Support Organizations

Boston Alliance of Gay Lesbian Bisexual and Transgender Youth · 617-227-4313 · www.bagly.org
For young people 22 and under.

Dignity Boston · 617-421-1915 ·
www.dignityboston.org
An inclusive community of LGBT Catholics.

Fenway Community Health · 7 Haviland St, Boston · 617-267-0900 · www.fenwayhealth.org
Provides high-quality medical and mental health care to Boston's gay and lesbian community; also a leader in HIV care.

Gay Men's Domestic Violence Project ·
800-832-1901 · www.gmdvp.org
Offers shelter, guidance, and resources to allow gay, bisexual, and transgender men in crisis to remove themselves from violent situations and relationships; also operates a 24-hour free-of-charge crisis center.

MassEquality · 617-878-2300 ·
www.massequality.org
Grassroots advocacy group defending equal marriage rights for same-sex couples.

The Network · 617-423-SAFE ·
www.thenetworklared.org
Provides information and resources for battered lesbian, bisexual, and transgendered women.

Annual Events

Boston Pride Week · 617-262-9405 ·
www.bostonpride.org
Begins on a Friday in June with a flag raising at City Hall; the parade and festival usually take place on the Saturday of the following weekend.

Boston Gay/Lesbian Film/Video Festival ·
617-267-9300 · www.mfa.org
Usually held in May at the MFA.

Mass Red Ribbon Ride · 617-450-1100 ·
www.massredribbonride.org
This bike ride across the state raises money for AIDS organizations. Takes place annually in August.

Venues – Lesbian

- **Aria** (Saturdays) · 246 Tremont St, Boston · 617-417-0186
- **Dyke Night Productions** · www.dykenight.com
- **Midway Cafe** (Sundays) · 3496 Washington St, Jamaica Plain · www.midwaycafe.com
- **Milky Way Lounge** (Sundays) · 401 Centre St, Jamaica Plain · 617-524-3740 · www.milkywayjp.com
- **The Modern** (Thursdays) · 36 Lansdowne St, Boston · www.lesbiannightlife.com
- **Toast** (Fridays) · 70 Union Sq, Somerville · 617-623-9211 · www.toastlounge.com
- **Tribe** (at Felt) · 533 Washington St, Boston · 617-350-5555 · www.tribenightclub.com

Venues – Gay

- **The Alley** · 14 Pi Aly, Boston · 617-263-1449 · www.thealleybar.com
- **Avalon** (Sundays) · 15 Lansdowne St, Boston · 617-262-2424 · www.avalonboston.com
- **Club Cafe** · 209 Columbus Ave, Boston · 617-536-0966 · www.clubcafe.com
- **Eagle** · 520 Tremont St, Boston · 617-542-4494
- **Flaunt** (Saint Nightclub) · 90 Exeter St, Boston · 617-236-1134
- **Fritz** · 26 Chandler St, Boston · 617-482-4428 · www.fritzboston.com
- **Heroes** (Saturdays at Toast) · 70 Union Sq, Somerville · 617-623-9211 · www.toastlounge.com
- **Jacques Cabaret** · 79 Broadway St, Boston · 617-426-8902 · www.jacquescabaret.com
- **Machine** (Thurs–Sat) · 1256 Boylston St, Boston · 617-226-2986 · www.ramrodmachine.com
- **Paradise** · 180 Massachusetts Ave, Cambridge · 617-868-3000 · www.paradisecambridge.com
- **Ramrod** · 1254 Boylston St, Boston · 617-226-2986 · www.ramrodmachine.com
- **Rise** (members only, after-hours) · 306 Stuart St, Boston · 617-423-7473 · www.riseclub.us
- **Shine Restaurant & Lounge** · 1 Kendall Sq, Cambridge · 617-621-9500 · www.shinecambridge.com
- **Venu** (Wednesdays) · 101 Warrenton St, Boston · 617-695-9500

After years of suffering from a shortage of hotel accommodations, Boston's hotel market has finally warmed up. Developers, encouraged by an improving economic climate and continued high demand for rooms, have moved forward with several large projects, most of which are located on or near the waterfront, where developers hope to leverage locations close to the Boston Convention & Exhibition Center. But it's not all just about harbor views and cafeteria-sized restaurants—boutique hotels are also popping up in various locations around town. Newcomers in the boutique market include **Hotel 140 (Map 6)** (a historic building in the shadow of the Hancock Tower), sleek **Nine Zero (Map 3)** (on Tremont Street), the **Bulfinch Hotel (Map 1)** (near North Station), and the **Beacon Hill Hotel (Map 1)** (on Charles Street, near the Common). **Jurys' (Map 6)** first Boston location has opened in the fully renovated former headquarters of the Boston Police Department. Another recently-opened property, the **Hampton Inn & Suites (Map 12)** (near Newmarket Square), may not be as luxurious as Jurys, but its suites are a decent option for long-term stays, and its proximity to I-93 and the Mass Pike make it easy to get to other locations. For visitors largely confined to happenings at the Boston Convention Center, the newly opened **Westin Boston Waterfront (Map 4)** and the **Seaport Hotel (Map 11)** are safe, convenient bets.

But Boston residents shouldn't let tourists have all the fun. Even if you're not staying the night, it's worth popping into one of Boston's classic hotels to soak up the atmosphere. The lobby of the **Fairmont Copley Plaza (Map 6)** exudes luxuriousness, as does its acclaimed restaurant, the Oak Room. For those looking for a respite from retail therapy on nearby Newbury Street, the **Eliot Hotel (Map 5)** on Commonwealth Avenue can rejuvenate even the weariest shopper. Genteel rivals the **Four Seasons (Map 3)** and

the **Taj Boston (Map 3)** (formerly home to the oldest Ritz Carlton in the country) both overlook the Public Garden. (The Bristol Lounge at the Four Seasons serves what many argue is the city's best-known high tea.) Across the Common, towards the financial district, the **Omni Parker House (Map 3)** stands as a Boston institution and a literary landmark (and has been known to flaunt its claim to fame as the birthplace of Parker rolls and Boston Cream Pies). The **Langham Hotel (Map 4)**, located smack dab in the middle of Boston's high-finance hub, offers a chocolate buffet on Saturdays that is To Die For. If you're killing time in Back Bay, check out the charming and cozy lobby of the **Lenox Hotel (Map 6)**. Playing up its proximity to techie heaven is the **University Park Hotel @ MIT (Map 26)**, decorated with tributes to the art of engineering. In Harvard Square, the **Charles Hotel (Map 20)** offers nightly jazz at the Regattabar as well as organic fine dining at Henrietta's Table. And if you're suffering from wanderlust of the spirit, ask about the weekend retreats at the **Monastery of the Society of St. John the Evangelist (Map 20)**.

Marriott's Custom House (Map 2) is located in one of Boston's most prominent historic landmarks, the Custom House Tower. The original Custom House building, completed in 1847, was described by Walt Whitman as "the noblest form of architecture in the world." The tower was added in 1915. The open-air observation deck on the 26th floor is open to the public and offers prime views of the harbor and the open spaces created by the demolition of the Central Artery.

See the average room rates listed below? Pretty expensive, huh? Whether you're booking for yourself or the in-laws, call the hotels to ask about specials and check websites such as hotels.com, Orbitz, Hotwire, Travelocity, and All-Hotels for discounts. Maybe you'll get lucky.

Map 1 • Beacon Hill / West End

Beacon Hill Hotel	25 Charles St	617-723-7575	$245
Bulfinch Hotel	107 Merrimac St	617-624-0202	$169
Charles Street Inn (B&B)	94 Charles St	617-314-8900	$250
Holiday Inn	5 Blossom St	617-742-7630	$200
John Jeffries House (B&B)	14 David G Mugar Wy	617-367-1866	$105
Onyx Hotel	155 Portland St	617-557-9955	$209
Shawmut Inn	280 Friend St	617-720-5544	$109
XV Beacon Hotel	15 Beacon St	617-670-1500	$375

Map 2 • North End / Faneuil Hall

Boston Marriott Long Wharf	296 State St	617-227-0800	$349
Golden Slipper (floating B&B)	Lewis Wharf	781-545-2845	$175
Harborside Inn	185 State St	617-723-7500	$129
Marriott's Custom House	3 McKinley Sq	617-310-6300	$429
Millennium Bostonian Hotel	26 North St	617-523-3600	$269

Map 3 • Downtown Crossing / Park Square / Bay Village

Boston Park Plaza Hotel	64 Arlington St	617-426-2000	$125
Courtyard Boston Tremont	275 Tremont St	617-426-1400	$179

Doubletree Boston	821 Washington St	617-956-7900	$189
Four Seasons Hotel	200 Boylston St	617-338-4400	$475
Hyatt Regency Boston	1 Ave de Lafayette	617-912-1234	$189
Milner Hotel	78 Charles St S	617-426-6220	$89
Nine Zero Hotel	90 Tremont St	617 772 5800	$206
Omni Parker House	60 School St	617-227-8600	$279
Radisson Hotel Boston	200 Stuart St	617-482-1800	$249
Ritz-Carlton Boston Common	10 Avery St	617-574-7100	$295
Taj Boston	15 Arlington St	617-536-5700	$275

Map 4 • Financial District / Chinatown

Boston Harbor Hotel	70 Rowes Wharf	617-439-7000	$275
Hilton Boston	89 Broad St	617-556-0006	$171
InterContinental Boston	510 Atlantic Ave	617-747-1000	$526
The Langham Hotel	250 Franklin St	617-451-1900	$185
Westin Boston Waterfront	245 Summer St	617-532-4600	$199

Map 5 • Back Bay (West) / Fenway (East)

436 Beacon Street	436 Beacon St	617-536-1302	$79
Central YMCA	316 Huntington Ave	617-536-7800	$46
Commonwealth Court Guest House	204 Commonwealth Ave	617-424-1230	$79
Eliot Hotel	370 Commonwealth Ave	617-267-1607	$275
Hilton Boston Back Bay	40 Dalton St	617-236-1100	$179
Hosteling International	12 Hemenway St	617-536-9455	$28 (dorm)
			$70 (private room)
Midtown Hotel	220 Huntington Ave	617-262-1000	$99
Newbury Guest House (B&B)	261 Newbury St	617-437-7666	$99
Oasis Guest House	22 Edgerly Rd	617-267-2262	$79
Sheraton Boston Hotel	39 Dalton St	617-236-2000	$249

Map 6 • Back Bay (East) / South End (Upper)

Boston Marriott Copley Place	110 Huntington Ave	617-236-5800	$199
Charlesmark Hotel	655 Boylston St	617-247-1212	$159
The College Club	44 Commonwealth Ave	617-536-9510	$90
Colonnade Hotel	120 Huntington Ave	617-424-7000	$234
Copley House	239 W Newton St	617-236-8300	$85
Copley Inn	19 Garrison St	617-236-0300	$105
Copley Square Hotel	47 Huntington Ave	617-536-9000	$168
Courtyard by Marriott Copley Place	88 Exeter St	617-437-9300	$179
Fairmont Copley Plaza Hotel	138 St James Ave	617-267-5300	$479
Hotel 140	140 Clarendon St	617-585-5600	$129
International Guest House	237 Beacon St	617-437-1975	$120 (single)
			$95 (dorm)
Jewel of Newbury	254 Newbury St	617-536-5523	$200
John Hancock Hotel & Conference	40 Trinity Pl	617-933-7700	$115
Jurys Boston Hotel	350 Stuart St	617-266-7200	$295
Lenox Hotel	61 Exeter St	617-536-5300	$179
Westin Copley Place	10 Huntington Ave	617-262-9600	$209

Map 7 • South End (Lower)

Chandler Inn	26 Chandler St	617-482-3450	$129
Clarendon Square Inn (B&B)	198 W Brookline St	617-536-2229	$155
Encore Bed & Breakfast	116 W Newton St	617-247-3425	$140
Hampton Inn & Suites Boston Crosstown Center	811 Massachusetts Ave	617-445-6400	$125
Rutland Square House	56 Rutland Sq	617-247-0018	$165
YWCA/Berkeley Residence	40 Berkeley St	617-375-2524	$60 (men & women)

Map 8 · Charlestown

Bunker Hill Bed & Breakfast	80 Elm St	617-241-8067	$135
Constitution Inn	150 2nd Ave	617-241-8400	$129
Marriott Residence Inn Boston Harbor	34 Charles River Ave	617-242-9000	$229

Map 9 · East Boston

Embassy Suites Boston at Logan	207 Porter St	617-567-5000	$206

Map 10 · South Boston (West) / Fort Point

Nolan House (B&B)	10 G St	617-269-1550	$95

Map 11 · South Boston (East)

Seaport Hotel	1 Seaport Ln	617-385-4000	$469

Map 12 · Newmarket / Andrew Square

Best Western Inn Roundhouse Suites	891 Massachusetts Ave	617-989-1000	$135
Holiday Inn Express	69 Boston St	617-288-3030	$104

Map 15 · Fenway (West) / Mission Hill

Best Western Longwood Medical	342 Longwood Ave	617-731-4700	$149
Brigham Guest House	698 Huntington Ave	617-566-8947	$48
Howard Johnson	1271 Boylston St	617-267-8300	$135

Map 16 · Kenmore Square / Brookline (East)

Anthony's Town House	1085 Beacon St	617-566-3972	$90
Beacon Inn	1087 Beacon St	617-566-0088	$80
Buckminster Hotel	645 Beacon St	617-236-7050	$104
Gryphon House (B&B)	9 Bay State Rd	617-375-9003	$149
Holiday Inn Boston at Brookline	1200 Beacon St	617-277-1200	$155
Hotel Commonwealth	500 Commonwealth Ave	617-933-5000	$293
Longwood Inn (B&B)	123 Longwood Ave	617-566-8615	$79

Map 17 · Coolidge Corner / Brookline Hills

Beacon-Plaza	1459 Beacon St	617-232-6550	$65
Bertram Inn (B&B)	92 Sewall Ave	617-566-2234	$99
Coolidge Corner Guest House	17 Littell Rd	617-734-4041	$69
Courtyard by Marriott Brookline	40 Webster St	617-734-1393	$179
Samuel Sewall Inn (B&B)	143 St Paul St	617-713-0123	$139

Map 18 · Brighton

Best Western Terrace Inn	1650 Commonwealth Ave	617-566-6260	$143
Days Inn	1800 Soldiers Field Rd	617-254-0200	$88

Map 19 · Allston (South) / Brookline (North)

Abercrombie's Farrington Inn	23 Farrington Ave	617-787-1860	$27.50
Days Hotel	1234 Soldiers Field Rd	617-254-1234	$116
Doubletree Guest Suites	400 Soldiers Field Rd	617-783-0090	$279

Map 20 · Harvard Square / Allston (North)

Charles Hotel	1 Bennett St	617-864-1200	$219
Harvard Square Hotel	110 Mt Auburn St	617-864-5200	$199
The Inn at Harvard	1201 Massachusetts Ave	617-491-2222	$259
Mary Prentiss Inn (B&B)	6 Prentiss St	617-661-2929	$184
Monastery of the Society of St John the Evangelist	980 Memorial Dr	617-876-3037	$50
Sheraton Commander Hotel	16 Garden St	617-547-4800	$219

Map 21 · West Cambridge

Best Western Hotel Tria	220 Alewife Brook Pkwy	617-491-8000	$189

Map 22 · North Cambridge / West Somerville

A Cambridge House, B&B Hotel Inn	2218 Massachusetts Ave	617-491-6300	$109
Meacham Manor	52 Meacham Rd	617-623-3985	$75
Morrison House (B&B)	221 Morrison Ave	617-627-9670	$65

Map 24 · Winter Hill / Union Square

Holiday Inn Boston/Somerville	30 Washington St	617-628-1000	$143
La Quinta Inn & Suites	23 Cummings St	617-625-5300	$119

Map 25 · East Somerville / Sullivan Square

Hampton Inn Boston/Cambridge	191 Monsignor O'Brien Hwy	617-494-5300	$152

Map 26 · East Cambridge / Kendall Square / MIT

Holiday Inn Express Hotel & Suites	250 Monsignor O'Brien Hwy	617-577-7600	$152
Hotel Marlowe	25 Land Blvd	617-868-8000	$224
Kendall Hotel	350 Main St	617-577-1300	$275
Marriott Cambridge	2 Cambridge Ctr	617-494-6600	$229
Residence Inn by Marriott - Cambridge	6 Cambridge Ctr	617-349-0700	$249
Royal Sonesta Hotel Boston	40 Edwin H Land Blvd	617-806-4200	$259

Map 27 · Central Square / Cambridgeport

Cambridge Bed & Muffin	267 Putnam Ave	617-576-3166	$75
Hyatt Regency Cambridge	575 Memorial Dr	617-492-1234	$179
University Park Hotel at MIT	20 Sidney St	617-577-0200	$259

Map 28 · Inman Square

A Bed & Breakfast in Cambridge	1657 Cambridge St	617-868-7082	$75
A Friendly Inn at Harvard (B&B)	1673 Cambridge St	617-547-7851	$97
Amory Guest House (B&B)	62 Amory St	617-308-4237	$70
Harding House (B&B)	288 Harvard St	617-876-2888	$85
Irving House at Harvard (B&B)	24 Irving St	617-547-4600	$75
Prospect Place (B&B)	112 Prospect St	617-864-7500	$85

And this is good old Boston.
The home of the bean and the cod.
Where the Lowells talk to the Cabots,
And the Cabots talk only to God.

—John Collins Bossidy (a toast given
at a Harvard alumni dinner in 1910)

Useful Phone Numbers

General Info	411
Emergencies	911
Boston Globe	617-929-2000
Boston Herald	617-426-3000
Boston Public Library	617-536-5400
Boston City Hall	617-635-4000
Brookline Town Hall	617-730-2000
Cambridge City Hall	617-349-4000
Somerville City Hall	617-625-6600
Boston Board of Elections	617-635-4635
Brookline Town Clerk	617-730-2010
Cambridge Board of Elections	617-349-4361
Somerville Board of Elections	617-625-6600, ext. 4200
Boston Police Headquarters	617-343-4200
Keyspan Energy Delivery	617-469-2300
NStar	617-424-2000
Comcast	888-633-4266
Verizon	800-256-4646
Red Sox Ticket Line	877-733-7699

Websites

www.notfortourists.com/boston.aspx—
  The Boston site written by the people, for the people.
www.cityofboston.gov—Boston government resources.
www.cambridgema.gov—
  Cambridge government resources.
www.ci.somerville.ma.us—
  Somerville government resources.
www.town.brookline.ma.us—
  Brookline government resources.
www.boston.com—Website of the *Boston Globe*.
www.boston.craigslist.org—
  Classifieds in almost every area, with personals, apartments
  for rent, musicians, job listings, and more.
www.boston.citysearch.com—
  Portal channeling the Yellow Pages.
www.boston-online.com—
  Forums and fun facts; guide to Boston English.
www. bostonist.com—
  About Boston and everything that happens in it.
www.universalhub.com—Info hub for the Hub.
www.beantownbloggery.com—
  Anything and everything beantown.

We're the First!!!

- America's first public park (Boston Common, 1634)
- America's first college (Harvard, founded in 1636)
- America's first public school (Boston Latin, 1645)
- America's first public library (Boston Public Library, 1653)
- America's first post office (Richard Fairbanks' Tavern, 1639)
- America's first regularly issued newspaper (*Boston News-Letter*, 1704)
- America's first lighthouse (Boston Harbor, 1716)
- First flag of the American colonies raised on Prospect Hill (January 1, 1776)
- America's first published novel (*The Power of Sympathy* by William Hill Brown, 1789)
- First demonstration of surgical anesthesia (1845)
- First telephone call (Alexander Graham Bell, 1876)
- America's first subway (1897)
- First person-to-person network email (BBN Technologies, 1971)
- First "First Night" New Year's celebration (1976)

Boston Timeline

A timeline of significant Boston events (by no means complete)

1620	Mayflower arrives in Plymouth.
1630	Dorchester founded by Gov. John Winthrop.
1630	City of Boston chartered.
1634	Boston Common, first public park in America, opens.
1636	Harvard College opens.
1639	America's first canal cut near Dedham.
1645	Boston Latin School, first public school in America, opens.
1692	Witchcraft trials begin in Salem.
1693	Society of Negroes founded.
1704	First regularly issued American newspaper, the *Boston News-Letter*.
1706	Benjamin Franklin born.
1716	First American lighthouse built (Boston Harbor).
1770	Boston Massacre.
1773	Boston Tea Party.
1775	Revolutionary War begins at Lexington and Concord.
1775	Battle of Bunker Hill.
1776	First flag of the American colonies raised on Prospect Hill in Somerville.
1776	British evacuate Boston.
1780	John Hancock becomes first elected Governor of Massachusetts.
1788	Massachusetts ratifies Constitution.
1795	The "new" State House built.
1796	John Adams, of Quincy, elected second president.
1806	African Meeting House, first church built by free African-Americans, opens.
1820	Maine secedes from Massachusetts.
1824	John Quincy Adams elected sixth president.
1826	Union Oyster House opens.
1831	William Lloyd Garrison publishes first abolitionist newspaper, the *Liberator*.
1837	Samuel Morse invents electric telegraph machine.
1845	Sewing machine invented by Elias Howe.
1846	Boston dentist William T.G. Morton publicly demonstrates the use of anesthesia in surgery.
1846	From 1846 to 1849, 37,000 Irish people flee the Potato Famine for Boston.
1860	From 1860 to 1870, the Back Bay is filled in, greatly increasing the landmass of Boston.
1863	University of Massachusetts at Amherst chartered.
1868	From 1868 to 1874, Boston annexes Charlestown, Brighton, Roxbury, West Roxbury, and Dorchester.
1872	*Boston Globe* prints its first newspaper.
1872	Great Fire.
1876	First telephone call by Alexander Graham Bell.
1877	Helen Magill becomes first woman Ph.D. in US (at BU).
1882	John L. Sullivan becomes bare-knuckle boxing champ.
1886	*Irish Echo* newspaper founded.
1888	Construction begins on new building for Boston Public Library.
1892	JFK grandfather John F. "Honey Fitz" Fitzgerald elected to state senate.
1894	Honey Fitz elected to US Congress.
1896	First US public beach opens in Revere.
1897	First American subway opens.
1900	Symphony Hall opens.
1901	Boston Red Sox play first game against New York Yankees.
1903	Red Sox (then the Americans) win first World Series.
1906	Honey Fitz becomes first Boston-born Irish-American mayor.

1912 Fenway Park opens.
1914 James Michael Curley elected mayor for the first time.
1915 Custom House Tower completed, tallest building in Boston at time.
1919 Great Molasses Flood kills 21 in the North End.
1920 Red Sox owner Harry Frazee sells Babe Ruth to Yankees for $100,000.
1920 Irish-Italian gang fights begin.
1924 Boston Bruins play first game.
1924 World's first mutual fund established.
1927 Sacco and Vanzetti wrongly executed for robbery shootings.
1928 Boston Garden opens.
1928 First computer invented at MIT.
1929 Bruins win their first Stanley Cup trophy.
1934 JFK's father, "Old Joe" Kennedy, named SEC chairman.
1941 Ted Williams hits .406, last player to hit over .400.
1942 Fire at Cocoanut Grove nightclub kills 491 people.
1946 JFK elected to Congress.
1946 Boston Celtics play first game.
1946 Red Sox lose World Series after tragic player error.
1947 Microwave oven invented at Raytheon.
1947 Polaroid camera invented.
1947 Dr. Sidney Farber introduces chemotherapy.
1950 Red Auerbach becomes Celtics coach.
1952 Boston Braves play final game in Boston, move to Milwaukee.
1956 Celtics draft Bill Russell.
1957 Massachusetts Turnpike opens.
1958 Celtics win first of 16 championships.
1958 Demolition of the West End neighborhood begins.
1959 Central Artery opens.
1960 Boston Patriots play first game.
1960 John F. Kennedy elected 35th president.
1960 Ted Williams homers in last at-bat for Red Sox.
1962 From 1962 to 1964, Boston Strangler kills 13 women. Albert DeSalvo is convicted and killed in prison.
1963 JFK assassinated in Dallas.
1964 Prudential Tower built.
1965 Havlicek steals the ball! Celtics win championship.
1966 Bobby Orr plays first game as a Bruin.
1966 Edward W. Brooke becomes first African-American elected to US Senate since Reconstruction.
1967 Red Sox's "Impossible Dream" season ends in defeat.
1971 First e-mail sent by BBN Technologies.
1973 John Hancock building, tallest in Boston, nears completion—giant windows start falling out.
1974 Federal court declares "de facto segregation" of Boston public schools; orders desegregation by busing. Demonstrations and violence ensue.
1975 Carlton Fisk hits 12th inning Game 6 homer, does baseline foul pole dance. Sox go on to lose Game 7.
1975 Gangster Whitey Bulger begins relationship with FBI agents, reign as Boston's biggest crime lord.
1976 First "First Night" New Year's celebration.
1978 Blizzard of '78 paralyzes Southern New England.
1978 Bucky Dent! Sox lose to Yanks.
1986 Celtics draft pick Len Bias dies of a drug overdose.
1986 Red Sox lose World Series Game 6 to Mets after excruciating 10th inning error, go on to lose Game 7.
1987 Big Dig construction begins in Charlestown.
1987 Cleanup of Boston Harbor begins.
1988 Governor Michael Dukakis runs for president, rides tank, loses to Bush HW.
1993 Celtics captain Reggie Lewis dies.
1993 Former Mayor Ray Flynn named ambassador to Vatican.
1993 Thomas M. "Mumbles" Menino elected Boston's first Italian-American mayor.
1995 Boston Garden closes; FleetCenter opens.
1995 Whitey Bulger goes on the lam after his FBI handlers are indicted.
1998 Boston Globe columnists Patricia Smith and Mike Barnicle fired over fabrications and plagiarism, respectively.

2001 Jane Swift becomes first female governor of Massachusetts.
2001 Planes that destroy NYC World Trade Center leave Logan Airport.
2002 After a 0-2 start, New England Patriots win their first Super Bowl.
2002 Ted Williams dies, cryogenically frozen in two pieces.
2002 Catholic clergy sexual abuse scandal explodes; Cardinal Bernard Law resigns amid controversy.
2003 Billy Bulger forced to resign as UMass president due to controversy about his gangster brother, Whitey.
2004 Supreme Judicial Court rules that gay couples have the right to marry.
2004 Demolition of Central Artery.
2004 Sox win World Series for first time since 1918.
2005 New England Patriots win their third Super Bowl in four years.
2006 Boston gets its first exciting new building in years with the opening of the ICA.
2007 Sox end three year drought by winning the World Series (again!).
2008 The Pats finish their almost perfect season 18-1.

15 Essential Boston Movies

The Boston Strangler (1968)	*Far and Away* (1992)
The Thomas Crown Affair (1968)	*Good Will Hunting* (1997)
Love Story (1970)	*A Civil Action* (1998)
The Paper Chase (1973)	*Monument Ave* (1998)
Between the Lines (1977)	*Next Stop, Wonderland* (1998)
The Verdict (1982)	*Mystic River* (2003)
The Bostonians (1984)	*The Departed* (2006)
Glory (1989)	*Gone Baby Gone* (2007)

15 Essential Boston Songs

"Boston" — The Byrds
"Charlie on the MTA" — The Kingston Trio
"Dirty Water" — The Standells
"Down at the Cantab" — Little Joe Cook & the Thrillers
"Government Center" — Jonathan Richman
"Highlands" — Bob Dylan
"I Want My City Back" — The Mighty Mighty Bosstones
"Massachusetts" — The Bee Gees
"Roadrunner" — Jonathan Richman
"Rock and Roll Band" — Boston
"Sweet Baby James" — James Taylor
"Tessie" — Dropkick Murphys
"The Ballad of Sacco & Vanzetti" — Joan Baez
"Twilight in Boston" — Jonathan Richman
"UMass" — The Pixies

15 Essential Boston Books

All Souls, Michael Patrick McDonald
The Autobiography of Benjamin Franklin
Black Mass, David Lehrer and Gerard O'Neill
The Bostonians, Henry James
Dark Tide: The Great Boston Molasses Flood of 1919, Stephen Puleo
Faithful, Stewart O'Nan and Stephen King
The Handmaid's Tale, Margaret Atwood
The House of the Seven Gables, Nathaniel Hawthorne
Infinite Jest, David Foster Wallace
John Adams, David McCullough
Johnny Tremain, Esther Forbes
Little Women, Louisa May Alcott
Make Way for Ducklings, Robert McCloskey
The Trumpet of the Swan, E.B. White
Walden, Henry David Thoreau

Overview

There's always something going on in Boston—the list below is just a smattering of the hundreds of annual parades, festivals, and wing-dings. Note that the dates indicated below for September through December reflect schedules for 2008, and the dates indicated for January through August reflect schedules for 2009. As always, it's a good idea to check an event's website when making plans. Now get out and enjoy!

- **First Night** · Dec 31/Jan 1 · www.firstnight.org · Family-oriented First Night got its start in Boston. Celebrate the new year with live performances, interactive events, and in most years, bitter cold. The purchase of a First Night Button gains you admission to participating performance centers.
- **Boston Wine Expo** · Late Jan/Early Feb · www.wine-expos.com/boston · Largest consumer wine event in the country, with a long bill of celebrity chefs to boot.
- **Anthony Spinazzola Gala Festival of Food & Wine** · Jan/Feb · www.spinazzola.org · Perhaps the premiere foodie festival in the USA, here's your opportunity to hob-nob with who's who in the Hub for only $200.
- **Chinese New Year** · Late Jan–Early Feb · Fireworks, parades, and special banquets in Chinatown.
- **Black History Month Music Celebration** · Feb · www.berkleebpc.com · A series of concerts at the Berklee Performance Center.
- **Winter Restaurant Week** · Early March · www.restaurantweekboston.com · Local eateries offer specially priced lunches and dinners. A chance to sample meals you could never otherwise afford!
- **New England Spring Flower Show** · Early March · www.masshort.org · Flower and craft exhibition at the Bayside Expo Center.
- **Evacuation Day** · Mar 17 · British troop withdrawal from Boston was the perfect excuse for infamous Mayor Curley to make St. Paddy's Day an official holiday for all Suffolk County municipal workers. Gotta love the Irish.
- **St. Patrick's Day Parade** · March· www.saintpatricksdayparade.com/boston · Marching through Southie since 1737.
- **Red Sox Opening Day** · Early Apr · www.redsox.com · Unofficial holiday.
- **Boston Marathon/Patriots Day** · Apr 20 · www.baa.org · Pseudo local holiday with the 111th running of the marathon and an early Red Sox game.
- **Wake Up the Earth Festival** · Early May · spontaneouscelebrations.org · Hippies and children alike enjoy stilt walking, puppets, live bands, and community bonding in Jamaica Plain.
- **Lilac Sunday at the Arnold Arboretum** · Early May · www.arboretum.harvard.edu · Follow the perfume of the lilac and the hippie in a Morris dancing outfit. Fun atmosphere at the Arnold Arboretum for families and friends.
- **MayFair 2008** · First Sunday in May · www.harvardsquare.com/mayfair/ · Harvard Square festival featuring everything from Literary tours to indie rock to Morris dancers.
- **Walk for Hunger** · Early May · www.projectbread.org · 20-mile walk whose proceeds fund over 400 emergency food programs each year.
- **Anime Boston** · Spring · www.animeboston.com · Japanese animation convention at the Hynes Convention Center.
- **Street Performers Festival** · Late May · Faneuil Hall carnival that's especially fun for kids. Magicians, sword swallowers, and lil' one activities like the Kid's Kazoo Parade.
- **Feast of the Madonna di Anzano** · Early June · www.anzanoboston.com · Procession and gala feast in the North End Italian community.
- **Scooper Bowl** · Early June · www.jimmyfund.org · World's biggest all-you-can-eat ice cream festival. Proceeds go to the Jimmy Fund.
- **Boston Gay Pride Parade** · Early/Mid June · www.bostonpride.org · New England's largest, capping a week of pride events.
- **Cambridge River Festival** · Mid June · Summer-starting festival along Memorial Drive between JFK Street and Western Ave, featuring music, food, art, kid-stuff.
- **Dragon Boat Festival** · Early/Mid June · www.bostondragonboat.org · Celebration of Chinese Dragon Boat racing at the Weeks footbridge, on Memorial Drive. Races, food, activities all day long.
- **Bloomsday** · Jun 16 · www.artsandsociety.org · Celebration of James Joyce's *Ulysses* at BU.

- **Bunker Hill Parade** · Around June 17 · www.charlestownonline.net · Celebration of Bunker Hill Day in Charlestown.
- **Boston Globe Blues and Jazz Festival** · Late Jun · Jazz and blues on the waterfront.
- **Boston Harborfest** · Early July · www.bostonharborfest.com · Over 200 events celebrating Boston's colonial and maritime history through reenactments, concerts, and historical tours.
- **Boston's Fourth of July** · Guess · www.july4th.org Ridiculously crowded Boston Pops concert and fireworks on the Esplanade.
- **Puerto Rican Festival** · Late July · Franklin Park goes loco for 5 days with amusement rides, food, and general fun in the name of Puerto Rico. Lots of live music.
- **Feast of St. Agrippina** · Early Aug · Featuring a procession, block party, and a giant tug-of-war.
- **August Moon Festival** · Mid Aug · At the Chinatown Gateway arch on Harrison Ave, celebrating Chinese culture and marked by tasty flaky pastries with an interesting history,
- **Feast of the Madonna del Soccorso** · Mid Aug · www.fishermansfeast.com · Boston's longest-running Italian festival.
- **St. Anthony's Feast** · Late Aug · www.saintanthonysfeast.com · With Italian-American festivals in the North End every weekend throughout late July and August, this is the one to get off your coolie on. True combination of kitsch and classic.
- **Summer Restaurant Week** · August · www.bostonusa.com · Discounted *prix-fixe* meals at scores of area restaurants—a terrific bargain.
- **Boston Carnival** · Late Aug · www.bostoncarnival.com · Celebration of Caribbean culture in Dorchester.
- **Khoury's State Spa Big Man Run** · Late Summer · www.clydesdale.org · A 4.8-mile race through Somerville during which runners stop three times to consume a hot dog and a beer.
- **Central Square World's Fair** · September · September is evidentially carnival month in Cambridge.
- **Boston Film Festival** · Mid/Late Sep · www.bostonfilmfestival.org · Plenty to please the most finicky cinephile.

- **Boston Tattoo Convention** · Early Sep · www.bostontattooconvention.com · Celebrating the newly legal (in Mass) art form.
- **Boston Freedom Rally** · Mid/Late Sep · www.masscann.org · That ain't freedom they're smoking.
- **Boston Folk Festival** · Mid Sep · www.wumb.org/folkfest · Pickin' and grinnin'.
- **Phantom Gourmet Food Festival** · Late Sep · www.phantomgourmetfoodfestival.com · $40 for the Landsdowne St Grand Bouffe that's unlike any other in Boston, featuring booths hand picked by the Phantom himself,
- **Opening Night at the Symphony** · Early Oct · www.bso.org · Kicks off Maestro Levine's second season at the BSO.
- **Harvard Square Oktoberfest** · Early Oct · www.harvardsquare.com · Don't expect liters of free beer.
- **Head of the Charles** · Late Oct · www.hocr.org · The world's largest two-day rowing event.
- **Belgian Beer Fest** · Late Oct · www.beeradvocate.com/fests · *Sluit je aan bij de Bierrevolutie!*
- **Boston Jewish Film Festival** · Nov · www.bjff.org · Now in its 17th season.
- **Boston International Antiquarian Book Fair** · Mid Nov · www.bostonbookfair.com · The country's longest running antiquarian book fair features autographs, photographs, maps, and more.
- **Black Nativity** · Weekends in Dec · www.blacknativity.org · One part Harlem Renaissance, one part folk music, dance, and verse celebration of the birth of Jesus Christ. Held at the Tremont Temple.
- **Prudential Center Christmas Tree Lighting** · Early Dec · www.prudentialcenter.com · Each year Nova Scotia thanks Boston for helping Halifax recover from a 1917 disaster by sending down a huge tree.
- **Boston Tea Party Reenactment** · Mid Dec · www.oldsouthmeetinghouse.org · A fine excuse to don your tri-cornered hat.
- **Boston Common Menorah Lighting** · Late Dec · www.cityofboston.gov/arts · Celebrating the first night of Hanukkah.

Television

2	WGBH	(PBS)	www.wgbh.org
4	WBZ	(CBS)	www.wbz4.com
5	WCVB	(ABC)	www.thebostonchannel.com
7	WHDH	(NBC)	www1.whdh.com
25	WFXT	(FOX)	www.fox25.com
27	WUNI	(Univision)	www.wunitv.com
38	WSBK	(UPN)	www.upn38.com
44	WGBH	(PBS)	www.wgbh.org
56	WLVI	(WB)	www.wb56.trb.com
66	WUTF	(Telefutura)	www.univision.com
68	WBPX	(PAX)	www.paxboston.tv

AM Radio

590	WEZE	Christian radio	www.wezeradio.com
680	WRKO	Talk	www.wrko.com
740	WJIB	Instrumental Pop/Light Oldies	
850	WEEI	Sports	www.weei.com
950	WROL	Religious	
1030	WBZ	News/Talk/Sports	www.wbz.com
1060	WBIX	Business Talk	
1090	WILD	Urban	
1120	WBCN	Financial Talk	www.moneymattersradio.net
1150	WJTK	Religious	
1260	WMKI	Radio Disney	www.radio.disney.go.com/mystation/Boston/
1510	WWZN	Sports	www.1510thezone.com
1600	WUNR	Leased-time/ethnic	
1670	Allston-Brighton Free Radio		www.abfreeradio.org

FM Radio

88.1	WMBR	MIT	wmbr.mit.edu
88.9	WERS	Emerson College	www.wers.org
89.7	WGBH	NPR News/Classical	www.wgbh.com
90.3	WZBC	Boston College	www.wzbc.org
90.9	WBUR	NPR/BU	www.wbur.org
91.5	WMFO	Tufts University	www.wmfo.org
91.9	WUMB	Folk/Jazz	www.wumb.org
92.9	WBOS	Modern AC	www.wbos.com
94.5	WJMN	Hip-Hop/R&B	www.jamn.com
95.3	WHRB	Harvard University	www.whrb.org
96.9	WTKK	Talk	www.wtkk.com
98.5	WBMX	Modern AC	www.mix985.com
99.5	WCRB	Classical	www.wcrb.com
100.1	WBRS	Brandeis University	www.wbrs.org
100.7	WZLX	Classic Rock	www.wzlx.com
101.7	WFNX	Modern Rock	www.wfnx.com
102.5	WKLB	Country	www.wklb.com
102.9	WCFM	Caribbean Music	www.choice1029.com
103.3	WODS	Oldies	www.oldies1033.com
104.1	WBCN	Modern Rock	www.wbcn.com
104.9	WBOQ	Soft Rock	www.northshore1049.com
105.7	WROR	Classic Rock	www.wror.com
106.7	WMJX	Soft Rock	www.magic1067.com
107.3	WAAF	Active Rock	www.waaf.com
107.9	WXKS	Pop	www.kissfm.com

Print Media

Bay Windows	www.baywindows.com	617-266-6670	LGBT newsweekly.
Beacon Hill Times	www.beaconhilltimes.com	617-523-9490	Newsweekly serving Beacon Hill.
Boston Business Journal	www.bizjournals.com/boston	617-330-1000	Business weekly.
Boston Globe	www.boston.com	617-929-2000	Daily broadsheet.
Boston Haitian Reporter	www.bostonhaitian.com	617-436-1222	Free monthly for Haitian-American community.
Boston Herald	www.bostonherald.com	617-426-3000	Daily tabloid.
Boston Irish Reporter	www.bostonirish.com	617-436-1222	News from and about the Irish in Boston.
Boston Metro	www.metropoint.com	617-338-7985	Weekday tabloid aimed at commuters.
Boston Magazine	www.bostonmagazine.com	617-262-9700	Glossy monthly.
Boston Phoenix	www.bostonphoenix.com	617-536-5390	Progressive news and entertainment listings.
Boston Review	www.bostonreview.net	617-258-0805	Leftish politics and culture magazine.
Boston Russian Bulletin	www.russianmass.com	617-277-5398	Russian community news, in Russian.
Brookline TAB	www.townonline.com/brookline	617-566-3585	Brookline newsweekly.
Cambridge Chronicle	www.townonline.com/cambridge	617-577-7149	Cambridge newsweekly.
Cambridge TAB	www.townonline.com/cambridge	617-497-1241	Cambridge newsweekly.
Charlestown Patriot-Bridge	www.charlestownbridge.com	617-241-8500	Charlestown newsweekly.
Dorchester Reporter	www.dotnews.com	617-436-1222	Dorchester news.
Improper Bostonian	www.improper.com	617-859-1400	Free entertainment and lifestyle magazine.
In Newsweekly	www.innewsweekly.com	617-426-8246	LGBT news and entertainment.
Jamaica Plain Gazette	www.jamaicaplaingazette.com	617-524-2626	JP news.
The Jewish Advocate	www.thejewishadvocate.com	617-367-9100	News about Boston's Jewish community.
Mass High Tech	www.masshightech.com	617-242-1224	Technology news.
Mattapan Reporter	www.bostonneighborhoodnews.com	617-436-1222	Mattapan neighborhood news.
Patriot Ledger	www.patriotledger.com	617-786-7000	Daily south shore news.
Pilot	www.thebostonpilot.com	617-746-5889	Catholic newsweekly.
Sampan	www.sampan.org	617-426-9492	Chinese/English bimonthly.
Somerville Journal	www.townonline.com/somerville	617-625-6300	Weekly Somerville news.
South Boston Tribune	www.southbostoninfo.com	617-268-3440	Weekly South Boston news.
Stuff@Night	www.stuffatnight.com	617-859-3333	Entertainment listings and "what's hot."
Weekly Dig	www.weeklydig.com	617-426-8942	Humor, news and nightlife.

WiFi

Starbucks	1 Charles St	617-742-2664	1
Starbucks	222 Cambridge St	617-227-2959	1
Starbucks	97 Charles St	617-227-3812	1
Boston Bean Stock Coffee	97 Salem St	617-725-0040	2
Starbucks	2 Atlantic Ave	617-723-7819	2
Starbucks	63 Court St	617-227-2284	2
Starbucks	84 State St	617-523-3053	2
Rachel's Kitchen	12 Church St	617-423-3447	3
Starbucks	12 Winter St	617-542-1313	3
Starbucks	143 Stuart St	617-227-7332	3
Starbucks	240 Washington St	617-720-2220	3
Starbucks	27 School St	617-227-7731	3
Starbucks	62 Boylston St	617-338-0067	3
Starbucks	1 Financial Ctr	617-428-0080	4
Starbucks	1 International Pl	617-737-4688	4
Starbucks	101 Federal St	617-946-0535	4
Starbucks	125 Summer St	617-737-0250	4
Starbucks	211 Congress St	617-542-4439	4
Espresso Royale	286 Newbury St	617-859-9515	5
Espresso Royale	44 Gainsborough St	617-859-7080	5
Starbucks	151 Massachusetts Ave	617-236-4335	5
Starbucks	273 Huntington Ave	617-536-6501	5
Starbucks	346 Huntington Ave	617-373-8860	5
Starbucks	350 Newbury St	617-859-5751	5
Starbucks	10 Huntington Ave	617-867-0491	6
Starbucks	165 Newbury St	617-536-5282	6
Surreal Image Café	300 Boylston St	617-244-3030	6
Starbucks	441 Stuart St	617-859-0703	6
Starbucks	443 Boylston St	617-536-7177	6
Starbucks	755 Boylston St	617-450-0310	6
Tealuxe	108 Newbury St	617-927-0400	6
Francesca's	564 Tremont St	617-482-9026	7
Starbucks	627 Tremont St	617-236-7879	7
Sorelle	100 City Sq	617-242-5980	8
Emack & Bolio's	736 Centre St	617-524-5107	14
Fiore's Bakery	55 South St	617-524-9200	14
June Bug Café	403A Centre St	617-522-2393	14
Sweet Finnish	761 Centre St	617-522-5200	14
Starbucks	283 Longwood Ave	617-277-5202	15
Espresso Royale	736 Commonwealth Ave	617-277-8737	16
Starbucks	148 Brookline Ave	617-867-6545	16
Starbucks	874 Commonwealth Ave	617-734-3691	16
Starbucks	15 Harvard St	617-232-5063	17
Starbucks	1655 Beacon St	617-232-5940	17
Starbucks	1660 Soldiers Field Rd	617-782-1325	18
Starbucks	277 Harvard St	617-739-3453	19
Starbucks	473 Harvard St	617-738-8005	19
Upper Crust	286 Harvard St	617-739-8518	19
Peet's Coffee & Tea	100 Mt Auburn St	617-492-1844	20
Simon's Coffee House	1736 Massachusetts Ave	617-497-7766	20
Starbucks	1662 Massachusetts Ave	617-491-0442	20
Starbucks	31 Church St	617-492-7870	20
Starbucks	36 JFK St	617-492-4881	20
Tealuxe	0 Brattle St	617-441-0077	20
Starbucks	220 Alewife Brook Pkwy	617-876-1070	21
Diesel Café	257 Elm St	617-629-8717	22
Starbucks	260 Elm St	617-623-4497	22
Starbucks	711 Somerville Ave	617-776-6783	23
Beantowne Coffee House	One Kendall Sq	617-621-7900	26
Starbucks	100 Cambridgeside Pl	617-621-9507	26
Starbucks	6 Cambridge Ctr	617-577-7511	26
1369 Coffee House	757 Massachusetts Ave	617-576-4600	27
Clear Conscience Café	581 Massachusetts Ave	617-661-1580	27
Starbucks	655 Massachusetts Ave	617-354-5471	27
1369 Coffee House	1369 Cambridge St	617-576-1369	28
Starbucks	468 Broadway	617-491-9911	28

Internet

FedEx Kinko's	2 Center Plz	617-973-9000	1
FedEx Kinko's	60 State St	617-523-8174	2
FedEx Kinko's	125 Tremont St	617-423-0234	3
FedEx Kinko's	10 Post Office Sq	617-482-4400	4
FedEx Kinko's	211 Congress St	617-482-0701	4
FedEx Kinko's	900 Boylston St	617-954-2725	5
FedEx Kinko's	187 Dartmouth St	617-262-6188	6
FedEx Kinko's	575 Boylston St	617-536-2536	6
FedEx Kinko's	715 Albany St	617-414-2679	7
FedEx Kinko's	415 Summer St	617-954-2203	10
FedEx Kinko's	115 Cummington St	617-358-2679	16
FedEx Kinko's	1370 Beacon St	617-731-3100	17
FedEx Kinko's	252 Washington St	617-723-7263	18
FedEx Kinko's	1 Miffin Pl	617-497-0125	20
FedEx Kinko's	600 Technology Sq	617-494-5905	26

Self Storage

Self Storage	Address	Phone	Map
Planet Self Storage	33 Traveler St	617-426-7229	7
Town & Country Moving & Storage	9 Appleton St	617-350-6683	7
William Lowe & Sons Moving & Storage	50 Terminal St	617-242-6800	8
A-Plus Moving & Storage	44 Border St	857-540-9531	9
Planet Self Storage	135 Old Colony Ave	617-268-8282	10
Castle Self Storage	39 Old Colony Ave	617-268-5056	12
Gentle Movers Moving & Storage Centers	25 Boston St	617-268-0500	12
Patriot Self Storage	968 Massachusetts Ave	617-541-5600	12
Planet Self Storage	100 Southampton St	617-445-6776	12
Public Storage	290 Southampton St	617-445-6287	12
U-Haul	985 Massachuetts Ave	617-442-5600	12
Extra Space Storage	3175 Washington St	617-323-1110	14
Extra Space Storage	235 North Beacon St	617-782-1177	18
EZ Storage	145 N Beacon St	617-779-0005	18
Road Warrior Moving & Storage	86 Lincoln Street	617-782-5400	18
Brighton Self Storage	1360 Commonwealth Ave	617-739-4401	19
Simply Self Storage	130 Lincoln St	617-787-4325	19
Yellow Brick Self Storage	138 Harvard Ave	617-254-5007	19
O B Gray Moving & Storage	200 Harvard Way	617-825-4416	20
Cambridge Self Storage	445 Concord Ave	617-876-5060	21
Extra Space Storage	460 Somerville Ave	617-625-1000	23
Extra Space Storage	14 McGrath Hwy	617-623-7690	25
Storage Bunker	420 Rutherford Ave	617-242-6400	25
Planet Self Storage	39 Medford St	617-497-4800	28
U-haul Center Of Somerville	151 Linwood St	617-625-2789	28

Van & Truck Rental

Van & Truck Rental	Address	Phone	Map
Budget	33 Traveler St	617-426-7886	7
Budget	95 Brighton Ave	617-497-3608	19
Budget	420 Rutherford Ave	617-242-8044	25
Ryder	280 W 1st St	617-269-8000	10
U-Haul	985 Massachusetts Ave	617-442-5600	12
U-Haul	1579 Columbus Ave	617-445-0405	14
U-Haul	240 N Beacon St	617-782-0355	18
U-Haul	844 Main St	617-354-0500	27
U-Haul	151 Linwood St	617-625-2789	28

Locksmiths

	Phone
ABC Lock & Keys Services	617-522-2646
Boston Lock & Safe	617-787-3400
Champion Locks	617-723-7000
Flying Locksmiths	617-720-4571
Greater Boston 24 Hour Lock Smith	617-254-8674
Mass Ave Lock	617-247-9779
MegaLockSmith	617-723-5433

Plumbers

	Phone
Beacon Hill Plumbing	617-723-3296
Drain Doctor	617-547-6969
Drain King	617-439-3929
John's (Brookline)	617-277-1447
Metro Sewer & Drain	617-426-8939
Plumbing Express	617-288-0777
Roto-Rooter	617-267-1489
Sudden Service	617-367-8300

Bowling (yes, bowling)

	Address	Phone	Map
Boston Bowl	820 Morrissey Blvd, Dorchester	617-825-3800	32

Convenience Stores

	Address	Phone	Map
Store 24	177 State St	617-367-0034	2
Store 24	141 Massachusetts Ave	617-353-1897	5
Store 24	717 Boylston St	617-424-6888	6
Store 24	140 Main St	617-241-7865	8
Store 24	684 Centre St	617-524-9893	14
Store 24	542 Commonwealth Ave	617-424-8856	16
Store 24	1912 Beacon St	617-738-4874	18
White Hen Pantry	462 Washington St	617-787-3719	18
Store 24	509 Cambridge St	617-782-3900	19
Store 24	957 Commonwealth Ave	617-783-5466	19
White Hen Pantry	1868 Massachusetts Ave	617-547-7255	23

Copy Shops

	Address	Phone	Map
FedEx Kinko's	2 Center Plz	617-973-9000	1
FedEx Kinko's	187 Dartmouth St	617-262-6188	6
Copy Cop	601 Boylston St	617-267-9267	6
FedEx Kinko's	1 Miffin Pl	617-497-0125	20

Pharmacies

	Address	Phone	Map
Walgreens	841 Boylston St	617-236-1692	5
CVS	587 Boylston St	617-437-8414	6
CVS	210 Border St	617-567-5147	9
Walgreens	1 Central Sq	617-569-5278	9
CVS	1426 Massachusetts Ave	617-354-4420	20
CVS	211 Alewife Brook Pkwy	617-661-6422	21
CVS	36 White St	617-876-5519	23
Rite Aid	14 McGrath Hwy	617-776-3003	25

Restaurants

	Address	Phone	Map
Bova's Bakery	134 Salem St	617-523-5601	2
IHOP	1850 Soldiers Field Rd	617-787-0533	18

Veterinary

	Address	Phone	Map
MSPCA Angell Memorial Animal Hospital	350 S Huntington Ave	617-522-7282	14

Hungry?

Seafood

Legal Sea Foods (Map 3, 6, 26) has the highest profile among local fishmongers and deserves its good reputation, despite its high prices. **McCormick and Schmick's (Map 2, 3)** excels in both raw and fried oysters. Worth the trip to Inman Square is **East Coast Grill & Raw Bar (Map 28)**, which also excels at barbecue. For something cheaper in Cambridge, try **Dolphin Seafood (Map 27)**; in Somerville, **Out of the Blue (Map 22)**. For lovers of Chinese food, some of the best seafood dishes can be found at **Peach Farm (Map 4)**. In the summer, get out of the city and eat your seafood by the seashore.

Italian

Boston is blessed with numerous outstanding Italian restaurants. In the North End, **Mamma Maria (Map 2)** and **Bricco (Map 2)** are two among many standouts. Or, if you are tight on cash and can make it to the North End on weekday afternoon, check out **Galleria Umberto (Map 2)**. For a fine Italian meal elsewhere in Central Boston, reserve a table at **Domani (Map 6)**, **Teatro (Map 3)**, or **Grotto (Map 1)**. Brookliners should look into **La Morra (Map 17)**. On the other side of the river, **Vinny's at Night (Map 25)** dishes out Southern Italian to a loyal following who swear the food is better than anything in the North End. And Roslindale's **Delfino (Map 30)** has legions of local fans.

Pizza

Few foods inspire as much passion (and contentiousness) as pizza; as such, identifying Boston's best pizza is a thankless task. Our favorites? In no particular order: **Penguin Pizza (Map 15)**, **Pizzeria Regina (Map 2)**, **Santarpio's (Map 9)**, **Emma's (Map 28)**, **Joe V's (Map 7)**, **Cambridge, 1 (Map 20)**, and **Armando's (Map 21)**.

East Asian

As with the North End and its Italian food, Chinatown has scads of high-quality restaurants. If you're looking for full-on dim-sum craziness, try **Chau Chow City (Map 4)**, **China Pearl (Map 4)**, or **Hei La Moon (Map 4)** for weekend brunch. If you want more sedate surroundings in Chinatown, try **King Fung Garden (Map 4)**, **Hong Kong Eatery (Map 4)**, or **Peach Farm (Map 4)**. Want Thai? Try **Rod Dee (Map 15, 17)** or **Dok Bua (Map 17)**. Korean? Try **Buk Kyung II (Map 19)**. Sushi? Try **Oishii (Map 7)** or

O Ya (Map 4). Cambodian? Try **Elephant Walk (Map 16, 22)**. Vietnamese? Try **Pho 2000 (Map 32)** or **Ba-Le (Map 32)** .

South Asian

Central Square (home to reliable standby **India Pavilion (Map 27)**) is no longer the only place to get good Indian food. Consider trying Brookline's **Rani Indian Bistro (Map 17)**, Harvard Square's **Tamarind Bay (Map 20)**, Jamaica Plain's **Bukhara (Map 14)**, Dorchester's **Shanti: Taste of Indian (Map 32)**, or Kenmore Square's **India Quality (Map 16)**. If you want top notch Indian food for dirt cheap, check out **Punjabi Dhaba (Map 28)**. For something different (and pleasant), try the Afghan cuisine at East Cambridge's **Helmand (Map 26)**.

Bars

Better known as drinking and meeting spots, but also serving damn good grub, are **The Asgard (Map 27)**, **Audubon Circle (Map 16)**, **B-Side Lounge (Map 28)**, **Blarney Stone (Map 20)**, **Grendel's Den (Map 20)**, **James's Gate (Map 14)**, **Matt Murphy's Pub (Map 17)**, **Miracle of Science (Map 27)**, **The Paradise (Map 19)**, and **Silvertone Bar & Grill (Map 3)**.

Grease

Diner enthusiasts should try **Mike's City Diner (Map 7)**, **Breakfast Club Diner (Map 19)**, or **Rosebud Diner (Map 22)**. For a big breakfast, consider **Sound Bites (Map 23)**, **Broken Yolk (Map 23)**, **Brookline Lunch (Map 27)**, or the slightly more civilized **Trident Bookstore & Café (Map 5)**.

Top-End

Want to celebrate a special occasion? Have your concierge reserve a table downtown at **Aujourd'hui (Map 3)**, **Excelsior (Map 3)**, **The Federalist (Map 1)**, **Mantra (Map 3)**, **No. 9 Park (Map 3)**, or **Radius (Map 4)**, in the South End at **Hamersley's Bistro (Map 7)** or **Masa (Map 7)**, around Back Bay at **Mistral (Map 6)**, **L'Espalier (Map 5)**, **Grill 23 (Map 6)**, **Great Bay (Map 16)**, or **Clio (Map 5)**, or over the river at **Harvest (Map 20)**, **Rialto (Map 20)**, **Oleana (Map 28)**, or **Rendezvous (Map 27)**.

Key: $: Under $10 / $$: $10–$20 / $$$: $20–$30 / $$$$: $30–$40 / $$$$$: $40+
* : Does not accept credit cards./ † : Accepts only American Express / †† : Accepts only Visa and Mastercard
Time listed refers to kitchen closing time on weekend nights

Map 1 • Beacon Hill / West End

75 Chestnut	75 Chestnut St	617-227-2175	$$$$	10 pm	Featuring a Sunday jazz brunch.
Artu	89 Charles St	617-227-9023	$$$	11 pm	Affordable Italian. Fresh ingredients. Take-out panini.
Beacon Hill Bistro	25 Charles St	617-723-1133	$$$$	11 pm	Elegant cooking in a cozy space.
The Federalist	15 Beacon St	617-670-2515	$$$$$	10 pm	A thoroughly top-end experience with an old Boston atmosphere.
Figs	42 Charles St	617-742-3447	$$$	10 pm	Beacon Hill outpost of upscale pizza chain.
Grotto	37 Bowdoin St	617-227-3434	$$$	10 pm	Good value Italian in a Beacon Hill basement.
Harvard Gardens	316 Cambridge St	617-523-2727	$$	11 pm	More for meeting and drinking than eating.
Hungry I	71 1/2 Charles St	617-227-3524	$$$$	10 pm	French. Cozy spot for intimate meals.
King & I	145 Charles St	617-227-3320	$$	10:30 pm	No-brainer for decent, inexpensive Thai.
Lala Rokh	97 Mt Vernon St	617-720-5511	$$$	10 pm	Alluring Persian in a pleasant Beacon Hill townhouse.
Ma Soba	156 Cambridge St	617-973-6680	$$$	11 pm	Sleek Asian fusion.
Panificio	144 Charles St	617-227-4340	$	9 pm	Paninis, pastries. Try the formaggio.
The Paramount	44 Charles St	617-720-1152	$$	11 pm	Popular local spot for all three meals. Fantastic brunch.
Phoenicia	240 Cambridge St	617-523-4606	$$	10 pm	Excellent grape leaves.
Pierrot	272 Cambridge St	617-725-8855	$$$$	10 pm	Authentic French bistro.
Upper Crust	20 Charles St	617-723-9600	$$	10:30 pm	Fancy schmancy, crisp-crust pizza.

Map 2 • North End / Faneuil Hall

Al's State Street Café	110 State St	617-720-5555	$††	2 am	Good sandwiches on the cheap, but order fast. You have been warned!
Antico Forno	93 Salem St	617-723-6733	$$$	10:30 pm	A home-style North End stand-out. Great pizza.
Billy Tse	240 Commercial St	617-227-9990	$$$	11 pm	Pan-Asian near the waterfront.
Boston Sail Loft	80 Atlantic Ave	617-227-7280	$$	11 pm	Good seafood with a great view.
Bova's Bakery	134 Salem St	617-523-5601	$*	24-hrs	Baked goods available 24/7!
Bricco	241 Hanover St	617-248-6800	$$$$	2 am	Boutique Italian cuisine. Rather popular.
Caffe Paradiso	255 Hanover St	617-742-1768	$	2 pm	Coffee and cannoli. Local landmark.
The Daily Catch	323 Hanover St	617-523-8567	$$$*	11 pm	For those who can stand the heat in the kitchen.
Galleria Umberto	289 Hanover St	617-227-5709	$*	3 pm	Tasty, dirt cheap, greasy Italian lunch.
Green Dragon Tavern	11 Marshall St	617-367-0055	$$	2 am	Pretend you're Sam Adams while having the same.
Haymarket Pizza	106 Blackstone St	617-723-8585	$*	7 pm	Enjoy a great slice in the company of pigeons.
Il Panino Express	11 Parmenter St	617-720-1336	$$	11 pm	Grab a quick bite of decent Italian.
L'Osteria	104 Salem St	617-723-7847	$$$	11 pm	Family style red sauce joint.
La Famiglia Giorgio's	112 Salem St	617-367-6711	$$	10:30 pm	Cheap family style Italian without any fancy pants.
La Summa	30 Fleet St	617-523-9503	$$$	10 pm	More low-key than most North End places, and it will leave your belly satisfied.
Lucca	226 Hanover St	617-742-9200	$$$$	12:15 am	Stylish Northern Italian.
Lulu's Bake Shoppe	227 Hanover St	617-720-2200	$	11 pm	The cupcakes cost more than a package of Twinkies, but they are worth it.
Mamma Maria	3 North Sq	617-523-0077	$$$	11 pm	High-end Italian in a charming townhouse.
Massimino's Cucina Italiana	207 Endicott St	617-523-5959	$$	11 pm	Out-of-the-way Italian, largely tourist-free
Maurizio's	364 Hanover St	617-367-1123	$$$$	10:30 pm	Tiny, yet amazing, Italian restaurant on the main drag
McCormick & Schmick's	Faneuil Hall Marketplace	617-720-5522	$$$	12 am	Enormous fresh seafood selection in steakhouse atmosphere.
Neptune Oyster	63 Salem St	617-742-3474	$$$	12 am	Great oysters, of course, and the most amazing lobster roll –worth every penny.
Pizzeria Regina	11 1/2 Thacher St	617-227-0765	$$*	11 pm	Local landmark. Worth the wait.
Prezza	24 Fleet St	617-227-1577	$$$$$	10 pm	High-end Italian. Don't forget to try the Key Lime Martini.
Sel de la Terre	255 State St	617-720-1300	$$$$	10 pm	A taste of Provence.
Taranta	210 Hanover St	617-720-0052	$$$$	11 pm	Delicious Italian food with a Peruvian twist.
Theo's Cozy Corner	162 Salem St	617-241-0202	$*	3 pm	Cozy diner. Killer hash browns.
Trani	111 Salem St	617 624-0222	$*	10 pm	Stunt pastries.
Union Oyster House	41 Union St	617-227-2750	$$$	10 pm	Oldest restaurant in America, saddle up to oyster bar.
Wagamama Faneuil Hall	Quincy Market Building	617-742-9242	$	11 pm	Wag the noodle. Fast food style Japanese noodle house.

Key: $: Under $10 / $$: $10–$20 / $$$: $20–$30 / $$$$: $30–$40 / $$$$$: $40+
* : Does not accept credit cards / † : Accepts only American Express./ †† : Accepts only Visa and Mastercard
Time listed refers to kitchen closing time on weekend nights

Map 3 • Downtown Crossing / Park Square / Bay Village

Aujourd'hui	200 Boylston St	617-351-2071	$$$$$	10 pm	Sublime French, delightful room.
Bonfire	50 Park Plaza	617-262-3473	$$$$	11 pm	More than a steakhouse. Go for gourmet tacos.
Buddha's Delight	5 Beach St	617-451-2395	$$	9 pm	All-vegetarian Asian.
Chacarero	426 Washington St	617-542-0392	$*	7 pm	Unique Chilean sandwich. Lunch, take-away only.
Dedo	69 Church St	617-338-9999	$$$	1 am	Rib-eye for the queer guy.
Emperor's Garden	690 Washington St	617-482-8898	$$$	10 pm	Dim sum for the masses.
Excelsior	272 Boylston St	617-426-7878	$$$$$	11 pm	Opulent food, room, crowd. Cool wine elevator.
Herrera's Mexican Grille	11 Temple Pl	617-426-2350	$*	4 pm	Good and cheap Cali-Mex.
Intermission Tavern	228 Tremont St	617-451-5997	$$	1 am	Drinks and burgers until 1 am.
Jacob Wirth	31 Stuart St	617-338-8586	$$	12 am	German-y. Local institution since 1868 with barroom sing-a-long on Friday nights.
Know Fat!	530 Washington St	617-451-0043	$	9 pm	Healthy-ish burgers and sandwiches.
Legal Sea Foods	26 Park Plz	617-426-4444	$$$	12 am	Fresh fish, famous chowder. Legal's sleekest space.
Locke-Ober	3 Winter Pl	617-542-1340	$$$$	11 pm	Worth it just for the ambiance and history although the food should be better.
Lu's Sandwich Shop	2 Knapp St	626-292-1453	$	7 pm	Delicious Banh Mi made fresh in back of a jewelry store!
Mantra	52 Temple Pl	617-542-8111	$$$	10 pm	French/Indian in a stylish setting.
McCormick & Schmick's	34 Columbus Ave	617-482-3999	$$$	11 pm	$2 "social hour" bar menu is a great deal.
Montien	63 Stuart St	617-338-5600	$$$	11 pm	If you don't like raw fish, you can always order a Pad Thai.
New Saigon Sandwich	696 Washington St	617-542-6296	$*	6:30 pm	Cheap sandwiches, boxed lunches. Delicious!
New York Pizza	224 Tremont St	617-482-3459	$$	3 am	Perfect for late night noshing.
No 9 Park	9 Park St	617-742-9991	$$$$$	11 pm	Consistently rated among Boston's best.
Penang	685 Washington St	617-451-6373	$$	11 pm	Well-established Malaysian out of NYC.
Pigalle	75 Charles St S	617-423-4944	$$$$	10 pm	Modern French cuisine in an intimate setting.
Rachel's Kitchen	12 Church St	617-423-3447	$*	3 pm	Friendly breakfast/lunch corner shop.
Sam LaGrassa's	44 Province St	617-357-6861	$$	3:30 pm	Monster sandwiches. Try the pastrami.
Silvertone Bar & Grill	69 Bromfield St	617-338-7887	$$*	12 am	Great after-work lounge with tasty home cooking.
Smith & Wollensky	101 Arlington St	617-423-1112	$$$$$	11 pm	The castle has been taken.
Teatro	177 Tremont St	617-778-6841	$$$	12 am	Sleek Italian next to Loews Cinema.
Tequila Mexican Grill	55 Bromfield St	617-482-8822	$*	4 pm	Muy sabroso hole-in-the-wall.
Via Matta	79 Park Plz	617-422-0008	$$$$	11 pm	Stylish Italian, stylish crowd.
Viga	304 Stuart St	617-542-7200	$	4 pm	Cheap and tasty take out.

Map 4 • Financial District / Chinatown

Chau Chow City	83 Essex St	617-338-8158	$$	4 am	Best known for their Dim Sum. Open late.
China Pearl	9 Tyler St	617-426-4338	$$	11 pm	Dim sum for beginners and experts.
Ginza	16 Hudson St	617-338-2261	$$$	3:30 am	Waitresses in kimonos, great sushi, Japanese people actually eat here.
Hei La Moon	88 Beach St	617-338-8813	$*	11 pm	Best Dim Sum in Boston!
The Hong Kong Eatery	79 Harrison Ave	617-423-0838	$*	10:30 pm	Mountains of pork and rice for just a few bucks.
J Pace & Son	1 Federal St	617-227-4949	$	5 pm	Hot and cold Italian for take-away.
Julien	250 Franklin St	617-451-1900	$$$	10 pm	Elegant French in the Langham Hotel.
King Fung Garden	74 Kneeland St	617-357-5262	$*	11 pm	Serving the best peking raviolis, scallion pancakes, and noodle dishes.
Les Zygomates	129 South St	617-542-5108	$$$	11 pm	French bistro. Comprehensive wine list, pleasant bar.
Mei Sum Inc	40 Beach St	617-357-4050	$	7 pm	Another tasty option for Bahn Mi and baked goods in the heart of Chinatown.
Meritage	70 Rowes Wharf	617-439-3995	$$$$$	11 pm	Serious about pairing food with wine.
Milk Street Café	50 Milk St	617-542-3663	$	3 pm	Dependable lunch option.
New Shanghai	21 Hudson St	617-338-6688	$$	11 pm	Critically acclaimed Shanghainese.
News	150 Kneeland St	617-426-6397	$$$	5 am	Leather District late-night spot.
Noodle Alcove	10 Tyler St	617-542-5857	$$	11 pm	Fresh, fresh noodles, knife-cut, and hand-pulled.
Ocean Wealth	8 Tyler St	617-423-1338	$$	3 am	Cantonese seafood specialists open late...very late...
Osushi	101 Arch St	617-330-1777	$$$	11 pm	Copley fave now open in the Financial District.
Peach Farm	4 Tyler St	617-482-1116	$$	3 am	Family-style Cantonese. Cool seafood tanks.
Pho Hoa	17 Beach St	617-423-3934	$	11 pm	Phat pho.
Pizza Oggi	131 Broad St	617-345-0022	$$	9 pm	Creative Pizzas and outdoor tables.
Pressed Sandwiches	2 Oliver St	617-482-9700	$	3 pm	Potential ironic indie band name.
Radius	8 High St	617-426-1234	$$$$$	11 pm	A Financial District jewel. Expensive, worth it.

Sakurabana	57 Broad St	617-542-4311	$$$	9 pm	Good bet for low-key sushi.
Shabu-Zen	16 Tyler St	617-292-8828	$$	12 am	Pay to cook your own food in a delicious broth? Yeah, it is worth it!
South Street Diner	178 Kneeland St	617-350-0028	$	24-hrs	Night shift dining excellence with a liquor license.
Sultan's Kitchen	116 State St	617-570-9009	$	4 pm	Terrific Turkish. A great lunch choice.
Taiwan Café	34 Oxford St	617-426-8181	$$*	1 am	For opponents of the PRC's "one China" policy.
Umbria	295 Franklin St	617-338-1000	$$$	12 am	Good food, but doubles as a dance club. Be ready to pay a cover charge.
Xinh Xinh	7 Beach St	617-422-0501	$$	10 pm	Exceptional Vietnamese. Not much ambiance.

Map 5 • Back Bay (West) / Fenway (East)

Bangkok City	167 Massachusetts Ave	617-266-8884	$$$	10 pm	Solid Thai served in a large, blue room.
Bhindi Bazaar	95 Massachusetts Ave	617-450-0660	$$		Go for the dinner, not the mediocre buffet.
Bukowski's	50 Dalton St	617-437-9999	$$*	1:30 am	Watering hole also has great chili, p.b.j. sandwiches, late hours.
Café Jaffa	48 Gloucester St	617-536-0230	$	11 pm	Affordable, delicious Middle Eastern.
Capital Grille	359 Newbury St	617-262-8900	$$$$$	11 pm	Arise, Sir Loin!
Casa Romero	30 Gloucester St	617-536-4341	$$$	11 pm	Mexican. Decent food, good atmosphere.
Chilli Duck	829 Boylston St	617-236-5208	$$	11 pm	Thai eatery with modern decor, slightly-elevated prices, and expectedly-tangy sauces.
Clio	370A Commonwealth Ave	617-536-7200	$$$$	11 pm	Sublime spot in the Eliot Hotel.
India Samraat Restaurant	51 Massachusetts Ave	617-247-0718	$$	10:15 pm	Good Indian food. Pretty good value. Great delivery!
Island Hopper	91 Massachusetts Ave	617-266-1618	$$	12 am	How can you not want to eat at a place with a name like this?
Kashmir	279 Newbury St	617-536-1695	$$	11 pm	Excellent murg saagwala.
L'Espalier	30 Gloucester St	617-262-3023	$$$$$	9:30 pm	One of Boston's best. If you want the experience and have the cash , spend it there.
Other Side Cosmic Café	407 Newbury St	617-536-9477	$	12 pm	Good for a bite and beer on their outdoor patio. Cheap PBR!
Pour House	907 Boylston St	617-236-1767	$	10 pm	Wonderful, cheap bar food. Opens at 8 am.
Sonsie	327 Newbury St	617-351-2500	$$$	1 am	People-watching mainstay. Nice French-doors street exposure.
Spike's Junkyard Dogs	1076 Boylston St	617-266-0909	$*	2 am	Perfect summer eats.
Tapeo	266 Newbury St	617-267-4799	$$$	11 pm	Tasty tapas. Sip sangria outside on warm days.
Top of the Hub	800 Boylston St	617-536-1775	$$$$	11 pm	Almost worth the price for the amazing view atop the Pru.
Trident Booksellers & Café	338 Newbury St	617-267-8688	$	11 pm	All-day breakfast in a cool bookstore.

Map 6 • Back Bay (East) / South End (Upper)

33	33 Stanhope St	617-572-3311	$$$$	11 pm	Enticing menu, snazzy digs. Patio too.
Abe & Louie's	793 Boylston St	617-536-6300	$$$$	12 am	Popular local steakhouse.
b.good	131 Dartmouth St	617-424-5252	$	10 pm	Healthy, quick lunches.
Bouchee	159 Newbury St	617-450-4343	$$$$	11 pm	Two-story French bistro, killer crème brulee.
Brasserie Jo	120 Huntington Ave	617-425-3240	$$$	11 pm	French brasserie near Symphony Hall. Usually very busy.
Charlie's Sandwich Shoppe	429 Columbus Ave	617-536-7669	$*	2:30 pm	A local institution with an old Boston feel. A good lunch choice.
Claremont Café	535 Columbus Ave	617-247-9001	$$$	12 am	(Too) popular for weekend brunch. Good scones, though. Delicious dinners!
Davio's	75 Arlington St	617-661-4810	$$$$	11 pm	Good food, but it's about the river view.
Domani	51 Huntington Ave	617-424-8500	$$$	11 pm	Eat like there's no, er, "tomorrow".
Grill 23 & Bar	161 Berkeley St	617-542-2255	$$$$$	11 pm	Classic steakhouse. Ideal for business dinners.
House of Siam	542 Columbus Ave	617-267-1755	$$	11 pm	If you are off to the symphony, this is a good bet.
L'Aroma Café	85 Newbury St	617-412-4001	$	10 pm	We're so glad that there is an alternative to Starbucks!
Laurel	142 Berkeley St	617-424-6664	$$$	10 pm	Five-star meals at two-star prices.
Legal Sea Foods	800 Boylston St	617-266-6800	$$$	11 pm	At the Pru, sporting a new look.
Mistral	223 Columbus Ave	617-867-9300	$$$$	11 pm	Superb. Great bar, too. Look sharp.
The Oak Room	138 Saint James Ave	617-267-5300	$$$	11 pm	Go for the old school Boston vibe, not the overpriced menu and mediocre martinis.
Osushi	10 Huntington Ave	617-266-2788	$$	11 pm	Good sushi in the Westin? You better believe it!
Parish Café	361 Boylston St	617-247-7777	$$	1 am	Inventive sandwiches. Full bar too.
Petsi Pies	285 Beacon St	617-661-7437	$	6 pm	Name a dinner or dessert pie…any pie…and they probably make it.
Shino Express Sushi	144 Newbury St	617-262-4530	$$††	9:45 pm	Cheap sushi (for Newbury Street). Great lunch specials.

Key: $: Under $10 / $$: $10–$20 / $$$: $20–$30 / $$$$: $30–$40 / $$$$$: $40+
* : Does not accept credit cards / † : Accepts only American Express / †† : Accepts only Visa and Mastercard
Time listed refers to kitchen closing time on weekend nights

Map 7 • South End (Lower)

Addis Red Sea	544 Tremont St	617-426-8727	$$	11 pm	Ethiopian. Get jiggy with some injera.
Appleton Bakery & Café	123 Appleton St	617-859-8222	$	5 pm	Melt-in-your-mouth muffins meet sandwiches with a twist.
Aquitaine	569 Tremont St	617-424-8577	$$$$	11 pm	A solid French bistro.
B&G Oysters	550 Tremont St	617-423-0550	$$$$	11 pm	Stylish oyster shop. Good wine list. Best lobster rolls in town!
Delux Café	100 Chandler St	617-338-5258	$$*	10 pm	Small, hip spot with good eats, music.
Dish	253 Shawmut Ave	617-426-7866	$$$	11 pm	Popular bistro. Outdoor seating.
El Triunfo	147 E Berkeley St	617-542-8499	$*	11 pm	Cheap tacos. Good tongue!
flour bakery + café	1595 Washington St	617-267-4300	$	9 pm	Beyond exceptional bakery. Also serves dinners for take-away.
Franklin Café	278 Shawmut Ave	617-350-0010	$$$	12 am	Delicious late-night option.
Garden of Eden	571 Tremont St	617-247-8377	$$	11 pm	Popular bruncheonette. Excellent veggie sandwiches.
Gaslight 560	560 Harrison Ave	617-422-0224	$$	12 am	Good French food. Stainless steel bar is a nice touch.
Hamersley's Bistro	553 Tremont St	617-423-2700	$$$$	11 pm	Outstanding. Deserves its reputation.
Joe V's	315 Shawmut Ave	617-426-0862	$$$	10 pm	Relatively unknown, people like their pizza, pleasant room.
Masa	439 Tremont St	617-338-8884	$$$$	11 pm	Tiniest $1 tapas specials that we've ever seen.
Metropolis Café	584 Tremont St	617-247-2931	$$$	11 pm	Try the cranberry pancakes for brunch.
Mike's City Diner	1714 Washington St	617-267-9393	$*	3 pm	A trusty not-too-greasy spoon.
Morse Fish	1401 Washington St	617-262-9375	$$	9 pm	The neighborhood's only fish shack.
Oishii	1166 Washington St	617-482-8868	$$$$$	12 am	The only place with better sushi is their other location.
Orinoco	477 Shawmut Ave	617-369-7075	$$$	11 pm	The South End puts a twist on Venezuelan food and it's delicious!
Pho Republique	1415 Washington St	617-262-0005	$$$††	12 am	Vietnamese gets the South End treatment.
Picco	513 Tremont St	617-927-0066	$$	11 pm	The gated community of ice cream. Serves pizza, too.
Red Fez	1222 Washington St	617-338-6060	$$$	12 am	Open late. Red fez not required for entry.
Sage	1395 Washington St	617-248-8814	$$$$	10 pm	Tasty Italian/American. Might cause claustrophobics.
Sibling Rivalry	523 Tremont St	617-338-5338	$$$$	11 pm	Fighting brothers serve up great food, outdoor dining when warm.
Stella	1525 Washington St	617-247-7747	$$$	11 pm	Too Stylish, whitish soul. Mostly Italian menu.
Tremont 647	647 Tremont St	617-266-4600	$$$$	10 pm	One of the South End's best.
Union Bar and Grille	1357 Washington St	617-423-0555	$$$$	12 am	Expensive and tasty!

Map 8 • Charlestown

Figs	67 Main St	617-242-2229	$$$	10 pm	Charlestown branch of upscale pizza chain.
Ironside Grill	25 Park St	617-242-1384	$$	11 pm	Formerly managed by Raymond Burr.
Jenny's Trattoria	320 Medford St	617-242-9474	$*	9 pm	Subs, too. Nice view of the, erm, Autoport.
Navy Yard Bistro & Wine Bar	One 1st Ave	617-242-0036	$$	11 pm	Mid-priced bistro fare near the ships.
Ninety Nine	29 Austin St	617-242-8999	$$	12 am	Take your step-kids.
Olives	10 City Sq	617-242-1999	$$$$	10 pm	Mediterranean mecca.
Paolo's Trattoria	251 Main St	617-242-7229	$$$	10 pm	Italian, including wood-oven-cooked pizzas.
Sorelle	1 Monument Ave	617-242-2125	$*	3 pm	Tasty sandwiches, baked goods, alcohol, too.
Sorelle	100 City Sq	617-242-5980	$	9 pm	Tasty sandwiches, baked goods, alcohol, too.
Tangierino	83 Main St	617-242-6009	$$$	11 pm	Rockin' Moroccan.
Warren Tavern	2 Pleasant St	617-241-8142	$$	10 pm	One of Paul Revere's favorite watering holes.

Map 9 • East Boston

Angela's Café	131 Lexington St	617-567-4972	$$	9 pm	By far the best Mexican food in town prepared by someone else's Grandma...
Café Belo	254 Bennington St	617-561-0833	$	10 pm	One of the many tasty Café Belo's serving up Brazilian food around Boston.
Café Italia	150 Meridian St	617-561-6480	$$	11 pm	For enjoying jazz with coffee and dessert.
Café Meridian	271 Meridian St	617-561-6622	$$	11 pm	Relaxing Colombian restaurant
El Buen Gusto	295 Bennington St	617-561-6333	$$	11 pm	Upscale Salvadoran taqueria.
El Chalan	405 Chelsea St	617-567-9452	$	11 pm	Finest pollo in Eastie.
Jeveli's	387 Chelsea St	617-567-9539	$$	10 pm	Italian. Has a bar.
La Frontera	290 Bennington St	617-569-8600	$*	11 pm	Mexican/Salvadoran hole in the wall.
La Terraza	19 Bennington St	617-561-5200	$*	11 pm	Straight-forward Colombian cooking. Try the flan.
Rincon Limeno	409 Chelsea St	617-569-4942	$	11 pm	Specializing in Peruvian rotisserie chicken.
Santarpio's Pizza	111 Chelsea St	617-567-9871	$*	12 am	Thin and crispy. Get a side of lamb and homemade sausage from the grill.

TacoMex	65 Maverick Sq	617-569-2838	$	11 pm	Tongue taco, a sign of real Mexican.
Taqueria Cancun	192 Sumner St	617-567-4449	$	11 pm	Don't count on tequila slammers.

Map 10 · South Boston (West) / Fort Point

6 House	28 W Broadway	617-268-6697	$$	11 pm	Open air, long bar.
Amrheins	80 W Broadway	617-268-6189	$$	11 pm	Has been here since Southie was mostly German.
Anthony's Pier 4	140 Northern Ave	617-482-6262	$$$$	3 pm	A Boston institution that has passed its glory days.
Barking Crab	88 Sleeper St	617-426-2722	$$	11 pm	Make a mess while viewing the harbor skyline.
The Daily Catch	2 Northern Ave	617-772-4400	$$$*	11 pm	Italian seafood specialists' Moakley Court-house spot.
Fresh Tortillas	475 W Broadway	617-269-0061	$	11 pm	Mexican take-out.
Lucky's	355 Congress St	617-357-5825	$$	12 am	Well-liked retro cocktail lounge. Music most nights.
Mul's Diner	80 W Broadway	617-268-5748	$		Three words. Grilled Blueberry Muffins.
R&L Delicatessen	313 Old Colony Ave	617-269-3354	$	10 pm	For large sandwiches.
Salsa's Mexican Grill	118 Dorchester St	617-269-7878	$$	10 pm	Legit Mexican.
Stadium	232 Old Colony Ave	617-269-5100	$$	1 am	Not into sports? Don't eat here.
Teriyaki House	32 W Broadway	617-269-2000	$	1 am	Japanese, some other Asian. Good value.

Map 11 · South Boston (East)

Aura	1 Seaport Ln	617-385-4300	$$$$	10 pm	Seafood for doing deals over.
Boston Beer Garden	732 E Broadway	617-269-0990	$$	11 pm	If you are looking for a place right by the game, this is it.
Café Porto Bello	672 E Broadway	617-269-7680	$$*	11 pm	Straight-forward, honest Italian.
Kelly's Landing	81 L St	617-268-8900	$$$	10 pm	The "original" is back, specializing in seafood.
L Street Diner	108 L St	617-268-1155	$	10 pm	Southie standby.
LTK (Legal Test Kitchen)	225 Northern Ave	617-330-7430	$$$	12 am	Hip cousin to Legal chain has attentive service, i-Pod docks.
No Name Restaurant	15 Fish Pier Rd	617-338-7539	$$	10 pm	Attracts tourists and waterfront workers alike.
Playwright	658 E Broadway	617-269-2537	$$	11 pm	For socializing and television watching.
Summer Street Grille	653 Summer St	617-269-2200	$$	11 pm	Undemanding American at the BAC.
Terrie's Place	676 E Broadway	617-268-3119	$*	1 pm	Home of the meatloaf omelet.

Map 12 · Newmarket / Andrew Square

224 Boston Street	224 Boston St	617-265-1217	$$$	11 pm	Big portions, good prices! Oh crap!
Alex's Pizza	580 Dorchester Ave	617-464-3663	$	12 am	Steak subs and pizza, late nights near the T.
Avenue Grille	856 Dorchester Ave	617-288-8000	$$	9 pm	Always something tasty here. A good choice.
Baltic Deli & Café	632 Dorchester Ave	617-268-2435	$	8 pm	Foods from the old country.
Café Polonia	611 Dorchester Ave	617-269-0110	$$	10 pm	Polish. Small, inviting, authentic. Have a Zywiec.
Restaurante Laura	688 Columbia Rd	617-825-9004	$$	10 pm	Scary outside, lovely Cabo Verde inside. Live music.
Singh's Roti Shop	692 Columbia Rd	617-282-7977	$	10 pm	Huge roti. Also try the channa doubles.
Taqueria Casa Real	860A Dorchester Ave	617-282-3135	$	8 pm	Mexican; good hot sauce options.
Venetian Garden	1269 Massachusetts Ave	617-288-9262	$$	1 am	A '60s time warp for Rat Pack Mexican food.
Victoria	1024 Massachusetts Ave	617-442-5965	$$	12 am	Diner. Good choice before hitting the highway.
World Seafood Restaurant	400 Dorchester Ave	617-269-1456	$$	8 pm	Fishmonger with fish, chips, and decent crab cakes.

Map 13 · Roxbury

Bob's Southern Bistro	604 Columbus Ave	617-536-6204	$$	12 am	For those needing a soul food fix.
Breezeway Bar and Grill	153 Blue Hill Ave	617-541-5400	$$	2 am	Decent American. Tasty wings. Occasional live music.
Merengue	156 Blue Hill Ave	617-445-5403	$$	10 pm	Dominican. Tropical vibe. Gets props from the Sox.
Pepper Pot	208 Dudley St	617-445-4409	$$	12 am	Jerk and ginger beer for dem belly a yawn.
Stash's Grille	150 Dudley St	617-989-0200	$	12 am	With a name like that, you expect more than pizza and subs.

Map 14 · Jamaica Plain

Alchemist Lounge	435 S Huntington Ave	617-477-5741	$$	10:30 pm	Go for the ambiance and the music. A little more effort would make the food better.
Alex's Chimis	358 Centre St	617-522-5201	$*	9 pm	How can you complain about a giant plate full of chicken and chicharrones?
Bukhara	701 Centre St	617-522-2195	$$	11 pm	Well-liked Indian bistro. Level of tastiness is like a mystery wheel.

Key: $: Under $10 / $$: $10–$20 / $$$: $20–$30 / $$$$: $30–$40 / $$$$$: $40+
* : Does not accept credit cards / † : Accepts only American Express / †† : Accepts only Visa and Mastercard
Time listed refers to kitchen closing time on weekend nights

Map 14 · Jamaica Plain—*continued*

Café D	711 Centre St	617-522-9500	$$$	11 pm	Dressed-up comfort food. Cool newspapered walls.
Centre Street Café	699 Centre St	617-524-9217	$$	10 pm	Groovy, particularly for brunch.
Cha Fahn	763 Centre St	617-983-3575	$$	10 pm	An unexpected spot for delicious tea sandwiches and sake martinis.
Dogwood Café	3712 Washington St	617-522-7997	$$	12 am	Enjoy your wood-fired pizzas while listening to an actual human playing an actual piano.
Doyle's Café	3484 Washington St	617-524-2345	$$*	12 am	The history and great atmosphere make up for the mediocre food.
El Oriental de Cuba	416 Centre St	617-524-6464	$$	10 pm	Always packed. So, be ready to wait for your cubano.
Fredy's Pastelito	3381 Washington St	617-524-4079	$	8 pm	A newcomer to Washington Street in JP does not disappoint. Delicious and inexpensive!
The Galway House	720 Centre St	617-524-9677	$	10 pm	Resisting the onion rings is futile.
Great Wall	779 Centre St	617-522-0277	$	11 pm	Cheap and tasty take-out featuring the Irish-influenced curry fries?
James's Gate	5 McBride St	617-983-2000			Enjoy the fireplace while getting busy on your Sheppard's & your Guinness.
JP Seafood Café	730 Centre St	617-983-5177	$$	10 pm	Some like it. Some don't. I don't.
La Pupusa Guanaca	378 Centre St	617-524-4900	$	9 pm	Little-known Salvadoran kitchen serving up some mighty fine food for cheap.
Miami Restaurant	381 Centre St	617-522-4644	$	11 pm	Go for the cubano ... don't leave without a beef patty.
Sorella's	388 Centre St	617-524-2016	$*	2 pm	Worth waiting for famous, diner-style breakfasts.
Tacos El Charro	349 Centre St	617-983-9275	$$	11 pm	Actual Mexican food enjoyed well getting down with some mariachi!
Ten Tables	597 Centre St	617-524-8810	$$$	10 pm	Short, precise, inspired menu. Delicious.
Vee Vee	763 Centre St	617-522-0145	$$	10 pm	One of JP's newest restaurants that not only cares about your eating experience but also where the food comes from. Menu changes with the seasons.
Wonder Spice Café	697 Centre St	617-522-0200	$$	10 pm	Tasty Cambodian/Thai. Well named. Get their Crispy Fish!
Yely's Coffee Shop	284 Centre St	617-524-2204	$*	10 pm	Coffee? The counter is stacked full of pork, chicken, sausages, and plantains.
Zon's	2 Perkins St	617-524-9667	$$		Home-cooking done right for hipsters and their families.

Map 15 · Fenway (West) / Mission Hill

Bravo	465 Commonwealth Ave	617-369-3474	$$$$	8:30 pm	At the MFA. Stick with the art.
Brigham Circle Diner	737 Huntington Ave	617-277-2730	$*	2 pm	Dirty & tasty. Good hash browns.
Brown Sugar Café	129 Jersey St	617-266-2928	$$	11 pm	Sometimes it is good, but too often it is mediocre.
Chacho's	1502 Tremont St	617-445-6738	$	9 pm	Pizza and subs.
El Pelon Taqueria	92 Peterborough St	617-262-9090	$	11 pm	Mmm...did someone say fish tacos!?
Huntington Pizza & Café	764 Huntington Ave	617-566-1177	$	11 pm	Pretty clear, huh?
Longwood Grille & Bar	342 Longwood Ave	617-232-9770	$$$	10 pm	Hotel restaurant serving the medical community; designed like a chain restaurant.
Mississippi's	103 Terrace St	617-541-4411	$	5 pm	Good for a hot lunch.
Penguin Café	735 Huntington Ave	617-277-9200	$	1 am	Recommended, and not just for the name.
Rod Dee II	94 Peterborough St	617-859-0969	$*	11 pm	So tasty that we wish that it was more than just a small take-out joint.
Solstice Café	1625 Tremont St	617-566-5958	$$	10 pm	Tasty, sort of hip, and friendly.
Sorento's	86 Peterborough St	617-424-7070	$$	12 am	Darn good pasta and pizza.
Squealing Pig	134 Smith St	617-566-6651	$$	1 am	Toasties served by indifferent staff.

Map 16 · Kenmore Square / Brookline (East)

Ankara Café	472 Commonwealth Ave	617-437-0404	$	12 am	Turkish place popular with student snackers.
Audubon Circle	838 Beacon St	617-421-1910	$$	11 pm	Chill out with tasty bar food.
Boston Beer Works	61 Brookline Ave	617-536-2337	$$	12 am	Cavernous suds across from Fenway Park.
Café Belo	636 Beacon St	617-236-8666	$	10 pm	Another Café Belo featuring great Brazilian food.
Cornwall's	654 Beacon St	617-262-3749	$$	12 am	Eat only to soak up pints.
Eastern Standard	528 Commonwealth Ave	617-532-9100	$$$	12 am	At the Commonwealth with lip-smackingly good drinks.
Elephant Walk	900 Beacon St	617-247-1500	$$$	11 pm	French-Cambodian local legend.
Ginza	1002 Beacon St	617-566-9688	$$$	1:30 am	Sushi/Japanese. Pompous, overpriced.
Great Bay	500 Commonwealth Ave	617-532-5300	$$$$	11 pm	Elegant seafood, exquisite desserts. Check out their ceviche menu.

India Quality	484 Commonwealth Ave	617-267-4499	$$	11 pm	Quality Indian. The name says it all.
New England Soup Factory	2 Brookline Pl	617-739-1899		9 pm	Creative, home-style soups. Recommended.
Noodle Street	627 Commonwealth Ave	617-536-3100	$	11 pm	Unexpected spices transcend everyday Asian fare.
O'Leary's Pub	1010 Beacon St	617-734-0049	$$	1 am	Try the Guinness stew.
Petit Robert Bistro	468 Commonwealth Ave	617-375-0699	$$	11 pm	Traditional bistro fare. Try the skate wing.
Taberno de Haro	999 Beacon St	617-277-8272	$$$	11 pm	Solid tapas spot with a great Sherry menu.
Uburger	636 Beacon St	617-536-0448	$††	11 pm	Burgers and frappes right by BU.

Map 17 • Coolidge Corner / Brookline Hills

Boca Grande	1294 Beacon St	617-739-3900	$	11 pm	Lots of good taqueria fare. Consider ordering carnitas.
Bottega Fiorentina	41 Harvard St	617-738-5333	$	8 pm	Tuscan sandwiches to die.
Brookline Family Restaurant	305 Washington St	617-277-4466	$$	11 pm	Top notch Turkish food.
Dok Bua	411 Harvard St	617-277-7087	$	11 pm	Tastiest Thai around! Their best dishes are not the noodle dishes.
Fireplace	1634 Beacon St	617-975-1900	$$$	11 pm	Warning: food also capable of inducing nap.
Fugakyu	1280 Beacon St	617-738-1268	$$$	1 am	Sushi, very popular. Be prepared to wait.
Gourmet India	1335 Beacon St	617-734-3971	$	10 pm	Fast food Italian.
Khao Sarn	250 Harvard St	617-566-7200	$	11 pm	Relax and enjoy excellent Thai.
La Morra	48 Boylston St	617-739-0007	$$$$	10:30 pm	Popular Northern Italian.
Martin's Coffee Shop	35 Harvard St	617-566-0005		3 pm	Brookline Village's own greasy spoon features breakfast, heavenly home fries.
Matt Murphy's Pub	14 Harvard St	617-232-0188	$$	11 pm	Stylish Irish pub with good food and occasional live music.
Michael's Deli	256 Harvard St	617-738-3354	$$	2:30 pm	Deli authenticity in Coolidge Corner.
Orinoco	22 Harvard St		$$$	11 pm	Make sure to make a reservation for their Saturday tasting table.
Pho Lemongrass	239 Harvard St	617-731-8600	$$	12 am	Pho, Brookline-style.
Rani Indian Bistro	1353 Harvard St	617-734-0400	$$	11 pm	Serving all your Indian favorites alongside some Hyderabadi specialties.
Rod Dee	1430 Beacon St	617-738-4977	$*	11 pm	So tasty that we wish it was more than just a small take-out shop.
Shawarma King	1383 Harvard St	617-731-6035	$*	11 pm	Excellent Middle-Eastern—informative service, fresh-fruit beverages, traditional desserts.
Village Fish	22 Harvard St	617-566-3474	$$	11 pm	Neighborhood standby.
Washington Square Tavern	714 Washington St	617-232-8989	$$$	11 pm	Good American food, but not as cheap as the name might suggest.

Map 18 • Brighton

Bamboo	1616 Commonwealth Ave	617-734-8192	$$	11 pm	Very good Thai at Washington Street.
Bangkok Bistro	1952 Beacon St	617-739-7270	$$	11 pm	Thai for the BC crowd.
Bluestone Bistro	1799 Commonwealth Ave	617 254-0309	$$	12 am	Pizza and pasta, small and hopping.
Café Mirror	362 Washington St	617-779-9662	$	5 pm	Sandwiches and small bites.
Cityside Bar & Grill	1960 Beacon St	617-566-1002	$$	11 pm	More for watching television than dining.
Devlin's	332 Washington St	617-779-8822	$$$	11 pm	A little better than other places around here.
Green Briar	304 Washington St	617-789-4100	$$	11 pm	Generic pub food. Stick with beer.
IHOP	1850 Soldiers Field Rd	617-787-0533	$	24-hrs	Pancakes anytime.
Jasmine Bistro	412 Market St	617-789-4676	$$$	10 pm	Hungarian-French-Lebanese. Somehow this works.
Roggie's	356 Chestnut Hill Ave	617-566-1880	$$	3 am	Hang out with BC kids, drink beer, and eat greasy food.
Soho	386 Market St	617-562-6000	$$$	12 am	Sleek, large dining spot-cum-nightclub.
Tasca	1612 Commonwealth Ave	617-730-8002	$$	12 am	Good (but not great) tapas for all budgets!

Map 19 • Allston (South) / Brookline (North)

Aneka Rasa	122 Harvard Ave	617-562-8989	$	11 pm	Top notch Malaysian food that is easy on the wallet.
Angora Café	1024 Commonwealth Ave	617-232-1757	$	12 am	Great wraps and not-to-miss fro-yo with exhaustive and surprising toppings.
Anna's Taqueria	446 Harvard St	617-227-7111	$*	11 pm	It doesn't mean much, but they roll up one of the best burritos in town.
Bagel Rising	1243 Commonwealth Ave	617-789-4000	$*	6 pm	Funky bagel joint.
Big City	138 Brighton Ave	617-782-2020	$$	1 am	For the beer and pool, not food and service.
Bottega Fiorentina	313B Harvard St	617-232-2661	$	8 pm	Tuscan sandwiches to die.
Breakfast Club Diner	270 Western Ave	617-783-1212	$$*	2 pm	The shiniest diner found outside New Jersey.
Buk Kyung II	151 Brighton Ave	617-254-2775	$	11 pm	Top-notch Korean food. Good luck finding a parking space on weekends.
Café Brazil	421 Cambridge St	617-789-5980	$$	11 pm	Authentic, home-style Brazilian.
Camino Real	48 Harvard Ave	617-254-5088	$$	10 pm	Good-value Colombian.
Charlie's Pizza & Café	177 Allston St	617-277-3737	$	11 pm	Best hummos around. Delicious kabobs too.
Coolidge Corner Clubhouse	307 Harvard St	617-566-4948	$$	1:15 am	Home of the Big Papi Burger.

Arts & Entertainment · **Restaurants**

Key: $: Under $10 / $$: $10–$20 / $$$: $20–$30 / $$$$: $30–$40 / $$$$$: $40+
* : Does not accept credit cards / † : Accepts only American Express / †† : Accepts only Visa and Mastercard
Time listed refers to kitchen closing time on weekend nights

Map 19 · Allston (South) / Brookline (North)—continued

El Cafétal	479 Cambridge St	617-789-4009	$$	10 pm	Co-yum-bian.
Gitlo's	164 Brighton Ave	617-782-2253	$	10:30 pm	Dim Sum for Dinner? It doesn't get any better than this!
Grasshopper	1 N Beacon St	617-254-8883	$$	11 pm	Hip Asian vegan.
Grecian Yearning	174 Harvard Ave	617-254-8587	$	3:30 pm	Classic diner with a good variety of sausages.
Indian Dhaba Roadside Diner	180 Brighton Ave	617-787-5155	$	11 pm	Curried goodness. Not actually a diner.
La Mamma Pizza	190 Brighton Ave	617-783-1661	$	1 am	Stick with the empanadas and Chilean specialties.
Mr Sushi Japanese Restaurant	329 Harvard St	617-731-1122	$$	11 pm	Good basic sushi with no frills.
Nori Sushi	398 Harvard St	617-277-3100	$$	11 pm	Among multitude of Brookline sushi options, this one's intimate and spot-on.
Paradise Rock Club & Lounge	967 Commonwealth Ave	617-562-8814	$$*	1 am	Major rock acts. Tasty food and smaller bands in Lounge.
Paris Creperie	278 Harvard St	617-232-1770	$$	11 pm	A variety of sweet and savory crepes.
Pho Viets	1095 Commonwealth Ave	617-562-8828	$	10 pm	Best Vietnamese subs (Bahn Mi) in town for just a few bucks.
Quan's Kitchen	1026 Commonwealth Ave	617-232-76175	$	2 am	Fast, cheap Chinese—open late, good lemon chicken, flat-screen TV.
Rangoli	129 Brighton Ave	617-562-0200	$$	11 pm	Emphasizes South Indian. Delicious!
Redneck's Roast Beef	140 Brighton Ave	617-782-9444	$††	3 am	Open til 3 am; great drunk food. Not sure how it tastes when sober.
Reef Café	170 Brighton Ave	617-202-6366	$	12 am	One of the best Lebanese joints in Boston.
Saigon	431 Cambridge St	617-254-3373	$$*	12 am	Pleasant Vietnamese, good value. Try the catfish.
Saray	1098 Commonwealth Ave	617-383-6651	$$	11 pm	Just the thought of their kabobs and eggplant dishes is making me drool.
Spike's Junkyard Dogs	108 Brighton Ave	617-254-7700	$*	1 am	Quick sausage fix.
Steve's Kitchen	120 Harvard Ave	617-254-9457	$*	6 pm	The best diner in Allston even though Lisa no longer works there.
Sumi	182 Brighton Ave	617-254-7010	$$††	11 pm	Tasty meats and fish on a stick for dirt cheap.
Sunset Grill & Tap	130 Brighton Ave	617-254-1331	$$	1 am	Huge Mexican platters and tons of great beer.
Super 88 Food Court	1095 Commonwealth Ave	617-787-2288	$*	8 pm	Boston's largest Asian food court.
Upper Crust	286 Harvard St	617-739-8518	$	11 pm	Fancy schmancy pizza with wifi.
Victoria Seafood	1029 Commonwealth Ave	617-783-5111	$††	12 am	Good food and dirt cheap prices! Great Chinese dinner options.
YoMa	5 N Beacon St	617-783-1372	$*	10 pm	Fantastic Burmese food finally arrives to Boston!
Zaftigs Delicatessen	335 Harvard St	617-975-0075	$$	10 pm	Comfort food for breeders who brunch.

Map 20 · Harvard Square / Allston (North)

Algiers	40 Brattle St	617-492-1557	$	11 pm	An excellent, and oddly tourist-free, lunch and coffee spot.
b. good	24 Dunster St	617-354-6500	$$	12 am	Healthier fast food.
Border Café	32 Church St	617-864-6100	$$	12 am	Feeding students sub-par Tex-Mex for years.
Café Pamplona	12 Bow St	617-492-0352	$*	12 am	Mellow Cuban hangout with outdoor patio.
Caffe Paradiso	1 Eliot Sq	617-868-3240	$	11 pm	For students getting their just desserts.
Cambridge, 1	27 Church St	617-576-1111	$$	12 am	Tasty innovative pizzas and salads. Relaxed, stripped-down space.
Casablanca	40 Brattle St	617-876-0999	$$$	11 pm	Still popular with the Harvard crowd.
Charlie's Kitchen	10 Eliot St	617-492-9646	$$	1 am	Old School at the old school. Best jukebox around!
Craigie Street Bistro	5 Craigie Cir	617-497-5511	$$$$$	10:30 pm	Acclaimed, award-winning, very French, very expensive, very good splurge.
Crazy Doughs	36 JFK St	617-492-4848	$	10 pm	Pizza in The Garage.
Daedalus	45 Mt Auburn St	617-349-0071	$$$	10:30 pm	Food with a nice patio.
Darwin's Ltd	148 Mt Auburn St	617-354-5233	$*	9 am	Hidden Harvard Square refuge.
Flat Patties	81 Mt Auburn St	617-871-6871	$	11 pm	Try their shredded pork sandwich and an order of fries.
Grafton Street	1230 Massachusetts Ave	617-497-0400	$$$	12 am	High-volume, high-end Irish restaurant offering an eclectic menu.
Grendel's Den	89 Winthrop St	617-491-1050	$	1 am	For the laid-back academic. Reasonable prices. Excellent after work specials.
Harvest	44 Brattle St	617-868-2255	$$$$	11 pm	Excellent. Nice garden terrace.
Hi-Rise Bread Company	56 Brattle St	617-492-3003	$*	5 pm	Tasty, but bring some extra cash.
John Harvard's Brew House	33 Dunster St	617-868-3585	$$	12 am	Large and loud, good for crowds.
Mr & Mrs Bartley's Burger Cottage	1246 Massachusetts Ave	617-354-6559	$*	9 pm	Classic burger joint across from the Yard. .
My Thai Vegetarian Café	404 Harvard St	617-739-8830	$$	11 pm	If you are looking for beef, chicken, or pork, you have come to the wrong place.

OM	92 Winthrop St	617-576-2800	$$$$$	10 pm	Super expensive.
Pho Pasteur	35 Dunster St	617-864-4100	$$	9 pm	Reliable Vietnamese. You can't go wrong here.
The Red House	98 Winthrop St	617-576-0605	$$$	11 pm	Seasonal menus served in an old red house.
Rialto	1 Bennett St	617-661-5050	$$$$$	11 pm	Probably Cambridge's finest restaurant.
Sabra Grill	20 Eliot Sq	617-868-5777	$*	10 pm	Tasty, cheap Greek food.
Sandrine's	8 Holyoke St	617-497-5300	$$$$	10:30 pm	Have a flammekueche—hard to say, easy to eat.
Shilla	57 JFK St	617-547-7971	$$$	12 pm	Quiet, subterranean Japanese/Korean.
Tamarind Bay	75 Winthrop St	617-491-4552	$$	11 pm	One of the best Indian restaurants in town. Try the bhuna paneer.
UpStairs on the Square	91 Winthrop St	617-864-1933	$$$$	11 pm	Neoclassical food in an expressionist room.
Veggie Planet	47 Palmer St	617-661-1513	$$*	10 pm	At Club Passim. Mostly for pizzas, some vegan.
Z Square Restaurant & Bar	14 JFK St	617-576-0101	$$	12 am	American comfort food with heated outdoor patio.

Map 21 · West Cambridge

Armando's	163 Huron Ave	617-354-8275	$*	11 pm	Cheap and delicious pizza.
Cheddars	201 Alewife Brook Pkwy	617-661-3366	$	8 pm	Fresh-from-the-oven pizza and sandwiches, complete with a local cult following.
Full Moon	344 Huron Ave	617-354-6699	$$	9 pm	For a night out with the children.
Hi-Rise Bread Company	208 Concord Ave	617-876-8766	$*	5 pm	Tasty, but bring some extra cash.
Il Buongustaio	369 Huron Ave	617-491-3133	$*	11 pm	Very good pizzas, calzones, paninis.
Trattoria Pulcinella	147 Huron Ave	617-491-6336	$$	11 pm	For those not going to the North End.

Map 22 · North Cambridge / West Somerville

Anna's Taqueria	236 Elm St	617-666-3900	$*	11 pm	Fastest burritos in town.
Antonia's Italian Bistro	37 Davis Sq	617-623-6700	$$	11 pm	Solid choice for the carb-starved.
Café Barada	2269 Massachusetts Ave	617-354-2112	$	9 pm	Relaxed Middle Eastern.
Dave's Fresh Pasta	81 Holland St	617-623-0867	$††	7:30 pm	Homemade pasta and sauces.
Diesel Café	257 Elm St	617-629-8717	$	1 am	Coffee and sandwich shop with an attitude.
Diva Indian Bistro	246 Elm St	617-629-4963	$$	1 am	Flashy and tasty, but pricey.
Elephant Walk	2067 Massachusetts Ave	617-492-6900	$$$	11 pm	French-Cambodian local legend.
Gargoyles on the Square	219 Elm St	617-776-5300	$$$$	10 pm	Deservedly popular Davis Square haunt with amazing apps and top-notch drinks.
House of Tibet	235 Holland St	617-629-7567	$$	9 pm	Delicious. But where's the yak butter?
Jasper White's Summer Shack	149 Alewife Brook Pkwy	617-520-9500	$$$	11 pm	Seafood. More a hangar than a shack.
Jose's	131 Sherman St	617-354-0335	$$	12 am	It's all about the Margaritas.
Joshua Tree	256 Elm St	617-623-9910	$$	10 am	Achtung, baby.
Martsa on Elm	233A Elm St	617-666-0660	$$	11 pm	Your meal is best accompanied by a Tibetan tea.
Namaskar	236 Elm St	617-623-9911	$$$	11 pm	Above-average Indian with good variety.
Out of the Blue	215 Elm St	617-776-5020	$$$††	11 pm	Good value for seafood, Italian. Colorful room.
Qingdao Garden	2382 Massachusetts Ave	617-492-7540	$	11 pm	Casual, delicious. Sells dumplings-to-go in bulk.
Redbones	55 Chester St	617-628-2200	$$*	12 am	Don't dig on swine? Go for the beers.
Rosebud Diner	381 Summer St	617-666-6015	$$	12 am	Wise choice for a comfort food fix.
Rudy's Café	248 Holland St	617-623-9201	$$	12 pm	Serving up generous Tex-Mex portions with a loco selection of tequila.
Sabur	212 Holland St	617-776-7890	$$$	10:30 pm	Food from Greece, North Africa, and the Balkans in a casbah-like atmosphere.
Sangra	400 Highland Ave	617-625-0200	$$$	10 pm	Rustic, eastern region Italian cuisine, great menu, small portions.
Soleil Café	1153 Broadway	617-625-0082	$	4 pm	Breakfast, lunch. Closed Sundays.
Spike's Junkyard Dogs	217 Elm St	617-440-1010	$*	1 am	Awsome veggie dogs and real ones too!

Map 23 · Central Somerville / Porter Square

Anna's Taqueria	822 Somerville Ave	617-661-8500	$*	11 pm	Fastest burritos in town.
Blue Fin	1815 Massachusetts Ave	617-497-8022	$$	10 pm	Not the best sushi, but close to the cheapest.
Broken Yolk	136 College Ave	617-628-6621	$	3 pm	Mmm, pancakes.
Café Mami	1815 Massachusetts Ave	617-547-9130	$	9 pm	It's amazing what they can do with a little ground beef and an egg.
Café Rustica	356 Beacon St	617-491-8300	$*	4 pm	Friendly neighborhood café.
Caffé Rossini	278 Highland Ave	617-625-5240	$*	10 pm	Comfy Italian.
Christopher's	1920 Massachusetts Ave	617-876-9180	$$	12 am	Good for relaxing on a wet day.
Kelly's Diner	674 Broadway	617-623-8102	$*	3 pm	Old-school greasy spoon known for its "Kiss My Grits!" service.
Lil Vinny's	525 Medford St	617-628-8466	$$	11 pm	Spin-off of East Somerville's Vinny's at Night.
Lyndell's Bakery	720 Broadway	617-625-1793	$	6 pm	Old-fashioned bakery.
Passage to India	1900 Massachusetts Ave	617-497-6113	$$	11 pm	Good Indian, served late. Try the curries.
RF O'Sullivan's	282 Beacon St	617-492-7773	$††	1 am	Quite possibly the best burgers in Boston.

Arts & Entertainment • **Restaurants**

Key: $: Under $10 / $$: $10–$20 / $$$: $20–$30 / $$$$: $30–$40 / $$$$$: $40+
* : Does not accept credit cards / † : Accepts only American Express./ †† : Accepts only Visa and Mastercard
Time listed refers to kitchen closing time on weekend nights

Map 23 • Central Somerville / Porter Square—*continued*

Sound Bites	708 Broadway	617-623-8338	$*	3 pm	For filling breakfasts.
Sugar & Spice	1933 Massachusetts Ave	617-868-4200	$$$	1 am	Thai food when you're not in the mood for the Japanese.
Tacos Lupita	13 Elm St	617-666-0677	$*	11 pm	Cozy Mexican and El Salvadorian hybrid is 100% authentic.
Tu y Yo	858 Broadway	617-623-5411	$$	10 pm	Authentic Mexican—no burritos here.
Wang's Fast Food	509 Broadway	617-623-2982	$	1 am	Best Mandarin hole-in-the-wall on this side of the river. Try the dumplings.

Map 24 • Winter Hill / Union Square

Café Belo	120 Washington St	617-623-3696	$	10 pm	Brazilian cafeteria.
Fasika Ethiopian Restaurant	145 Broadway	617-628-9300	$$*	1 am	Best Ethiopian in town in the oddest setting.
Great Thai Chef	255 Washington St	617-625-9296	$$††	10 pm	It's Thai, it's great, there's a chef.
Leone's	292 Broadway	617-776-2511	$*	11 pm	Meatball subs that are To-Die-For.
Machu Picchu	25 Union Sq	617-623-7972	$	10 pm	Peruvian. Definitely worth trying.
Neighborhood Restaurant & Bakery	25 Bow St	617-623-9710	$*	4 pm	Big, good breakfasts + patio = summer morning bliss.
Sherman	257 Washington St	617-776-4944	$*	7 pm	Good lunch spot; comes recommended by Mr. Peabody.
Taqueria la Mexicana	247 Washington St	617 776 5232	$	10 pm	The real deal. Terrific flautas.

Map 25 • East Somerville / Sullivan Square

Beijing Taste	99A Cambridge St	617-241-5077	$	12 am	For emergencies only.
Mount Vernon	14 Broadway	617-666-3830	$$	11 pm	Sleepy spot with occasional lobster specials.
Vinny's at Night	76 Broadway	617-628-1921	$$	10 pm	Quality home-style Italian tucked behind a deli.

Map 26 • East Cambridge / Kendall Square / MIT

Aceituna	605 W Kendall St	617-252-0707	$$	8 pm	Mediterranean for lunch at the Genzyme building.
Bambara	25 Land Blvd	617-868-4444	$$$	11 pm	Hit-or-miss at Hotel Marlowe.
Black Sheep Café	350 Main St	617-577-1300	$$	10 pm	In the Kendall Hotel. Go for breakfast.
The Blue Room	One Kendall Sq	617-494-9034	$$$$	11 pm	Terrific food, popular. Somehow elegant and casual.
Court House Seafood	498 Cambridge St	617-491-1213	$$	8 pm	One step removed from bobbing for fish.
Desfina	202 Third St	617-868-9098	$$	1 am	Greek for geeks.
Helmand Restaurant	143 First St	617-492-4646	$$	11 pm	Delightful, authentic. Family ties with Afghanistan's president.
Legal Sea Foods	5 Cambridge Ctr	617-864-3400	$$$	10 pm	Another Legal Seafoods for your fishy pleasure.
Second Street Café	89 Second St	617-661-1311	$$*	3:30 pm	Plenty of fresh, inexpensive choices.

Map 27 • Central Square / Cambridgeport

Asgard	350 Massachusetts Ave	617-577-9100	$$	2 am	Enormous "Celtic" gastropub.
Asmara	739 Massachusetts Ave	617-864-7447	$$	11 pm	Once was the only Ethiopian restaurant in Cambridge.
Brookline Lunch	9 Brookline St	617-354-2983	$*	4 pm	Popular diner. For food, not service.
Café Baraka	80 1/2 Pearl St	617-868-3951	$$*	10 pm	A tiny restaurant serving up some good Morrocan cuisine.
Carberry's Bakery & Coffee House	74 Prospect St	617-576-3530	$	8 pm	Bakery items and good sandwiches.
Central Kitchen	567 Massachusetts Ave	617-491-5599	$$$	11 pm	Simple Mediterranean menu featuring incredibly flavorful dishes with great wines to match.
Cuchi Cuchi	795 Main St	617-864-2929	$$$	11 pm	You either love this place or hate it. Find out for yourself!
Dolphin Seafood	1105 Massachusetts Ave	617-661-2937	$$	10 pm	Unpretentious fish house.
Green Street Grill	280 Green St	617-876-1655	$$$	10 pm	Great Caribbean food with a slow burn. Mellow bar.
Hi-Fi Pizza & Subs	496 Massachusetts Ave	617-492-4600	$	3 am	Soak up the beer you drank at T.T.'s.
India Pavilion	17 Central Sq	617-547-7463	$$	11 pm	Reliable Indian that's been a part of Central Square forever. A decent value.
La Groceria	853 Main St	617-497-4214	$$$	10 pm	Still there. Still good.

Arts & Entertainment • **Restaurants**

Mary Chung	464 Massachusetts Ave	617-864-1991	$$*	11 pm	This Central Square institution is still going strong.
The Middle East	472 Massachusetts Ave	617-864-3278	$$	12 am	Cheap and tasty food before going to see a show.
Miracle of Science	321 Massachusetts Ave	617-868-2866	$$	1 am	Energetic neighborhood mainstay. Great burgers, quesadillas.
Moody's Falafel Palace	25 Central Sq	617-864-0827	$	3 am	Located in what was once a White Castle.
Picante Mexican Grill	735 Massachusetts Ave	617-576-6394	$	11 pm	Cali-Mex. Pretty good salsas.
Pu Pu Hot Pot	907 Main St	617-491-6616	$	11 pm	Chinese. Much better than it sounds.
Rendezvous	502 Massachusetts Ave	617-576-1900	$$$$	11 pm	Fancy restaurant pops up in what was once a Burger King. No dollar menu anymore.
Salts	798 Main St	617-876-8444	$$$$	10 pm	New ownership, higher prices. Tasty.
Zoe's	1105 Massachusetts Ave	617-495-0055	$	10 pm	Retro-ish diner food, breakfast of the day.
ZuZu!	474 Massachusetts Ave	617-492-9181	$$$	1 am	Funky, colorful. Make a meal of maza.

Map 28 • Inman Square

All-Star Sandwich Bar	1245 Cambridge St	617-868-3065	$*	10 pm	Old-fashioned favorites like Mom used to make.
Amelia's Trattoria	111 Harvard St	617-868-7600	$$$	10 pm	The best Italian in this area.
Atasca	50 Hampshire St	617-621-6991	$$$	11 pm	Nothing better than bacalhau with a Portuguese red.
B-Side Lounge	92 Hampshire St	617-354-0766	$$$	1 am	Hip spot that deserves its reputation.
Café Kiraz	119 Hampshire St	617-868-2233	$	11 pm	Subs and shwarma.
City Girl Café	204 Hampshire St	617-864-2809	$	9 pm	Comfy and cool. Try the lasagna.
Dali	415 Washington St	617-661-3254	$$$	11 pm	Fun taparia. Worth the wait. Usually worth the price.
East Coast Grill & Raw Bar	1271 Cambridge St	617-491-6568	$$$	11 pm	Awesome seafood, barbecue. Try the Hell Sausage.
Emma's Pizzeria	40 Hampshire St	617-864-8534	$$	10 pm	Design your own gourmet pie. Worth waiting.
EVOO	118 Beacon St	617-661-3866	$$$$	11 pm	Creative cuisine. One of Somerville's best.
Koreana	154 Prospect St	617-576-8661	$$	12 am	Cooking tasty Bulgogi right at your table.
Magnolia's	1193 Cambridge St	617-576-1971	$$$	10 pm	Southern. Try the fried chicken.
Midwest Grill	1124 Cambridge St	617-354-7536	$$$	12 am	Brazilian sword-play.
Montien	1287 Cambridge St	617-868-1240	$$$	11 pm	Thai in the Theater District with giant yummy sushi.
O Cantinho	1128 Cambridge St	617-354-3443	$$	11 pm	NFT approved Portuguese spot. Easy on the wallet.
Ole Mexican Grill	11 Springfield St	617-492-4495	$$	11 pm	Delicious guacamole made right at your table.
Oleana	134 Hampshire St	617-661-0505	$$$$	11 pm	Top-notch Mediterranean. Patio seating in warm weather.
Pho Lemon	228 Broadway	617-441-8813	$	10 pm	Vietnamese. Not fancy, but good value.
Punjabi Dhaba	225 Hampshire St	617-547-8272	$*	12 am	Some of the best Indian food for dirt cheap.
S&S Restaurant	1334 Cambridge St	617-354-0777	$*	12 am	Serving deli, comfort food for eighty years.
Toscanini and Sons	406 Washington St	617-666-2770	$*	7 pm	Scrumptious café food and, of course, great ice cream.

Map 29 • West Roxbury

Himalayan Bistro	1735 Centre St	617-325-3500	$$$	11 pm	Nepali for your inner sherpa.
MaSoNa Grill	4 Corey St	617-323-3331	$$$$	10:30 pm	Euro-Peruvian eclectic grill, West Roxbury's best
Real Deal	1882 Centre St	617-325-0754	$	9 pm	Imagine a typical sub shop with creative fixin's.
Samia Bakery	1894 Centre St	617-323-5181	$	8 pm	Absolutely delicious kabobs.
Vintage	1430 VFW Pkwy	617-469-2600	$$$$	11 pm	Pricey steakhouse for locals unwilling to drive downtown for a better deal.
West on Centre	1732 Centre St	617-323-4199	$$$	11 pm	Casual American; plenty of brick and mahogany.

Map 30 • Roslindale

Birch Street Bistro	14 Birch St	617-323-2184	$$	10 pm	Inviting place to kick back for dinner.
Delfino	754 South St	617-327-8359	$$$	10 pm	Tiny, popular spot serving good-quality Italian.
Diane's Bakery	9 Poplar St	617-323-1877	$*	1 pm	Croissant sandwiches, snack cakes.
Geoffrey's Café	4257 Washington St	617-325-1000	$$$	12 am	South End, Back Bay transplant, brunch rocks.
John's Bakery	31 Poplar St	617-323-9465	$	2 pm	Famous hideaway for pizza. Arbitrarily open.
Pleasant Café	4515 Washington St	617-323-2111	$$	11 pm	Pizza and other basics. Don't be scared of the sketchy exterior.
Primavera	289 Walk Hill St	617-522-1186	$$††	9 pm	Cheap Italian that occasionally hits the spot.
Sophia's Grotto	22 Birch St	617-323-4595	$$	10:30 pm	Cozy family trattoria. Enjoy the mussels in the courtyard.
Village Sushi & Grill	14 Corinth St	617-363-7874	$$	10 pm	Japanese and Korean.
Yucatan Tacos	1417 Centre St	617-323-7555	$	8 pm	Authentic Mexican food, apparently.

Key: $: Under $10 / $$: $10–$20 / $$$: $20–$30 / $$$$: $30–$40 / $$$$$: $40+
* : Does not accept credit cards / † : Accepts only American Express / †† : Accepts only Visa and Mastercard
Time listed refers to kitchen closing time on weekend nights.

Map 31 • Mattapan / Dorchester (West)

Ali's Roti	1188 Blue Hill Ave	617-298-9850	$	10 pm	You have not experienced life until you dive into a delicious roti.
Bon Appetit	1138 Blue Hill Ave	617-825-5544	$$	10:30 pm	Haitian food supposedly makes you a better lover.
Brothers	1638 Blue Hill Ave	617-298-5224	$	5 pm	Southern. Huge side portions.
Flames	461 Blue Hill Ave	617-989-0000	$$	11 pm	Unusually stylish for this neighborhood.
Flames	663 Morton St	617-296-4972	$$	11 pm	Jamaican. Serves ackee!
Lenny's Tropical Bakery	1195 Blue Hill Ave	617-296-2587	$*	9 pm	Double parking for the patties.
P&R Ice Cream	1284 Blue Hill Ave	617-296-0922	$	2 am	Nothing beats a beef patty followed by a scoop of Grape Nut ice cream.
Picasso Creole Cuisine	1296 Blue Hill Ave	617-296-1300	$	10 pm	Haitian home-style cooking.
Pit Stop Bar-B-Q	888A Morton St	617-436-0485	$	12 am	A rib shack, literally. Stick to the ribs.
R&S Jamaican Restaurant	770 Blue Hill Ave	617-287-8600	$	11 pm	More Goat Curry than you can eat in two sittings for $12.
Simco's on the Bridge	1509 Blue Hill Ave	617-296-3800	$*	1:30 am	Boston's best hotdogs since the 1930s.
Tastee Jamaican Restaurant	522 River St	617-296-1935	$*	11 pm	Pretend you're not in Boston with tasty jerk chicken and a ginger beer.
United House of Prayer	206 Seaver St	617-445-3246	$*	6 pm	Friendly soul food in basement of Boston's old stadt shul.

Map 32 • Dorchester (East)

Ashmont Grill	555 Talbot Ave	617-825-4300	$$$	11 pm	Bringing flair to Peabody Square.
Ba-Le Restaurant	1052 Dorchester Ave	617-265-7171	$*	10 pm	Wonderful crisp Vietnamese sandwiches.
Blarney Stone	1505 Dorchester Ave	617-436-8223	$$	11 pm	Hodgepodge of good pub-type food.
Blasi's Café and Fat Belly Deli	762 Adams St	617-825-4566	$	10 pm	Sit down or take out. Big, fat portions.
CF Donovan's	112 Savin Hill Ave	617-436-6690	$$	1 am	Friendly neighborhood restaurant/bar.
Charlie's Place	1740 Dorchester Ave	617-265-3111	$	10:30 pm	Pizza and steak sandwiches.
Chef Lee's II	554 Columbia Rd	617-436-6634	$$	8 pm	Second location of Boston soul food institution.
dBar	1236 Dorchester Ave	617-265-4490	$$$	10 pm	So chic, you could be in Downtown Crossing.
Ka' Carlos	33 Hancock St	617-282-4616	$$*	10 pm	Cape Verdean and Portuguese food under the same roof!
Lucky Café	1107 Dorchester Ave	617-822-9888	$*	9 pm	Chinese BBQ. Meat-elicious.
Phillips Old Colony House	780 Morrissey Blvd	617-282-7700	$$$$	10 pm	Brunch to impress your grandmother visiting from Iowa.
Pho 2000	198 Adams St	617-436-1908	$$	10 pm	Serving a delicious 7 course beef dinner.
Pho Hoa	1356 Dorchester Ave	617-287-9746	$	11 pm	Phat pho.
Restaurante Cesaria	266 Bowdoin St	617-282-1998	$$	11 pm	Something for everyone—grilled octopus to chicken parmesean.
Shanti: Taste of India	1111 Dorchester Ave	617-929-3900	$$	11 pm	Popular spot, good quality.
Sunrise	1157 Dorchester Ave	617-288-7314	$	10 pm	Pho and other ethereal delights.

Map 33 • Hyde Park

African Cuisine	1248 Hyde Park Ave	617-364-9999	$	11 pm	Sketchy from the outside, but step inside for great food.
Dottie's Deli	5 Fairmount Ave	617-364-9814	$*	3 pm	An old fashioned breakfast joint with its original charm.
Rincon Caribeno	18 Fairmount Ave	617-361-3210	$	10:30 pm	A new addition to Fairmont that serves predominately Puerto Rican food.

It's not quite the city that never sleeps, but Boston's nightlife is vast and varied, catering not only to teeming masses of college students but young professionals and aging hipsters alike. Unable to completely cast off the heavy cloak of its Puritan past, however, Boston tries its darndest to make sure you don't have too much fun by forcing the bars to close by 1 or 2 am. But what's dumber. This blue-law hangover or putting the T to bed for the night even earlier? After-hours joints exist, but are for members-only. As bartenders are fond of saying, "You don't have to go home, but you can't stay here." Despite these best efforts, though, the variety of bars, dance clubs, and live music venues keep growing, so you'll be able to find just the right spot to be seen, be picked up, dance, throw some spears, or sit and share a pint with a friend while you catch a live band. Remember that clubs are always in flux, so it makes sense to call ahead and confirm what's up before rounding up your crew and hitting the town.

Beer

Like Dunkin' Donuts shops, you can't throw a shillelagh in this town without hitting an Irish pub. Some of the best Guinness this side of the Atlantic can be found (usually poured by authentic Irish hands) at many of these fine establishments. If stout is not your thing, there are several good microbreweries around town including **Boston Beer Works (Map 2)**, **Cambridge Brewing Company (Map 26)**, and **John Harvard's Brew House (Map 20)**. Large (we mean large) beer selections can be found at **Sunset Grill & Tap (Map 19)**, **Bukowski's (Map 5, 28)**, **Roggie's (Map 18)**, and, to a smaller degree, **Christopher's (Map 23)**, **Pour House (Map 8)**, **Cambridge Common (Map 20)**, and **Doyle's (Map 14)**. Redbones (Map 22) barbecue joint has a beer wheel you can spin if you're having trouble making up your mind. If you insist on going straight to the source, take a tour and quaff some samples at the **Harpoon (Map 11)** and **Sam Adams (Map 14)** breweries.

Sports

Almost every bar in Boston becomes a sports bar when the Sox or Pats are playing. It's a good thing, too, since tickets to actual games are prohibitively expensive and the Sox decided to broadcast their games only on cable. If you're desperate to see your (non-Boston) team or follow every March Madness game, try **Sports Depot (Map 19)**, **The Four's (Map 1)**, **Stadium (Map 10)**, **Champions (Map 6)**, **Game On! (Map 16)**, **Tequila Rain (Map 16)**, or **Lir (Map 5)**.

Elegant and Nice

Sometimes you just need to dress up and treat yourself to see how the other half lives. For a change of pace from drunken sports fans and bottles of Bud, or for a good way to impress a date, sip a cocktail in the refined elegance of **Parker's Bar (Map 3)**, **City Bar (Map 6)**, or **Rowes Wharf Bar (Map 4)**. Have a nice romantic evening taking in the view of the Boston skyline at **Top of the Hub (Map 5)** in

the Prudential Center. Or don your coolest duds for some cocktails and dancing at **Whiskey Park (Map 3)** or **Sonsie (Map 5)**. For exotic drinks in a far-out futuristic setting, don't miss **Diva Lounge (Map 22)** in Davis Square. The newest nightlife destination that has created quite a stir is **The Beehive (Map 7)**. This spot has a fantastic old-timey, speakeasy feel to it that has folks flocking back every weekend. Wear your hippest duds and bring the latest issue of Artforum.

Dive

The smoking ban threatened the livelihoods of many a beloved Boston dive, and while some have revamped their image to draw in different crowds, the few hardy stalwarts are still alive and still dives. Go get lost at **Sullivan's Tap (Map 1)**, **Pete's Pub (Map 2)**, **Silhouette Lounge (Map 19)**, **Punter's Pub (Map 15)**, or **T.C. Lounge (Map 5)**, or more upscale dives that feature live bands like the **Midway Café (Map 14)** and **Abbey Lounge (Map 28)**. While not quite dives, good local color can be absorbed at the **Sligo Pub (Map 22)**, **Beacon Hill Pub (Map 1)**, and the **People's Republik (Map 27)**.

Live Music

For such a small city, Boston has a thriving live music scene, its local community of musicians nurturing each other and able to get lots of exposure in a wide array of venues. The Cars, The Pixies, Jonathan Richman, J. Geils, and Aerosmith are just a few decent names to come out of this town. On the flip side you can thank Beantown for torturing us with New Kids on the Block in the late '80s and early '90s. And on behalf of all Bostonians we apologize for their recent reunion tour. Whether you're in the mood for rock, blues, roots, punk, folk, rockabilly, jazz, or yes, even bluegrass, somebody in Boston is playing it. Pretty much everything but country.

While huge national acts play at the Garden and Tweeter Center, many also opt for smaller venues like the 2,800-seat Orpheum Theater for its great acoustics. Berklee College has graduated the likes of Branford Marsalis, Melissa Etheridge, and Donald Fagen, and at its Berklee Performance Center (www.berkleebpc.com, 617-747-2261) you can catch performances by big names and famous alumni or cheap concerts by teachers and students. Who knows? You may be watching the next John Mayer. Other places to catch national acts in a club atmosphere are the spacious **Roxy (Map 3)**, **Axis (Map 16)**, and **Avalon (Map 16)**. Avalon shows usually start early at 7 pm, so they can clear the room in time for the 10 pm clubbers. Rumor has it they once forced Bob Dylan off the stage to make way for a DJ.

For jazz, you can grab dinner and a show at the classy **Regattabar (Map 20)** or **Scullers (Map 19)**. Both in Cambridge, they host world-class performers. If you're on a budget, check out smaller venues like **Ryles (Map 28)** in Inman Square, **Good Life (Map 4)** in

Downtown Crossing, and **Wally's (Map 5)** in the South End, a tiny neighborhood bar where you'll sometimes find Berklee students sitting in with the evening's combo.

Rock 'n rollers head to **Paradise Rock Club (Map 19)**. If the downstairs is packed, go upstairs for a bird's-eye view of the band. If you get tired of moshing, the adjoining **Paradise Lounge (Map 19)** features smaller bands and food in a more relaxed setting. In Central Square, lines form out the door for **T.T. the Bear's Place (Map 27)**. At next door's **Middle East (Map 27)**, one of the coolest clubs around, you can grab some grape leaves before heading to one of its three rooms of music. **Harper's Ferry (Map 19)** gets a good mix of rock, blues, and New Orleans funk. And if you're pining for some old school blues and rock, head to the **Cantab (Map 27)** on the weekend for the still standing Little Joe Cook and the Thrillers. Smaller bars to catch a good groove include **Sky Bar (Map 23)**, O'Briens **(Map 19)**, **Midway Café (Map 14)**, **PA's Lounge (Map 24)**, **Great Scott (Map 19)**, and **Abbey Lounge (Map 28)**.

Folkies and singer-songwriters worship at the altar that is **Club Passim (Map 20)**, a 40-plus-year-old landmark dedicated to promoting independent musicians. Joan Baez, Bob Dylan, and Muddy Waters have all graced its stage. Be warned that they do not sell drinks, just coffee, tea, and vegetarian meals. And if you're dying to dust off that old banjo of yours, return to the **Cantab (Map 27)** on Tuesday nights for its bluegrass pickin' party.

You can find reggae, hip-hop, and afrobeat at **Western Front (Map 27)**. Latin music and salsa dancing heat up **Green Street Grill (Map 27)**, **Mojito's Lounge (Map 3)**, and **Milky Way Lounge (Map 14)**, which also hosts a popular karaoke night and candlepin bowling.

Can't decide what mood you're in? For every kind of musical act, both local faves and national legends, **Johnny D's (Map 22)** in Somerville reigns supreme. The **Lizard Lounge (Map 20)**, a laid-back neighborhood hang in Cambridge, hosts an eclectic mix of music and performances seven nights a week, ranging from punk to acoustic, rock and roll, experimental, and poetry slams.

Many pubs and bars feature local bands or musicians, often for free or a minimal cover charge. It's a great way to get to know the scene. Check weekly listings for schedules.

Some worth paying a visit to are **The Plough and Stars (Map 27)**, **Sally O'Brien's (Map 24)**, and **Atwood's Tavern (Map 28)**. Probably the best of these is **Toad (Map 23)**. The room is small, and you usually have to sneak past the bass player to get to the bathroom, but the wide variety and high quality of bands make this a popular gathering place.

Clubs

If you're new to Boston clubbing, start with the strip of clubs situated along Lansdowne Street. These clubs draw a huge student and Euro crowd and, as they're all behind Fenway Park, get particularly busy when the Sox are in town. Among the many good clubs on Lansdowne is **Avalon (Map 16)** which for years has hosted a huge, very popular gay night on Sundays. Central Boston has smaller clusters of clubs in the Theater District (such as the **Roxy (Map 3)**, **Aria (Map 3)**, or **Venu (Map 3)**), around Faneuil Hall (such as **Boston Rocks (Map 2)**, **Vertigo (Map 2)**, and **Parris (Map 2)**), and in Downtown Crossing (the self-important **Felt (Map 3)** or the salsa heaven **Mojito's Lounge (Map 3)**). If you're in Cambridge, check out **Phoenix Landing (Map 27)**, which morphs from an Irish pub into a dance club on most nights. **Jacque's (Map 3)** is Boston's oldest drag club, with shows on most nights. Many clubs have 18+ nights and gay nights, so check their schedules.

Karaoke

It seems like this fad is never going to die, and many bars and pubs still have a karaoke night at least once a week. For the truly diehard fanatics, there are a few notable venues for you to prove your vocal mettle. At the **Milky Way Lounge and Lanes (Map 14)** you can sing with the percussive accompaniment of falling candlepins. The new **Limelight Stage and Studio (Map 3)** applies pitch correction technology so you can sound just like Christine Aguilera. You can perform on stage in front of a large crowd or rent a private studio. Other worthy spots include the college-oriented **An Nua Tua (Map 16)**, after-work **Elephant & Castle (Map 4)**, Harvard Square's **Tommy Doyle's (Map 20)**, and the touristy **Purple Shamrock (Map 2)**.

Map 1 · Beacon Hill / West End

21st Amendment	150 Bowdoin St	617-227-7100	Favorite of the State House crowd.
6B	6 Beacon St #B	617-742-0306	Martinis and snacks for the after-work crowd.
Beacon Hill Pub	149 Charles St	617-625-7100	Dive popular with young Hill residents.
Cheers	84 Beacon St	617-227-9605	If you must.
The Four's	166 Canal St	617-720-4455	Sports tavern across from the Garden.
Greatest Bar	262 Friend St	617-367-0544	Big deal.
The Harp	85 Causeway St	617-742-1010	Pack in after an evening at the Garden.
Hill Tavern	228 Cambridge St	617-742-6192	Middling Beacon Hill hangout.
Seven's	77 Charles St	617-523-9074	Sturdy Beacon Hill local.
Sullivan's Tap	168 Canal St	n/a	Dive. Proper before Celtics and Bruins games.

Map 2 · North End / Faneuil Hall

Bell in Hand Tavern	45 Union St	617-227-2098	Welcoming thirsty travelers since the 18th century.
Black Rose	160 State St	617-742-2286	Tourist-crowded, unremarkable. Try somewhere else first.
Boston Beer Works	112 Canal St	617-896-2337	Cavernous suds shop near the Garden.
Boston Rocks	245 Quincy Market	617-726-1110	Generic nightclub.
Boston Sail Loft	80 Atlantic Ave	617-227-7280	Big outside deck on the water, good crowds.
Green Dragon Tavern	11 Marshall St	617-367-0055	Pretend you're Sam Adams while having the same.
The Hong Kong	65 Chatham St	617-227-2226	Scorpion bowl anyone?
McFadden's	148 State St	617-227-5100	Eek!
Paddy O's	33 Union St	617-263-7771	The name tells you it's Oirish, you know.
Parris	Quincy Market	617-248-8800	Tucked inside the less impressive Ned Devine's.
Purple Shamrock	1 Union St	617-227-2060	Giggly and bland.
Sanctuary	189 State St	617-573-9333	For the young and fashion-aware.
Tia's on the Waterfront	200 Atlantic Ave	617-227-0828	Warm-weather party house.
Vertigo	126 State St	617-723-7277	Downtown hot spot.

Map 3 · Downtown Crossing / Park Square / Bay Village

Aria	246 Tremont St	617-338-7080	DJs Tuesday through Saturday.
Felt	533 Washington St	617-350-5555	Club/upscale pool hall. DJ most nights.
Jacque's	79 Broadway	617-426-8902	Drag, but all welcome. Nightly cabaret.
Limelight Stage and Studios	204 Tremont St	617-423-0785	Karaoke on a grand scale; private studios available.
Matrix	275 Tremont St	617-542-4077	Large dance club.
MJ O'Connor's	27 Columbus Ave	617-482-2255	Large Irish pub. Outdoor seating when warm.
Mojitos Lounge	48 Winter St	617-817-2533	For those who like their salsa hot.
Parker's Bar	60 School St	617-227-8600	Elegant. Try the Boston Creme martini.
Roxy	279 Tremont St	617-338-7699	Large, popular dance club. Matrix is downstairs.
Rumor	100 Warrenton St	617-442-0045	Tuesday's the big night here.
The Tam	222 Tremont St	No phone	Local dive.
Venu	100 Warrenton St	617-338-8061	Always changing; check before you go.
Whiskey Park	64 Arlington St	617-542-1483	Swank, popular. Dress up.

Map 4 · Financial District / Chinatown

An Tain	31 India St	617-426-1870	For after work; DJs on Thursday, Friday.
Aqua	120 Water St	617-720-4900	Nice glass walls, anyway.
Elephant & Castle	161 Devonshire St	617-350-9977	Large pub handy for groups. Skip the food.
Good Life	28 Kingston St	617-451-2622	Martinis and jazz.
JJ Foley's	21 Kingston St	617-338-7713	Attracts a big after-work crowd.
Jose McIntyre's	160 Milk St	617-451-9460	Casual DJ and dance spot. Popular and simple.
Les Zygomates	129 South St	617-542-5108	Comprehensive wine list, pleasant bar.
Mr Dooley's Boston Tavern	77 Broad St	617-338-5656	Irish. Popular after-work drinking spot.
News	150 Kneeland St	617-426-6397	Leather District late-night spot.
Rowes Wharf Bar	70 Rowes Wharf	617-439-7000	Relax with scotch and an armchair.
Times Restaurant and Bar	112 Broad St	617-357-8463	Irish. Live music and DJs.
Umbria	295 Franklin St	617-338-1000	Italian restaurant goes club at night.

Map 5 · Back Bay (West) / Fenway (East)

Bukowski's	50 Dalton St	617-437-9999	100+ beers served with loud, eclectic music.
Crossroads	495 Beacon St	617-262-7371	Dive popular for its late last call.
Dillon's	955 Boylston St	617-421-1818	Revisiting the Roaring '20s.
Kings	10 Scotia St	617-266-2695	Bowling, pool, TV sports. Goofy but fun.
The Last Drop	421 Marlborough St	617-262-5555	Supposed latest last call in Boston.
Lir	903 Boylston St	617-778-0089	Upscale Irish. Large, handy for sports watchers.
Match	94 Massachusetts Ave	617-247-9922	More for cocktails than food. Stylish.
Our House East	52 Gainsborough St	617-236-1890	Branch of Allston college-kid hangout.
Pour House	907 Boylston St	617-236-1767	Wide beer selection, cool bartenders.
Sonsie	327 Newbury St	617-351-2500	People-watching mainstay. Nice French-doors street exposure.
TC's Lounge	1 Haviland St	617-247-8109	Dive for Berklee people and locals.
Top of the Hub	800 Boylston St	617-536-1775	Great view from the top of the Pru.
Wally's Café	427 Massachusetts Ave	617-828-1754	Cramped jazz landmark. For everyone at least once.

Map 6 · Back Bay (East) / South End (Upper)

Anchovies	433 Columbus Ave	617-266-5088	Easy-going neighborhood joint.
Champions	110 Huntington Ave	617-937-5658	Sports. Food wins no trophies.
City Bar	61 Exeter St	617-933-4800	At the Lenox Hotel.

Arts & Entertainment · **Nightlife**

Map 6 · Back Bay (East) / South End (Upper)—*continued*

Clery's	113 Dartmouth St	617-262-9874	Bar with food. Location is its best attribute.
Club Café	209 Columbus Ave	617-536-0966	Gay: restaurant in front, scoping in back.
Flash's	310 Stuart St	617-574-8888	Casual South End eatery and cocktail spot
Rattlesnake	384 Boylston St	617-859-8555	Hit the roof deck in the summer.
Rise	306 Stuart St	617-423-7473	For clubbing after 2 am. Arrive with a member.
Saint	90 Exeter St	617-236-1134	Nitery for aspiring Paris Hiltons.
Vox Populi	755 Boylston St	617-424-8300	Strangely soulless.

Map 7 · South End (Lower)

Beehive	541 Tremont St	617-423-0069	There's an old-timey, speakeasy feel to this place.
Delux Café	100 Chandler St	617-338-5258	Small, hip spot with good eats, music.
Eagle	520 Tremont St	617-542-4494	Casual gay local, mostly denim and leather.
Franklin Café	278 Shawmut Ave	617-350-0010	Mainly a restaurant, but a good bar choice too.
Pho Republique	1415 Washington St	617-262-0005	Fave of South End drinking set.

Map 8 · Charlestown

Goody Glovers	50 Salem St	617-367-6444	Irish drinks in a seas of Italian.
Sullivan's Pub	85 Main St	617-242-9515	Relaxed pub off of Thompson Square.
Tavern on the Water	1 Pier 6 at E 8th St	617-242-8040	Good on a warm afternoon. Skyline view.
Warren Tavern	2 Pleasant St	617-241-8142	One of Paul Revere's favorite watering holes.

Map 9 · East Boston

Kelly Square Pub	84 Bennington St	617-567-4627	Neighborhood local, try the ribs.
Trainor's Café	127 Maverick St	617-567-6995	Neighborhood local.

Map 10 · South Boston (West) / Fort Point

Blackthorn Pub	471 W Broadway	617-269-5510	Real Irish. Pours a mean Guinness.
The Cornerstone	16 W Broadway	617-269-9553	Broadway Square, erm, cornerstone. Parking in rear.
The Junction	110 Dorchester St	617-268-6429	Low-key neighborhood spot.
Lucky's	355 Congress St	617-357-5825	Well-liked retro cocktail lounge. Music most nights.
The Quiet Man	11 W Broadway	617-269-9878	Pub. Try the steak tips.
Shenanigans	332 W Broadway	617-269-9509	Popular watering hole.
Stadium	232 Old Colony Ave	617-269-5100	Two parts sports bar, one part dance club.

Map 11 · South Boston (East)

Boston Beer Garden	732 E Broadway	617-269-0990	Had a makeover recently. Long wine list, too.
Corner Tavern	645 E 2nd St	617-269-9891	Locals only.
Harpoon Brewery	306 Northern Ave	617-574-9551	Brewery tours, seasonal special events.
L Street Tavern	658 E 8th St	617-268-4335	No nonsense local. Appeared in *Good Will Hunting*.
Murphy's Law	837 Summer St	617-269-6667	Occasional live acoustic acts.
Playwright	658 E Broadway	617-269-2537	For socializing and television watching.

Map 12 · Newmarket / Andrew Square

Aces High	551 Dorchester Ave	617-269-7637	Check out their "new drinks and decor."
Dot Tavern	840 Dorchester Ave	617-288-6288	Neighborhood local.
Sports Connection Bar	560 Dorchester Ave	617-268-4119	Featuring "a big screen TV."

Map 13 · Roxbury

C&S Tavern	380 Warren St	617-442-7023	Neighborhood local.
El Mondonguito	221 Dudley St	617-522-3672	A decent dive bar.
Slade's	958 Tremont St	617-442-4600	Dancing, mostly R&B and hip-hop.

Map 14 • Jamaica Plain

Brendan Behan Pub	378 Centre St	617-522-5386	Well-liked Irish local. Relaxed atmosphere.
Costello's Tavern	723 Centre St	617-522-9263	Friendly JP tavern; decent food and darts.
Doyle's Café	3484 Washington St	617-524-2345	Trusty Irish landmark. Good grub and a mean Bloody Mary
Drinking Fountain	3520 Washington St	617-522-3424	Locals bar. Cheap beer, pool in the back.
James's Gate	5 McBride St	617-983-2000	Order the mussels, drink the best Guinness. and sit by the fire on winter nights.
Jeanie Johnston Pub	144 South St	617-983-9432	Darts, karaoke, live music, local flavor.
Midway Café	3496 Washington St	617-524-9038	Local watering hole featuring a variety of live bands.
Milky Way Lounge & Lanes	403 Centre St	617-524-3740	Hipster lounge with colorful décor, live music, candlepin bowling.
Samuel Adams Brewery	30 Germania St	617-368-5080	Tours and samples.

Map 15 • Fenway (West) / Mission Hill

Baseball Tavern	1270 Boylston St	617-867-6526	Sports tavern with a focus on Fenway.
Flann O'Brien's	1619 Tremont St	617-566-7744	Spirited Brigham Circle local.
Machine	1256 Boylston St	617-536-1950	Large gay club.
Punter's Pub	450 Huntington Ave	n/a	Student dive.
Ramrod	1254 Bolyston St	617-266-2986	Gay denim-and-leather crowd; various theme nights.

Map 16 • Kenmore Square / Brookline (East)

An Tua Nua	835 Beacon St	617-262-2121	Pub and dance club popular with twenty-somethings.
Audubon Circle	838 Beacon St	617-421-1910	Chill out with tasty bar food.
Axis	13 Lansdowne St	617-262-2437	DJs, occasional live acts.
Bill's Bar and Lounge	5 1/2 Lansdowne St	617-421-9678	Predominantly student crowd. Mostly rock.
Boston Billiard Club	126 Brookline Ave	617-536-7665	Capacious, down the street from Fenway Park.
Cask 'n' Flagon	62 Brookline Ave	617-536-4840	Just behind the Green Monster. Nothing special.
The Dugout	722 Commonwealth Ave	617-247-8656	Babe Ruth's basement dive bar of choice.
Embassy	36 Lansdowne St	617-536-2100	Dress to impress. Mostly hip-hop.
Foundation Lounge	500 Commonwealth Ave	617-859-9900	For sake connoisseurs.
Game On!	82 Lansdowne St	617 351 7001	Yet another sports bar near Fenway.
Lucky Strike Lanes	145 Ipswich St	617-437-0300	Über gaming and lounge establishment.
The Modern	36 Lansdowne St	617-536-2100	Dress to impress.
Tequila Rain	3 Lansdowne St	617-437-0300	Woooo! Woooo!
Who's on First?	19 Yawkey Wy	617-247-3353	Fun Fenway dive.

Map 17 • Coolidge Corner / Brookline Hills

Matt Murphy's Pub	14 Harvard St	617-232-0188	Popular Irish pub. Good food and music.
The Publick House	1648 Beacon St	617-277-2880	Focus here is on the beers.
Washington Square Tavern	714 Washington St	617-232-8989	Pub/restaurant with slightly overpriced food.

Map 18 • Brighton

Cityside Bar & Grill	1960 Beacon St	617-566-1002	Hit the patio if it's nice outside.
Green Briar	304 Washington St	617-789-4100	Pub with frequent live rock.
Irish Village	224 Market St	617-787-5427	Popular, relaxed local.
Joey's	416 Market St	617-254-9381	Don't ask for Joey.
The Last Drop	596 Washington St	617-787-1111	Sibling of Marlborough Street bar.
Mary Ann's	1937 Beacon St	n/a	BC student dump.
Roggie's	356 Chestnut Hill Ave	617 566 1880	52 beers, televised soccer.
Soho	386 Market St	617-562-6000	Sleek, large dining spot-cum-nightclub.

Arts & Entertainment • Nightlife

Map 19 • Allston (South) / Brookline (North)

Avenue Bar & Grille	1249 Commonwealth Ave	617-782-9508	Cheap drafts and college kids.
Big City	138 Brighton Ave	617-782-2020	For beer and pool, not food and service.
Bus Stop Pub	252 Western Ave	617-254-4086	Townie bar with sports.
Common Ground	85 Harvard Ave	617-783-2071	Defending Allston.
Great Scott	1222 Commonwealth Ave	617-566-9014	Loud, live music in a small, dark place.
Harper's Ferry	156 Brighton Ave	617-254-9743	Good place for live, unthreatening rock and blues.
Harry's Bar & Grill	1430 Commonwealth Ave	617-738-9990	Casual and roomy, with a mostly neighborhood crowd.
Joshua Tree	1316 Commonwealth Ave	617-566-6699	Red lights, leather seats…yawn.
The Kells	161 Brighton Ave	617-782-9082	Now with revamped Asia-by-way-of-Ikea theme.
Model Café	7 N Beacon St	617-254-9365	Allston staple, with all the usual suspects.
O'Brien's	3 Harvard Ave	617-742-6245	Live rock, mostly local acts.
Our House	1277 Commonwealth Ave	617-782-3228	So mellow that patrons fall asleep on the couches.
Paradise Rock Club & Lounge	967 Commonwealth Ave	617-562-8814	Major rock acts. Tasty food and smaller bands in Lounge.
Scullers Jazz Club	400 Soldiers Field Rd	617-562-4111	Live jazz most nights. In the Doubletree.
Silhouette Lounge	200 Brighton Ave	617-254-9306	A room full of darts and drunks.
Sports Depot	353 Cambridge St	617-783-2300	Good choice for March Madness drinking.
Sunset Grill & Tap	130 Brighton Ave	617-254-1331	Hundreds of beers to choose from, food until 1 am.
T's Pub	973 Commonwealth Ave	617-254-0807	An institution; free champagne on your birthday.
White Horse Tavern	116 Brighton Ave	617-254-6633	Always hopping, great for sports.
Wonder Bar	186 Harvard Ave	617-351-2665	Wannabe Soho, patronized by wannabe yups.

Map 20 • Harvard Square / Allston (North)

Cambridge Common	1667 Massachusetts Ave	617-547-1228	Local restaurant hang above the Lizard.
Charlie's Kitchen	10 Eliot St	617-492-9646	Old School by the old school. Great jukebox.
Club Passim	47 Palmer St	617-492-7679	Folk singer-songwriter landmark and vegetarian restaurant.
The Comedy Studio	1238 Massachusetts Ave	617-661-6507	A few scorpion bowls and you'll laugh at anything.
Grendel's Den	89 Winthrop St	617-491-1050	Harvard Square mainstay.
John Harvard's Brew House	33 Dunster St	617-868-3585	Large and loud, good for crowds.
Lizard Lounge	1667 Massachusetts Ave	617-547-0759	Great spot to kick back to live music.
Noir	1 Bennett St	617-661-8010	More pretentious than sophisticated.
Redline	59 JFK St	617-491-9851	A decent spot, but too often cramped.
Regattabar	1 Bennett St	617-661-5000	Serious jazz club.
Shay's Lounge	58 JFK St	617-864-9161	Lo-fi wine bar and pub with outdoor seating.
Temple Bar	1688 Massachusetts Ave	617-547-5055	Popular and impressed with itself.
Tommy Doyle's	96 Winthrop St	617-864-0655	Two-story Harvard hangout.
West Side Lounge	1680 Massachusetts Ave	617-441-5566	For those who find Temple Bar too pretentious.

Map 22 • North Cambridge / West Somerville

The Burren	247 Elm St	617-776-6896	Well-known Irish; live music.
Diva Lounge	246 Elm St	617-629-4963	Sprung from the loins of adjacent Diva Restaurant.
Johnny D's Uptown	17 Holland St	617-776-2004	Music nightly, wide variety.
PJ Ryan's	239 Holland St	617-625-8200	Brick and beer bar.
Redbones	55 Chester St	617-628-2200	Don't dig on swine? Then come spin the beer wheel.
Sligo Pub	237A Elm St	617-625-4477	A landmark of sorts.
Somerville Theatre	55 Davis Sq	617-625-5700	Occasional live music.

Map 23 • Central Somerville / Porter Square

Christopher's	1920 Massachusetts Ave	617-876-9180	Large selection of drafts, friendly staff, warm food.
Newtowne Grille	1945 Massachusetts Ave	617-661-0706	Divey, but lively.
Olde Magoun Saloon	518 Medford St	617-776-2600	Nicer than it looks neighborhood favorite with good beer and Sox games
On the Hill Tavern	499 Broadway	617-629-5302	DJs Thursday through Saturdays.
Samba Bar & Grill	608 Somerville Ave	617-718-9177	Brazilian vibe.
Toad	1912 Massachusetts Ave	617-497-4950	Cramped but fun. Live music nightly.

Map 24 • Winter Hill / Union Square

11th Chapter Saloon	366 Somerville Ave	n/a	Hard to find, tiny corner bar.
The Independent	75 Union Sq	617-440-6022	Irish pub on one side, upscale bar on the other.
Khoury's State Spa	118 Broadway	617-776-0571	Large, easy-going joint. Pool, darts.
PA's Lounge	345 Somerville Ave	617-776-1557	Cool spot for live, modern rock.
Sally O'Brien's	335 Somerville Ave	617-666-3589	Local bands, local sports, decent pub food.
Toast	70 Union Sq	617-623-9211	Basement lounge. DJs most nights.

Map 25 • East Somerville / Sullivan Square

Good Time Emporium	30 Assembly Square Dr	617-628-5559	Enormous. TVs, arcade games, batting cage, etc.
Night Games	30 Washington St	617-628-1000	Party at the Holiday Inn, yo!

Map 26 • East Cambridge / Kendall Square / MIT

Cambridge Brewing Company	One Kendall Sq, Bldg 100	617-494-1994	Decent microbrews. Some outdoor seating.
Flat Top Johnny's	One Kendall Sq, Bldg 200	617-494-9565	Cambridge's best large pool hall.
Pugliese's	635 Cambridge St	617-491-9616	Cambridge's oldest family-owned bar.

Map 27 • Central Square / Cambridgeport

All Asia	334 Massachusetts Ave	617-497-1544	Restaurant squeezes in live bands most nights.
Cantab Lounge	738 Massachusetts Ave	617-354-2685	Legendary quasi-dive. Little Joe Cook still plays.
The Cellar	991 Massachusetts Ave	617-876-2580	Stuck between Central and Harvard? Here you go.
Enormous Room	567 Massachusetts Ave	617-491-5550	Trendy couch lounge with tasty bar food.
The Field	20 Prospect Ave	617-354-7345	Dark and gritty Irish pub.
Green Street Grill	280 Green St	617-876-1655	Great Caribbean food with a slow burn. Mellow bar.
The Middle East	472 Massachusetts Ave	617-864-3278	Venerable venue that gets high-profile music bookings.
Middlesex	315 Massachusetts Ave	617-868-6739	Rotating DJ line-up, form modular seating.
Miracle of Science	321 Massachusetts Ave	617-868-2866	Energetic mainstay, always playing cool music.
People's Republik	880 Massachusetts Ave	617-492-8632	Toast 'til 2:00.
Phoenix Landing	512 Massachusetts Ave	617-576-6260	Irish pub with club music every night.
Plough & Stars	912 Massachusetts Ave	617-441-3455	Well-loved local. Frequent live music.
River Gods	125 River St	617-576-1881	Hipster house. DJs spin frequently.
TT the Bear's Place	10 Brookline St	617-492-2327	Live rock nightly. Showcases local bands.
Western Front	343 Western Ave	617-492-7772	Mostly reggae and world, occasional hip-hop.

Map 28 • Inman Square

Abbey Lounge	3 Beacon St	617-864-2792	Boston's "best dive bar"? You decide. Music nightly.
Atwood's Tavern	877 Cambridge St	617-354-0766	Food 'til late and live local music.
B-Side Lounge	92 Hampshire St	617-354-0766	Comfortably hip, well-loved local. Free hard-boiled eggs.
Bukowski's	1281 Cambridge St	617-497-7077	100+ beers. More chill than its Boston brother.
The Druid	1357 Cambridge St	617-497-0965	Well-liked Irish pub.
Ryles Jazz Club	212 Hampshire St	617-876-9330	Two-level club with jazz, world, Latin.
Thirsty Scholar Pub	70 Beacon St	617-497-2294	Laid-back neighborhood local. Good food, too.

Map 30 • Roslindale

JJ Foley's Fireside Tavern	30 Hyde Park Ave	617-338-7713	A great old man bar that is slowly being taken over by the young'uns

Map 32 • Dorchester (East)

Banshee	934 Dorchester Ave	617-436-9747	Irish pub.
Boston Bowl	820 Morrissey Blvd	617-825-3800	Open 24 Hours. Family fun all night long.
dBar	1236 Dorchester Ave	617-265-4490	Hip, gay bar. Food till 10pm, then the dancing starts.
Eire Pub	795 Adams St	617-436-8974	Politicians and sports fans welcome.
Harp & Bard	1099 Dorchester Ave	617-265-2893	Patio makes this a summertime Irish standout.

It's difficult to typecast Boston shoppers. This is due in part to the varied levels of crazy inhabiting its people—ranging from the Burberry-sporting, Beacon Hill-dwelling elite to the thrift shop-shopping Cambridge funksters in Doc Martens. The city's extremes of climate (the adage being, "if you don't like the weather, wait five minutes") compel most Bostonians to spend their weekends popping into climate controlled shops that range from uncomfortably exclusive to quietly quaint to downright weird. And, in addition to the extreme consumerist lifestyle of many of its dwellers, the city also has its fair share of psychotic, year-round outdoor athletes, for whom purveyors of gear spread evenly throughout the city. The fleet of moving trucks clogging this college town on the first of every month from March through October keeps the furniture-and-housewares hawkers in business. Despite the few malls that have weaseled their way onto the scene, the dependable disparity and constant movement of the city results in a throbbing, colorful, and sometimes shocking mass of consumers.

Clothing: New, Used & Vintage

For the labradoodle-walking yuppies in our midst, the Boston shopping scene certainly delivers. Start in the Back Bay on Newbury Street at **Louis Boston (Map 6)** then head across the street to **Brooks Brothers (Map 6)** and similar venues. More reasonably priced but still plenty preppy is **Eddie Bauer (Map 3)** downtown. On the other side of the coin, Boston has a ton to offer those seeking funkier duds–you just need to know where to look. The **Garment District (Map 28)** in Cambridge is a gargantuan thrift/vintage store with everything from '60s sweaters to contemporary second-hand treasures—contrary to New York, it's a store, not a neighborhood. Poke around the North End's tiny shops and you'll eventually stumble onto the treasures to be found in **Karma (Map 2)**. Around the corner, **Poor Little Rich Girl (Map 22)** in Davis Square has a great selection of vintage duds. Even upscale Newbury Street has its share of vintage chic—the **Army Barracks (Map 5)** is an old fave. And Boston is really a walking city (you know, when it's not hailing), so outfit your feet with shoes from **Berks (Map 20)**, **The Tannery (Map 20)** in Back Bay and Harvard Square, or **DSW (Map 2)** in Downtown Crossing.

For the Home/Apartment/Dorm

Though driving through Brookline and Beacon Hill on September 2—after most apartments have been vacated and their perfectly usable furniture is left on the curb—is a fabulous way to outfit your own digs, you may wish to take a gander at the furniture 'n' stuff offered throughout a city that's constantly turning over. Despite the terrific selection and prices offered by the obvious **Crate and Barrel (Map 6, 20)**, beware the slalom of newly-engaged couples registering for gifts. **Bowl and Board (Map 17)** is similar, but more diverse as far as neat little whosits for every room in the home. Crowded, annoying, one-stop house shopping can be achieved at the wicked huge **Bed Bath & Beyond (Map 16)** in Kenmore. **Economy Hardware (Maps 5, 16, 19, 27)** is always a safe—albeit pricey—bet for furniture, gadgets, even paint (oh, and hardware). Check out counter-intuitive spots like **Urban Outfitters (Map 20, 5)**, **Absolutely Fabulous (Map 28)**, or even **TJ Maxx (Map 3, 19)** and **Marshall's (Map 3, 6, 12)** for finishing touches like pretty pillows, cool lamps, and funky artwork. Antique hunters will be kept happy at **Cambridge Antique Market's (Map 26)** five floors of yesteryear.

Sports

Ready, set…Cross-country ski? Whatever the season, you can find what you're looking for at **City Sports (Map 3, 6, 19, 20, 23)**. Boston's also a biker city (but more the Schwinns than the Harleys). Riders can get tune-ups, gear, and honest advice at **International Bicycle Center (Map 19)**. **REI (Map 16)** is also good for bikes along with anything you might need for a cliff-hangin' good time. **Marathon Sports (Map 17)** in Brookline lets you test drive the sneakers on the sidewalk and makes sure you leave with exactly the right pair.

Computing Machines

Thanks to its many universities, hospitals, and research facilities, Boston is awash with computer-loving dweebs. **Micro Center (Map 27)** is swarmed on the weekends. Two centrally located **Best Buys (Map 16, 26)** feature their usual merchandise and crowds. The PC-user-repellant **Apple Store (Map 26)** in the Cambridgeside Galleria is one stylin' geek boutique.

Music Maniacs

The rise of the iPod has given Bostonians yet another excuse to keep eyes forward and not interact with fellow human beings that dare cross their path. But there are still plenty of options for those in search of disks and vinyl. **Newbury Comics (Map 2, 5, 20, 21)** delivers on their offer of "a wicked good time" with not only music, but movies, novelties, and general craziness. For those in search of vinyl, vintage, and generally hard-to-find tunes, stroll along Mass Ave in Cambridge to find **Cheapo Records (Map 27)**, **Massive Records (Map 27)**, **Stereo Jack's (Map 20)**, and a number of others. Comm Ave near BU and Harvard Square are also places to troll for rare stuff with stores like **In Your Ear (Map 19)**, **Nuggets (Map 16)**, and **Planet Records (Map 20)**.

Foodie Fanatics

You simply cannot go wrong once you set foot in the North End. **Mike's Pastry (Map 2)**, **Modern Pastry (Map 2)**, and the 24-7 **Bova's Bakery (Map 2)** are just three of about a thousand places to try for sweet goodies. For savory Italian treats try **Salumeria Italiana (Map 2)** or **Salumeria Toscana (Map 2)**. Equally tempting treats can be found at **Athan's Bakery (Map 17)** in Brookline or **Cremaldi's (Map 27)** and **Central Bakery (Map 28)** in Cambridge. If ever you lived abroad and are feeling nostalgic, **Cardullo's (Map 20)** in Harvard Square are a fun place to grab imported anything, from Branston Pickle to real Italian gelato. For ice cream, **Christina's Homemade (Map 28)** in Inman Square is a favorite. For a hot fudge sundae you can't beat **Herrell's (Map 20)**. Other Popular spots also include JP Licks (Maps 5, 14, 19), Toscanini's (Map 27), and **Emack & Bolio's (Maps 5, 17, 30)**, all with lines out the door in warmer months. **Lionette's (Map 7)** in the South End, well known for their local, grass-fed meats, also carries a mix of specialty and standard items, sandwiches, prepared foods, and fresh bread.

Malls and 'hoods

If you're going to make an afternoon of it, you might as well hit up a neighborhood with a lot to offer—including a bite in between stops and plenty of people—watching for when the cash runs out. Downtown Crossing is a high-energy center of rabid consumerism, very convenient to the T, and boasting the gigantic department store **Macy's (Maps 3, 19)** (which has recently gobbled up the beloved Filene's), discount stores (**Marshall's (Maps 3, 6, 12)**, TJ Maxx (Map 3)), and other joints like **H&M (Map 3)** where you can get lost for hours. Clothes aren't the only thing for which to shop here—there are jewelers, shoe stores, and street vendors and performers. It's also within walking distance of **Faneuil Hall (Map 2)**. One could easily spend a solid afternoon wandering around Harvard Square. **Newbury Comics (Map 20)** and **Little Tibet (Map 20)** are great for gift shopping (for yourself or anyone else). Stop for a snack at **Cardullo's (Map 20)**, or recharge at **Tealuxe (Map 20)**, and while you're sipping or munching, flip through a book at the **Coop (Map 20)** or **Harvard Book Store (Map 20)**. Walk the length of **Newbury Street (Map 5)**, and you'll find everything from bookstores (**Trident Booksellers and Café (Map 5)** is a must) to house stuff (**Kitchen Arts (Map 6)**) to

ice cream (**Emack & Bolio's (Map 5)**) to art (**International Poster Gallery (Map 6)**), plus clothes and clothes and clothes. Though most of what's found on Newbury is decidedly pricey, things do get more reasonable as you get closer to Mass Ave. **Boylston Street (Map 6)** runs parallel to Newbury with offerings like **Anthropologie (Map 6)**, **City Sports (Maps 3, 6, 19, 20, 23)**, **Tweeter Etc. (Map 6)**, and **Shreve, Crump & Low (Map 6)**. And yes, as much as we hate to admit it, Boston does have a few "malls"—though they are well camouflaged and the word "mall" does not actually appear in their titles. **The Shops at Prudential Center (Map 5)** include **Sephora (Map 5)**, **Lord & Taylor (Map 6)**, and several others and also cuts through to the even higher-end **Copley Place (Map 6)**. The **CambridgeSide Galleria (Map 26)** is a multi-leveled mecca where MIT kids, Biotech execs, and European tourists flock to where the **Apple Store (Map 26)** to satisfy their Mac addictions.

Map 1 · Beacon Hill / West End

Black Ink	101 Charles St	617-723-3883	Amusing tchotckes, quirky gifts, purty paper.
DeLuca's Market	11 Charles St	617-523-4343	Good deli, pricey fruit, wine, and beer downstairs.
Eugene Galleries	76 Charles St	617-227-3062	A treasure chest of old maps, prints, books.
The Flat of the Hill	60 Charles St	617-619-9977	Quirky gifts. Lots of pink.
Good	88 Charles St	617-722-9200	Lovely gifts
Hilton's Tent City	272 Friend St	617-227-9242	Four floors of outdoors needs since 1947.
Moxie	51 Charles St	617-557-9991	Shoes, bags, accessories.
The Red Wagon	69 Charles St	617-523-9402	Pricey kids' clothes and toys.
Savenor's Market	160 Charles St	617-723-6328	For a variety of gourmet goodies.
Wish	49 Charles St	617-227-4441	Trendy, upscale women's clothing and accessories.

Map 2 · North End / Faneuil Hall

Bova's Bakery	134 Salem St	617-523-5601	Pastries, also deli and pizza. Open 24 hours.
Brooks Brothers	75 State St	617-261-9990	Branch of venerable Back Bay clothier.
Dairy Fresh Candies	57 Salem St	617-742-2639	Big selection of candy imported from Italy.
Fresh Cheese	81 Endicott St	617-570-0007	Also sells dozens of oils and vinegars.
Green Cross Pharmacy	393 Hanover St	617-227-3728	Old-world pharmacy. Also sells Italian sundries.
Holbrows Flowers	100 City Hall Plz	617-227-8057	Convenient to Government Center T stop.
Karma	26 Prince St	617-723-8338	Upscale consignment shop.
Maria's Pastry Shop	46 Cross St	617-523-1196	Sweet tooth heaven.
Mike's Pastry	300 Hanover St	617-742 3050	The most famous of the North End Italian bakeries.
Modern Pastry	257 Hanover St	617-523-3783	Boston's best cannoli? You decide.
Monica's Salumeria	130 Salem St	617-742-4101	Homemade takeout and Italian groceries.
Newbury Comics	1 Washington Mall	617-248-9992	Downtown location of successful music/novelties chain.
Salumeria Italiana	151 Richmond St	617-523-8743	Well-regarded Italian specialties store.
Salumeria Toscana	272 Hanover St	617-720-4243	Imported Italian specialties, heat-and-serve meals.
Stanza dei Sigari	292 Hanover St	617-227-0295	17-year-olds take note: hookahs available.
Staples	25 Court St	617-367-1747	Printer ink and other more reasonably priced supplies.

Map 3 · Downtown Crossing / Park Square / Bay Village

Beacon Hill Skate Shop	135 Charles S St	617-482-7400	Rentals available. Also has hockey gear.
Borders	10 School St	617-557-7188	All you've come to expect, plus sidewalk sales.
Bromfield Camera & Video	10 Bromfield St	617-426-5230	Decent selection of new and used cameras.
City Antiques	362 Tremont St	617-423-7600	Used furniture and furnishings.
City Sports	11 Bromfield St	617-423-2015	Covers all the basics in apparel and equipment.
DSW	385 Washington St	617-556-0052	Oodles and oodles of sho[od]les.
Eddie Bauer Outlet	500 Washington St	617-423-4722	Good deals on quality clothes.
H&M	350 Washington St	617-482-7001	Disposable chic from Swedish mega-merchant.
Lambert's	Washington St & Summer St		Fruit and veggie stand in the heart of Downtown Crossing.
LJ Peretti	2 1/2 Park Sq	617-482-0218	Oldest family-run tobacconist in the country.
Macy's	450 Washington St	617-357-3000	Once Jordan Marsh. Big outdoor "holiday" tree in December.
Marshall's	350 Washington St	617-338-6205	Discount clothing and other stuff.
Roche-Bobois	2 Avery St	617-742-9611	Très trendy interior design and furnishings.
Staples	25 Winter St	617-426-2290	Good deals with the Court Street branch.
TJ Maxx	350 Washington St	617-695-2424	Put on your bargain-hunting hat. Off-price apparel and housewares.
Windsor Buttons	35 Temple Pl	617-482-4969	A crafter's delight. And buttons for every mood.

Arts & Entertainment • **Shopping**

Map 4 • Financial District / Chinatown

Anna's Dessert House	66 Harrison Ave	617-542-7903	One of Chinatown's newer bakery/dessert shops.

Map 5 • Back Bay (West) / Fenway (East)

Army Barracks	328 Newbury St	617-437-1657	Surplus store. Knives, canteens, T-shirts, and all things cammo.
Back Bay Bicycle	366 Commonwealth Ave	617-247-2336	Accurately monikered.
Bön Bön	197 Massachusetts Ave	617-904-0770	Gorge yourself on amazing gelato and other sweet treats.
The Compleat Strategist	201 Massachusetts Ave	617-267-2451	Gaming paraphernalia.
Daddy's Junky Music	159 Massachusetts Ave	617-247-0909	Comprehensive store serving the Berklee community.
DeLuca's Market	239 Newbury St	617-262-5990	Good deli, pricey fruit, wine, and beer downstairs.
Economy Hardware	219 Massachusetts Ave	617-536-4280	Hardware, household needs, cheap furniture. Very popular.
Emack & Bolio's	290 Newbury St	617-536-7127	Innovative ice cream flavors.
Firefly Jewelry & Gifts	270 Newbury St	617-375-5885	Unique jewelry, friendly service.
John Fluevog	302 Newbury St	617-266-1079	Indulge the hipster in you with these funky shoes.
Johnny Cupcakes	279 Newbury St	617-375-0100	Trendy T-shirts. Not cupcakes.
Johnson Artist Materials	355 Newbury St	617-536-4065	Tony. Also a selection of stationery.
JP Licks	352 Newbury St	617-236-1666	Local ice cream chain.Try the warm peanut butter topping.
Luna Boston	286 Newbury St	866-910-3900	Lotsa handbags.
Matsu	259 Newbury St	617-266-9707	Inviting boutique, unusual clothing and accessories.
Newbury Comics	332 Newbury St	617-236-4930	Now featuring a large DVD section.
Orpheus	362 Commonwealth Ave	617-247-7200	Focusing on classical music.
Sephora	800 Boylston St	617-262-4200	A makeup wonderland—play before you buy.
Sweet-N-Nasty	90 Massachusetts Ave	617-266-7171	Saucy cakes for all [adult] occasions.
Trident Booksellers & Café	338 Newbury St	617-267-8688	Busy, independent bookstore/cafe with tons of magazines.
Urban Outfitters	361 Newbury St	617-236-0088	Funky clothes, apartment stuff and novelties.
Utrecht Art Supply Center	333 Massachusetts Ave	617-262-4948	Serious art store near Symphony Hall.

Map 6 • Back Bay (East) / South End (Upper)

All Things Chocolate	31 St James Ave	617-423-9400	For that funny valentine of yours.
Amazing Express	57 Stuart St	617-338-1252	Sex; a vestige of the erstwhile Combat Zone.
Anthropologie	799 Boylston St	617-262-0545	Clothes, accessories and colorful objets d'home.
Best of Scotland	115 Newbury St Ste 202	617-536-3048	Cashmere outlet from the olde country.
Brooks Brothers	46 Newbury St	617-267-2600	Flagship store of company operating since 1818.
City Sports	480 Boylston St	617-267-3900	Covers all the basics in apparel and equipment.
Crate & Barrel	777 Boylston St	617-262-8700	Back Bay location of Chicago behemoth.
First Act Guitar Studio	745 Boylston St	617-226-7899	Guitars made, guitars played, in-store concerts.
Hempest	207 Newbury St	617-421-9944	Don't ask if they sell screens.
International Poster Gallery	205 Newbury St	617-375-0076	Prints and posters from around the world.
Kitchen Arts	161 Newbury St	617-266-8701	Broad range of kitchen needs for the serious cook, and the dabbler.
Lindt Master Chocolatier	704 Boylston St	617-236-0571	Nifty gifts for your Swiss miss.
Lord & Taylor	760 Boylston St	617-262-6000	Featuring new façade.
Louis Boston	234 Berkeley St	617-262-6100	High-end men's and women's designer clothing.
Luna Boston	205 Newbury St	866-910-3900	Lotsa handbags.
Lush	166 Newbury St	617-375-5874	British cosmetics merchant.
Marc Jacobs	81 Newbury St	617-425-0707	Will he make it in fashion-challenged Boston?
Marshall's	500 Boylston St	617-262-6066	Discount clothing and other stuff.
Neiman Marcus	5 Copley Pl	617-536-3660	Needless Markup?
O & Co.	161 Newbury St	617-859-8841	Worship at the wall of oil.
Paper Source	338 Boylston St	617-536-3444	DIY paper crafts and quirky gifts.
Saks Fifth Avenue	1 Ring Rd	617-262-8500	A posh shopping experience.
Second Time Around	176 Newbury St	617-247-3504	Pre-owned chic.
Shreve, Crump & Low	440 Boylston St	617-267-9100	Boston jewelers since 1796.
Stil	170 Newbury St	617-859-7845	Au courant clothes and accessories.
Teuscher Chocolates	230 Newbury St	617-536-1922	For the Swiss chocoholic in you.
Tweeter Etc	350 Boylston St	617-262-2299	Audio and video equipment.
Winston Flowers	131 Newbury St	617-266-1058	This is how the well-heeled say "I love you" in Boston.

Map 7 • South End (Lower)

Aunt Sadie's	18 Union Park St	617-357-7117	Fabulous candles, other gifts.
Bobby from Boston	19 Thayer St	617-423-9299	Vintage clothing.
Brix Wine Shop	1284 Washington St	617-542-2749	Upscale wine shop.
The Butcher Shop	552 Tremont St	617-423-4800	Neighborhood meat shop. Also a wine bar serving specialties.
Community Bicycle Supply	496 Tremont St	617-542-8623	South End bike shop.
Ilex	73 Berkeley St	617-422-0300	Florist.
Lekker	1317 Washington St	617-542-6464	Unique, modern home furnishings.
Lionette's	577 Tremont St	617-778-0360	Food shop associated with Garden of Eden.
Picco	513 Tremont St	617-927-0066	Ice cream handy to the BCA.
Posh	557 Tremont St	617-437-1970	Gifts, home furnishings and accessories.
South End Buttery	314 Shawmut Ave	617-482-1015	Churning out the treats.
South End Formaggio	268 Shawmut Ave	617-350-6996	Cheese, cured meats, dry goods, and wine.
Uniform	511 Tremont St	617-247-2360	Top clothes for lads.
Urban Living Studio	58 Clarendon St	617-247-8150	Cheery home accessories store.

Map 8 • Charlestown

A Wild Flower	73 Main St	617-242-4214	Florist.
Bunker Hill Florist	1 Thompson Sq	617-242-2124	Florist.
Doherty's Flowers	223 Main St	617-242-1300	Main Street florist.
The Joy of Old	85A Warren St	617-242-6066	Coming soon: "The Joy of Gay Old."
Serenade Chocolates	5 Harvard Sq	617-739-0795	Tastes of Vienna.

Map 9 • East Boston

Brazilian Soccer House	110 Meridian St	617-569-1164	The place to get your soccer kit.
Globos y Fiesta	52A Bennington St	617-569-4908	Order your piñatas here.
Lilly's Flower Shop	512 Saratoga St	617-567-5177	Day Square florist.
Lolly's Bakery	158 Bennington St	617-567-9461	Quality pañería.
Studium Spanish Bookstore	268 Bennington St	617-569-1253	Los libros en Español.

Map 10 • South Boston (West) / Fort Point

Machine Age	645 Summer St	617-464-0099	Modern furniture in a huge space.

Map 11 • South Boston (East)

EP Levine	23 Drydock Ave	617-951-1499	High-end photo shop.
Ku De Ta	663 E Broadway	617-269-0008	A slice of Newbury St prices, in Southie.
Miller's Market	336 K St	617-268-2526	Apparently, the coldest beer in town.
Stapleton Floral	635 E Broadway	617-269-7271	Florist.

Map 12 • Newmarket / Andrew Square

Home Depot	5 Allstate Rd	617-442-6110	Got wood?
Marshall's	8D Allstate Rd	617-442-5050	Discount clothing and other stuff.

Map 13 • Roxbury

Bikes Not Bombs	18 Bartlett Sq	617-522-0226	Shop for bikes and be socially responsible.

Map 14 • Jamaica Plain

Boing! JP's Toy Shop	729 Centre St	877-264-6400	Friendly toy shop.
Boomerangs	716 Centre St	617-524-5120	Used clothing and housewares.
Canto 6	3346 Washington St	617-983-8688	Baked goodies and a good cup of joe.
City Feed and Supply	66 Boylston St	617-524-1657	Popular neighborhood grocery, meeting spot.
Eye Q Optical	7 Pond St	617-983-3937	Designer eyeglasses.
Fat Ram's Pumpkin Tattoo	380 Centre St	617-522-6444	Skilled ink artists with degrees in fine art.
Ferris Wheels Bicycle Shop	66 South St	617-522-7082	JP bike shop.
Fire Opal	683 Centre St	617-524-0262	Upscale craft gallery.
Gadgets	671 Centre St	617-524-6800	Kitchen stuff, mostly.
Honeyspot	48 South St	617-524-2444	Shop for mom, your hipster cousin, and yourself.
JP Licks	659 Centre St	617-524-2020	Popular ice cream shop.
Petal & Leaf	461 Centre St	617-524-2227	Friendly staff, fun gifts, and fresh flowers.
Salmagundi	765 Centre St	617-522-5047	Check out the coolest selection in the city.

Map 16 • Kenmore Square / Brookline (East)

Bed Bath & Beyond	401 Park Dr	617-536-1090	For when holes are growing in your towels.
Best Buy	401 Park Dr	617-424-7900	Awful, annoying electronics retailer.
Blick Art Materials	401 Park Dr	617-247-3322	Art-supply megashop.
Boston Bicycle	842 Beacon St	617-236-0752	Selection geared toward messengers, plenty of fixies.
Economy Hardware	1012 Beacon St	617-236-1510	Hardware, household needs, cheap furniture. Very popular.
Guitar Center	750 Commonwealth Ave	617-738-5958	Also has drums, keys, etc.
Hunt's Photo and Video	520 Commonwealth Ave	617-778-2222	Good selection of used cameras.
Japonaise Bakery	1020 Beacon St	617-566-7730	Mmm...curry donut.
Nantucket Natural Oils	508 Commonwealth Ave	617-437-9800	Aromatherapy and perfumes.
Nuggets	486 Commonwealth Ave	617-536-0679	Sells only used recordings. Quite fun to browse.
REI	401 Park Dr	617-236-0746	Seattle co-op for the gearhead.
Ski Market	860 Commonwealth Ave	617-731-6100	Skis or bicycles depending on the season.
University Computers	533 Commonwealth Ave	617-353-1800	BU store; ask about student discounts.

Map 17 • Coolidge Corner / Brookline Hills

Athan's Bakery	1621 Beacon St	617-734-7028	Exquisite baked goods, chocolates, gelato, and espresso.
Bowl & Board	1354 Beacon St	617-566-4/26	Home furnishings and housewares.
EC Florist & Gifts	224 Washington St	617-232-3693	Florist.
Emack & Bolio's	1663 Beacon St	617-731-6256	Innovative ice cream flavors.

Eureka Puzzles	1349 Beacon St	617-738-7352	Old-timey gamers' heaven.
Madras Masala	191 Harvard St	617-566-9943	Indian Grocery store with a good selection of chutneys and prepared food.
Marathon Sports	1638 Beacon St	617-735-9373	Run! Run! Run!
Paper Source	1361 Beacon St	617-264-2800	DIY paper crafts and quirky gifts.
Party Favors	1356 Beacon St	617-566-3330	Satisfies your sweet tooth and your inner party animal.
Petropol	1428 Beacon St	617-232-8820	Russian books and cds.
Pier 1 Imports	1351 Beacon St	617-232-9627	Brought to you by Fat Actress Kirstie Alley.
Russian Village	1659 Beacon St	617-731-2023	Foodstuffs, DVD/videos.
Ten Thousand Villages	226 Harvard St	617-277-7700	Free-trade, handmade crafts from around the world.
Wild Goose Chase	1431 Beacon St	617-738-8020	Crafts, gifts. A flea market, Brookline-style.

Map 18 · Brighton

Amanda's Flowers	347 Washington St	617-782-0686	Florist.
CompUSA	205 Market St	617-783-1900	Has the basics, but service could be sharper.
New Balance Factory Store	40 Life St	877-623-7867	Running gear for cheap runners.
Staples	1660 Soldiers Field Rd	617-254-4822	Printer ink and other more reasonably priced supplies.

Map 19 · Allston (South) / Brookline (North)

Berezka International Food Store	1215 Commonwealth Ave	617-787-2837	Russian goods for the slavophile.
Bicycle Bill's	253 N Harvard St	617-783-5636	Quality, no-attitude, neighborhood bike shop.
Bob Smith's Wilderness House	1048 Commonwealth Ave	617-277-5858	Everything for your outdoor adventures.
Brookline News and Gifts	313 Harvard St	617-566-9634	Since 1963, chances are they have what you're looking for.
Catering by Andrew	402 Harvard St	617-731-6585	Shabbot bakery, Thursdays and Fridays only.
City Housewares	434 Harvard St	617-278-6333	Inexpensive yet stylish kitchen goods.
City Sports	1035 Commonwealth Ave	617-782-5121	Covers all the basics in apparel and equipment.
Clear Flour	178 Thorndike St	617-739-0060	Lines out the door for Boston's honest bread.
Coco Cosmetics	192 Harvard Ave	617-782-1547	Trendy bright shop seems out of place. The future of Allston?
Eastern Mountain Sports	1041 Commonwealth Ave	617-254-4250	Gear for the New England outdoor enthusiast.
Economy Hardware	144 Harvard Ave	617-789-5552	Hardware, household needs, cheap furniture. Very popular.
Herrell's Ice Cream	155 Brighton Ave	617-782-9599	Attracts a loyal following.
In Your Ear	957 Commonwealth Ave	617-787-9755	Good selection of independent, experimental music.
International Bicycle Center	89 Brighton Ave	617-783-5804	Two floors of bikes, one of Boston's largest.
Israel Bookshop	410 Harvard St	617-566-7113	Books in Hebrew.
JP Licks	311 Harvard St	617-738-8252	Popular Boston ice cream institution.
Kolbo Fine Judaica	437 Harvard St	617-731-8743	Good place for Jewish gifts.
Kupel's Bake & Bagel	421 Harvard St	617-566-9528	Old school bagel joint.
New England Comics	131 Harvard Ave	617-783-1848	Study break reading material, some independent comics.
Re: Generation Records and Tattoo	155 Harvard Ave	617-782-1313	Good addition to the Allston punk scene.
Richman's Zipper Hospital	318 Harvard St	617-277-0039	The place to go for fixing zippers and tailoring.
Staples	214 Harvard Ave	617-566-8605	Printer ink and other more reasonably priced supplies.
Stingray Body Art	1 Harvard Ave	617-254-0666	Huge tattoo parlor with sassy boutique.
TJ Maxx	525 Harvard Ave	617-232-5420	Off-price apparel and housewares.
Urban Renewals	122 Brighton Ave	617-783-8387	Thrift shop with clothes, gifts, and kitsch.
Vespa Boston	22 Brighton Ave	617-254-4000	Imagine you are in Italy with its better drivers.
Wulf's Fish Market	407 Harvard St	617-277-2506	Respected fishmonger.

Map 20 · Harvard Square / Allston (North)

Abodeon	1731 Massachusetts Ave	617-497-0137	Retro housewares.
Alpha Omega	1380 Massachusetts Ave	617-864-1227	Jewelry, large selection of watches.
Berk's Shoes	50 JFK St	888-462-3157	Arm yourself with the right kicks for the neighborhood.
Black Ink	5 Brattle St	617-497-1221	A blend of quirky and handy gifts.
Bob Slate	1288 Massachusetts Ave	617-547-1230	Popular stationery store. Art supplies, too.
Brattle Square Florist	31 Brattle St	617-547-7089	Delphinium paradise.
Cardullo's Gourmet Shoppe	6 Brattle St	617-491-8888	Craving Swedish ginger cookies? International, gourmet goodies.
Colonial Drug	49 Brattle St	617-864-2222	Unbeatable old-school, family run shop.
City Sports	44 Brattle St	617-492-6000	Moved from Dunster Street.
Crate & Barrel	48 Brattle St	617-876-6300	Harvard Square location of Chicago behemoth.
Harvard Bookstore	1256 Massachusetts Ave	617-661-1515	An independent bookstore selling new, used, and remainders.
Harvard Coop	1400 Massachusetts Ave	617-499-2000	Good for books, maps, and school stuff.
Herrell's Ice Cream	15 Dunster St	617-497-2179	Try the hot fudge.
Hidden Sweets	25 Brattle St	617-497-2600	Bulk candy and other crap.
LA Burdick Homemade Chocolates	52D Brattle St	617-491-4340	Sublime confections and some killer hot chocolate.
Leavitt & Pierce	1316 Massachusetts Ave	617-547-0576	Best tobacconist in Cambridge. Chess sets too.
Little Tibet	1174 Massachusetts Ave	617-868-1030	Far-eastern clothing, jewelry, incense, and more.
Lizzy's Ice Cream	29 Church St	617-354-2911	Homemade.
Lush	30 JFK St	617-497-5874	British cosmetics merchant.
Museum of Useful Things	49 Brattle St	617-576-3322	Museum/shop celebrates the Beauty of Function.
Newbury Comics	36 JFK St	617-491-0337	A zoo on weekends.
Nomad	1741 Massachusetts Ave	617-497-6677	An eclectic mix with a Mexican bent.
On Church Street	54 Church St	617-497-7070	Replaced CD Spins here.
Oona's	1210 Massachusetts Ave	617-491-2654	Nifty little vintage shop.

Out of Town News	0 Harvard Sq	617-354-7777	The sensible Harvard Square rendezvous spot.
Planet Records	54B JFK St	617-492-0693	CDs, some vinyl. Grab a $1 "mystery bag."
Proletariat	36 JFK St	617-661-3865	Cool clothes and other fun nonsense.
Staples	57 JFK St	617-491-1166	Printer ink and other more reasonably priced supplies.
Stereo Jack's	1686 Massachusetts Ave	617-497-9447	Specializing in jazz, blues, and the like.
Tannery	11A Brattle St	617-491-0810	Known for huge selection. Hit-or-miss service.
Tcaluxe	0 Brattle St	617-441-0077	Good spot to hide from Harvard Square crowds.
Tennis and Squash Shop	67 Mt Auburn St	617-864-8800	Serious gear for those who like to wear white.
Tess and Carlos	20 Brattle St	617-864-8377	Well-chosen selection of pricey designer clothing and accessories.
Twisted Village	12B Eliot St	617-354-6898	Focusing on experimental, modern psychedelic music.
Urban Outfitters	11 JFK St	617-864-0070	Funky clothes and apartment stuff. Great bargain basement.
ZIPA Jewelry	1316 Massachusetts Ave	617-491-6991	Some tobacco with your jewels?

Map 21 • West Cambridge

Formaggio Kitchen	244 Huron Ave	617-354-4750	Cheese and other gourmet imports.
Henry Bear's Park	361 Huron Ave	617-547-8424	Chi-chi toy store.
Newbury Comics	211 Alewife Brook Pkwy	617-491-7711	Fresh Pond location of successful music/novelties chain.

Map 22 • North Cambridge / West Somerville

Bicycle Exchange	2067 Massachusetts Ave	617-864-1300	Porter Square bike shop.
Black & Blues	89 Holland St	617-628-0046	Laid back duds, friendly shopkeepers.
CD Spins	235 Elm St	617-666-8080	A good choice for selling back CDs.
China Fair	2100 Massachusetts Ave	617-864-3050	Inexpensive kitchen gear and housewares.
Chinook Outdoor Adventure	93 Holland St	617-776-8616	Sporty, stylish. Clothes for him and her.
Cibeline	85 Holland St	617-625-2229	Party clothes, whatever your mood.
Magpie	416 Highland Ave	617-623-3330	Featuring over 150 indie crafters and artists.
McKinnon's Choice Meat Market	3300A Elm St	617-666-0888	Smart choice before a barbecue.
Modern Brewer	2304 Massachusetts Ave	617-498-0400	Everything for your home-brewing needs.
Nellie's Wildflowers	72 Holland St	617-625-9453	Florist.
Poor Little Rich Girl	255 Elm St	617-684-0157	Good spot to shop for fun clothes.
Staples	186 Alewife Brook Pkwy	617-547-3948	Printer ink and other more reasonably priced supplies.

Map 23 • Central Somerville / Porter Square

Ace Wheelworks	145 Elm St	617-776-2100	Davis Square bike shop.
Big Fish, Little Fish	55 Elm St	617-666-2444	Pet store with more than just fish.
Bob Slate	1975 Massachusetts Ave	617-547-8624	Popular stationery store. Art supplies too.
Cambridge Music Center	1906 Massachusetts Ave	617-547-8263	Sells instruments and hard-to-find sheet music.
Cambridge Naturals	23 White St	617-492-4452	Quality selection of all things yogi.
City Sports	1815 Massachusetts Ave	617-661-1666	Covers all the basics in apparel and equipment.
Greenward	1776 Massachusetts Ave	617-395-1338	Unique, eco-friendly somethings.
Joie de Vivre	1792 Massachusetts Ave	617-864-8188	Silly gifts, nostalgic toys, good stocking stuffers.
Lyndell's Bakery	720 Broadway	617-625-1793	Tasty pastries.
Paper Source	1810 Massachusetts Ave	617-497-1077	DIY paper crafts and quirky gifts.
Porter Square Books	25 White St	617-491-2220	Fiercely independent!
Roach's Sporting Goods	1957 Massachusetts Ave	617-876-5816	100 years of sporting goods, camp supplies, and guns.

Map 24 • Winter Hill / Union Square

Bombay Market	359 Somerville Ave	617-623-6614	Good Indian grocery, Bollywood movies.
Bostonian Florist	92 Highland Ave	617-629-9300	Florist.
Christmas Tree Shops	177 Middlesex Ave	617-623-3428	Everything including the kitchen sink.
Mudflat Studio	149 Broadway	617-628-0589	Pottery classes and studios.
Reliable Market	45 Union Sq	617-623-9620	Overflowing East Asian grocer.
Ricky's Flower Market	9 Union Sq	617-628-7569	Great outdoor market. Mind the traffic, though.

Map 25 • East Somerville / Sullivan Square

Home Depot	75 Mystic Ave	617-623-0001	Got wood?
Vinny's Superette	76 Broadway	617-628-1921	Damn good Italian cold-cuts.

Map 26 • East Cambridge / Kendall Square / MIT

Apple Store	100 Cambridgeside Pl	617-225-0442	Mac heaven in the Galleria.
Best Buy	100 Cambridgeside Pl	617-577-8866	Awful, annoying electronics retailer.
Calumet Photographic	65 Bent St	617-576-2600	High-end photo shop.
Cambridge Antique Market	201 Monsignor O'Brien Hwy	617-868-9655	Five floors to keep you busy.
Mayflower Poultry	621 Cambridge St	617-547-9191	Live poultry, fresh killed.

Map 27 · Central Square / Cambridgeport

Buckaroo's Mercantile	5 Brookline St	617-492-4792	Kitsch niche.
Cambridge Bicycle	259 Massachusetts Ave	617-876-6555	Bike shop near MIT.
Cheapo Records	538 Massachusetts Ave	617-354-4455	A treasure trove of older tunes.
Cremaldi's	31 Putnam Ave	617-354-7969	Gourmet shop.
Economy Hardware	438 Massachusetts Ave	617-864-3300	Hardware, household needs, cheap furniture. Very popular.
Great Eastern Trading Company	49 River St	617-354-5279	Like the Garment District's little sister on crack
Hubba Hubba	534 Massachusetts Ave	617-492-9082	Focusing on the naughty bits.
Looney Tunes	1001 Massachusetts Ave	617-876-5624	Records covered with the finest dust.
Micro Center	730 Memorial Dr	617-234-6400	Computer have-it-all. Avoid going on Saturdays.
Pearl Art & Craft Supplies	579 Massachusetts Ave	617-547-6600	Arts and crafts, Central Square style.
Shalimar	571 Massachusetts Ave	617-868-8311	Huge selection of spices.
Ten Thousand Villages	694 Massachusetts Ave	617-876-2414	Free-trade, handmade crafts from around the world.
Toscanini's	899 Main St	617-491-5877	In our opinion, Boston's best ice cream.
University Stationery	311 Massachusetts Ave	617-547-6650	A friendly little shop near MIT.

Map 28 · Inman Square

Boston Costume Company	200 Broadway	617-482-1632	Rentals and sales.
Boutique Fabulous	1309 Cambridge St	617-864-0656	Inman Square maxi-boutique.
Central Bakery	732 Cambridge St	617-547-2237	Unembellished interior and a menu with nothing over $3. Perfect.
Christina's Homemade Ice Cream	1255 Cambridge St	617-492-7021	Clever flavors; good spice shop next door.
The Garment District	200 Broadway	617-876-5230	Vintage threads, costumes, clothing by-the-pound.
Inman Square Market	1343 Cambridge St	617-354-8697	Independent quickie mart.
Royal Pastry	738 Cambridge St	617-547-2053	Caters to a devoted clientele.
Sadye & Company	121 Hampshire St	617-547-4424	Good antiques store.
Target	180 Somerville Ave	617-776-4919	Oh, you know.
Urban Oasis	243 Hampshire St	617-491-0176	Get hydrated in the community hot tubs.
Wine Cask	407 Washington St	617-623-8656	Wine, cheese, specialties.

Map 29 · West Roxbury

Irish Cottage	1898 Centre St	617-323-4644	Food, kitsch. Gag us with a shamrock.
Jack Davis Florist	2097 Centre St	617-323-6006	Florist.

Map 30 · Roslindale

Atlas Liquors	591 Hyde Park Ave	617-323-8202	Sousing the locals since 1933.
Boston Cheese Cellar	18 Birch St	617-325-2500	Free samples. European stinkies for $12.99/lb.
Droubi Bakery	748 South St	617-325-1585	Cheap veggies and fruit along with delicious Middle Eastern baked goods.
Emack & Bolio's	2 Belgrade Ave	617-323-3323	Innovative ice cream flavors.
Exotic Flowers	609 American Legion Hwy	617-247-2000	Florist.
Fornax Bread Baking Company	27 Corinth St	617-325-8852	Sandwiches, too.
Joanne Rossman: Purveyor of the Unnecessary & the Irresistible	6 Birch St	617-323-4301	Curios for the rich. Cool stuff, nice lady.
Pazzo Books	4268 Washington St	617-323-2919	Used and rare books with skeeball in the basement.
Roslindale Fish Market	38-39 Poplar St	617-327-9487	Come early for fresh fish.
Solera	12 Corinth St	617-469-4005	Wine.
Thrift Shop of Boston	17 Corinth St	617-325-5300	A small thrift store packed with tons of possible treasures and the friendliest staff!
Village Books	751 South St	617-325-1994	Beloved community bookstore.

Map 31 · Mattapan / Dorchester (West)

Dark Horse	2297 Dorchester Ave	617-298-1031	Antiques. Friendly.
Le Foyer Bakery	132 Babson St	617-298-0535	Long lines for patties at this Haitian bakery.
Taurus Records	182 Blue Hill Ave	617-298-2655	Small shop is best source for reggae, tons of singles.

Map 32 · Dorchester (East)

Asian Bookstore	1392 Dorchester Ave	617-822-9996	Tidy bookstore specializing in Vietnamese books.
Coleen's Flowershop	912 Dorchester Ave	617-282-0468	Cute florist on Dot Ave.
Greenhill's Irish Bakery	780 Adams St	617-825-8187	Soda bread, scones and sandwiches with blood pudding.

Map 33 · Hyde Park

Capone Foods	14 Bow St	617-629-2296	All your specialty food shop needs.
Marascio's Market	1758 River St	617-361-6847	Italian specialties.
Ron's Gourmet Ice Cream	1231 Hyde Park Ave	617-364-5274	Candlepins too!
Tutto Italiano	1893 River St	617-361-4700	Deli. A mayoral favorite.

Arts & Entertainment • **Movie Theaters**

There was a time when Bostonians could duck into the Cheri on Dalton Street for a flick, or take a movie-break where Barney's is now located after spending all their money at the Copley Plaza. These days the City of Boston has just two theaters showing the new Matt Damon vehicle or Pixar whimsy: **AMC Loews Boston Common (Map 3)** and **Regal Fenway 13 (Map 16)**. Both offer stadium seating and all the Milk Duds you can afford. Or head to Davis Square for popular first and second-run movies at the **Somerville Theater (Map 22)**.

To see a movie not primarily marketed to teenagers, check what's on at **Landmark Kendall Square Cinema (Map 26)**, **Brattle Theatre (Map 20)**, the **Harvard Film Archive (Map 20)**, the **Museum of Fine Arts (Map 15)**, or the Art Deco landmark **Coolidge Corner Theatre (Map 17)**.

From the end of June through the end of August, check out Free Friday Flicks at the **Hatch Shell (Map 6)** on the Esplanade. Movies start at sundown, but arrive early to get your spot on the grass. And for heaven's sake, don't forget to bring some wine and cheese.

Huge-screen freaks should hit the **Mugar Omni Theater (Map 1)** at the Museum of Science and the **Simons IMAX Theatre (Map 2)** at the New England Aquarium. If you just *have* to shop for furniture before seeing a movie, you owe yourself a trip to **Jordan's Furniture** (1 Underprice Wy, 508-424-0088) out in Natick where, for reasons we're still struggling to determine, there's an on-site 3-D IMAX theater. (Coming soon: Bernie & Phyl retaliate by building a drive-in behind their Saugus showroom…)

Movie Theater	Address	Phone		Map
AMC Loews Boston Common	175 Tremont St	617-423-3499	Blockbusters.	3
AMC Loews Harvard Square	10 Church St	617-864-4580	Get your *Rocky Horror* fix here.	20
Brattle Theatre	40 Brattle St	617-876-6837	*Casablanca*. Every year.	20
Coolidge Corner Theatre	290 Harvard St	617-734-2500	Theme nights and film festivals.	17
Entertainment Cinemas Fresh Pond	168 Alewife Brook Pkwy	617-661-2900	A bit sticky.	22
Harvard Film Archive	24 Quincy St	617-495-4700	Films you won't see at Boston Common.	20
Institute of Contemporary Art	100 Northern Ave	617-266-5152	Arty flicks, no Milk Duds.	10
Landmark Kendall Square Cinema	One Kendall Sq	617-499-1996	Movies for smart grown-ups.	26
Mugar Omni Theatre	Science Park	617-723-2500	Don't move your head, you'll puke.	1
Museum of Fine Arts	465 Huntington Ave	617-369-3770	Ever changing array, filmmaker Q&A.	15
National Amusements Circle Cinemas	399 Chestnut Hill Ave	617-566-2170	Numbinus buminus.	18
Regal Fenway Stadium 13	201 Brookline Ave	617-424-6266	On-site parking. Video games in the lobby.	16
Simons IMAX Theatre	Central Wharf	866-815-4629	Wicked big screen.	2
Somerville Theatre	55 Davis Sq	617-625-5700	Now serving beer and wine.	22

Newbury Street has Boston's largest and densest concentration of art galleries. You've probably passed by the several dozen galleries on Newbury Street many times without taking a look at what's inside, but popping into just a few of them will give you some idea of the broad scope of what's on offer (even if your budget means you're more likely to be striking deals at the MFA's gift shop). Commercial art fans should check out **International Poster Gallery's (Map 6)** expansive collection of Italian, travel, and Soviet-era posters. The gallery of the **Copley Society of Boston (Map 6)**, also on Newbury Street, hosts several competitions over the course of the year, including showcases of student work.

While Newbury Street galleries may have the city's most established spots, the interesting developments are happening in the South End, where a number of galleries have opened or relocated. The center of the action is the converted warehouse at 450 Harrison Avenue between Thayer Street and Randolph Street. (Take the Silver Line to East Berkeley Street, walk one block to Harrison Avenue, and hang a right.) Big names at the "SoWa Building" include **Bernard Toale Gallery (Map 7)**, **Kingston Gallery (Map 7)**, and **Genovese/Sullivan (Map 7)**. If you're interested in what's emerging in Boston's contemporary art scene, head to SoWa on the first Friday of the month to see the new exhibits. (At the very least, it's an excuse to get dressed up and consume some free wine.) Elsewhere in Boston, consider seeing what's on display at **Axiom Gallery (Map 14)** in Jamaica Plain's Green Street T station, the **Fort Point Arts Community Gallery (Map 10)**, Roxbury's **Hamill Gallery of African Art (Map 13)**, and Kenmore Square's **Panopticon Gallery of Photography (Map 15)**. Cheaper rents continue to attract artists to East Boston, where the newly reopened **Atlantic Works Gallery (Map 9)** holds regular exhibitions and potluck get-togethers.

In addition to standard galleries, many of the city's neighborhoods put on "open studio" events where you can satisfy your nosy streak by poking around the studios of artists willing to open them up to the public. Go to www.cityofboston.gov/arts.

Map 1 · Beacon Hill / West End

Gurari Collections	91 Charles St	617-3G7-9800
Judith Dowling Asian Art	133 Charles St	617-523-5211
Keiko Limited	121 Charles St	617-725-2888

Map 2 · North End / Faneuil Hall

Mayor's Art Gallery	1 City Hall Plaza, 3rd floor	617-635-3245
Scollay Square Gallery	1 City Hall Plaza, 3rd floor	617-635-3245

Map 3 · Downtown Crossing / Park Square / Bay Village

Barbara Krakow Gallery	10 Newbury St	617-262-4490
Comenos Fine Arts	9 Newbury St	617-262-9365
Howard Yezerski Gallery	14 Newbury St	617-262-0550
Miller Block Gallery	14 Newbury St	617-536-4650
Tepper Takayama Fine Arts	20 Park Plz	617-542-0557

Map 4 · Financial District / Chinatown

Gallery Anthony Curtis	186 South St	617-988-8119
JMW Gallery	144 Lincoln St	617-338-9097

Map 5 · Back Bay (West) / Fenway (East)

Kaji Aso Gallery	40 St Stephen St	617-247-1719
St George Gallery	245 Newbury St	617-450-0321

Map 6 · Back Bay (East) / South End (Upper)

Acme Fine Art	38 Newbury St	617-585-9551
Alfred J Walker Fine Art	162 Newbury St	617-247-1319
Alpha Gallery	38 Newbury St	617-536-4465
Arden Gallery	129 Newbury St	617-247-0610

Artful Hand Gallery	100 Huntington Ave	617-262-9601
Axelle Fine Arts Galerie Newbury	91 Newbury St	617-450-0710
Beth Urdang Gallery	129 Newbury St	61/-424-5550
Chase Gallery	129 Newbury St	617-859-7222
Childs Gallery	169 Newbury St	617-266-1108
Copley Society	158 Newbury St	617-536-5049
DTR Modern Galleries	167 Newbury St	617-424-9700
Eclipse Gallery	164 Newbury St	617-247-6730
French Library and Cultural Center	53 Marlborough St	617-912-0400
Galerie d'Orsay	33 Newbury St	617-266-8001
Gallery NAGA	67 Newbury St	617-267-9060
Guild of Boston Artists	162 Newbury St	617-536-7660
International Poster Gallery	205 Newbury St	617-375-0076
Judi Rotenberg Gallery	130 Newbury St	617-437-1518
Judy Ann Goldman Fine Art	14 Newbury St	617-424-8468
Kidder Smith Gallery	131 Newbury St	617-424-6900
L'Attitude Gallery and Sculpture Garden	218 Newbury St	617-927-4400
Lanoue Fine Art	160 Newbury St	617-262-4400
Martha Richardson Fine Art	38 Newbury St	617-266-3321
Martin Lawrence Galleries	77 Newbury St	617-369-4800
Mercury Gallery	8 Newbury St	617-859-0054
Newbury Fine Arts	29 Newbury St	617-536-0210
Nielsen Gallery	179 Newbury St	617-266-4835
Pepper Gallery	38 Newbury St	617-236-4497
Pucker Gallery	171 Newbury St	617-267-9473
Robert Klein Gallery	38 Newbury St	617-267-7997
Rolly-Michaux Gallery	290 Dartmouth St	617-536-9898
Royka's Gallery	213 Newbury St	978-582-8207
The Society of Arts and Crafts	175 Newbury St	617-266-1810
Victoria Munroe Fine Art	179 Newbury St	617-523-0661
Vose Galleries	238 Newbury St	617-536-6176

Map 7 · South End (Lower)

Allston Skirt Gallery	65 Thayer St	617-482-3652
Ars Libri	500 Harrison Ave	617-357-5212
BCA Mills Gallery	539 Tremont St	617-426-5000
Berenberg Gallery	4 Clarendon St	617-536-0800
Bernard Toale Gallery	450 Harrison Ave	617-482-2477

Boston Sculptors Gallery	486 Harrison Ave	617-482-7781
Bromfield Art Gallery	450 Harrison Ave	617-451-3605
Gallery AA/B	535 Albany St	617-574-0022
Gallery Kayafas	450 Harrison Ave	617-482-0411
Genovese/Sullivan Gallery	450 Harrison Ave	617-426-9738
Jules Place	1200 Washington St	617-542-0644
Kingston Gallery	450 Harrison Ave	617-423-4113
Laconia Gallery	433 Harrison Ave	617-426-5303
MPG Contemporary	450 Harrison Ave	617-357-8881
OHT Gallery	450 Harrison Ave	617-423-1677
OSP Gallery	450 Harrison Ave	617-778-5265
Qingping Gallery Teahouse	231 Shawmut Ave	617-482-9988
Samson Projects	450 Harrison Ave	617-357-7177
Soprafina	450 Harrison Ave	617-728-0770
Space Other	63 Wareham St	617-451-3500

Map 9 · East Boston

| Atlantic Works | 80 Border St | n/a |

Map 10 · South Boston (West) / Fort Point

| Fort Point Arts Community Gallery | 300 Summer St | 617-423-4299 |
| Studio Soto | 63 Melcher St | 617-426-7686 |

Map 11 · South Boston (East)

Artists Foundation	516 E 2nd St	617-464-3559
Crump McCole Gallery	200 Seaport Blvd	617-330-1133
Diana Levine Art Gallery	1 Design Ctr Pl	617-338-9060

Map 12 · Newmarket / Andrew Square

| Cambridge Mulitcultural Art Center | 41 Second St | 617-577-1400 |

Map 13 · Roxbury

| Hamill Gallery of African Art | 2164 Washington St | 617-442-8204 |

Map 14 · Jamaica Plain

| Axiom | 141 Green St | n/a |
| JP Art Market | 36 South St | 617-522-1729 |

Map 15 · Fenway (West) / Mission Hill

| Grossman Gallery at School of the Museum of Fine Arts | 230 Fenway | 617-369-3718 |

Map 16 · Kenmore Square / Brookline (East)

| Boston University Art Gallery | 855 Commonwealth Ave | 617-353-3329 |
| Boston University Sherman Gallery | 775 Commonwealth Ave | 617-358-0295 |

| Brookline Arts Center | 86 Monmouth St | 617-566-5715 |
| Panopticon Gallery of Photography | 502 Commonwealth Ave | 617-267-8929 |

Map 17 · Coolidge Corner / Brookline Hills

| Artana | 1378 Beacon St | 617-879-3111 |
| Gateway Gallery | 62 Harvard St | 617-734-1577 |

Map 20 · Harvard Square / Allston (North)

Baak Gallery	35 Brattle St	617-354-0407
Cambridge Artists Cooperative	59A Church St	617-868-4434
Hurst Gallery	53 Mt Auburn St	617-491-6888
University Place Gallery	124 Mt Auburn St	617-876-0246

Map 21 · West Cambridge

| Kathryn Schultz Gallery | 25 Lowell St | 617-876-0246 |
| Mobilia Gallery | 358 Huron Ave | 617-876-2109 |

Map 22 · North Cambridge / West Somerville

| 38 Cameron | 38 Cameron Ave | 617-492-2848 |
| Nave Gallery | 155 Powderhouse Blvd | 617-625-4823 |

Map 24 · Winter Hill / Union Square

| Scat Gallery | 90 Union Sq | 617-628-8826 |

Map 25 · East Somerville / Sullivan Square

| Brickbottom Gallery | 1 Fitchburg St | 617-776-3410 |

Map 26 · East Cambridge / Kendall Square / MIT

| MIT List Visual Arts Center | 20 Ames St | 617-253-4680 |

Map 27 · Central Square / Cambridgeport

| Art Interactive | 130 Bishop Richard Allen Dr | 617-498-0100 |
| Gallery 263 | 263 Pearl St | 781-393-0000 |

Map 28 · Inman Square

Cambridge Arts Council Gallery	344 Broadway	617-349-4380
Out of the Blue Gallery	106 Prospect St	617-354-5287
Zeitgeist Gallery	186 Hampshire St	617-876-6060

Even bad books are books and, therefore, sacred.
—Gunther Grass (*The Tin Drum*)

Big

As in so many other US cities, **Barnes & Noble (Map 5, 16, 19)** and **Borders (Map 3, 26)** are the big dogs on the Boston bookstore scene. If you're shopping for a book, but not also for a low-fat latte or a high-fat chocolate croissant, get familiar with the large independents **Brookline Booksmith (Map 19)** and the 75-year-old **Harvard Book Store (Map 20)** (unaffiliated with the university). Both focus on new titles but have cellars that handle used books.

Used

Davis Square's **McIntyre & Moore Books (Map 22)** sells an array of used books, with a bent toward school textbooks. When in Roslindale, stop by **Pazzo Books** (4268 Washington St, 617-323-2919, Map 30) for used and rare books and a round of skee-ball on the old machine in the basement. Some people think **Raven Used Books (Map 20)** in Harvard Square delivers the best bang for your buck. A good place to find used guidebooks and fiction is **Rodney's Bookstore (Map 17, 27)**, with locations in both Central Square and Brookline. Downtown Crossing's **Brattle Book Shop (Map 3)** is a well-known used book specialist—check out the outdoor book racks on dry days. Also in Central Boston, and worth checking out for antiquarian books, are **Lame Duck Books (Map 20)** and **Commonwealth Books (Map 3, 16)**. There's also the **Boston Book Annex (Map 16)**, sloppy but well stocked, a fun place for cat lovers and long-term browsing.

Specialty

Quantum Books (Map 26) is the best computer bookstore in the city. The **MIT Press Bookstore (Map 26)** is the best for social sciences, philosophy, economics, and sciences—pretty much everything MIT is best for. For little kids, take a look at Brookline's **Children's Book Shop (Map 17)**. Slightly older kids

who dig gaming will enjoy **Pandemonium (Map 27)**. **Ars Libri (Map 7)** has an exemplary collection of rare and out-of-print fine art books. The only remaining LGBT bookstore in Boston is **Calamus (Map 4)**, near South Station. A big tip of the chapeau is due to **Schoenhof's Foreign Books (Map 20)** for its broad selection. **James & Devon Grey Booksellers (Map 20)** specializes in books printed before 1700. **Lucy Parsons Center (Map 6)**, in the South End, stocks many progressive titles. **Trident Booksellers & Café (Map 5)** stocks books and a good variety of mainstream and alternative magazine titles, in addition to serving a mean breakfast.

Cambridge

Several years ago there were more than 25 bookstores in Harvard Square, the greatest concentration of bookstores in the city (and perhaps the country). No longer. Blame high rents, online retail, large chains dominating the market, or a general waning interest in the printed arts, but the sad fact is that many fine shops have packed it in. That being said, there are still a lot of friggin' bookstores and they range from the nuanced to the Coop. Headlining the niche category is NFT's favorite travel bookshop, **Globe Corner Travel (Map 20)**—it fits into the "glad it exists" category (note the new location). **Grolier Poetry Book Shop (Map 20)**, a national poetry landmark, is nothing less than a beacon of art in its tiny space on Plympton Street. Another Harvard Square stalwart is **Revolution Books (Map 20)**, a bookstore particularly conducive to raging against the machine. **The Harvard Coop (Map 20)** is managed by Barnes & Noble and unaffiliated with the school. The previously mentioned Raven, Schoenhof's, James & Devon Grey's, and probably three or four others round out a full day of page flipping. If the clogged walkways and impossible parking makes Harvard Square more trouble than it's worth, there's always **Porter Square Books (Map 23)** and Inman Square's **Lorem Ipsum (Map 28)**, the latter being one of the best resources for used fiction and literature in the area. Now get going, you bookworm.

Map 1 · Beacon Hill / West End

Commonwealth Books	2 Milk St	617-292-0065	Scholarly, used, antiquarian.
Suffolk University Bookstore	148 Cambridge St	617-227-4085	Schoolbooks and campus merchandise.

Map 2 · North End / Faneuil Hall

Newbury Comics	1 Washington Mall	617-248-9992	Comics.

Map 3 · Downtown Crossing / Park Square / Bay Village

Black Library Booksellers	Washington St & Summer St	617-442-2400	African-American literature.
Borders	10 School St	617-557-7188	General.
Brattle Book Shop	9 West St	617-542-0210	Used; outdoor racks when warm.
Commonwealth Books	134 Bolyston St	617-338-6328	Scholarly, used, antiquarian.
Emerson College Bookstore	114 Bolyston St	617-824-8696	Schoolbooks and campus merchandise.
Peter L Stern & Co	55 Temple Pl	617-542-2376	Antiquarian, especially first editions.
Suffolk Law School Book Store	110 Tremont St	617-227-8874	Schoolbooks and campus merchandise.

Map 4 · Financial District / Chinatown

Barbara's Best Sellers	2 S Station	617-443-0060	In South Station.
Calamus Bookstore	92 South St	617-338-1931	Gay & lesbian.
Central China Book Co	44 Kneeland St	617-426-0888	Chinese.
FA Bernett	144 Lincoln St	617-350-7778	Rare and scholarly art and architecture.
Tufts Medical Bookstore	116 Harrison Ave	617-636-6628	Schoolbooks and campus merchandise.
World Journal	216 Lincoln St	617-542-1230	Chinese.

Map 5 · Back Bay (West) / Fenway (East)

Barnes & Noble	800 Boylston St	617-247-6959	General.
Berklee College of Music Bookstore	1080 Boylston St	617-267-0023	Schoolbooks and campus merchandise.
Newbury Comics	332 Newbury St	617-236-4930	Now featuring a large DVD section.
Trident Booksellers & Café	338 Newbury St	617-267-8688	Independent; eclectic.

Map 6 · Back Bay (East) / South End (Upper)

Borders	511 Boylston St	617-236-1444	General.
Brentano's at Copley Place	100 Huntington Ave	617-859-9511	General.
Bromer Booksellers	607 Boylston St	617-247-2818	Fine, rare, and unusual.
Buddenbrooks Fine & Rare Books	31 Newbury St	617-536-4433	Fine, rare.
Lucy Parsons Center	549 Columbus Ave	617-267-6272	Progressive.

Map 7 · South End (Lower)

Ars Libri	500 Harrison Ave	617-357-5212	Rare and out-of-print books on art.
Boston University Medical Center Bookstore	700 Albany St	617-638-5496	Schoolbooks and campus merchandise.

Map 9 · East Boston

Avila's Christian Book Store	112 Chelsea St	617-569-2252	Religious.

Map 13 · Roxbury

Roxbury Community College Bookstore	1234 Columbus Ave	617-442-8150	Schoolbooks and campus merchandise.

Map 14 · Jamaica Plain

Boston Book Co	705 Centre St	617-522-2100	Antiquarian.
Jamaicaway Books & Gifts	676 Centre St	617-983-3204	Multicultural.
Rhythm & Muse	470 Centre St	617-524-6622	Independent.

Map 15 · Fenway (West) / Mission Hill

Emmanuel College Bookstore	400 The Fenway	617-264-7697	Schoolbooks and campus merchandise.
Mass College of Pharmacy & Art Bookstore	625 Huntington Ave	617-739-4772	Textbooks.
Medical Center Coop	333 Longwood Ave	617-499-3300	Schoolbooks and campus merchandise.
Northeastern University Bookstore	360 Huntington Ave	617-373-2286	Schoolbooks and campus merchandise.
Simmons College Book Store	300 The Fenway	617-521-2054	Schoolbooks and campus merchandise.
Wentworth Book Store	103 Ward St	617-445-8814	Textbooks.

Map 16 · Kenmore Square / Brookline (East)

Barnes & Noble at Boston University	660 Beacon St	617-267-8484	General/schoolbooks and campus merchandise.
Boston Book Annex	906 Beacon St	617-266-1090	Used.
Comicopia	464 Commonwealth Ave	617-266-4266	Comics.

Map 17 · Coolidge Corner / Brookline Hills

Book World	77 Harvard St	617-739-5768	Russian.
Children's Book Shop	237 Washington St	617-734-7323	Children's.
Horai-san	242 Washington St	617-277-4321	New age/spiritual.
New England Comics	316 Harvard St	617-566-0115	Comics.
Petropol	1428 Beacon St	617-232-8820	Russian.
Rodney's Bookstore	1362 Beacon St	617-232-0185	General.

Map 19 · Allston (South) / Brookline (North)

Barnes & Noble	325 Harvard St	617-232-0594	General.
Brookline Booksmith	279 Harvard St	617-566-6660	Independent; used book cellar.
Cheetah Trading	214 Lincoln St	617-451-1309	Chinese.
Harvard Business School Co-op	117 Western Ave	617-499-3245	Business.
Israel Bookshop	410 Harvard St	617-566-7113	Judaica.
The Kabbalah Center	14 Green St	617-566-0808	Religious.
Kolbo Fine Judaica	437 Harvard St	617-731-8743	Judaica.
Korean Book & Video (Korean & Japanese)	156 Harvard Ave	617-782-8874	Korean.
New England Comics	131 Harvard Ave	617-783-1848	Comics.

Map 20 · Harvard Square / Allston (North)

Ahab Rare Books	5 JFK St	617-547-5602	Antiquarian, rare books.
Atherton Antiquarian	5 JFK St, 4th Floor	617-547-2664	Old, rare books.
Curious George Goes to Wordsworth	1 JFK St	617-498-0062	Children's.
Globe Corner Book Stores	90 Mt Auburn St	617-497-6277	Travel.
Grolier Poetry Book Shop	6 Plympton St	617-547-4648	Poetry books.
Harvard Book Store	1256 Massachusetts Ave	617-661-1515	Independent, with an academic bent.

Harvard Coop	1400 Massachusetts Ave	617-499-2000	General/schoolbooks and campus merchandise.
Harvard Law School Coop	14 Everett St	617-499-3255	Law.
James & Devon Gray Booksellers	12 Arrow St	617-868-0752	Pre-18th-century.
Lame Duck Books	12 Arrow St	617-868-2022	Rare books, manuscripts, art.
Million Year Picnic	99 Mt Auburn St	617-492-6763	Comics.
New England Comics	14A Eliot St	617-354-5352	Comics.
Raven Used Books	52-B JFK St	617-441-6999	Scholarly used.
Revolution Books	1158 Massachusetts Ave	617-492-5443	Revolution.
Robin Bledsoe Books	1640 Massachusetts Ave	617-576-3634	Out-of-print books on horses and art.
Schoenhof's Foreign Books	76A Mt Auburn St	617-547-8855	Foreign languages.

Map 21 • West Cambridge

Bryn Mawr Book Store	373 Huron Ave	617-661-1770	Used and rare, stocked by donations.
Newbury Comics	211 Alewife Brook Pkwy	617-491-7711	Comics.

Map 22 • North Cambridge / West Somerville

Kate's Mystery Books	2211 Massachusetts Ave	617-491-2660	New and used mysteries.
McIntyre & Moore Books	255 Elm St	617-629-4840	Scholarly used.

Map 23 • Central Somerville / Porter Square

Barefoot Books	1771 Massachusetts Ave	617-349-1610	Picture books for the wee.
Barefoot Books	2067 Massachusetts Ave	617-576-0660	Picture books for the wee.
Comicazi	380 Highland Ave	617-623-2664	Comics.
Porter Square Books	25 White St	617-491-2220	Fiercely independent!

Map 24 • Winter Hill / Union Square

CPAD Bookstore	100 Washington St	617-625-1234	Brazilian.

Map 25 • East Somerville / Sullivan Square

Bunker Hill Community College Book Store	250 Rutherford Ave	617-241-5161	Textbooks.

Map 26 • East Cambridge / Kendall Square / MIT

Borders	100 Cambridgeside Pl	617-679-0887	General.
MIT Co-op	3 Cambridge Ctr	617-499-3200	Schoolbooks and campus merchandise.
MIT Press Bookstore	292 Main St	617-253-5249	MIT Press authors and quality trade.
Quantum Books	4 Cambridge Ctr	617-494-5042	Computer, technical.

Map 27 • Central Square / Cambridgeport

Bookmarx	550 Massachusetts Ave	617-354-2876	At the Center for Marxist Education.
Pandemonium	4 Pleasant St	617-547-3721	Sci-fi, fantasy, and gaming.
Rodney's Bookstore	698 Massachusetts Ave	617-876-6467	Used, out-of-print, remainders.
Seven Stars	731 Massachusetts Ave	617-547-1317	New Age.
Stratton Center Co-op	84 Massachusetts Ave	617-499-3240	Schoolbooks and campus merchandise.

Map 28 • Inman Square

Lorem Ipsum	157 Hampshire St	617-497-7669	Used.

If you're familiar with every painting at the **Gardner (Map 15)**, every print in the **MFA (Map 15)**, every fish in the **Aquarium (Map 2)**, and every cobblestone on the **Freedom Trail** (pg 189), then it's time to take it to the next level by ferreting out some of the city's hidden treasures and discovering something new about some old favorites.

The new facility of the **Institute of Contemporary Art (Map 10)**, whose design evokes a laptop, opened in the winter of 2006. If you're looking for a reason to make your way over to Fan Pier, here it is.

Release your inner child on a Friday night at the (newly expanded and renovated) **Boston Children's Museum (Map 4)**—from 5 pm to 9 pm, admission is just $1. Or, engage your inner adult at the **Museum of Science (Map 1)** with a cocktail (yes, a real cocktail), a movie in the Mugar Omni Theater, or free stargazing at the Gilliland Observatory.

If you want to take in some art during a drive out of town, check out the **DeCordova Museum and Sculpture Park** in Lincoln (not far from Route 2 and Route 128). The DeCordova's 35 acres of woodlands is the largest sculpture garden in New England. The contemporary American outdoor sculpture park changes its exhibitions on a regular basis. Admission to the sculpture park is $9 for adults, $6 for students, seniors, and children ages 6–12. Children five and under, as well as active duty military personnel, are admitted free. For more information, visit www.decordova.org.

And if all of those museums are just too good to be true, check out the **Museum of Bad Art (MOBA)** way out in Dedham (580 High St, 781-444-6757). Contemplate art so bad, it can't be ignored.

Museum	Address	Phone	Map
Ancient and Honorable Artillery Company	Faneuil Hall, 4th Fl	617-227-1638	2
Arthur M Sackler Museum	485 Broadway	617-495-9400	20
Boston Athenaeum	10 1/2 Beacon St	617-227-0270	1
Boston Children's Museum	300 Congress St	617-426-8855	10
Boston Tea Party Ship & Museum	Congress St Bridge	617-269-7150	10
(closed for renovations, scheduled to re-open fall 2008)			
Busch-Reisinger Museum	32 Quincy St	617-495-9400	20
Carpenter Center for Visual Arts	24 Quincy St	617-495-3251	20
Commonwealth Museum	220 Morrissey Blvd	617-727-9268	32
Fogg Art Museum	32 Quincy St	617-495-9400	20
Gibson House Museum	137 Beacon St	617-267-6338	6
Harrison Gray Otis House	141 Cambridge St	617-227-3956	1
Harvard Mineralogical & Geological Museum	24 Oxford St	617-495-3045	20
Harvard Museum of Comparative Zoology	26 Oxford St	617-495-3045	20
Harvard Museum of Natural History	26 Oxford St	617-495-3045	20
Institute of Contemporary Art	100 Northern Ave	617-473-3100	10
JFK National Historic Site	83 Beals St	617-566-7937	19
John F Kennedy Library and Museum	Morrissey Blvd & Columbia Pt	617-514-1600	32
Larz Anderson Auto Museum	15 Newton St, Brookline	617-522-6547	n/a
The Loring-Greenough House	12 South St	617-524-3158	14
Mapparium/Christian Science Museum	200 Massachusetts Ave	617-450-7000	5
MIT List Visual Arts Center	20 Ames St	617-253-4680	26
MIT Museum	265 Massachusetts Ave	617-253-4444	27
Museum of Afro-American History	46 Joy St	617-725-0022	1
Museum of Bad Art (MOBA)	580 High St, Dedham	781-444-6757	n/a
Museum of Fine Arts	465 Huntington Ave	617-267-9300	15
Museum of Science	Science Park	617-723-2500	1
National Center for Afro-American Artists	300 Walnut Ave	617-442-8614	13
New England Aquarium	Central Wharf	617-973-5200	2
Nichols House Museum	55 Mt Vernon St	617-227-6993	1
Old South Meeting House	310 Washington St	617-482-6439	3
Old State House	206 Washington St	617-720-1713	3
Paul Revere House	19 North Sq	617-523-2338	2
Peabody Museum of Archaeology and Ethnology	11 Divinity Ave	617-496-1027	20
The Semitic Museum at Harvard University	6 Divinity Ave	617-495-4631	20
Somerville Museum	1 Westwood Rd	617-666-9810	23
The Sports Museum	150 Causeway St	617-624-1234	1
USS Constitution Museum	Charlestown Navy Yard	617-426-1812	8
Warren Anatomical Museum	10 Shattuck St	617-432-6196	15

General Information

NFT Map: 10
Address: 100 Northern Ave
Phone: 617-478-3100
Website: www.icaboston.org
Hours: Tues, Wed, Sat, Sun: 10 am–5 pm; Thurs, Fri 10 am–9 pm; closed Mon, except on Martin Luther King, Jr. Day, Presidents' Day, Memorial Day, Labor Day, Columbus Day, and Veterans' Day. Closed Thanksgiving, Christmas, New Year's Day, and July 4.
Admission: $12 for adults, $10 for seniors; free to members and children under 17.

Overview

In 2006, the city's stodgy art scene got a royal kick in the rear when the Institute of Contemporary Art unveiled its new digs on South Boston's waterfront. The building's architecture by itself—an awe-inspiring modern masterpiece that offers a spectacular view of the harbor, an outdoor grandstand, and open gallery spaces—is well worth the museum's pricey $12 cover charge. Founded in 1936 as The Boston Museum of Modern Art, the original space was a cramped laboratory where artists were encouraged to make works that both inspired and provoked. Renamed in 1948, the ICA continued to push the envelope with a cavalcade of media, ranging from visual arts, film, video, performance, and literature. While many viewed video and digital media as the art scene's bastard stepchild in the '90s, the ICA embraced the marriage of visual design and technology.

In the past, the ICA offered Boston itself as a landscape for artists working on site-specific works. In 1998 for example, the museum hosted a collection of taped interviews featuring local mothers of murdered children.

The MoMA-ized new space continues the site-specific tradition with its Art Wall, located along the eastern interior of the museum's glass-enclosed lobby. Recent exhibitor Chiho Aoshima unleashed her digitally manipulated monster mural, "The Divine Gas," on the wall. Illustrated on a Macintosh G4 and printed on adhesive vinyl, the installation is a brazen statement with a Gothic sensibility. From Aoshima's mixed-media piece, it's almost like the ICA is shooting a metaphorical middle finger at those who doubted the impact digital media would eventually have on our cultural landscape.

What to See

While getting to the museum in South Boston is a bit of a pain (seriously, who takes the Silver Line?), the experience you'll have at the new site is worth the trek. The museum offers audio tours—narrated by exhibiting artists and ICA curators—you can easily download to your MP3 player. Don't have an iPod? They'll rent them out for a small fee. It's interesting to be able to listen to the inspiration behind something as vexing as Misaki Kawai's "Momentum 7," a free-floating home of the future inhabited by puppets juxtaposed with the voices from the ICA's permanent collection, with luminaries like Nan Goldin, Cornelia Parker, Thomas Hirschhorn, and Paul Chan.

Nestled beneath the museum's larger-than-life cantilever is the Poss Family Mediatheque where you have access to some of the museum's 18 computer stations. Here's where you can download clips with the art and artists featured at the ICA and check out the museum's footage-archive collection which offers a glimpse of exhibitions from the museum's past. Also, the Mediatheque is where you can experience the dramatic, horizonless view of the Boston Harbor.

Amenities

The museum is handicapped accessible. All bags (including your laptop) will be checked and stored in the lobby. The ICA has limited space to hang coats and it does not have its own parking garage. However, there's a paid lot immediately adjacent to the museum. Both the men's and women's restrooms are located on the first floor.

As far as food, Wolfgang Puck's Water Café offers another stellar view—not to mention some great French-bistro cuisine—where you can open the restaurant's glass doors for outdoor dining. For those who want to skip the art and head straight for the yummy pastries, museum admission is not required to dine.

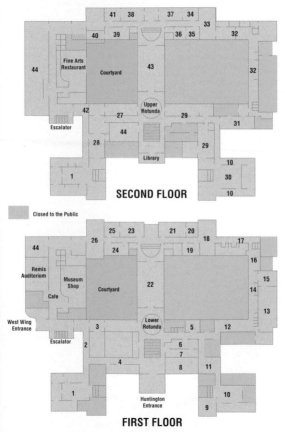

SECOND FLOOR

FIRST FLOOR

West Wing Entrance

Huntington Entrance

Closed to the Public

MAP
15

1. Japanese Art
2. Islamic Art
3. Brown Gallery
4. Indian Art
5. Egyptian Mummies
6. Graphics
7. Musical Instruments
8. Nubian Art
9. Etruscan Art
10. Greek Art
11. Near-Eastern Art
12. 18th-Century American Furniture
13. 18th-Century French Art
14. 18th-Century Boston
15. English-Silver
16. 19th-Century American
17. American Federal
18. Copley & Contemporary
19. American Neoclassical & Romantic
20. American Folk Painting
21. 19th-Century Landscape
22. American Modern
23. American Masters
24. Early 20th-Century American & European
25. Chinese Art
26. Egyptian Art
27. Roman Art
28. Medieval Art
29. Euro Decorative Arts
30. Impresses
31. 19th-Century French & English
32. Post-Impressionism
33. Coolidge Collection
34. 18th-Century Italian
35. Dutch & Flemish Art
36. Renaissance
37. Spanish Chapel
38. Baroque Art
39. Himalayan Art
40. Tapestries
41. Special Exhibitions

General Information

NFT Map:	15
Address:	465 Huntington Ave
	Boston, MA 02115
Phone:	617-267-9300
Website:	www.mfa.org

Overview

The Museum of Fine Arts is Boston's largest and most famous art institution. The extensive permanent collection of paintings and sculpture, as well as the various lectures, films, concerts, and special traveling exhibitions, offer something for one-time sightseers and regular visitors alike. While you're there soaking up a little sophistication, enjoy a meal at one of the museum's three restaurants, and buy an artifact from the gift shop or some of their little postcards with the pretty paintings on them. Why? Because the museum needs the money. Though it's one of the largest art museums in the country, it receives little public funding. This, in part, accounts for the high admission fee. But don't worry: You get what you pay for.

The MFA is in the middle of a mammoth project that will increase the size of the museum by 28%, with an expected finish date sometime in 2010. To replace the old east wing of the museum, the MFA is building a new, 60,000-square-foot four floor addition featuring the massive Art of the Americas collection. The new wing will focus heavily on the museum's peerless colonial art of New England collection, and will feature a gallery devoted entirely to John Singer Sargeant. Check the MFA's website for project details including the exciting-sounding Ruth and Carl J Shapiro Family Courtyard.

Hours

The museum is open Mon, Tues, Sat, and Sun 10 am–4:45 pm, and Wed–Fri 10 am–9:45 pm. Special exhibitions close 15 minutes before the museum closes. The gift shop is open until 5:30 pm on Saturdays and Sundays.

Admission Fees

Admission to the MFA costs $17 for adults, $15 for seniors and college students, and $6.50 for kids 7–17 on school days until 3 pm (free at all other times). School group visits are discounted but must be scheduled in advanced.

Paid admission entitles visitors to one free visit within ten days of ticket purchase. On Wednesday evenings 4 pm–9:45 pm, admission is by voluntary contribution.

Tickets for entry can be purchased at the museum. Tickets for concerts, films, lectures, or special exhibitions can be purchased at the museum or online at www.mfa.org.

How to Get There—Driving

From the north, take I-93 S to Exit 26 (Storrow Drive). From Storrow Drive, take the Fenway/Kenmore exit. From the exit, take a left at the first traffic light, heading toward Boylston Street inbound. At the second traffic light, bear right onto The Fenway and proceed to the next set of lights. After passing through two stone gates, take the first right onto Hemenway Street and proceed to the end of the street. Take a left onto Forsythe Way and then a right onto Huntington Avenue. The museum is located a few lights down and on your right. Go past the museum and turn right onto Museum Road to reach the museum's parking lots.

From the south, take I-93 N to Exit 18 and follow the signs for Massachusetts Avenue. Turn right on Massachusetts Avenue, go past Columbus Avenue, and then turn left onto St. Botolph Street. Drive one block and turn right onto Gainsborough Street. Drive one block and turn left onto Huntington Avenue. The museum will be a couple of blocks down on your right. Go past the museum and turn right onto Museum Road to reach the museum's parking lots.

From the west, take the Mass Pike (I-90) E. Upon approaching the Boston city limits, look for Exit 22 (Prudential Center/Copley Square), the first exit after the Cambridge/Brighton toll plaza. You will enter a tunnel and Exit 22 will be on your right. Once on the exit ramp, get into the left lane (Prudential Center) and follow the exit to Huntington Avenue. Follow Huntington Avenue past the Christian Science Center (go through the underpass) and Northeastern University. The museum is located a few lights down on the right. Drive past the museum and turn right onto Museum Road to reach the museum's parking lots.

Parking

There is limited parking available at the museum, including two parking lots on Museum Road. Museum members pay $3.00 for each half-hour, $12 maximum. Non-members pay $4.00 for each half-hour with a $22 maximum for the day. A far cheaper option is public transportation.

How to Get There—Mass Transit

The museum is close to the Green Line's Museum stop (E train only) or the Orange Line's Ruggles stop. You can also take the 39 bus to the Museum stop or the 8 bus, 47 bus, or CT2 bus to the Ruggles stop.

Children's Museum of Boston

General Information

Address: 300 Congress Street
Boston, MA 02210

Phone: 617-426-6500

Website: www.bostonchildrensmuseum.org

Hours: Daily 10 am–5 pm; Fridays 10 am–9 pm.
Closed Thanksgiving and Christmas

Admission: General Admission $10, Seniors $8,
Children (Aged 2–15) $8,
Children (Under 2) $2;
Members are free.
Friday nights 5 pm–9 pm, $1 for everybody.

Overview

A word of advice to adults visiting the Boston Children's Museum: Bring earplugs. The sound of children delighting in scientific wonder can be deafening, and this interactive hands-on museum tends to be very crowded, even on weekdays. The exhibits are fun even for adults, who most likely have forgotten everything they learned in middle school science classes, but if you've ever driven the mean streets of Boston you'll appreciate how difficult it is to fight for space at many of the activities.

Created by a group of teachers in Jamaica Plain in 1913, the Boston Children's Museum moved to its current location near Fort Point Channel on the waterfront in 1979. The goal of the original museum was to teach kids about nature, cultural diversity, and science through hands-on experiences. In the 1960s, the museum expanded and became an innovator in the concept of interactive exhibits, and today there are over 16 permanent learning areas.

Now occupying a former wool factory on the prized Boston waterfront, the small and crowded Children's Museum went through a much needed renovation and expansion in 2007. A new glass-paneled addition borders the newly expanded Harborwalk, with open spaces for additional outdoor exhibits, summer concerts, and special events. More space means more exhibits, including a 3-story climbing maze (New Balance Climb), a health and fitness area with bikes, basketballs, and interactive dance activities in Kid Power, and a brand new 160-seat theater at the Kid Stage. Popular areas include the Science Playground, where kids can engage in scientific exploration, the Japanese silk merchant's house, which is an actual house transported to the museum, the Arthur exhibit, where kids can become a part of the famous children's book and TV series, and the PlaySpace for kids under three.

The outdoor area is still being developed, but there is a Nature trail, boulders to climb on, and a waterfront park to eat lunch, escape the kids, or just sit by the water with a view of the Boston skyline. Disconcertingly, a museum promoting kids' education and healthy development once housed a McDonald's, but since the renovation, it has been replaced by the somewhat healthier Au Bon Pain. The museum is a nonprofit institution which also offers workshops, seminars, and classroom kits for teachers in their Teacher Leadership Center. Check its Website or call about special events and concerts during the summer.

How to Get There—Driving

From the north: Take I-93 South to Exit 23 "Purchase Street." At the first set of lights, take a left onto Seaport Boulevard. At the next light, take a right onto Sleeper Street. The museum is on your right.

From the south: Take I-93 North to Exit 20 "South Station/I-90." Follow signs for I-90 East, and once in the tunnel, take the first exit, labeled "South Boston." At the end of the ramp, go straight onto East Service Road. At the next intersection, turn left onto Seaport Boulevard. At the first set of lights, turn left onto Sleeper Street. The museum is on the right.

From the east: Take I-90 West to Exit 25 "South Boston." At the end of the ramp, go straight onto B Street. At the next light, take a left onto Seaport Boulevard. At the third set of lights, turn left onto Sleeper Street. The museum is on your right.

From the west: Take I-90 East towards Logan Airport. Once in the tunnel, take Exit 25 "South Boston." At the top of the ramp, bear left towards "Seaport Boulevard." At the next set of lights, stay straight onto East Service Road all the way to the end. At the next light, turn left onto Seaport Boulevard. At the second set of lights, turn left onto Sleeper Street. The museum is on your right.

Parking

The museum doesn't have its own lot or garage, but there are discounted prices for nearby lots. Both the Farnsworth Street Garage (two blocks away) and the Stillings Street Garage (four blocks away) are $9 on weekdays and $6 on weekends with museum validation. Farther away is the Moakley Courthouse Parking Lot. Street parking is hard to find and not recommended.

How to Get There—Mass Transit

Commuter rail and the MBTA Red Line and Silver Line drop you off at South Station, which is about a five minute walk away. The MBTA Silver Line stop at Courthouse Station is only a block away. Bus #4, 6, 7, and #11 all stop at South Station.

Boston may not have the Great White Way, but the theater scene—including musical venues—is alive and vibrant; you just might have to look a little harder for it. Where to start looking? Well, the most enthused patron of theatre in the region is Larry Stark of www.theatermirror.com. If there's a production taking place anywhere within 100 miles, Larry and his cast of writers are all over it. The *Boston Phoenix* and *Dig* will also point you to good productions.

Broadway in Boston runs popular mainstream shows (e.g. *Wicked, Swan Lake, Les Miserables*) at Boston's flagship theaters such as the **Wang Theatre (Map 3)**, neighboring **Shubert Theater (Map 3)**, and the newly-restored **Opera House (Map 3)**. These theaters also produce readings, dance, and a wide variety of performances. Also of note in the Theater District: **Tribe Theatre (Map 6)** which hosts a mix of improv and irreverent performances, Emerson's **Cutler Majestic Theatre (Map 3)**, and the **Charles Playhouse (Map 3)**, with long-running favorites *Blue Man Group* and *Shear Madness*.

Away from the clamor of the Theater District down Tremont Street, you'll find the newly expanded **Boston Center for the Arts (Map 7)**, containing four performance spaces that accommodate fare ranging from *Forbidden Broadway* to one-man shows. **The Lyric Stage Company (Map 6)** nearby on Clarendon Street showcases wide-ranging seasons. The **Huntington Theatre (Map 5)** attracts top-name actors in local productions, while the **American Repertory Theater (ART) (Map 20)** in Cambridge features renowned innovative stagings.

For something a little different, check out the **Puppet Showplace Theater (Map 17)** in Brookline. For laughs, try Inman Square's **ImprovBoston (Map 28)** or the North End's **ImprovAsylum (Map 2)** (both, despite the names, do more than just improv). Scattered, smaller theaters worth a look include **Boston Playwrights' Theatre (Map 19)**, associated with BU, and the **Publick Theatre (Map 19)**, which stages open-air Shakespeare productions by the Charles River. If you like a real local flavor in your theater, check out a performance at **Jimmy Tingle's Off-Broadway Theater (Map 22)**, especially if the man himself is performing.

If you're more of a choir and orchestra person, keep your eye on what's playing at the **Sanders Theatre (Map 20)**, which also hosts the occasional play, film, or roots concert. Located in Harvard's Memorial Hall, Sanders Theatre offers terrific acoustics in a classic interior. Built to offer a 180-degree perspective for the audience, the theater was inspired by a Christopher Wren design. And of course, the Boston Symphony Orchestra at **Symphony Hall (Map 5)** has a thing or two to offer as far as classical music goes. The acoustics just can't be beat.

You can pick up half-price, same-day tickets at the BosTix booth in Copley Square or at Faneuil Hall Marketplace (both accept cash only). You can find out performances for which tickets are available at www.bostix.org.

Theater	Address	Phone	Map
BCA Plaza Black Box	539 Tremont St	617-426-5000	7
Berklee Performance Center	136 Massachusetts Ave	617-747-2261	5
Blackman Auditorium/Studio Theatre	360 Huntington Ave	617-373-2247	15
Boston Center for the Arts	527 Tremont St	617-426-5000	7
Boston Children's Theater	321 Columbus Ave	617-424-6634	6
Boston Opera House	539 Washington St	617-259-3400	3
Boston Playwrights' Theatre	949 Commonwealth Ave	617-353-5443	5
Charles Playhouse	74 Warrenton St	617-426-6912	3
Colonial Theatre	106 Boylston St	617-426-9366	3
Cutler Majestic Theatre at Emerson College	219 Tremont St	617-824-8000	3
Devanaugh Theatre at The Piano Factory	791 Tremont St	617-247-9777	13
Footlight Club	7A Eliot St	617-524-3200	14
Huntington Theatre Company	264 Huntington Ave	617-266-0800	5
ImprovAsylum	216 Hanover St	617-263-6887	2
ImprovBoston	1253 Cambridge St	617-576-1253	28
Jorge Hernandez Cultural Center	85 W Newton St	866-811-4111	7
Kresge Little Theatre	48 Massachusetts Ave	617-253-6294	27
Loeb Drama Center	64 Brattle St	617-547-8300	20
Lyric Stage Company	140 Clarendon St	617-437-7172	6
Nancy and Edward Roberts Studio Theater	539 Tremont St	617-426-5000	7
Orpheum Theatre	1 Hamilton Pl	617-679-0810	3
The Publick Theatre	1400 Soldiers Field Rd	617-782-5425	19
Puppet Showplace Theatre	32 Station St	617-731-6400	17
Remis Auditorium	465 Huntington Ave	617-369-3770	15
Sanders Theatre	45 Quincy St	617-496-2222	13
Semel Theatre at Emerson College	10 Boylston Pl	617-824-8364	3
Shubert Theatre	265 Tremont St	617-482-9393	3
Stuart Street Playhouse	200 Stuart St	617-426-4499	3
Symphony Hall	301 Massachusetts Ave	617-266-1492	5
Theater at Zero Arrow Street	0 Arrow St	617-547-8300	20
Theatre Cooperative	277 Broadway	n/a	24
Tower Auditorium	621 Huntington Ave	617-879-7000	15
Tribe Theater	67 Stuart St	617-510-4447	6
Virginia Wimberley Theatre	539 Tremont St	617-266-0800	7
Wang Center for Performing Arts	265 Tremont St	617-482-9393	3
Wang Theatre	270 Tremont St	617-482-9393	3
Wheelock Family Theatre	180 The Riverway	617-879-2000	16
Wilbur Theatre	106 Boylston St	617-423-4008	3

BOSTON POPS SEATING

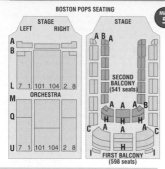

BOSTON SYMPHONY ORCHESTRA SEATING

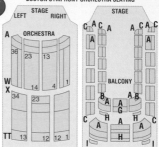

MAP 5

General Information

NFT Map: 5
Address: 301 Massachusetts Ave, Boston, MA 02115
Website: www.bostonsymphonyhall.org
Phone: 617-266-1492
Tickets: 617-266-1200; www.bso.org

Overview

Boston Symphony Hall, home of the Boston Symphony Orchestra and Boston Pops, is regarded as one of the finest concert halls in the world. Modeled after the German Leipzig Gewandhaus and the old Boston Music Hall, Symphony Hall was the first American hall designed to maximize acoustics, thanks to Harvard physics professor Wallace Clement Sabine (and to think you slept through your physics class!). Classical music connoisseurs recognize the hall as a space that produces a near-perfect sound experience, thanks to the sloping walls and floor of the stage and the alignment of the recessed Greek and Roman statues. The Hall, designed by New York architects McKim, Mead, & White, opened in 1900, replacing the Boston Music Hall, which was in the way of the burgeoning subway system. The hall seats 2,625 people in the Boston Symphony Orchestra (BSO) season and 2,371 in the Boston Pops Orchestra season (in the original leather seats from 1900). Don't leave without checking out the Aeolian-Skinner organ with 67 stops and 5,130 pipes. Free tours offer an insight into the history and features of Symphony Hall.

Symphony Hall contains dozens of museum-like items documenting notable events in its history. You can learn just what was so revolutionary about the acoustics and famous composers. Excitement and pride leaps from a reprinted *Boston Globe* article documenting the first performance. A 2006 renovation of the concert floor rebuilt it using the original processes, equipment manufacturers, and the exact same materials, in order to retain its premium acoustic properties.

In the past the Hall has hosted auto shows, mayoral inaugurations, meetings of the Communist Party, and a performance by Harry Houdini. You can also celebrate New Year's in style here as the orchestra performs in the background. (Bring your tux.) The tradition of hosting non-traditional events looks set to continue. In recent years, the US Open Squash Tournament has been held at Symphony Hall, using portable glass courts placed just below the stage.

If you're looking to throw your own Diddy-like party, function rooms and hall spaces can be rented for your own private shindig.

But unless you're making Manny Ramirez-style money, you probably can't afford it. Renting out Symphony Hall for a night costs between $4,700 and $6,200. Five different function spaces are available for rent and cost between $700 and $2,700 per night.

How to Get Tickets

You can purchase tickets to any of the Symphony Hall performances online at www.bso.org, in person at the Symphony Hall box office, or by phone on 617-266-1200 or 617-638-9283 (TDD/TTY).

How to Get There—Driving

From the north, take I-93 to Storrow Drive (Exit 26). Once you're on Storrow Drive, bear left towards Copley Square/Back Bay. Turn right onto Beacon Street. Turn left onto Clarendon Street. Turn right onto St. James Avenue. Bear left onto Huntington Avenue. Symphony Hall is on the corner of Huntington Avenue and Massachusetts Avenue.

From the south, take I-93 to Exit 18 and follow signs toward Massachusetts Avenue. Turn right onto Massachusetts Avenue.

From the west, take the Mass Pike (I-90) to the Prudential Center/Copley Square (Exit 27) and merge onto Huntington Avenue. Symphony Hall is on the corner of Huntington Avenue and Massachusetts Avenue.

Parking

There are two pay parking garages on Westland Avenue, another parking garage on Gainsborough Street next to Jordan Hall at the New England Conservatory, and very limited street parking. The Prudential Center Garage offers discount parking with the presentation of a performance ticket stub from the same day if you enter the garage after 5 pm.

How to Get There—Mass Transit

The Green Line's E train stops at Symphony Hall. Other Green Line trains that stop at the Hynes Convention Center will get you close. Another option is to take the Orange Line to the Massachusetts Avenue stop.

The #1 bus, which runs down Massachusetts Avenue from Harvard Square to Dudley Square, stops mere feet from Symphony Hall.

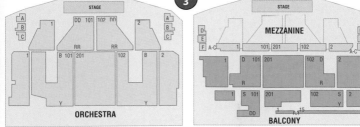

General Information

NFT Map: 3
Address: One Hamilton Pl, Boston, MA 02108
Website: www.ticketmaster.com/venue/8318
Phone: 617-679-0810
Ticketmaster: www.ticketmaster.com

Overview

The Orpheum has been around since 1852, and despite renovations, it can still feel like its age, which many consider part of the charm. (Apparently, they have not heard of this thing called The Internet either...) The Orpheum originally had an eye on high-brow stuff: Tchaikovsky along with the Boston Symphony Orchestra made debuts there. Now, it packs in close to 3,000 people to witness an eclectic lineup of acts ranging from Larry the Cable Guy to Norah Jones to Nine Inch Nails, and tickets often sell out quickly. Bands love the Orpheum for its premium acoustics (several live albums have been recorded here), and view-wise there isn't a bad seat in the house, though leg room is notably sparse.

How to Get Tickets

Tickets can be purchased from the Orpheum Theater Box Office Mon–Sat, 10 am–5 pm. Tickets can also be purchased online at www.ticketmaster.com or by calling 617-679-0810.

How to Get There—Driving

From the north, take I-93 S to Exit 24A (Government Center). At the bottom of the ramp, bear right onto New Chardon Street. At the second set of lights, take a left onto Cambridge Street. Stay on the right-hand side of Cambridge Street, which will become Tremont Street as soon as you pass City Hall Plaza (on your left). Drive two blocks down Tremont Street. The Orpheum will be on your left on Hamilton Place.

From the south, take I-93 N to Exit 23 (Government Center). At the end of the ramp, follow signs for Government Center/Faneuil Hall. At the set of lights, make a left onto North Street. Drive a quarter-mile to the end of North Street, then make a left onto Congress Street. Take your first right onto State Street, which turns into Court Street after a few feet. Follow Court Street to the end, then make a left at the fork onto Tremont Street. Drive two blocks farther on Tremont Street. The Orpheum will be on your left on Hamilton Place.

From the west, take the Mass Pike (I-90) E to Exit 24B, which will dump you onto I-93 N. From there follow the directions above for driving from the south.

Parking

Street parking will be scarce, especially during event hours. The closest parking lots are on Tremont Street, under Boston Common, and on Washington Street.

How to Get There—Mass Transit

Take the Red or Green Line to the Park Street stop or the Orange Line to Downtown Crossing. The theater is just a short walk from both stops. It's directly across from the Park Street Church.

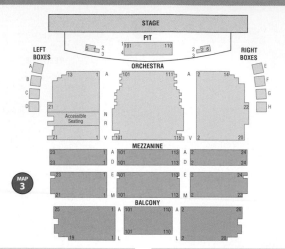

General Information

NFT Map: 3
Address: 270 Tremont St, Boston, MA 02116
Website: www.citicenter.org
Phone: 617-482-9393
Tele-charge: www.telecharge.com, 800-447-7400

Overview

The Shubert Theatre is the "Little Princess" to the Wang Theatre's "Grand Dame." The 1,600-seat venue opened in 1910 and has since undergone two major renovations. The theater's elaborate entranceway was destroyed during the widening of Tremont Street in 1925, and in 1996, $6 million was spent restoring and improving the theater's original ornate French Renaissance architecture. The intimacy within the Shubert remained intact, and the theater is now the home of the Boston Lyric Opera, many Boston arts organizations, as well as several touring companies. Broadway shows, including such classics as The King and I and South Pacific, debuted at the Shubert before making their way to New York. Once part of the not-for-profit Wang Center for the Performing Arts, both theaters have sadly had to sell off naming rights in an attempt to stay solvent. The Wang and Shubert are now owned by the Citigroup umbrella and carry the Citi moniker in front of their traditional names.

How to Get Tickets

You can purchase tickets for the Shubert Theatre online at www.telecharge.com or by calling Tele-charge at 800-447-7400.

How to Get There—Driving

From the north, take I-93 S to Exit 23 (South Station), which dumps you onto Purchase Street. Immediately after the Chinatown Gate (on your right), take a right onto Kneeland Street. Go straight for several blocks and then turn left onto Tremont Street. The Shubert Theatre is on your right.

From the south, take I-93 N to Exit 20 (South Station) and immediately get into the left-hand lane. The sign overhead will read "Detour South Station via Frontage Road." Take this left exit off the ramp and follow Frontage Road north to South Station. Turn left onto Kneeland Street. Go straight for several blocks, and then turn left onto Tremont Street. The Shubert Theatre is on your right.

From the west, take the Mass Pike (I-90) E to Exit 24A. Turn left onto Kneeland Street. Go straight for several blocks and then turn left onto Tremont Street. The Shubert Theatre is on your right.

Parking

Your best bets are the parking lot on the corner of Tremont and Stuart Streets, the lot at the Radisson Hotel on Stuart Street, the Kinney Motor Mart on Stuart Street, or the Fitz-Inn lot on Kneeland Street.

How to Get There—Mass Transit

The Orange Line's New England Medical Center stop and the Green Line's Boylston Street stop are both one block away from the theater. The Red Line's Park Street stop on Tremont Street is three or so blocks from the theater.

General Information

NFT Map:	3
Address:	270 Tremont St, Boston, MA 02116
Website:	www.citicenter.org
Phone:	617-482-9393
Tele-charge:	www.telecharge.com,
	800-447-7400

Overview

Surviving several name changes and heavy renovation over the years, the Wang Theatre has remained a prominent feature of the Boston theater scene. With 3,600 seats, it is the larger of the two performance spaces once operated by the Wang Center for the Performing Arts and now owned by Citigroup (the other is the famous Shubert Theatre) across the street). Though the Wang and Shubert keep their names, the complex is now known as the Citi Performing Arts Center.

Opened in the "Roaring Twenties" (1925) as the Metropolitan Theatre, the venue was considered to be a "magnificent movie cathedral" with its ornate interior resembling something from Louis XIV's palace. Renamed the Music Hall in 1962, the theater became home to the then-fledgling Boston Ballet. As the years passed, the shiny gem began to lose some of its luster and relevance. Some minor renovations were made, but it wasn't until 1983, when Dr. An Wang stepped in to resuscitate the theater, that things took a turn for the better. Since the restoration, the theater has played host to such classics as *Les Miserables*, *The Phantom of the Opera* , and *Spamalot*, and still houses one of New England's largest movie screens. Although the Wang has expanded its repertoire to include pop concerts and comedians. The *Nutcracker at the Wang* (snicker...) holiday tradition is no more (it moved to The Opera House), replaced by the very un-Boston "Radio City Christmas Spectacular" featuring high-kicking Rockettes wearing reindeer antlers.

How to Get Tickets

You can purchase tickets for the Wang Theatre online at www.telecharge.com or by calling Tele-charge at 800-447-7400. The Wang Theatre Box Office, open Monday through Saturday from 10 am until 6 pm, sells tickets without the nasty service charges levied by external vendors.

How to Get There—Driving

From the north, take I-93 S to Exit 20A (South Station), which dumps you onto Purchase Street. Immediately after the Chinatown Gate (on your right) take a right onto Kneeland Street. Go straight for several blocks and then turn left onto Tremont Street. The Wang Theatre is on your left.

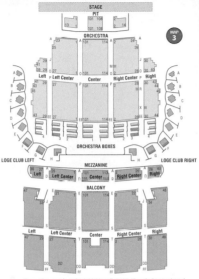

From the south, take I-93 N to Exit 20 (South Station) and immediately get into the left-hand lane. Follow signs for South Station and take the left exit for South Station/Chinatown. At the second light, turn left onto Kneeland Street. Go straight for several blocks, turn left onto Tremont Street. The Wang Theatre is on your left.

From the west, take the Mass Pike (I-90) E to Exit 24A. Turn left onto Kneeland Street. Go straight for several blocks and then turn left onto Tremont Street. The Wang Theatre is on your left.

Parking

Your best bets are the parking lot on the corner of Tremont and Stuart Streets, the lot at the Radisson Hotel on Stuart Street, the Kinney Motor Mart on Stuart Street, or the Fitz-Inn lot on Kneeland Street.

How to Get There—Mass Transit

The Orange Line's New England Medical Center stop and the Green Line's Boylston Street stop are both one block away from the theater. The Red Line's Park Street stop on Tremont Street is about three blocks from the theater.

WHAT IS *THAT?!*

HUH? OH, IT'S
WWW.NOTFORTOURISTS.COM

BUT WHY?!
WHY WOULD YOU
USE ANYTHING
OTHER THAN ME?

WELL, THE WEBSITE
JUST OFFERS A FEW THINGS
THAT YOU DON'T: DAILY
CONTENT, FUN PHOTOS,
SEARCHABLE DATABASE...
COOL STUFF LIKE THAT.

DEVASTATED

OH...
I SEE...

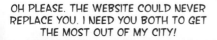

...unexpected necessities...

Black Ink
Harvard Square
5 Brattle Street
Cambridge

Black Ink
Beacon Hill
101 Charles Street
Boston

www.BlackInkBoston.com

LIFE,
LIBERTY
AND THE
PURSUIT OF
HAPPY HOUR
>JOIN THE PARTY
SVEDKA
Imported Swedish
VODKA
Product of Sweden

Where do you go when your desire to help is larger than your zip code?

You go to Morocco, Mongolia, or 71 other countries. And when you return, your own community will benefit in ways you can't imagine.

PEACE CORPS

800.424.8580
www.peacecorps.gov

Life is calling.
How far will you go?

Street Index

Street Index

Street Index

Street Index

Street Index

Street Index

Cambridge

Street Index

Beech St	23	B1/B2
Bell Ct	27	B1
Bellevue Ave	20	A1
W Bellevue Ave	20	A1
Bellis Cir	22	B1
Bellis Ct	22	B1
Belmont Ct	22	A1
Belvidere Pl	27	A1
Bennett St	20	B1
Bent St	26	A1/A2/B1
Berkeley Pl	20	A1
Berkeley St	20	A1
Berkshire Pl	28	B2
Berkshire St	28	B2
Bigelow St	27	A1
Binney St	26	A1/A2/B1
Birch St	21	A1
Bishop Richard Allen Dr	27	A1/A2
Blackstone St	27	A1
Blair Pl	22	B1
Blake St	23	A1
Blakeslee St	21	A2/B2
Blanche St	27	A2/B2
Boardman Pl	28	B2
Boardman St	28	B2
Bolton St	22	B1
Bond Ct	20	A1
Bow St	20	B2
Bowdoin St	20	A1/A2
Boyle Ter	21	A2
Bradbury St	20	B1
Brattle Sq	20	B1
Brattle St		
(1-147)	20	A1/B1/B2
(148-227)	21	B1/B2
Brewer St	20	B1
Brewster St	21	B2
Bristol St	28	B2
Broadway		
(1-189)	26	B1
(190-472)	28	A1/B1/B2
(473-501)	21	B2
Broadway Ct	28	B1
Broadway Ter	28	B1
Brookford St	22	A1
Brookline St	27	A2/B1/B2
Brown St	20	A1
Bryant St	20	A2
Buckingham Pl	20	A1
Buckingham St	20	A1
Buena Vista Park	22	B2
Burns Ct	20	A1
Cadbury Rd	21	A2
Callender St	27	A1
Cambridge Ctr	26	B1
Cambridge Pky	26	A2
Cambridge St		
(1-703)	26	A1/A2/B2
(704-1724)	28	A1/B1/B2
(1725-1899)	20	A2/B2
Cambridge Ter	22	B2
Cambridge Park Dr	22	B1
Cambridgeside Pl	26	A2
Camden St	20	B1
Camelia Ave	28	A1
Camp St	20	B1
Canal Park	26	A2
Cardinal Medeiros Ave	28	B2
Carleton St	26	B1
Carlisle St	28	B2
Carver St	20	A2
Cedar Sq	22	A1
Cedar St	22	A1/B1
Central Sq	27	A1
Centre St	27	A1
Chalk St	27	A1/B1
Channing Cir	21	B2
Channing Pl	21	B2
Channing St	21	B2
Chapman St	20	B1
Charles St	26	A1/A2/B1
Chatham St	28	A1
Chauncy Ln	20	A1
Chauncy St	20	A1
Chauncy Ter	20	A1
Cherry Ct	27	A2
Cherry St		
(1-94)	27	A2
(95-199)	26	B1
Chester St	22	B2
Chestnut St	27	B1
Chetwynd Rd	21	A2
Chilton St	21	A1/A2
Church St	20	B1/B2
Churchill Ave	22	A1
Citizens Pl	28	B2
Clary St	28	B2
Clay St	22	A1
Clement Cir	21	A2
Cleveland St	28	B1
Clifton St	22	A1
Clinton St	27	A1
Cogswell Ave	22	B2
Cogswell Pl	22	B2
Columbia St		
(1-124)	27	A2
(125-152)	26	B1
(153-599)	28	A2/B2
Columbia Ter	27	A2
Columbus Ave	22	A1
Concord Ave		
(1-103)	20	A1
(139-578)	21	A1/A2
Concord Ln	21	B2
Coolidge Hill	21	B2
Coolidge Hill Rd	21	B1
Copley St	21	A2
Corliss Pl	21	A2
Cornelius Way	26	B1
Corporal Burns Rd	21	A1
Cottage Ct	27	A1
Cottage Row	27	A1
Cottage St	27	A1
Cottage Park Ave	22	A1
Cowperthwaite St	20	B2
Craigie Cir	20	A1
Craigie St	20	A1
Crawford St	28	B1
Creighton St	22	B2
Crescent St	20	A2
Cresto Ter	26	A2
Cross St	27	A1
Crossland St	28	B2
Cutler Ave	20	A1
Cypress St	22	B2
Dana Pl	27	A1
Dana St		
(1-21)	27	A1
(22-99)	28	A1/B1
Davenport St	23	B1
Davis St	28	B2
Day St	22	A2/B2
Deacon St	26	B1
Decatur St	27	B1
Dewolfe St	20	B2
Dinsmore Ct	20	B1
Divinity Ave	20	B1
Doane St	20	A1
Dock St	26	B1
Dodge St	27	A1
Donnell St	21	A2
Douglas St	21	A2
Dover St	22	A2
Drummond Pl	22	B2
Dudley Ct	22	A1
Dudley St	22	A1
Dunstable Rd	21	B2
Dunster St	20	B2
East St	26	A2
Eaton St	22	A1
Edmunds St	22	A1
Education St	26	A2
Eliot St	20	B1
Ellery Pl	28	B1
Ellery Sq	28	B1
Ellery St		
(1-27)	20	B1
(28-199)	28	A1/B1
Ellsworth Ave	28	A1/B1
Ellsworth Park	28	B1
Elm St	28	B2
Elmer St	27	A1
Elmwood Ave	21	B1
Emily St	27	B1
Emmet Pl	26	A1
Emmons Pl	28	A1
Endicott St	27	B2
Erie St	27	B1/B2
Essex St	27	A2
Eustis St	23	B1
Evereteze Way	28	B2
Everett St	20	A2/B1
Exeter Park	23	B1
Fainwood Cir	28	B1
Fair Oaks St	22	A2
Fairfield St	22	B2
Fairmont Ave	27	A1
Fairmont St	27	A1/B1
Fallon Pl	21	A1
Farrar St	20	A1
Farwell Pl	20	B1
Fayerweather St	21	A1/A2/B1
Fayette St	28	A1/B1
Fayette Park	28	B1
Felton St	22	B2
Fenno St	21	A2
Fern St	21	A2
Fernald Dr	20	A1
Field St	21	A1/A2
Fisk Pl	27	A2
Flagg St		
(1-77)	27	A2
(78-99)	20	B2
Florence St	27	B1
Foch St	22	A1
Follen St	20	A1
Forest St	20	B1
Fort Washington Pl	27	B1
Foster Pl	20	A1
Foster St		
(1-121)	20	A1/B1
(122-199)	21	B2
Frances Pl	22	B1
Francis Ave	20	A1
Franklin Pl	27	A1
Franklin St	27	A1/A2/B2
Fresh Pond Ln	21	B1
Fresh Pond Pky	21	A1/B1
Frisbie Pl	20	A2
Front St	27	A2
Frost St		
(1-65)	23	B1
(66-99)	20	A2
Frost Ter	23	B1
Fulkerson St	26	A1

Street Index

Street Index

Street Index